Introduction to
THE DRAMA OF SOCIAL WORK

MARTIN BLOOM

Virginia Commonwealth University

Rutgers University

F. E. PEACOCK PUBLISHERS, INC.

Itasca, Illinois

Cover Painting, *Intermission*, by Robert Amft

Contents | *brief*

v

Contents | *detailed*

Figures and Tables

FIGURES

TABLES

Preface

Hamlet, Prince of Denmark, is moody and distraught over the recent death of his father, the King. Moreoever, he has had a disturbing conversation with his father's ghost who accused Hamlet's mother and uncle-now-stepfather of murder. But Hamlet is not so crazy as to believe what any old ghost has to tell him, and so he concocts a test, a little scientific experiement if you will, to see whether or not his uncle (the new King) and mother are guilty of this terrible crime. A troupe of players has come to the castle, and Hamlet asks them privately to add some lines to a standard play. The new lines simulate the murder of his father.

> . . . *The play's the thing*
> *Wherein I'll catch the conscience of the king.*
>
> —HAMLET, Act II, Scene II, from Edwards edition, 1985, p. 143

Why does Hamlet do this? He is not just an aspiring playwright—he knows the power of drama to involve people in the course of action, to move their emotions, and possibly, to influence the course of events that involves them. Hamlet hypothesizes that if the King flinches at recognizing how close the play comes to replicating the events of murder—which, of course, only the murderers would know—then Hamlet will know that the King is guilty. So William Shakespeare tells us in this famous play within a play.

This book is about social work, the profession par excellence that tries to put all the pieces of a client's life and times together in helping to solve a problem or to fulfill a potential. I use some major dramas, part of the great liberal arts foundation of this helping profession, to involve you in the course of some particular human events, to stimulate your ideas and feelings with regard to these situations, and possibly, to influence your choice of a life career in social work.

It is a challenging task to help people help themselves. It requires knowledge of human thoughts, feelings, and actions; skills to influence these in appropriate ways; and values to help make the tough choices about what ought to be done, given scarce resources and conflicting points of view. It is important to know the history of helping efforts of those who preceded us—so we won't repeat their trials and errors, and so we may benefit from their successes. It is equally important to know the mission and values of the profession as our guide through an unclear and uncharted future.

This book introduces students to a range of traditional and not so traditional topics social workers need to know. These include the following:

Major social problems, such as
- Poverty and wealth
- Health and illness, physical and mental
- Alienation: studies in suicide, homelessness, and joblessness

Major theories that guide practice, such as
- Cognitive-behavioral
- Psychodynamic
- Humanist

Major methods of practice (preventive and interventive), such as
- Direct practice with individuals
- Work with groups and families
- Work with neighborhoods and communities

Major fields of practice, such as
- Child and family welfare
- Criminal justice
- Occupational social work

Special problem areas, such as
- Concerns about gender, race, and age
- The many faces of violence: war, child abuse, rape, and post-traumatic stress disorders
- Human sexuality, overpopulation, and AIDS

Special tools assisting social work research and practice, such as
- Observational skills
- Precision information retrieval skills
- Skills in the evaluation of one's own practice

In addition to using dramas to connect the reader with work-like situations, I also employ a conceptual model—called the configuration approach—to provide a road map to the actions and interactions of persons and social systems within their environmental contexts. I describe each part of the social work enterprise by reference to this conceptual model so that the reader can see how the several chapters and parts fit together.

I would like to acknowledge with deepest thanks the help many people have given me in the course of writing this book. This is an appreciation without obligation—they need not bear the burdens of this text, although I hope that they may take delight in whatever parts they helped to create. I am especially pleased to acknolwedge some social work colleagues in other countries—Great Britian, Sweden, Israel, and South Africa—from whom I have learned how universal are the values and arts of helping.

My thanks go to Jane Reeves, Betsy Elliot, Linda Miyake Brandeis, Craig Winston LeCroy, Maricarmen Asiota, Mitchell Spero, Mario Jardon, Clarke Chambers, Carolyn Wells, William E. Buffum (and five other unnamed reviewers), Patrick Dattalo, Ronna I. Saunders, Jane Ramsay, Ingrid Bermeus, Kerstin Lindholm, Margareta Dysting, Jennifer D. Smith, Peter Day, Benyamin Chetkow Yanoov, Wilfred Van Delft, Holly Levinson, Caryle Neal, Lewis Powell, David Saunders, Dennis Poole, Sheila Kleff, Te Roth, Stanford Schwartz, Adrienne Chambon, David Antebi, Ludwig Geismar, Leslie Muchmore, Stephen M. Aigner, Frederic G. Reamer, and the late Mark Overvold, as well as to generations of beginning social work students who endured, if not prevailed, through the development of these materials. I also want to thank the deans at Virginia Commonwealth University (Grace Harris) and Rutgers University (Paul Glasser, Elfriede Schlesinger) for providing an environment conducive to thinking and writing about social work in its many faceted expressions. My debt to the libraries at Virginia Commonwealth University, Rutgers University, and the University of Connecticut is enormous, even though I sampled only a tiny portion of their holdings.

I feel especially fortunate to be able to work on this book with Ted Peacock, publisher, gentleman, and lover of literature, and his helpful colleagues, especially Leo Wiegman.

Now, dim the houselights, sound the trumpets, and open the curtains on the dedication: There, at the center stage of my life, is Lynn and our two sons, Bard and Laird. They have contributed to this book directly (Lynn read countless drafts) and indirectly (as our scientist sons engaged in wonderfully endless discussions on the nature of science and scientific method). They are part of an exciting and loving family drama running for over three decades.

I must add a special dedication, with love, to the newest member of the cast, Sara Miron, who will co-star with Laird in a new family series of their own construction.

PART

I.

INTRODUCTIONS

The three chapters in this Part introduce social work as a scientific practice by the use of theater drama as a vicarious experience for what it is like to help people help themselves. We have all attended plays that have gripped our imaginations because of the intensity of the conflicts in feelings and ideas. So it is with some social work situations. We have experienced the satisfying insight that comes from seeing how the pieces of the drama all come together at the end. So it is sometimes with social work. We have become deeply involved with one or another character on the stage perhaps because that person's experiences were like those we or our friends have known. So it is with some clients in the social work situation.

But we leave the theater after an hour or two to return to the real world. We have many obligations in everyday life. We cannot long remain tied up with one person's dilemmas. Yet the drama remains as a stirring memory. We return in our mind's eye to savor the mysteries and the understandings we experienced. We may learn some new perspectives on fundamental human concerns. We may add something to our stock of practical wisdom by participating in the universal experiences expressed through individual actors and specific situations.

So it is with some client situations, particularly when we may have contributed to solutions of common human concerns. Social work can be a very satisfying and engaging enterprise, but it is also hard work. This introductory Part begins the process of engaging your imagination while it exercises your mind. We discuss how to begin—perhaps in a volunteer capacity—to meet with clients, to understand what their concerns are, and, perhaps, to begin the helping process. We also discuss the more abstract tools, such as concepts and theories, by which helping professionals make constructive contributions. These are the basic tools for the helping professional.

OUTLINE

Introduction: The Configural Approach

Ibsen's *An Enemy of the People:* Helping at the Community and Organizational Level

Shaffer's *Equus:* Helping at the Individual and Family Level

Where is the Drama in Your Life?

CHAPTER ONE

Introduction to the Helping Professions

This first chapter uses drama to introduce social work practice in several different social welfare settings. The stage has long been the place where individual and collective ideas, actions, and emotions have been presented in controlled and concentrated forms and where audiences have laughed or wept or wondered at these scenes of human behavior. Drama will be used here to help us gain insight into the human condition and about those who would help ease that condition or raise it to new heights. Social work is continually filled with dramas every bit as stimulating and meaningful as those of our greatest playwriters. The chapter ends with the question: Where is the drama in your life? Consider social work as your career choice.

INTRODUCTION: THE CONFIGURAL APPROACH

There are few experiences in life that are as fascinatingly dramatic or as satisfying as helping other human beings. It is a fascination that appears to be a perennial aspect of human society. We have records of people becoming "people-helpers" from the dawn of time. Yet, helping is fresh and new, drawing you to read this book or to take a class that introduces you to one particular helping profession, so as to stimulate your interest or reaffirm your commitment to join that host of others who have helped their neighbors, friends, strangers, and even their enemies.

Helping means many things to different people. For some, it means helping to solve problems, to adapt to or to cope with disabling illnesses or accidents, or to overcome multiple stresses. For others, helping involves enhancing people's potentials, preventing predictable problems, or achieving a better quality of life. I will try to give equal emphasis to treatment and rehabilitation and to the preventive aspects of helping. Society needs both.

This book introduces readers to the profession of social work and to the programs and services that constitute the nation's social welfare system. Here are definitions of basic terms:

Social work consists of the activities of persons trained to help individuals, groups, or communities to enhance or to restore their capacity for effective social functioning and to create the societal conditions that are favorable to this goal.

Social welfare refers to society's organized ways to provide for the persistent needs of all people—for health, education, socio-economic support, personal rights, and political freedom. Social welfare is manifested through many programs and services from public (governmental) and private sources.

Because most students will have some guided experiences with clients in the community—as volunteers or as student interns in field placements—this book also provides some direction on what to do to help clients. Thus there are chapters on the nature of social work (Chapters 1, 2, 3, and 5), the activities that social workers engage in (Chapters 2, 6, 7, 8, and 9), the fields (or types of settings) in which these activities are practiced (Chapters 14, 15, and 16), and some of the problems they deal with in both their individual and collective aspects (Chapters 11, 12, 13, 17, 18, 19, and 20).

There are chapters on the social welfare system and how we came to have the present service system, as well as some brief reviews of the history of several minority groups in America (Chapters 4, 17, and 18). Additional chapters provide tools for the helping professional—how to observe carefully (Chapter 21), how to locate information effectively (Chapter 22), how to monitor and evaluate practice during the course of its delivery (Chapter 23), and how to begin thinking about resolving the almost inevitable value conflicts that emerge in practice (Chapter 10).

This book also has a central theme. It is presented in detail later, but it can be briefly summarized here. The distinctive emphasis of social work as a helping profession is its breadth of vision, seeing "the person in his or her environment." I want to expand this vision while making it more explicit. I use the term *configural approach* to mean seeing the individual in his or her various environments, each of which interacts with the others, influencing and being influenced by them. Whenever I discuss a person or group as a target of social work efforts, I will put them into a configural context, as indicated in Figure 1.1.

This configural approach may be illustrated with two examples, one from an individual perspective, the other, from a community point of view. Suppose that a young man has performed a bizarre act that has led him to be locked up in a psychiatric clinic for treatment. How should we begin to think about this case? From the configural perspective, one would place this individual in the center of a figure (1.1) in which his problems would be indicated on one side of the figure, his strengths on the other. Of course, this person has several important primary groups that have influenced his life and currently are highly important to him—such as his family, friends, and some others. Suppose that this young man works and belongs to other large organizations that make up what social scientists call secondary groups, those that have specialized claim on certain parts of the individual's interests and labors. These secondary contexts also influence what he has done and how he has done it. Beyond these primary and secondary groups are the socio-cultural contexts, the ethnic heritage, and the societal order in which he lives. These too are powerful determinants of his life, particularly if he is in any minority groups

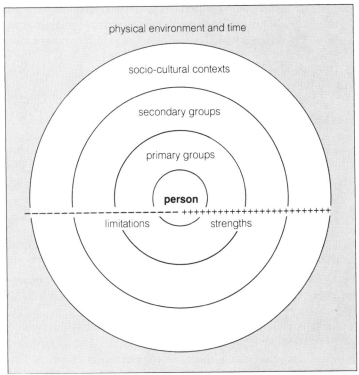

physical environment and time

socio-cultural contexts

secondary groups

primary groups

person

limitations   strengths

Ingredients of the model

person—cognitive, affective, and behavioral dimensions.

primary groups—for example, family, peer group, close work groups.

secondary groups—for example, workplace, school system.

socio-cultural contexts—for example, laws, social mores, ethnic heritage, subcultural life style.

physical environment—for example, natural environmental conditions, environments and environmental conditions made by people whether intended or not.

time—used with joint reference to the life cycle of the person, relevant primary and secondary groups and organizations, and changes in the socio-cultural context.

FIGURE 1.1   Configuration of factors to be considered in the study of any human problem or challenge

that experience direct or indirect forms of discrimination. And finally, beyond the cultural and societal context, are the physical environment and the historical age in which we live. All of these factors influence the individual, as I show in later chapters; that individual, moreover, may influence all of these other factors to some degree as well. Obviously, in certain cases, some factors are more relevant and more useful than others in a helping context. We have to think about helping within such a broad framework because all of the factors are potentially important. Helping professionals check out each new situation to see which of the factors is important in a given case.

Likewise, when one begins with a complex situation, for example, a whole community that is trying to revitalize itself by developing a recreation area to attract tourists, we can also use the conceptual frame of reference to guide our thinking. We would again begin with the configural arrangement and place this "target group"—the community—within its context. We would examine the larger contexts of the culture and the society, as well as the physical environment and the times. We would also look at what relevant secondary groups are influential, such as businesses, unions, mass media, and schools, since they would likely be involved in any effort to modify the community. Likewise, we would look for specific individuals and their primary support groups, those who were most concerned about the problem, most affected by the proposed changes. These are the people who will ultimately be a part of whatever collective action might occur.

Here is a youngster happily playing amid the rubble in a ghetto in South Bronx, New York. It is a bittersweet play, a mixture of optimism about the possibilities of life and pessimism about life's brutal limitations. Social work shares this same bittersweet perspective, recognizing the many complicated challenges ahead, while at the same time comprehending the underlying strength that exists in every people, every time, every place.

Jim Hubbard

In general, every helping professional has his or her frame of reference with which to make sense of the complex problems to be resolved. By beginning with a very broad frame of reference, the configural approach, we can be certain of at least considering all of the potentially relevant factors in a case situation. The facts of the matter will make some aspects of the configuration more or less relevant, and we would then use the relevant ones in specific ways as directed by our theories of behavior change (described in Chapter 9). So, keep in mind this configural figure as we approach any topic in social work.

To get a good perspective on the many forms of helping, I have chosen to use that mirror of humankind, the dramatic arts. The many faces of helping and of being helped are portrayed in dramas. You will recognize many of them, and you will doubtless have seen others on the stage or on television. Thus you know how gripping a good play can be, how involved you can become with the characters and the issues they are facing.

The play is, of course, different from real life; nothing happens so inexorably or with such concentration as in the theatrical production. But the experience of helping and of being helped is perhaps most nearly approximated in vivid dramas that capture our imaginations, intelligence, and feelings. The words are not always sweet, for there is often bitterness in helping or in trying to help when it is too late or when we have too little to offer. But for whatever bittersweet experiences being a professional may bring, helping another human being or group is still a perennial fascination.

A play is a unique work. It seeks to represent the singularity of the individual characters and the universality of what we learn by understanding their lives. Science seeks to understand patterns in human behavior. Its theories and empirical generalizations attempt to present uniformities among the diverse instances of everyday life. One of the central tasks of a scientific practitioner is to apply this general knowledge with the particular individual or group in need. For this purpose, the liberal arts may play a significant role because in art there is nothing as universal as the clearly comprehended plight or the potential of one unique human being. As social psychologist Kurt Lewin noted, nothing is as practical as a good theory.

IBSEN'S AN ENEMY OF THE PEOPLE: *HELPING AT THE COMMUNITY AND ORGANIZATIONAL LEVEL*

Let us then use the experience of drama to introduce the helping arts. Imagine yourself in a theater, the lights dim, and the curtain opens. You observe an ordinary and familiar scene, a living room of a home, and as if you were an invisible guest, you hear the actors speak their lines. Soon, you are drawn into the plot, and you forget that you are sitting on a hard seat in a crowded theater. The scenery and the props hint at what lies beyond the stage, a door leading outside to the world. The words and actions transport you to another time and place as you become part of that drama, a witness to life.

Henrik Ibsen's play *An Enemy of the People* is more than one hundred years old, but it seems contemporary because it presents issues of human greed and vested interests that are still with us. Our concern is with the character of Dr. Thomas Stockmann, a medical officer at the recently opened Baths (a kind of public health spa) in a small town in Norway. The play is simple to describe, but it can be best appreciated, perhaps, by audiences familiar with the Chernobyl incident that involved nuclear accidents of immense proportions, or the controversies surrounding acid rain that spans continents and nations, or the debates about Love Canals (toxic waste deposits) past and future.

As the play opens, great excitement is in the air. The town is beginning to look prosperous as a result of building the Baths over the past several years because great crowds of tourists are expected soon. Indeed, it was Dr. Stockmann's original idea to build the Baths, although he had suggested a different way to construct them than was actually done. The Baths Committee and the city fathers prevailed, and now the Baths are about to open.

The leading city father happens to be Peter Stockmann, the doctor's elder brother. Mayor, Chief Constable, and Chairperson of the Baths all rolled into one, Peter is the man of action who turned the doctor's idea into a practical reality. The brothers are vastly different in personalities. Thomas is a self-proclaimed scientist with a lively and liberal mind and imagination. For him, committees and bureaucracies in general are necessary evils to achieve what the creative mind directs. Peter, the Mayor, is a cautious businessman, ever aware of money, power, and status.

The crux of the play is soon arrived at: The doctor has been secretly conducting some tests on the water to be used in the Baths, and he finds that the water is contaminated by the tanneries upstream. This had resulted in the past in some isolated complaints of typhoid and of gastric and other troubles. Were the health Baths to open, the doctor concludes, many people might become sick. The doctor reports his findings to the editor of a liberal newspaper, who promises to print them. Then the doctor sends a copy to his brother, the Mayor, fully expecting praise for his discovery that will likely save many lives and the reputation of the community.

There is more to life than pure medical and public health issues, however. The state of the economy is fully invested with the plan to put the Baths into operation soon. The repairs the doctor has called for will take several years to complete and will cost a large amount of money. The reputations of the leaders of the community are also at stake.

But the liberal newspaper editor has vowed to take on these local bureaucrats, and the leader of the tradespeople (who also happens to be the head of the local temperance society) has also volunteered to assist Dr. Stockmann. The workers' livelihood depends on the work from this project. The forces of good and evil appear to be lined up for dramatic confrontation. The first skirmish takes place when the Mayor tries to convince the doctor to suppress his findings for the good of the community. News of this "rumor" of poisoned waters would ruin the town as a health resort. Should some people become ill, then the doctor could just treat them individually and not connect their cases to a common cause. The doctor is an employee of the Baths, moreover, and this is an order.

The doctor, in scientific-righteous indignation, will not back down. So the Mayor gets to work. He talks to the leader of the tradespeople and says that he will be forced to raise taxes that will fall most heavily on the tradespeople. That puts a "completely different face" on the situation for their leader. The liberal newspaper editor decides not to risk financial ruin by printing the doctor's reports. So, with his support collapsing, the doctor seeks to take his case directly to the citizens of the community. He will give a public speech at the home of a friend because he is not permitted to use public places.

The night of the public speech is crackling with tension. But in a bureaucratic world, the evening is set within strict rules of procedure, complete with a chairperson (the same leader of the tradespeople we met just a moment ago) and a recording secretary. The chair first permits the Mayor to speak. He repeats the economic facts of life and how they will affect each citizen. This turns the crowd against the doctor, even before he tries to speak. Yet, speak he does. He tells them that he has discovered an even more important truth than the fact that the Baths are poisoned—the tyranny of the majority committed to a comfortable status quo: "A community that lives on lies deserves to be destroyed." And to this the crowd shouts, "He is an enemy of the people." The bureaucracy makes it official: "I move that we embody this opinion in a resolution. . . ." And so it is done. (Even great drama is not without humor.)

This is not the end of the play, although it is a dramatic high. I leave the drama to your direct enjoyment while I comment on the fate of those who choose to serve the best interests of the community. Sometimes a community worker has at his or her disposal such scientific methods, which can determine that some invisible things (such as bacteria in the water) will cause personal and social harm. Another type of collective implication can be made by a community worker who draws inferences from visible events to predict invisible harm (such as smoking cigarettes increases the probability of lung cancer and other illnesses). But no fact exists in isolation, and society, as well as individuals, knowingly trades off a degree of risk for a degree of comfort.

The whistle blower (a person who calls public attention to a social problem, particularly one created and maintained at a public agency) is rarely received with enthusiasm by the powers that be, regardless of the esteem and praise that the public at large may provide. The masses speak in muffled voices, while one's immediate superior speaks loud and clear. Yet whistle blowing goes on; there are always Dr. Stockmanns willing to risk fame and fortune for the truth as they know it. Society is ultimately benefited by their perseverance, but society has a short memory, and the bureaucracy lives long and sometimes vindictively. These are the social facts that one must contemplate when risking to be "an enemy of the people." Yet, the social problems we face will never be resolved by treating their victims one by one. We must go to the socio-cultural sources of the problems, and in our organizations and communities make the changes that will address the basic causes of the conditions that affect individuals. This is also the truth recognized by the Dr. Stockmanns of our day.

Where can you start right now? Ask your city health department about the level of lead found in the blood of the school-aged children in your community. Chances are that it will be higher than recommended levels (Lin Fu, 1979) because we live in a lead-saturated society, and the children are the most vulnerable to it. Lead is not only present in lead-based paint that is peeling off the walls in slum housing but it is also found on toys, on newsprint, and in the air near busy highways. As the thousands of city workers commute to their suburban homes, they pass through densely crowded neighborhoods and school playgrounds. (Children living on lower levels of public housing projects, for example, get poorer grades in school than those living at higher levels, a finding probably associated with how much lead they breathe from highway dust and fumes.) This is not an isolated social problem that can be handled one victim at a time. We are in the middle of an epidemic, a collective health problem with strong socio-cultural overtones. Lead poisoning produces a range of effects, from stomachaches and irritability, to severe mental retardation and death. Lifetime institutionalization of one victim who becomes mentally retarded costs more than one million dollars (Wisconsin Department of Health and Social Services, 1978). Why is not something being done about this? Whose vested interests are being threatened? Ask the Dr. Stockmanns.

Or, perhaps an example closer to home. Do you or any of your good friends smoke? You doubtless know the relevant facts about the correlates of cigarette smoking, just as Dr. Stockmann knew the facts about the poisoned waters. Why cannot people simply accept the facts and do the rational thing, even if it requires some pain in the transition period? Ask the Dr. Stockmanns.

What we learn from the drama of Dr. Stockmann is that helping requires cooperation from the persons helped, even when the facts are incontrovertible. It does not matter whether the facts are medical or psychological or social. We all face the challenge of being "an enemy of the people" at some point in our lives as we seek to be of service to the whole community. Is it worth the fight?

SHAFFER'S EQUUS: HELPING AT THE INDIVIDUAL AND FAMILY LEVEL

In considering Peter Shaffer's drama *Equus* (1974), we will examine a variety of types of helping professionals even while focusing on one young man and his therapist. If we are treating an individual for a mental disturbance, we must perforce consider his physical existence and the meanings he attaches to the events in life. That life, moreover, has to be viewed in relation to the lives of important other persons because it is the action and reaction among them that constitutes the life we seek to understand, and where possible, to change in positive directions. If we pull on the strings of one life, we animate the lives of others, for good or for ill, knowingly or not. This interconnectedness is embodied in the configural approach.

Equus is a psychological murder mystery. No one is actually killed, but the play raises the disturbing question of the meaning of curing the mind of a strange passionate obsession. What is the meaning of being normal? What is the meaning of psychological pain? How are other people involved in the bizarre actions of one person? Implicated in this psychological maelstrom are the parents and the co-workers of a 17-year-old youth, Alan, who has been committed to a psychiatric clinic because of his behavior—he blinded six horses with a metal spike. But eventually, the therapist becomes equally involved in Alan's mind by discovering forgotten experiences, and inferring ones that may not be consciously available to the youth. Piecing this information together, the therapist is able to help Alan relive a trauma and transcend it. Now, to the play.

A court worker who is also an old friend of the therapist makes a special request that the therapist take on a difficult case of a youth who has blinded six horses. Public opinion was so strongly against the youth that his chance of obtaining justice was very slim. The therapist is already too busy, but he accepts his friend's request. "One great thing about the adjustment business: you're never short of customers."

The patient, Alan Strang, comes in, singing TV commercials, "Double your pleasure, double your fun, with Doublemint, Doublemint, Doublemint gum." The therapist acts unperturbed by this and goes on with his rational questioning.

Alan continues singing until the therapist says, "Now that's a good song. I like it better than the other two. Can I hear that one again?"—a therapeutic double bind, although the playwright does not present any such jargon. If the patient does what the therapist asks, he is obeying the therapist. If the patient does not do what the therapist asks (in this case, he would have to stop singing eventually), then he is obeying the therapist's implicit command. In either case, the client loses—which is to say, one step has been made toward a therapeutic objective. Sometimes it works, sometimes not. It depends on whether the patient's mind can find another avenue of escape to maintain the bizarre behavior.

Then, by some unexplained leap of insight, the therapist asks Alan which parent it was who did not allow him to watch TV. Alan goes off with the nurse to his room without answering. If you find this question a little mysterious, then think about it. Think about what you know and where this question might have come from.

Several days later, Alan bursts in on the therapist, saying "Dad"—and gives the answer to the question asked two days earlier. Intervening were nights filled with nightmares for Alan, building pressure on him to cooperate in seeking solutions for his perplexing behavior. Alan's father hates TV because it steals the mind while pretending to provide entertainment, and he ordered the set to be removed from the home. The father said that it was a disgrace that a son of a printer like himself never opens a book.

Alan is proud of his mother, a former schoolteacher. She came from an upper-middle-class family and brought a strong religious orientation to the family. In contrast, her working-class husband had an atheistic perspective. In the class-conscious English setting of the play, such distinctions may make a greater difference than they might in a typical American city.

The various characters in the play come forward in good dramatic sequence to supply more pieces to the puzzle about Alan's strange behavior toward the horses. From his mother we learn that Alan loved stories about horses when he was very young, and that she associated riding horses with her middle-class background—"all dressed up in bowler hat and jodhpurs." It was the former schoolteacher who told him the word equitation comes from *equus*, the Latin word for horse.

Alan's father tells the therapist in a private conversation that he thinks the mother poisoned their son's mind with too much religious talk about torture (crucifixion) and "kinky rituals." Alan cried bitterly when his father took down the picture of Jesus in chains at Calvary, until it was replaced with a photograph of a horse viewed head on, its great eyes staring straight at him.

Alan begins to answer the therapist's questions, although with a twist that adds another dimension to the play. Alan insists on being able to ask the therapist a question for every one that the therapist asks him. He thereby enters the therapist's life—a dull, unfulfilled life relieved only by reading books on Greek mythology.

Alan tells of his earliest memories of horses. At age six, he was playing on a beach when a horse and rider came galloping by and stopped to give Alan a ride—but his hysterical parents pulled him off, much to Alan's dislike. Alan begins to build up his mental world around horses, substituting images of horses for his religious images whose open demonstrations produce family conflicts. "Cowboys are free; parents don't nag them." "God sees you, Alan. God's got eyes everywhere," Alan says mimicking his mother.

The owner of the stable where Alan worked enters. In his opinion, Alan should be in prison, not in a hospital at the taxpayers' expense. (We meet that opinion again in our study of the welfare system.) But the owner does tell the therapist about Jill, the girl who also worked at the stable, and how she introduced Alan to him. Alan learned quickly, and was very good at grooming the horses and cleaning the stables, but he never wanted to ride the horses, which the owner thought very strange. But maybe Alan did ride. The owner mentions his suspicion that perhaps Alan was riding the horses at night, but he never could prove it.

In the course of the play, the therapist introduces several methods to help Alan get at buried truths. One hypnotic device enables Alan to relate how he worships the horses at the stables. He tells how he secretly put sacks on a horse's hooves so as not to waken the stable owner and went into the big field for a midnight ride in the nude. Horse and rider become one in a combination of religious and sexual ecstasy. The therapist compares Alan's approach to life with his own dry existence: "I sit looking at pages of centaurs trampling the soil of Argos—and outside my window (Alan) is trying to become one in a Hampshire field."

Yet even knowing this secret does not permit the therapist to penetrate the full reaches of the mind, to know what particular experiences in life so came together as to explain fundamentally why a person does what he or she does. As he ponders this, the nurse rushes in to report that the mother has visited Alan and has upset him greatly. After she is ousted from her son's room, she complains bitterly to the therapist of being misunderstood and blamed for his bizarre behavior: "You call it a complex, I suppose," the mother says. "But if you knew about God, Doctor, you would know about the Devil." There are many who still use this ancient explanation to find meaning in irrational behavior.

A crisis is coming. Alan is upset by the deepening revelations that he is making and tries to deny them. But in his own fright, he presents the therapist with his strongest tool. Alan believes the hospital rumors that the doctor uses a truth serum, so people "can't help saying things." The therapist offers Alan a placebo (a harmless pill that a patient believes has a certain effect), and sets the stage for a reliving of a traumatic experience. Alan takes the pill and waits for the miracle drug to work.

The therapist asks about Jill, and learns that Alan felt strongly attracted to her and her beautiful eyes. But he never did anything about it, "until one night." Thus we enter the climatic mystery of the play: Until one night Jill asked Alan to take her out to the skinflicks (porno movies) just because neither of them had ever seen them. And so they made arrangements (lying to their parents) and went. The movie hall was full of men, and the film was a dull thing that eventually showed a girl taking a shower. All of a sudden Alan sees and is seen by his father! Embarrassed, Alan, Jill, and Alan's father leave the movie. After several moments of awkward silence, the father informs Alan that he was just discussing some poster business with the movie theater owner and happened to peek inside to see what was being shown. After this transparent lie, he orders Alan to come home, but Alan refuses so that he can take Jill home. The father acquiesces and leaves.

Walking Jill home, Alan thinks about what has happened and gains a number of insights. He sees men leaving the pubs and realizes that they are not "just Dads," but they all have penises and they use them. Then he thinks about his mother and recognizes that she probably does not "give" her husband any sexual gratification. "She likes Ladies and Gentlemen. Do you understand what I mean?" he asks Jill, who says, "Ladies and Gentlemen aren't naked?"

"That's right! Never! . . . Never! That would be disgusting! She'd have to put bowler hats on them!"

Alan is freed by this insight of the sexual commonality among all people, even though some do things at night in secret. "There's no difference," Alan observes, "he's just the same as me." So Alan is freed to do anything, and Jill's gentle seduction is his initiation into sex.

The only available place turns out to be the stables. Jill's mother does not allow Jill to bring boys home, and going to Alan's house would be impossible. But the stable is Alan's "Holy of Holies." They find a small room away from the horses and lock the door. After some necking, Jill suggests going all the way: "I will, if you will."

In a dramatic nude scene, the teenagers try to make love. But Alan is unable to perform because he senses the presence of the horses and all that they mean to him. Although Jill is understanding without really understanding his motivations, Alan repulses her. She dresses hastily and leaves. Alan, still naked, takes the metal spike to his beloved equus gods. He blinds their all-seeing eyes that have prevented him from achieving human love.

A summary never accomplishes what an entire dramatic experience can achieve. For present purposes, however, it is sufficient to note the parallels between actors who deliver prepared lines and gestures to one another, and what helping professionals do. They, too, deliver planned lines and gestures, but entirely in response to what clients say to them. The therapist in *Equus* was almost always right. That is unrealistic in the course of real-life professional helping.

The therapist was also self-critical and philosophical about the broader implications of his attempts to make Alan "normal" like himself. He recognized that in reality his life and passions were pale imitations of the ones that Alan led. Unfortunately, such self-criticisms and philosophical musings are all too rare among professional helpers. No theory is true. It is merely helpful or not to some degree. We have to test ourselves constantly at being helping professionals. The professional cannot impose any absolute standards of what is right, good, or true. All of these goals are relative to the people involved, and the social-cultural worlds in which they live.

We may learn about some idealized version of helping from drama. We may recognize the great poetic insights that are possible by means of a concentrated and intense experience. Yet we rarely are as perceptive, as quick, or as successful as are the players in ninety-minute dramas. Drama is an experience that probably most nearly approximates what it is like to be a professional helper, who focuses on one individual in the context of his family and his work situation. A helping professional must not only be one's own person. He or she must also be involved in helping others become their own persons, reasonably free of problems and reasonably able to attain their life objectives. They become the topics of courses in human behavior in the social environment, on policy, and on practice methods and field experiences. In a word, this is the menu for programs in the helping professions.

WHERE IS THE DRAMA IN YOUR LIFE?

I make no pretense about my trying to encourage you to consider a career in the helping professions. I began this book with dramatic incidents from literature to illustrate some of the various ways of professional helping. I want to encourage your consideration of a most fascinating and meaningful life employment, ever changing, ever gratifying, ever helpful. It isn't easy, but then neither is life itself. Where will the drama in your life be? I invite you to consider the helping professions.

OUTLINE

CHAPTER TWO

Starting Points—
How To Begin Helping as a Professional

This chapter presents a general orientation to professional helping. Called the configural approach, it enables the worker or the volunteer to keep the many aspects of helping in mind as he or she talks with a client. Inexperienced students should not begin their social work careers, of course, as "junior psychiatrists." It is important even for beginners, however, to talk with clients and to exhibit appropriate empathy and understanding of their condition and the social context. (Later chapters present a generalist approach to problem solving.) This chapter describes the starting points for professional practice, with particular reference to the core professional attributes of warmth and respect, accurate empathy, and facilitative genuineness.

TOWARD A CONFIGURAL APPROACH TO PROFESSIONAL HELPING: A DRAMATIC ILLUSTRATION

Suppose that you are going to begin your social work education by trying to understand the problems a client brings to the agency where you are doing your field work or volunteering. We know from personal experience that life is very complicated, with pushes and pulls coming from every direction. How are we to make sense of all these happenings? We may never come to understand the problems and potentials of one client's life as thoroughly as that person who has directly experienced them. So what do we have to offer clients, especially when we are rank beginners?

Let us approach that question through another dramatic example. Imagine that you are on stage in a theater-in-the-round. The theater lights are dim, but you can see the shadowy images of the audience all around you. A table and a few chairs, your only props, stand nearby on stage.

Then, the spotlight turns on you, and a middle-aged woman and a young teenage boy come bursting into the light, talking rapidly in Spanish as they come. They see you and stop talking, an eerie silence. Mother and son have come together to the office of a community mental health center, two volcanos awaiting eruption. The silence continues.

"What am I supposed to say? I never saw the script. I don't even know what play this is," you sputter to yourself. But the other actors are now squarely in front of you, waiting. Panic! Anxiety! What in the world is going on here? Then you see a flicker of a smile from the other actor and you relax. He's just another human being, like me, you think. You breathe deeply as you say, "Hello, I'm ———, a social worker with this agency. Can you tell me what brings you here today? And the play, the drama of life, begins—Act I Scene I.

Shakespeare said it: "All the world's a stage, and all the men and women merely actors. They have their entrances and their exits." Philosopher Edmund Burke used the drama as a total metaphor for his analysis of the human condition. I, too, want to use the dramatic metaphor for scientific purposes, to help us understand and change portions of the world. By looking at what is manifestly artificial—the play—we can look at simple constructed situations, lines, even props, to examine the effects portrayed as well as the effects on us, the audience. As we identify with the characters and the dramatization, we gain something, a kind of perspective and hence, a kind of intellectual and emotional experience.

Another of Shakespeare's memorable remarks: "The play's the thing." But what kind of thing is it? Let's look more closely at its elements, as they serve to introduce the helping professions. First, the actors. There are two types of actors immediately present: the client (who may be an individual or a group of some type) and the worker (you—and possibly a team of colleagues). But inevitably there will be other actors, nearer, or farther away from the client, waiting for their signal to enter the stage. A second dramatic element is the stage itself and the props that indicate the objects associated with our everyday life. But, offstage, there will be other stage props, pieces of the furniture of the universe that influence what the actors do and how they do it. These may, or may not, get moved to center stage. The third dramatic element is the atmosphere that is created by means of the actors' lines and is supported by the stage props. It provides a culture or context for making sense of the play; it provides the basis for making judgments about good and evil, humor and seriousness, meaningfulness or confusion.

You recall your opening lines: "Mrs. Armello, Julio, please come into my office and have a seat." The three of you shift around the table and chairs, turning some simple props into a clinical office at a community mental health center in the deep South where the drama is set. They know their lines: Mrs. Armello begins by accusing her 13-year-old son of trying to kill her with a pair of large scissors; Julio says it was only a joke. He says she is always nagging him, "do this, do that," and that she never lets him do what he wants to do. She agrees to this, but says he is abusing drugs and alcohol, and she wants him to stop. And also, Julio never goes to school anymore, so the truant officer is after him. "I don't like school," Julio says and turns away, dejected.

The mother gets up and in effect turns the stage into her home; the spot lights turn on the woman and boy: "Julio, listen to me! You never do anything around the apartment to help me. Look at that pile of dirty clothes. Why don't you put them in the laundry box? Why don't you ever help around the house? I work so hard. . . . "

Julio rises and faces his mother: "You never worked a day in your life. You're always sponging off your relatives or the welfare department. Why should I do your work for you?"

"Don't you talk to me like that, young man. You show me some respect."

"Then you show me why I should respect you."

Mother and son come menacingly close together, and there is a moment of silence as the stage lights come on, and you (the social worker) are back in the picture. Mother and son circle around and return to their chairs in the social worker's "office."

"Yes," Mrs. Armello admits, "we do have to get money from my brother and sometimes from the welfare office to make ends meet. It's been that way ever since my husband deserted us when Julio was five years old. And I've been . . . ill. I can't work. And I wanted to stay home and take care of Julio."

"You're well enough to go to plenty of parties," Julio says haughtily. Mrs. Armello bursts into tears, and Julio, with an impish grin on his face, gets up and stalks out of the office (that is, he walks off stage into the shadows).

Sounds like a "masterpiece theater" drama to you? Unfortunately, it is not a theatrical piece; it is a real case presented here (in a disguised form) to illustrate some of the basic concepts and starting points of social work practice. But more than that, it illustrates a larger conceptualization of the helping process. Once you can take hold of the whole picture, you will be able to see how the smaller pieces fit together more easily. I am not suggesting that beginning social workers will be able to handle cases like this, but I start with realistic situations in order to motivate your study of the components of any practice.

The term *configuration* will be used here to represent a system of elements (three at minimum): they are the individual, some relevant primary groups like a family or close friends, and some relevant secondary groups such as a school, a job situation, or a social agency. These three elements are themselves set within three contexts: the socio-cultural and the physical environment plus a time dimension. Thus a configuration contains at least three psycho-social elements and three environmental contexts. (See Figure 1.1, page 7.)

This configuration of psycho-social elements and environmental contexts functions as a checklist of factors to be considered in any case situation. These are the kinds of factors that *could be* relevant to the particular events the client presents. Not all of them will necessarily be active in a given situation, of course, but this is what the worker has to determine by talking with the client and observing the context in which client events take place. The configural checklist is also helpful to hear and to observe what is *not* said, as well as what is. Thus, overall, the configural approach is an expansion and specification of the basic social work perspective: the person-in-the-environment.

The concept of the configuration as a generic frame of reference will be used in discussing how social workers provide professional help. Return to the stage—now recognized as a stage of life for the real clients. We have come to know something about Mrs. Armello through the lines she spoke and the way she spoke them, as well as by nonverbal means of communication—her tears, her voice intonations, her hand gestures of frustration. We also have learned much about her in the way she speaks to her son, and how he responds, as well as what he says about her.

The fragment of their family life we have seen represents the whole, a high tension field in which two combatants fight. We get hints that there is a brother somewhere in the picture who gives Mrs. Armello money—and presumably has other, as yet unspecified, contacts with them. Far distant, perhaps entirely out of the picture forever, is the husband who left the mother and child eight years ago.

So far, others are conspicuous by their absence. No peers have been mentioned, no neighbors or friends, no association with a church, although the worker knows the Armellos live in a poor Hispanic neighborhood with a large Catholic church nearby. Looking again, we may see that Mrs. Armello is wearing a small gold crucifix on a necklace, which presumably symbolizes her relationship to her church. Symbols and metaphors abound.

When you stop to consider these, you will notice the three psycho-social elements (person, small groups, large groups) and the three environmental contexts (the physical, the socio-cultural, and the time dimension). It is not difficult to see aspects of all these elements in the configuration of Mrs. Armello's life. The point is to keep this configuration in mind because it represents both the possible problems and challenges and the probable strengths and resources to be used in the intervention.

You will be playing your part correctly, from the point of view of the configural approach, if, whenever you meet a client "on stage," you see not merely the person before you, but as many primary groups and secondary groups as are relevant, as well as the physical and socio-cultural contexts and time dimension that are inevitable aspects of your client's life. This configuration is always present, if you have the orientation to see the drama before you in its holistic, life-in-the-round perspective. This is, I believe, the meaning and the spirit of the traditional social work axiom of viewing the person in his or her environment.

What do social workers do? The best way to find out is to watch social workers in action and then talk with them later to find out why they did what they did. This gives you both the immediate impressions from your perspective, as well as the interpretation by the worker. Also available are films or tapes of live sessions such as the "Gloria" films in which Carl Rogers, Albert Ellis, and Fritz Perls all interview the same client, Gloria. It might also be useful to ask clients what their impressions were of the events, thus giving a third perspective, like Kurosawa's magical film version of *Rashomon*. (See also Mayer and Timms, *The Client Speaks*, 1970.) Another way to discover what social workers do is to read about their accounts of cases. An excellent example is Carolyn Cressy Wells' *Social Work Day-to-Day: the Experience of Generalist Social Work Practice* (1989).

My approach to helping you see what social workers do is to present cases as dramatic situations, so as to put you into the scene as far as possible. During the rest of the Armello case, we will stop at dramatic points to reflect on one or another aspect of the case. This chapter presents the starting points. Please note that there are other major topics to be considered in later chapters. These include a generic problem-solving approach, values applied to practice, and the evaluation of practice.

Julio was not a stranger to this community mental health center, located in the heart of a large Hispanic community. He had been referred there by the school social worker for his acting out behavior almost from the time he entered school at the age of six. Recently, he was brought to the attention of both the court and the community mental health staff for his persistent absences. A psychiatrist associated with the school system saw him several years ago, after which he described Julio as aggressive, distrustful, and angry at all authority figures—especially his mother.

Technically, in terms of the descriptive categories of the *Diagnostic and Statistical Manual,* (third edition, revised, 1987, known to the clinical world as the DSM IIIR), Julio was characterized as exhibiting a conduct disorder, with social aggressive components, and some hallucinations probably related to his abuse of mixed substances (such as marijuana, cocaine, and alcohol). It was also noted that he had an underlying depressive condition. A second aspect of his DSM IIIR rating noted that he had some learning disability. Indeed, he was doing poorly during the rare times he was attending school. He had been moved into special education classes after the fourth grade, where he found his more severely handicapped classmates disturbing and resented having to go to class with them.

There are three other aspects, or axes, of the DSM IIIR, having to do with prior physical or medical problems, severity of stressors acting on the client, and the highest level of functioning in the past year (as sort of a marker to attain in any rehabilitation process). A prognosis or prediction of what is likely to occur is based on these known facts. For Julio, there were no significant prior medical problems; the level of stress seemed to be very high; and over the past year, he showed persistent poor impulse control, which was a discouraging point of reference. Overall, his prognosis was pessimistic. The psychiatrist's recommendation was for institutionalization, both to control his abuse of drugs and to deal with his serious psychiatric problems of aggression and depression. Julio later received tranquilizers from the staff physician to help reduce the stress he felt in his life.

At another time, Julio saw a school psychologist who gave him a set of tests that enabled her to describe her view of his functioning. He scored 93 on a standard intelligence test, on the low side but within the range of the majority of people. This score has to be further interpreted within a cultural context in which the items on the test may not have been familiar in his home and life experience, putting him at a disadvantage compared with children from the dominant culture on whom test norms are fixed. Because of these cultural factors, Julio's score of 93 may suggest a much higher real intelligence. He also was given the Minnesota Multiphasic Personality Inventory (MMPI) and a child's version of the thematic apperception test (TAT), which indicated no thought process disturbances. But his test scores were similar to those individuals who experience strong feelings of inferiority, inadequacy, and lack of drive. The psychologist attributed these characteristics to Julio's feelings of abandonment or rejection by his father years earlier.

All of these background events took place offstage, so to speak. They were events involving other helping professionals and Julio at an earlier time, but the implications were that these personality trends continue. Yet Julio was developing and changing. Although records from the past influence interpretations of present behavior, we must always be on the lookout for significant changes.

Julio is an early maturing youth, not yet as tall as his mother, but growing rapidly. Thin, not particularly handsome, Julio is struggling with his self-image in a socio-cultural context that rewards macho characteristics. He refuses to go swimming at any of the inviting beaches near his home because he feels embarrassed by his body. Yet, he is sexually active, not with his age-mates, but with older dropouts (men and women) who now lead derelict lives and who exchange sexual favors for drugs. Julio not only uses drugs, but he also sells some.

This is a good point to stop and to reflect on all that has been said about Julio and his mother. Review these materials and try to organize them into the configural categories: Which are the facts that seem to describe the specific individuals (Julio or his mother)? Which describe the patterns of interaction between these two that reflect their family pattern? Which factors involve the extended family, including the deserting father, the mother's mysterious brother (and his family)? What about Julio's friends, particularly the dropouts? Does the mother have any close friends or confidants? All of these people—or lack of such persons—represent the inner circle of significant associations, the relevant primary groups.

But there are other relevant secondary groups involved. Can you list them? Again, some are agencies that have been directly involved in Julio's and Mrs. Armello's lives, but there may be others that are not yet visible, and may not be involved, although there could be need for them (such as an institution of the type recommended by the psychiatrist). One must raise questions with oneself about why some secondary groups are not present; why can't Mrs. Armello get a job, for example? Is there anything about the job market in her home area that contributes to her unemployed status? Or are there some personality factors contributing as well?

The socio-cultural context of this case is vitally important, as it is in every situation, even though it may be taken for granted for members of the majority culture. Growing up in a Hispanic culture has some distinctive meanings for a young man whose genetic inheritance and rate of growth may not be entirely supportive. Julio does not look macho, merely disheveled in his torn blue jeans, tee shirt, and sneakers. But this cultural factor is as important to the understanding of the entire case as is the biological stage of development Julio is going through.

The physical environment also plays a part. Although the Armellos live in a poor part of the city, the climate is mild, and when the apartment gets hot in the summer, there are parks and shopping malls to go to. The buildings may look somewhat dreary, but the skies are often brilliant blue. Yet the signs of obvious wealth in the larger community are visible, in contrast with the poor surroundings of the Armellos. They are not blind to that contrast, although little is said about it. What impact do you think the physical environment has on this situation?

When I use the phrase time dimension in the configural context, I am calling attention to something that we rarely see because we are literally surrounded by it and tend to take it for granted. However, social critics and historians often call attention to the temper of the times, as compared with the general mood of the populace of other times. In the Armellos' case, the time is the present. Given the location in the deep South, where Hispanics are becoming an increasing fraction of the population, there is a beginning recognition of their potential political power as well as an increase in awareness of the discrimination directed toward them and their lack of achievement of the American dream in proportion to their numbers. The times (the late 1980s) have been termed conservative, reflecting the greater attention given to supporting individualistic entrepreneurial activities and the national defense, as contrasted with the 1960s, which were more liberal with regard to social welfare. The historic times must be considered in developing possible plans, as contrasted with an ideal plan of intervention, unless we "oppose our times" and seek major social changes.

Much more could be said about the Armellos. The more we understand, the more nearly complete is the picture of their lives. But there is a point of diminishing returns. Spending more energy to get new facts may not be worth the time spent in obtaining them. They may not add significantly to the body of knowledge we have about these clients. How do you know when you have reached this point of closure? Compare your answers to those questions with what follows, as the social workers involved report their experience of the events.

Back to the stage. Scene two. As we ended Scene one, Julio left with his mother in tears. Now we see the social worker trying to help Mrs. Armello regain her composure. Mrs. Armello is standing, as is the worker. Mrs. Armello seems to be wavering, whether to go or to stay. The social worker is not pressuring her, but speaks in a calm voice and reviews the situation and what options they have. Mrs. Armello stands and listens.

The social worker was struck by the rather sudden changes in Julio in the few months since she has last seen him. Not only have the interpersonal problems escalated, as in the incident with the scissors, but Julio's appearance seems to have changed too. His face has a hard look, augmented by bruises, which we later learn were received in clashes with drug dealers and buyers. He's growing up; the problems are becoming more serious. The social worker felt the sense of urgency. Somehow, Julio recognized this too, and after a few minutes, he returns to the stage and sits down. The two women tower over him. There is a moment of silence, until the worker snaps her fingers as an idea comes to her. She excuses herself for a moment and returns with a new staff member, a young man who has recently earned his MSW and is sensitive to the life and life-style of teenagers like Julio. Not a word is spoken as the scene ends, but everyone present understands what is about to happen—and why.

The third scene between Julio and the young male social worker, Mr. Raoul, a muscular, dark-haired man in his late twenties, took place several weeks after the scissor incident. Julio came in alone, and reported that he was "clean," meaning that he had gotten very upset by that potentially dangerous encounter with his mother and had voluntarily stopped using hard drugs. He was scared, but he still put up a strong macho front and tested the patience of the worker by throwing bits of paper toward the wastebasket while he talked. The worker said nothing about this annoying behavior. He was slightly in the line of fire, but he knew Julio's mother and his teacher would have gone into tirades over such actions. Mr. Raoul clearly separated himself from the "establishment," those people in authority who were trying to get Julio to do specific things. The worker recognized that these outside forces were present, but he tried to emphasize that it was Julio himself who had to make the choices of what he was to do about them.

When Julio started to talk about his sexual exploits, Mr. Raoul did not criticize or condone his actions but instead talked about Julio's choices and responsibility to know about birth control and safer sex methods. When Julio tried to impress the worker with his florid use of multiple drugs, Mr. Raoul reminded him that it was not illegal to talk about being high on drugs, but it was illegal to use or to sell them, and that Julio was realistically endangering himself and others. When Julio threatened to bash in his mother's car with his baseball bat, the worker calmly pointed out that he would not be able to help Julio if he lost his control because then it would be a legal violation, and the case then would be in the hands of the police. At that point, Julio got very angry and picked up the box of tissues he had been playing with and threw it at the wall opposite Mr. Raoul. There was a loud thud. Mr. Raoul looked at Julio, then leaned over and picked up the box and put it back on the desk near the youth, and said, "Well, I guess better this than a baseball bat, hey, Julio?"

The testing continued for several more sessions, but each time the worker tried to accept Julio's anger and frustrations, some of which were realistic, and yet tried to redirect them into more effective ways of handling the stresses so as not to get him into trouble. Then something unexpected began to happen. Julio would walk into the office without an appointment, and if Mr. Raoul was free, would come to talk for a short time, describing a current stressful event and how he was trying to get control over it. All the while, the worker supported these small gains in control, and suggested that Julio think about others nearly like them. If Mr. Raoul was busy, Julio would talk with the other staff members. He volunteered to help the secretaries stuff envelopes. He asked whether there was anything else he could do. He became increasingly cheerful and outgoing.

More important than this burst of altruism was Julio's claim that he was increasingly free of drugs and that this made it easier for him to keep in control when his mother nagged. (This was the very point that Mr. Raoul was making in a variety of ways.) Julio was not going back to school for any greater periods of time than before, but at least he was not getting into violent arguments. Mr. Raoul said that he believed that Julio was clean (off drugs) but that he would need more evidence if Julio should ever be brought before the court again. He had had several contacts earlier over some alleged thefts of money. Julio volunteered to provide specimens for a urinalysis that would become part of the official record, and Mr. Raoul agreed to make arrangements. (The test required the worker to be present to certify that it was the client's urine.) Julio had to be off drugs for about 30 days to show that he was clean. This procedure was done every week or two when they met. Julio was smoking continuously, and while that would show up as nicotine addiction, it was not considered a hard drug. The evidence began to accumulate: Julio was definitely off hard drugs during this time. The subjective evidence corroborated this. Julio was increasingly proud of his reports of keeping himself under control. He received considerable praise, but with the added reality factor that he had to keep this up. The worker had "every confidence that a man like Julio could manage very well." Julio beamed at such statements.

In view of the grim prognosis generated from the psychiatric interviews and the psychological tests, to the effect that Julio would need institutionalization to get his impulses and his use of harmful drugs under control, what brought about these constructive changes in Julio? Hard drugs are definitely addictive. How is it that Julio simply willed himself to stop using them and was able to sustain this?

The workers involved in this case attributed these remarkable events to several factors. As you read these reasons, note which categories of the configural model are illustrated—characteristics of the individual, the primary group, the secondary group, the physical and the socio-cultural environments, all viewed over time. First, Julio knew he had a stable source of support from the nearby community health center and its staff; indeed, he became attached to some of the staff. Second, he was smart enough to realize what might become of him if he persisted in his destructive and self-destructive ways. He heard what people were telling him, even if he did not seem to show it. Third, he found an adult male whose character he could admire—Mr. Raoul's cool self-control, his strong mastery of situations that troubled Julio, and his physical charisma. Here was a man! Julio was willing to discuss personal feelings with the male worker, something he could not do with the many women in his life (his mother, the teacher, and the first social worker). Another factor was the medication prescribed by the staff physician that seemed to help reduce the perceived stresses of family life. Finally, the staff realized that they were just lucky to this point; they were not sure why Julio had made the constructive changes that he did. Perhaps, they wondered, it might have something to do with the fact that many of the workers at the agency were deeply religious and were themselves members of the community of which Julio was a part. The cultural closeness of worker and client, the understanding from having been close to the problems, all seem to be part of this outcome.

The lights come on, signaling the end of Act I. So far, so good, but don't be fooled. There are many difficult scenes to follow. Let us go into the lobby where people are milling around and discussing the drama. What are the basic terms or the starting points illustrated in this professional helping situation?

STARTING POINTS: THE BEGINNING OF GENERIC PROBLEM SOLVING

By having you imagine yourself on stage with other actors in a life drama, I have tried to convey what one experiences as one begins professional helping. These are not magical or mysterious behaviors, but they are consciously considered. One uses knowledge, skills, and values in achieving purposeful objectives on behalf of the client. This *planfulness* is what distinguishes a professional's actions from the ministrations of well-meaning lay friends, relatives, and strangers. It is time to identify the specific concepts and principles by which you may be guided.

This chapter presents the beginnings of a parallel set of activities that constitute professional practice at any level (that is, with individuals, groups, or communities). Generic problem solving refers to those basic steps and relationships that are typically employed by workers dealing with any size of cli-

TABLE 2.1   The generic problem-solving process

TASK FUNCTIONS Sequence of activities related directly to solving problems	RELATIONSHIPS Activities related directly to developing and maintaining rapport
1. Identify the configuration of strengths and limitations of the client system. What are the client's problems and goals? In what ways do others in the social and physical environments help or hinder the client's situation?	A. Use core professional conditions of *warmth/respect, accurate empathy,* and *facilitative genuineness*
steps 2–7 are developed in chapter 6	*factors B–G are developed in chapter 7*
2. Identify alternative theories of behaviors relevant to the client's situation	B. Clarify worker's and client's roles, expectations, and the issue of confidentiality
3. Prioritize long-term goals and short-term objectives	
4. Make joint decisions on a plan of action and specify contractual obligations (for example, who does what for whom)	C. Respond with sensitivity to differences between worker and client on race, gender, or other factors
	D. Encourage joint participation on all aspects of the problem-solving process
5. Implement and concurrently evaluate the process and outcome of the intervention	E. Continually check on client reactions to the helping process
6. Compare present state of client with case objectives in order to modify services as needed	F. Introduce early the objective of termination
7. Conduct follow-up	G. Assist client toward independent problem-solver status

ent system. There will be differences among individuals, groups and communities, to be sure, but the similarities are what concern us in this chapter.

Table 2.1 divides the generic problem solving process into two columns. The one entitled TASK FUNCTIONS refers to the sequence of logically planned considerations and actions that make it likely that you will be able to deal effectively with client problems. Tasks refer to the business at hand. The second column is entitled RELATIONSHIPS and refers to a collection—not a sequence, that is, not a string of logically interconnected actions—of ways the worker and client get along with each other while engaged in the business at hand. Workers have to establish some minimal level of rapport with clients. They must feel able to trust workers with personal and often embarrassing matters.

Paradoxically, professional helping has to proceed along both columns. It must deal with tasks and establish and maintain relationships, even though the worker who is engaged in the one cannot easily engage in the other. Professional helping often involves the alternation of achieving tasks and rapport building.

This chapter takes up the first item on each list and then points out how we have already experienced them in the case of the Armellos. Thus what appears as an abstract guideline to practice may be seen as behaviors that you are fully capable of at this time. Like any set of skills, one may learn how to use the guidelines with increasing effectiveness.

TASK FUNCTIONS

Step 1: Identify the Configuration of Strengths and Limitations of the Client System

The practice wisdom of the helping professions urges the worker to begin where the client is. This means that we must take seriously the topics the client brings up to discuss as being most important at that moment. But such topics must themselves be brought into some comprehensive frame of reference. In doing so, you begin to make sense of what is a confusing or troubling assortment of happenings to the client. Where is the client within the configuration of events in his or her life, both those that help the client to achieve desired objectives and those that hinder these actions?

The configural approach can be used as a checklist of the categories of experience that may be involved in the case. These categories will have to be considered in understanding both the problems and the potentials in this situation from the perspectives of the client and of other relevant people or groups.

How much information will you need about the client's problems and potentials, and about the stresses and resources from the client's social environments? No one can answer that question specifically. It will depend on the relative importance of each factor in the particular case, as we shall see with the Armellos. Since both client and environment may need to change, it is important to know enough about all parts of the configuration so as to decide with the client which specific parts require further discussion.

Step 1 is just the first in a logically interrelated set of steps in the problem-solving sequence. We consider the other steps in Chapter 6. Now, turn to the relationship side of Table 2.1, where discrete factors are discussed (as contrasted with the interrelated sequence of task functions).

RELATIONSHIPS

Factor A: Meet the People Who Are Your Clients by Active Listening

The task of the helping professional is to understand as completely and clearly as possible the problems and needs of the client. This information is obtained by listening to the client, but not simply listening as one might do with a friend in the course of chattering back and forth with each party speaking about equal amounts of the time. Professional listening is sometimes termed "active listening," exhibited by a range of verbal and nonverbal means to indicate to the client that you are listening carefully and thoughtfully to what he or she is saying.

The emphasis is on the worker's *listening*, and thus speaking considerably less than half the time. There is no precise proportion of speaking time when one is actively listening. The worker initiates a topic on which information is wanted—unless the client has already started some topic. Then the worker is to listen to what the client is saying. Sometimes this involves waiting in silence

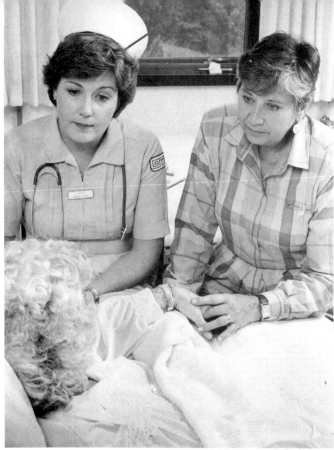

How do helping professionals begin to help? By being there with the client. By listening actively, patiently, and carefully. Sometimes helping begins with a touch of the hand, which communicates something that cannot easily be said in words. There is no magic in this; it is a skill that almost anyone can learn.

for the client to complete some thought-reaching closure on a given topic. Other times listening actively may involve brief probes to get further information. One might repeat a phrase that the client has just said, for example, but intone the phrase as a question, indicating the worker wants more information on it. Or the worker might ask short questions under the general topic being discussed. But the point of speaking is to get more information on a given subject, and these questions indicate the degree of carefulness and attentiveness of the listener.

From communication theory, we know that messages being sent from, say, the client to the worker contain several components. First, there is the *message* itself, presumably some indication about the client's perception of facts in the world—"this is how the world looks to me." A second component is an affective component or *metacommunication* that comments about the message, "this is how I feel about that fact." These two components are inextricably intertwined; it is impossible to send one kind of message without also communicating the other. However, these components need not be aligned; for example, some clients may relate what is a difficult situation in joyous terms. "Well, the divorce proceedings have started" (spoken strongly with a slight upturn of the last word and a smile on the lips). In such a case, the worker might want to sort out the two components and respond to them separately: "So, you say the difficult proceedings have started in the divorce court," *and* "I gather from how you expressed this, that you are happy or relieved that it has begun." The client may or may not be aware of the fact or feeling aspects of his or her speech, and sorting them out may prove to be insightful for that client.

A major part of conversations in professional contexts involves giving feedback to the client on what has been said or unsaid, and how the client has expressed him or herself. It informs the client that the worker is listening carefully, and it also encourages the client to expand on given themes.

There is a considerable body of research on professional interviewing skills (Ivey and Authier, 1978; Carkoff, 1969). The general thrust of the findings is that helping professionals who can convey three characteristics will have a better chance of being effective than those who do not demonstrate them. These three factors, termed by Fischer (1978) the core professional conditions, are *warmth/respect, accurate empathy,* and *facilitative genuineness.* (The terms originated in a somewhat different form from the clinical theories and research of Carl Rogers and his colleagues. The terms used here reflect more recent research.)

Table 2.2 summarizes the major aspects of performing these three factors. Note that there are both beginning and advanced aspects of these factors. Advanced applications require training and experience from guided field experiences and is beyond the scope of this introductory book.

Schools of social work frequently offer laboratories in communication skills in which guided practice in each of these components of the core professional skills are discussed, demonstrated, practiced, critiqued, and practiced again. While we may do many of these things naturally, we also may fidget with a pencil, chew gum, smoke, or in other ways distract the client. These need to be brought to our attention so as to improve the client's perception of our interest, understanding, and empathy.

The core professional skills cited in Table 2.2 are useful in their own right, but they also provide another benefit. One point that frequently is brought up by beginning students going into volunteer or field settings is the feeling of being nervous and anxious. These are natural feelings. They may be present whenever you meet a new client, but probably in decreasing levels as you gain confidence and experience. There are several ways to reduce anxiety: First, be prepared. Read the background materials so you have some idea about what you will be facing and what general directions you may want to follow. (Use the generic problem-solving approach as one set of general directions.) Second, take a big breath and release the air slowly. This tends to calm one. (Any tensing of muscles and then relaxing them will achieve the same effect.)

Third, have some standard lines prepared—"Hello, Mrs. X, I am ———. Please come in and sit down. Can you tell me why you've come here today?" (Or, for clients with whom you have been meeting: "How have things been going for you in the past week?") If you have a set of beginning lines such as these, it will make it easier to get into the business of active listening. Notice that these standard opening lines do not label the person as having problems, a label that some clients find offensive. Also, these standard lines do not promise that you will provide any special help that you may not yet be able to deliver.

Fourth, remember that you do not have to talk all the time. You are to listen and encourage the clients to talk about topics important to them. Silence (from you) is a powerful encourager for the client to continue talking, developing the topic further. Silence is also a time to think about what has been said and to plan new directions. Do not be in a rush to start solving the client's problems before you understand enough of the contextual factors to know what might be done. A great deal of your "talking" will take the form of brief probes, paraphrases, or gestures that urge the client to continue discussing the topic.

A fifth point about controlling your own nervousness is to get settled into a comfortable position. By your posture (leaning forward slightly), relaxed eye contact, and occasional nodding that you understand, you tell the client that you are relaxed, whether you are or not. This reassuring attitude of ease should make the client feel more relaxed. Thus both worker and client are more able to talk about important topics in a trusting and accurate way.

Active listening uses the entire range of core professional conditions— showing respect, exhibiting accurate empathy, and being a genuine person. This encourages the client to tell his or her story as fully and accurately as possible. The problem that the client has brought has not been solved after some time of trying, and it would be unreasonable to expect the worker to solve it in an instant. Active listening shows that you are seriously engaged in hearing the problem and in thinking about various aspects of it. This is the necessary starting point of any professional helping.

Examples in textbooks tend to be very neat and simple, while events in real life are more likely to be complex and messy. Many clients are able to discuss their situations in a rational way, but many others may not ever be able to do that. Therefore, a nice clear problem statement may never appear, and the worker may be left to construct a best guess about what is happening in the situation. Such guesses make even more important than usual the continual testing in the client's world. Many social workers, especially B.S.W.s, do not work in specialized therapeutic settings. Social workers are found in the middle of the flow of life, on hospital wards, in schools, in group homes. We have to adapt generic problem solving to the context, as the next case situation demonstrates.

PRACTICE USING THE CORE PROFESSIONAL CONDITIONS: A NEW CASE ILLUSTRATION

It is evening and you enter the downtown City Emergency Shelter in a large metropolis where you are working as a volunteer. Activities are slow since the Shelter's beds filled up with the homeless and the transient earlier in the day. It is after supper and the people have settled in their rooms. The living room of the Shelter is dreary, filled with second-hand mismatching furniture and old magazines. You switch on the TV to break the monotony, but just as you get a program, an elderly black man stumbles in, looking dazed, and trembling. He says he has just been mugged, but since he had no money or anything of value, the mugger just roughed him up a little and ran away. His clothes are poor and ill-fitting, and he looks like many of the deinstitutionalized people who wander around the ghetto area surrounding the university.

He does not want you to call the police. He just wants to sit there quietly for a while, catch his breath, and then be gone—to where, you are not able to discover. You do not know whether or not he has a home to return to. You notice that he does not appear to be seriously injured from what you see of his

TABLE 2.2   Introduction to the core professional conditions: Warmth/respect; accurate empathy; facilitative genuineness

In spite of the natural feelings of anxiety we experience when we first meet a new client, there is evidence that if we follow some relatively simple steps, we will be more likely to conduct a good interview, overcome our own anxiety, and be convincing to the client that we are interested and competent. But, like any other skill, these core professional conditions take practice. Interviewing someone in a role-playing situation and then looking critically at what you did and how you did it is often very helpful. (The steps in demonstrating three core professional conditions are set forth below in elementary form. For further details, see Ivey and Authier, 1978; and Fischer, 1978.)

Warmth and respect for the client is communicated by:

- A warm tone of voice.
- Postures and gestures that convey warmth and interest, like leaning slightly forward toward the client and maintaining a friendly and interested eye contact.
- Saying in various ways that the worker respects the client as a person, regardless of the client's behaviors that may be causing problems.
- (*Advanced*: Recognizing that the client is responsible for his or her own actions at whatever maturity level is expectable for a person of that age and circumstance. The worker accepts this client responsibility and does not approve or disapprove of the client's choices that are within socially approved limits.)
- (*Advanced*: Sometimes touching the client's hand or shoulder can convey the worker's feelings of concern or closeness. But different cultures accept or reject physical contact of this sort, so that the worker must recognize when touching or putting an arm around the client's shoulders is appropriate or not.)

Accurate empathy for the client is communicated by:

- Showing awareness for the client's expressed *ideas* by reflecting back in various ways what the client has said. ("You're saying that xxx is the case." "Am I correct that what you've been saying is xxx?")
- Showing awareness for the client's expressed *feelings* by reflecting back in various ways the perceived effect ("I sense that you're feeling XXX about xxx." "I can understand that xxx would make you feel XXX.")
- (*Advanced*: Showing awareness for unexpressed ideas—the patterns among events that are emerging from comments the client has made—and for unexpressed feelings—the underlying affective theme that appears in various instances. These unexpressed ideas and feelings are often summarizations of the underlying problem. For instance, it might be that a client gets angry with various people all of whom are in authority positions. Relationship to authority may be the underlying problem, not simply fights with A or B.)

Facilitative genuineness for the client is expressed by:

- Responding to the client naturally as a person, not as a "bureaucrat" in the sense of giving mechanical, rigid answers. Show personal interest in the client and respond to the client's unique characteristics and conditions.
- Continually aiding the client to understand the situation, and exploring it until a sense of closure is reached. (*Closure* involves the perception that you have enough information for the time being to be able to understand and to deal with a given issue.)
- (*Advanced*: Sharing a self-disclosure may be helpful when appropriate. If the worker has gone through an experience comparable to the client's, then it both establishes the worker's depth of experience and sensitivity to the client's problem to share this fact. Such sharing should not take the focus away from the client's experience.)

face and hands. But he continues to tremble and his speech is not always understandable.

You consider what you can offer him by way of help. The Shelter is filled for the night, but you could inquire about nearby places where he might stay. You think about letting him sleep for the night on the couch in the living room of the Shelter, but you recall a stern lecture on following the rules of the agency that prohibit this. No meals are served at the Shelter. But there is a small snack area for the staff in the back office, with cookies, tea, and coffee. You have had only some beginning courses in psychology and social work, and you are not sure what mental state the man is in. You do have the home phone number of the agency director, which you were told to use in cases of emergency. Is this an emergency? What are the starting points in this case?

One way to think about this is to look at the two starting point questions, and then to translate them to this present case situation. Consider some possible actions. Which of these would you consider good starting points with this old man at the City Shelter?

1. I would help him to a chair, and after speaking with him for a few minutes just to assess quickly the nature of the problem, I would offer him a cup of coffee and some cookies.

Critique: A reasonable beginning. Clearly, you want to get him to a comfortable chair to be able to talk, assuming that this is medically possible. Offering food has many advantages. It supplies nutrients to a person who might need them in an emergency; it signals an act of friendship and trust; it gives you and the client a little time to catch one's breath and to think about what to do next.

2. You cannot hear clearly what he is saying, so you turn off the TV and throw away the gum you were chewing. He can now hear you more clearly too.

Critique: Good. These noise factors can easily be changed. There are others that may not be as easy. You may not be used to the dialect of an elderly black man. He may not be speaking clearly because of his mugging or for other physiological or psychological reasons, as yet unknown. Make it as easy as you can for both you and him to talk.

3. As you hear him describe the mugging, you get angry that someone would pick on an old man like him and in spite of what he said, you decide to call the police, whose number is well-placed by the phone.

Critique: Your own outrage at this instance of injustice is understandable, but in fact, it may not be helpful to call the police. What would they do? The assaulter has by now escaped. The old man is not able to provide much detail, and he seems as much frightened by the thought of the police (for reasons yet unknown) as by the attack. It probably is not worth adding one more statistic on mugging for the sake of the records.

4. You wonder whether he is drunk, and so you lean forward a little to detect any odor on his breath. You think he may have been drinking, but your private breathalyzer test is not conclusive. You ask him directly whether he has been drinking tonight.

Critique: The information could be helpful, and you tried at first to get it without disturbing him directly. That part is reasonable, but if he is not obviously drunk—and he's not—then this probe seems premature. There are other things to consider before investigating his drinking history, which, by the way, might explain why he is shy about the police.

5. You ask him about his life history, where he is from, whether he has a family or not, what sort of work he has done, and similar questions. You get some vague answers, and you are not sure whether they are the truth, or the whole truth. This makes you a little annoyed because here you are trying to help him by learning about his background, and he is not cooperating with you.

Critique: Sometimes clients do resist cooperating with the workers, but probably much apparent resistance comes when the worker tries to explore paths that seem to the client not on target, or too much on target too soon, before the client knows and trusts the worker. In any case, it might be too soon to ask these broad questions about personal history, especially since the man will not be a long-term client of this worker. The point is to focus on the here and now in this kind of context.

6. You ask whether he would like to talk about the mugging, or whether there is something else that is more important to discuss, something he needs immediately, like a place to stay.

Critique: To ask is fine, but there are other ways to get into the topic without having to make the first move. For example, you can ask if he is feeling better, or you might comment that he must have felt upset by the mugging. Each of these kinds of actions, a question or a comment, can lead to the mugging, if the old man wants to talk about it. However, it may be premature to try to get to new topics before the immediate one has been resolved to your and his satisfaction.

7. He seems to have calmed down and has finished his second cup of coffee. You ask whether there is anything else you can do for him, and he says no but does not move to leave. You wonder what to do next, and you decide to ask whether he would like to watch TV with you.

Critique: This probably will not do any harm, but it is not particularly helpful either. It may enable the old man to rest, but if the TV were off, and you and he were "just talking," it might have proved to be more helpful. Perhaps he is not yet ready to trust discussing serious concerns. An extended conversation might firm up his relationship with the worker.

Clearly there is no one right answer on how to start helping in a professional manner. Among the ways that might lead to productive paths of present or future conversations, those actions that convey respect for the client, show empathic understanding of his or her problem, and present the worker as a human being trying to facilitate the resolution of a problem are a good start. Taking a configural view of the client's situation as a whole, as a person in multiple socio-cultural and physical environments, is a useful way to begin to understand the case in sufficient detail and to make an informed decision on how to help. Start by listening actively and see where the events lead.

OUTLINE

CHAPTER THREE

Philosophy of Scientific Practice—
The Translation of Theory for Practice

This chapter tackles a difficult but important topic on how we know. Bertolt Brecht's vivid drama Galileo *introduces the view that sometimes what we see clearly may not be the way things are. Rather, we need concepts and theories—abstractions—to help see reality clearly. In the case study, we observe two ways of looking at a given problem from the individual and the collective perspectives. Brief theories are presented and then several steps are given to translate from the conceptual language to the actions social workers take that are guided by these theories. We are never free of concepts. The question is: How are we to use them effectively and humanely?*

BRECHT'S GALILEO: PIONEER IN KNOWING HOW WE KNOW

Few individuals are ever placed in a position in which they can move the world. Bertolt Brecht's drama *Galileo* poses this 17th-century physicist-mathematician at the tangent between two incompatible world views, the religious versus the scientific. The centuries-old religious view determined that the Earth is the center of the universe, around which the sun and the moon move. The stars are fixed to eight great crystal spheres. At the pinnacle of it all—Man, God's greatest creation. Underlying this system is religious doctrine and the testament of the senses. As Galileo's housekeeper's son, Andrea, says:

> I can see with my own eyes that the sun comes up in one place in the morning and goes down in a different place in the evening. It doesn't stand still. I can see it move. (Gassner and Dukore, 1970, p. 873)

Opposed to this long-held religious view are the opinions of a handful of 17th-century scientists who, using only the available crude telescopes, some simple mathematical formulas, and the slow accumulation of evidence, disputed the obvious. The implications of this scientific view of the universe are heretical—Giordano Bruno had recently been burned at the stake for his astronomical views. Cautiously, other scientists still persisted in their studies.

The result was that mankind was transferred from a pinnacle to the sidelines of the universe, on a small planet warmed by accident by a second-rate star. People were left to wonder anxiously about when they would be pushed from their divinely-enthroned height into a meaningless abyss.

Let us return to Brecht. Galileo dramatically demonstrates his planetary thesis to the boy, Andrea, by seating him in a chair beside the iron washstand in the middle of the room. This washstand represents the sun, now on the boy's left. Then, by picking up the boy and chair and by swinging them around the washstand, the "sun" is now on the boy's right. The chair, with a viewer seated on it, represents the earth, "seeing" the immobile sun "move."

But doctrine dies hard. The leading authorities of the time would not even look through Galileo's wondrous telescope to see with their own eyes proof of the errors of their doctrine. Speaking to an assemblage of secular leaders and university professors, Galileo said:

> (Galileo): I can only beg you to look through my eyeglass.
> (Mathematician): If I understand Mr. Galilei correctly, he is asking us to discard the teachings of two thousand years.
> (Galileo): For two thousand years we have been looking in the sky and didn't see the four moons of Jupiter, and there they were all the time. Why defend shaken teachings? You should be doing the shaking (p. 899).

The old Pope dies in 1633, and in his place a mathematician, Cardinal Barberini, becomes Pope Urban VIII. Suddenly there is hope for science. Just as suddenly a summons comes from the Holy Inquisition to force Galileo to renounce his heretical doctrines. The new pope caves in to the demands of his office, even though he tries not "to set [himself] up against the multiplication tables (p. 890)." Urban recognizes Galileo's genius, "the greatest physicist of our time. He is the light of Italy." But the religious pressure is overwhelming. Urban gives his final consent to the Inquisitor:

> (Pope): It is clearly understood: he is not to be tortured. At the very most, he may be shown the instruments.
> (Inquisitor): That will be adequate, Your Holiness. Mr. Galilei understands machinery (p. 890).

Will the "light of Italy" renounce his fundamental discoveries about the universe? Will 1633 be the beginning of the age of reason—or the ending? As Andrea, now a young man and assistant to Galileo, says:

> The earth moves, spinning about the sun. And he showed us. You can't make a man unsee what he has seen (p. 891).

But Brecht's Galileo does understand the machinery of the Holy Inquisition and renounces his doctrines. Galileo descends into the oblivion of house arrest, while his students and assistants flee to other parts of Europe. Galileo's religious daughter and the clergy monitor his research and writings carefully.

Time passes. Galileo is an old man. Andrea, now a university teacher in Holland, passes through Italy and stops to inquire about Galileo's health. When Galileo's daughter leaves the room momentarily, Galileo tells Andrea that he has finished his book on motion—secretly, writing at night—and asks Andrea to take it and get it published abroad. Andrea, who had deserted Galileo at the time of his recanting, now sees how wise Galileo was—to gain

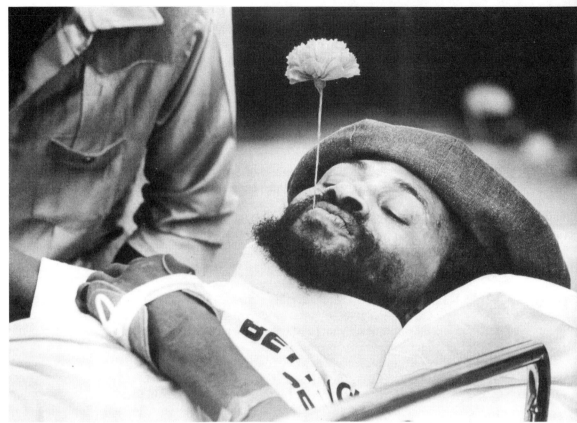

Much of what we make of a situation depends on our perspective—the way we understand whether or not a problem exists, how we construct the nature of the problem itself, the possible solutions we are willing to consider, and how we choose to act. This man being transported on a stretcher has chosen to redefine the nature of his problem—and himself—by the act of holding the carnation. This chapter deals with perspectives in scientific practice, the way we choose to define the world around us. Perspective is old in history but ever new in practice.

his life and to write his great book in secret. Brecht's Galileo is not that simple, however. Galileo breaks Andrea's illusion of the great and noble scientist. Galileo recanted out of fear of physical pain. There was no plan for secret writings. Galileo says he betrayed his profession, science, in spite of his contributions to it. Andrea replies for all of us, for all times, that that analysis is perhaps not the last word on the subject of Galileo. It depends on what one knows and the perspective from which it is known.

A PHILOSOPHY OF SCIENTIFIC PRACTICE

What do you know? This is a strange question, but when you stop to think about it, it turns out to be a very important one, especially when you are trying to help a client. What do you know? Certainly, you *know* lots of things (direct experiences during which you have seen, heard, felt, and in other ways apprehended something that is now embedded in your memory). You also know *about* many more things (indirect experiences of others who have seen, heard, or felt things that they reported to you by words or written symbols). You may be aware that while you are learning many new things all the time, you are also forgetting a lot of other things.

What we know is constantly changing. We have to live with that fact, but we still really have not answered the question, What do we know? The Greek philosophers of twenty-five hundred years ago were fascinated with this inquiry, termed *epistemology*, as scholars have been ever since. The long-time dominant idea of what we know has come from Newtonian science and supporting philosophical positions. This point of view suggests that there is a world external to our perception of it, and that something is true to the extent that it conforms to what really exists "out there." With this orientation, we could happily look for what researchers call "independent variables" (those that could be changed by the experimenter) so we could see what effect these changes had on some other factor, the "dependent variables." We have a hunch that x causes y, and we test this hunch or hypothesis in certain ways. We could study, for example, whether "broken homes" (independent variable) caused "delinquency" (dependent variable).

It was almost inconceivable—literally, "not seen"—that the beginning acts of delinquency might have produced problems in the family that escalated to the point of becoming a "broken home." Or more likely, that delinquent-like behaviors, family problems, and many other events were occurring at the same time, all of which acted together on each other to generate the observed outcomes. To see or to think about problems from this more complex perspective requires an enormous jolt out of our established way of thinking, what Kuhn (1970) calls a paradigm shift, such as the one from the early Ptolemic (earth-centered) astronomy to the Galilean (sun-centered) astronomy.

This more recent (post-Newtonian) way of thinking, stemming from Einstein and many other field or systems theorists, presents an alternative perception of what we know. (See, for example, Bateson, 1975; Gurman, Kniskern, and Pinsof, 1986; Keeney and Sprenkle, 1982; Dell, 1982; Allman, 1982; Coyne, Denner, and Ranson, 1982.) This point of view not only suggests that each element in the system affects and is affected by every other element, but also that the act of knowing something is itself an influence on the thing known; in effect, the viewer is also a participant in constructing the reality viewed. The viewer is intrinsically part of the system being studied. This removes the certainty about what exists, but makes intensely visible the part that the values and orientation of the viewer add to what is perceived.

This book emphasizes the more complex systems perspective because it is more useful than the simpler Newtonian perspective in understanding human interactions. However, we will try to move in steps so that we do not get flooded with too many pieces of the system all at once. Every statement could be qualified to the effect that this is only a part of the whole, and that as other pieces are added, they will change what we have said about the interaction of the previously named parts. But this would make the writing burdensome. Please keep this qualification in mind as we continue.

The therapist in *Equus* always seems to know what he is doing, where he is trying to go with the client (Chapter 1). How does he know? The social workers trying to get Julio to cease endangering his life with drugs and to regain some equanimity with his mother seem to know what they are doing, where they are trying to go with Julio and his mother (Chapter 2). How did they know?

I think that any honest social worker would quickly tell you that, in the beginning, he or she did not know—in the sense of having a clear mental picture of what was going on with the client. Rather, the social worker began with a receptive frame of mind and took in what the client chose to reveal. (That would be the active listening stage described in Chapter 2.) Indeed, an honest therapist would consciously try to avoid beginning by imposing some given set of answers automatically, regardless of the facts of the case. This does not mean that the worker's or therapist's mind is a total blank; we simply cannot erase what we know. We have to work with the body of our previous experiences.

Students ordinarily do not have a large body of experiences of helping others, so what do they bring to the helping situation? Beginners bring perhaps the most powerful of any human experience, a naive common sense, an ability to "see" the emperor in his "new clothes" without the frills of jargon. What a beginning training in professional service asks of the new student is simply to put oneself in the place of the client and to think about what it would be like. What alternatives would you have if you were in a like situation?

This common-sense approach to the first stages of professional helping is another aspect of active listening. By drawing out the client and listening actively to the client's story, we hear what the client wants to tell us. By imagining what these events would mean to us, and what alternatives we might see in resolving them, we gain some perspective on the client's story. It is this common sense, I believe, that gives most students of the helping professions their first taste of helping in high school or college when friends and acquaintances come to them for assistance.

Common sense is a fragile thing. As soon as we think we have some special gift of helping, we may lose our common sense—in favor of repeating some technique or gimmick that worked in one particular situation. The challenge of the beginning student is to remain open to experiences with a common-sense orientation and to begin to assemble a body of experiences that offer useful ways of understanding people's problems. This chapter begins the process of offering that body of experiences (crystallized in theories of behavior and behavior change), but do not overlook the importance of keeping receptive to your good common sense as the touchstone of any theory.

A CASE STUDY: FATHERS AND SONS

One gray fall day, Mr. Landsma came to the office of a social worker, Mr. Willard, and began a sad story of his troubles with his son, Richard. For the past several years, but especially in the past few months, Richard had become almost unmanageable at home. He was drinking and smoking to excess, doing poorly in school, and swearing at his parents. These signs of disrespect were unusual in the country in which the events were taking place, South Africa.

Richard, at age 17, was becoming a young adult in ways his parents found most unpleasant and conflictive. His disrespect for all forms of authority was creating problems at home and at school.

In succeeding sessions with the father and the mother, the social worker discovered many other aspects of the problematic home situation. Mrs. Landsma was worried about Richard's sexual behavior. She thought the group of boys he hung around with might be getting into some sort of trouble with girls, but she was not sure. Richard did not talk much with his parents, and he refused to go to the counseling sessions.

How informed was Richard about sexuality, Mr. Willard asked? There was a long and uncomfortable silence. Finally, Mr. Landsma said that he did not know, since he never got around to talking to his son about it, and now he thought it was too late. He never had been able to have that kind of conversations with his son.

The social worker arranged to visit the Landsmas at home at a time when Richard was likely to be there. Richard was tall, nicely groomed, and everyone's typical teenager. He was momentarily angry at being trapped at a family counseling session. There were angry words exchanged, and the father shouted an order that was strongly authoritative. Richard sat down with his parents and the social worker. Richard expressed his anger at his parents, especially his father, in no uncertain terms. Mr. Landsma was barely able to contain himself as his son was speaking about how his father never let him finish his sentences to say what he wanted to say. The son nervously explained that his parents were too hard on him. They never let him do the things that his friends could do, and he was fed up. He said he was going to do just what he and his friends wanted to do. Mr. Willard asked what he wanted to do. Richard broke into a big smile and said, "Just things the guys do." While the problems became clearer, the solutions seemed farther away.

First Analysis: The Individual

Let us stop here to explore what was going on in the mind of the social worker during these early sessions. Several people were clients in this case: Richard, the young man whose behavior was causing distress to his parents; Mr. Landsma, the father who initially sought help because of his feelings of inadequacy in handling his son; and Mrs. Landsma, the mother who felt inadequate to assist either her son or her husband out of this vicious cycle. The worker could have focused on any one of these people or the whole family as a unit. In his initial thinking, he considered Richard first because of the immediacy of his problems. Conflicts with the family and difficulties at school were placing him in a position of being expelled.

Richard, a 17-year-old male, was experiencing some of the challenges of growing up, including becoming independent while maintaining an adult-level relationship with his parents. His attempts at both were flawed. Independence for him involved superficial behaviors like drinking, smoking, and cursing "like the other guys do," without working on a clear sense of self or what he wanted to do with his life. He was sexually active. This distressed his mother very much, although his father remained silent at that revelation. Yet his angry battles with his parents (and they with him) indicated he had not yet worked out an effective relationship with them as equals (as adults). He wanted to "get away," but it was quite clear that he was unready and unable at present to do so.

With these thoughts in mind, the social worker began to formulate a mental map for thinking about these events. One set of events (the bio-social ones) were here; another set of events (the family relationships) were there; and the conflict involved the clash of these two sets of events. The bio-social events involved inevitable developments in sexual maturation and physical growth, as well as the individual changes in cognitive and moral developments. Also, there were culturally determined events in how these and other adult manifestations were expressed. Getting to know Richard well involved understanding where he was in his developments in these various aspects.

In addition, the social worker had to know where the family was in its life cycle. The father was clearly the dominating figure in this family, but his position of authority had been increasingly challenged by his teenage son. It was not that the teenager was "bad," but the son would always point out how so-and-so's son was getting to stay out later than he could, and why couldn't he stay out later? An interesting fact the worker also noted was that the social status of the other youths with whom Richard compared himself was generally higher than his family's status.

Thus, combining these developmental factors, the worker decided to open up for discussion some problematic factors. He assumed that when the facts were known, they could be dealt with rationally through compromise. The young man was growing up and needed independence in his choice of actions. The family and their values were very much a part of his life, however, and he had to select actions that did not violate family rules. It all seemed quite reasonable to the worker, who assumed that these people were rational and in favor of the best outcomes for all concerned. However, as the worker soon discovered, he could not have been more wrong. No amount of direct challenge of the youth's actions or the parents' counteractions seemed to be able to move either a significant distance toward compromise. Something else seemed to be interfering with constructive change.

Second Analysis: Groups and Institutions

Let us continue with developments in the Landsma case. One day, as the worker came to realize that the common-sense rational approach was not working, he visited the Landsma family at their home for their family counseling session. He learned that Richard was not there. Where was he? The parents did not know. After a brief talk with the parents, Mr. Willard went looking for the son. He drove around the suburban community aimlessly at first, and then he drove to some sites where teenagers hang out. Not there. He continued to drive around in the apartment house area, and there he thought he saw Richard's motorbike. Mr. Willard stopped and walked around the apartment house. He was immediately attracted to one area from which the sounds of loud music were emanating. And there, through the open door, he saw Richard sitting on the floor among seven or eight youths, including a single girl wearing only a pair of jeans. The youths, talking loudly over the music, smoking, and passing around a bottle of liquor, suddenly became quiet as Mr.

Willard knocked and stuck his head through the door. He recognized several of the boys, sons of some prominent businessmen in the small community. The attractive girl was the daughter of a professor who was away on sabbatical. The youths recognized Mr. Willard and invited him in. The social worker told the girl to get dressed and asked the boys what they were doing. Some were drunk but all of them insisted that nothing was going on, just some friendly talking and playing of music. Clearly the solidarity of the peer group was strong.

When thinking about this happening later, Mr. Willard began to recognize one of the hidden forces acting on Richard to produce his rebellious behaviors. The peer group was a tough nut to crack. Mr. Willard thought about what resources he had to counter these pressures on Richard. His train of thought was: First, individually, the fathers of the youths in that room were all men of some status in the community. Each teenager had manipulated his father by saying that so-and-so received more allowance than he did. The fathers were unaware that the youths were using the money for wine, woman, and song, or that a young sex goddess was behind the boys' pleas for more money. Each time the ante was raised to purchase her favors, the youths' fathers were being subtly, and without their knowledge, manipulated as well. If X (a father of a higher social position than Y) let his son have some object or privilege, it was hard for Y to say that his son could not have something equivalent. And so, one by one, the fathers were being manipulated in ways that involved ordinary father-son dynamics combined with the social status element.

The social worker thought that if he could get a fathers' group together and make them aware of the subtle manipulation that was taking place among the boys, then the fathers could unite to hold the line on acceptable behaviors. He contacted the boys' fathers, each of whom admitted having some difficulties with his son, and arranged a group meeting. That gathering did not go as Mr. Willard expected, however. The fathers began by blaming each other for giving in to their sons, which in turn made the others' sons demand more. As these grievances were aired, the fathers began to recognize that they were being manipulated. As Mr. Willard expected, a group norm developed for establishing limits—reasonable enough to permit growth, but not so extreme as to allow the disrespectful and disruptive behaviors most of the families were experiencing. The fathers also realized that many of their sons were in jeopardy of being expelled from school.

Mr. Willard continued to meet with the Landsmas, and found that his plan was quite successful with Richard. Taking empowerment from the group, Mr. Landsma began to set limits and hold firm to them. And more important, all of the other fathers in the group did likewise. Each father was supported for his firmness and fairness—they, too, remembered what it was like to become an adult when still considered a child by their parents. Each father knew the general guidelines of permissions and was able to say, in effect, "Your father instructed me to send you home at midnight. It is 12:00 p.m. now. Go home. He'll be expecting you."

The spread of the effect of this plan was unexpected. First, the fathers continued to meet to clarify for themselves what methods worked best in the encouragement of controlled growth into adulthood. They also began to express some feelings among themselves—something men in this culture do not do easily—about their families and the way society was forcing them to "keep up" with the Joneses when they did not like what the Joneses were letting their children do. Fathers and sons began to talk more—not argue—and it was difficult to decide who benefited more from this exchange.

Most unexpectedly, the school administrator heard about this program and invited the social worker to discuss it. The administrator and his board invited the worker to introduce a related program to identify youth at risk and to invite parents to get involved with a similar self-help group. Thus what was a concern for one parent expanded into programs for parents with common concerns. This is an expansion of an effective intervention that is supported by the configural approach. Where else in the social configuration can experiences with one client be used effectively with others sharing the common problems?

HOW TO TRANSLATE AN ABSTRACT THEORY INTO CONCRETE ACTIONS

The social worker had two quite different theories in mind as he worked first with the individuals in the Landsma family with a rationally-based approach, and second, with the group of fathers using an approach based on small group theory. It will serve the purposes of this chapter to discuss just the group theory and how it was translated for practice because the process is the same for all social theories. The basic steps of translation are these:

1. *Identify the major concepts and propositions contained in the theory.* You should find a series of interrelated ideas that (1) describe a portion of reality, (2) explain how these events change, and (3) predict what future states are likely to be. These three are the major functions of any theory. The third point is especially important in professional helping because it permits workers to predict what will occur if they take certain actions. Then they can measure or observe whether that predicted change takes place, and modify their interventions accordingly.

2. *Identify how the specific behaviors exhibited by the client fit the abstracted classes of events described by the theory.*

3. *Specify what the worker has to do.* What specific actions should the worker perform to follow the conceptual suggestions of the theory with regard to making constructive changes in the situation?

Step 1 requires that the worker knows the abstract ideas (concepts and propositions) used by a given theory. For example, the theory involving social group norms offers the following abstract and general ideas: Groups that remain together for a considerable period of time inevitably form rules (norms) about what members should and should not do vis-à-vis the group's goals and the means to attain them. These norms act to draw members more closely to the group. They provide sanctions, both positive ones regarding what one is to do and negative ones, those that specify what one is not to do. People may belong to several groups whose norms demand contradictory behaviors from one individual, in which case that person acts according to the norms of the group that has the most power over him or her.

Assume that this set of sentences describes one version of a theory about social group norms. Then Step 2 directs us to look for norms that influence the behaviors of individuals. In particular, we should look for situations where one individual is under contradictory pressures (conflicting norms) from two or more groups of which he or she is a member. With the Landsma family, we noted that the worker observed several family norms, including the power of the father in the family, the family value system, such as children should show respect to parents, and so forth. The worker also inferred some peer group norms that involved smoking, drinking, and competitive sexual activity as well as resistance to efforts by parents to manage their sons' time, energy, or activities. Thus the worker recognized conflicting norms. In answer to Step 3, the brief theory described above also suggests a way to resolve these conflicts, by empowering one group's norms over another—that is, to make the norms of one group more powerful for the overlapping member than the power of the norm of the other group. This obviously demands making a value judgment, an issue discussed further in Chapter 10.

Perhaps some diagrams would help to clarify this theoretical interpretation. In Figure 3.1, the Landsma family is represented by a large circle that contains smaller circles of the Father (F), Mother (M), and Son (Richard). The peer group is also indicated by a circle that includes the Landsma's son, Richard, as well as other families' sons (e.g., Peter, John, Paul). As determined

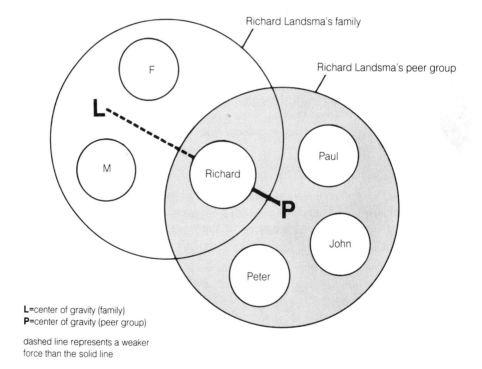

L=center of gravity (family)
P=center of gravity (peer group)

dashed line represents a weaker
force than the solid line

FIGURE 3.1   **The Landsma family and son Richard's peer group, showing the relative strength of the two sets of forces acting on Richard from the Landsma family and the peer group "centers of gravity"**

by clinical observation, it appears that the peer group exerts a more powerful influence over Richard than does his family. To represent this idea, I want to use a phrase that stems from the configural approach, "center of gravity," meaning the point assumed to exist among a group of persons that exerts the greatest force on its members to conform to group norms. The closer one is to this center of gravity, the greater is its influence over the individual. In Figure 3.1, the center of gravity of the family (indicated by the letter L) is at a greater distance from the son than is the center of gravity of the peer group (P), which indicates that Richard is more influenced by the peer group norms than by family norms at this time and place. Conditions change, obviously. The family exerts great influence early in the child's life, but over time others may come to exert greater influence. Adolescence is a transition period for many functions, including social influence, but it is not inevitable that families lose their influence on major values and choices. Adolescents may come to incorporate these values into their own personality systems.

In Figure 3.2, the fathers' group (FG) is represented by the outer irregular circle. The major function of this group is to empower fathers to move the centers of gravity of the individual families closer to the sons, thus increasing the influence the families have over the sons' actions. This empowerment involved fathers' rethinking together what sort of parents they wanted to be, and what sort of sons they wanted to have. As they verbalized these goals and sought ways to bring them into being, they were aided to recognize that these teenagers were at once members of the peer group as well as members of the family. The influence of this peer group had to be taken into consideration as plans were made for raising adolescents.

Notice that we are talking about entities, configural centers of gravity, that are invisible, just as gravity and other solar phenomena were invisible to the scientists who originally conceived them. When considering invisible phenomena, some conceptual entity had to be present to make sense of what could be seen. If the planets were making their long elliptical orbits around the sun, something had to be holding them to their course—the invisible concept of gravity. So it is in dealing with human behavior. We conceptualize about invisible entities that help to explain what we are witnessing and, possibly, help to predict and control those behaviors. There is nothing that says we will guess correctly about the nature of that invisible entity. After all, Ptolemy had inferred that the earth was the center of the universe, and he had made elaborate maps of how this was so, including predictions of solar events, most of which were accurate (cf. Burtt, 1932)! Copernicus and Galileo and others conceptualized another set of explanations for these same phenomena, concepts that ultimately proved to be more useful and accurate in directing our understanding and actions, such as flying to the moon. But there is much we do not yet understand; there are anomalies, events that do not conform to how we imagine the world to work. In the future, another Galileo will teach us how to see the world in yet another way, resolving the anomalies that now exist, even as new ones may appear (cf. Hawking, 1988).

The fathers' group that the social worker created was designed to increase the reasonable authority of fathers with reference to their adolescent sons. This is a difficult task to specify since different people will have different ideas about what limits and methods of disciplining are appropriate. Through dis-

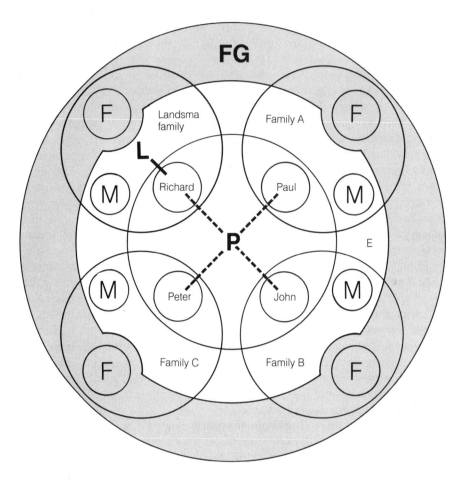

FG=fathers' group
L=center of gravity (Landsma family)
P=center of gravity (peer group)
E=environment

dashed line represents a weaker
force than the solid line

FIGURE 3.2   **The Fathers' Group (FG) represented in connection with their members'
families and their sons' peer group (P), in a common physical environment (E)**

cussion, group norms develop, are tried out, and perhaps readjusted, depending on the collective experiences. All of this is a predictable expectation of
support groups, such as the one the social worker created with the fathers.
The developing group norms for setting fair limits and encouraging appropriate behaviors gained strength and specificity as the fathers tried them out
with their sons. But it was the uniformity among family rules that proved to be
most powerful in opposing the destructive patterns of the peer group. Individual families had their own center of gravity, so to speak, but they were empowered by the collective center of gravity of the support group.

This case brings up another important issue for the helping professions, the *involuntary client*. In an important sense, all clients are involuntary to some degree. They would no doubt prefer to deal with their own concerns by themselves, instead of turning to strangers to help them. Frequently, we observe this resistance to admitting the need for help. Most people do not ask for the forms of welfare that would be available to them under the laws of the land. There is a special group of clients, perhaps the end of the continuum of involuntariness, who have no choice but to see and be seen by professionals. Sometimes people are seen because of a court order, backed up by the police power of the state, at other times because of their own lack of competence to deal with reality by themselves. In any case, the usual rules for gaining rapport and working mutually to solve problems is strained, as in the case of Richard, who neither asked to have the help of the social worker, nor much wanted it even when it was offered to his family.

The configural approach offers some opportunities to the involuntary client. When a person cannot be directly approached or when rapport is not likely, the model suggests approaches that influence the several relevant environments surrounding that client—primary and secondary groups, the sociocultural contexts, and even the physical environment. Activating changes in these environments is a way of trying to bring that person into the problem-solving context. The appeal to broader social factors in which the client is naturally embedded is a general principle of practice with involuntary clients. In effect, one looks for centers of gravity that naturally affect the individual client but do not depend solely on that person's voluntary participation for their impact. (See also Genevieve Oxley's discussion on promoting competence in the involuntary client through the use of the ecological or life-model approach, 1981; Germain, 1979; Maluccio, 1981.)

SUMMARY

Once a Galileo makes a point clear—such as that the earth circles around the sun or, on a more modest scale, that the closer one is to a support group's center of gravity, the stronger its influence is over one—it is hard to imagine that we could have seen it any other way. These theoretical statements are arbitrary as well as abstract, however. We must recognize that we can imagine them in other ways because there may be many other ways to conceive of any given batch of events. Indeed, knowing what to include in a given batch may be part of our conceptualizing. A fathers' support group was not within the experience of any of the fathers until it was created.

Even when a Galileo formulates a brilliant conceptual idea, we must be on guard against reifying it into an unchangeable notion. This was part of the problem with the Ptolemaic version of the solar system. Especially with social science concepts, we must be on guard continuously against believing too much in our own wisdom. We must test whether or not these arbitrary ideas are good guides to practice and toward achieving the outcomes that we want for our clients. If the guides work, then continue to use them. If they do not work, then try something else. Sometimes it is hard to abandon our conceptual ideas after we have devoted so much attention to their birth and development.

In the end, however, we must use concepts. We cannot *not* conceptualize. It is a matter of what concepts we use and how we use them. We must be cautious because many of the "theories" we have formulated are inaccurate, stereotypic, or biased. We conduct our personal lives according to their dictates without too many problems ("Knock wood"). As helping professionals, we must consciously pick and choose among theories that offer the best ideas about how the world is organized and run, and what we can do about it. Some theories are simple, clear, and wrong; others are complex, elegant, and wrong. In fact, all theories are "wrong" in the sense that they must be incomplete guides to reality. Human beings, nonetheless, appear to be wired genetically to use conceptual maps to organize their lives. This is also true of helping professionals in performing their specific duties.

Where do we stand? With Galileo or with our common sense? I have tried in several ways to argue that both common sense and an uncommon sense are necessary to the scientific practitioner. Science is a system of abstract interrelated concepts and propositions. The methods for determining their usefulness in the real world should account for the raw observations of our common-sense world. We "see" the sun moving from its morning rising to its evening setting. However, we "know" that the sun does not move in the way we see it. Yet for the scientific theory to be humanly useful, it has to account for the reasons we "see" the sun as we do. Theory has to account for the phenomenon even when it goes beyond the phenomenon to explain its actions.

Social workers have to account for their clients' human experiences even when the workers' concepts go beyond the visible aspects of those experiences to find causal patterns that are invisible to the naked eye. However, there are many such theories that purport to account for the very same phenomenon by emphasizing one set of factors or another. They cannot all be right—or can they?

Almost all theories may be partially right in the sense of guiding us to different but useful events in the real world that we may influence to help clients solve problems and achieve objectives. Some theories may be more useful than others. This would be indicated by empirical research that shows which theories have led to more effective outcomes.

At the present state of knowledge of human and social nature, we may best treat all logically sound and reasonable theories as potential guides to action. Then we must test them in action. Do they tell us clearly what to expect when we follow their recommendations and do these events in fact occur? If so, continue using them as guides. If not, and if there are no major problems with our measurements, then consider changing to new guides.

For a theory to be partially right, it must also be partially wrong. It may not work as an effective guide on all occasions. The theory itself does not tell us when it is most applicable, and so we had better keep track of situations where it has been applied to see if we can determine for ourselves why it might work here but not there. Hold all theories as systems of hypotheses to be tested and not believed without critical reservations.

As you do this, note that you have moved from a Newtonian position (assuming one clear cause and one clear effect) to an Einsteinian position (assuming a system of forces acting together in a common arena, each influencing and being influenced by the others). The task of the helping professional is to determine which forces are more powerfully affecting some particular reference point or target, like the client. As we will see, this will also mean that we discover how the client affects others, including us, and how we as helpers begin to affect these others as well.

A theory will help us identify the ingredients of this system of interacting elements more clearly. But each theory is a selective grouping of concepts; no one theory accounts for the whole of the human experience. This is why it is useful to read or attend great dramas. They have the capacity for transforming the whole web of a particular life situation into a manageable experience. We can see the whole even though we sometimes cannot express what it is that we see entirely. We "know" something significant, and as we try to understand the dramatic experience and put it into words, we may develop our capacity for scientific understanding as well.

PART

II.

THE
PROFESSION
OF
SOCIAL WORK

W hat we are today is strongly influenced by what we have been all the yesterdays of our collective experience. So it is necessary that we understand something of that collective history. Chapter 4 presents some highlights of the American experience in health, education, welfare, employment, justice, and civil liberties, from the colonial days down to the present. Many human dramas, large and small, are represented in this historical sketch.

Chapter 5 introduces social work as a profession, that is, as a disciplined way of thinking and acting that has its own historical development. To personalize this chapter, I report the reasons my students have given for why they are entering this helping profession, brief reflections about their personal histories and how they find the profession of social work to be the best stage for their life's work. The question is: Will the historical tasks and challenges of the social work profession fit your own interests and values closely enough to make it your life's work?

OUTLINE

Introduction: The Raw Materials and the Making of History

Selective History of Social Welfare in America
   1600 to 1776: Colonial Days to Independence
   1776 to 1860: From the Revolutionary War to the Civil War
   1860 to 1900: Reconstruction, Expansion, and Crises
   1900 to 1930: Prosperity, War, More Prosperity, Then Depression
   1930 to present: The New Deal to the Bush Administration
   To year 2000: Beginning the 21st Century

The More Things Change, the More They Stay the Same

CHAPTER FOUR

A Brief History
of Social Welfare
in America

This chapter presents some historical materials about social welfare. Some actual documents initially challenge the reader to learn how "historical facts" come to be generated. This analysis helps the reader to be not only more skeptical about the fullness and accuracy of any fact, but also more understanding of the difficulties involved in generating any historical statement. The main part of the chapter is an extensive tabular history of social welfare in America. It is divided into eight categories: Demographics, health conditions, mental health conditions, education, work, crime and justice, civil rights and religion, welfare. Notice that these categories represent aspects of the social configuration. Each topic is discussed for given periods of history so that categories for one period can be studied all together, or given topics like mental health can be followed over time.

INTRODUCTION: THE RAW MATERIALS AND THE MAKING OF HISTORY

The philosopher George Santayana once remarked that those who were ignorant of history were doomed to repeat its errors. Unfortunately, knowledge of history is no guarantee that the future will be error free, but at least we might try to avoid the classes of errors that bedeviled people from the past (cf. Muller, 1952). That is no small order because we have every reason to believe that the ancients were no less wise nor virtuous than are our leaders of today or tomorrow. Historian Barbara Tuchman (1985) presents the disheartening thesis that governments often pursue policies that are knowingly self-destructive, even when feasible alternatives are available. Her penetrating examples extend from the Trojan Horse to America's involvement in the Vietnam War.

Yet history also records successes. The Constitution of the United States, for example, has survived for more than 200 years as a clear and flexible instrument that maintained relatively consistent values throughout the centuries of social change. Knowing where we have been gives us some perspective on where we are at present and on directions we might like to go in the future.

But many view history as being composed of old dry facts in dusty books. Just what is it that history is supposed to teach us? And how are we to learn?

Let us go directly to some historical information and see for ourselves. The following paragraphs present excerpts from articles in major newspapers in America; each article is disguised slightly. If we can approach these articles openly and discover not only what each says, but also whether they have anything in common, then we will be doing a small historical analysis. On one level, this is an easy task. On another, there are some difficulties and traps that I fully expect you to fall into, even though you are forewarned. I am not making up a "tricky" test. These following documents are real; they are also the raw material of history.

> *Article 1.* Special officers X and Y of the Z Street police station had been working on a chainstore break-in since Wednesday, when word was passed to them yesterday that it might be worth their while to question a young man living on P Street.
>
> They went to his home early in the morning. He was asleep. His wife was asleep. Their baby was wide awake. The officers tiptoed around the apartment and found the missing loot. It included 48 cans of milk.
>
> After piling all of it at the foot of the bed, the officers awakened the man and his wife.
>
> They were gratified when the man confessed, but they were hardly exultant when they took him away. He explained he had been out of work, needed milk for his baby and food for his wife, had broken into the store to get it, had broken into another store previously for the same purpose, and probably would have done it again.
>
> *Article 2.* Two-year-old Lenny H and his 4-year-old brother Alan were sleeping in the back of the old black Ford with the dingy stuffed duck hanging from the rearview mirror when the policeman rapped on the window.
>
> Lenny started crying.
>
> His mother and father quickly woke up, startled in the dark by the noise. They asked what was wrong. The policeman told them they couldn't sleep in the park.
>
> Lenny's and Alan's daddy told the policeman that the family didn't have anywhere else to sleep—they didn't have any money. The policeman told their daddy that he would have to take the boys and their mother out of the park.
>
> That night the family slept uneasily on a side street in a strange neighborhood.
>
> A few days later, after their money for food had run out, Lenny wanted milk. Alan watched as his father gave blood to get $8.
>
> *Article 3.* Officer R arraigned in police court yesterday a twelve-year-old girl, Lisa S, whom he had arrested Tuesday night for selling papers at a late hour along a major thoroughfare in the city.
>
> Investigation showed that she was the oldest of five children, who lived with their father, Charles S, and their mother in two rooms at XXX West Thirty-Seventh Street. Their father was slowly dying of a respiratory disease and their mother had met with an accident that had left her deaf. Their father's illness made it impossible for him to speak above a whisper, and he and his wife could only communicate by writing.
>
> To save the family from starvation, Lisa had taken to selling papers and the money she earned was all they had had for some time. The officer said that the father had been industrious until he became too weak to work.

What is your reaction to these excerpts? They are all rather sad stories, being about poor families with young children who are hungry. This is not the kind of "What are we having for dinner?" hunger. It is, "Are we going to be able to have anything for dinner tonight?" hunger, which most of us have never known. That is the explicit message from each of the excerpts, but there is an important implicit message that careful reading reveals. Each principal person involved is a fighter, no matter whether the form of the fight is to steal, to sell blood, or to work past curfew to get money to buy the necessities of life. Can it be that we have observed a strength common to the poor, as well as a problem? As we look at three instances of human behavior from an historical perspective, we attempt to discover both the explicit and the implicit patterns of behavior and the correlative conditions surrounding them. Once we make the generalized statement, that the poor face many difficult problems in ordinary living and exhibit certain strengths to overcome them, we have an historical hypothesis that will guide our future thinking and acting, and which we can subject to further tests. We should expect probabilistic evidence, for example, that in nine cases out of ten, we find strengths in poor families. Nothing in human affairs is ever 100 percent certain except death and taxes. The importance of having such hypotheses is to alert us to be on the lookout for these characteristics, strengths as well as weaknesses, because it is by making use of strengths that helping professionals can hope to affect such situations in constructive ways.

What else did you notice about these three excerpts? Perhaps you recognized that police were involved in each of the three cases, which leads to the hypothesis that the police are frequently the front line in social service situations. That is true, even if it is not widely recognized. The police provide a great many basic social services, ranging from providing information to resolving interpersonal problems. There are, of course, other front-line helping professions in different contexts such as medical emergencies, educational or family crises, and crises of the spirit.

If you were reading especially carefully, you probably noticed a flaw in the behavior of the police in the first excerpt (the milk thief), namely, that they appeared to enter his home without a search warrant or invitation. Isn't that illegal? You are to be congratulated for having recognized this event, but you are excused from making an incorrect inference because you did not know that the event took place in 1941. Here are the dates of each of the three excerpts: The first article is from the *Boston Herald*, August 24, 1941, p. A 1; the second from the *Washington Post*, June 9, 1985 (Williams, 1985), p. A 1; and the third from the first page of the second section of the *New York Times*, January 16, 1896, p. 9. That's correct—1896.

The reason it is important to know the dates of each excerpt is that the legal context of the events may be different. You perhaps assumed that the federal law against unauthorized search and seizure would have required the use of a search warrant in this case. In fact it was only in 1966, in the case of *Mapp* v. *the State of Ohio*, that the Supreme Court ruled that certain of the protections found in Constitutional Amendments applied to states as well as to the federal government. The point is worth emphasizing that we tend to assume that today's hard-won civil liberties always existed. Even more perilously, we tend to assume that these fragile civil rights always will exist. That is why John Philpot Curran's immortal line, "Eternal vigilance is the price of liberty," should be recited once a day and twice on Sundays. Actually, the good Mr. Curran said: "The condition upon which God hath given liberty to man is eternal vigilance" (his Speech on the Right of Election, 1790).

Now that you know that there are about 100 years between the earliest and the latest excerpt, you might make some additional observations. In spite of my disguising them slightly, you can probably pick up some differences in styles of reporting the news. Perhaps you noticed that bit of paternalism in the third article when the police officer commented that the father had been "industrious" until his illness made it impossible to work. What is the implication of that comment? Clearly, the officer was making the case that the father was a worthy individual, not just an idle loafer. That sort of moralizing was common in the late 19th century. Do you detect any similar moralizing in the 1941 and the 1985 excerpts? In the full story from the 1985 article, you will see another form of moral analysis, as the author skillfully blends observations about the H family and the state of welfare in which they are seeking to survive. Clearly, the villain of the piece is the economy. There was a massive shutdown of jobs in the H family's home state, and after fruitless searching for work, Mr. H took his family to a new state that was reputed to be in need of workers. Unfortunately, others had gotten there before him, and there was no work to be had. Moreover, the state welfare system had been exhausted by the waves of unemployed migrants, and only a bit of private charity and a commercial employment office saved the H family—or prolonged the agony. The full-time job Mr. H found did not pay enough to keep his family above the poverty line.

The main point here is that we have to know a considerable amount of information to make sense of outward behaviors. It would be all too easy to see Mr. H, an able-bodied young man who was not working, and make some comments like:

> If he really wanted to, if he really had enough motivation, he could get a job.
> He may not be intelligent enough to figure out how to get a job.
> He may be morally corrupt so that he is taking advantage of the welfare system, trying to get something for nothing.

Each of these comments blames the victim (cf. Ryan, 1976; 1981). The individual holds full responsibility for his fate. There are other types of remarks that emphasize another villain:

> He's an innocent victim of a cruel socio-economic system that uses people for its own purpose and then discards them.
> He is just another superfluous person in an impersonal socio-economic system that hasn't yet figured out how to incorporate these marginal people into the mainstream of cultural life, either through work or through welfare.

These remarks put the blame on the larger social system without much thought about what the individual contributes to the problem. The social work perspective recognizes contributions that both the environment and the person make to any given event. In some situations, it is clear that socio-economic events contribute the lion's share, but we must not overlook how individuals respond to these large-scale events. Most important, we must recognize that how people interpret events frequently determines how they

Martin Luther King, Jr., eminent leader in America's historical struggle for civil liberties and human rights, lived and died for his dream of a democracy with "liberty and justice for all." Part of every social worker's mission in society, beyond such daily routines as obtaining someone's missing welfare check or resolving a family conflict or promoting a neighborhood day care center, is to help fulfill that fundamental dream.

David Antebi

respond to them. If policymakers see the problem with the H family as stemming from personal defects as contrasted with socio-economic breakdowns, their plans of response will be widely different.

It gets frustrating, at times, to try to explain these historic patterns of poverty to those who are not closely associated with the social welfare scene. There are always counterexamples—such as the story in a newspaper of the welfare cheater who signed multiple names in order to get thousands of dollars. The sociological fact is that fewer than one percent of all people on welfare are able-bodied persons like Mr. H. The overwhelming majority of welfare recipients are either the very young, the very old, the disabled, or people caring for persons in those categories. The majority never seem to make as much impact as the single welfare fraud. But that is one of the other benefits of knowing your history. You will recognize the problems of credibility we face in discussing welfare and in making plans for suitable responses each time anew.

The final point about the three excerpts concerns what is not present in any of them. In historical analysis, it is sometimes as important to notice what is not present as to observe what is. In each of these situations, what do you observe that is not present and that could have been? One answer is that no public or private social service agencies are there to respond to the crisis conditions of each of these families. And while the availability of such agencies differed over the one hundred years represented by these newspaper articles, there were such services at each of the three times. What does it mean that we, as a nation, are facing the same kind of problems over the course of a century? Has there been no progress in dealing with the conditions that generate and perpetuate poverty and hunger in America? In a word, where are the social workers?

Table 4.1 provides an extended answer. The response has to be as complex as are the persisting social problems we face. In the end, we still must ask, where are the social workers? Notice that several categories used here—health, mental health, education, work, crime and justice, civil rights and religion, welfare—are aspects of the total configuration of which our lives are composed. These categories represent the major sources of influence on the lives of individuals, both historically and at present.

TABLE 4.1   A selective history of social welfare in America

DEMOGRAPHICS		
1600–1776	**1776–1860**	**1860–1900**
The population of the territory that would become the United States was estimated to be under one million Europeans in 1750, including a small number of Spaniards in the far west. There were about two million Indians. In the period between 1619 to 1776, more than 250,000 Africans were brought to the country as slaves. The colonies differed in how they were settled. The northern and some middle colonies were established mainly by whole families, often for reasons of seeking religious freedom in their own permanent settlements. The other colonies began with men explorers, or other nonfamily groupings. Social organizational differences added to geographic ones to create distinctive cultures.	Population increased rapidly aided by a quickening flow of immigration, especially during the mid-19th century. By the time of the Civil War in 1860, there were about 31 million Americans, including 4 million slaves and a small number of free blacks living in the North. The invention of the cotton gin in 1797 had made slavery even more important to the agrarian society of the South. The industrial revolution in America began during this time period, stimulating the movement of workers from farms to city factories. There was continuing westward expansion to the great frontier. In spite of periodic economic depressions, optimism pervaded many areas of life in America.	In the last half of the 19th century, the population of the United States more than doubled, from about 31 million to 76 million. Of these, a sizable proportion were immigrants, mainly from northern and western Europe—nearly 14 million people. Another 9 million were blacks. Orientals brought over to work the mines and build the railroads were still relatively few in numbers, and they were to remain so because of the first restrictive immigration laws that were passed in 1882 against the Chinese. The population of Native Americans decreased as a result of wars and disease. The proportion of persons living in urban areas doubled during these years to 40 percent of the population by 1900. This demographic change corresponded with a downward shift in agricultural workers, from 60 percent in 1860 to less than 40 percent of the total number of gainfully employed workers by 1900. Axinn and Levin (1975, pp. 75–80) note that the gross national product rose two and a half times, in spite of several serious depressions, raising the standard of living for most citizens with it. By 1900, there were 45 states in the Union. The frontier was, in effect, gone.

DEMOGRAPHICS

1900–1930	1930 to present	To year 2000
The population continued to grow rapidly, from 76 million in 1900 to 123 million 30 years later. The trend toward urbanization continued; now 56 percent of the citizens lived in urban areas. There were 20 million immigrants during this period, most of whom settled in urban areas and in the North. They came largely from southeastern Europe as unskilled, illiterate, and non-English speaking peoples, which posed new acculturation challenges for Americans. Black Americans and Hispanic peoples also grew in numbers and proportions of the total population.	When the nation was two hundred years old, its population was more than 215 million people, including some 26 million blacks, 14 million Hispanics, and several million Asian and Native Americans. What is noticeable about this total population, in addition to the large minorities, is the average age of the people. The proportion of persons who are 65 years of age or older is nearly 12 percent and growing, up from 4 percent at the beginning of the century. Implications are momentous for who is going to support these elderly in their retirement years. Ozawa (1986) points out that the growing segment of nonwhite children will be heavily involved in this support. It behooves the current white majority to provide quality education and job potentials for the low-income children for selfish reasons if not for humanitarian ones. War periods create population balloons, such as the baby boomers. The sudden increase in population that occurs when soldiers return from war then proceeds through the social cycle and imposes predictable strains, first on the schools, then on the job market, and finally, on retirement support. Changes in life-style, particularly in the wake of the women's movement, have produced other demographic changes such as delays in having children and larger numbers of childless couples. Also, the increased rate of cigarette smoking by women now is beginning to have its fatal demographic impact; 50 years ago male smoking habits led to the large surplus of widows (Waldron and Johnston, 1976).	The overall population growth is expected to reach about 268 million by the beginning of the 21st century, but it will include larger proportions of nonwhite peoples. Hispanic peoples (Mexican Americans, Cubans, South Americans, Puerto Ricans, and others) may overtake blacks as the largest minority group. The characterization of people living in the urban area will take on new meaning as minority groups continue to be the majority groups in some major cities such as Chicago, Houston, and Los Angeles, which affects many aspects of the political and sociocultural climates of those places. Other trends are also likely to be important in the life of the nation. The average age of the population is increasing, as public health and private life habits combine to enable people to live longer. By 2000, about 15 percent of the population will be over the age of 65, including a rapidly increasing number of persons over the age of 85. The trends toward single-parent families and nonfamily households probably will continue; divorce rates will probably remain high.

HEALTH CONDITIONS

1600–1776	1776–1860	1860–1900
Health conditions world-wide were poor because of the limited knowledge of sanitation, personal hygiene, nutrition, and medicine. There were few trained doctors in the colonies; home care and folk medicine had to suffice. There were high rates of infant and maternal mortality. For instance, Puritan minister Cotton Mather saw many children die in infancy and many mothers (including his own wife) die in childbirth. Her death may explain his fanaticism about witchcraft that fanned the Salem mania. Contagious diseases were prevalent and were contained only by quarantine and evacuations; one-fifth of the population of Philadelphia, for example, hurriedly left during the yellow fever epidemic of 1733 (Schlesinger, 1983). The first general hospital in America, the Pennsylvania Hospital, was built in 1751 in part through the good offices of Benjamin Franklin. Epidemics, war injuries, and illnesses often devastated the early colonies. The precariousness of health and life was an ever-present reality. The first medical school in the colonies was founded in Philadelphia in 1765 on the eve of the Revolutionary War.	Some important changes that affected the health of large numbers of people were occurring. In England, major sanitation reforms were improving the lot of the urban factory workers. In America, public health measures were beginning. They ranged from introducing public sewers in New York in 1703 to instituting boards of public health with police powers to act on individual and collective health problems (Duffy, 1968). Lemuel Shattuck's Report of the Sanitary Commission of Massachusetts of 1850 established a general plan for promoting public health that was widely adopted. Canning, invented in 1809 by Nicolas Appert, made it possible for a more nearly adequate food supply year around. The invention of cotton underwear resulted in greater freedom from lice because it could be washed easily. While there were some scientific advances in understanding health and illness, common medical practices of the day included bleeding and purging patients. Medical training was still limited in America, and barbers continued to act as surgeons in some areas. Almshouses became, by force of circumstances, the first public hospitals for the poor; the rich were cared for at home. Use of the almshouse infirmaries as separate quarters for the growing numbers of people with contagious diseases led to the creation of true hospitals. Hospitals began to serve the wealthy as well as the poor because contagious diseases did not respect social class lines. This is how Bellevue Hospital in New York began in 1794. Early in the 1800s the first free medical clinic, the Philadelphia Dispensary, was founded by Dr. Benjamin Rush.	This was a golden age of health discovery. The identification of specific disease organisms and their control, for example, through the wide-scale application of vaccinations (Pasteur; Koch), anesthetics (Long and Morton). Antiseptics (Lister), and the pasteurization of milk, were other memorable events. Mortality rates from contagious diseases tumbled, although differentially for the poor and the nonpoor and for white and nonwhite. Public health activities flourished. The U.S. Sanitary Commission, a private voluntary organization, operated effectively during the Civil War to reduce needless suffering and loss of life from diseases by improving sanitary conditions and distributing needed supplies more effectively. These lessons in community public health efforts were not lost because boards of health adopted similar practices.

HEALTH CONDITIONS

1900–1930	1930 to present	To year 2000
The major health developments came as part of public health, the recognition that the social and physical environmental contexts affected the health and well-being of individuals. Indeed, the interrelationships between ill health and poverty were becoming better understood: not only that illness of the breadwinners caused much poverty, which produced devastating effects on all aspects of family life, but also that being poor was associated with higher rates of illness. It was a vicious cycle. Sanitation efforts continued to make major reductions in mortality and morbidity rates. Social workers and public health personnel were deeply involved in setting up milk depots to distribute free pastuerized milk to the poor. They also worked together to counter contagious diseases such as tuberculosis, influenza, diphtheria—the major killers in 1900—and also venereal diseases (Folks, 1912). One important, though short-lived, federal action during this period, the Sheppard-Towner Act of 1921, set up some 3,000 child and maternal health centers, mostly in rural areas. Passed only after several years of acrimonious struggles, that Act, for the first time, brought the federal government into the field of health and welfare of children and their mothers. It died on the eve of the Great Depression, only to be brought back as part of the Social Security Act of 1935 in a different form.	The Social Security Act of 1935 did not directly address health. Bills related to a national health insurance were introduced each succeeding year, but they were not successful until 1965 when amendments to the Social Security Act established two systems that provided for parts of the nation's health care needs. One amendment (Title XVIII) created Medicare, with its two main parts—Part A, a compulsory plan for hospital coverage, extended care in nursing homes, and some home health care, and Part B, a voluntary plan covering doctors' fees, outpatient services, and the like. This program is financed by obligatory contributions from employees and employers. A completely different part of the amendment (Title XIX) established Medicaid to provide some health care for the medically indigent. Medicaid is financed by matching funds from the federal government and the 50 states; each state can choose what level or scope of coverage it wants, within some general federal guidelines. (Chapter 12 discusses these amendments further.) The costs of health care have skyrocketed without a corresponding increase in overall health benefits (Hilbert, 1977). Threats to financial solvency caused by major illnesses still exist, and not merely for older persons. Discussions continue regarding catastrophic illness insurance and how to pay for it. Efforts also continue toward a full health coverage program, as does opposition to proposals for such a national health plan. Prevention of predictable health problems has emerged as critical on the national agenda. For example, cigarette smoking over a lifetime is estimated to kill more than 300,000 persons annually. Many life-style changes are being promoted, not merely for good health, but also for a renewal of quality of life. Likewise, new health risks appear, such as AIDS, and the search for answers continues.	With concerted efforts in research in cancer, heart disease, and chronic illnesses, the decade of the 1990s should see some advances. It is uncertain whether breakthroughs will occur, such as the kind that effectively eliminated polio, because of the complex nature of the current major killers and disablers. Medical technology will continue to develop to new heights. However, a major ethical dilemma will have to be faced in the coming decades: Medical technology is becoming extremely expensive, while facts about basic nutrition, medical care of ordinary minor problems, and information on life-style activities are widely and cheaply available. Is it worth the great expense to extend life artificially for short periods of time? (The spotlight on spectacular heart transplant operations tends to divert attention from a more rational, broad-based emphasis on healthful living that could often prevent the need for these expensive treatments.) Should everyone have equal access to these expensive methods of treatment? Who is going to pay the bill?

MENTAL HEALTH CONDITIONS

1600–1776	1776–1860	1860–1900
On the one hand, Europeans coming to the new world saw this as a land of opportunity (religious for some, economic for others), challenge, and change. This view led to a general sense of optimism. On the other hand, life was continually stressful, and understanding or tolerance of mental disorders was minimal. Insanity was confused with possession by the devil. "Witches" were hanged or crushed to death in 1692 at Salem Village, Massachusetts, in the wake of a mass hysteria brought on by a group of adolescent girls who claimed they were bewitched by some old women. (For a literary interpretation of these events, see Arthur Miller's *The Crucible* (1949), discussed in Chapter 10.) At first the various almshouses, houses of correction, and other social institutions mixed the insane with the criminal and the destitute. Later, beginning at the Pennsylvania Hospital, the mentally ill were separated from the physically sick, although treatment was harsh and often punitive. Williamsburg, Virginia, was the site of the first publicly supported hospital in America solely for the mentally ill (1769). Its building and its implements of "treatment" have been restored at Colonial Williamsburg.	Theories of the causes of mental illness changed; demons were replaced by physical causes that led to physical treatments and restraints. A more humane form of treatment was adapted from the work of Philippe Pinel in France and perhaps from the village of Gheel, Belgium, which had for centuries treated patients by taking them into the homes of villagers and showing them kindness and firmness as the form of treatment. This was termed Moral Treatment and was reported to have high recovery rates (Black, 1977; Bockoven, 1963). It was used in some mental hospitals in America for a time, but as the rise of immigrants brought new kinds of foreign-speaking patients and as the population began to rise, it became less possible to use Moral Treatment, and again, institutional solutions were adopted. Institutions for the mentally ill were never pleasant places, but Dorothea Dix found extraordinary misery and cruelty in her visits to institutions for the insane. She mounted a campaign for humane treatment in appropriate state institutions that was occasionally successful. In 1848 she even succeeded in convincing Congress to set aside 5 million acres for mental institutions—Congress raised the figure to 10 million—but President Pierce vetoed the bill on the grounds that such welfare measures properly belonged to the states and not to the federal government. The effect of his veto dampened federal welfare efforts for nearly 75 years.	There were only faint glimmerings of advancement in the mental health area. Socially speaking, mental illness was clearly seen as a situation for which the state, as contrasted with local or federal efforts, had important responsibilities. These responsibilities were largely translated into state mental hospitals. Because of the numbers of patients involved, however, there was a transition from a rehabilitative to a custodial orientation, with much frustration on the part of the medical professionals, the reformers, and the general public. The chronically mentally ill became an increasing proportion of patients at mental hospitals as the elderly and the poor were institutionalized for long periods of time. With the limited understanding of the causes and effective treatment of mental illness, there were persisting conflicts between the professionals and administrators who wanted to maintain control over the hospitals and the general public who, aroused by exposes of inhumane treatment and high costs, demanded appropriate changes through their elected representatives.

MENTAL HEALTH CONDITIONS

1900–1930	1930 to present	To year 2000
New theories about the nature of mental health and illness began to become influential during this period. Sigmund Freud's model of unconscious conflicts, Adolf Meyers' holistic approach to psychiatry, and a behavioral approach in the form of "habit clinics" (Orme and Stuart, 1981) were developed with varying degrees of success.	The optimism of Americans was profoundly shaken by the Great Depression of the 1930s. The richest nation in the world suddenly had nearly 40 percent unemployed and suffered the consequent stresses on health and mental health. The conservative response was to rely on market forces to regain prosperity, as they had done before in earlier but weaker recessions. Some private practitioners in social work continued to treat individuals on a one-to-one paying basis. The vast numbers of stressed and distressed unemployed persons were left to their own devices.	The stresses of modern life probably will increase, as natural resources are reduced and the population grows. Preventive methods of dealing with predictable problems should increase in demand, as the limitations of treatment and rehabilitation are recognized by taxpayers. New organizational methods of treatment are likely to emerge, partly because of economic factors and partly as a result of developments in methods of therapy. (Therapies that are empirically based, but ecological in orientation, will flourish in the coming decades.) Genetic research may provide new medical approaches of revolutionary dimensions, raising the possibility of genetic engineering to prevent biological-chemical problems. These changes will also create new ethical controversies as people move closer to god-like decision making (Rauch, 1988). Self-help groups of all types will continue to develop as people come to recognize their own strength and competency to help themselves while helping others.
Exposes of the horrors of mental hospitals, such as in Clifford Beers' *A Mind That Found Itself* (1908), led to the formation of a national mental hygiene movement. It was based on the premises that mental illness was curable, and that the stigma of having been mentally ill was inappropriate and harmful.	Reactions to the dominant psychoanalytic tradition came from diverse sources, such as alternative professional approaches to treatment, and from minority and women's groups who objected to the white, middle-class oriented, male-dominant methods. Mental health became viewed as integrated with life in the community, rather than separated from it. The Community Mental Health Act of 1963 began the process of recognizing that health and illness are partly functions of social forces. Comprehensive preventive and interventive efforts were both needed and possible (Albee, 1983; Bloom, 1981).	
In 1910 an outpatient clinic was developed in Massachusetts to serve people who had mild or incipient forms of mental distress. The year 1921 saw the beginnings of child guidance clinics. They were originally intended to serve preventive functions related to reform of community programs, but attention soon switched to focus on treatment of individual children. This reflected the overall trend, away from the social reforms of the 1890s and early 1900s, to the post-World War I conservative mode with its individualistic orientation. The clientele changed from immigrants and working class people to the more affluent middle classes who could afford the fee-for-service treatment of private practitioners, social workers included.	Tranquilizers and other drugs were introduced on a large scale in the middle of the 1950s. These drugs radically altered the way mentally ill persons were treated. Tranquilizers did not cure mental illness, but they made it possible for afflicted persons to live more nearly unagitated lives in the community. Large numbers of former patients were discharged in rapid order, before appropriate arrangements for follow-up care could be made in the community. This created a new challenge for mental health personnel and community leaders. Large numbers of homeless individuals, and even whole families, were sleeping on hot air grates at night. The plight of those people began to prick at the moral senses of Americans. The country is still struggling to find solutions.	As the level of education continues to rise in the population, we might expect to see more sophisticated consumers of mental health information who will make greater demands of professional helpers to help solve problems. These problems will be seen to involve larger environmental contexts, particularly in the work place as stresses there have repercussions in family and private life. The problems of the 21st century will continue to deal with chronic mental illnesses, along with issues of the deinstitutionalized and the homeless.

EDUCATION

1600–1776	1776–1860	1860–1900
The colonies differed in their approach to public education. In Massachusetts there was a high proportion of university-trained persons, mainly ministers, who encouraged the setting up of schools in towns where concentrations of children made classes feasible. Education was viewed as promoting a defense against idleness, unemployment, and poverty—three evils of the Puritan religion in whose support these schools were to be established. Harvard University was established in 1686, followed slowly by a handful of other colleges and universities. By 1647 Massachusetts laws set up a system of public education, although it was noncompulsory. Boys who were apprenticed to craftsmen were required to be taught to read and write. Girls were required to read only. Missionary schools for the Indians began early (such as at the College of William and Mary in 1693) but were largely ineffective. Slaves were educated in some northern locations as early as 1707, but education of slaves was not permitted in the South. Indeed, southern colonies did not promote educational systems, in part because of their sparse population and the agrarian nature of their society. The wealthy employed tutors in their homes.	The new nation needed educated citizens and began the long road toward compulsory public education. In 1813 Connecticut law required compulsory school attendance even for the increasing numbers of children employed in factories. Rural people insisted that the school calendar conform to the farming calendar, and so we have our extended summer "vacation." It was initially the time to plant and harvest. The rapid increase in population made it difficult for children to be apprenticed or indentured. Particularly in view of the large numbers of foreign immigrants, a free public education was seen to be a socializing force that helped to mold diverse people into loyal citizens of the United States. During this pre–Civil War period, the South continued to outlaw education of slaves. The Northwest Ordinance of 1785, among other important provisions, made federal lands available to provide for the establishment of public schools in the new territories. This precedent was to be used in other ways to extend federal support for public welfare.	Many difficult educational issues faced the nation after the Civil War. The Freedman's Bureau was established in 1865 (but ended by 1872) to address the critical needs of the newly freed slaves and others displaced by the war. It spent about half of its funds on the education of blacks. The Bureau was the first federal effort in public education, but there was no national educational policy, even though a Department of Education had been set up in 1867. Education was effectively controlled by the several states. After the war, public high schools were introduced, reflecting the need for more educated citizens and efforts to acculturate the continuing waves of immigrants. In spite of the apparent victory of anti-slavery forces in the Civil War, the place of blacks in America was still unsettled. After the Reconstruction period, integration was resisted formally in the South through Jim Crow laws. It was also resisted, but less formally, in the North. The Supreme Court decision in *Plessy* v. *Ferguson* (1896) established the doctrine of racial separation through "separate but equal" educational institutions. Many black leaders, among them Booker T. Washington, promoted vocational training so that blacks could gain immediate entry into the job market and later gain economic and social progress. That position was strongly opposed by other black leaders, including scholar and writer W. E. B. DuBois, who pressed for the full measure of rights and opportunity for all. An emphasis on vocational training was also made for Native Americans. The boarding schools set up for Indian children required that they be removed from their families for long periods of time. That course was destructive to Indian culture as well as a practical failure in education. The results were only barely perceived by white Americans by the turn of the century.

EDUCATION

1900–1930	1930 to present	To year 2000
The progressive education movement began somewhat before the turn of the century, criticizing rote teaching methods and ideological indoctrination. It proposed methods to further the development of the child's potentials (Dewey, 1899). Thus education, like the child welfare and the legal system, began to view the individual child as a person with rights and potentials to be nourished and protected. This was a time of many educational experiments including the forming of closer relationships between school and community and a furthering of athletics and the arts along with traditional educational content.	While education is still largely in the hands of state and local governments, momentous changes did occur as a result of national events. *Brown* v. *Board of Education* (1954) made school segregation unconstitutional—"Separate educational facilities are inherently unequal"—but ending the residential patterns of de facto segregation remains a continuing challenge.	Educational philosophy and technology will undergo continued scrutiny and experimentation, but will probably not yet be linked with the natural educational environment—the family, the neighborhood, and the socio-economic community in which out-of-school learning neutralizes or accentuates the lessons from the class. Until such time as the school is truly embedded in the structures and forces that predominantly educate the child, no major improvements are likely. As was recognized in studies of Head Start, the economic, social, medical, and environmental contexts must be put in order before the modest efforts of a Head Start can be fully effective. Remedial education necessitated by the collective assaults of an impoverished, discriminatory, and unhealthy environment is doomed from the start. As more people live longer, there will be increasing demands for life-time education, for variable entry and exit points in education, and for different types and deliveries of knowledge.
The development of public high schools continued. But classes were large in urban areas, and there was rapid turnover of students and teachers. A school social worker role (originally called a visiting teacher) emerged in 1906 in an attempt to link students, families, and the school system. Night school was an important vehicle toward acculturation of immigrants and to their economic progress.	School dropout rates finally went below 50 percent during this period and in the late 1980s fluctuated in the 20 to 25 percent range. Average figures do not reveal that minority youths drop out at much higher rates than white students, however, a disadvantage that continues to plague their life chances and the health of society.	
	Federal aid for veterans' education was very successful as a societal investment. It provided the mental set for a program that helped prepare the very young to take advantage of public schooling—the Head Start Program that began in 1964 (see Richmond, Zigler, and Stipek, 1975)—and others, including work-study programs to assist poor college students.	
	The quality of American education has been the subject of criticism for many years, particularly after the Russians launched Sputnik and before the Americans got their space program successfully off the ground. In spite of fantastic successes in certain technological spheres, the overall effectiveness of American education in supplying the quality of mind citizens of the future will need is still very much debated (A. Bloom, 1987; E. D. Hirsch, 1987).	

WORK

1600–1776	1776–1860	1860–1900
In the New World, work was necessary from all hands—men, women, and children. Work was sanctified by religion while idleness was castigated as evil, and various laws required work as a condition of citizenship. Indentured persons were transported to the country and were to work out their contract for a specified number of years in exchange for their transportation and room and board. The European immigrants were pioneers who faced enormous challenges in the new land. The scarcity of labor and the possibility of moving farther west changed the status of workers in the colonies. Few worked for wages; most were independent workers such as farmers, artisans, and small business people. The rugged individualistic life has become an enduring theme in the American tradition. Children worked at home with their parents or were apprenticed out, in which case the master undertook full control of the child's work, education, and behavior. Boys so worked until they were 21 and girls until they were 18 or until they married. Children were "imported" from the almshouses of England, relieving the English of the expense of keeping the children while providing new workers for the colonies. The transatlantic crossing was long and arduous, and many died in transit.	The need for workers grew as industrialization developed in urban areas. Economic conditions were harsh, especially from 1819 to the Civil War. At times nearly one-third of the work force was unemployed and there was no system of unemployment insurance. Labor unions were formed, but they were ineffective in the face of a mobile work force—"Go west, young man, go west"—and small-sized businesses. There were no protections from industrial injuries or bad working conditions for men, women, or children. Hours were long and the pay was low. Religious sanctification of work—idleness was called the handiwork of the devil—provided justification for the harsh conditions and the exploitation of labor. Gone were the master/apprentice relationships of personal care and education; factory bosses had no such obligations to their employees. Slowly, some laws protecting child labor were enacted, but the enforcement was weak. In England, the New Poor Law of 1834 tightened and hardened the social response to poverty and destitution, probably because of the increased rate of taxation levied for poor relief. Coll (1966) notes that the evidence on which this major revision of the Old Elizabethan Poor Laws was based was improperly interpreted. Its pronouncements, nevertheless, influenced welfare thinking for decades in both England and America. The doctrine of "less eligibility" (that financial assistance given to the poor must be less than the lowest wage of workers) was particularly pernicious, especially as it was discovered that large proportions of the working poor themselves were not able to make it above the poverty line (a figure estimated for minimal survival). The tax rate did go down in England, but indicators of mass misery rapidly increased.	The Civil War was a stimulus to industrialization, by encouraging the trend toward urbanization and expanding the ruthless competition and exploitation that early capitalism brought. The post-war period was the era of the self-made man and of growth of large-scale organizations. A large proportion of the wealth of the nation was in the hands of a very small number of persons and families. Corruption and scandal were all too common, and even federal efforts, such as the Sherman Anti-Trust Act of 1890, were too weak to reduce the inequalities and the prevailing unfair practices. Depressions reoccurred in 5- to 20-year cycles that hit urban workers particularly hard. The unemployed had few resources to fall back on. The Freedman's Bureau had provided jobs for blacks, primarily through the construction of federally financed schools. Unemployed ex-soldiers went westward to look for work and ousted Orientals from jobs they were brought over to do. Racial tensions were fanned and violence occurred. The culture of the Plains Indians had been destroyed with the passing of the buffalo herds that whites had recklessly slaughtered by the mid-1880s. The Homestead Act of 1862 allowed farmers to purchase western Indian lands cheaply. Numerous problems—natural disasters, social and political upheavals—brought poverty to many hardworking white Americans. Even so, President Grover Cleveland vetoed a drought-relief bill in 1887 in accord with an ideology that disapproved of relief by the federal government for individual suffering. Populist political movements emerged to challenge such examples of unrelenting capitalism. Child labor grew enormously during this time. By 1900 one out of six children between the ages of 10 and 15 was employed, 40 percent in industries such as textiles and millinery. Concern over working conditions mounted rapidly.

WORK

1900–1930	1930 to present	To year 2000
By the end of World War I, the United States became one of the leading countries in the world in agriculture and industry. And it was the richest. Its wealth was due in part to the bounty of the land and to its hardworking citizens but also to a new form of organization, the large corporation. Through monopoly conditions, the corporation could amass large amounts of capital and labor, and generate great amounts of products and profits. Wealth was increased and concentrated in the very rich; large proportions of the working class were unable to manage on the wages of one worker. President Calvin Coolidge epitomized the era by observing that "the business of America is business." The government generally promoted this business orientation through protective tariffs, a Supreme Court that supported the capitalistic ideology, and the absence of an income tax—although one was eventually imposed after a constitutional amendment in 1913. Farmers fell behind in their purchasing power as the Gross National Product of the whole nation increased. Women and children worked long hours for low wages and with few safeguards. National efforts to protect them were generally unsuccessful during the early part of this period.	The Great Depression of the 1930s was a turning point in many ways for American labor. A series of laws brought into existence real protection for workers. The National Labor Relations Act of 1935 permitted elections to determine workers' bargaining agents and heard complaints of unfair labor practices. The Fair Labor Standards Act of 1938 established a minimum wage of 25 cents an hour, but, of course, prices were correspondingly low at that time, and a 44-hour work week (to be reduced to 40 hours by 1941). Unskilled industrial workers organized in the Congress of Industrial Organizations (CIO), and the craft union (AFL) continued to expand as well.	The rise of the electronic cottage (a home containing computers and other telecommunication devices) will be a major change in the workplace, particularly as traditional (smoke stack) industries in America are gradually replaced in favor of a world trade system (Toffler, 1980). New activities, barely understood at present (such as genetic engineering), will probably emerge and develop as significant parts of the new world of work. Presumably, these will use renewable resources rather than the nonrenewable ones currently employed. Many new and existing work settings will undertake new organizational arrangements such as "flextime" schedules, on-the-job training programs, and factory- or office-based day-care centers, so that a wider array of workers can participate in satisfying and remunerative activities. Married women will continue to enter the labor market in increasing numbers, but even so, there is expected to be only three working people to support every retired individual in the year 2000.
Labor unions had emerged in the late 19th century but were not effective. The American Federation of Labor (established in 1881), a union of craft workers of different types, was successful in bringing the collective force of many individual workers against the powerful organization for which they worked. There were thousands of strikes and lockouts during this period as labor and management jockeyed for the right to influence working conditions and workers' rights. By the beginning of the 20th century, the AFL had been instrumental in achieving the eight-hour day, workmen's compensation, and factory inspections, among other advances (Schlesinger, 1983).	The various emergency work relief programs of Roosevelt's New Deal administration produced mixed results. The Works Progress Administration (WPA) built fine public structures but employed relatively few workers. The Civil Works Administration and the Civilian Conservation Corp (CCC) attempted to put large numbers of persons to work on any sort of project. Some projects were less than useful, and thus did not maintain the dignity of the workers involved as they were intended to do. It was World War II that really put Americans back to work again.	
	Technological change created wholly new kinds of work that were unforeseen in earlier decades. The computer industry sprang up after World War II and has become extremely important in every facet of modern life. Another major development has been the impact of multinational organizations and the international scene in general. As other countries develop more modern industrial plants with more effective managerial arrangements, American "smoke stack" industries (steel, automobiles, etc.) are being cut down and eliminated, with predictable consequences to the large numbers of workers employed, as well as to the U.S. economy. In the face of such pressures, both labor unions and national companies are hard pressed to help their constituencies survive.	

CRIME AND JUSTICE

1600–1776	1776–1860	1860–1900
All things considered, the colonies were rough and unsafe places, especially as the diversity of people began to increase. There were at first no special places for controlling, correcting, or preventing crime and delinquency. Punishment was harsh. Confinement in public stocks, physical punishment, and fines were used for lesser offenses and capital punishment for serious crimes. Children were not separated from adults in almshouses, workhouses, or houses of correction, although the problems with this were recognized. Later, houses of refuge were established for juveniles, some who had committed crimes, others whose major "crime" was being poor.	Crime was a shadow that grew with the growing society. It was not until 1837 that Boston supplemented its watchmen and constables with paid policemen. The middle classes tended to avoid certain districts of the cities while lower-class persons struggled with rough environments.	This was the era of the robber barons, whose aggressive business practices rode roughshod over people and laws. There were few cases of the very wealthy going to jail for white collar crimes, however, even those who operated on a grand scale.
Imprisonment for even small debts was common; some offenders were put in prison for owing pennies. Debtors' positions were made even more difficult because they had to pay for their own upkeep while in prison. The Quakers of Pennsylvania had a different approach to "criminal" behavior. Instead of placing responsibility for the antisocial behavior on the individual, as did most of the other colonies, the Pennsylvania Quakers recognized the role the environment played. William Penn removed small debts as grounds for imprisonment, and he restricted the use of capital punishment to cases of murder and treason. Quaker prisons were viewed as rehabilitation units in which prisoners should meditate in silence and isolation on their evil actions.	The dual presence of increasing numbers of crimes and the growing humanitarianism led to new developments in dealing with criminals and delinquents. The Pennsylvania model prison focused on isolation and meditation as a way of rehabilitation. The Auburn, New York, model prison used congregate prison workshops in the daytime to pay some of the costs of the prisons and individual cells at night. The Auburn model came to predominate across the country, largely because it was cheaper.	Perhaps the most significant events of the last half of the 19th century in criminology concerned juvenile justice. There had long been the need to separate juveniles from adult criminals, but facilities were lacking at first. Eventually, separate quarters were built, but more than that, a new philosophy was developing. In 1869 the Elmira (New York) Reformatory began to use indeterminate sentencing whereby a person's behavior at the institution determined the length of stay there.
The most common problem among youth was running away from harsh masters. Benjamin Franklin recounts his running away from his domineering half brother and making a new life for himself in another colony. In general, the early colonies tried to avoid problems by forcibly ejecting from town persons who made trouble or who could not support themselves.	In 1841 the germinal idea of probation emerged from the personal efforts of a shoemaker, John Augustus. The virtue of trying to rehabilitate an offender outside prison made considerable headway later in the century. Juvenile corrections institutions emerged. In 1825 the New York City House of Refuge was founded. A public state reform school for boys began in 1847 in Massachusetts; one for girls, started seven years later, featured the use of cottages to house small groups of inmates. As with any organizational innovation, other states soon followed suit.	Methods to divert juveniles from the prison system also emerged. Some, such as probation, continued earlier developments. Others, such as the George Junior Republic (founded in 1895), were private attempts to socialize predelinquent youths into a socially appropriate work orientation. The Republic's plan was that youths should earn their keep by hard work, the level of luxury of life at the Republic being determined by the quality and quantity of the work they did. The Republic is still going strong (Kohlhepp, 1986).
		Another major development was the juvenile court, established after long years of effort in Chicago (1899). Going beyond simple separate court hearings for children, which had been done in Massachusetts in 1870, the juvenile court was constructed to be a noncriminal court of equity. This meant that the court itself was acting in the best interests of the child by exercising parental rights, and thus it did not need to employ the regular legal process as did the criminal courts. The court's first probation officer was a social worker recruited from Hull House.

CRIME AND JUSTICE

1900–1930	1930 to present	To year 2000
The 18th Amendment to the U.S. Constitution, passed in 1919, on the prohibition of the manufacture, sale, and distribution of alcoholic beverages, created conditions leading to large-scale law breaking in America during the post-war years. Crime organizations provided illegal liquor. Al Capone, alcohol and vice lord of Chicago, was broken only by his conviction for federal income-tax evasion, not for his many other illegal activities. Developments in juvenile courts that had begun at the end of the 19th century were further expanded in the early years of the 20th. The Chicago social experiment and its philosophy was repeated across the county.	America has had the unfortunate reputation of being a violent nation. It dates from the lawless frontier days that still get glorified in the mass media to the gang wars of the 1930s and extends to contemporary life, many aspects of which are pervaded by large criminal associations. Many times more costly but largely invisible to the average American is white collar crime. The 1986 stock market trembled at the revelations of insider stock manipulations that netted millions for the perpetrators. Crimes against person and property get the major attention from the public and the politicians. Crime in the streets and in homes is dreaded by many, especially the elderly. The myriad of programs aimed at reducing these threats, such as neighborhood crime watches, do have some impact, but the problems continue. Perhaps the unrelenting pressure to attain what is perceived as the good life, even with illegal short cuts, caused the continuation of problems. The international dimension of crime continues to grow because of the highly profitable business associated with importing illegal drugs. In spite of the pressures to get tough, to smash the criminal in the street (but rarely the crime rings that have diversified into quasi-legal enterprises while amassing enormous fortunes), the past 50 years have seen changes in criminal law that protect the rights of the accused. They also provide the poor with suitable legal defense and monitor outcomes. There has been a rise in legal assistance to the victim, but some critics suggest that it is not proportional to that for the accused. Status offenses of young persons have been decriminalized in some areas. Each modification in the retributive orientation in criminal justice in favor of rehabilitation or prevention is widely viewed as "coddling the criminal." Voters tend to respond to the slogan, especially when they or a friend have been victims of crime.	White collar crime may expand as technological opportunities for manipulation of wealth increases. Crimes against property and person are also likely to increase in urban areas as mixes of populations, more by socio-economic class than by race, begin to cause frictions and perceived needs. The next decades should see continued interest in the plight of the victim, so that changes in the justice system will not be so much reductions in justice toward criminals but increases in restitution for their victims. Private action groups, such as Mothers Against Drunk Driving (MADD) or Action on Smoking and Health (ASH) will continue to stimulate public action and legislative changes. New forms of diversion should emerge to redirect the flow of juveniles who might otherwise enter the justice system. Whether they achieve a significant portion of their goals will depend on whether the correlative problems in society—economic, educational, and social—are viewed and resolved in their ecological connectedness.

CIVIL RIGHTS AND RELIGION

1600–1776	1776–1860	1860–1900
The church and the state were not clearly separated in colonial times. Although some colonists, such as the Puritans, had come to the New World to escape religious tyranny, they often created intolerant and rigid societies and excluded dissenters. Only white males could vote or hold office, and even those rights were limited to property owners. Sometimes church attendance was compulsory, and public taxes were levied to support the church. These requirements were relaxed eventually, but the religious connection has remained strong throughout American history. Other colonies were more liberal in their interpretation of the relation between religion and the state.	The Constitution was a delicate compromise on many of the issues that divided the former colonies. White male property holders first gained the power of the franchise. Women, minorities of color, and Indians (Native Americans) were excluded from many basic civil rights. For example, women could not vote, hold title to property, establish businesses, or testify in court while their husbands had total control over the wife's property. However, women began to become involved in both the abolition of slavery and the temperance movement. A momentous national convention on women's issues held at Seneca Falls, New York, in 1848 added women's rights to these social causes. The humanitarian and Enlightenment movements, together with some religious groups, began to put together an antislavery movement, particularly in the North, where slaves were less useful than in the South. Some Northern states abolished slavery, although this did not necessarily create equality between the races in those states. Other economic and political concerns were combined with the moral issue of slavery as pressure mounted toward a civil war that even the many legislative compromises of the day could not hold back indefinitely.	New social inventions, like the juvenile court, raised difficult issues for civil libertarians. Was the removal of due process or indeterminate sentencing actually in the best interests of the child? There were numerous other assaults on civil liberties in the last half of the 19th century, such as the Jim Crow laws in the South, a new form of social bondage, that codified discrimination all over again. Women also pressed without success for the same rights of the franchise as had been given to former male slaves. Women did enter new professions such as nursing, which was permitted only because of wartime exigencies, and proved themselves capable in spite of the doubts of dominant males. Yet, in spite of these continuing forms of injustice, progress was being made with regard to the protection of individual rights. The federal government began to set limits on the state's intrusion on the rights of citizens, and began some redistribution of wealth to the poor as well. There was also a reaction against the extreme individual-centered economic structure, in favor of a growing social concern that expressed itself in religious groups (such as the Salvation Army and the Ys) that emerged to serve the poor.

CIVIL RIGHTS AND RELIGION

1900–1930	1930 to present	To year 2000
The Russian Revolution of 1917 cast an international specter and generated a "Red Scare" in America after World War I. There were many labor strikes, and the label "Red" was applied to communists, anarchists, pacifists, union organizers, and reformers indiscriminately. Attorney General A. Mitchell Palmer created the FBI and organized illegal raids, using information assembled by J. Edgar Hoover, that led to the imprisonment of some 4,000 people who were denied counsel (Norton et al, 1982, p. 659). Public reaction to these civil liberties violations led to organized attempts to monitor and promote constitutional rights. There were many fronts to monitor.	The civil rights movement has taken various forms in the past 50 years. Generally, there has been a growing activism, even militancy, on behalf of the rights presumably long guaranteed to "We the People." Blacks won their citizenship after the Civil War. They may be said to have won their personhood a hundred years later in a struggle to overcome institutional and personal racism and to attain not only a sense of personal and racial pride but also relatively equal access to most career opportunities. Many gaps remain.	Continuing headway will be gained by all types of minorities including fundamentalists seeking to preserve their valued ways of acting. Some major decisions will have to be faced in the coming decades, decisions that will determine the direction the nation takes on matters such as individual choice of sexual behaviors and the possible offspring therefrom. The increased trend in pill-protected premarital sex probably will continue, though with more selectivity, assisted by the condom, which offers some protection against AIDS. People may require evidence of freedom from AIDS to gain sexual partners.
In 1915 the Ku Klux Klan was revived—"Native, white Protestant supremacy" was their motto—intimidating their opposition to prevent "mongrelization" of the white race. By 1923 the KKK claimed 5 million members, but in 1925 it was weakened by internal scandal when a Grand Dragon (its highest leader) was convicted of kidnapping and raping his secretary. Many civil rights groups opposing the KKK also grew in strength.	Women won their voting rights about 70 years ago. The attempt to pass the Equal Rights Amendment failed, however, and they will have to continue to struggle for their personhood against institutional and personal sexism if they are to attain not only a sense of personal and gender pride but relatively equal access to career opportunities. Many gaps remain for them too, and the goals of full civil rights may be many years away.	The Constitution, it may be predicted, will prove remarkably durable in preserving the basic civil liberties, even in the face of opposing forces, but eternal vigilance remains the price of liberty as new ways of reducing civil liberties emerge. The issue of censorship of reading materials for schools will remain a problem until national standards are set, for example, because standards are usually established by local option.
There were many other challenges to civil liberties. One important case occurred in 1925 in Dayton, Tennessee, when a high school teacher, John Scopes, violated a new state law prohibiting the teaching of evolution. The trial pitted William Jennings Bryan, a three-time presidential candidate, against a group of civil liberties lawyers headed by Clarence Darrow. As a test of fundamentalist religion against modern science, it ended when Scopes was convicted and fined, but the secular forces claimed an overall victory in public opinion.	Other minorities of color, origin, and religion are nearer the beginnings of their struggles. They are taking a page from the experiences of blacks and women, and thereby may be able to move more rapidly into the light of justice and civil liberties. Their smaller numbers may make it more difficult to pressure society to take the full measure of action. Other groups, such as those who are handicapped and those who have different life-styles, are also at the beginning of their quest for full civil liberties.	Religion may be expected to remain relatively hardy in the coming decades, but with more gains for extremist sects than for mainline groups. Sects provide for emotional expression regarding alienation and stress. Because of the threat of global destruction from nuclear war or other means, we might expect more introspective meditation on the meaning of life and thus more personalized religious activity.
	Religion remains an important dimension in the lives of many Americans. Televangelism brings the power of modern communications to the aid of fundamentalist religion, and creates a whole new style of orthodoxy that has national political implications. The civil religion of contemporary democracy is a faint reflection of the earlier puritanical traditions, but occasional issues like abortion, and the election of a Roman Catholic president (John F. Kennedy), stir a religious element into the cauldron of political thought and action.	

WELFARE

1600–1776	1776–1860	1860–1900
The many and varied risks that faced the new immigrants required a spirit of cooperation. The families worked together to build each other's homes, and they opposed common perils, such as Indian raids, by collective action. The concern for the welfare of others was literally a concern for the common good of all to protect and improve everyone's quality of life because everyone's efforts were needed. The help given to the poor was no longer merely a religious duty that was of more benefit to the giver than to the receiver (Trattner, 1984). This neighborly benevolence, however, conflicted with the growing tradition of rugged individualism; neighbors had to be worthy to receive the help.	The population began to concentrate in urban areas as the new nation took shape. Institutional solutions to welfare problems, primarily through state and local governments, became commonplace. The Constitution was silent on specific federal responsibilities for social welfare other than the general statement that "Congress shall have power to lay and collect taxes, duties, imposts and excises, to pay debts and provide for the common defense and general welfare of the United States. . . ." (Article I, Section 8).	During the last half of the 19th century, Americans saw the beginnings of many major social welfare efforts, both public and private. The majority of these efforts were based on the premise of personal responsibility for one's poverty, but some saw the wider socio-cultural context as a primary cause of personal distress.
This important value conflict emerged from the English Poor Law tradition codified in the Act of 1601 (the 43d Elizabeth), and it embodied several major points: (1) There was to be public, tax-supported aid to the poor; (2) there would be local financing and administration to residents of the town or parish; (3) aid would be given differentially, direct aid to the worthy poor, the aged or the disabled, and to children too young to work, and forced work would be required for the able-bodied idle, the unworthy poor; (4) people would have responsibilities to aid their relatives as far as possible; (5) children of the poor would be apprenticed to artisans for their care and education. From the beginning of the new nation, and continuing to the present, veterans have received special aid from the whole community as grateful compensation for services rendered in wartime.	The conditions of the immigrants—among them overcrowded boats, medical problems, and the need for housing and employment—demanded attention. The first state welfare agency was the New York State Board of Commissioners of Emigration, created in 1847, to protect the immigrants and to assist them to take advantage of the opportunities to better themselves through their own efforts. History records that the great majority of them succeeded. During this time, the major instrument of public welfare was the almshouse. Services to the ever increasing numbers of poor were designed to have resident paupers do some of the necessary labors of the almshouse so as to reduce the costs of operations. Over time, almshouses deteriorated to overcrowded, mismanaged, and miserable places. Dickens portrayed the evil images that the poorhouse had in England. Similar attitudes were held by Americans.	The Freedman's Bureau was established as a response to a desperate need to aid dispossessed blacks and whites. While it came into being only after several years of petitioning, the Freedman's Bureau became a model federal agency. It was headed by Otis Howard, an effective administrator who made this the first federal welfare program that did not require residency for eligibility. It offered comprehensive family-centered community services to provide emergency relief; established medical facilities for the ill; provided supplies and jobs in the building of homes and schools; and, as its major contribution, promoted education through the support of teachers. The Bureau was terminated as being too costly and as contributing to the dependence of the recipients.
	At the same time, there was a spirit of benevolence current in America. It manifested itself in the forming of many charities, most with highly specialized, often parochial, purposes. One interesting example was the New York Society for the Prevention of Pauperism, founded in 1817 to deal with causes of poverty. Although they generally accepted the prevailing view that poverty stemmed from some defect of the person's character, these associations marked the beginning of the development of professional welfare agencies.	Veterans, but only northern soldiers, received federal aid; Confederate veterans were given whatever the impoverished Southern states could afford. This veterans' relief, and the extensive benefits arising later, were always seen as earned rights, never as public welfare. President Lincoln signed into law a program to set up military hospitals that evolved into the extensive veterans' health and welfare system.
(continued on page 76)	(continued on page 76)	(continued on page 76)

WELFARE

1900–1930	1930 to present	To year 2000
The first 20 years of the new century saw the development of some of the most powerful ideas on the nature of poverty and welfare in the history of social work. Regional or societal-scale socioeconomic causes were largely responsible for the fate of individuals whose poverty was often completely beyond their control. As knowledge from the social sciences grew, some observers began to believe that these social structures and forces could be understood and influenced so as to mitigate their destructive effects on individuals. This would promote a more nearly just society. People at the settlement houses would work for community-level changes—and beyond to the state and the nation. Jane Addams was an influential member of the pacifistic Women's International League for Peace and Freedom. Their successes and their leadership promoting other social welfare causes left a clear mark in this golden age of reform.	These were the best of times, these were the worst of times. From the days of the New Deal to the end of the Reagan administration, we have done significant searching for answers to perennial questions on how to aid the poor and disabled while stimulating the nonpoor and differently abled to be productive citizens. The initial New Deal programs dealt with a nation in crisis and represented some significant experiments in every aspect of public welfare.	The nation will be paying off its bad debts—poor health of its citizens, particularly the poor and nonwhite, inadequate education, and insufficient economic opportunities—for many years to come. The pendulum of social beneficence will swing back and forth—between a more liberal and a more conservative orientation—depending on the state of the economy, both in the nation and in the world at large. Large scale "wars on poverty" are not likely to be attempted again, at least until carefully planned model programs are tested in different contexts across the nation. These new models, it may be predicted, will be preventive and promotive in nature, sensitive to the strengths of minority peoples, to the stresses they face, and the consequent limitations they possess. As President Johnson's War on Poverty met defeat on the battlefields of Vietnam, so President Reagan's attempts to revitalize the capitalistic system of free enterprise may be scuttled by the enormous expenditures for the military and an accumulated national debt of exorbitant proportions.
The White House Conference on Dependent Children (1909) placed the problems of children on the national agenda and involved social workers as they had never been involved before. A Children's Bureau was established in 1912 over the vituperative objections of conservatives. It was the first federal entry into social services, although on a small scale. Its work influenced a variety of social efforts, including the Sheppard-Towner Act of 1921, and the Social Security Act of 1935.	The Social Security Act of 1935 and subsequent modifications represent the cornerstone of current welfare policy and practice. It contains (1) an unemployment insurance program financed by employers only; (2) an old-age and survivors insurance program that, with the addition of disability insurance, has come to be known as OASDI, the heart of "social security"—financed by worker and employer contributions; (3) various public assistance programs such as aid to the aged and the blind, which have been collected together under the title of Supplemental Security Income (SSI); and (4) various other provisions that deal with specific populations such as those concerned with the health of mothers and children, crippled children, and child welfare services. The largest of these programs was Aid to Dependent Children, which eventually became Aid to Families with Dependent Children (AFDC).	
(continued on page 77)	(continued on page 77)	

WELFARE (continued)		
1600–1776	**1776–1860**	**1860–1900**
Initially, welfare was provided by boarding the sick or the poor with families in the community who would be paid to take care of them. As the population grew, the colonies moved toward an institutional solution for these welfare concerns. The first almshouse (poor house) was established in New York City in 1657. The first orphanage appeared in New Orleans in 1729. A workhouse was constructed in Boston about 1739. The institutional solution spread rapidly, as other colonies followed the leaders. Friendly societies, specialized self-help groups, emerged as early as 1657 in Boston among Scottish immigrants. However much promise the New World held out to immigrants, there were always unmet human needs—food, shelter, work, friendship—common to large numbers of persons; and concerned citizens of every age struggled to figure out ways of meeting those needs.	Another memorable beginning was the Association for Improving the Conditions of the Poor (AICP). Established in 1843, it attempted to organize existing charities in some rational manner. The AICP also planned services for families through local male volunteers (and later, through paid agents, some of the first paid social workers). Under its director, Robert Hartley, AICP also attempted to improve social conditions that led to the problems of the poor. Even this organization, with a broad array of social services to individuals, the community at large, and other social agencies, floundered, however. It maintained a rigid view on poverty beyond its usefulness to the community. Friendly societies were developed. The Philadelphia Free African Society in 1787 became the earliest known black mutual aid organization. Religious groups like the Little Sisters of the Poor, founded in 1840, cared for the poor elderly. Special institutions for the differently abled appeared, such as an institution for the deaf in Hartford, Connecticut, in 1817, and later for the retarded, the blind, and other special groups. Day care started in 1854 in New York with the establishment of the Nursery for Children of Poor Women. As society became more complex, so emerged the specialized organizations to provide needed public welfare.	Philanthropy changed from being randomly given to being given on a more orderly planned basis. An important organization, the Charity Organization Society (COS), was founded in Buffalo, New York, in 1877. Like its predecessor, the Association for Improving the Conditions of the Poor (AICP), COS used volunteers (women as well as men) and paid workers to be friendly visitors to the poor, to detect what personal defect was the cause of their problems, and to help correct them. Relief was to be separated from the personal services. Thus a case method evolved as a way of dealing with poverty. At the same time, the settlement house movement began in America. It grew out of its English origins a decade or more earlier. Jane Addams' Hull House started in 1889 in Chicago, for example, in a house in the midst of a crowded immigrant area. Settlement houses were directed at promoting the strengths of basically healthy people, although some troubled people also sought aid. The settlements worked with an ecological unit, the neighborhood or the community, to deal with the configuration of interlocking problems and challenges. They provided education, from the kindergarten level to classes for adult immigrants, as well as art classes for all ages of people. They were involved in community-wide and state-level actions in connection with child labor issues, sanitation, and occupational safety, to name only a few of their multifaceted efforts. The settlements became training grounds for various social reformers, especially women and artists; among them was the writer Upton Sinclair, who gathered materials for his muckraking novels. Other service organizations emerged or gained stature during this period: the YMCA (1851) and the YWCA (1866); Boys Clubs (1860); the Salvation Army (1865); child protection agencies such as the New York Society for the Prevention of Cruelty to Children (1875), and the Children's Aid Societies.

WELFARE (continued)		
1900–1930	**1930 to present**	**To year 2000**
A conservative and individualistic reaction set in after the horrors of World War I. Normalcy, a focus on individualistic profit making through a strong capitalistic arrangement, returned. Suggestions of any collective solutions to common human problems—such as health insurance, child and maternal health centers, and the like—were labeled "Bolshevist" (Communistic), which made passage of such bills impossible. Even social work turned from the reforms of the settlement houses to the new forms of the Charity Organization Society, namely, the private family agency providing services for fees.	This welfare package, extended by the Great Society program of President Lyndon Johnson, reached its greatest extent in the War on Poverty. It was a multifaceted attempt to provide significant means to reduce poverty—as contrasted with merely alleviating it—through job training, education, health care, legal services, and community development with citizen participation. In fact, poverty rates for the aged did fall sharply, mainly as a result of social insurance programs. Overall, poverty rates went from 22.4 percent in 1959 to 11.1 percent in 1973 and back up to 15.2 percent in 1983, reflecting the cutbacks in various forms of welfare. President Ronald Reagan sought cutbacks as one way to strengthen the basic foundations of society—by reducing taxes and by stimulating investment so that the overall rise in productivity in the nation would ultimately benefit all citizens. His program provided a "safety net" for the "truly poor", but Reagan's critics claimed too many of the poor were falling through the holes. Poverty and misery were again on the rise as the presidential administration of George Bush began in 1989.	

THE MORE THINGS CHANGE, THE MORE THEY STAY THE SAME

History pushes us into looking for the universal or group experiences, with only an occasional excursion into the lives of specific individuals. As helping professionals you will reverse this. You will have to look at the specific Lisas, Lennys, and Alans, as well as the classes of children of which they are members. It was only when Lisa was taken to court that the mitigating circumstances of her curfew violation were recognized. Helping professionals look for the circumstances, the socio-cultural and physical contexts, of any given behavior to understand the meaning of that behavior. As anthropologists Kroeber and Kluckhohn (1952) noted, in some ways each of us is like everyone else; in other ways we are like some other persons, and in yet other ways we are like no one else—we are unique. We are like everyone else in sharing basic biological attributes, needs, and drives, and have probably been so since the days of the cave dwellers (Rensberger, 1987). We are like certain groups within the common mass of humanity because we share a limited gene pool that generates certain attributes such as color, sex, and the like, along with a common experience in growing up with others in our shared culture. But how we experience both the universal and the collective aspects of our lives and what we make of them is ours and ours alone.

Each of us reading the same history will come from that experience with different reactions and responses, just as much as people will differ in constructing that record of past human events. But helping professionals must know something about the collective and the individual aspects of any situation if they are to determine what is likely to be the most effective action. A perspective of history that best serves the helping professional is one that recognizes that interventive actions must be both individual and collective, crisis oriented and preventive, for the immediate and for the long term. Professional helping is complex; many persons must necessarily be involved in different aspects, but somewhere some integrated perspective should arise to give meaning to the whole. This is where history provides another aid, to show where we have been and what we have made out of raw materials.

We continue the stories introduced at the beginning of this chapter to see what happened. The newspaper account from 1896 says that Lisa was acquitted, and "a little purse was raised for her" by people at the courtroom. How nice. How nice of these people to bestow their charity on Lisa, who is so admirable and deserving. But nowhere is there any mention of disability insurance for the parents, medical assistance, public housing, or public welfare on a continuing basis for such a destitute family after that little purse runs out. Do you suppose if she were picked up again for breaking the curfew selling newspapers that the court would acquit her and give her another little purse? The 19th-century mind seems focused only on the individual and immediate needs. What happens about 100 years later?

The story of Lenny, Alan, and their parents is far different in many ways, as noted earlier. Juan Williams (1985) completes the story: Mr. H is a veteran who has been out of work for the past three years, even with the mechanical skills he learned in the army. The family stayed around their hometown hoping to get work but nothing was available. So they took their food-stamp money and cash and drove to another state where they heard jobs were available. But others had arrived before them and there was no work. The federal and local funds for the homeless had run out well before the year was up. Their own money ran out, but the parents tried to manage as best they could to keep the children clean and orderly. They continued to get some state welfare money, and a little help from the father's parents when they could afford it. The H family also was allowed to stay at a temporary church home until they could get on their feet. Eventually, the father did get a job through an employment agency, but he earned only the minimum wage, not enough to keep above the poverty line. Also, the residency requirement of the new state was long, and the father did not qualify yet for food stamps or other forms of welfare. And then the father was injured on his job. No sick leave or benefits were provided, so they were once again without aid. The only "good" thing that happened is that another poor family was evicted from a house owned by a parochial social service agency in town, and the H family got permission to stay in the house for several months. Nothing is mentioned about what happened to the other poor family.

The story of the H family is ably reported by Williams, who blends personal narration with societal events such as the overall poverty rates—one child in every four under six years of age lives in poverty—and the state of poverty of working heads of households—2.5 million of the 13.8 million poor children live in families where at least one person has a full-time job. The helping professional also must see each unique story as set within the context of socio-cultural and political-economic events and trends, and act so as to influence portions of them. Whole groups of helping professionals, each taking somewhat different actions, have to coordinate their efforts toward personal and social change. History is nothing but change. The question is: Who is to influence what changes occur? And that is a personal question!

APPENDIX 4.1

Books of Documents on American History

There are many sources of documents that historians use, but some have been collected conveniently in books for study by nonhistorians. Selected collections of interest to students of social work follow:

Robert H. Bremner (Ed.), *Children and Youth in America: A Documentary History.* Cambridge, Mass.: Harvard University Press, 1970–1974.

A three-volume collection of writings presented in five books by the famous and the unknown persons who make up a history of the nation. Topics covered include health, mental health, welfare, juvenile delinquency, and justice, education, and work during historic periods in American history.

Rosalyn Baxandall, Linda Gordon, and Susan Reverby (Eds.), *America's Working Women: A Documentary History—1600 to the Present.* New York: Random House, 1976.

Covers a neglected area of history, the role of working women. Divided by historical periods, one volume presents materials and commentary on work, slavery, work in the home, and the feminine mystique and reality.

Judith Papachristou (Ed.), *Women Together: A History in Documents of the Women's Movement in the United States.* New York: Knopf, 1976.

Focuses on the history of the women's movement, through its various emphases (abolition, temperance, and the vote), using historical documents and interpretative commentary.

Gerda Lerner (Ed.), *Black Women in White America: A Documentary History.* New York: Random House (Vintage Books), 1972.

From slavery to freedom, presents documents on the many issues of life in America from the perspective of black females.

Herbert Aptheker (Ed.), *A Documentary History of the Negro People in the United States*. New York and Secaucus, New Jersey: Citadel Press, 1951–1974.

Three-volume series (Volume I, from the colonial times to 1910; Volume II, 1910 to 1932; and Volume III, 1932 to 1945), dealing with all phases of life, work, slavery, resistance, and movements toward freedom.

Jonathan Katz (Ed.), *Gay American History: Lesbians and Gay Men in the U.S.A.* New York: Thomas Y. Crowell, 1976.

Emphasizes more recent times, since there are relatively few documents surviving from the beginnings of the nation. Documents present negative attitudes that straight people (and some gays as well) hold toward homosexuals and history of the discriminations against them.

OUTLINE

CHAPTER FIVE

The Profession of Social Work

The profession of social work as we know it today is a very recent phenomenon, just a little more than a century old. Yet it has undergone many changes of emphasis. They range from a rigid concern for the morality of individual clients, to assertive efforts on behalf of social reform, use of group methods, and actions affecting whole neighborhoods and communities, as well as keeping a continuing interest in individual clients. Education for this profession has grown from a six-week summer course to beginning-level practice programs—requiring the baccalaureate or BSW degree—and beyond through advanced-practice programs—the master's or MSW degree—and advanced research programs—the doctoral or PhD degree. While there has always been concern for the helping triad of prevention, treatment, and rehabilitation, the dominant concern has been in treating acute problems. Recent developments in primary prevention and work with the chronically ill may represent a fundamental restructuring of social work concerns. With all of these changes in the profession, prospective students should ask themselves whether their beliefs and values are generally congruent with contemporary social work. To be successful and happy with one's life career requires a reasonable goodness of fit between the individual and the profession.

HISTORY OF SOCIAL WORKERS IN SEARCH OF A PROFESSION

Social work, in a form that we can clearly recognize, is just about a century old. Some earlier ancestoral forms appeared another century before that. There were always people helping people, but efforts were largely by enthusiastic people without clear directions or methods for providing their help. Sometimes it helped, sometimes it did not. There were the "lady bountiful" types giving indiscriminant aid without adequate information or follow-through. There were the religious or philosophical zealots who were driven to give aid to others (whether or not they needed or wanted their kind of aid) on the grounds that the giver knew more—or "better"—than the receiver.

As complex social problems cumulated with the coming of the industrial revolution and its crowded urban areas, dangerous working conditions, poverty and sickness, crime and delinquency, to say nothing of the lack of public health and sanitation, a need arose for better ways of dealing with these problems, individually and collectively. In current terms, there was need for people-helpers with a body of systematic scientific knowledge, a set of efficacious techniques to influence human behavior, and a code of values and ethics that would guide the helpers along socially accepted and just ways. Knowledge, skills, and values regarding effective and humane ways to help others were to be integrated and conveyed to those seeking to become helpers. These basic dimensions of a profession slowly came into being in the middle of the 19th century.

The American Social Science Association (founded in 1865) discussed scientific questions related to social problems, and about a decade later some charity organization leaders who were members of the ASSA met and formed a special subgroup to discuss the particular issues related to charity. That group came to be known as the Conference of Charities and broke off from the parent group in 1879. Later, in 1884, the new group became known as the National Conference of Charities and Corrections. It published Proceedings of its annual meetings and generated a sense of a beginning profession by bringing together people who worked to help others in various ways. The emphasis was on practical applications rather than on theories and research (as in the ASSA).

At that time two fundamental developments were taking place independently. One was the development of special methods in charity organizations that became what is now casework—helping individuals adjust to their social environments and their inner demands. The early workers, known as friendly visitors (at first, volunteers working at these charity organizations, but later paid workers—men initially, later women) met with clients and tried to distribute their charity on the basis of "scientific philanthropy." It consisted of what they thought was scientific diagnosis of problems, professional skills in helping people to change, and democratic and entrepreneurial values of individual responsibility and hard work. Critics charged that the scientific basis was at that time very slender and the values were very narrow, even when the individual workers were sensitive to human difficulties.

The other major event was the beginning of the settlement houses in America, an idea borrowed from England. Educated young adults, like Jane Addams and her friends at Hull House (1889) in Chicago, rented buildings in the centers of crowded immigrant communities. There they tried to provide whatever they thought was needed—nursery schools, adult literacy courses, various forms of recreation, and job training, among other services. They later engaged in actions pointed toward social reforms in child labor, sanitation, and a variety of contemporary issues such as women's suffrage.

There was considerable tension between these two ways of dealing with human problems, from the individual perspective or from a social and community perspective. Many observers, however, saw that both were necessary aspects of the fledgling profession. It soon became apparent that training was needed for people to be effective in these kinds of helping approaches. In 1898 the New York Charity Organization organized the first school of social work, a six-week summer program. This "school" later became the Columbia University Graduate School of Social Work. Other schools of social work quickly emerged, some in connection with universities, others as independent organizations. The tension between science and the helping arts remain to this day, between wanting to incorporate empirical and conceptual knowledge in planning how to help clients as contrasted with emphasizing the individual and subjective relationship formed between worker and client as the primary basis for effecting personal change.

The social workers were very proud of their new educational programs. In 1915 they invited a noted medical educator, Dr. Abraham Flexner, to comment on their efforts. They were shocked when he concluded that social work was not a profession in the sense that medicine was since it lacked a theoretical foundation and clear transmission of methods. This led social work educators to develop such tools, for example, Mary Richmond's important text, *Social Diagnosis* (1917), which attempted to fill gaps identified by Flexner.

In 1920 a group of directors of schools of social work met to discuss ways to maintain standards among the products of these educational institutions. And so was born the Association of Training Schools of Professional Social Work (1920), which in 1952 became the Council on Social Work Education (CSWE). This organization continues to accredit schools of social work and provides a forum for educational discussions.

At about the same time, another group of professionals met (as part of the National Conference of Charities and Corrections) to discuss professional matters such as employment. This group eventually evolved into what is now the National Association of Social Workers (NASW) (1955). It combined several large specialist organizations, among them Medical Social Workers, School Social Workers, and Psychiatric Social Workers. The purpose of NASW has remained the same: to develop standards and a code of ethics, to encourage development and professional education, and to offer various services to members such as publications, annual conferences where new ideas and critical issues can be discussed, and, later, political action and lobbying.

Like any watchdog, the NASW acted to protect its members, and restricted membership to those with graduate Master of Social Work (MSW) degrees. But because many people were involved in delivering social work services, and baccalaureate (BSW) programs were emerging to provide training for those positions, the NASW elected in 1970 to expand membership to BSW graduates of programs approved by the Council on Social Work Education (CSWE). By 1974 CSWE programs had evolved into a BSW accreditation program, like the MSW one. By 1989 there were more than three times as many accredited undergraduate programs as there were graduate ones (288 to 88, as well as 51 doctoral degree–granting schools) (Rosen, Fanshel, & Lutz, 1987).

The Basic Professional Level requires an accredited BSW degree for beginning or generalist practice. Such formal social work training is distinguished from knowledge and skills obtainable in day-to-day work experience by being based on conceptual knowledge and in training in the disciplined use of self in working with clients. (This and the following three levels of professional practice are based on the NASW Standards for the Classification of Social Work Practice: Policy Statement 4, 1981).

The Specialized or Expert Professional Level requires an accredited MSW degree. Such training may be focused on micro-practice (therapy with individuals and groups) or on macro-practice (administration and planning). The former involves demonstrated mastery of at least one knowledge and skill method, as well as a general knowledge of human development in a sociocultural context. The latter involves a broad conceptual knowledge of research, administration or planning methods, and social problems.

The Independent Professional Level requires an accredited MSW degree and at least two years of post-master's experience under appropriate professional supervision. MSWs working part-time have to complete 3,000 hours of such supervised experience. This level applies both to solo practice and to practice within a social work agency. The independent professional level is certified by the Academy of Certified Social Workers (ACSW).

An Advanced Professional Level is usually indicated by a doctoral degree in social work or in a closely related social science discipline. It represents either practice involving major organizational responsibility for professional policy development and research, or it involves advanced conceptual contributions to social work knowledge.

Most states (46 of the 50) set the criteria for who may work in social service settings, and these may or may not agree with professional social work views on such matters. So, social workers are often engaged in efforts to obtain standards of licensing to prevent unqualified persons from taking sensitive positions where social services are offered. (The LCSW (licensed clinical social worker) is a state standard of competence, while the ACSW is a professionally set standard. State licensing permits social workers to receive third-party payments, which are paid to professionals by an organization on behalf of the insured client. See Standards for the Regulation of Social Work Practice, NASW, 1976, and State Comparison of Laws Regulating Social Work, NASW, 1989.)

As part of the same issue, states may declassify some civil service positions, in effect reducing the requirements for holding these positions. This, of course, dilutes the value of a professional degree, and so social workers seek to maintain quality standards, which in turn guarantee jobs for those qualified.

Thus social work as a profession is acting to ensure quality services for society through maintaining the educational standards and seeking to maintain social-service positions that require certain levels of training. Like other professions, it is open to attack as seeking to provide monopoly advantages for its members. Perhaps the ultimate question is to ask whether professionally trained individuals deliver more effective and humane services at an acceptable cost, as compared with untrained individuals (cf. Feldman, Capinger, Wodarski, 1983).

PATHS TO SOCIAL WORK: WHY WOULD ANYONE WANT TO BE A SOCIAL WORKER?

The reasons people enter the helping professions are as varied as the individuals themselves. Yet, students respond with common themes over the years when asked what brought them to this profession. Here is a sampling that blends some comments from a large number of students (all disguised):

Ann responded to a question about the factors that led her to social work as a career by noting that she was at first unsure about what to do with her life. "I considered a number of different majors, each with its good and bad points. But in the end, social work seemed to be the place for me because I am a person who loves working with people."

Betty continued this same theme by adding that in high school, "many of my friends came to me to ask for my advice. I generally found myself concerned and interested in what these people were saying about their daily lives. And I think I was helpful in many instances, but there was so much I didn't know. . . ."

Cary was in the same boat, Uncertainty, and after a short excursion as an English major, she became disenchanted with reading about life. She took off a year to work in a social agency as secretary. "This was the turning point in my life. I worked with people who honestly seemed to enjoy their work. There were always a variety of things to do. There was organization but no dull routine. The important thing for me was that social work seemed real, not made up. What the workers did had consequences in people's lives."

Don had worked in a volunteer setting during the summers. He wrote about being on a teen suicide hotline, and how deeply moved he was about the stories he heard. Some of the teenagers were runaways; others were youngsters with serious family or personal problems. Still others were kids who just wanted to give their parents a message. There were so many people with problems. What a waste of human potential, unless they could get some useful help.

Ellen had a different introduction to social work. Like many students, she herself needed some help at an earlier stage in her life. Her story was of a life-threatening illness. For others, it was violence at home, arising from an alcoholic parent or a physically or a sexually abusing parent. Several students mentioned problems such as suicide of a sibling or close friend. When Ellen was at the hospital, she and her family were "helped" by a social worker who apparently failed to understand or deal with the intensity of this difficult medical problem. Ellen vowed to become a social worker who would be caring and considerate. And indeed, she has chosen to work in the health area.

There have been many stories of poverty, of discrimination, of hardship, in which the path to social work represents an important step toward personal and social respectability, a worthwhile and honorable career. Frank's story surprised me. He had been involved in some criminal activities as a teenager, as part of a gang he went around with. He was eventually caught and taken to the police station, where his parents arrived soon thereafter. He reported feeling absolutely miserable for letting everyone in the family down, as well as being scared to death about becoming a criminal. His parents were very supportive of him through this ordeal, however, and he wanted to give to others what he had learned from his parents—a second chance.

Geraldine came to social work on the rebound. She was in the school of business (or the SOBs as they proudly described themselves), and was doing very well. She knew that she could have made lots of money, but " . . . the more I became involved in business, the more uncomfortable I felt. There was so much greed and corruption. Then, along the way, I discovered that I genuinely liked people, and I wanted a career where I could do things to help them.

I considered several other helping professions, but I didn't feel I could do enough in any profession but social work."

Hal reported that as he became aware of the depth and extent of the social problems facing the country, he looked through the college catalogs for different fields of study in which he could do something about these problems. He ended in social work because he thought it seemed most relevant to these kinds of issues. "Frankly, I didn't know then exactly what a social worker did, but I was fascinated with the ideas discussed in the social work texts and the methods they used. I also liked the idea of field training, in addition to classroom education."

Irwin's parents were social workers and so he had lots of exposure to these ideas at home. June's strong religious background made it natural that she would search for ways to help her fellow creatures. Karen's alternative lifestyle led her to seek ways of helping others who faced similar discriminations in an occupation that was tolerant of such diversity. Lenore rebelled against her (librarian) parents' demands that she go into library science. So she was making a difficult choice, but one that she felt better suited her. Mary was not clear why she was exploring social work as a career choice, but she was satisfied with getting information and facing some challenges that were forcing her to make up her mind.

It is interesting to read these remarks, the personal dramas in the lives of students. They are remarkable because of their diversity—and yet, there is a sense of similarity as well. There are many ways that a profession like social work can be "right" for a person, even though there may be many legitimate doubts along the way. Sometimes students have found their commitment all at once; at other times, students may slowly come to the decision based on many small separate experiences. Sometimes it is "right" for a student to choose another profession that better expresses the fit between his or her personality and the demands and tasks of that career choice.

GOODNESS OF FIT BETWEEN THE STUDENT AND THE PROFESSION: A CHALLENGE

For the student considering a career in social work, it is useful to compare the correspondences between the individual and the major attributes of the profession on such matters as values, actions, knowledge orientation, and the like. All things being equal, it is likely that persons who have a close fit to the profession's values and other attributes will be more inclined to enter the field, enjoy the work, and stick with it. Where there are significant discrepancies between one's values and those typically representative of the profession, the individual should consider carefully whether or not to go forward in social work. It is not that one must agree with every rule and norm of the profession. There is always room for differences of opinion. When one's personal orientation runs counter to significant portions of the profession's orientation, however, it is likely that person would encounter continual frustrations in everyday dealings with colleagues who hold different views.

In short, the following discussion is intended to produce a kind of soul searching that may lead you away from a field filled with frustrations—or en-

David Antebi

Social work is composed not only of individuals; it also involves a national organization, with state chapters, which acts to express the collective sentiments of its members. As people helpers in every aspect of social life, as lobbyists in the halls of federal or state legislatures, or as communicators in the mass media, social workers seek to manifest in their lives the values expressed in their Code of Ethics concerning "the worth, dignity, and uniqueness of all persons as well as their rights and opportunities."

courage you to enter one that fits very closely the deepest aspirations you hold. Consider carefully:

Values

The chapter on values indicates some substantive values held by social workers—such as valuing the self-determination of clients so far as possible and treatment delivered in dignity to all persons regardless of personal or social backgrounds. On an abstract level, social workers face value conflicts—such as whether it is right to put the well-being of one person ahead of the freedom of another, e.g., an abused child against the rights of privacy of the parent. Indeed, NASW's *Code of Ethics* (see Chapter 10) specifies thoroughly many of the procedural relationships and substantive goals suitable for the professional who is trying to maintain a balance between the rights of the individual client and responsibilities toward the society of which all are members. A code of ethics for radical social work such as Galper's (1974) offers another set of guidelines that emphasizes the well-being of the community or people in general over the well-being of any given member.

For the student who is coming to identify his or her own values with increasing clarity, there are decisions to be made. The predominant value orientation in social work is probably represented by the NASW *Code of Ethics,* but even it may be too liberal or too radical for some persons who hold a more conservative and individualistically-oriented perspective. For others, the Code may be too conservative, with little recognition of the need for radical social changes to provide some degree of equality and equity for all. Regardless of your personal value orientation, it is important to recognize any differences from the main stream of social work values, and whether, given such differences, a career in social work offers the best way to express them. There is much latitude within the social work profession, but it is not infinitely forgiving.

Knowledge

The knowledge base of social work is extensive. It includes human growth and development, research, and policy, as well as practice methodology and many specialized topics. But more important than the scope is the depth of knowledge required. The knowledge base of social work is highly complex, and results from interrelating many bodies of theory, research, and practice wisdom. The attribute necessary in a successful social worker is one of cognitive complexity, the capacity to integrate potentially large clusters of different portions of knowledge on demand. This is not simply a matter of intelligence; most needed is the kind of intelligence that permits and enjoys integrating complex materials toward the end of solving problems. The general hypothesis would be that those people who exhibit a high degree of cognitive complexity would be most challenged by the complexity of tasks that social work presents.

Motivations

There are several types of motivations relevant here, those related to one's immediate job, and those related to one's long-term goals in life. I would argue that some common motives people bring to social work are not vibrant enough to last them through a career, and they might therefore be better used in other pursuits. For example, if one honestly recognizes that he or she likes it when people are dependent on him or her for information or affection or whatever, then the dependence may become the chief reason for the continuing relationship rather than the real goal, healthy independence, and well-being. Likewise, when one honestly discovers that he or she likes being in control of others, then sometimes that controllingness becomes the end rather than the means toward achieving some other desired outcome. (Consider the motives of Nurse Ratchet in Kesey's *One Flew Over the Cuckoo's Nest*.) When such stuck-in-place motives emerge through routinization, this reflects being burned out rather than being professional (Gillespie, 1986).

Likewise, motives that reflect some vague long-term duty, like "helping one's fellow man," sustain only the most saintly over the long run. Such duties may be those imposed early in life before one has had the mental tools to consider one's options, and may not be sustained as worldly experiences increase. Such general motives, one might hypothesize, require substantial supports that involve more specific values and interests that recognize what growth and stimulation one receives for oneself in addition to those of helping others. One has to be able to answer for oneself the saints' litmus test: If you believe in equality, justice, and the like, why don't you give up all of your worldly goods to more nearly attain these values? (See Chapter 10 for some interesting answers to this question.)

Action

Wide varieties of actions are required of social workers, although some kinds of actions and services are more likely in one context than in another. Working with the poor, the deprecated, and the ill means to come into contact with these conditions of life and to face and take action against them. Frankly, that is not everyone's cup of tea. It is true that one can find great depths of humanity in humble situations and wonderful persons among the most despised. But can you go to those situations, interact with these people, and find meaning in your life for so doing?

Psychological Equilibrium

This point is difficult to express, but in some fashion, the social work profession needs workers who paradoxically are calm but compassionate, quiet but actively listening, stable but dynamic forces in social settings. In short, one must have one's self "together," not necessarily free of doubts and worries, but capable of putting them into perspective and dealing with them appropriately in one's own time, rather than letting personal concerns interfere with helping others. A professional helper should not come to social work or another clinical field seeking to understand his or her own problems. That is the work of therapy, not education. One will grow in self-insight as a result of thinking about the contents of social work, but it should be in the sense of promoting a more fulfilling life (partly through the service of others), not in putting mixed up pieces back together.

Therefore, for whatever quasi-professional status is to be derived from the role of social worker, for whatever modest wages are to be paid, and for whatever gratifications can be obtained by helping people who may not wish to be helped as well as those who do, the interested reader might be well advised to "go for it." But please recognize the importance of the goodness of fit between personal characteristics and the demands of the profession that are necessary to be an effective social worker—and human being.

THE FUTURE OF SOCIAL WORK AND SOCIAL SERVICES

The social services a society provides are a reflection of the political, economic, and social structures and values of the times. By all measures during the late 1980s we were in a strong retrenchment phase, if not a major reorienting phase, in the history of social work. And yet, the opportunities for constructive social services have never been greater. Consider some background to this apparent paradox.

The 1960s were a time for rediscovery—of poverty, of the political and social will to face serious social problems and attempt to resolve them. But as rapidly as social services were encouraged—by federal law (Title XX of the Social Security Act, Revised) that provided matching grants to the states to initiate needed social welfare programs—they were in effect being undermined by national involvement in costly and destructive foreign wars and ventures. In the mid-1970s and the 1980s, the political leadership and perhaps national values shifted. They returned to a traditional stance favoring individual initiative and moved away from a collective responsibility for persons excluded from the mainstream of American life, even when it was due to reasons beyond their control, such as racial discrimination, regional unemployment, and the like.

Social work has been a traditional defender of the underprivileged and the socially excluded, based on its values stance of the intrinsic worth of all individuals. As "conscience" to the nation, social work repeatedly tried to bring back concerns for human services and social welfare to the national agenda or, at least, tried to contain the reductions that presidential administrations had initiated (particularly during the Reagan era). There was ample evidence that social welfare cutbacks were producing grave hardships for many of the poor and the disadvantaged.

It would be unwise, however, to ignore what the political climates, from Presidents Nixon through Bush, were trying to accomplish. Generally speaking, it is not hard-heartedness that seeks to remove public assistance from the weak and the poor. It is rather a different vision of what constitutes help for the poor. First, there was an attempt to gain some fiscal control over welfare spending by introducing to the human services field the management approaches used successfully in industry. Such attempts at fiscal responsibility have been a perpetual challenge in the social services field from the time of the first Community Organization Societies (1880s). The more recent version in management control was combined with both an emotional exaggeration of "welfare cheating" and a philosophy that emphasizes the overall growth of the total economy as being the most fundamental aid to those at the bottom. The view is that as the whole ship (of state) rises, everyone rises with it. Thus governmental policy encouraged those who are likely to contribute to national growth, through personal incentives such as capital gains incentives, tax breaks for the wealthy, and deregulation of industries (to increase competitiveness and efficiency, so more profits may be made, which, in turn, stimulates growth of the industry).

Unfortunately, the reality has not entirely followed this scenario. In the late 1980s the rich were indeed getting much richer, and the poor were getting much poorer—all without the entire ship of state rising appreciably. World conditions and new technological events have contributed, once again, to the failure of economic schemes to provide accurate guidance to national events. This is not simply a Republican versus Democratic Party issue. Many members of both parties hold relatively conservative and relatively liberal views on how to influence the society to reach high levels of economic productivity and a strong national defense, while providing for the health, education, and welfare of its citizens. The cumulative difficulties, including enormous federal debt and trade deficits generated during the Reagan era, even when the Democrats controlled both houses of Congress, have meant a slowing down of innovative efforts to help the disadvantaged. Thus we face many difficulties, regardless of the succeeding presidential administrations.

The real challenge is to reconstruct our programs for the world not only as it is but as it can be. Recognizing the realities of limited resources, what can be done to help people help themselves? How will these changes affect social welfare and the education of social workers?

One professional response is to encourage primary prevention programs, those that seek to aid healthy individuals to prevent predictable problems, to retain their healthy functions, and to promote the achievement of desired objectives. Prevention can be much less costly than treatment, but it is not in itself an inexpensive helping service (Bloom, 1987). Moreover, while there are many preventive/promotive programs that work (Bond & Wagner, 1988), there is much yet to be learned on how to institute effective preventive programming. On the other hand, we have not integrated the preventive knowledge base into social work education effectively. Thus the profession tends to react to social problems on a pathology/treatment, rather than a proactive/ preventive, basis.

Another professional response would be to encourage self-help programs in which affected individuals and their families have banded together to provide support and encouragement to either solve the problem (as in Alcoholics Anonymous) or to live with it (as in organizations of parents with children who have certain diseases). Self-help groups have arisen partly because no other form of service was available. Their organization emphasizes their strengths, people with some special experience helping those who are just entering a situation. Very little structure or financing seems necessary. All that is needed is the enthusiasm of many volunteers who can show the newcomers the ropes that they have learned through hard experiences. It might be useful for helping professionals, however, to learn whether they have anything to contribute to such self-help groups. We should not assume—certainly the self-help group members do not assume—that helping professionals necessarily make positive contributions to their programs. We have to earn the right to be helpful—a new orientation that should be added to the curricula of schools of social work in a time of austerity.

Yet another way social work may fit into the future realities of austerity is to work with existing organizations who stand to benefit from services to their members. For example, occupational social work can make important contributions to the lives of workers, both as members of the industry or business and as members of families. But social work has to accommodate this change of perspective—both where to conduct its services and the value context in which it is employed. An educational program has to inform students of the culture and values of nontraditional work settings, as well as ways of cooperating with other professions and occupations. Social workers might become private or corporate providers to industry and business, requiring yet other changes in teaching and orientation.

Social workers should also observe the changing demographic profiles. The growth of the numbers of older citizens, for example, will mean the development of services for the aged. Some will be traditional services, but there will be some innovations as well, in which social workers might take the lead in developing effective and humane services, in both community and institutional contexts.

High interest remains in various direct-service careers such as family and marriage counseling, as well as newer developments like divorce counseling. This reflects, however, another change in traditional social work: away from working class and poor clients to those in the middle and upper middle classes who are aware of these helping services and have the money to pay for them.

TABLE 5.1   Comparison among helping professions

SOCIAL WORK (BSW, MSW, PhD/DSW)			
Populations served	**Major emphases**	**Worker roles**	**Client roles**
Individuals, families, groups, neighborhoods, communities, and society at large	Person-in-environments (configuration of target individuals within sociocultural and physical environments) Self-determination and social empowerment of oppressed groups Treatment primarily but also prevention and rehabilitation	Advocate for the powerless Broker or case manager linking resources and clients Enabler or teacher promoting client strengths Problem solver or therapist helping clients solve problems Mediator or negotiator in resolving conflicts Research Administration and planning	Client (voluntary or involuntary) or consumer

CLINICAL PSYCHOLOGY (MS, PhD)			
Individuals, families, groups	Treatment primarily but also rehabilitation and prevention	Therapist or problem-solver Diagnostic testing Research	Patient

COMMUNITY PSYCHOLOGY (MS, PhD)			
Neighborhoods and communities; society at large (populations at risk and with potential)	Prevention primarily but also treatment and rehabilitation	Enabler or teacher Advocate Research	Consumer

PSYCHIATRY (MD plus psychiatric)			
Individuals, families, groups	Treatment primarily but also prevention and rehabilitation	Therapist or problem-solver Medical treatment including the use of drugs Research	Patient

COUNSELING (BA/BS; MS; PhD)			
Individuals, families, groups	Treatment primarily but also rehabilitation and prevention	Therapist or problem-solver Diagnostic testing Aptitude testing Research	Client, consumer

There would be little need to change social work curricula in this area (marriage and the family), as it has been a staple for many years.

And finally, as a review of history reveals (Chapter 4), America has frequently applied institutional solutions to social problems. We live in a period of deinstitutionalization, however, at least with regard to some types of clients (the mentally ill primarily). We still use social institutions and policies as instruments of social control. There will probably be an increase in social control services, from detention and probation to family planning services. The social work contribution to these mechanisms of social control is to provide some degrees of freedom of choice and encouragement of human potential, a difficult task in an era of repressive law and order.

Regulation is finding its way into social work services at many junctures. For example, medical social workers have to work within the financial constraints of the DRGs (diagnostic-related groups: federal reimbursement categories) as they provide their services in hospital settings (see Chapter 12). Likewise, extensive use of the *DSM IIIR (Diagnostic and Statistical Manual,* third edition, revised, of the American Psychiatric Association) for insurance payments for care of the mentally ill imposes another kind of restraint on practice. Even accountability, however desirable it is in the abstract, is putting pressure on social workers and others to demonstrate their effectiveness and efficiency. These changing conditions present either crises or challenges to the profession, depending on one's position. As crises, they may be seen as destructive and restrictive to traditional methods of practice. As challenges, they represent the current conditions of practice with which we have to accommodate, modify where they are harmful, and benefit from when possible (as in demonstrating effectiveness).

The needs of individuals and groups continue to grow as society and the international community become more complex. But likewise, the potentials of individuals and groups also grow. Both await creative solutions and adaptations from the coming generations of social workers and other professional helpers (see Table 5.1 for a comparison of social work and several other related professions).

PART

III.

THE
HELPING
PROCESS

The chapters in this Part have two purposes. First, Chapters 6 and 7 present a generic problem-solving approach. It is composed of several steps that can be applied to a wide variety of problems and possibilities in working with individuals or groups. These steps include identifying the presenting problem, framing alternative explanations for what causal factors seem to be present, and deciding what might be done to deal with these factors. Then as some intervention is implemented, the social worker monitors both the process and the outcomes of the service so as to know when client objectives are attained and when to terminate service. Equally important are the relationships of trust and respect generated and used throughout this helping process. Indeed, it is through the rapport one gains with clients that the service aspect of the intervention is often conveyed.

Chapters 8 and 9 present specific methods of helping by means of extended case examples. Work with individuals, small groups, community organizations, and administrative social work are illustrated. Social workers employ a variety of theories of human behavior to guide their thinking about client problems and strengths. They also use a variety of theories of behavior change to guide their interventions. A number of these theories are presented throughout the book, but Chapter 9 lists them in one place (and also gives brief statements of several theories) so that students can recognize the tools they have to work with. Sketches of theories are poor substitutes for reading the primary sources, but as an introduction, these short discussions may be useful.

OUTLINE

Introduction to the Helping Process

A Case Study: A Military Family at War with Itself

The Generic Problem-Solving Approach
  Get Ready!
  Get Set! Go!

Task Functions: The Problem-Solving Sequence
  Step 1: Identify Problems and Strengths in the Client/Situation
  Step 2: Identify Alternative Theories about Causal Factors
  Step 3: Identify Goals and Objectives
  Step 4: Make Decisions and Contracts
  Step 5: Implement and Evaluate the Plan of Action
  Step 6: Change Interventions as Needed
  Step 7: Follow Up

Summary

A Generic Problem-Solving Approach—
Part I: Basic Tasks

This chapter presents a flow diagram of the helping process, along with discussions that expand each point in the diagram. At the heart of professional helping is a generic problem-solving approach that is applicable as a guide to helping in almost every context. (Recall that the beginning points in problem-solving are discussed in Chapter 2. The problem-solving process is continued in Chapter 7.)

INTRODUCTION TO THE HELPING PROCESS

Every novel or play contains some dramatic tension such as a conflict involving sex, violence, or simply a clash of ideas. This is a reflection of life itself. There is no peace this side of heaven. Life is composed of pressures and tensions, some of which are pleasurable, while others are unpleasant, sometimes to the extreme. To make one's way through life, one must learn to balance the pressures and to orchestrate the various pushes and pulls so as to attain a meaningful and satisfying life.

People present themselves to a social work agency because they have been unable by themselves to bring about that positive balance among the forces acting on them and within them. What the social worker brings to this situation is a fresh and informed perspective that sorts out the potential resources and refocuses them on the resolution of a problem and the attainment of desired ends. There is no miracle here. We use whatever is available. Sometimes the social worker is able to see strengths and resources in the person or the environment or both that the client has not been able to see or to use effectively. How this is done is the subject of this chapter.

Do not expect The Answer, a magic formula for every occasion. Rather, what this chapter contains is the distillation of a common approach used by case workers, group workers, community workers, and many other helping professionals, as an orderly and reasonable analysis of problems and strengths so as to deal with the client's concerns. The problem-solving approach fits no particular case situation perfectly, but it will be a useful beginning guide for almost every situation.

We introduced the helping process in Chapter 2 with some beginning points. In this and the following chapter, we complete the survey. Other books focus exclusively on this topic for practice-methods classes. Some of the advanced texts will be cited when the occasion calls for it, but this introductory overview is intended as a snapshot of the big picture; it covers both the helping process and the social work context in which it occurs.

A CASE STUDY: A MILITARY FAMILY AT WAR WITH ITSELF

Meet Mrs. Rogers and her family. Their life drama will be our illustration in examining the nature of the helping process. By following the events of this actual (but disguised) case, and generalizing from the ideas and actions the social worker used in helping to resolve some of the problems, we will be able to construct a generic approach to work with almost any psycho-social difficulty.

The Eastern Seaboard Family Agency serves large numbers of families from the nearby military bases. This small agency is just off a major highway that is crowded with car dealers, fast-food establishments, and "adult stores" around the edges of a large shopping mall. It is centrally located—if one has access to an automobile. A five-story brick building houses the family agency and an intriguing assortment of other United Way agencies for family planning, for sickle-cell anemia prevention and treatment, and for adult literacy, a substance abuse drop-in center, and many agencies. An elevator ride to the fourth floor reveals the history of previous passengers. Graffiti and counter-graffiti express some violent feelings for the world to see.

A week before, Mrs. Rogers rode this elevator to the fourth floor on an impulse. She was shopping in the area and saw the sign for the family agency. She came in to inquire about whether anyone would be able to help her. An intake worker obtained enough information to recognize that she did indeed have some serious troubles that she seemed unable to handle on her own. She made an appointment with a regular staff social worker for a week later. The intake worker also discussed with her the general philosophy of the agency, a task-centered form of short-term counseling with individuals and families. She also discussed fees, which were based on a sliding scale according to income. Mrs. Rogers said she understood these terms.

Mrs. Joyce Miller was reviewing the brief notes of the intake worker about Mrs. Rogers just before she and her family were due to arrive. With her were Joey, her 12-year-old son around whom the problems seemed to focus, and Lucy, her 7-year-old daughter. Mr. Rogers, a career navyman, was at sea on maneuvers. Mrs. Miller's reverie is broken by the intercom: "Mrs. Rogers to see you, Joyce."

The reception desk is immediately off the elevator, and the waiting room is just down the hall. In the waiting room are the usual utilitarian chairs and tables and a large assortment of wilting periodicals—*Time, American Baby, People*, and others. When Mrs. Miller arrives to fetch her clients, she finds Mrs. Rogers sitting on the edge of the couch with a very taciturn daughter sitting next to her, holding her hand. Mrs. Rogers is a 32-year-old black woman, very nicely dressed in a green woolen skirt and matching sweater. Lucy is wearing a white dress with a small apron and looks much older than her seven years. Joey is off in the corner of the room fidgeting with the radiator controls and looking out the window at the traffic speeding by. He is dressed in corduroy pants and a dress shirt with a tie; he looks uncomfortable and tugs occasionally at the knot around his neck.

After introducing herself to the Rogers family, the social worker invites them to come to the family room. She leads them into a large room with a homey arrangement of comfortable furniture. The walls are brightened by bold wallpaper, and there are some lemon trees in tubs in the corner. Mrs. Miller invites the Rogers to sit down, but Joey makes a beeline for the television camera on its tripod and starts to examine it. Mrs. Rogers shouts at him to "stop that and sit down." He ignores her and Mrs. Miller goes over to Joey and explains that sometimes they make video recordings of how people talk together and work at solving problems together so that they can look at themselves afterward to discover whether there are better ways of talking and solving problems. The camera is used only with the permission of the people involved. "Could we use it sometime?" Joey asks. "I'm sure we can once we get an idea of what we'll be doing here," she replies, and that seems to satisfy Joey for the time being. He returns to the couches and chairs that form a square in the center of the room.

The worker repeats her name and asks the children about their grade in school and what sorts of things they like best to do at school and at home. The children answer perfunctorily at first, but they seem to grow more relaxed as Mrs. Miller relates some similar stories about her own children, two of whom are slightly older than Joey. Mrs. Rogers sits back in her chair, crumpled over, as if exhausted. She watches with considerable interest as Mrs. Miller gets some smiles from Lucy and even has Joey asking her some questions about her sons. Then the worker turns to her and says in a warm and sincere voice that she knows Mrs. Rogers has had some problems and would she like to tell the worker about them.

Like a cork pulled from a shaken bottle, Mrs. Rogers erupts, spouting angry words, waving her hands, crying. It is all Joey's fault, she says. He never obeys. He takes things. In fact, one of the problems Mrs. Rogers had mentioned to the intake worker last week was that Joey had been caught stealing money from the locker of another student at school. And he is mean and talks back to her. All the time Mrs. Rogers is reciting about Joey's faults, he is shaking his head, making negating statements. Finally, he gets up and walks to the window and stares out as the stream of invectives continues.

The worker is a little overwhelmed by this flood of strong feelings and the events they describe. She takes advantage of a short break in the declamation, as Mrs. Rogers wipes away some tears, to sympathize with how difficult it must be to raise a family when her husband is away at sea for long periods. (This recognizes Mrs. Rogers' feelings, but does not take sides in the family dispute. It also takes the focus of the monologue away from Joey, who is getting very upset, and it leads Mrs. Rogers to an important new topic.)

Mrs. Rogers takes a deep breath, regains a bit of composure, and says, "Yes, it is difficult to raise the family almost alone." She describes her situation, more or less stuck at home, a small and uncomfortable house on the navy base. She does not get along well with her neighbors, she explains, because they are all city folk, mostly white, and they talk about trivial things all the time. Mrs. Rogers and her husband are from the rural South, and went to a local college on scholarships. They met there, soon married, and started their family. After graduation, he went into the Navy, and was away on many long tours of duty. Mrs. Rogers returned to her parents' town to raise the children. Only in the past few years had Mrs. Rogers moved the children to be with her husband—and away from her family and relatives.

Mrs. Rogers had tried to raise her children as she had done before, but it did not seem to go smoothly. When Joey was caught stealing money from school, it brought to a head a growing conflict between mother and son. He seemed to be growing unmanageable; he talked back to her and stayed out late at night with a 16-year-old neighbor whom she thought was a bad influence. Money was always a problem, and though Navy pay was regular, she always felt pressured to pay the bills near the end of the month. She had taken a job at a fast-food place nearby, and had progressed to be head cashier, a job she felt had more status and responsibility. It helped with the money, but it kept her away from the children when they returned from school. Her husband complained, another source of family conflict. Now she felt overwhelmed and out of control.

THE GENERIC PROBLEM-SOLVING APPROACH

We break off the narrative of this case for a moment, and begin to look at what is happening, with an eye toward generalizing and reaching a more generic model of problem solving. Table 6.1 summarizes the main headings of the helping process. The points made in the table are illustrated by the Rogers' case.

Get Ready!

Professional workers never walk into a helping situation cold. They have much background information that will serve them in a variety of situations. One general type of information comes from their training. They have studied the behavioral and social science literature for materials relevant to practice. They have learned how to translate this information into practice skills. And they have struggled with the value conflicts that so frequently arise in solving client problems. Knowledge, skills, and values are forged together on the anvil of professional education into an integrated professional self, which is continually renewed with new information and experiences.

A second type of information concerns knowledge of the available services in the community and outlying areas, should referral to other programs become necessary. Many larger communities develop "community services directories" that aid in learning about the network of available services. The modern welfare system is a remarkably complex entity so that workers need to devote some time to keeping everything in mind, or knowing where to find such information.

TABLE 6.1   The generic problem-solving approach

GET READY:
1. General knowledge of social behavior
   and development
2. Knowledge about systems of helping services
   in the community
3. Knowledge about one's own agency
4. Available information about the specific client

GET SET:
1. Free oneself of personal matters so far as possible
2. Mentally review the values of the helping professions
3. Get set to listen actively as a social worker

GO: on TASK FUNCTIONS and *simultaneously* . . . on RELATIONSHIPS

The problem-solving sequence:	Developing and maintaining rapport:
1. Identify the configuration of strengths and limitations of the client system (the person-in-the environment). What are the problems and what does the client want to occur?	A. Use core professional conditions of *warmth/respect, accurate empathy,* and *facilitative genuineness*
2. Identify alternative theories of behavior that describe, explain, and predict states of the configuration of client events	B. Clarify worker's and client's roles with regard to the responsibilities and contributions to the helping process, expectations regarding desired outcomes, confidentiality
3. Identify long-term goals and short-term objectives; prioritize in terms of their value and feasibility	C. Respond with sensitivity to differences between worker and client on race, gender, or other factors
4. Make decision (joint where possible) on a configural plan of action; specify a contract (written or verbal) of who does what specific action in what time frame—as guided by theories of behavior change	D. Encourage joint participation on all aspects of the problem-solving process
5. Implement and concurrently evaluate the process and outcome of the intervention	E. Continually check on client reactions to the helping process and to changes that may be occurring, especially client resistance
6. Compare the present state of the target of intervention with objectives for it so as to decide whether to continue, modify, go to a maintenance-training phase, or terminate, as appropriate	F. Introduce early the objective of eventual termination. Encourage growing autonomy and self-directed skills.
7. Conduct follow-up, after termination, to measure long-term effects of service; be prepared to offer "booster" shots as needed. Remember your professional obligation to share useful discoveries with others through publications and presentations.	G. Assist client to move from a client to that of a "graduate," one who has learned how to solve problems and who is likely to be able to deal with new challenges as they emerge.

A third type of knowledge is related to one's agency, its mission, rules, and guiding practice principles. It is important to know what one is *required* to do according to agency rules, as well as what one is *permitted* to do without violating these rules. Social workers ordinarily have a great deal of discretion, but agencies do set realistic limits and these must be honored, if one intends to continue working in these settings.

The fourth general type of background information concerns the individual client, as reported in the intake interview or in prior records. The worker gets a sense of what the intake person or prior workers thought was happening in the situation, but because of the changing times and the interpretations the other workers may have made, the present worker recognizes this background information as a beginning picture of the client, something akin to a hypothesis to be tested, not a truth to be permanently accepted.

With these GET READY points in mind, return to the case example as an illustration. Mrs. Miller had earned her MSW some ten years before, and so her general knowledge is probably condensed in scope, although certain features begin to become more prominent as she finds the need to use some parts of her training more frequently than other parts. She keeps up as much as possible with professional journals and books, and she attends conferences now and then to stay current. But she would readily admit that she would not care to sit down to a final exam in your class at this moment. On the other hand, she has had considerable experience in thinking about problems and in knowing where to look to find specific information about things she does not know. (That is the most valuable lesson to be learned from advanced education: specific facts change over time, but strategies on how to learn about something and find information about that something are always useful. Chapter 22 is devoted to the topic of information retrieval.)

Having worked for more than five years at this agency, the social worker is familiar with most of the agencies in town to which she might refer clients. She also knows what she can do and what she cannot do according to her family agency policy book, although there are some gray areas in which she uses her own discretion. Her supervisor has agreed with her on almost every gray-area choice she has made. She read the intake worker's report, but it was too brief to give more than a sketch of possible problems. (It was a "walk in" client, and the intake worker was busy with several clients at the same time.)

Even the general background information in the GET READY section is subject to personal variation, but there must be enough of this knowledge to be a working basis to be a professional helper.

Get Set! Go!

The next major section of Table 6.1 is GET SET. One must shake loose of all the distractions from one's personal life to the extent possible and get into a mental set to listen actively and single-mindedly to what the client has to say and how the client says it. It also helps to recall the major values of the profession—promoting the dignity of the individual, the health of the society, and the compatibility of personal and collective needs. These values also include the goal of helping the clients to help themselves, to assume responsibility for coping with the strengths and limitations of their situation, while seeking to make appropriate changes in the social environments to facilitate such adaptations.

In addressing the Rogers' case, the social worker has no particular conflicts in her personal affairs or with social work values. Oh, yes, her car is in the garage for what might be costly repairs, and her daughter recently wrote home from college that she met a "Mr. Right"—again. But worrisome as these are, the worker could put them out of her mind temporarily and concentrate on being professionally helpful to the client. Thus Mrs. Miller was set to GO when the call came to meet her clients. In spite of a bit of nervousness at meeting a new client, the worker appears calm, friendly, and interested—just the thing to encourage the client to reduce her nervousness at being in a strange situation.

TASK FUNCTIONS: THE PROBLEM-SOLVING SEQUENCE

The major part of Table 6.1 comprises the double columns labeled GO: ON TASK FUNCTIONS—and simultaneously—ON RELATIONSHIPS. This part of the table is constructed on the assumption that every social communication contains simultaneously a task function (trying to accomplish some objective for the speaker) and a relationship function (maintaining workable relations between the speaker and other participants).

The TASK FUNCTION column is further enclosed in a box to emphasize the integrity of this ordered sequence of steps in the problem-solving approach. It is true that problem solvers may go back to repeat steps on occasion, but there is still an order among the steps. The RELATIONSHIP column is not so ordered because relational matters can occur in any order and at any time; they are likely to be in need of renewal—"Do you trust me?"—like a daily dose of vitamin C. Notice in the RELATIONSHIP column that the worker would be well advised to discuss termination with the client very early in the contact (more details on this shortly).

The most important point to understand about Table 6.1 is that it is an *orienting table*, giving an overview of the entire problem-solving process.

The most difficult part of the GO section might appear to be the *simultaneous* directive: Deal with some task problem at the same time one attempts to sustain a good relationship with the client. Actually, this is not a difficult combination to attain. Simply remember that every step of the problem-solving sequence has to be accomplished in a relationship with the client. Most of the time, these relationships will be rational, open, and constructive. However, there may be times when confrontation and conflict will be involved. For example, the *simultaneous* part of Table 6.1 begins with the TASK instructions to identify problems and strengths while at the same time relating in an empathic, warm, and genuine manner that will encourage client participation in the helping process and the other considerations involving RELATIONSHIP. To get into the process of problem solving, the worker will need to activate first one and then another of these task and relationship considerations as the situation demands. Much of the time developing a good relationship will simply involve active listening with empathy, warmth, and genuineness. At other times it will involve discussing some procedural matters like the role

Professional helping at every level of social work enterprise begins in the dual obligation to help solve some problem while at the same time maintaining a trusting relationship through which to help the client solve his or her problems. Whether it is through play therapy or street drama, individual efforts or collective actions, every professional service combines task and relationship functions.

expectations of both client and worker. What Table 6.1 offers is a basic outline of beginning considerations of relationship in connection with the problem-solving steps.

Consider again the Rogers case to illustrate this point. To begin to understand the Rogers family's problems and strengths, the worker has to establish a working relationship with the clients. As the worker shows interest in these people, as she asks them questions in a warm, empathic manner, she is also demonstrating her role and what she expects from the clients as well. If she felt that their racial difference seemed to make a difference to the client (or herself), the worker would be likely to raise that point as part of the discussion, another consideration of relationship. So any one statement or gesture may serve a variety of task and relationship functions. Or, to put it another way, any task action also requires some consideration of the relationships involved as client and worker strive to complete that activity.

Examine the events in the Rogers case in relation to the GO section of Table 6.1. We have already seen how the worker tried to build up a sense of trust with the children. She asked simple questions about themselves and reported some personal anecdotes about her own children. This also established her as a sensitive person with Mrs. Rogers and as a person who shared such attributes as being a working mother with early teenage children. But in the course of establishing a relationship, the worker also gained information about the family and the individuals who composed it because these are the ingredients that will likely make up a major part of the problems and the resources to be used in resolving the problem. A detailed explanation of the seven steps in the problem-solving sequence follows:

Step 1: Identify Problems and Strengths in the Client/Situation

How should the worker identify the problems and strengths of the clients and the environments in which they live? There are an infinite number of ways of doing this, and there is no absolute right way. However, there are probably many wrong ways. The important point to notice is that Mrs. Miller did not ask a long list of structured questions. She let the conversation flow naturally, with occasional probes to stimulate needed information. In effect, the worker was mentally ticking off relevant factors about the mother's life configuration: first, about some personal characteristics, then about interactions with her children and her husband. She later broadened the discussion to the neighbors and to her extended family; and finally, she explored some issues related to the children's schools and to the mother's job and her husband's position in the Navy.

The social worker's questions appear to flow naturally and they did, but they were systematic in the sense of filling in information from the relevant systems and subsystems of the configural model (Figure 1.1). Sometimes there were many facts related to a given system, and the worker would encourage the mother to continue until some sense of closure emerged. Other times, it may have seemed as if there were no resources coming from some quarters, such as when Mrs. Rogers could not find anything constructive to say about her neighbors, although when pressed to think about it, she smiled and said that the woman next door did loan her a car to come to this appointment when her own would not start. Sometimes it takes effort and persistence to find sources of support in some areas of the psycho-social map. To ask about these topics at random is to risk overlooking something that may be important. Mrs. Miller did not have to ask any formulaic questions at all. She simply set the client off to tell her own story and quite naturally many pieces of her life configuration were mentioned.

Clients feel themselves embedded in multiple systems even though they are blessedly free of the professional's jargon. But a client may omit some factor too embarrassing to tell to a stranger or because it is "too unimportant," whereas the worker can see from another perspective how these omitted elements might be very influential. Having a framework for a systems check is very helpful, but it is not to be used mechanically. It tells the worker what categories to explore; it does not say how much information may be present in any given category. To get this information requires a good working relationship—again reinforcing the simultaneity of TASK and RELATIONSHIP functions.

Viewed as a whole, the Rogers case illustrates the fact of life that there is a configuration of forces and structures, some positive, some negative, operating in the lives of everyone. But it is also clear that these factors are of uneven size and importance in reference to the problems facing the family. How are we to make sense of this array of factors?

Step 2: Identify Alternative Theories about Causal Factors

This question leads to the second step of the problem-solving sequence in Table 6.1, which seeks to identify alternative theories (and supporting empirical generalizations) that describe, explain, and predict something about the configuration of events surrounding the client. If the worker were to decide that Joey's behaviors were the critical problem, then she might wish to consider the theories and research relevant to changing behaviors. If the worker thought that the problems were essentially reflections of the family dynamics, then she might want to consider theories that guided actions in family therapy. Sometimes there may be several foci of interest in a given client situation, and so several theories might be employed, which requires that their coordination be worked out. (Chapter 9 describes briefly a dozen basic theories to get the reader started in having some conceptual guides to practice.)

To return to the case illustration, the worker notes that Mrs. Rogers is having a difficult time controlling Joey. This may be caused by any number of factors, from lack of parenting skills regarding a teenage boy who is pushing for more autonomy to some unidentified, perhaps unconscious, conflicts emerging in the dynamics of the family. There is no way to know the causes of any particular human event unequivocally, so the worker makes some tentative best guesses by considering theories that purport to describe and explain general patterns of human behavior. Let us say, for example, that the worker thinks the lack of parenting skills idea accounts for a large number of the known factors in this case: Mrs. Rogers is away from her husband and parents who might offer advice on child rearing; she is not on good terms with neighbors either. She seems to use yelling as a method of control, and appears insensitive to Joey's feelings or point of view.

Step 2 merely identifies what appears to be the best conceptual explanation for the known set of client events. It does not tell the worker what to do about these events. That is the business of *theories of behavior change*, which we will discuss in Step 4. Notice that more than one theory may be useful in our understanding. For example, it might also be the case that Joey is the scapegoat for problems that are part of the family system. He may be acting unconsciously in ways to gain more attention from his parents who are fighting over the demands of their jobs and the family needs (Minuchin, 1974). This explanation also seems to account for many of the known facts, but because it assumes unconscious conflicts, a concept difficult to verify in empirical research, the worker may choose to give priority to the other explanation, at least initially. Theories are neither right nor wrong, true or false; they are simply guides to thinking about how pieces of the human configuration are fitting together.

Step 3: Identify Goals and Objectives

The third step in the problem-solving process concerns *identifying long-term goals* and the *short-term objectives* that will act as stepping stones to those goals. A client's goals and objectives often belong to the realm of wishes and dreams; some are realistic, others border on the impossible. But this is often why the client has come for assistance, to sort out goals and objectives and to obtain help in achieving some of them. So we begin with the client's dreams and wishes.

Any objective will have repercussions on other people, however. The worker is obliged to consider the effects attaining the client's goals and objectives will have on others. The worker again does a systems check to anticipate the effects of the client's fulfilled wish (or value) on members of the family, peers, co-workers, and the like. For example, if the mother's wish for a more compliant son were granted, what would this do to the boy's chances for learning how to become an independent adult? Particularly when financial support by the government is involved, the worker must consider the community's and the society's values.

The implication of considering multiple value perspectives is that some negotiation in problem solving seems inevitable. The client generally views the matter from his or her own point of view; the worker is obliged to reflect the perspectives of others, should the client's desired changes come to pass. Change may be needed for all of the individuals and systems involved. Of course, it is easier to change individuals than systems (like the school system or the Navy), but sometimes one must seek to change those systems because they may be the basic cause of the problems, not merely for one client but for many people.

Mrs. Rogers is not very clear about her goals—"I just want to have peace in the family and have my children grow up to be good people." The worker will have to help her clarify what "peace in the family" means to her, and what "good people" means. When pressed, Mrs. Rogers explains that she wants her children to keep out of trouble with the law—she seems to be thinking of Joey's recent stealing incident and what might follow from that. Also, she does not want to always be arguing with her husband about money or Joey's problems. She wistfully recalls the days when the children were younger and she could ask her parents how to handle a small incident on the spot. She wonders whether their family life would be a great deal better if Mr. Rogers were home more of the time. But, shaking her head sadly, she recognizes that as long as he is in the military, they are likely to have periods of extended separations.

All of this conversation makes sense, but the worker feels uneasy about directions. Toward what goals should the family be working? What specific objectives should come first? As she listens to Mrs. Rogers talk, the worker comes to realize that part of the difficulty in establishing family goals and objectives is that Mr. Rogers' views are necessary for a complete picture to emerge, and he was not due to return for some months. So the worker shifts to some more immediate objectives around crisis problems, putting off discussion of long-range goals until Mr. Rogers returns. Mrs. Rogers decides that the most pressing concern to her is the fact that Joey has stolen money at school. She wants to stop this behavior. The social worker aids Mrs. Rogers to expand on this objective to include understanding the causes of this type of behavior.

The social worker then presents a small scenario: "If we want to understand why Joey took the money from the other student's locker, we have to try to understand that situation at school from his perspective. Then, if we can understand why he felt he had to steal, we might be able to take some steps to change those reasons so he doesn't have to do it again." Mrs. Rogers nods that this is a reasonable approach. Mrs. Miller notes that Joey is very attentive and is nodding approval, too. Note that what the worker has done is to work backward from some known event (the theft) to antecedent events until it becomes possible to make some changes in the antecedents that might prevent another incident like the theft.

The social worker turns to Joey and asks him in a calm but warm manner what was going on in his mind when he took the money from the student's locker. Joey gulps, looks down, and says it was because he needed some money and he never gets any at home. Mrs. Rogers interrupts and says, "That's not true. I do too give you money." And Joey yells at her, "No, you don't." Mrs. Rogers speaks in an angry tone to Mrs. Miller: "See, see, how he is?" And she begins to cry. Lucy looks with fearful concern at her mother and holds on to her hand more tightly, but Mrs. Rogers pulls free so as to wipe her eyes.

The social worker senses the high tension, but does not diffuse it. She says calmly that yelling back and forth doesn't seem to get to the bottom of things. (She is aware that both mother and son seem to be engaged in an immature shouting match, which has to be broken into if they are to get anywhere. Note that the worker is in effect engaging in counseling at this point, not to solve problems as such but to enable the clients to clarify what it is they want to work on.) Mrs. Miller then asks Mrs. Rogers whether Joey gets a regular allowance. She responds that he is supposed to, but sometimes she doesn't have the money, especially near the end of the month. Joey says that he doesn't get his allowance most of the time. Lucy speaks up, very hesitantly, that she doesn't get her allowance either. There is a very long silence. (The worker does not rush to break the silence; great pressure is building up on the Rogers family.)

Mrs. Rogers speaks first. She speaks very quietly, as if she were talking aloud as she thinks: "Can it be that Joey took that money just because I didn't give him his allowance?" Mrs. Miller then says that this may be one factor, but perhaps there are others as well. The important thing is that the matter of allowances represents a clear objective for some family problem solving. Joey shakes his head in agreement, but even he seems stunned by the insight his mother has had. "I tried to tell you that, I did try," he says, tearfully. Mrs. Rogers reaches across the couch and puts her hand on Joey's arm, but is unable to say any words.

Mrs. Miller asks about how Mrs. Rogers budgets the family income. Mrs. Rogers admits that she does not have any particular system. She is good with figures but tends to buy things on impulse, and so sometimes there's only enough money for the bare essentials. Mrs. Miller suggests that perhaps talking about budgeting money might be helpful in general, but also to provide some assurance to the children that they will get a regular allowance. The social worker goes on to say that this is an element in the growing autonomy that children need, and Mrs. Rogers nods in agreement, but says that sometimes she just feels like she has to have something; it makes her feel better when she's feeling blue. Then she laughs and says, "It's better than drinking, like some wives do." Mrs. Miller nods in agreement.

TABLE 6.2   Comparison of the probabilities and values related to a given course of action, from the point of view of one actor

Value attached to a given action	Probability of outcome (Joey's good behavior) of a given action, from the point of view of Mrs. Rogers		
	HIGH	MID	LOW
POSITIVE	Giving Joey regular allowance		Talking to Joey about values
NEUTRAL			
NEGATIVE			Punishing Joey for each new violation

Let us examine the two factors related to Joey as short-term objectives: the problem of not having regular allowances and the problem of budgeting the family income in the face of impulsive buying habits that are used to deaden the mother's feelings of unhappiness. Regarding the allowance question, the worker wonders whether Mrs. Rogers can face Joey's (and Lucy's) growing independence represented by having money of their own to spend at their discretion. The other question of allocating only a few dollars in advance seems like a small task, unless it is part of a larger problem such as the state of finances in the family.

The value implications of the allowance issue involve Joey's growing independence and Mrs. Rogers' sense of control over her son. She values both, but they appear contradictory in this instance. Giving the allowance on an irregular basis is like a compromise, pleasing neither party. Facing the values involved might help Mrs. Rogers to clarify which has priority. Let's say that Mrs. Rogers admits that she would like to retain control over her son, but recognizes that it is far more desirable to let him grow up, even if this entails his making some mistakes along the way.

Regardless of the value preferences, there is the additional and joint consideration of how probable it is that any given solution will result in one's desired outcomes. If allowance were given regularly, would this indeed eliminate Joey's future thefts? Or if Mrs. Rogers could maintain firm control over her son by punishing each new violation, would this stave off more delinquencies? What about talking with Joey about basic values (Kohlberg, 1983)? No one can say for certain, but the worker guesses that giving an allowance that permits graduated steps into teenage independence might be more likely to lead to nondelinquent behavior than tighter controls by the mother. (See Table 6.2.)

If these guesses as to the probability of outcome for given paths of action are combined with the relative weighting of the values attached to each path, then we have the basis for making a choice in terms of priorities in short-term objectives. In this case example, the choice is easy because both values and pragmatics favor the provision of regular allowance as a more likely as well as more valued way of achieving the objective of no further theft. It is no guarantee because other factors probably influenced such an action in the past.

We considered here only a portion of this case for illustrative purposes. In the actual case, the worker discussed her approach to dealing with objectives on a short-term, task-centered focus. She recognized that the Rogers could handle these plans once they gained some skills in doing so, and the brief series of meetings also kept the service fees low. The actual case dealt with several objectives over a specified three-month period, with the possibility of renegotiating for some other issues that emerged along the way. (We will return to the Rogers in the next chapter.)

Step 4: Make Decisions and Contracts

The next step in the problem-solving sequence involves making mutual decisions about what to do regarding specific objectives, and putting this understanding into a written or verbal contract. This step is a relatively recent addition to the traditional problem-solving sequence; it is based on a conceptual model and supporting empirical findings that clients who are clear about who is to do what, when, and where are more likely to perform these behaviors correctly (Reid, 1985; Fortune, 1985; Meichenbaum, 1977; Schinke, Gilchrest, & Small, 1979; Epstein, 1988).

As to the mutual decision making, the worker can probably sense the degree of agreement present, and put this feeling into words to the effect that "I sense that we agree that we should work on arrangements to give Joey and Lucy allowances regularly." If this sense of agreement is not strong and clear, the worker might be wise to ask, "Where are we now with regard to what objective is to be our top priority to achieve?"

Notice that the decision has to be mutual. If the worker were to choose the objective apart from the client, there would likely be little client motivation to work on the practitioner's objective, however much the client might say it is a good idea. But also, if the worker does not agree with a client's objective— perhaps it violates the worker's sense of values, or agency policy, or society's laws—then the worker as a professional cannot be a party to that objective.

Assuming that a mutual decision has been reached, then the social worker is to present the contract, verbally or in written form. The following summary of steps for developing a contract is derived from the work of Reid and Epstein (1972) and their colleagues. First, the client is motivated to select some objective to be worked on. Then, the tasks involved in accomplishing that objective are specified in the client's own words as a sequence of behaviors that the client is able to perform:

1. Who?
2. Does What? (Make sure the client understands and can actually perform the steps required.)
3. With Whom?
4. Where?
5. When?
6. Under what circumstances? (This includes the frequency, intensity, and duration of the actions.)
7. Given what socio-cultural and physical contexts? (assuming that these contexts may make a difference in what is to be done)

8. How will you know when the action has been done as intended? (This is an evaluation question that is discussed in Chapter 23.)

The worker also anticipates possible barriers to the client's implementing the task and attempts to find ways to minimize any barriers. Then the client and worker practice performing these steps (with the worker providing corrective feedback as needed) so that the client will feel more comfortable and knowledgeable when he or she actually performs it. Finally, the worker summarizes what has been covered, which should both motivate and provide a brief checklist for the whole set of activities. (Sometimes a checklist is written out for the client's benefit.)

In the Rogers case, the worker believes the motivation is high on everyone's part to work on the problems, and they seem receptive to her encouraging comments that these problems can be resolved. Then she goes to the second step where she discusses the "Who?" "Does what?" details. She talks out the steps with the family and writes down notes as she talks—these notes will be copied so that both family members and the social worker have copies. Who does what to whom? Mrs. Rogers will give Joey and Lucy their agreed upon allowances. Where and when? Saturday morning at the desk in the living room where Mrs. Rogers keeps the financial papers. Under what circumstances? Each Saturday will be an allowance day, with money set aside initially from the family paychecks at the beginning of the month. The children will be allowed to spend their money on anything they want up to a given amount ($2.00 for Joey; $.50 for Lucy). If they want something that costs more than that, they must consult with a parent to permit a purchase. (Mrs. Rogers requests this restriction; she still is not able to give up some control over the children, but neither child sees this as a problem. The social worker anticipates this will change relatively soon.)

There is a special clause for Joey regarding receiving allowance. Joey is not permitted to take any money unlawfully. At his request, the contract is amended to permit him to earn money at part-time jobs. Mrs. Rogers is surprised at his even thinking about earning money—"he's so young." But she concedes to the amendment. If on special occasions he needs more money than he gets in allowance, he is to discuss this with a parent. This ties Joey's allowance to other behaviors, and thus becomes a parenting tool. How will they know if this behavior occurs? Joey will construct a chart that indicates the dates and how much allowance he and his sister get. Parent and child are to initial the chart as public confirmation of giving/getting allowance. With regard to theft, the parents will have to rely on the school authorities.

This may seem like a lot of work just to get an allowance, and this may in fact be a problem that could be a barrier. But the irregularity of allowances and the unclarity of when it was bestowed suggest that this degree of specification is necessary until the process gets routinized. The practice step involves both allocating money to the children at the beginning of the month, and then signing off on the chart to indicate that the allowance has been delivered. Once these practice steps have been completed, the worker compliments the family members and tries to put this whole process into perspective: "We are making these detailed arrangements about allowances for the children so as to eliminate one possible factor that may be influencing Joey to get into trouble at school. This is not the only thing we have to work on, but it is something that we can start with as we try to work together on some of the other concerns you all may have."

There is another important body of information that the worker is using at this point: theories of behavior change. In contrast to the theories used earlier (in Step 2) that offered descriptions and explanations about certain behaviors, the theories of behavior change involve how and why certain interventive actions are supposed to produce specific changes in the behaviors or circumstances of the clients and their environments or both. The positive reinforcement concept from behavioral theory, for example, proposes that people will tend to repeat some specific behavior if the consequences are perceived to be desirable. Thus this theory of behavior change directs us to arrange for, or to deliver some consequence after, the specified behavior that is perceived by the recipient as desirable. This specific behavior change principle is stated at an abstract level. The worker has to learn what is considered as desirable by a given client in specific contexts—not everyone finds the same things rewarding, even from one time to the next.

Assume that the social worker was using this principle of behavior change (positive reinforcement) as the underlying rationale for having the mother give regular allowances. In effect, the allowance Joey gets is dependent on his not getting into trouble at school. This idea of "not getting into trouble" is expressed in a negative way, but it is clear to both parent and child. Note that the theory of behavior used in thinking about the theft and the allowance involves a developmental notion concerning growing independence, while the theory of behavior change involves positive reinforcements of desired behaviors. They are different but they also are compatible. (If the worker had used a theory of behavior that employed unconscious conflicts, and then used a theory of behavior change that involved behavioral reinforcements for conscious behaviors, some conceptual gaps might have arisen in the reasoning when one thinks about the unconscious conflicts and then uses consciously controlled behaviors.)

Step 5: Implement and Evaluate the Plan of Action

Notice in Step 5 that the worker is directed both to implement the plan of action (the behavior changes outlined in the contract) and to evaluate objectively what changes occur in the client's situation after the intervention is in place. This is no accident: scientific practice is evaluated practice. Not to evaluate objectively what a practitioner is doing is like flying blind. There is a strong tendency to interpret positive changes as being due to the worker's efforts and to overlook negative changes. That may be in accord with human nature, but it is destructive to building a sound helping profession. The profession requires objective evidence about what works under what conditions.

The implementation of a plan of action involves a set of factors. From a configural perspective, the worker has to orchestrate the positive forces that are moving a client toward an acceptable objective while decreasing or neutralizing the negative forces or barriers that prevent the client from attaining the objective. Matters get complicated when a given activity that might result in

TABLE 6.3   Comparison of the probable effects of one planned action on one party for other parties involved

Probable effects on targeted client	Probable effects on other parties (mother, sister, father, school situation, law agents)		
	POSITIVE	NEUTRAL	NEGATIVE
POSITIVE (Joey getting regular allowance)	Promotes sister's development to independence; may reduce stealing at school and contact with law enforcement agencies	No effect on father	Mother loses some measure of control
NEUTRAL (Mother discusses values with Joey)	Mother feels more in control	No effect on school as such	Children may feel more pressure on them
NEGATIVE (Mother punishes Joey for each new violation)	Mother feels more in control	More thefts at school or elsewhere	Joey may become hardened in stealing; Lucy may become more fearful of independence

desired outcomes for the client produces undesired outcomes for relevant others. The worker's orchestration has to concern the whole configuration: client, relevant primary and secondary groups, as well as salient aspects of the physical and socio-cultural environments. (See Table 6.3)

Mrs. Rogers has to change, for example, how she allocates the monthly income checks into fixed categories, such as rent, payment charges, insurance, and the like. She now is to add children's allowances as a fixed category. The main effect of this change is on the family, giving the children more flexibility and independence. There may be an effect on the school, reducing the likelihood of future theft and making it easier for Joey to keep in good graces at school. But notice the possibility that giving Joey, in particular, more independence might produce some negative consequences as he tries out the limits of his new freedom. It might also have a negative effect on reducing the mothering function Mrs. Rogers has long served, and which she may see as tied up with her feelings about herself as an effective adult. The worker may be willing to take the risk of these latter negative outcomes. She may even provide anticipatory counseling about these effects because on balance, and with continuing watchfulness, this set of decisions (budgeting and regular allowances) seems like the optimal combination of actions.

Is it? Rather than just assume it will be successful, let us measure what we mean by success on this given target of intervention. Note that we are measuring outcomes—a complete cessation of behavioral problems at school and no new problems at home. We might observe whether the intervention—having the mother and children indicate on a public chart whether or not she provided the allowances regularly—has been done as promised. This is a measure of interventive effort, not of the ultimate outcome. But theft is a rare occurrence, and so it might be worthwhile to monitor in an ongoing way some other behaviors that might be indicators of possible problems; for example, it may be that the number of yelling arguments between mother and son might be positively affected by a regular allowance that removes the need for many such arguments. If this is the case, then the worker might aid the mother and son to monitor their yelling arguments as well as reported thefts from the school (or elsewhere). If the arguments do not abate, or even get worse, after several weeks of trying the new approach, this might be a signal to reconsider what has been tried. One of the presumed indicators of the problematic configuration of events is not changing according to expectation. Chapter 23 presents the steps in evaluations of the worker's own practice during the time it is occurring in field conditions.

Step 6: Change Interventions as Needed

The Rogers continued in treatment with Mrs. Miller for more than two months before Mr. Rogers returned from naval maneuvers. During this period, Mrs. Rogers had provided allowances for the children on a regular weekly basis. There was a reduction in the number of yelling arguments between mother and son, Mrs. Rogers reported from notations she made on her calendar following the social worker's suggestion. This was quite remarkable she thought, given the level and regularity of their fights before they went to the agency. Mrs. Miller noted both of these changes on charts she was keeping from their weekly meetings. Moreover, there were no reports of any school-related problems. So the social worker had to consider whether to continue work on the budgeting/allowance objectives, or to turn their attention to other matters.

In general, the worker has to decide whether to continue the intervention as before, whether to modify it (up or down), or whether to go into a maintenance phase (teaching the client new skills to maintain the attained level of success), or simply to terminate. The decision depends in part on the initial objectives, but it also depends on the context in which the actual events have occurred. There may be differences from what was originally anticipated, thus changing the meaning of changes in the target behaviors. (If, for instance, the 16-year-old boy who Mrs. Rogers thinks of as a bad influence on Joey involves him in drinking beer the youth obtained from his parents' supply, then the allowance factor may become irrelevant.) Mrs. Miller decided to move into a maintenance phase by discussing how the Rogers could continue their success in budgeting and providing regular allowances. A monthly budget allocation book was constructed and this proved successful in reminding Mrs. Rogers to provide the month's worth of allowances for the children. After this method seemed to be going well, everyone agreed to terminate discussions on that objective. They also agreed to turn their attention to some other difficult issues.

Step 7: Follow Up

Looking only at the budget/allowance objectives, let's say that there is a mutual decision to terminate services. What remains is to conduct a follow-up contact (or contacts) with the clients, both to assess the long-term staying power of the changes that have occurred in the family and to provide "booster shots" as needed. The very understanding that the worker will be calling on the clients every once in a while as a friendly check to see how things are going may help the clients to rehearse what they have learned so as to be ready for that call. A brief chat might also bring up recollections of that learning, another benefit. And if new problems arise, the worker might suggest how the old skills can be applied to the new situation, or the clients can be invited back to the agency for some further work.

Everything went smoothly on budgeting and allowances in the Rogers case. The problem was quite specific and the solution was relatively simple. At the same time, arguments between mother and son were reduced at home, and there were no incidents at school. But as the time grew near when Mr. Rogers was to return, Mrs. Rogers reported an increase in tensions in her family. Mrs. Miller wondered what was going to happen when Mr. Rogers came home. She reminded Mrs. Rogers of how the family had worked together to solve one problem, and she felt confident that they could resolve the remaining ones too. Mrs. Rogers smiled weakly, and Mrs. Miller wondered what was behind that ambivalent expression.

SUMMARY

Chapter 6 has introduced one of two basic aspects of social work practice—dealing with the tasks necessary to attain some objective or resolve some problem. As we will see in the following chapter, we must also engage clients in a trusting relationship to the greatest extent possible, at the very same time we are addressing task issues.

There is a logic inherent in dealing with tasks that is applicable to almost every kind of social psychological problem or objective you might encounter. These problem-solving steps direct us to define the problems or objectives, to identify what factors are influencing them, to decide what plan of action we can feasibly and ethically perform that has a chance of attaining the client's goals. We are further directed to implement these plans and to evaluate concurrently whether or not events are changing with reference to desired outcomes. This feedback influences decisions on continuation, modification, or termination of the intervention. Post-service follow-up informs us of the staying power of the outcome.

These simple steps are powerful tools in problem solving. To connect these general statements with the particulars of a given case situation requires much practice and experience. But everyone begins with these same basic steps.

OUTLINE

Relationship Considerations

Summary

CHAPTER SEVEN

A Generic Problem-Solving Approach—
Part II: Basic Relationships

This chapter continues the discussion of the generic problem-solving approach begun in Chapter 2 (starting points) and continued in greater depth in Chapter 6 (task functions). The present chapter focuses on relationships with clients that go on continuously while tasks are being addressed. The new worker has to learn to balance efforts directed toward maintaining a good rapport with the client while at the same time working on resolving problems. It is not difficult. It does take practice.

RELATIONSHIP CONSIDERATIONS

The second major part of the GO section of Table 6.1 on page 105, involves relationships between the worker and the client. While there is some natural ordering among the seven items listed there, considerations of relationship can take place at almost any time. For example, rapport building efforts naturally come very early in the helping process, but they may be brought up repeatedly over the course of the entire association. Moreover, it may be very useful to begin considering termination from the very start, especially if one is involved with time-limited types of therapy. This wonderfully focuses the mind on the tasks at hand, and it sets up an expectation that the client is going to be able to resolve the problem and continue on his or her own in some relatively short period of time. Let us examine these seven considerations regarding relationship.

Factor A: Core Professional Conditions of Warmth/Respect, Accurate Empathy, and Facilitative Genuineness

As discussed in Chapter 2, there is considerable evidence, both from research and from clinical experience, that these three core professional conditions greatly facilitate the helping process (cf. Ivey & Authier, 1978; Meador and Rogers, 1984, but also see Barber (1988) to the contrary). As a brief review of that discussion, please recall the following:

The core professional conditions are roughly equivalent to the basic acting instructions for a beginning actor. They instruct one in how to position oneself physically vis-à-vis the client—namely, a culturally-defined polite conversational distance, about three to six feet apart. They teach one how to communicate nonverbally one's interest and compassion—by such gestures as leaning forward slightly, maintaining a good but relaxed eye contact, and by removing interferences to attention, such as playing with a pencil, smoking, or other distractions. And the core professional conditions provide the fundamental ground rules of talking with clients—be aware and reflect back your understanding of the client's thoughts and feelings regarding the problems and potential solutions he or she is discussing. (See Table 2.2, in Chapter 2, for a summary of how one can perform the core professional conditions.) Performing basic "acting instructions" will not make you into a great actor. But not performing them will almost certainly destroy whatever good you could have done for your client.

In the Rogers case, Mrs. Miller had to address three people, including Joey, who was moving around at times. But the same considerations hold for professional relationships in groups: A comfortable arrangement of furniture made it easy to be close to the clients, to maintain a steady but relaxed eye contact, and to speak in a warm but serious voice. Yet, these conditions may be modified; one therapist reportedly does consulting when jogging with clients!

Factor B: Worker and Client Roles and Responsibilities

While you might readily assume that the worker's role in the helping process is of vital importance in its outcome, you should not be surprised to learn that research has also emphasized the client's contribution to the success or failure of the intervention, regardless of personal attributes or presenting problems. For example, clients from different social classes tend to expect different things from the helping process, and these expectations may or may not be fulfilled in the actual intervention. Less sophisticated clients may prefer concrete actions and less "talking" as the focus of treatment, especially if the conversations focus on feelings and events that occurred in their distant childhood. It seems irrelevant and a waste of time and money. Thus there is a built-in problem for therapists with a psychodynamic orientation that places so much emphasis on the origins of current problems as stemming from unresolved conflictful relationships from a client's infancy and childhood.

The work of Heitler (1976) and others suggests that pre-therapy training of clients to understand the reasoning behind a therapeutic strategy before they actually begin counseling is conducive to better therapeutic results. Trained clients have more successful outcomes than nontrained ones. The notion of training clients to be receptive to one's brand of professional helping is very general. All professional helpers implicitly train their clients to understand the problems and proposed solutions within the linguistic and cultural context of the worker. With regard to the role of client and worker, however, it might be useful if the worker were sensitive to the client's cultural perspective too.

Kleinman (1978) argues effectively that clients—who always bring their socio-cultural backgrounds with them as they seek help—may make some important assumptions about the helping process that are at odds with those assumptions made by the helper. This spells trouble. For example, the chief concern of most clinicians schooled in the medical model (in which some underlying factor like a bacterium or a specific emotional trauma is viewed as the cause of the illness) is to recognize and to treat the disease, which is considered to be a malfunction of the bio-psychological processes. On the other hand, the chief concern of the patient and his or her family is with the illness, which involves the personal and social problems generated by their experience with the sickness. Correspondingly, clinicians tend to emphasize curing or producing technological fixes of the causal factors, whereas patients evaluate the treatment they receive according to the healing that occurs, that is, in the provision of personal and social meaning and the management of life problems that stem from the sickness.

From a systems or configural perspective, both dimensions, disease/illness and curing/healing, must be taken into consideration. It is the extra responsibility of the professional, however, to understand the client's sickness or problem from the client's perspective, as well as from his or her own.

Confidentiality in the helping process requires some further amplification. Both parties to the helping process must understand that personal topics will be directly and openly discussed, topics that may be embarrassing to the client, actions that show the client in unflattering light, even discussions of what might be illegal behavior. Concerning the matter of illegality, the social worker is subject to the law regarding the reporting, for example, of suspected child abuse. If the client talks about contemplated actions harmful to self or others, the worker has the responsibility to inform the client about the legal status of such actions, and where needed, to report these to the authorities who are empowered to take appropriate actions.

The client must understand that a wide range of information will be needed by the worker to assist in an effective solution of problems—basic facts needed to complete application forms or whatever, personal feelings and ideas, full disclosure of past and current behaviors, one's associations with others, and the like. (You can see a checking off of relevant configural systems.) Before a client is willing to remove his or her psychosocial facade, like a patient stripping down for a physical exam, that person has to trust the professionalism of the worker. This sense of trust is usually earned through testing. Delicate information may be revealed gradually with the client watching to see what effect it has on the worker. Some clients think they alone have had aggressive, sexual, or antisocial thoughts or actions, which can be a terrible burden on them and very difficult for them to discuss. A worker's discussion of confidentiality may help to develop trust.

At the same time, the worker has to be prepared to hear and see things that may be unsettling and uncongenial. Indeed, the worker has to invite the open communication and exploration of these things by being sensitive to the hints of what may have been long-hidden experiences, and by being willing to discuss what are ordinarily taboo topics, such as substance abuse, sexual explorations, or violent acts. The worker has to know the language as well as the substance of these topics so as to understand what the client is saying—

without showing shock at four-letter words and their equivalent. The worker's calm reaction to the recitation of these events, which rarely reach the heights or depths of the average soap opera, may go far in establishing the rational atmosphere in which the discussion on resolving problems may occur.

But clearly, all such information must be kept confidential within the helping context. The worker should discuss at the outset the confidential nature of their discussions. Some agencies request blanket consent forms that permit agencies to receive and to give out confidential information related to the helping process. For a professional to share information with other professionals sounds sensible, but it also opens up the possibility that clients may become part of health information data banks without their realizing it (Wilson, 1978, p. 961). Professional confidentiality is not the same as personal confidentiality. The worker must inform the client if supervisors or other specialists may read some of the material describing the case. Never is a case to be discussed casually among friends or acquaintances. Never is the client's personal identity to be made known in professional publications or conferences. Never are any written materials about the case to be left in unsafeguarded places. This is a statement of honor that the worker must give the client and must fulfill to the letter.

Wilson (1978) discusses the complexities of the confidentiality issue from the legal point of view. Many social workers assume that the information they obtain in private sessions is secure from being subpoenaed by the court should a legal suit emerge. In fact, only 15 states have privileged communication—giving clients the right to prohibit their social workers from disclosing in court, in response to a subpoena, information gathered during the course of their professional relationship. Malpractice litigation is becoming a significant problem for many social workers, especially those in private practice. In general, both practitioner and client must be well informed about confidentiality and its limits.

Factor C: Biases and Stereotypes

Biblical literature and written history ever since remind us of the biases and discrimination that different peoples have borne toward one another. Scientific literature does little more than confirm these discouraging facts. For example, the writings of Hollingshead and Redlich (1958) note that the lower socioeconomic classes generally are rated as having more serious psychiatric conditions and are given what was thought to be poorer treatment by less experienced workers in large inadequate public institutions, as compared with their wealthier contemporaries. Later reports of the underutilization of health and mental health facilities by minorities is another aspect of cultural bias and discrimination (cf. Miller, et al, 1982; Siegel, 1974; Green, 1982; Lum, 1986).

Brown (1981) notes that even some socially sensitive social workers have maintained sexist practices by encouraging excessive dependence in female clients and by discouraging assertive behavior because it goes against the feminine ideal held by many in this society. Such systematic discrimination must be described as institutional classism, racism, or sexism, when whole categories of persons are subjected equally to unequal treatment merely because of their membership in a socially devalued category.

While headway against these institutional forms of discrimination are possible through organized efforts of groups and associations opposed to inequality, individuals commit another form of discrimination toward other individuals because of their class, race, sex, or other distinguishing feature. Often the forms of individual discrimination are subtle. The discriminator may not be aware of his or her own biased views and actions. Lacking this perspective on their own stereotypes, workers must challenge themselves about what services are usually offered majority and minority persons with the same type of problem.

Biases and stereotypes may be recognized more clearly and efforts engaged in to diminish their effect on helping actions. The more clearly one recognizes one's own biases and stereotypes, the more likely is one to challenge them effectively. Colleagues can be helpful to provide feedback on one's own actions that might be seen as biased in particular minority settings. Supervisors might be able to suggest ways of self-challenging these learned holdovers from one's own early developmental experience.

Clients also have biases and stereotypes about social workers, and these may get in the way of clients benefiting fully from service. Solomon (1976) notes that "social workers" are generally viewed by many black clients as "welfare workers," the kind of helpers they are likely to have had experience with in the distributing of financial assistance, food stamps, housing subsidies, and the like. Such a worker is not expected to deliver "talking" services, especially those that may stress client deficits. Solomon urges white workers to develop a rapport with black clients that involves entering into their culture and life space so as to understand the language, the challenges, and the strengths that come of surviving in white America—as well as the individual limitations a given person might have.

This brief discussion of class, race, and gender issues involved in biased and discriminatory behaviors suggests the need for a model of social work practice that is sensitive to these concerns. The general problem-solving model has to be adapted to identify the strengths of various types of clients as well as their limitations. Such a model has to recognize the part that the sociocultural and physical environments play in causing and relieving such stresses on minority groups and special populations. Fortunately, some conceptualizations offer useful guides to that end. They are summarized in Table 7.1.

As in the Rogers case, when the client and worker were of different races, the potential for stereotypic beliefs and discriminatory behavior is always present, regardless of how liberated one feels from one's past. The worker recognized not so much racial bias, but a rural one, and she had to keep reminding herself that although Mrs. Rogers came from a poor rural background, she was in fact an intelligent and educated person. Yet, she was continually reminded of the client's rural background by the slow cadence of her speech patterns that might be mistaken for the pattern of a retarded person. The words she used were apt and clear. So the worker was conscious of keeping a perspective on Mrs. Rogers' words in spite of the way she said them. She wondered what Mrs. Rogers thought of her crisp New England way of speaking, but she never asked. It might have been appropriate to do so, perhaps at the time when she was asking Mrs. Rogers where her home was, and what differences there were in the two regions.

TABLE 7.1   Promoting socio-cultural sensitivity in social work practice

Steps in the problem-solving sequence	Sensitivity considerations relevant to minority and other special populations, as additions to other relationship considerations
STEP 1 Identify the problems and strengths of the client and situation	1. Begin where the client is in his or her personal, social, and cultural context, and consider how these affect the presenting (and other) problems. 2. Use bilingual/bicultural workers who are competent and experienced with the challenges and strengths of this client population whenever possible. 3. Use accessible locations and methods of communication appropriate to the client population, such as sign language for the deaf. 4. Client dignity must be maintained at all times. Use surnames and other culturally appropriate forms of address. 5. Listen with warm interest to what the client is saying and let him or her feel at ease with the worker before getting into the problem. 6. Admit to one's own cultural limitations and seek the client's (and client's family's) help to understand nuances of the presenting events. 7. Recognize appropriate strengths of clients, family, and friends.
STEP 2 Identify alternative theories of behavior	1. Recognize that any theory must be translated into different cultural contexts. An item that is reinforcing or valued in one culture may not be in another. 2. The roles we play may be interpreted in different ways. For example, a young female worker may run into cultural problems from an older male client who is not used to taking advice from either the young or from females. 3. Clients may hold folk theories about their problems or illnesses, and may be comforted by the presence of their folk healer. If the folk belief conflicts seriously with the scientific view, seek a broader cultural value under which both might fit with suitable modifications (without compromising its major interventions), rather than be drawn into an argument.
STEP 3 Identify long-term goals and short term objectives STEP 4 Make joint decision on plan of action	1. Help clients formulate goals and objectives with reference to the multiple cultures in which they live. Accept client goals unless laws or good practice dictate otherwise. 2. Aid empowering of the powerless by developing personal skills needed to perform valued social roles. 3. Recognize and support the realistic goals of handicapped persons and the constructive function such goals play in their lives. 4. Identify all the relevant parties affected by the clients' value choices, but recognize the culture's relative weighting of the persons involved (such as the weight some cultures assign to the elders). 5. Be careful of one's own biases and stereotypes when forming goals and objectives and determining who is to do what under terms of the contract. The worker is the learner in regard to the client's culture and personalized style. The client must "own" the values to be fully involved and motivated.
STEP 5 Implement and concurrently evaluate the process and outcome of the intervention	1. Work with the client's strengths and the environment's resources, rather than trying to remediate based on deficits in both. Do not ignore deficits and problems, but show respect by using and valuing the client's strengths. 2. Be careful not to use any techniques that blame the victim, but do not ignore the client's contributions to the cause or maintenance of the situation. Cultural sensitivity does not mean blindness to client limitations, but rather it means an understanding of how these problems came to be under socio-cultural pressure. 3. Observe strict equality in dealings with clients at one's agency. Have high standards for all.
STEP 6 Compare the present state of client with case objectives STEP 7 Conduct follow-up	1. Comparing the client's current state with goals and objectives should include the cultural contexts in which these events are viewed. It is never enough to have resolved one problem; there should be no new problems emerging in its place. 2. Are the overall costs of coming for service less than the benefits derived from that service? Costs include not only money for transportation and baby-sitting but also the effort to communicate with a person from another culture. 3. Leave the clients with a sense of self-competence to deal with new challenges by reinforcing the strengths in their lives, but stand ready to offer "booster shots" as needed.

Sources: These practice suggestions for socio-culturally sensitive social work are derived from various sources, including Lum (1986); Green (1982); Brown (1981); Siegel (1974); Devore and Schlesinger (1987); Solomon (1976); Ryan (1976).

Factors D and E: Joint Participation and Checking Client Reactions

Beginning professional helpers want to do everything for their clients, but overzealous altruism, though well-intentioned, is often more harmful than helpful. No one can live another person's life. Helping professionals should not try to make value decisions that clients are uniquely able to do for themselves. As long as the clients' choices do not have negative effects on the lives, well-being, and freedoms of others, workers should not try to impose their own values on their clients. Instead, workers can identify a range of available options, and can help their clients think through the implications of each alternative to see which is most appropriate for them.

Joint participation refers to the contributions of both client and worker, recognizing that on some topics one will take the lead—for example, the client's goals and objectives are the main determiners of the direction of intervention—while on other topics, the other will—for instance, the social worker will have special expertise on methods of behavior change. Each has to feel a part of the whole helping process to keep involvement at a high level. A new group or team has been created. Each member (client and worker) is involved in understanding the other's views and values, and in trying to accomplish the mutually agreed upon objective through means acceptable to all concerned.

The social worker has a special obligation in working with clients to encourage their full participation at every step of the problem-solving sequence, to the extent clients are able. This reflects not only the professional value of the intrinsic dignity and worth of each individual, but also pragmatic reasons. Clients have knowledge and skills that are vital to the solution of their own problems. Perhaps the ultimate lesson to be learned from any professional helping experience is that clients can learn to help themselves. It is a lesson learned particularly well when the client in fact participates continuously in the helping process.

In the Rogers case, all family members present participated, even though the mother and worker were the responsible parties. Joey's versions of the problem were solicited and Lucy made some points at times. During the talk back and forth about some critical incident, such as the discussion of irregular allowances, the participation became clear. The client had identified important objectives to be worked on, and the worker was proposing a logical way to approach one objective. There were no orders, no demands. There was an atmosphere of openness and of willingness to discuss problems that had resisted solution at home. Along with the content of those discussions there was also a lesson in the process of talking effectively about common concerns.

Resistance: Barriers to Effective Interventions.   There will frequently be barriers to resolving problems, some of which are largely internal to the client. Other barriers are largely external to the client and may include the worker as well. Let us examine each of these:

Sometimes the client may appear to be doing things that hamper the flow of the intervention, for example, by not arriving on time or at all, by arriving but not responding well to questions or comments, or by responding in ways that confuse, run away from, or argue with what the worker is trying to do.

Doug Buerlein/Virginia Commonwealth University

Social work has long recognized the importance of forming a helping relationship with the client, regardless of what helping actions are taken in the context of this relationship. It is sometimes difficult to put into words this sense of connectedness with our clients, but we may often see it in their expressions and actions. Once a relationship is formed, it must be sustained throughout the helping process by actions sensitive to the unique needs, interests, and cultural background of the client.

The client may or may not be aware of doing these things, but if attention is called to them, the client may get defensive about the behaviors.

If it is really the client's resistive behaviors, and not one of the other two types, then the worker should try to focus on this behavior as a special case in the overall task of resolving the client's presenting difficulty. The worker may have to go back to discussions of client objectives and the plans and the contract for attaining the desired outcomes. It may also require exploring the client's feelings and thoughts about the topics that appear too hot to handle at this moment. On the other hand, as Gottman and Leiblum (1974) point out, the resistance may arise from the client's not knowing how to deal with the current issue; it may be a knowledge or skill deficit and require additional training and discussion to get moving again on problem solving.

Other forms of resistance involve the environmental context, including the workers themselves. Sometimes circumstances reward negative behaviors. A client about to terminate a satisfying contact with a worker, for example, suddenly has a profusion of new symptoms and thus requires more aid. Although the symptoms are not pleasant, the possibility of losing a valued helping relationship may be worse, and so new problems emerge. The solution to this would be to make being an effective person more rewarding than any therapeutic relationship, connecting the client with his or her ordinary social networks that provide intrinsic rewards and stimulation. The worker might lose sight of the objective—client autonomy—by enjoying the relationship too much.

Some persons are, by definition, *involuntary clients*—they would resist the helping or controlling situations in which they find themselves if they could. Examples are encountered while working in the criminal justice setting, or with involuntarily hospitalized persons, or with spouses who do not wish to join their partners in therapy. They do not want to be with you and they see little reason to cooperate. The only result they can foresee is more trouble for themselves. Frequently, persons forced to be "clients" or inmates may conform superficially to the requirements of the superior police or legal force that brought them to their situation. They have no intention of conforming to others' expectations when not under direct police or legal control.

It is obviously difficult to work with involuntary clients. One approach is to gain their personal respect and trust, based on your personal characteristics, not institutional roles. Then you can try to move from there to interventive objectives on the (honest) basis that you believe that such action is in their best interests—and you stand ready to figure out with them how to make the best of a limited (controlled) situation. This approach involves use of any of several bases of power or influence you have with the resistive/involuntary client. French and Raven (1959; Bloom, 1984, pp. 217-220) have described several such bases, in addition to being liked for oneself. The worker can reward the client for good behavior or punish bad behavior. The worker has expertise that the client needs. The worker is a legitimate authority under the circumstances and deserves obedience.

Another approach is to appeal to some more basic value such as honor, family, or self-interest. From this broader value base, the specific details of what the intervention is seeking to accomplish may be derived. "If you behave and can get out of prison sooner, then you will be able to care for your family yourself rather than leave them drifting on welfare and charity." The worker's basic concern is whether any of the observed changes of behavior are real and likely to continue or a ploy. For the most part, only time will tell. Evaluations of predicted behaviors may be helpful, but it is difficult at this late stage of "treatment."

Sometimes nothing works, and we fail at encouraging the client to do what we believe would be most helpful. All that we can do is to try again, learning, one hopes, from what did not work before.

Factors F and G: Introducing Termination and "Graduation"

Plans for termination are frequently discussed at the same time as the client and worker plan goals and objectives. The two types of plans are opposite sides of the same coin. However, as worker and client struggle together to resolve problems, they inevitably form some quality of relationship that must come to an end when the professional association ends. Termination always involves strong feelings, often a sense of loss or separation as well as gain and advancement with the solution or amelioration of the problem and the understanding of problem-solving skills in general.

Hellenbrand (1987) and others describe termination as a kind of graduation, when the client changes to a new role as successful problem solver. To be sure, not every client will be successful, either in the sense of resolving the presenting problem or learning how to be a problem solver of future challenges. But enough clients will be successful to require careful consideration of the termination process.

Hellenbrand describes a number of types of terminations. One is called a natural termination in the sense that the client achieves the planned objectives to a sufficient degree that both client and worker agree to end their relationship. This is, of course, the ideal ending. A worker-forced termination is one in which circumstances other than case progress require the end of the client-worker relationship. For example, the student may come to the end of the field work semester, or the worker may take another job. There are some ethical issues involved when workers take the initiative in terminating a contact for their own reasons. Care must be taken not to harm the client in the process. In cases of a worker-originated change, the agency may substitute a new worker for the old. The issues of termination must still be resolved before the new worker takes over.

A third type is the client-imposed termination, for example, when the client leaves an institution or the agency, and the worker cannot follow up on progress. A final type is unplanned termination, when the client or worker dies, or when the client stops coming for unknown reasons. Also called client dropout, it represents an unfortunately high proportion of terminations.

Termination planning will be handled differently depending on the type of clients (for instance, children who may form strong ties with a worker and who are thus hard-hit when the professional contact ends) or the type of service (for example, short-term therapy in which an arbitrary end point is set so that specific tasks may be engaged in a defined sequence of events). Different settings also address the issue of termination in different ways. Work with the elderly tends to be on-going, so that termination may not be addressed but only understood as occurring at the death of the client.

Whether the client is young or old, in a brief or extended service contact, in a concrete service or insight-oriented program, the ending of a significant relationship that frequently occurs in social work often will be difficult for both client and worker. But viewed in the positive light of working toward graduation as a successful problem solver, the client and the worker can feel some gratification about their accomplishments. It helps to know too that the door of the agency is always open, should new problems require additional help.

One might take the opportunity in planning termination to address the issue of maintenance. Assuming a client has resolved the problems that have brought him or her to the agency, then another set of skills, those having to do with maintaining the learning and applying them to novel circumstances, become very important. In some situations, this may move the client to a new role, that of helper (with regard to new problems he or she may face). Reissman (1965) describes the important concept of the helper therapy principle: one client who helps another who is on a more elementary level not only provides the assistance for that other person, but also strengthens his or her own skills and knowledge and self-esteem at the same time. Sometimes a client may be able to help others by drawing on his or her service experience. Indeed, family life education is based on this premise of the transfer of learning to new persons and in new contexts.

Thus a discussion of endings is important. It provides the perspective and the expectations that are healthy contributors to the very ends that both client and worker seek. It is probably preferable to be quite clear about termination, provided the client is able to tolerate the information, both as to when it is to occur (time period or competence level attained by the client) and how the transitions are to be arranged back to daily life without the worker. Again, such information will be made less threatening by pointing out that the agency remains ready and able to respond to other requests of aid, should that be necessary. Still, clients may respond to the termination in many ways, anger or happiness, a rapid improvement or a sudden burst of new symptoms, denial or acceptance.

In the Rogers case, we have seen how the worker introduced the time-limited notion during the discussions of the allowance matter in connection with the crisis problem of the theft. This case was complicated by Mr. Rogers' absence. He would be returning, however, and no specific termination was set until the whole family could be present. Then they could define together what problems were to be resolved—and hence when a natural termination would be called for.

SUMMARY

At the dramatic climax of the play, everything begins to make sense. All the pieces are put back together again, and the playgoers return home with a sense of the whole drama in their mind's eye. This sense of the whole is very important because once you have it, individual actions seem to belong together as part of a larger pattern. We have to look for the larger perspective in everything we do, whether we are counseling an individual client, making choices about graduate education, or reading a chapter in a book.

We are at the end of two long and detailed chapters introducing the generic approach to professional helping. Ideally, you take with you that sense of the whole that playgoers take as they leave the theater. If you take hold of the large overall pattern, then the details will eventually fall into place. That large picture is presented in Table 6.1, the problem-solving sequence.

So, learn the plot outline, then how the actors are to relate to one another and to their audiences (their gestures, motions, and positions, so to speak). Then study the specific lines to be recited in the various scenes. These are not to be memorized, but they are to be used as outlines from which you adapt your actual words and gestures to meet the conditions of specific people and places. Obviously this will take practice, but a good performance as a helping professional is worth the effort.

OUTLINE

Introduction

Helping Individuals in Group Contexts
  The Alverez Case
    Communication Theory: Virginia Satir
    Family Structural Therapy: Salvador Minuchin
    Individual Session with Ricardo
    Natural Helping Networks: Collins and Pancoast
    Analysis of Types of Groups Illustrated in the Alverez Case

Community Organization Methods: Jack Rothman
  A Case Illustration: The Neighborhood Association
    Analysis

Administration of Social Services
  The Bureaucratic Model: Max Weber
  The Human Relations Approach: Rensis Likert
  A Case Study in Administration: Services for the Deaf

Summary

CHAPTER EIGHT

Methods of Helping Individuals in Small Groups and Communities

Chapter 8 presents and illustrates materials on the major modes of professional helping at the group or organizational levels—group work, community organization, administration, and planning. In each of these collective modalities, there are many occasions when a worker will interact with a single client, but the context always involves other persons who are part of families, peer groups, or neighborhoods or who live throughout a community but who share a common problem such as deafness. Brief statements of theories to guide practice at these levels are introduced, and case studies clarify applications of each theory.

INTRODUCTION

In many contexts of helping, more than one client is involved, either in the aggregate (that is, individuals unrelated to one another except in sharing a common characteristic) or organized into some group such as a family, a set of friends, or a neighborhood organization. In each of these multi-person configurations, social workers have to be prepared to provide help when needed. This chapter deals with several such contexts; it illustrates traditional methods of professional helping: working with groups, community organization, and administration.

In some ways, these methods should be familiar to you—we all have had some type of family experience and some peer-group and other associations. But when we view these familiar contexts from the point of view of helping, something happens. The professional helper has to break in on some intimate grouping or some formal structures to identify problems and offer considered solutions. This is the application of the generic problem-solving approach, but there are important modifications of the approach when the actions and reactions of many people are involved in a situation.

This chapter considers three extended case studies, each focused at one level of intervention—work with groups of various types, community organi-

zation, and administration—although it will be obvious to you that there is a
great deal of overlap. These actual (but disguised) cases are easy to grasp, but
it is important to look for the theoretical ideas guiding practice in each case.
Because community organization and administration are probably less familiar to some readers, we put the theoretical materials before the case illustrations, whereas with work with groups the conceptual discussions are
embedded in the story itself. In either case, keep your eye on the theories that
guide practice, not only for the examples presented here, but also for ways in
which these same general ideas might be used by a helping professional in
new situations.

HELPING INDIVIDUALS IN GROUP CONTEXTS

The Alverez Case

To his Anglo friends at the high school, he was known as Al (shortened for
Alverez), a very shy Hispanic youth who was always near the bottom of the
class in every subject. To his parents, he was known as Ricardo, a stubborn
youth who was the source of yet another generation of problems because he
was skipping school, just as his older brothers had done. To his Hispanic
friends, he was Rick, a lively, talkative youth, full of energy and determination. But his characterization depended on the group from which he was
viewed.

The Alverez family came to the Desert City Family Services agency to try
to resolve the problem of Ricardo's school absences before he joined his four
older brothers as dropouts. Ricardo was thought to be brighter than his older
brothers, and therefore had a greater chance of making it out of the poverty
that held the Alverez family in a viselike grip. The six younger brothers and
sisters were watching the outcome of this domestic battle as if their own desti-
nies were being worked out. And perhaps they were.

The Desert City Family Services agency knew about the Alverez family in
a variety of contexts. The children had been involved in their summer programs for the past nine years. There were some "fresh air" camps that took
poor children away from the hot city up to mountain retreats for two weeks.
The Alverez children loved these outings, in part to get away from a crowded
home situation. Not that their home lacked love—Mrs. Alverez was an extraordinary nurturing mother—but 11 children and 2 adults make any house
crowded, especially if it is only modest in size.

On one of the camping occasions Mrs. Alverez noticed an announcement
of a series of free workshops on "ordinary family concerns"—how to discipline children, how to talk with teenagers about topics like drugs and sexuality, and a variety of other topics that were not quite as salient to her at the
moment. She went to the discipline workshop and enjoyed it very much. She
learned about some new ways of disciplining, but she was not able to convince her husband of their efficacy. Nor was she able to persuade him to attend the workshop.

Possibly a more important lesson for her was the realization that there
were people available with whom she could talk over her many concerns. She

realized at the workshop that it was not natural to feel as depressed as she did. After much hesitancy, she mustered up the courage to talk with the social worker who was leading the workshop. He suggested that she come in for a discussion in private with someone at the agency. So it was that she had been receiving individual counseling for several months, in spite of her husband's objections. The worker had suggested strongly that she try to have Mr. Alverez come in as well, but he was always "too busy."

When the school social worker insisted that the parents both come in to discuss Ricardo's absences, she convinced them (especially Mr. Alverez) to get some family counseling. After much foot-dragging, Mr. Alverez joined his wife and Ricardo at the Family Services Agency. Mr. Johnathan Lee, an experienced MSW, spoke limited Spanish and was not able to catch all of the side comments Mr. Alverez was making to his wife. Mr. Lee understood enough, however, to recognize something about the power structure in this family.

Mr. Lee welcomed them at the office door and ushered them inside. There were five or six chairs in an arc, and a small desk was against one wall. In the middle of the chairs was a small coffee table. Mrs. Alverez sat next to her husband, Ricardo sat far opposite. Mr. Lee sat between them. He leaned forward slightly and looked at each of the family members as he talked. He began by saying that he understood they had come about a problem arising at school, but he would like to hear more about it from them. Mrs. Alverez glanced at her husband, but he turned slightly away from her and the others to look out of the window. She began to recount the visit to the school social worker. She also touched on the dropping out of the older four boys, but Mr. Alverez said something in Spanish that made her change that topic.

Throughout the session, Ricardo spoke almost not at all. Even when directly questioned, he mumbled monosyllabic answers, which infuriated his father, who almost shouted for him to speak up. He then launched into a lecture on his son's stubbornness and the futility of this meeting.

Mr. Lee tried to get the family to talk about specific factors: How was Ricardo doing at school? (Average, but his test scores showed that he should be doing much better.) How did Ricardo feel about school? Were there any special problems? (School was "O.K." There were no special problems.) Ricardo was staring at his tennis shoes. What sorts of aspirations did Ricardo have for his life? Did he have any particular plans for a certain kind of career? (No, he never thought much about it, except—and here Ricardo looked at Mr. Lee for the first time—he was going to do right well for himself. He wasn't going to be poor.) Mr. Alverez gave Ricardo a withering glance, and then he turned on his chair and stared out the window at the hot dusty scene outside.

Mr. Lee asks Mr. Alverez whether talking about money makes him uncomfortable. Mr. Alverez replies with a raised voice that he is not uncomfortable and folds his arms across his chest and stares at the floor. Silence. Then Mr. Alverez continues in a quieter voice: He makes a good wage as foreman of the city sanitation crews, but he has a big family, and it is just hard to make ends meet. More silence.

Then Mr. Lee tried to involve Mrs. Alverez in the conversation. He asked her how she saw the situation. She began to say something about another son, Carlos, who apparently was also very quiet and a school dropout, but he started to cry uncontrollably one day and was eventually taken to the state mental hospital. Mr. Alverez broke into the conversation, saying that was not why they were here now. And Mrs. Alverez said no more.

There was an uneasy silence. The hour was coming to an end, and Mr. Lee tried to put the best face possible on this first family session. He offered some hope even in the recognition of the difficult work ahead. Although he saw that this was a family in trouble, he also recognized that he would have to see Ricardo alone if he was to obtain any useful information from the boy, who was inhibited in the presence of his parents, especially his father. In concluding the session, Mr. Lee suggested that he would like to speak with Ricardo alone for a time, and possibly Mr. and Mrs. Alverez as well. He would invite the family back together as matters progressed. The family left with grim expressions on their faces. Mr. Lee wondered whether he would ever see any of them again.

Communication Theory: Virginia Satir.   There are many ways to analyze any family session. Different family theorists and therapists would reconstruct the events according to their guiding conceptions of how disturbed families operate. One widely used approach, associated with the work of Virginia Satir (1964), is based on a communication model that views information flowing from one source to another, then back again, so as to keep all members of the group working together in harmony among themselves and with relation to the group as it deals with the larger world. Part of this information flow is carried by words that express some belief about the world. Another part of that information flow is carried by nonverbal means (gestures, intonation, etc.) that qualify or modify the belief statement according to how the speaker feels about it. People can communicate what they think and feel about a situation, or they can disguise their true feelings or thoughts in various ways—by sending only partial information or by presenting some noncongruent information between their message and the way they say it. (Consider the parent who is smiling broadly at his sons who have brought home some toys stolen from the store while saying to them, "You shouldn't do that sort of thing.") Satir assumes that people, especially members of families, learn a pattern of interpersonal communication that resolves some of the tasks the group has to perform, even though it may not solve others.

Satir identifies the patterns of communication going on in the family that is experiencing problems so that what is troubling them can be identified in turn. She looks for unclear messages, verbal statements, and nonverbal communications that are not congruent and family rules or norms that develop from these kinds of destructive communications. Such family rules concretize the roles each member plays vis-à-vis the others. For example, one family rule may be that no family problem should be discussed with strangers. This may be why Mr. Alverez stopped conversation at various points. The other members of the family were "breaking rules." Satir hypothesizes that disturbed families contain people with poor senses of self-esteem, and thus they are unable to say what they really feel and believe. Speaking obliquely about what one wants, rather than saying it directly, defends the fragile self-esteem against rejections, but it also tends to increase the communications that fail to attain their desired ends.

Another form of communication problem Satir and other advocates of the communication approach identify is the *unhealthy double bind.* This is a communication pattern in which two contradictory expectations are sent to one person who is damned if he does and damned if he doesn't. For example, Ricardo is told to speak up by his father, who also says "shut up" when Ricardo starts to tell things that family rules prohibit. This happens even in a family therapy session, which requires discussion of matters troubling them. When the stress of this communication bind gets very intense, the victim may try to escape by not talking at all—at least he does not get blamed for taking one or the other action—or through some other symptomatic behavior. (The communication theorists, such as Bateson, Watzlawick, and Jackson, use the double-bind hypothesis as one cause for schizophrenic behavior. The older Alverez son seems to have exhibited this behavior.) Typically, the people involved in the double bind refuse to see their communication behaviors as the cause of problems. Rather, the identified patient (Satir, 1964) is the problem to them and family therapy seems superfluous. Such people tend to blame the scapegoat instead of being aware of their own feelings and actions. They tend to speak in terms of "you" messages rather than "I" messages that provide clear communications about these feelings.

The objectives of Satir's version of communication theory is to increase clear and congruent messages that express what each of the members is feeling and thinking so that the family can develop more successful problem-solving methods and constructive family rules in dealing with common concerns. One method for achieving these goals is to break into the dysfunctional pattern of communication to make the destructive family rules visible and subject to rational change. (For example, a worker might say: "Mr. Alverez, do you recognize that every time your wife or son begin to talk directly about issues that are bothering them, you tell them, in one way or another, to stop talking about that?" It is sometimes useful to have a videotape of the family session to play back scenes to verify such observations. Mr. Alverez might dispute this. He might say that his intention was quite different. The worker, however, can point to the actual effect on the behavior of the others, regardless of Mr. Alverez's intention.)

In brief, this model proposes both an analysis of problematic conditions embedded within the family communication structure and methods that can be used to change disturbed forms of communication. (For further details on this form of therapy, see Satir, 1964; Haley, 1963.)

Family Structural Therapy: Salvador Minuchin.   Another widely used form of family therapy has been developed by Salvador Minuchin, who focuses on the structural systems of the family. Each subsystem—spouses, parents-to-children, and siblings—has its natural functioning within the healthy family (although what this is in actual behavioral patterns will differ in different families). The spousal subsystem involves the functions of emotional and intellectual support, sexual fulfillment, social engagement with outsiders, and financial efforts. Note that these functions include external tasks and internal affective (emotional) components and require some division of labor. Problems can occur when views about who is to do what or what is to be accomplished do not meet the expectations of each spouse.

The parental subsystem has functions related to the children, including physical and psychological nurturing and acting as a protective buffer from, or a stimulus to engage, the outside world and the individual child. Again, there are some task and affective components.

The sibling subsystem occurs when there are two or more children. Each is supposed to be able to relate easily to the others, to gain some support and stimulus from them, and to avoid conflicts.

For each subsystem, there are some characteristic traps, things that can go wrong between or among the subsystem functions. As a form of therapy, Minuchin seeks to identify the workings of each subsystem and to correct dysfunctional parts. For example, Mr. Alverez feels the pinch of finances, but he does not allow his wife to work. This creates some tension between them, even though within their subculture, this pattern is common and acceptable. Also, as parents, the Alverezes want to encourage their sons to become independent adults, but they do not permit them much expression of individuality and autonomy. As for the siblings, Mrs. Alverez puts Ricardo in charge of the younger children when she goes to see the counselor—thus giving him the responsibilities of an adult role—but neither she nor her husband credit Ricardo with adult-like privileges. They put him in a difficult position with regard to his younger siblings. In short, the therapist from the structural perspective would try to identify what features of family subsystems are not working well, and then the worker would try to help the family to change them.

One technique used on occasion is the *therapeutic paradox* (or a *healthful double bind*): the clients are instructed to perform what is the problematic behavior. By instructing them to do so, the therapist shows that the behavior is in fact under their control. For example, a structural therapist might have instructed Mr. Alverez to do some "homework" for the next couple of weeks—cutting off Ricardo whenever he tries to speak, and criticizing his behavior regardless of what it is. If Mr. Alverez does the assignment, he has to recognize that he is in control of his actions, and that he is cutting Ricardo off or unjustly criticizing his behaviors at times, something he is not aware of. If Mr. Alverez refuses to comply, and does not criticize or cut off his son, then he again has admitted having control over these behaviors. Presumably, whichever horn of the therapeutic dilemma Mr. Alverez chooses, he will be advancing the cause of family problem resolution. This is a difficult technique to use in practice, and is presented here for illustrative purposes only. Be cautious about creating paradoxes, especially when clients exhibit self-destructive behavior, or when they have little attachment to the helping process and are liable to drop out of treatment.

Generally speaking, Minuchin's model directs workers to be aware of the natural patterns that exist within and between subgroups in the family, and to act so as to reinforce the natural patterns that provide support for individual and group functioning. (See Minuchin, 1984.)

Individual Session with Ricardo.   Group work can be conceived as dealing with individuals in collective situations (as a matter of economy), or it may be seen as dealing with a distinctive entity, the group, in which problems develop and through which changes must be made. This chapter has been taking the second point of view. However, individuals can still be seen apart from the group, to make plans for how to use the resources of the group on their behalf. For that reason Mr. Lee saw Ricardo alone.

Ricardo came in as shy as ever, still studying his tennis shoes. Mr. Lee began to ask short questions that had concrete answers, and soon established a flow of conversation. By listening actively and by responding accurately to Ricardo's statements and their underlying feelings, Mr. Lee soon earned some trust. Little by little, he opened up the questions and encouraged Ricardo to say more—"Hey, call me Rick, O.K.? Like my friends do."

It became clear that Rick was troubled by many things. First, with regard to his home, he revealed that his father found fault with everything he did, and he criticized him regardless of what he did or did not do. Everything was a new attack. Rick described how this pattern had been applied to one of the older brothers, Carlos, who started to cry and then went mute, before being taken to the state mental hospital for treatment. Even though he is home now, he hardly says anything to anyone. This was very frightening to the other siblings, and, Rick believes, helped to precipate Mrs. Alverez' own breakdown, for which she was seeking counseling help. Mr. Alverez blamed the boy himself, and the harsh criticisms continued, but they have tended to be focused more on Rick. He was deeply frightened and did not know what to do.

School, on the other hand, was not really so bad. (Note that the presenting problem does not seem to be the central concern for Rick as it was for his parents.) It was just that the large high school seemed so unpleasant and uncaring compared to his small neighborhood grade school. No one talked to him, and the classes were so large that he felt he was being pushed around. By whom? Rick hesitated but then said by the Anglos. Mr. Lee, an Anglo, nodded indicating understanding and Rick went on. He said that even the other Hispanic kids seemed too busy for him. He had only a few friends, and some of them had already dropped out of school. They told him it was easier than fighting the system. That got Rick to thinking—and truanting. (Group influences, we recognize, of course, can be destructive as well as constructive.)

What did Rick do for fun? Not much. There was not much fun to be had, partly because he could not get a job to earn money, and his parents did not give him an allowance—just occasional handouts when they could. So he would talk on the phone for long periods—until one or the other parent would chase him off. He did not talk about anything in particular, just "stuff." But that was the only thing he could think of that he liked.

Mr. Lee reflected back to Rick about how he saw Rick's situation, and wondered whether it might be possible to involve Rick's friends in something that might help him make it through school. He asked Rick about just the friends who were sticking it out at school, what were they like? Rick said that they had strong career aspirations, just as he had. That was one thing they talked about on the phone at times (when no one was around). They were hassled by the school system, but they did not seem to get as upset or frustrated as Rick did. Why was that? He didn't know. Maybe it might be helpful to invite his friends to the agency and talk about these things. Sort of a conversation among friends, not like the therapy session. Maybe it might lead to some specific ideas about how Rick can get through, too. He grew silent as he thought about the suggestion. He nodded assent. Yes, yes, that would be fine. Yes, he would ask them to come with him. Yes.

Natural Helping Networks: Collins and Pancoast.   It was Friday, the day of the peer appointment. Before the boys arrived at his office, Mr. Lee could hear the loud joking and carrying on by the three young Hispanic teenagers. Mario and Freddy (Fernaldo) came bursting through the door with Rick, and they plastered themselves around the furniture still joking and talking rapidly. Mr. Lee tried to join the "fun." Then there was a moment of awkward silence. Another nervous laugh. Mr. Lee offered the boys some potato chips and juice. Then he introduced the reasons why they were there, and the three boys grew quiet and serious.

Earlier, the social worker had asked Rick whether he could discuss some of his school problems at this group session, and he agreed. Rick had told them as much already. So Mr. Lee began by saying that Rick's parents had come to this agency to help Rick in staying at school. In talking about school, Rick had mentioned that he had some friends—loud cheers—who were managing to get through things that were causing him difficulties. Mario agreed, and commented that a lot of Latino kids were having these difficulties, but he was determined not to let it get to him. He wanted to be a lawyer, and he knew he had to get through school. Freddy nodded, but did not say anything. Mr. Lee complimented them for being so observant about the structures at school that were causing troubles and how they were handling them.

Then Mr. Lee asked what they could think of to help Rick stay in school. Dead silence. Mr. Lee thought for a moment that he had lost the battle. Then he decided to prime the pump. "For example," he said with a smile, "you guys could tie a rope around Rick's leg and pull him from class to class." Freddy obviously enjoyed thinking about this idea when Mario suggested another idea, something about having a sign-in system so that when Rick was at school, they would know it, and they could meet him at the cafeteria for lunch. Rick did not think a sign-in system was necessary, but he liked the idea of having some regular lunch buddies.

Then Freddy suggested that they get together after school sometimes, but Mario pointed out—with a punch to Freddy's shoulder—that doing so would not necessarily do anything to keep Rick in school. Silence. More thinking. Mr. Lee said that he thought they were on the right track. More thinking. Mr. Lee was beginning to wonder to himself whether the boys would be able to come up with a workable idea.

Mario put it together this way: First, they would meet at school in the morning, and then they would meet at lunch time, since they all ate at the same time. And then they would meet either at afternoon study hall or after school some days. Rick liked that idea, but Freddy said that Rick might not ever get to school in the first place, so they had better walk to school together. Everyone liked that idea immediately (even though it later proved to be difficult because of where they lived). But they fell to figuring what time they would have to get up to make it in time.

Mr. Lee said that time was up for today and that he thought the boys had done an excellent job of figuring out how to solve this problem. The boys were noisily congratulating themselves for their brainstorm as well, and were physically patting each other on the back as they left, still chattering and joking. (See Collins and Pancoast, 1976, for other forms of natural helping networks. See also Garvin, 1987, for an overview on group work.)

Analysis of Types of Groups Illustrated in the Alverez Case.   Somewhat to his surprise, Mr. Lee met with the Alverez family on a regular basis for the next several months. Mr. Alverez was as uncommunicative as earlier, but he still attended. One of the possible reasons for their returning was that Ricardo was now attending school quite regularly, with the help of his friends, and this reduced a certain amount of tension at home. Mr. Alverez recognized the progress, and Mrs. Alverez pointed out that it was just the beginning. So they returned and were working on their difficulties, which they all began to see as a family problem, not just an individual one.

In between sessions, Mr. Lee arranged to call Rick on occasion to see how the plan was working out. He knew that his attendance was much better, and that his grades had improved somewhat as well. When Mr. Lee got through the long busy signals at the Alverez household, he talked to a surprised Ricardo.

"How are things going?"

"Fine."

"Are Mario and Freddy meeting you in the mornings?"

"Yeah."

"Do you get together at lunch times?"

"Yeah."

Mr. Lee recognized the slow start and fed Rick a string of questions that were simple to answer before switching over to more open-ended ones. "What sorts of differences do you see in the way you are handling school stresses these days, compared to before?" Rick began to warm up to the conversation, and soon was talking rapidly about some exciting event of the day. Mr. Lee listened with pleasure to a youth who had become involved with his education, despite the difficult family situation. At least this part of the battle seemed to have gone well. The rest would have to wait until another day.

As you have probably observed, the Alverez family was involved in several kinds of groups. First, the children attended summer camp, one instance of recreational groups planned simply to offer pleasurable and healthy environments for young people. They might learn some social skills or other kinds of information, but they are probably incidental to the recreational purpose.

Second, Mrs. Alverez attended a family-life educational workshop, an example of an educational group in which specific content is being transmitted so that the participants can apply it in their own lives. A form of adult education, workshops provide approaches different from those associated with the formal education of children in schools, reflecting the different levels of maturity and responsibility adults bring to their learning situation. The particular workshop she attended was both treatment and prevention oriented. It was intended to aid here-and-now problems parents were having, but it also provided an approach to prevent future problems.

The third type of group the Alverezes were involved with was the family therapy situation. This is also one instance of many types of group therapy, but with the special twist that members of only one family attended. (It is possible to form groups with numbers of families present as well. Or groups of strangers sharing common problems might be involved in a group therapy. The combinations of types of clients are almost limitless.) It has been noted that even with one type of therapy group, it is possible to use a number of theories of family therapy to guide or analyze practice. The techniques of group therapy and family therapy are numerous. (See, for example, Zastrow, 1990.)

The fourth type of group illustrated by the Alverez case is a natural helping network, a kind of self-help group in which people with like stresses work together to overcome common problems. There is less structure in these groups—that is why they are "natural"—but it is still possible for practitioners to stimulate participants to consider solutions to common problems. In Rick's case, the problems were common to all of the boys, but only he was having particular difficulty. The worker was careful not to suggest a plan. Rather, he wanted something workable to come from the boys themselves, so that their motivation and energy would be directed toward implementing it. Again, this is one example of a large category of self-help groups.

Garvin (1987) distinguishes two major types of groups: Socialization groups involve enhancing "the social development of members who have joined the group voluntarily and whose development is viewed as proceeding normally"; resocialization groups seek "to remedy the social development of members whose previous socialization is viewed, in a sociological sense, as deviant, and where group participation is often a consequence of some form of social pressure (p. 3)." For example, socialization groups provide opportunities to enhance social skills; to increase self-confidence; to do preventive or promotive work (like water safety, rape prevention, child-rearing skills); or to do remotivation work, as with elderly in nursing homes. Resocialization might include work with groups in transition, such as assisting people about to be released from prison in adjusting to civilian life; therapeutic groups (for instance, to help institutionalized mental patients to work on their problems), or deviant groups (such as help given to young prostitutes to develop healthy sense of self and independence from sexual victimization).

Sensitivity or encounter groups are a special form of socialization group. They differ in intensity, by meeting for brief but concentrated periods of time in some isolated setting, and having nothing on the agenda except how each person affects and is affected by others. (Sartre's *No Exit* is a drama that gives the flavor of an encounter group but with a special twist: it takes place in Hell.) Such experiences often give participants candid feedback about how their style of communicating affects others. Such feedback, of course, may be stressful to the persons involved.

All of the above examples describe work with individuals in groups. However, group work, as a specific form of professional practice, is an entire study in itself. (See the writings of the major contributors to this study: Garvin, 1987; Northern, 1969; Middleman and Goldberg, 1974; Rose, 1972; and others.) Group work involves the planned use of a group of selected persons to influence both the objectives of the individual members and the group's collective goals. A group viewed from this perspective helps members to become a mutual-aid system. A group worker, using a variety of methods, in general seeks to facilitate this key function of the group. The mutual aid system seeks to prevent predictable problems and breakdowns in the group or its members; to maintain current states of health and requisite resources; and to ameliorate members' problems through treatment or rehabilitation.

Most theories of group work involve some form of problem solving, although they may differ on how best this general strategy is to be accomplished. Careful attention is given to how a group is to be composed (what members with what problems and what strengths?) and organized (what are to be the roles for the leaders and the followers? How are changes in these roles to be handled?). The specific purposes of the group are often carefully identified so that members and leaders can know where they are vis-à-vis their mutual objectives. There is often careful assessment or evaluation of the process and the outcome of the group's efforts.

COMMUNITY ORGANIZATION METHODS: JACK ROTHMAN

The community may be the most taken-for-granted aspect of our lives, in spite of the many important influences it exerts over us. Perhaps this is due to the size of the community. We can interact with members of our family every day. We see most of our neighbors on the block every week, but we rarely comprehend, let alone see, the social structures that make up a community and determine where we are to live, who will live near us, and many other aspects of the quality of our lives.

Professionals who work at the community level have to make special efforts to observe individuals and groups whose actions constitute "the commu-

Although we may believe that we lead private lives, groups are everywhere and are involved in every part of our lives. Here, for example, is a neighborhood association block party. Social workers can use this fundamental fact of social life to good advantage because through groups and larger social structures, people obtain a sense of belonging and meaningfulness. Some groups and crowds may be oppressive, even dangerous. But social workers can construct and maintain helpful and stimulating social environments.

Elizabeth Hamlin/Stock, Boston

nity." We examine here some conceptual tools that enable workers to engage the community. We will begin with the theoretical materials and then apply them in practice.

There are three major approaches to social work practice at the community level (Rothman, 1979): (1) a *social planning approach,* in which an expert assembles some information about a problem and then constructs a plan of action to resolve it; (2) a *community development approach,* in which a worker facilitates local citizen involvement in determining the problems and solving them in their own way; and (3) a *social action or reform approach,* in which the worker helps a victimized group mobilize strong collective action against entrenched power interests. While Rothman makes the distinctions among these three approaches as distinct as possible, he recognizes that in real life, more than one approach may come into play at different times in dealing with one complex problem.

In the following case study, consider what appears to be happening at various stages as the story unfolds. People working at the community level recognize the importance of the many social structures that the rest of us usually take for granted, assuming that we are aware of them at all. For example, the street in front of your house is jointly and continually considered by the road building and maintenance department, the police, the fire department, the sanitation crews, and the various utility companies, to say nothing of the political bodies in your community, neighborhood associations, and many others. Your street is not all they think about, of course, but it is part of the complex whole of community life. It is only when something goes wrong or when something is not right (is not what it could be) that we notice an everyday thing as mundane as the street in front of our home.

Because these various institutions and organizations of a society are involved in every facet of community life, social workers engaged in practice at the community level often must be assertive. Social work is the wrong occupation for wallflowers. Many times a community worker has to speak up, confront powerful people or organizations, and even help mobilize large numbers of citizens who may have been passive or submissive all their lives. This does not mean that community workers must all speak like Demosthenes, throw their weight around like Rambo on the Rampage, or exude the charisma of a Gandhi or a Martin Luther King. What is generally needed is a person who, after carefully analyzing a collective problem, is willing and able to be assertive in seeking its resolution. Ideally, the assertive professional is a person who speaks out in a reasonable, calm, and firm manner for the fair rights of others and who continues to speak out (although perhaps with rising intensity at the right moments) until just actions are performed. But equally important is the ability of the community worker to be *socially assertive,* that is, able and willing to work together with others in seeking a common social good. Let's observe one community worker in action.

A Case Illustration: The Neighborhood Association

"Midweston" is a city of about one half million in a conservative and largely rural state. The city center is beginning to show signs of life, with new construction and a revitalization of the downtown business section. Surrounding the business center is a poor inner-city residential area, and then rings of suburbs. The particular neighborhood in which this event occurred is at the edge of the inner city, in a racially mixed, lower-middle-class settlement. It is a lovely old part of town, with many good-sized houses and large oak trees shading the narrow streets. The garages are small—people did not own cars when most of these houses were built—and are set in the backyards with openings facing the alleyways behind the houses. The houses are in generally good repair. The residents are proud of their homes and lawns, especially since many have worked their way to this neighborhood from the inner city.

Recently there has been an in-migration of minority groups of color. These people are largely young family groups, and the schools have become quite crowded. The streets are jammed with cars parked overnight. (These families generally contain multiple-wage earners who need two cars.) There has been a lot of turnover, as new families arrived and some of the older people moved away. Consequently, there is not a strong feeling of community among current residents. For that reason, among others, a neighborhood association has emerged, to try to recreate a sense of community among the new young residents as well as the older residents.

One of the early leaders of the neighborhood association was Micheal Benjamin, a resident who was a social worker by profession. He was appointed block captain for several years, and people in his area got to know him and called on him for various questions and problems. Mrs. Washington is new to this neighborhood. A former AFDC mother with two high school children, she took secretarial courses and now is working full-time and has been able to move to a better school district.

When Mrs. Washington returned home one evening to find her street torn up by a road construction company, leaving big chunks of cement lying around, the sidewalks gone, and the large holes in the road beds filled with rainwater, she was very upset. She did not call the neighborhood association representative because she did not know about the organization. Instead, she asked her neighbors what was going on. No one knew. Some of the people who were home that day asked the workmen what they were doing, and had gotten rude and uninformative answers: "I don't know; I just do like I'm told." No one thought to call the city government or any other organization—until Mrs. Washington took the initiative.

Early the next morning, she called the city's Human Relations Department because she recalled reading something about it in the newspapers recently. The agent who spoke to her suggested she call her local neighborhood association to make some formal complaint since it would be better coming from a group of persons rather than one individual. The agent explained that his organization could not act because there was no apparent civil rights violation. But he did locate the name and phone number of the president of her neighborhood association. Mrs. Washington called this person and told her what had occurred. The president in turn called the city engineer to get more facts. Beyond the fact that the city had decided to extend the one-way traffic pattern through this neighborhood by widening the streets and removing overnight parking, all the president got was a clear message of annoyance for bothering the engineer. This infuriated the neighborhood association leader, who then called Mike Benjamin, the social worker-block captain. She directed Mike Benjamin to "do something," carte blanche, provided it did not cost anything (since the association was invariably broke).

Before going to work, Mr. Benjamin drove over to Mrs. Washington's home—or tried to. He found the streets torn up and cars parked in every possible place, making driving near the area very slow going. As Mr. Benjamin walked to Mrs. Washington's house, he spoke to residents he recognized. All expressed anger but also passivity. One of them said, "You can't fight city hall."

Mr. Benjamin introduced himself to Mrs. Washington, and they discussed the situation to that moment. Before Mr. Benjamin had arrived, Mrs. Washington had been on the phone with the local NAACP office to see what they could do. The office manager sympathized with her and pointed out other happenings that he interpreted as a general strategy to put down blacks and other minorities in this city. But he was not certain what he could do at this moment. Mrs. Washington understood the limitations of the groups she had called for aid, but she was interested in pursuing the matter, so Mr. Benjamin asked what other organizations could she think of that might be induced to get involved in this challenge. She thought a moment, and mentioned her church. It turned out, however, that she was still going to her old church in the inner city, and it was probably too far away for them to get involved. She remembered that she had volunteered at a poverty coalition group to get neighborhood health clinics for the inner city, and even though that was several years ago, she knew that some of these people had been hired by the mayor's office. She mentioned some names, and Mr. Benjamin recognized a couple of people who were also prominent in the local Democratic Party.

This led to an idea. Elections were coming up soon, and so Mr. Benjamin called one of his acquaintances who was an assistant in the Mayor's office. He summarized the situation on Mrs. Washington's street. He concluded with the remark that the community's displeasure might well lead to the loss of several hundred votes in the up-coming elections. There was a moment of silence on the other end of the phone. Mr. Benjamin's friend said, "Keep the lid on for a little while longer" until she was able to call the city engineer directly from her office.

Later that day, Mr. Benjamin called the city engineer and received a much more polite answer than had the president of the neighborhood association. He stated that there had been a public hearing on the question of the one-way streets through that section of the city—no one had showed up from the neighborhood—so legally speaking, everything that had to be done was done. However, he did promise that someone from the department would be out the next afternoon to talk to the residents.

Two days later, Mr. Benjamin called Mrs. Washington, who reported that nothing had happened, no one from the city engineer's office had come. He asked her to wait another few days to see if anyone showed up. At the end of the week, she called him to report no change. So Mr. Benjamin called the city engineer again, but he was "not available." Eventually, he called back late in the day and repeated that he had done what was legally necessary. But he also said that if he had to respond to every question or request any citizen made about his department's work, he would not be able to get anything done. He had an angry tone in his voice that made Mr. Benjamin angry, but he tried to respond calmly that the city engineer's office was a civil service, and it had better respond appropriately to every citizen, or else. With that implied threat, he hung up. He did not know what the "or else" would be, but he knew that he had to come up with something.

Mr. Benjamin called his friend in the mayor's office again. He reported the "progress" and added that the residents were getting increasingly upset. He was considering going public with the whole matter by calling the local newspapers about the attitude and efforts by the city government. The mayor's assistant uttered a disparaging remark about the city engineer and then proposed a special meeting with the Democratic Party chieftains to see what could be reclaimed from this situation. She said she would "lean" on the city engineer again to be more responsive to citizens. She noted that he did some very good engineering work, but she wished he were half as good with people.

Later that night, Mrs. Washington called in a happy tone of voice to say that the city engineer had called her and volunteered to respond to any questions that she and her neighbors wished to put into writing. She said that the city engineer sounded as if the mayor or someone was breathing down his neck as he was talking, but at least he called and she was pleased. Mr. Benjamin suggested that she collect these questions quickly. He would consolidate them and make copies for all of the neighbors. They turned out to be good tough questions, but what was most impressive was that there were questions from so many of the neighbors. As he passed out copies, Mr. Benjamin recognized that people were getting some sense that "we" can do things when we stick together.

Early next week, a meeting was held at the mayor's assistant's home. Six of the Party leaders were present, including one lawyer who speculated as to whether there might be some violation involved when he heard how the construction crews tore up the sidewalks and lawns. The upshot of that meeting was that the local Party leaders (some of whom were candidates for reelection) were to go door to door and explain the situation to people. They were to urge them to attend a new formal hearing at City Hall that would be set up shortly, when the city engineer would respond in person to questions.

Two days later, Mr. Benjamin got a call from the lawyer who found the evidence he was looking for: the city had violated its right-of-way limits by tearing up the sidewalks and lawns. He had talked with the city engineer but had gotten a runaround, until he got steamed up and made his point very loudly—the city was in legal violation of its own codes and a lawsuit might be in order. A chastened city engineer ended the conversation with the statement that he would have to see about all of this.

The day of the formal hearing came. Although it was set for early morning when many of the residents could not attend, a group of some 25 neighbors attended and heard their questions read and answered. They also learned that they could ask more questions from the floor, which they did, after some hesitancy. The city engineer, the vice mayor, and several officials from the Board of Public Works were present—half of them were candidates for reelection in this largely Democratic precinct—and they apologized over and over again, and listened with great attentiveness, making notes as people spoke. Moreover, the officials promised compensation for damages to private property. They announced that new street lights would be installed, and proposed that the alleys behind the houses be refurbished so that more parking space might be made available. The meeting ended on a happy note, and Mr. Benjamin could see that Mrs. Washington and her neighbors were satisfied. But he cautioned them to wait for concrete results before they had any victory celebration.

Indeed, several weeks went by and nothing happened. Even the street construction had stopped. During that time, the local papers reported another neighborhood was having problems similar to those of Mrs. Washington's group. Mr. Benjamin suggested that the neighborhood association write a formal letter to the Board of Public Works and summarize the problem and the proposed solutions at the public hearing. He went on to note that a similar problem in a new neighborhood suggested that the Board might wish to consider the development of regular procedures for effective neighborhood participation in their own local affairs. Doing so might avert crises and lawsuits while expediting the important work of their office. The letter indicated that copies were to be sent to the Democratic Party leadership.

Still nothing happened. Then one night a child fell into a hole in the street and cut herself on some rusty equipment left there. She had a fast visit to the emergency room to get stitched up. The residents were extremely angry and called an emergency meeting with Mr. Benjamin. Although the child was not seriously injured, Mr. Benjamin called the Democratic Party chief and said: "How many kids have to be maimed or killed before the city will get around to enforcing what it had promised a group of responsible citizens a month ago?" The chief asked Mr. Benjamin to calm down, and he said that he would handle it personally from now on.

Mr. Benjamin never did find out what the Party leader did, but the facts are that within a few weeks the entire street reclamation project was completed, sidewalks, trees, lights, everything. The construction company seemed to be working overtime. The crews had become almost solicitous, and they cleaned up all of their debris. At a block party some weeks later, the residents were congratulating themselves for a job well done, and Mr. Benjamin was supporting this—up to a point. He reminded them that other neighborhoods were still not getting what they were entitled to, and perhaps this group might want to support their more distant neighbors with ideas, energy, and moral support. Mrs. Washington summarized the mood of the crowd that evening: "You know, there's more in this business of loving thy neighbor than I realized from church. When you get to work with people, all sorts of people, on a common cause, you get to like them as well." She was soon much in demand in various neighborhoods around the city, helping empower average citizens through their own collective efforts.

Analysis.   The three basic approaches to community activities are illustrated in this case. First, *social planning* was apparently done by the city engineer's office as a response from the mayor and other policy-making groups who were looking at the transportation needs of the entire community. They came up with a plan to facilitate rapid movement from the downtown business district to the bedroom communities through the inner city to the suburban fringes. The plan met its specific objectives, but it did not take into full consideration the implications for neighborhoods in the path of the change. Only a part of the entire social configuration had been considered.

There was an element of *social action* as well. Community power was unevenly distributed, and according to some of the residents of the affected neighborhood, the city government leaders and the wealthy suburbanites were not about to share much of it. There was talk of lawsuits against the city officials. Some people wanted to picket the mayor's office and invite the local TV news team to televise the confrontation. The more frustrated the neighbors got with unfulfilled promises, the more often confrontation measures were discussed. Unseen by the residents was another form of conflict, that involving the several officers in the city government. Mr. Benjamin suspected that the Democratic Party leaders, realizing how seriously community unrest might affect the local election, in which handfuls of votes can make powerful differences, ganged up on the insensitive city engineer and forced him to do what was requested. City officials control lots of resources that department heads need, so they are inclined to be responsive when threats to those resources are made. But we do not know what actually occurred.

For the most part, this case illustrates *community development*—large numbers of citizens, who individually may be powerless, joined together and learned how to describe their problems and their rights, and how to take the facts to the relevant powers. The social worker in this case was mainly a facilitator, even though he was himself a resident in a nearby neighborhood. Mrs. Washington and her neighbors were able to sustain the assertive pressures and followed through on their own problems. They also later provided assistance to others with similar concerns.

A community worker, man or woman, needs skill in communicating at two levels—with the powerful and the powerless. Such a worker has to know how to reach the media, as well as how to use (or threaten to use) the resources the community has in the given situation.

ADMINISTRATION OF SOCIAL SERVICES

In *An Enemy of the People*, Ibsen's drama discussed in Chapter 1, you will recall that a town health spa had been built at the suggestion of Dr. Stockmann, although not according to his plan. He later discovered that the public baths were using contaminated water and would be a health hazard. That discovery led to the dramatic confrontation.

A point that was mentioned but may not be remembered is that the leaders of the community took Dr. Stockmann's vague idea and translated it into a reality, using the efficient organizational structure of the town council and related agencies. We take for granted the efficiencies of bureaucratic organizations—until their inefficiencies come to annoy us sufficiently enough to take action. We consider in this section a disguised service situation that involves a difficulty experienced by a particular handicapped group in a community. It required some effective problem solving, but with sensitivity to the limitations of the parties involved. These two challenges—efficiency and sensitivity—sometimes appear to demand contradictory behavior from the people involved. Yet, for human service organizations, it is obvious that both are necessary. First, consider some administrative and organizational theories that address these issues. Then we will turn to a case study.

The Bureaucratic Model: Max Weber

Why do people create the types of arrangements for working together that they do? Consider a broad approach to organizational theory, drawing on the pioneering work of Max Weber (1864-1930), whose analysis of bureaucracy still influences a large portion of contemporary organizational and administrative theory. Briefly put, Weber identifies a number of characteristics of an ideal organization or bureaucracy that he conceives as a rational problem-solving machine dealing with social and economic problems.

We have all known many specific bureaucracies. It is impossible to live in today's society without being part of some and being influenced by others. Some of our experiences have been satisfactory. The streets in front of our homes are kept in reasonable repair. We eventually get our health insurance to pay the major part of the doctor's bill, and the mail usually gets delivered on time. So satisfactory are such bureaucratic services that we tend to forget them until something happens to call our attention to the red tape and bungling that occur.

Weber, who was well aware of the deficiencies of bureaucratic services in daily life, defined bureaucracy *in ideal terms* as a *formal social machine* composed of parts (positions) in relationship to one another (the social structure), each part having certain functions (roles) that are interrelated to all the others in a hierarchical "organization chart" detailing the flow of influence/control (down) and information/obedience (up). The purpose of this arrangement is to solve some problem or achieve some goal in the most orderly and efficient manner possible. This purpose requires predictable relationships between elements of the organization. Therefore, qualified people are presumed to be recruited for various positions based on their merits for fulfilling the required functions. Measures like civil service exams test the applicants' competency, while eliminating extraneous influences (such as being the nephew of the boss). All persons of a like rank are given equal rewards for quality work, and they progress along a known merit system of advances. Once in place, workers are protected from arbitrary discharge or harassment as long as they perform their duties as specified in both cases by impersonal and formally written rules of the organization. The business of the organization is conducted through appropriate channels (regarding who is required and permitted to talk with whom); and records are kept (in duplicate) of each step along the way. While personality differences and the operation of small informal groups are recognized, the emphasis is on the rational organization solving problems.

The Human Relations Approach: Rensis Likert

A second type of organizational theory can be termed the *human relations approach* (Likert, 1961). In reaction to the formal bureaucratic model, the authors of human relations theory emphasized that the personal beliefs and attitudes of workers about each other, their work, and their employers influenced how well they worked, and what kind of environment existed at the work site. Thus the informal group of immediate peers came to exert a powerful leverage on productivity, even though it never appears on organizational charts as such. Based on some provocative research by Roethlisberger and Dickson (1939) (the famous Hawthorne studies), social scientists began to recognize the importance of the informal but real relationships workers had with each other. Norms on how fast one should work and other matters limiting or promoting productivity were set by informal groups. Such norms were, of course, influenced powerfully by the rules and structures of the organization, but not always in positive ways.

By involving the workers in some aspects of the work that concerned them, management could encourage constructive informal group norms. But the price was giving up the prerogatives of power, the top-down giving of orders, and some of the abstract efficiency that bureaucracies were presumed to achieve. According to the human relations model, the workers, who saw the production process more closely, were often able to give insight into arrangements that were both satisfying to themselves and yielding as much or more productivity in many cases than the management-prescribed systems.

In the following case study concerning the deaf, as well as that of the preceding example of the neighborhood association, we will examine social organizations that operate more like the human relations model than like a formal bureaucratic model. In place of the pyramid of power of the typical bureaucracy, there is a two-level structure that consists of a temporary governing council and the rest of the membership. There may be some committees to carry out some of the formal aspects of these organizations, but anyone can volunteer to take part. Much of the business of these types of organizations takes place informally, among friends or colleagues who are currently directing the organizations.

The major purpose of the typical neighborhood organization is to create opportunities to stimulate a sense of community among residents. Whenever a task arises that requires effective problem solving, the association may form some structures (like committees and chairpersons) to perform the job. Thus, more of the bureaucratic elements emerge as people are called upon to do specialized tasks toward advancing some specific common cause. Records are usually kept, especially on contributions or dues collected and expended, in spite of the informality that characterizes the occasional meetings of such voluntary organizations.

A special feature of both neighborhood organizations and charity organizations is that they can use the participatory zeal of their members as fuel for their work. The contributions of all members should be equally valued, even while recognizing the differences in native talents in performing certain roles. Various kinds of rewards, tangible and intangible, are given for team efforts and achievements. A great many services of modern life are provided by unpaid volunteers working in concert.

It might be useful to think of the bureaucratic model and the human relations approach as being opposite poles of one continuum, the formal and the informal ways people arrange themselves to solve external tasks, while maintaining satisfying internal relationships. Current thinking on organizational theory seeks to balance both aspects in relation to the larger systems context in which interdependent units contribute to the task functions of the whole as well as to relationships within subgroups (Hasenfeld, 1983).

Behind all of the individual casework, the group work, and even the efforts that go into community development, there must be an agency that organizes personnel and resources to achieve goals in an effective and humane manner. How that agency is organized and run is a critical factor in the successful or unsuccessful delivery of social services. This is yet another perspective using the configural approach relating system components to one another.

This section of Chapter 8 presents an example on the administration of a specific project over the course of its development. As you read the case, observe the ways a bureaucratic organization provides social services. It seeks to identify problems; collect materials relevant to its solution; and plan a program to resolve that problem. It engages in the nitty-gritty of bringing an idea into reality, including making personnel decisions (what tasks are to be performed and by whom?) and working out budgets. It then implements the program and evaluates its functioning in order to routinize the successful solution to a common human need. These are the kinds of problem-solving activities involved in administration.

The contemporary administrator of a social agency is more than a bureaucrat who thinks only of delivering a product. How the product (the social service) is given is half of its meaning. As leader of the organization and a major influence in the structures that provide for the delivery of its services, the administrator plays a large part in creating the atmosphere for efficient and humane social work. Given the nature of the social services, largely autonomous dealings with many different individuals over long periods of time, it is necessary to establish some sense of order in providing workers with necessary resources. But equally important, given the individualistic nature of human problems, is the stimulation of a creative environment so that workers can feel supported in trying new and innovative—that is to say, "risky"—endeavors to solve intransigent problems. Routinization is both the boon and the bane of bureaucratic life. If routines and rigid rules are all there are to the organization, then services will soon become stilted and inhumane because they do not fit well the changing individualized needs of clients.

Administrators have to deal not only with the professional staff of the agency but also with many others. Others include the administrator's board or whatever the governing body of an agency is called. It may consist of a group of distinguished citizens who are concerned about the agency goals and means but are not paid employees of that agency. They do not stand to benefit from its functioning. Or the person governing a given agency may be an administrator at a higher level in the organization. Boards typically provide general policy determination and guidance on broad operational programs, as well as oversight of the agency as a whole. They may hire, and evaluate the performance of, the agency director or administrator. They are typically much involved in general budgetary matters: Where are funds to come from and are they sufficient for the need? What new plans and programs are suitable to the agency's mission? Are the established programs working adequately?

Administrators also have to deal with other agencies or organizations whose work is related to his or her own agency's because the need for cooperation and sharing of scarce resources requires that such agencies work together for some common social goals. Sometimes this interaction results in shared projects; at other times it is simply a matter of obtaining the goodwill and support of others, or the exchange of information on current efforts and future plans.

Administrators perform public relations duties in the community at large, to keep the good image of the agency visible and to solicit support for its programs and funding (such as through United Charities Appeals). Contacts should also be made between the administrator and professional groups and organizations that conduct research and provide guidance on professional and policy issues, including ethics, the professional's employment conditions and benefits, and other concerns.

Usually administrators come to their positions after much experience in the different aspects of agency practice, as well as with special education in social work administration. However, it is worth noting that many direct-practice social workers end up in administrative positions of various types. They may become supervisors, participate in various levels of management, help frame policy, or engage in planning, research, or overall direction of a department or an agency. So it is worthwhile to study some of the basics of administration, both to understand the context in which much social work practice occurs as well as to prepare for the day you might be running some part of an agency.

A Case Study in Administration: Services for the Deaf

Bill Braden was sick yesterday and wanted to notify his employer that he would not be at work—but he could not do so. There was a telephone at the Braden home, and he was not so sick that he could not reach the phone, but Mr. Braden cannot do what most of us take for granted a dozen times a day. Mr. Braden is deaf, and no one was at home with him to make the call. There are many persons with hearing impairments of various degrees, invisible burdens that frequently get ignored by the helping professions because they are not easily seen. This case study concerns one agency's response to the challenge of deafness.

About a dozen years before, the community college had established a communications center for the deaf. They provided such services as information and referral about treatment, problem-resolving assistance, and something new—a message relay service. In the relay service, a hearing person provided the linkage between a deaf person and another hearing person. It could take place by the deaf person's going to the center and communicating in sign language that the staff person would read and then communicate by a regular voice telephone to the other hearing person. Or the deaf person might use a telecommunication device from his or her home: a typed message would be communicated to the staff person who would then make the voice telephone call.

Over the next decade, this service was available to people all over the community, and while no records were kept, observers felt that the needs of the hearing impaired were being met. However, financial pressures on the community college forced it to phase out the center's message relay activities, and the community deaf lost a valued resource. There were hardships, as in Bill Braden's case, but for about two years, there was no voice raised on behalf of the deaf. The invisible burden remained invisible.

The state government had a division that provided information and services regarding the deaf in pursuance of state regulations. A young community worker, Leroy Patton, was hired by this division to coordinate community services for the deaf. As part of his on-the-job learning, the worker visited various agencies in the community that had provided services for the hearing impaired. In the course of his travels, he stumbled upon the gap in services once provided by the message relay center. He also noticed that the Community United Way had no services for the deaf on its roster of supported activities. It was probably an oversight, as the staff of the Community United Way was zealous in trying to support organizations to remedy needs.

The question was raised in the mind of the community worker: Is there a need for a message relay station in this community, and if so, how can such a station be created and maintained?

Administrators follow a problem-solving process in ways similar to other social workers. Leroy began with a definition of the problem and the identification of the parties involved. It was not simply that there were people with hearing impairments. That was understood, even though there were no reliable counts of the numbers of people affected. Experts in the field of hearing impairment point out that such persons are frequently poor, and their educational and socialization experiences may be limited. They live in a silent culture, and face the relentless challenge of dealing "equally" with a hearing environment (see Higgins, 1980; Nash and Nash, 1981). Leroy was fascinated to learn that there were, in effect, different dialects among users of sign language, corresponding in part to the quality of their training as well as of their native talents. Communicating with and between the deaf was no easy business.

Once Leroy felt he had a sense of the characteristics of the hearing impaired, he then began to determine the goals and objectives of a message relay center. After consulting with experts and some deaf acquaintances, Leroy developed a goal statement that involved equal access to the phone system. Short-term and intermediary objectives would include the provision of services or devices that enable the hearing-impaired person to participate equally in this public communication system. Since deaf persons differ in their acceptance and use of mechanical devices, reflecting different levels of experience and sophistication with such machines, equal access was operationally defined as having options on ways to use the message relay service. Leroy observed that the black community in this city was relatively poorer than the larger white community and less well educated. They would be less likely to purchase telecommunication devices and might be less inclined to use such objects, even if they were provided free. However, if a message relay center or centers were centrally located and accessible, Leroy predicted that blacks would make greater use of the personal walk-in and signing services than would whites.

Leroy also made an important administrative decision—to add a new service unit to an existing organization that was functioning effectively instead of starting from scratch. The existing organization would have to be able to expand to accept additional staff and equipment to conduct the innovative project, but having the routine systems for housing, supplying, and supporting programs already in place should simplify the new service. Here is Leroy's story, in his own words:

As administrator of this project, I knew I had to get some basic supports: Money to start up a program; the technical knowledge and equipment with which to provide the service; the locations to house the workers and the equipment; and publicity that the service was available.

Since United Way did not have a specialized service for deaf people, I thought they might be open to accepting the concept of a message relay service, but I wasn't sure. There is always a lot of competition for charity dollars. The possibility of getting some start-up money from a fund-raising organization, such as the Lions Club (which has had a long-time commitment to the sensorily impaired in their service programs) seemed like a way to begin. I thought we might be able to run a pilot project to prove to the United Way that the message relay center was a workable concept.

The State Division for the Deaf would be able to provide expert services, a program design, the selection of equipment, and the recruitment and training of workers, but it couldn't raise the money to run the program. That meant that I had to coordinate these aspects of the State Division for the Deaf as well as arrange cooperation with the Lions Club, all in connection with the United Way. This took careful planning, and, as it turned out, a bit of luck.

I first got clearance from my supervisor at the office concerning the overall concept; this was exactly what he had intended me to be doing, and so gave full approval to a meeting between the State Division on the Deaf and the local Lions Club in order to persuade them to provide some start-up money for this project. At this meeting, I spelled out my proposal, which involved a partnership between our two organizations; with their seed money and our provision of expertise, we would both approach the United Way with a plan to offer a pilot project lasting 18 months, after which the United Way could decide whether or not it wanted to continue the service.

The Lions Club officials were delighted to hear about the project, and promised to cooperate with the fund raising. Moreover, they pointed out, many of their members were either on the Board of the United Way, or were close personal friends with Board members. "Ah," I thought to myself, "this is how the informal side of bureaucracies operate. I'll bet the message relay center will be a sure thing to get United Way support."

But it wasn't. There were many good proposals that United Way had to consider when we went to present our proposal. They listened politely, even enthusiastically I thought, but they did not offer any commitment at that time. The "carrot" had been well presented: a gift of start-up funds, the offer of technical expertise, training, and the like. All the United Way had to do was to monitor the project themselves so as to decide whether or not they wished to take it over after 18 months.

On the way out of the meeting, I was talking with the president of the Board of United Way and one of the Lions Club executives. The Lions executive was talking about the law that recipients of federal funds had to make their services accessible to the deaf. The president of the United Way said he knew about this, but his funds were either voluntary or from the state. I pointed out that the state got these funds from a block grant from the federal government, and so I thought that any recipient would be subject to the same federal regulations about accessibility. And even though the United Way was doing a fine job of supporting many service programs, many deaf people couldn't use them as they currently exist. "Ah," I thought to myself. "Here is the stick." I allowed as how I thought a message relay center would be just the thing to bring United Way into compliance with federal regulations. The Lions Club executive allowed as how he agreed with me. The president of the United Way looked at us for a moment, and then departed.

Not only was the message relay center approved, but within two months the new Communications Center for the Deaf appeared on the United Way brochure of sponsored agencies—with no mention that this was a pilot project.

Implementation of the project went relatively smoothly, given the numerous details that had to be attended to, everything from coordinating the various existing personnel and technical services, to hiring new personnel, and setting up budgetary and operational guidelines, as well as dealing with publicity. As predicted, the two aspects of the message relay center were differentially used. Although the average white deaf person was poor, the average hearing-impaired black person is much poorer. Blacks were the predominant users of the walk-in services in which the half-time staff person received the message in sign language and then made the appropriate phone calls, while whites were more likely to own and use the telecommunication devices.

I performed several types of evaluation, knowing that these would be required in the future deliberations about maintaining the service. First, I had some descriptive information collected. It turned out that about 75 percent of the requests for message relays came by way of telecommunication devices, and the rest from walk-ins. A survey of user satisfaction showed considerable approval of the system, particularly the two modes of making contact. In terms of volume, there were about 10 calls a day, a heavy load for a half-time staff person when you realize that each hearing-impaired communication takes about four times as long to process as normal phone calls. The incoming sign language message had to be received and then translated, and then it had to be sent out to a hearing person who makes a reply to the staff person, who then has to return the reply through signs to the deaf person.

However, as news spread among the hearing-impaired community, the requests began to increase. Soon there was need for a three-quarter time staff person, and then a full-time person, then one full-time and one half-time person, and now, five years later, two full-time staff members. There are between 30 and 40 communications a day, on the average; this level has held steady for many months, suggesting that a plateau has been reached. The administrative procedures were put into place, modified slightly as experience dictated, and have been relatively constant ever since. I did institute annual reviews to make sure we weren't overlooking anything in the delivery of the service or the kinds of new services we might provide.

The long-term outcome is that the United Way adopted the pilot project fully as its own funded project. However, the original alliance among the Lions Club, the State Division on the Deaf, and the United Way is still maintained, with the Lions making contributions to special projects, and the State Division still offering technical advice. This advice has been much needed, as the range of services to the hearing impaired has expanded. The Center now coordinates requests for sign interpreters; for offering training on services to the deaf for various social agencies; for information and referral (such as where can I send my hearing-impaired daughter to college so she will be able to participate as fully as possible in the educational experience?); for advocacy on behalf of the deaf (such as when a landlord with a "no pets" restriction refused to accept a deaf renter who had a "hearing dog." The staff member was able to convince the landlord that the dog was as essential as a guide dog is to a blind person. The state law reinforced this similarity, and the renter got her apartment).

Any service agency sensitive to the needs of its clients will adapt projects suitable for their needs. The Communications Center for the Deaf expanded its program to include funding of visual smoke alarms; baby-crying visual systems for deaf parents; and a loaner service when a hearing-impaired person's telecommunication device needed repair, something that took as long as two months. New projects included trying to persuade elderly black hearing-impaired persons to use telecommunication devices for their own convenience and safety. Bill Braden has not been sick much in the past few years, but whenever he is, he no longer worries about not being able to communicate with his boss.

SUMMARY

This chapter has reviewed several ways that individuals may be helped—in small groups, in the neighborhoods and the community at large, and through the administration of the policies and programs of organizations and the government. One might argue that it is always individuals who are the ultimate beneficiaries of these efforts. And there is some truth to this.

On the other hand, it is inconceivable to think about helping many individuals in a modern society without going through various groups and organizations to do so. Even the private practitioner speaking with one individual depends on a host of social organizations and natural helping groups to supplement his or her individual efforts. It is fully appropriate to deliver services to groups as such, regardless of what individuals are members. For example, there are employee-assistance programs at the workplace that provide services to workers (and sometimes family members) exclusively because of their work roles.

Thus this chapter, with its three case studies and different theoretical approaches, is really describing portions of the total helping configuration. It is important to observe that all of the workers described in this chapter are following the general outlines of the generic problem-solving process, applied to the unique situations of the persons, groups, or communities involved. The differences among them are easy to see, but it is the similarities that should attract our attention. There are many ways to be a helping professional.

OUTLINE

Introduction

True Believers and Honest Self-Critics

A List of Core Theories

Summary and Critical Discussion

Individual Level Theories
  Psychoanalytic Theory
  Learning Theories
  Humanist Theory

Group Level Theories
  Small Group Theory
  Communication Theory (Virginia Satir)
  Family Structural Therapy (Salvadore Minuchin)
  Natural Helping Network Theory (Alice Collins and Diane Pancoast)

Community Organization Level Theories (Jack Rothman)
  Social Planning Approach
  Community Development Approach
  Social Action Approach

Administration and Planning Level Theories
  Bureaucratic Theory (Max Weber)
  Human Relations Theory (Rensis Likert)

General Systems Level Theory
  Configural Model

Summary

CHAPTER NINE

Working Theories—
Toward a Workable Practice

One of the major distinguishing features of a helping professional, as contrasted with lay persons, is that the professional makes systematic use of theories of human behavior to guide practice. A scientific theory contains no magic; it is simply a systematic statement of how its originator believes a certain portion of the world works.

But there are different theories that purport to explain the same set of client behaviors in different ways. A helping professional has to assess critically each proposal and test the outcomes against the predictions. This chapter presents a list of the theories discussed throughout the book and goes into detail on several, so that readers will have some beginning understanding of these conceptual road maps for professional helping. Remember: Read critically and be critical of what each theory proposes the worker do. Make sure the objective results are in accord with what the theory predicts. Otherwise, consider changing to another theory.

INTRODUCTION

This chapter presents a brief overview of theories to guide practice at the individual, small group (including family), community, and organizational levels. Obviously, this can only be an introduction to these theories. Students will want to take advanced courses and guided field instruction before they can feel confident of their knowledge and skills in translating these abstract sets of ideas into workable practice principles.

But we can begin here to get a sense of the whole of a given theory and to learn the unique terms associated with one or another model. We can then understand what others are saying as they discuss cases, and we can come to appreciate the power that these abstract sets of ideas can provide in (1) describing a situation economically, (2) explaining how the events have come to be as they are, (3) predicting what events will occur—particularly so that we might act to prevent predictable problems, treat existing ones, and rehabilitate people whose conditions have run their course.

Again, this is an *introduction* to several theories. There are many additional aspects of each model, many critical analyses and research studies that call for modifications of each of the theories, and many value issues left unreported in this chapter. So, with that caveat, welcome to the first steps of thinking about theories for practice.

TRUE BELIEVERS AND HONEST SELF-CRITICS

The first major hurdle in understanding how to use theories for practice is to *believe* that theories—systems of fragile abstract ideas—can be useful in the rough and tough everyday world in which we live. Note that I did not say that theories are true or false; only propositions derived from them can be tested for truth or falsity. Theories only have to be useful as guides to effective and humane outcomes, which means that eventually you must evaluate their usefulness in the real world, rather than simply as an interesting or logical story. A second major hurdle is *not to believe* too strongly the theories we employ, that is, we must be honest self-critics in their applications. Are they really useful or not?

Social psychologist Kurt Lewin once remarked that nothing is as practical as a good theory. Even though helping professionals deal with very concrete human problems, such as physical injuries, psychological distress, and institutional forms of discrimination, we still need some perspective to guide our helping actions. Theories are logical networks of abstract ideas (concepts) that enable us to benefit from the systematic experiences of others so as to guide our own practices in like situations.

Courtesy Virginia Commonwealth University

Belief and criticalness are two aspects important for keeping perspective on using theories for practice. Do not let one get very far ahead of the other. You have to believe a theorist's claims to get started testing a theory in practice, after which you will probably become critical of one or another aspect of the theory, and may modify the theory or look for another that promises to be a better guide to practice. Then the cycle of believing (tentatively) and being critical begins again.

A LIST OF CORE THEORIES

Readers of earlier chapters have already been introduced to some theories. And other theoretical materials will be introduced later in the book. All of these theoretical materials are listed here for reinforcement so that you can become aware of what you will have studied by the conclusion of the book. The theories are divided by level, although sometimes a general theory may be applicable to more than one level; also indicated are the chapters where the theories are discussed.

INDIVIDUAL LEVEL
Psychoanalytic Theory (Chapter 9)
Learning Theories (Chapter 9)
Humanist Theory (Chapter 9)

SMALL GROUP LEVEL
Small Group Theory (Chapter 9)
Communication Theory (Virginia Satir) (Chapter 8)
Family Structural Therapy (Salvadore Minuchin) (Chapter 8)
Natural Helping Network Theory (Chapter 8)

COMMUNITY ORGANIZATION LEVEL
Social Planning (Chapter 8)
Community Development (Chapter 8)
Social Action (Chapter 8)

ADMINISTRATION AND PLANNING LEVEL
Bureaucratic Theory (Chapter 8)
Human Relations Theory (Chapter 8)

GENERAL SYSTEMS LEVEL
Configural Model (Illustrated throughout this text)

SUMMARY AND CRITICAL DISCUSSION

These theories or conceptual approaches represent a small portion of the many theories that exist, but because they are the original theoretical formulations, they may be used as the basis for understanding more recent variations or adaptations. The concepts discussed in the core theories and approaches constitute a large portion of the common language of the applied social sciences.

INDIVIDUAL LEVEL THEORIES

Psychoanalytic Theory

We examine here one of the most influential theories of human behavior to come from the work of one individual, Sigmund Freud (1856–1939) and later developed or modified by large numbers of followers and opponents. This and other theories are presented as a series of separate statements for more careful consideration of the parts of the theory.

ASSUMPTIONS

1. All social and psychological behavior is caused by knowable antecedent events. Even seemingly irrational behavior has systematic causes, when a thorough analysis is made of antecedent events, including many that happened in a client's early childhood and are not present in the person's conscious awareness.

2. The human personality may be conceptually described along five major dimensions; complete understanding of the structure, functioning (and dysfunctioning), and development of the individual requires that these five dimensions or approaches to human personality be combined. The first dimension is termed the *topographic* or *depth approach,* which refers to the accessibleness to consciousness of any thought or feeling. The largest portion of human personality is composed of *unconscious* thoughts and feelings. In the ordinary course of everyday events, these thoughts and feelings cannot gain access to the conscious awareness because they are anti-social and would lead to censure if they were made public. (Thus there has to be some mechanism that prevents them from reaching consciousness—it is called *repression.*)

Another aspect of human personality is the awareful portion termed the *conscious.* It is like a spotlight in a dark room; whatever it focuses on is brought to awareness, meaning that one can think about that topic, make decisions, and act. The third aspect of personality is the *preconscious,* that which can be brought to awareness by mental effort.

3. Freud later developed what he called a *structural dimension* to his personality theory. This overlaps somewhat the typographic dimension in that the several structural elements—*id, ego,* and *superego* (including the *conscience* and the *ego ideal*)—have unconscious and conscious aspects. Specifically, the id represents a hypothetical portion of personality that is largely unconscious whose function is to express sexual and aggressive drives or impulses. (See section 6, the dynamic dimension.) The id is present at birth, and it is from the id that other structures of the mind eventually emerge.

The ego is the term for a group of functions operating largely in the conscious realm that connect the person to reality. Included would be such functions as perception, cognition, decision making, mobility, and the like. The ego thus connects the unconscious id demands to the opportunities and barriers of the real world. The superego splits off from the ego in the course of development, and contains, sometimes at an unconscious level, the values, expectations, and sanctions internalized from the parents' behavior toward the young child—this would be called the conscience. Another aspect of the superego is the ego ideal, the aspirations and potentials for oneself, which are formed by observing a variety of models, including the parents, but not limited to them.

4. Another aspect of the structural view of personality is that the id operates by means of *primary process,* a form of functioning in which one seeks pleasure and avoids pain (the pleasure principle) by means of imagining whatever one desires. The powerful but irrational forces of the id thus imagine some desired object, such as food, but it requires the ego to negotiate with reality to obtain that objective. Thus the id surrenders some of its energies to the ego, after being frustrated in obtaining them on its own, in exchange for obtaining reductions of its tensions (desires). The ego develops *secondary process,* a form of problem solving in which reasoning is employed to negotiate with reality to meet basic needs.

5. A basic point to note is that the person always has unconscious demands from the id seeking expression. But equally, antisocial forces are opposed in a civilized world. (One has to eat, sleep, excrete, and so on, in certain socially permitted ways.) Thus the world of the person is intrinsically conflictful for Freud. Antisocial unconscious forces are always seeking expression, only to be kept down, indeed, tricked by the ego, to receive some portion of gratification in some socially tolerated fashion. When the conflict becomes more than ego can handle, we will see symptoms such as the classic neurotic or psychotic behaviors.

6. The *dynamic dimension* involves an analysis of the forces within the unconscious of the id that pressure the ego to perform certain actions. Freud first suggested a generalized pleasure-seeking drive, termed the *libido,* that sought sexual gratification in both the broadest (any pleasure seeking) and the narrowest (specific genital pleasure) senses of the word. He later added a general *aggressive drive,* so that his final dynamic version of personality included a life and a death force acting, often in conflict, within the individual. All behaviors are thus expressions of pleasure-seeking and death-seeking drives. These are not usually directly expressed, but are symbolically or indirectly expressed in ways that are socially tolerated.

7. Another dimension to personality is called the *developmental* or *genetic.* This focuses on the *psychosexual stages* of human development: the *oral, anal, phallic, latency,* and *genital.* Each such phase represents the chief form of gratification for the individual at that time, around which his or her life seems to focus.

   a) The oral phase (from birth to about 18 months) involves various forms of oral gratification using the mouth, lips, and such. Obviously the infant needs to suck to survive, but Freud recognized that the infant was also exploring his or her world at the same time.

   b) The anal phase (from about 18 months to 3 years or so) refers to the child's source of fascination, gratification, and control connected with excretory functions. Such antics may not thrill the caretakers who are trying to get the child toilet trained during this time, and so a power struggle may develop between parents and child.

c) The phallic phase (roughly from 3 or 4 to about 5 or 6) involves gratifications located at the genitals. Freud assumes that the penis becomes the chief object of fascination for both boys and girls, but for different reasons, and with different outcomes. Boys of this age, Freud asserts, literally seek to love their mothers, and they hate their fathers as competitors to the mother's love. (Note working of the libidinal and aggressive drives.) This uneven battle ends because the little boy, who has discovered that girls lack penises, fears *castration* if he were to persist in the competition. And indeed, he tries to ingratiate himself with his father, becoming a "little man" like his dad (technically called *identification*).

The little girl has a more difficult road to follow on the way to resolving this phallic challenge. She knows she lacks a penis and by some childish logic blames her mother for this, and turns toward the father as love object. However, she too cannot compete with her mother, and thus turns away from the father as love object. But the little girl cannot return to the mother completely, and thus is left seeking some future psychological anchor. This is the period of time when the superego is being formed, which explains for Freud why women have weaker superegos and poorer self-esteem than men.

These stories of the intricate girations of children to form their eventual sexual identities are labeled the *Oedipal Complex* for boys and the *Electra Complex* for girls, analogs of the ancient Greek tales.

d) The latency period is not a literal psychosexual stage as much as it is a quiescence in libidinal and aggressive drives after the Oedipal/Electra Complex resolutions. Biological drives appear to calm down just as children get involved in school and other extra-family activities.

e) The genital phase emerges when biology once again stirs during puberty. The libidinal drive frequently finds expression in masturbation, and the renewed sexual conflicts require another resolution, this time involving outside choices of sexual objects as a person's sexual identity and social role become increasingly clear.

8. The fifth dimension of personality is called the *economic*, referring to the supposition that there is a fixed amount of *psychic energy* which an individual has to invest in various choices in life. The term *cathexis* means the investment of libidinal energies in some object. (There is no parallel term for investments of aggressive energies.) The young infant forms some image of what he or she desires to satisfy a need, and immediately invests emotional energies in that object. But for the infant, energy is not clearly focused in action, and so frustration is inevitable. The infant learns to delay the discharge of this psychic energy, and thus forms the ego.

The infant is very self-centered—*narcissistic*—and focuses his or her cathexes on the self. Soon, the infant recognizes that others become sources of gratification, and some of the infant's psychic energies get invested in mental images of those significant others. They are called love objects, or just objects. When a child has poor object relations, severe problems might occur, among them character disorders (narcissistic type), borderline states, and psychoses.

9. *Defense mechanisms* are the various kinds of mental maneuvers a person takes to deal with experiences of anxiety that signal the emergence of an

antisocial impulse that is seeking expression. Initially, the young infant performs some maneuvers that deny the reality of the situation, but these are costly temporary reliefs from the stress because they do not change the problem. Later, the child learns more complex maneuvers that change either the feeling state (from *I love* to *I hate*, for example), the object of the feeling (from *you* to *me*, for example), or the actor involved (from *me* to *you*, for example). More complex defense mechanisms may change two or more of these elements. Examples follow (see Anna Freud, 1936):

> Given a starting condition, I love you, defense mechanisms may change one or another element:
> a. I don't love you. (*Repression*, the unconscious ejection from awareness of impulses that are painful)
> b. I love some logically lovable object. (*Rationalization*, the unconscious process that justifies conduct by use of reasonable, but not the real, reasons)
> c. I hate you. (*Reaction formation*, the development of an affect or action opposite to the original unconscious one)
> d. You love me. (*Projection*, the unconscious attribution of one's own affects or actions to another)
> e. I write love poetry. (*Sublimation*, unconscious transformation of an unacceptable affect or action into a socially acceptable, even valued, one)

THEORY

Combining these five dimensions that Freud evolved over the course of a lifetime of work is difficult. There are many concepts and propositions (assumptions) involved, and these get changed over time. However, as a tentative brief statement of the main point of the theory, we might suggest the following: Every aspect of human behavior is an expression of unconscious conflicts (learned within the first six years of life) battling against societal sanctions against improper sexual or aggressive impulses. The ego's state of balance represents how this conflict resolution is proceeding. Each stage of psychosexual development provides opportunities for growth into maturity, but also points where an individual may *fixate*, that is, get psychologically stuck even though he or she continues to grow chronologically.

Learning Theories

There are three major forms of learning theories and many variations. Altogether, they represent the most general approach in American psychology, and perhaps the most widely practiced forms of clinical approaches. These approaches are most closely associated with specific theorists: Ivan Pavlov (1849–1936), classical conditioning; B.F. Skinner, operant learning; and Albert Bandura, social learning.

DEFINITIONS

1. *Behavior* includes not only observable physical actions but also reportable feelings and thoughts.

2. *Learning* refers to the relatively stable changes that occur in a person's behavior, which take place in the course of psychosocial experiences and not because of genetic or chemical causes.

ASSUMPTIONS

3. The major ingredients of psycho-social experience include (cf. Kanfer & Phillips, 1970):

a) *Stimuli*—either internal thoughts, feelings, or tissue changes of which the individual may be unaware; or external stimuli from physical environmental sources or social environmental sources. Stimuli (especially the physical and social ones, but also the internal ones that have a physical basis) have an independent existence from what a person perceives them to have.

b) *The Person,* both the physical person who perceives events in the world and from within and the psychological-social person who has built up a set of organizing frames of reference that expect some object of perception to be a certain kind of thing, that value these objects in certain ways, that organize the perceptions to fit within existing knowledge. Some learning theorists may make more of these cognitive aspects of the person than others. Skinner would not use any of these cognitive functions of the person; for Skinner, the person is simply the sum of prior learning experiences. Bandura, Meichenbaum, Lazarus, and other learning theorists and therapists make much greater use of the cognitive dimensions of the person, which mediate how the stimuli "out there" are to be interpreted and used.

c) *Response.* Again, responses can be externally observable actions, or internal feelings and thoughts that can be reported. Responses are simply behaviors that follow after some stimuli. (Note that it is possible for a response to occur to some future hope or expectation, but the hope or expectation is an internal action occurring prior to the response.)

d) *Consequence,* the response the world makes to one's own response. If an infant wakes up hungry in the middle of the night, its cries are a response to bodily hunger pains, but a parent gets up to feed the infant, and this would be the environmental consequence to the crying. Note that it is the linking of one party's response to another party's behavior that represents social consequences.

e. *The contingency relation* between the response and the consequence. The contingency is the pattern of the relationship between response and consequence. There are several basic types:

i. *Continuous*—every time the response happens, the consequence occurs.

ii. *Intermittent*—sometimes when the response happens, the consequence occurs. The intermittency may be based on regular sequences (for example, every other response gets the reinforcement) or irregular ones (only when a certain behavior occurs is there the positive reinforcement) or a timed consequence (every ten minutes a reinforcement whether or not the person has performed as desired).

4. People tend to seek positive consequences and avoid negative consequences by their own definition of what is positive or negative to them.

5. Behavior may be increased, decreased, or kept constant. This is all that can be done to any learned behavior. Moreover, any behavior that has been learned can be unlearned and something else learned in its place. In practice,

learning differs by degree of experience; some things are strongly learned and are highly resistent to being erased. But some traumatic experiences may produce amnesia of strongly learned materials, like one's name.

EMPIRICAL STATEMENTS

6. The following relationships generally occur with regard to increasing, decreasing, or leaving the behavior in question as is:
   a) Increasing desired behavior can be accomplished by
      (1) *positive reinforcement,* that is, any consequence that follows a response such that the response is made more likely to reoccur. (Note that nothing is intrinsically a positive reinforcer; the rewarded behavior must reoccur for the consequence to be identified as a positive reinforcement. This is a circular definition, but a necessary and useful one.) Generally speaking, common pleasant stimuli act as positive reinforcers.
      (2) *negative reinforcement,* that is, the removal of an unpleasant stimulus if a desired behavior increases.
   b) Decreasing undesired behavior can be accomplished by
      (1) *positive punishment,* or *aversive consequences,* that is, the presentation of an unpleasant stimulus if an undesired behavior is exhibited.
      (2) *negative punishment,* or *response cost,* that is, the removal of a desired stimulus when the person performs some undesired behavior.
      (3) *extinction,* the removal of any response (desired or undesired) to a given stimulus. One instance of this is called "time out," in which an offending individual is removed from the presence of others for a short time, to cool off and stop the undesired behaviors and the receiving of positive reinforcement because of them, before being readmitted back to the group.
   c) Keeping behavior at its present level by
      (1) carefully orchestrating the small steps of increasing and decreasing behavior, as needed.
      (2) building into people certain habitual modes of performing across settings. (People tend to develop habitual styles and they tend to possess inborn temperaments, but because of the press of the external world, one cannot assume that these patterns of behavior will continue in every context.)
   d) Role of cognitions in increasing, decreasing, or keeping behavior constant. Note that these methods of producing changes of behavior essentially ignore the place of cognition in the process. However, as a general rule, the more aware a person is of the consequences of his/her responses, the more likely is learning to occur and to be maintained over time.

THEORIES

7. *Classical conditioning.* One set of concepts and propositions emerging from the above involves emphasis on the control of the initial external stimuli to influence the response by conditioning or teaching specific associations to

the learner. Pavlov's initial statement involved presentation of some unconditioned (or natural) stimulus which evokes its unconditioned (or natural) response. (Milk to a hungry infant has the natural response of satisfying hunger.) Then, presentation of a conditioned stimulus (or really, a stimulus to be conditioned) slightly ahead of, but in conjunction with the unconditioned stimulus, leads eventually to that conditioned stimulus generating a weaker form of the same response as the first (natural) stimulus did. (The caretaker is always associated with the milk, and eventually, seeing the caretaker is enough to give the infant some relief from hunger, even though no food is given.) If the caretaker feeds the infant with a certain baby blanket always present, then eventually that blanket may become conditioned and serves to reduce the hunger pangs or increase the expected security of being satisfied. (This is the origin of a child's "security blanket.") Likewise, it is possible for words to become conditioned in a way akin to things, and thus, according to a Pavlovian view, every aspect of behavior may be accounted for in this way. (This type of learning has been thought to occur in various types of phobias, sexual problems, and perversions.)

8. *Operant learning.* A second major conceptual formulation in learning theory is Skinner's operant learning approach, whose major assumption is that behavior is determined by the consequences it receives in the present time frame. (This time unit includes whatever learned habitual pattern is present. How a behavior came to be is not important; what patterns of consequences currently maintain it in its present form are important.) Initially, the infant "freely emits" random behaviors, some of which get positively reinforced and thus tend to be repeated. Moreover, the consequences received become more rigorously focused; the infant has to say "Mama," not "nana," to get a strong positive response. Eventually, the child learns clear discriminations to certain stimuli so they bring predictable positive reinforcements. (The process of teaching to be more discriminating is called *discriminant learning;* when it occurs, the behavior is said to be under specific stimulus control.)

For complex learning, the operant approach suggests that by judicious reinforcement the person can be moved by small steps toward a novel desired behavior pattern. Obviously, the complex behavior can be broken down into smaller units and then recombined. But all of these actions would follow the same basic set of rules. *Generalization* refers to the spread of one learned behavior into different but similar situations. (This is vitally important to therapists who often work in offices with clients, but where the important outcomes of their helping efforts are whether the clients can perform them outside the office. Care must be taken to insure the similarities of the therapeutic learning to situations outside the office.)

Life development consists, from this perspective, of the growth of strings of consequential learnings. The learned response of one unit becomes part of the stimulus for the next. This determinism vitiates concepts like free will and human dignity because it is the environmental consequences that ultimately shape behavior. However, this does not make us less human, according to Skinner; we simply have greater responsibility to determine what consequences will be given for what actions.

9. *Social learning.* Bandura points out that if we had to learn how to cross a

busy intersection at the rush hour by operant learning, we would all be dead. The point is that we have to use some cognitive awareness of the larger situation, some understanding of complex wholes rather than specific stimulus/response pairs, some comprehension of what happens to people if they do certain things without our having to repeat the experiences ourselves. In short, we have to learn by *vicarious* means, *modeling* the behaviors of others, in person or through the mass media, benefiting from the patterns of learning that others tell us about or exhibit to us (without telling us).

Social learning involves complex wholes, frequently with regard to what we have witnessed happening to others. Social learning may occur with no immediate stimulus or no reinforcement occurring directly to the learner. What is involved is an expanded view of cognition. Stimuli are received internally that are processed in connection with related memories, and decisions are made about how to respond, even though no reinforcements have been directly received. The person is able to imagine a "what if" situation in which he or she is the receiver of the experiences of some model. This imagination is sufficient basis for deciding to act in a given way. (Note that this seems to restore free will to the human being, but it also requires many inferences of unseen conceptual entities to explain events.)

Bandura (1977) describes a concept termed *self-efficacy* as a summary of these internal processes—the thoughts and feelings about oneself as being able or unable to perform in certain ways required by a situation. One has to attribute to oneself the ability to cope, to respond appropriately to the demands of a situation, in order to adapt effectively.

PROPOSITIONS

10. Procedural steps in the use of behavioral therapy [cf. Gambrill, Thomas, and Carter (1971); Gambrill (1983)].

a) *Contact with client and determination of roles:* This step includes meeting with the client and establishing whatever professional relationship is needed to get the helping process started. It is helpful to clarify to the client his or her part in the process, especially that he or she must be involved in making the changes, must understand what is expected, and must work at bringing the changes about.

b) *Problem identification:* This involves an intensive understanding of the scope of the presenting problem, its literal measurement, as well as what antecedent, concurrent, and consequent events occur in its presence. In a formulaic statement, this assessment of the problem involves the following: Who is involved? What happens? How often and when does it happen? Where does this occur? These who/what/how/when/where questions are a direct translation of the concepts stimuli, person, response, contingency, and consequences. In general terms, problems will be excesses or deficits of behaviors in given contexts. Abstract problems, like "poor self-esteem," have to be translated into specific steps or components of behaviors that are accessible to intervention.

Presenting problems may not be either the entire problem or the actual problem. The worker must search out what events are seen as problematic by which persons under what conditions. When there is some uniformity of opinion of significant people in a given context, then it is safe to proceed. When there is difference of opinion as to whether some specific behavior is problematic, then the worker must continue problem identification until closure is achieved.

c) *Functional analysis of probable controlling conditions:* Once a target problem has been identified, then the worker and client have to figure out what factors are likely to be controlling the continuing existence of the problematic action. Patterns in the antecedent, concurrent, and consequent events are observed, and counteractions are devised.

These counteractions involve personalized variations on the methods to increase certain desired behaviors (e.g., by positive or negative reinforcement, or by modeling and role playing, or by training in the necessary skills). At the same time, one would have to take steps to decrease certain undesired behaviors (e.g., by positive and negative punishment, or by extinction, as well as by training the person to engage in behaviors that are desirable at the same time undesired behaviors might have been performed). These methods are general approaches; the specific interventive actions have to be fine-tuned to the particular situation. For example, what may be positively reinforcing to one person may not be for another. Moreover, the worker may have to use reinforcements of successive approximations toward some long-term objective that cannot be attained all at once.

d) *Determination of priorities in intervention:* Given the predicted patterns of causal factors, and the likelihood of their interrelationships, along with the limitation of resources in conducting the interventions, some priority actions must be established. Sometimes it is best to perform those interventions that deal with the riskiest, most dangerous problem first; or it might be wise to start with the easiest problem that will likely achieve a good solution so that the client will be more willing to move to more difficult problems; or it might be useful to let the client make the selection of what is most important to him or her to have resolved. Whatever is selected as highest priority, the worker would be wise to keep the whole set of targets in mind; sometimes changing one key factor might bring along with it several other desired changes as well.

e) *Ongoing monitoring:* Since the problematic behaviors have been measured in their baseline or preintervention states, continuing measurement offers the worker knowledge about how well the intervention itself is proceeding. It is possible to notice turns for the worse that are not expected by the theory (for example, in extinction, ignoring bad behavior is likely to produce an increase in bad behavior at first, to attain some reaction, but eventually, the bad behavior will be reduced. But if the unwanted behavior continues, something is going wrong.) In either case, positive or negative change, it is necessary to keep clear track of the progress of the case.

f) *Matching of objectives and actions:* As the client's behavior continues to change, presumably in the direction of one's objectives, the worker and client have to determine the goodness of fit between the behavior and the objectives set in the case. The match must also include continuity, so that merely reaching some numerical objective (say, reduction in weight) is not enough; the person must demonstrate a staying power as well.

g) *Maintenance and termination:* Once the client has attained a stable objective, it is necessary to consider how to build into the natural environment those sets of forces that will maintain this desired outcome in the face of hostile and uncertain opposing forces. Maintenance involves an entirely new added set of training experiences, like the intervention itself, but different in the sense that the client has to be the ultimate and continuing reinforcer of desired behavior, in most instances. A problem-solving orientation has to be accepted for dealing with novel pressures. When client and worker are convinced this state has been achieved, then termination is called for.

Humanist Theory

A humanist may be defined as one who asserts the dignity and worth of the individual above all other values and who believes that the person has the capability of becoming all that he or she potentially can be. Carl Rogers is the originator of what has come to be called person-centered therapy. It evolved from nondirective therapy to client-centered therapy and to this present version. Rogers was an unsinkable humanist whose valuing of the dignity and worth of any client was so strong that he was able to communicate this faith to almost every one—a silent schizophrenic patient, members of a weekend marathon group, or students in the helping professions.

DEFINITIONS

1. *Self-actualization* refers to "the inherent tendency of the organism to develop all its capacities in ways that serve to maintain or enhance the organism" (Rogers, 1959b, p. 196). The growing individual tries to translate this tendency into action.

2. The tendency toward self-actualization soon conflicts with the *conditions of worth* that significant others, like parents, impose on infants and children as the price of being civilized into society. Some of these conditions of worth are assimilated into the developing person, even though they are contrary to the tendency toward self-actualization.

ASSUMPTIONS

3. Over the course of time, the infant or child develops a *self-concept,* an awareness of one's own physical and psycho-social being and functionings, particularly in relationship to others' view of this self, and the values attached to these perceptions (Meador & Rogers, 1984, p. 158). The term *self-structure* is also used, but primarily when the self of a person is looked at from an external perspective. The self-concept is influenced by a number of factors. First, there is a universal need in people that Rogers terms the *need for positive regard.* Second, the imposed conditions of worth influence the self-concept.

4. Out of the lifetime experiences of receiving or not receiving positive regard, the person learns to develop a sense of self-regard. When a person's tendencies to self-actualization (and the real life actions based on this innate

tendency) are in accord with experiences from others about the conditions of self-worth, then the person will feel positive self-regard. When a person receives messages from significant others that his or her actions are not congruent with their conditions of worth, then that person may feel the conflict, tension, and confusion of the resulting incongruence, and thus may be estranged from his or her true nature. This incongruence may be experienced as psychological maladjustment, or neurotic behavior.

Rogers also speaks of the concept *vulnerability,* which is a state of incongruence between a self and his or her experience which leaves that person open to anxiety and disorganization.

DEFINITION

5. *Therapy* is defined as a condition in which a certain person (therapist) conveys three basic attitudes—*congruence, positive regard,* and *empathic understanding*—to another person (client) so that a "growthful change" will take place in the client who has the total and sole capacity for correcting the problems. The therapist is a catalyst for the client to heal himself or herself; the therapist does not do the healing for the client.

    a) *Genuineness (or congruence)* refers to the ability of a therapist to be himself or herself, not to hide behind a facade of professional jargon. The therapist's own feelings should be congruent with his or her words and actions toward the client.

    b) *Accurate empathic understanding* emerges as the therapist uses his or her own experiencing of what the client is apparently experiencing. The therapist reports what he or she understands and feels regarding the client's words and situation at the moment, so as to check whether the therapist is accurate in understanding what the client is trying to express.

    c) *Unconditional positive regard* is a nonpossessive caring for the individual (based on the belief that every person has the capacity to self-actualize into a better or higher state, regardless of what past actions may have been).

ASSUMPTION

6. The goal of therapy is to put the individual back in touch with his or her natural tendency toward self-actualization, to an openness to experience (in contrast to being defensive against threats to the self), which the individual can incorporate into his or her self as desired. *Maturity* resides in being able to be open to experiences but not to be dominated by them (especially the conditions of worth from others).

EMPIRICAL STATEMENT

7. There are many studies of the importance of the core triad of therapist qualities, empathy, warmth, and genuineness (see Ivey and Authier, 1978; Fischer, 1976). Being trained to exhibit these characteristics represents a basic beginning point for therapists. (See Chapter 2.)

EMPIRICAL NOTE

8. Rogers pioneered use of technological devices in evaluative research

(such as taping sessions) and also developed the use of standardized tests and scales (such as the Q-sort) as part of the evaluative process.

GROUP LEVEL THEORIES

Small Group Theory

DEFINITIONS

1. A *small* or *primary group* may be defined as two or more individuals having relatively persisting face-to-face communications such that the behaviors (including thoughts, feelings, and actions) of one affects and is affected by the others, forming some norms and roles shared by them.

Social roles involve a set of behaviors that are expected of a person in a given social structure. Such roles are independent of the individual who is performing these behaviors at a particular time, even though he or she may give a distinctive twist to these behaviors.

Social norms are affective expectations that develop around roles in given social contexts. In effect, these norms involve a given group's awareness of the positive and negative sanctions related to acceptable or nonacceptable ranges of behaviors. Norms are independent of the individual who is aware of their sanction.

Social structures are the relatively stable system of relationships among roles and norms at a given time and within a given culture.

ASSUMPTIONS

2. Groups are distinct entities, separate from the individual members who compose it. There is something added by the fact of a number of persons interacting together in some fashion compared to the same number of individuals acting alone (and without considering the others as they act). In a word, the whole is more than the sum of the parts. For groups with three or more members, a given member may leave or be pushed out, and the remaining members would still constitute that group, although roles and norms might be modified. Likewise, if new members join a group, the essential nature of that group remains, although it may accommodate to the new members to some degree.

3. The added component of the group over individual members is the emergent structure that inevitably forms as the people interact and form relationships with one another. Several structural features usually emerge, following from the basic functions of any group. These basic functions are termed *task* (or *external* or *instrumental*) *functions* and *integrative* (or *socio-emotional* or *relationship*) *functions*. The task function involves the group's overall relationship to other groups and the physical environment in which it exists. An example of a task function is when a member of a family (a special type of group) works at a job which brings in money that can be spent on family needs (internal integrative needs).

Integrative functions (also known as internal, socio-emotional, or relationship functions) include doing those things that will insure that the group itself stays together in good working order. It is necessary to insure that each member of the group gets some minimum of basic human needs met—food, clothing, shelter, social approval, and the like. There is also an assumption that individuals need others (including groups of others) to facilitate their own growth and development. *Conflicts* are also assumed to be present in all groups to some degree because there are differences of opinion in how and what the members should be doing, so integrative functions are always needed.

4. The *size* of the group affects its functioning (Simmel, 1950). Assuming we are speaking first about members who have the same degree of power and status, the following statements are broadly descriptive of any group. When members of the group differ intrinsically in power and status, as in adult parents with infants and children, then further qualifications must be made on these statements. The *dyad* (two persons in a relationship that is significant to them) is the most fragile of groups, but it can generate intense feelings and intimacy. Relationships in the dyad may be diffuse with no division of labor, or it may have a precisely defined set of roles, or anything in between. The *triad* may reduce the intensity of the relationships by dividing the affect among the members. However, a third member may exploit the differences between the other two members, for his or her own benefit. Coalitions (two against one) may develop, adding new sources of strain, especially for the minority member. Additional role differentiation is likely, but the overall structure may still be diffuse.

Four members of a group permit several forms of coalitions to form. Three against one presents great pressure on the one, while two against two presents problems in solving group problems. There can be more division of labor, with sharper definitions of norms and sanctions. Five member groups permit majority/minority subgroup coalitions, and further division of labor, norms, and sanctions. Some researchers have suggested "ideal" sizes of groups for various purposes. For example, Slater (1958) suggested that groups with five members were effective in dealing with complex mental tasks that required sharing of information. Osborn (1957) suggested groups with five to ten members as being most effective for brainstorming groups. But smaller groups may be more satisfying to the members because they can participate more fully.

EMPIRICAL GENERALIZATION

5. There are several patterns of *communication networks* among the groups, corresponding roughly to size. The two-person group has the opportunity for equal exchange of information, although when the characteristics of the individuals involved are considered, the two-way flow may not occur.

Three-person groups may have full equal flows of communication, or messages may get filtered through one or two members for the other(s). The fact of centrality in the flow of communication automatically adds some status within the group. Four-person and larger groups have more combinations of ways in which communication may flow. Whenever equal communication opportunities do not occur, there will be unequal access to resources that provide status, power, and resources (cf. Shaw, 1981).

ASSUMPTIONS

6. Each pattern of persisting communications within a group creates different types of *power structures* (the way members are mutually expected to relate to one another), and hence, the ways groups attempt to meet their task and integrative functions. However, when cultural factors are added to natural family groups, as contrasted with artificial groups in laboratories from which most of these observations are based, there are sharp differences. For example, Strodtbeck (1951) found differences in Mormon, Navajo, and Protestant Texan couples following religious and cultural differences. Mormon husbands and Navajo wives were the more powerful members of their families, while the Protestant Texans divided power between them. In cultural triads, fathers, mothers, and adolescent sons, it turns out that Italian fathers were more powerful than their wives and sons, while Jewish parents shared power and had more power than their sons.

7. Groups can be distinguished by the kinds of leadership, followership, and specialized roles that emerge in the course of persisting communications.

EMPIRICAL GENERALIZATIONS

8. Early research on traits of leaders was frustrating because there were few reliable personal characteristics that held up across studies. Later research has tried to link some functions that leaders performed with the contexts in which their behaviors occurred. (This emphasizes a social work orientation of always viewing the person in the total situation.) Fiedler (1967) connects the motivating factors of the person in a group who gets or is given the responsibility for directing the group's efforts in achieving its tasks, with three situational factors: (a) how well this person gets along with other members (an integrative function); (b) the nature of the task itself, its clarity and familiarity; and (c) the authority and power inherent in the position the leader holds. In this view, every member of a group with some division of labor has some leadership functions with regard to some tasks, although some may have more than others, and these latter will be the visible leaders. (Cf. Wrightsman and Deaux, 1981.)

ASSUMPTIONS

9. Group movement involves a process of *unfreezing* a given system of roles and norms, moving the group to some new set that are presumed to be more effective in achieving their goals, and refreezing the new norms and roles in place (Lewin, 1951). Depending on the problem chosen for change, the number of elements may be large or small and require, consequently, more or less in the elements to be considered for the change.

10. There may be *role conflict* or *norm conflict* among the members of the group, both as to *within-group conflicts* (differences of opinion or value as to who should do what to whom and with what priority in use of group resources), or *out-group conflicts* (as when a person is a member of several groups, each of which make demands on his or her loyalties and behaviors, but whose norms and behavioral expectations differ).

11. As a member's behavior varies from group norms, he or she will be subjected to *pressures toward conformity* with common group values (based on the valued status that belonging to the group can command). But a point will be reached where that deviate's behavior is so extreme that he or she may be ejected by the group.

GROUP LEVEL THEORIES (continued)

Communication Theory (Virginia Satir)
  See Chapter 8 for a brief summary.

Family Structural Therapy (Salvadore Minuchin)
  See Chapter 8 for a brief summary.

Natural Helping Network Theory (Alice Collins and Diane Pancoast)
  See Chapter 8 for a brief summary.

COMMUNITY ORGANIZATION LEVEL THEORIES

Social Planning Approach (Jack Rothman)
  See Chapter 8 for a brief summary.

Community Development Approach (Jack Rothman)
  See Chapter 8 for a brief summary.

Social Action Approach (Jack Rothman)
  See Chapter 8 for a brief summary.

ADMINISTRATION AND PLANNING LEVEL THEORIES

Bureaucratic Theory (Max Weber)
  See Chapter 8 for a brief summary.

Human Relations Theory (Rensis Likert)
  See Chapter 8 for a brief summary.

GENERAL SYSTEMS LEVEL THEORY

Configural Model
  Discussed throughout this book, especially in Chapter 24.

SUMMARY

This chapter has listed 13 theories of various degrees of sophistication and logical development; four are actually covered in this chapter—the others may be found in the designated chapters of this book. For the uninitiated, 13 may seem a very large number of theories to know; for the more experienced reader, 13 is only a sample of what is available. Please remember the caveat cited earlier: each presentation in this chapter (and elsewhere in this book) is intended only as an *introduction* to principles and highlights of the given theory. More study is needed before one can say that one fully understands any of these theories, or before one can legitimately call on them to guide professional decisions in one's daily practice.

Yet, it must be added, these brief statements have offered major propositions for your study. Only two things are required of the reader: (1) That you try to understand what it is the theorist is saying and that you try to connect the system of abstract ideas to the concrete world in which social workers practice; (2) that you examine carefully the theory before, during, and after you apply it as a guide to practice—in other words, that you be *critical*, especially if you "like" the theory. Each theory deserves a careful study to understand it—and an equally careful critical analysis to recognize its limitations.

Every one of the theories presented here has received considerable criticism in the scientific and professional literature. Every one of the theories presented here embraces arbitrary constructs, interconnected according to the subjective impressions and guesses of the theorist, however scientific and objective they may sound. Every one of the theories presented here stands as a general hypothesis or assumption on how one portion of the world appears to work, and thus each one requires testing and modification of the "grand hunch." Every one of the theories presented here is finite, historically limited, and changing. Every one of the theories presented here is culture-bound, seeing problems and solutions in relatively limited ways; the great majority have been developed by men, making it probable that they are also gender-bound. Every one of the theories presented here is in some sense of the term wrong, an imperfect guide to understanding or influencing behavior in some circumstances.

In spite of these true limitations of each theory (to say nothing of the imperfect and very introductory presentations of these theories), this collection of conceptual road maps provides about the best intellectual core tools we have available for understanding human behavior and trying to make appropriate changes as needed. Each of these theories is borrowed from the behavioral and social sciences, and has as advocates some contemporary writers, many of whom have made important modifications in the theories' conceptual and applied dimensions.

This brief encounter with the 13 theories presented in this book will, it is hoped, challenge you to appreciate and understand them, to modify them as your practice dictates, and to develop new theoretical ideas of your own, ideas that will guide other helping professionals in the future.

PART

IV.

VALUES AND ETHICS IN THE PROFESSIONAL CONTEXT

This Part contains only one chapter that deals specifically with values and ethics in social work. However, the issue of values in practice is discussed throughout the book. The present chapter on values calls special attention to the nature of values and, in particular, to the problems and possibilities related to resolving value conflicts. Social work is filled with situations in which the worker is faced with choices between two or more desired objectives. There are few guidelines for making professional decisions between conflicting actions. This chapter examines four major ethical theories as guides to our thinking on conflict resolution. It then challenges us to formulate our own reasoned approach: By what rules will we be fair and just in our dealings with clients, colleagues, and members of the community?

OUTLINE

Arthur Miller's *The Crucible:* A Dramatic Representation
of a Conflict in Values

Definitions of Values, Norms, Ideology, Ethics, and Related Terms

The Place of Values in the World of the Helping Professional: Three
Case Examples
Case 1
Community Allocation of Funds
Case 2
Guardians of a Severely Retarded Girl
Case 3
Social Work with Mixed Groups of Pre-Delinquent
and Non-Delinquent Children

A Strategy for Analyzing Value Choices and Conflicts

Four Ethical Statements
Statement 1
Ensuring the Greatest Good for the Greatest Number: The
Utilitarian Theory of John Stuart Mill and Jeremy Bentham
Statement 2
Ensuring Fairness for the Least Advantaged Persons in Society:
John Rawls' Liberal Theory of Justice
Statement 3
Ensuring Fair Exchanges Among Free, Autonomous,
Protected Individuals in a Minimal State: Robert Nozick's
Conservative Theory of Justice
Statement 4
Ensuring the Freedom and Well-Being of Others as Well as
Oneself: Alan Gewirth's Logical Theory of Ethical Choice

Analysis of Three Test Cases Using Four Ethical Theories

A Social Work Paradigm for Resolving Value Conflicts:
The Configural Perspective

The NASW Code of Ethics
Preamble
Summary of Major Principles

CHAPTER TEN

Social Work Ethics—
Resolving Value Conflicts

Every action or nonaction by a social worker represents a value choice. Moreover, in a world of scarcity, what one party receives, another party cannot have. Thus actions usually present conflicts in values. This chapter deals with the difficult topic of how social workers justify their choices of action. It involves understanding the nature of value terms, having a systematic way of looking at the values of all the parties involved, and then making a value choice based on some explicit and defensible principles. The chapter concludes with a configural perspective on resolving value conflicts.

ARTHUR MILLER'S THE CRUCIBLE: *A DRAMATIC REPRESENTATION OF A CONFLICT IN VALUES*

The Devil is loose in Salem, Massachusetts, in the year 1692. Arthur Miller's fascinating play *The Crucible* (1953) presents a dramatic version of the known historical events. The conflicts that can be seen with extraordinary clarity in the play may help us visualize the subtler value differences in everyday life.

Massachusetts, at the end of the 17th century, was a highly repressive theocracy, where religious purists practiced their beliefs with such utter conviction that any deviation was suspect. The villagers watched each other closely to make sure none sinned where there were so many ways to sin. Church attendance was practically required and no frivolities were permitted. Miller notes the paradox in all this, that in order to create a heavenly city on earth, the Puritans were obliged to suppress freedom of expression.

The scene opens in the spring, at the end of a raw, dark winter; strange events are occurring. Several young teenage girls have taken to their beds unable to speak or to eat. They are some of the girls who had been discovered dancing in the forest—one of them naked—by the Reverend Samuel Parris, chief protector of every religious virtue. One of the girls is his own daughter, another his niece. This was no ordinary sickness. Word spreads quickly in the small village that it is the Devil's work.

The girls gather at the bedside of young Miss Parris, and when the Reverend Parris leaves the room, the girls excitedly and fearfully discuss the growing temperature in the village. One girl, Mary Warren, urges her friends to tell the truth about the dancing, because "Witchery's a hangin' error" while dancing merits only a beating. But the ringleader, a beautiful and somewhat older girl, Abigail, forces the lot of them to be quiet and let matters proceed. She has her private reasons. It turns out that she has had an affair with a man she worked for, John Proctor, a well-respected farmer. After that liaison, his wife, Elizabeth, somehow sensed what was happening and forced John to confess and send the girl away. Abigail now sees the possibility of getting rid of Elizabeth, an honorable but cold woman, and taking her place with John.

Later, egged on by witch-hunting officials of the church, the girls begin to act bizarrely, and point to various people in the village as their bedeviling tempters. At first, the vulnerable are accused, such as a senile old woman. But matters escalate. One man accuses a woman of selling him a pig that dies shortly thereafter, and when he complains, she says, "if you haven't the wit to feed a pig properly, you'll not live to own many." Sure enough, his bad luck with pigs continues and he accuses the woman of bewitching them. Even the strong, upright people are accused—after all, who would be better as unsuspected servants of the Devil?

The court of inquiry is called and the deputy governor comes to Salem to conduct the investigations, along with other ministers who are to help root out the Devil, wherever he might be. Many good citizens are imprisoned, including Elizabeth Proctor. Tortures extract confessions from some, and the hangings begin.

Mary Warren, one of the original clutch of girls who named witches, presently works for the Proctors. She is overcome with guilt and confesses to John that she and the other girls, led by Abigail, made up the witchery story to cover their dancing crime. John insists she tell this confession to the court, which Mary Warren is eager to do. The confession throws the entire proceedings into doubt, including the hangings, and so the judge seeks more evidence. John is driven to confess in court about his affair with Abigail and how she is using these trials to get rid of John's wife, Elizabeth. This monstrous fact would destroy the entire proceedings—but is it true? Ask Elizabeth. She never lies; she is well known as an upright, religious woman.

In a climactic scene, Elizabeth is brought to the court room. On the right side is her husband, John. On the left, Abigail, her accuser. In the center is the judge who orders John and Abigail to turn their backs to Elizabeth as he asks her questions. Did Abigail once work for the Proctors? (Yes) Why was she dismissed? (Elizabeth explains how, when she was sick after her last baby, she saw her husband turn from her toward the servant girl.)

Judge:	Your husband—did he indeed turn from you?
Elizabeth (*in agony*):	My husband—is a goodly man, sir.
Judge:	Then he did not turn from you.
Elizabeth: (*starting to glance at Proctor*):	He—
Judge:	Look at me! To your own knowledge, has John Proctor ever committed the crime of lechery? (In the crisis of indecision, she cannot speak.) Answer my question. . . .

There is a long and powerful moment of silence. Let us ponder what is going through Elizabeth's mind. If she says "yes," she will be labeling John as a lecher, identifying him as a person inordinately indulgent in sexual activity, a high crime in Puritan times. If she says "no," she will be guilty of lying, which is a sin to Elizabeth.

But the value conflict is raised to a much higher degree as well. Although Elizabeth does not know the particulars, she must guess that her answer will have a bearing on the witch trials themselves, and thus on the fate of many other innocent people in the jails. Beyond that, she may fear for her whole community and her religion, which allows the Devil's accomplices to be so easily chosen by hysterical children or by adults seeking advantage from another person's loss (for example, taking over another person's land). Thus, beyond the personal level, Elizabeth's answer will have a social impact: A "yes" answer will provide evidence against the entire witchcraft trials and will disgrace the judges who have already hanged innocent people. A "no" answer will support the proceedings against the Devil's handiwork by showing that even a good, strong man like John Proctor is under demonic control.

What this dramatic moment illustrates is the intensely personal matter of a sexual relationship becomes at the same instant a significant social matter that indicates the work of the Devil in the village of Salem. No wonder that Elizabeth pauses long before she answers.

The main point of this dramatic illustration is that every value has both personal and collective implications, although perhaps not as life-threatening as Elizabeth's. If we would be pushed, as she was, to think through the implications of our choices, we would also see the collective dimensions of every personal action. As one commentator pointed out with regard to the implications of AIDS, every time you go to bed with some Jack or Jill, you sleep with everyone that Jack or Jill has slept with as well. This is the intersection of decisions that are personal and collective in implications. Veritably every significant decision is embedded in a configuration of effects. One factor contributing to human problems, it may be hypothesized, is the lack of consideration given to the full set of effects of any action. We tend to select those we hope will occur, and neglect giving full weight to those we hope will not happen.

In most contexts, we are able to confront those involved in our value choices, unlike Elizabeth Proctor. Certainly, our role in helping others face difficult challenges is to encourage them to face all of the significant implications of their choices. This is not easy to do, but this is what has to be done. If a client recognizes the full range of options and understands what might follow from one or another action, then that person is more nearly able to make an informed choice. This does not guarantee that the choice will be wise and successful, but it does improve the chances, and that is about all we can ask of the helping professions.

By the way, Elizabeth answered "no." Her lie, to protect her husband's good name, eventually costs him his life. But, as Miller interprets the ultimate ending, the people of the Massachusetts colony revolted against the witchcraft trials when they heard of the mockery of justice that had occurred, which effectively ended theocracy in Massachusetts. While that may be a "good" outcome, it stretches the meaning of a positive value choice to ask that

Elizabeth lie, and that many good citizens of Salem are hanged, to achieve this good end.

Value choices appear to the people involved to be centered in their immediate configuration of events, their "center of gravity." When larger configurations are considered—in this case, several other villages revolted after they heard about the trials in Salem—then it appears that the sacrifice of some lives unknowingly served to give new freedom to the larger number of the living. But this raises all sorts of questions: at what point in the social configuration should one stop to consider relevant parties to any social action—and thus to the ethics of any given act? Is it ever just or right or fair to sacrifice some people for the betterment of others? On what basis ought one to make moral decisions?

These are not simply abstract philosophical questions to be debated in ethics classes at the university. They are the guts of everyday decisions in any helping practice. And when you and I are involved in influencing other people's value decisions, we had better be as clear as possible to ourselves about the bases of choices. Constructing a working model for analyzing value choices is the task of this chapter.

DEFINITIONS OF VALUES, NORMS, IDEOLOGY, ETHICS, AND RELATED TERMS

The term "value" has been defined in hundreds of ways, reflecting its importance in human life (Kluckhohn, 1953). For purposes of this discussion, let us use the word *value* to mean an enduring belief system (one's thoughts, feelings, and predispositions to behave in a certain way with regard to a given topic) that holds that a specific mode of conduct or end-state (goal) is personally or socially preferable to some alternative modes of conduct or end-states (cf. Rokeach, 1973). More briefly put, *values are persistent preferences for certain goals* (what one ought to seek) *and certain means* (how goals ought to be attained).

Values are shared among some group of persons. First, they are learned over the course of one's life education (especially the early years), and thus they tend to reflect the arbitrary nature of those experiences. Then values are reinforced in group situations throughout life. Technically, the term *social norm* refers to these shared expectations of what ought to be done by a member of that group and how he or she ought to do it. Groups have sanctions to reinforce conformity to their norms and to punish deviations from them. As the child matures, he or she is able to conceptualize values and sanctions in abstract and general rules, and comes to have an individual commitment to the collective beliefs about means and ends of conduct. However, there are many teachers of values—parents, peers, media heroes, and the like—so that the set of values any one person holds may not be internally consistent.

In spite of these inconsistencies, most people have learned some hierarchy of values, those that are most important to their lives and actions and those that are, by steps, less important although still influential. These hierarchies help to resolve possible conflicts between values. Research by Rokeach and others has suggested that some common patterns among hierarchies exist in

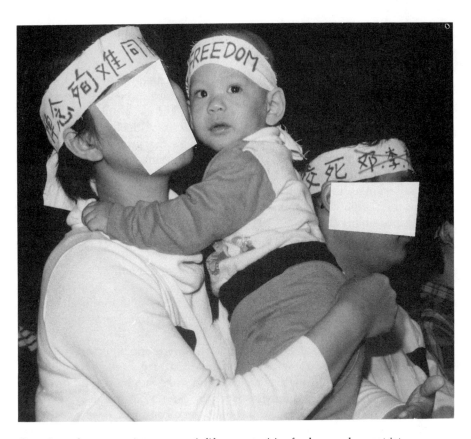

Sometimes there comes into a person's life a great crisis of values, such as patriotism for a beloved country versus belief in the universal rights of people. (Because of the fear that this picture may identify people and put them at risk, I have disguised the adults.) But it is important to recognize that crises of values come into our lives everyday in one form or another, especially when we are involved in professional actions. Thus, we must understand the nature of values and value conflicts, and our own professional stance in resolving them. This is the task of this chapter.

and across different cultures. When large numbers of persons share similar sets of values, we can speak of a *societal or cultural value* (the common theme or trend among specific shared values that organize major portions of what ends this larger group seeks and the means considered acceptable to do so).

Americans hold a range of views about preserving life in times of medical crisis, for example, whether or not a person can pay for it. But the dominant cultural theme is that life should be preserved—this is the goal—through available medical technology—this is the means. However, there are debates about these means, whether everyone should receive the best that medicine can offer regardless of costs. An interesting coming challenge to this cultural value is raised as people realize that it costs about $150,000 to care for an AIDS victim through the terminal years. As numbers of victims rise, the total costs will strain the cultural value regarding free medical care for those in need, an example made more complicated by the association of AIDS and alternative life-styles (most victims of AIDS are currently found among gays and intravenous drug users). Likewise, organ transplants are very expensive.

The Oregon state legislature voted to spend the state's limited health care funds on prenatal care for 1,500 needy pregnant women, rather than pay the same amount of money for 30 organ transplants (Specter, 1988; Gross, 1989).

When these societal or cultural values are combined with other pervasive ideas (or myths—nothing says that these ideas have to be accurate, merely that they are believed) about what a society ought to be doing and how it ought to be doing it, then we can speak of an *ideology*. Ideologies are systems of interrelated beliefs and values held by a large social group (which may include whole nations or groups of nations) that describe, rationalize, and support a particular cluster of institutionalized behaviors that have evolved to deal with ordinary life concerns. Some societies, for example, hold an ideology that the nation itself should provide basic health care for all its citizens, regardless of ability to pay.

Other societies hold an ideology that individuals should take care of their own health needs as far as possible and that government should supply a system of backup supports. These broad differences in orientation to the health of one's people reflect pervasive ideologies about what are good objectives (health—the same goal in both ideologies) and what are appropriate means (either socialized health programs or capitalistic health programs such as fee-for-service approaches).

Are there any universal values with which any rational person would always agree? Some philosophers (such as Kant, Bentham, and, as we shall see, some contemporary philosophers as well) and some religious traditions have attempted to offer universal maxims, such as "Do unto others as you would have them do unto you." These would seem, on a common sense basis, to be universal, until one reflects on exceptions such as masochists who take pleasure in receiving pain, or in the terrible facts recorded annually by Amnesty International that some governments systematically torture some of their own citizens and foreigners, often in the name of religious principles (Amnesty International, 1977). The valuing of human life and liberty may be a universal theme, but it is not universally honored.

Values, norms, cultural themes, and ideologies represent a continuum of value terms. Looking again at norms, we can identify some different types of values common to different groups. In particular, let us examine codes of ethics of helping professions. Veatch (1981) presents a fascinating discussion of the history and current status of medical ethics. In his view, any medical ethics includes a set of ethical standards, principles, and rules or codes for health care workers, generated and adjudicated when necessary by the profession itself (pp. 82–83). He describes the Hippocratic Oath—or perhaps, more correctly, the Hippocratic tradition, since the various writings of Hippocrates or his school been reinterpreted many times over history—as the core of medical ethics. The original statement, in *The Epidemics*, is translated in this form: "As to diseases, make a habit of two things—to help, or at least to do no harm" (Veatch, 1981, p. 22). This core meaning is equally applicable to social work.

The social work Code of Ethics (see Appendix 10.1) is intended to perform similar functions. Most of the Code involves general principles to guide everyday conduct of members vis-à-vis their clients, colleagues, the employing agency, the profession itself, and society. It is not detailed nor totally inclusive, but is to be used to guide the spirit as well as the letter of normative behavior for social work professionals. It also attempts to identify inappropriate deviations from the standards implied in the Code, but recognizes that actual cases must be judged within the contexts in which they occur. Ultimately, the Code requires that the individual worker accept a personal commitment "to help, or at least to do no harm" in the many and varied situations where social work occurs.

The Preamble to the Social Work Code of Ethics asserts that it is based on the fundamental values of the profession, including "the worth, dignity, and uniqueness of all persons as well as their rights and opportunities." But these fundamental values are not discussed in the Code. Nor are rules offered to decide between values in cases where they may conflict. So we have to look further in the literature to help us begin to formulate a way of analyzing values and of making professional decisions in the face of inevitable value conflicts.

THE PLACE OF VALUES IN THE WORLD OF THE HELPING PROFESSIONAL: THREE CASE EXAMPLES

Where do values and value conflicts emerge in the everyday world? Everywhere. Consider the following three situations.

Case 1

Community Allocation of Funds. In a small community, the town council discovered that it had a surplus of $10,000 and debated how to use the money. Four proposals were made. First, it was suggested that the money simply be returned to the taxpayers proportionately to what taxes they paid to the city. Second, it was proposed to give the money to a local program for the gifted and talented in the public schools. About 200 of the town's 2,000 students might benefit.

The third proposal was to expand services of a small program that used a rented house as temporary shelter for abused wives and their children. About 25 families (wives alone, or mothers with one or more children—50 people altogether) used the facility over the year. Funds were needed to make the house livable, while crisis intervention and support group work were conducted on the premises, and for supplies and additional clothing, now provided principally by charitable donations. Most of the participants, but not all, came from the poorer areas in the town.

The fourth proposal to spend the windfall $10,000 concerned a residence for discharged mental patients. There was a small group of such persons in town (about 10 or 12 people) who were essentially homeless. They drifted in and out of the few available cheap apartments, without any relative or friend to look out for them. The public welfare worker connected to the local government had suggested setting up some common accommodations for these people—perhaps the most down-and-out citizens of the community.

Because the funds were not large, the council decided on the ground rule to give all the money to one project (or all of it back to the taxpayers). The questions are not only where should the money go, but why? What value principle directs us to choose one alternative among several good alternatives? (Cf. Veatch, 1981, p. 252–3.)

Case 2

Guardians of a Severely Retarded Girl.   Mr. and Mrs. C are an elderly couple on welfare who also receive Medicaid for their serious chronic illnesses. They have taken on the care of a 15-year-old granddaughter, Doris, who is severely mentally retarded and who is able to do only minimal activities of daily living (eating, toileting, and bathing, and so on). The girl's father is dead and her mother has been committed to a state mental institution; there are no other relatives able to take care of Doris. The C's believe institutional care of the retarded is very poor in their state and so have accepted this burden. Doris has a pleasant disposition, watches TV most of the time, and wanders around the neighborhood on nice days, but always close to home.

One day, while helping Doris bathe, Mrs. C notices her swollen stomach, and later a doctor confirms that the girl is five months pregnant. The C's are dismayed and ask the doctor for advice. He counsels them not to tell the girl about the pregnancy (since it might upset her) and to have the offspring placed for adoption (since the C's are neither physically nor financially able to care for another child). Doris is not aware of her pregnancy, nor does she understand how conception takes place. The C's also talk with their welfare worker, who strongly advises them to tell the girl about what is happening to her (since she has a right to know about her own bodily changes) and to let her participate in decisions about her future child and herself to the extent she is able to do so (since her sense of trust of her grandparents might be otherwise shaken).

What do you think the grandparents should do, and why? What ethical principles are at stake, and which principle has priority over the others? (Cf. Reamer, 1982.)

Case 3

Social Work with Mixed Groups of Pre-Delinquent and Non-Delinquent Children. The staff of a family service agency was discussing proposals for improving their services to young (age 8 to 11) pre-delinquent children in their community. Fiscal constraints required consideration of group services if this group was to be served at all, and a literature search revealed one study in which a small number of pre-delinquent children were mixed in recreational groups with larger numbers of non-delinquents without identifying the problem children. By keeping the ratio of pre-delinquents to non-delinquents low, the researchers discovered that the pre-delinquents improved in their social behavior, while their non-delinquent peers suffered no apparent harm. Unfortunately, the family service agency could not afford the same low ratios of pre-delinquent to non-delinquent children, so their proposed program was somewhat more risky. The group worker was to facilitate the group's formation of healthy or pro-social goals and norms, in anticipation that the pre-delinquent children would learn to conform to these constructive peer rules.

The staff disagreed among themselves about this proposal: Should the agency form mixed/recreational groups of pre-delinquents and non-delinquents without informing participants of this mixture?

A STRATEGY FOR ANALYZING VALUE CHOICES AND CONFLICTS

The three case examples described above are representative of the thousands of cases social workers deal with every day. In addition to the manifest content each deals with—surplus funds, the pregnancy of a retarded teenager, delinquency—each case raises implicit values and value conflicts. How is one to consider the value conflicts in these cases from the point of view of the helping professional? We are not at this moment raising the question of which is the right intervention or action to choose but how does one think about making any kind of value choice under conflict of values conditions?

Some helpful ideas may be adapted from the work of Tymchuk (1981) and Reid and Billups (1986). The suggested strategy consists of dealing with a set of questions:

1. *What is the value issue?* As Reid and Billups (1986) note, most social work situations involve the redistribution of things or symbols of value to the individuals involved. One must look at the manifest events in the clients' situations and identify the values implicit in them. This involves finding out what each party lacks and what each party has in undesired excess, and how these lacks and excesses are interrelated among parties, before and after the proposed intervention. (Note that an intervention is viewed not only as redistribution of things, but changes in the values associated with these things.)

2. *Who is involved in this value situation?* Tymchuk (1981) suggests that it is critical to look not only at the identified client, but to consider all parties who are appreciably affected by the action or inaction in this situation. Note one potential conflict in the social work Code of Ethics, which states that a worker has been legally authorized to act on behalf of clients, and so should always act with those persons' best interests in mind. The point here is that a "client" is an arbitrary designation. From a configural point of view, all persons involved in a situation are clients, and it is the task of the worker to grasp the whole picture and act in some way to the optimal benefit of them all without harm being done to any. The configural view suggests considering at minimum the identified individual, the relevant primary groups, such as family or friends, and relevant secondary groups, such as school or workplace. Often the community is a relevant partner in some value conflict.

3. *To what degree are persons involved in the value situation?* Obviously, some people are more strongly affected by the value conflict than others. Some are affected sooner than others (especially when intergeneration transfers are concerned), and some are more knowingly and personally affected in contrast to an impersonal and collective impact in other cases (for example, an act that offends the community's sensibilities may have an impersonal and collective affect). Remember that the social worker is an agent of the community and state, as well as someone who acts on behalf of the client. There will

have to be some weighting of the values involved based on the degrees of directness of personal or group involvement.

4. *What are the "goods" to be distributed among people?* Broadly speaking, we can consider three classes of goods: life, liberty, and the pursuit of happiness or well-being. As stated in the Declaration of Independence (and deriving from the ideas of the Enlightenment), these are inalienable human rights. No one can impinge on them as such. (Note that the pursuit of happiness means that there should be equal opportunity before the law for all to pursue well-being; it does not guarantee equal distribution of such goods.) However, value conflicts also involve various goods and services as well as the opportunity to gain them.

5. *On what ethical ground or principle is each distribution of goods to be based?* After the various details of the events and associated values are identified, the major basis for making a decision depends on one's theory of values or ethical decisions. There are, as I will describe shortly, several major points of view that provide, more or less clearly, some rules for making decisions among values—the utilitarian theory of Bentham and Mill, the theory of duty of Rawls, the theory of entitlement of Nozick, and the theory of logical decisions of Gewirth. Each of these theories is argued persuasively by its authors, and is also soundly attacked by its critics. How does one decide among them? The following four ethical statements are not a technical analysis of theories of ethics but merely a summary aimed at producing principles that could guide social work practice. Each statement is made as comprehensible and persuasive as possible, but the reader should recognize the limitations of conveying a complex philosophy in a few paragraphs. If one or some combinations of views appeals to your sense of values, read the original sources for further understanding. Our first task is to understand the ethical theories themselves, and it is to this that we now turn.

FOUR ETHICAL STATEMENTS

Statement 1

Ensuring the Greatest Good for the Greatest Number: The Utilitarian Theory of John Stuart Mill and Jeremy Bentham.   Like the philosophers of old, the classical utilitarian thinkers, whose leaders included John Stuart Mill and Jeremy Bentham, sought happiness as the goal of life. For some philosophers, this meant the presence of pleasure and the absence of pain (Bentham), while for others it also included other ideal ends such as truth and beauty (Mill). But in either case, the rightness of any action was simply the rational calculation of the overall ratio of good (hedonic pleasure or intellectual/aesthetic ends) and evil. As a general formula, the utilitarians would assert that people ought always to do what is believed will promote the greatest balance of good over evil in the world. The overall ratio is the basis of justice since the net happiness of the people is what preserves order in society. The preservation of order is a critical function of justice.

Bentham's hedonic calculus provides the rules for choice (in what is termed act-utilitarianism): (1) add up the value of each pleasure for a given individual, (2) then add up the value of each pain for that individual, (3) then compare the two; (4) repeat these operations for each relevant party; and (5) take the overall or net balance of aggregated pleasures over pains to determine which class of actions is most useful for the people involved. Critics soon pointed out that a net balance might require that one person would suffer greatly while others benefited. Some people had views of justice that made such a net outcome unacceptable. Even when the calculus is made more complicated (in what is called rule-utilitarianism)—when rules are established on the basis of their overall utility so that individual acts can be compared to the rule, rather than the specific outcomes of the act itself—there are still problems, such as conflicts between rules, or whether the goal is to maximize *good outcomes* or the *numbers of persons involved* in good outcomes (goods and numbers can vary independently). Contemporary problems of this sort are found in cost/effectiveness studies that seek to determine which method or program is better based on the ratio that emerges between costs of the program and benefits or effects of the program (translated into common units of exchange such as dollars).

In spite of these serious problems with the calculation aspect, and thus with the operational definitions of the concepts of the theory, utilitarianism still represents a grand strategy of a just outcome that merits consideration: doing what produces the greatest utility for the largest number of citizens. This does not help in determining specific case situations, however, and even policy issues are unclear because of the vagueness of the terms of the theory.

Statement 2

Ensuring Fairness for the Least Advantaged Persons in Society: John Rawls' Liberal Theory of Justice.   Justice, according to Rawls (1971), involves the way in which major social institutions distribute fundamental rights and duties of people in a society and influence their life prospects (p. 7). Thus a theory of justice involves a formulation of principles by which a well-ordered society [that is, a generally cooperative venture for mutual advantage, in which conflict is effectively regulated by a public conception of justice (p. 4–5)] may be described in which each person acts fairly toward everyone else. [Rawls is enunciating a type of social contract theory, following Locke and Rousseau (p. 11).] Justice is fairness among fellow citizens, assuming social conditions of moderate scarcity that make cooperation advantageous.

What are these principles of justice? To make a rational determination of these principles, Rawls creates a hypothetical setting in which to imagine what rules a group of free, equal, and rational persons who are concerned to further their own interests would accept as defining the fundamental terms of their society (p. 11). But none of them knows what his or her place, assets, or characteristics will be in this society—they are operating as if under a "veil of ignorance"—so everyone is equal in this "original situation," which makes the choices more likely to be fair or just for everyone (p. 12). Like a rational form of the Golden Rule, the individual generalizes to others as he would have them do to him.

From this hypothetical context, Rawls derives his two basic principles of justice:

1. *Equal liberties for all:* "Each person is to have an equal right to the most extensive total system of equal basic liberties compatible with a system of liberty for all" (p. 302). Except under extreme emergencies, there is to be no compromising of these basic liberties, and no trade-offs for specific goods.

2. *Inequalities of the goods composing well-being:* This principle is the conflict-resolving heart of Rawls' theory of justice. If society were static, then the good things of life could be divided purely equally. But society is not static, so the distribution of goods has to be sensitive to changes in social conditions. The utilitarian philosophy of "the greatest good for the greatest number" led to situations in which specific individuals might suffer, even though the majority might profit. Since the people in Rawls' "original condition" recognize that they could be that one person to suffer, they would rationally choose to prevent that by generating a principle whereby inequalities in distribution of goods would be just only if they resulted in compensating benefits for everyone, and in particular for the least advantaged member of society (pp. 14–15). Formally, this is expressed as follows: "Social and economic inequalities are to be arranged so that they are both a) to have the greatest benefit of the least advantaged, consistent with the just savings principle where each generation will carry their fair share of the burden of realizing and preserving a just society" (p. 289) . . . and b) "attached to offices and positions open to all under conditions of fair equality of opportunity" (p. 302). Rawls states his general conception: All social primary goods—liberty and opportunity, income and wealth, and the bases of self-respect—are to be distributed equally unless an unequal distribution of any or all of these goods is to the advantage of the least favored (p. 303).

Thus fairness is guaranteed if any distribution of goods has to favor the least advantaged person, although inequalities may exist. In the long run, this creates a trend toward a socially-generated equality, while individual differences continue to generate a trend toward inequality. To distribute the goods of life in a just and fair manner requires a strong government, such as in the modern welfare state. [See Beverly & McSweeney (1987) for a social work policy perspective broadly based on a Rawlsian approach.]

Statement 3

Ensuring Fair Exchanges Among Free, Autonomous, Protected Individuals in a Minimal State: Robert Nozick's Conservative Theory of Justice. Justice, according to Nozick (1974), involves the way in which a minimal state [(that is, one whose only concerns are to protect or compensate citizens against force, theft, fraud, breaking of contracts, etc. (p. ix)] facilitates the fundamental rights of individuals (freedom from harm, freedom of choice and action, and the right to private property) without violating or putting constraints on any of their rights (p. 149). Using Kant's principle that individuals are always ends and not merely means, Nozick asserts that "they may not be sacrificed or used for the achieving of other ends without their consent" (p. 31). Essentially, this governmental facilitation is limited to overseeing the fair exchanges between citizens. "Whatever arises from a just situation (of the original acquisition of a given holding) by just steps (in the transfer of holdings) is itself just" (p. 151). Nozick asserts that any particular outcome of transfers (such as the utilitarianists' "greatest good for the greatest number" or Rawls' "justice for the least advantaged persons in society") is arbitrary.

Nozick is seeking a content-free set of procedures by which the infinite variety of possible desired outcomes may be fairly attained by the people involved. He finds this mechanism essentially in the competitive market place viewed historically, that is, "past circumstances or actions of people can create differential entitlements or differential deserts to things" (p. 155). Sometime in the past, a person has "mixed his labor" with a (previously unowned) thing and that gives him property rights over it, provided others have enough and as good left for them, as Locke argued (p. 175). People are entitled to what they have justly made, earned, or had transferred to them so long as this does not harm other people who are to be treated as ends in themselves or if one compensates these others so their situations are not worsened (p. 178). Also, it follows from the fundamental rights of freedom of choice and action, people are entitled to resist governmental encroachments to be forced to have their goods and money taxed so as to be transferred to the less well-endowed. Such taxation would be, to Nozick, like "forced labor" (p. 169), treating people as means to others' ends.

The status quo (existing entitlements resulting from historical events) may be flawed by unfortunate monumental imbalances of poverty and wealth, but this does not make the situation unjust, nor does it demand redistribution of holdings except those people make in the name of voluntary charity. Needs have no place in Nozick's view of justice.

Moreover, in the best of all possible worlds, such a minimal state would be the ideal basis for a utopia reflecting the diverse tastes that people have. Any group of compatible souls would be able to set up communities of like-minded persons, as long as the rules of fair exchange held. This is a framework of a society that some could go to the barricades to defend, suggests Nozick, thinking perhaps of conservative political administrations in the United States with their emphasis on individual achievements within a context of free competition and governmental deregulations.

Statement 4

Ensuring the Freedom and Well-Being of Others as Well as Oneself: Alan Gewirth's Logical Theory of Ethical Choice.   Moral principles, according to Gewirth (1978), involve actions that maximize freedom (a person's voluntary control over his/her behavior) and well-being (the achieving of one's purposes or goals). Gewirth describes three classes of well-being, that is, three kinds of goods people seek:

1. *Basic goods* include those aspects of well-being that are necessary preconditions for the performance of any other action; these include life itself, health, food, shelter, and mental equilibrium.

2. *Additive goods,* those which enhance one's ability to fulfill his/her purposes beyond those listed under Basic goods; these include knowledge, self-esteem, income, and education.

3. *Nonsubtractive goods,* those goods whose loss or lowered occurrence in relation to a person would diminish his/her ability to fulfill his/her purposes.

These goods include the quality of one's living and working conditions, and the honesty and confidentiality one experiences in dealing with others.

By a complex logical argument, Gewirth derives a basic principle of ethical decision-making from these givens: An ethically responsible person believes that he or she has a fundamental right to freedom and the fulfillment of his/her well-being, and that all other ethically responsible people share these rights. Indeed, one ought to act so as to maximize the freedom and well-being of others as well as of oneself. This sounds like a version of the Golden Rule, but Gewirth goes further by specifying what good things should be done unto others and oneself under what conditions.

Each aspect of the basic principle has its related duties for the social worker (see Reamer, 1982):

1. With regard to clients' freedom, the worker has the duty not to interfere by use of coercion, deception, or force. Moreover, the worker should promote the clients' freedoms as long as they will not restrict others' freedom or well-being.
2. With regard to the clients' well-being:
   a) Workers are not to interfere with clients' basic goods—life itself, health, food, etc.—but are to assist clients to acquire these basic factors (as long as such assistance can be provided without taking away these same basics from oneself or others in the process).
   b) Additive goods should be fostered, and compensations made for individuals' handicaps or for past interferences that diminished the ability of groups of individuals to fulfill their purposes.
   c) Workers have the duty not to break promises (confidentiality), cheat, or lie.

Moral statements are never absolute, however. There may be extenuating circumstances that suspend a given moral duty on that occasion. Thus Gewirth derives some guidelines for moral professional behavior, but these have to be considered in light of the existing situation. Reamer (1982) summarizes Gewirth's guidelines in a useful fashion for social work practitioners. Here is a brief adaptation:

1. Threats to basic goods (life, health, etc.) take precedence over additive or nonsubtractive goods (such as education or not being lied to). (So, for example, one can break the confidentiality rule if a client's life or health is at stake.)

2. One individual's right to basic well-being (such as life or health) takes precedence over another individual's right to freedom. (For instance, a child's health and safety takes precedence over a parent's right to discipline that child.)

3. One individual's right to freedom takes precedence over his/her own right to basic well-being. (For example, one has the right to decide to commit suicide, if no one else is affected by the act.)

4. The obligation to obey rules and laws to which one has voluntarily and freely consented (as when one chooses to work for a given agency) ordinarily overrides one's right to engage in ways that conflict with those rules. (For in-

stance, if one has agreed to work at an agency, one should follow its policies, say, on abortion or birth control, regardless of one's personal opinions.)

These guidelines are illustrative of the formulations Gewirth (and Reamer) provide helping professionals who have to make such decisions on reasonable grounds every day. Difficulties emerge, from the configural perspective, because of the definition of client. For Gewirth, there appears to be just one client in a situation. All of the ethical guidelines are made from one point of view. From the configural perspective, everyone involved is the client to some extent and must be considered in value decisions. Different outcomes emerge when one changes the client from whose perspective Gewirth's value analysis is made.

The very fact that some reasonable guidelines can be offered as points of departure for ordinary ethical decisions by workers in the community is a very impressive accomplishment, however, and one that should be studied carefully.

ANALYSIS OF THREE TEST CASES USING FOUR ETHICAL THEORIES

Examine the three test cases drawing on the value principles derived from the four ethical theories presented above. My analysis is not necessarily "right" or "true"; you are welcome to agree or disagree, so long as you can support your own choices using the constructs from the various ethical theories.

First, case one, involving the allocation of surplus community funds. The Utilitarians, we may assume, would opt for allocating the funds to the gifted and talented program, not merely because of the greater numbers involved (200), but also because of the potential spread of its effect to the community and state. Rawls would support allocation of the funds to the homeless because they are the least advantaged and the most in need of uplift toward equality. The abused spouses are in need, but they have some potential resources, including their homes and relatives. Nozick would probably suggest that the surplus taxes be returned to the taxpayers, since there is no necessity to support any of these social programs. Gewirth would probably select the spousal abuse program as most needing the extra allocation of funds, on grounds that people who are at immediate risk of loss of life or safety should be given precedence over increased educational experiences or shelter for the homeless, who appear to be managing to survive in spite of their lack of homes.

Each conclusion is different even though each theory purports to be a reasoned exercise in values. How convinced you are of one or another rationale may reflect not so much the logic of the ethical theories as it does your ideological position.

The second case involves a question, whether to tell or not to tell the retarded teenager about her pregnancy and thus involve or not involve her in the decisions on what to do with the baby. The Utilitarians would probably opt not to tell her and not to involve her, as she might want to keep the child and thus would create problems for numbers of persons—the C's, the baby, and the girl herself. However, no abortion is contemplated, since the pregnancy has gone too long to be considered safe for the mother. Abortion would definitely have been considered earlier as being for the greater good for the greater number. Rawls might suggest telling the girl because she is the least advantaged person in the situation and should participate in the proceedings. (Rawls is most appropriately applied to macro-level or policy decisions, and not to individual cases. In either case, the notion of "least advantaged" is vague. One might argue that the C's are the most burdened in this situation.) Nozick would probably suggest telling the girl about the pregnancy and the forthcoming child, since she is entitled as a human being, though a limited one, to know about her body and the changes that are occurring. Gewirth would probably choose to tell the girl about her pregnancy as well as the prospective adoption because her knowing will not jeopardize the life of the child, even though the girl may be made unhappy by this information. She has her right to well-being as would any individual.

Again, a variation arises in bases or justifications for value choices, even though the same choice is presumably made by three theoreticians. The reasoned principle for making the choice is the focus of ethical theory.

The third case—whether or not to mix pre-delinquent and non-delinquent children in recreational groups without informing participants—splits the theorists into two groups. The theorists who would choose to form the mixed recreational groups make this value choice for different reasons. Rawls would observe that the pre-delinquents were the less advantaged of the children in this situation, and thus deserved special consideration. Based on information from the literature, it seems that forming mixed groups is a reasonable way to help the less advantaged while not harming the others. The Utilitarians would concur in the value choice but for different reasons. They might argue that preventing delinquency would constitute the greatest good to society, even though some non-delinquent children might be hurt in the process (such as in fights with the pre-delinquents). On a cost-effectiveness basis, it is better to prevent a problem than treat its victims, and mixed groups offer a possible way to do this.

On the other hand, Nozick might argue that the deception—not telling parents of the non-delinquents that their children will be mixed with pre-delinquents—is unethical. The children who are lawbiding are entitled to good social services, without their having to do "social work" with their pre-delinquent peers. Gewirth might agree with the decision not to form mixed groups, but he might argue that because the pre-delinquent/non-delinquent ratio is higher than in the study from the literature, this current situation is more risky. It is not fair to expose the non-delinquent children to any threats of harm (e.g., fights, theft, etc.) merely as a device to educate or treat others.

A SOCIAL WORK PARADIGM FOR RESOLVING VALUE CONFLICTS: THE CONFIGURAL PERSPECTIVE

It is not possible to present an all-encompassing model for resolving every value conflict you might encounter. However, it is useful to present some preliminary ideas on how helping professionals might approach complex value issues. The following represents a configural view on values within the helping context. The points presented below represent a recommendation for a checklist of value considerations that the worker has to address in one fashion or another.

1. To paraphrase Hippocrates, the first issue social workers should seek to address is how to help their clients and the society they serve, viewed as a single configuration of interrelated systems. A related issue is that if social workers do not possess the knowledge, skills, or resources in needed particular cases, then they should at least act to do no harm to anyone in those situations.

2. Helping involves assisting in making changes in the things or symbols people possess or desire. For example, the textile workers in Worcester, Massachusetts, went on strike in 1912 for "bread and roses," that is, not merely for a livable wage and decent working conditions (bread), but for some quality of life as well (roses). Values were attached to things and symbols by the people involved. Thus the second task of the helping professional is to ask what are the values of the persons and groups involved in a given situation. This may be operationalized approximately by identifying what each party wants and needs, and what each party has in unwanted excess.

3. The configural or systemic principle is employed when the several needs and wants of one party are compared with those of other parties. Given the condition of moderate scarcity that exists in our society, it is likely that one party's needs involve another party's possessions and vice versa. (For example, strikers want livable wages and certain benefits, while employers want workers in their factories.) Some accommodations are necessary, such as exchanges of things valued by the other party for goods valued by one's self.

   How is the social worker to facilitate an ethical exchange from the configural perspective? A worker enters a helping system through contact with a given client—but also with the knowledge of the existence of other clients and the rest of the people in the community who are not in need. Indeed, the others may provide the wealth of the nation from which social welfare draws its resources. Given this context, I believe an ethical configuration would include the following actions:

   a) First, begin with the least advantaged client within the present social system for whom there is a clear-cut life/health-threatening need. Attempt to provide for that party, provided other clients and the community in general are not directly harmed in the process. That is, one should not take food away from one party to feed another when the action would leave the first party hungry. However, taking proportional amounts of everyone's wages to feed those without money is not a direct harm, even though it indirectly limits free choice on how to spend one's earnings.

   b) Recognize that the "least advantaged client" approach (Rawls) represents a drain on the total social system, since it involves a transfer of goods from the better endowed to the less well-off. This approach must be balanced by other actions that promote the immediate vitality of the currently productive and contributing members of society, while waiting for the current welfare beneficiaries (or their offspring) to begin to make their contributions to the society in the future (utilitarianism; Gewirth; Nozick).

Thus a configural view on conflict resolution strategies involves both immediate treatment/rehabilitation and long-term preventive/promotive services. The immediate treatment involves crises or existing problems, while the long-term preventive/promotive effects involve such structural changes in society that will make it possible for all parties to take advantage of the equal opportunities presumed to exist in a democratic nation.

It may not be possible for each social worker to perform both kinds of services (treatment and prevention/promotion). However, what is important is that social workers provide a balance of these services through the social welfare system as a whole. Receiving assistance to promote the development of human potential is "not for the poor alone" (to quote the title of an important book by Kahn and Kamerman, 1977). Yet it is equally ethical for social workers to engage in preventive/promotive actions for the less and the more advantaged members of society, when viewed from a perspective of the whole over time. Thus the justification of ethical choices involves not only one client or case situation but the whole social network of case situations as well as efforts on behalf of ordinary citizens in the community. Resolving value conflicts from this perspective clearly requires careful social planning at every point in the helping continuum, from the individual worker to community-wide services. This is not an easy task, but it is a necessary one in order to distribute scarce resources equitably for all members of society.

We have come a long way from Elizabeth Proctor's life and death decision in *The Crucible*, but in another sense, we have returned to that situation again. Every decision involves the individuals, their family and friends, their neighbors in the community, and perhaps the nation and world as well. No man or woman is a value island unto him or herself alone.

APPENDIX 10.1

The NASW Code of Ethics*

Preamble

This code is intended to serve as a guide to the everyday conduct of members of the social work profession and as a basis for the adjudication of issues in ethics when the conduct of social workers is alleged to deviate from the standards expressed or implied in this code. It represents standards of ethical behavior for social workers in professional relationships with those served, with colleagues, with employers, with other individuals and professions, and with the community and society as a whole. It also embodies standards of ethical behavior governing individual conduct to the extent that such conduct is associated with an individual's status and identity as a social worker.

This code is based on the fundamental values of the social work profession that include the worth, dignity, and uniqueness of all persons as well as their rights and opportunities. It is also based on the nature of social work, which foster conditions that promote these values.

In subscribing to and abiding by this code, the social worker is expected to view ethical responsibility in as inclusive a context as each situation demands and within which ethical judgment is required. The social worker is expected to take into consideration all the principles in this code that have a bearing upon any situation in which ethical judgement is to be exercised and professional intervention or conduct is planned. The course of action that the social worker chooses is expected to be consistent with the spirit as well as the letter of this code.

In itself, this code does not represent a set of rules that will prescribe all the behaviors of social workers in all the complexities of professional life. Rather, it offers general principles to guide conduct, and the judicious appraisal of conduct, in situations that have ethical implications. It provides the basis for making judgements about ethical actions before and after they occur. Frequently, the particular situation determines the ethical principles that apply and the manner of their application. In such cases, not only the particular ethical principles are taken into immediate consideration, but also the entire code and its spirit. Specific applications of ethical principles must be judged within the context in which they are being considered. Ethical behavior in a given situation must satisfy not only the judgement of the individual social worker, but also the judgement of an unbiased jury of professional peers.

This code should not be used as an instrument to deprive any social worker of the opportunity or freedom to practice with complete professional integrity; nor should any disciplinary action be taken on the basis of this code without maximum provision for safeguarding the rights of the social worker affected.

The ethical behavior of social workers results not from edict, but from a personal commitment of the individual. This code is offered to affirm the will and zeal of all social workers to be ethical and to act ethically in all that they do as social workers.

---

*1980, National Association of Social Workers, Inc., NASW CODE OF ETHICS, as adopted by the 1979 Delegate Assembly. Reprinted with permission.

Summary of Major Principles

I. The Social Worker's Conduct and Comportment as a Social Worker

A. *Propriety.* The social worker should maintain high standards of personal conduct in the capacity or identity as social worker.

B. *Competence and Professional Development.* The social worker should strive to become and remain proficient in professional practice and the performance of professional functions.

C. *Service.* The social worker should regard as primary the service obligation of the social work profession.

D. *Integrity.* The social worker should act in accordance with the highest standards of professional integrity.

E. *Scholarship and Research.* The social worker engaged in study and research should be guided by the conventions of scholarly inquiry.

II. The Social Worker's Ethical Responsibility to Clients

F. *Primacy of Clients' Interests.* The social worker's primary responsibility is to clients.

G. *Rights and Prerogatives of Clients.* The social worker should make every effort to foster maximum self-determination on the part of clients.

H. *Confidentiality and Privacy.* The social worker should respect the privacy of clients and hold in confidence all information obtained in the course of professional service.

I. *Fees.* When setting fees, the social worker should ensure that they are fair, reasonable, considerate, and commensurate with the service performed and with due regard for the clients' ability to pay.

III. The Social Worker's Ethical Responsibility to Colleagues

J. *Respect, Fairness, and Courtesy.* The social worker should treat colleagues with respect, courtesy, fairness, and good faith.

K. *Dealing with Colleagues' Clients.* The social worker has the responsibility to relate to the clients of colleagues with full professional consideration.

IV. The Social Worker's Ethical Responsibility to Employers and Employing Organizations

L. *Commitments to Employing Organizations.* The social worker should adhere to commitments made to the employing organizations.

V. The Social Worker's Ethical Responsibility to the Social Work Profession

M. *Maintaining the Integrity of the Profession.* The social worker should uphold and advance the values, ethics, knowledge, and mission of the profession.

N. *Community Service.* The social worker should assist the profession in making social services available to the general public.

O. *Development of Knowledge.* The social worker should take responsibility for identifying, developing, and fully utilizing knowledge for professional practice.

VI. The Social Worker's Ethical Responsibility to Society

P. *Promoting the General Welfare.* The social worker should promote the general welfare of society.

The following codified ethical principles should guide social workers in the various roles and relationships and at the various levels of responsibility in which they function professionally. These principles also serve as a basis for the adjudication by the National Association of Social Workers of issues in ethics.

In subscribing to this code, social workers are required to cooperate in its implementation and abide by any disciplinary rulings based on it. They should also take adequate measures to discourage, prevent, expose, and correct the unethical conduct of colleagues. Finally, social workers should be equally ready to defend and assist colleagues unjustly charged with unethical conduct.

The NASW Code of Ethics

I. The Social Worker's Conduct and Comportment as a Social Worker

A. *Propriety.*   The social worker should maintain high standards of personal conduct in the capacity or identity as social worker.

1. The private conduct of the social worker is a personal matter to the same degree as is any other person's, except when such conduct compromises the fulfillment of professional responsibilities.

2. The social worker should not participate in, condone, or be associated with dishonesty, fraud, deceit, or misrepresentation.

3. The social worker should distinguish clearly between statements and actions made as a private individual and as a representative of the social work profession or an organization or group.

B. *Competence and Professional Development.*   The social worker should strive to become and remain proficient in professional practice and the performance of professional functions.

1. The social worker should accept responsibility or employment only on the basis of existing competence or the intention to acquire the necessary competence.

2. The social worker should not misrepresent professional qualifications, education, experience, or affiliations.

C. *Service.*   The social worker should regard as primary the service obligation of the social work profession.

1. The social worker should retain ultimate responsibility for the quality and extent of the service that individual assumes, assigns, or performs.

2. The social worker should act to prevent practices that are inhumane or discriminatory against any person or group of persons.

D. *Integrity.*   The social worker should act in accordance with the highest standards of professional integrity and impartiality.

1. The social worker should be alert to and resist the influences and pressures that interfere with the exercise of professional discretion and impartial judgement required for the performance of professional functions.

2. The social worker should not exploit professional relationships for personal gain.

E. *Scholarship and Research.*   The social worker engaged in study and research should be guided by the conventions of scholarly inquiry.

1. The social worker engaged in research should consider carefully its possible consequences for human beings.

2. The social worker engaged in research should ascertain that the consent of participants in the research is voluntary and informed, without any implied deprivation or penalty for refusal to participate, and with due regard for participants' privacy and dignity.

3. The social worker engaged in research should protect participants from unwarranted physical or mental discomfort, distress, harm, danger, or deprivation.
4. The social worker who engages in the evaluation of services or cases should discuss them only for the professional purposes and only with persons directly and professionally concerned with them.
5. Information obtained about participants in research should be treated as confidential.
6. The social worker should take credit only for work actually done in connection with scholarly and research endeavors and credit contributions made by others.

II. The Social Worker's Ethical Responsibility to Clients

F. *Primacy of Clients' Interests.* The social worker's primary responsibility is to clients.
   1. The social worker should serve clients with devotion, loyalty, determination, and the maximum application of professional skill and competence.
   2. The social worker should not exploit relationships with clients for personal advantage, or solicit the clients of one's agency for private practice.
   3. The social worker should not practice, condone, facilitate, or collaborate with any form of discrimination on the basis of race, color, sex, sexual orientation, age, religion, national origin, marital status, political belief, mental or physical handicap, or any other preference or personal characteristic, condition, or status.
   4. The social worker should avoid relationships or commitments that conflict with the interests of clients.
   5. The social worker should under no circumstances engage in sexual activities with clients.
   6. The social worker should provide clients with accurate and complete information regarding the extent and nature of the services available to them.
   7. The social worker should apprise clients of their risks, rights, opportunities, and obligations associated with social service to them.
   8. The social worker should seek advice and counsel of colleagues and supervisors whenever such consultation is in the best interest of clients.
   9. The social worker should terminate service to clients, and professional relationships with them, when such service and relationships are no longer required or no longer serve the clients' needs or interests.
   10. The social worker should withdraw services precipitously only under unusual circumstances, giving careful consideration to all factors in the situation and taking care to minimize possible adverse effects.
   11. The social worker who anticipates the termination or interruption of service to clients should notify clients promptly and seek the transfer, referral, or continuation of service in relation to the clients' needs and preferences.

G. *Rights and Prerogatives of Clients.* The social worker should make every effort to foster maximum self-determination on the part of clients.
   1. When the social worker must act on behalf of a client who has been adjudged legally incompetent, the social worker should safeguard the interests and rights of that client.

2. When another individual has been legally authorized to act in behalf of a client, the social worker should deal with that person always with the client's best interest in mind.

3. The social worker should not engage in any action that violates or diminishes the civil or legal rights of clients.

H. *Confidentiality and Privacy.* The social worker should respect the privacy of clients and hold in confidence all information obtained in the course of professional service.

1. The social worker should share with others confidences revealed by clients, without their consent, only for compelling professional reasons.

2. The social worker should inform clients fully about the limits of confidentiality in a given situation, the purposes for which information is obtained, and how it may be used.

3. The social worker should afford clients reasonable access to any official social work records concerning them.

4. When providing clients with access to records, the social worker should take due care to protect the confidences of others contained in those records.

5. The social worker should obtain informed consent of clients before taping, recording, or permitting third party observation of their activities.

I. *Fees.* When setting fees, the social worker should ensure that they are fair, reasonable, considerate, and commensurate with the service performed and with due regard for the clients' ability to pay.

1. The social worker should not divide a fee or accept or give anything of value for receiving or making a referral.

III. The Social Worker's Ethical Responsibility to Colleagues

J. *Respect, Fairness, and Courtesy.* The social worker should treat colleagues with respect, courtesy, fairness, and good faith.

1. The social worker should cooperate with colleagues to promote professional interests and concerns.

2. The social worker should respect confidences shared by colleagues in the course of their professional relationships and transactions.

3. The social worker should create and maintain conditions of practice that facilitate ethical and competent professional performance by colleagues.

4. The social worker should treat with respect, and represent accurately and fairly, the qualifications, views, and findings of colleagues and use appropriate channels to express judgements on these matters.

5. The social worker who replaces or is replaced by a colleague in professional practice should act with consideration for the interest, character, and reputation of that colleague.

6. The social worker should not exploit a dispute between a colleague and employers to obtain a position or otherwise advance the social worker's interest.

7. The social worker should seek arbitration or mediation when conflicts with colleagues require resolution for compelling professional reasons.

8. The social worker should extend to colleagues of other professions the same respect and cooperation that is extended to social work colleagues.

9. The social worker who serves as an employer, supervisor, or mentor to colleagues should make orderly and explicit arrangements regarding the conditions of their continuing professional relationship.

10. The social worker who has the responsibility for employing and evaluating the performance of other staff members, should fulfill such responsibility in a fair, considerate, and equitable manner, on the basis of clearly enunciated criteria.

11. The social worker who has the responsibility for evaluating the performance of employees, supervisees, or students should share evaluations with them.

K. *Dealing with Colleagues' Clients.*   The social worker has the responsibility to relate to the clients of colleagues with full professional consideration.

1. The social worker should not solicit the clients of colleagues.

2. The social worker should not assume professional responsibility for the clients of another agency or a colleague without appropriate communication with that agency or colleague.

3. The social worker who serves the clients of colleagues, during a temporary absence or emergency, should serve those clients with the same consideration as that afforded any client.

IV. The Social Worker's Ethical Responsibility to Employers and Employing Organizations

L. *Commitments to Employing Organization.*   The social worker should adhere to commitments made to the employing organization.

1. The social worker should work to improve the employing agency's policies and procedures, and the efficiency and effectiveness of its services.

2. The social worker should not accept employment or arrange student field placements in an organization which is currently under public sanction by NASW for violating personnel standards, or imposing limitations on or penalties for professional actions on behalf of clients.

3. The social worker should act to prevent and eliminate discrimination in the employing organization's work assignments and in its employment policies and practices.

4. The social worker should use with scrupulous regard, and only for the purpose for which they are intended, the resources of the employing organization.

V. The Social Worker's Ethical Responsibility to the Social Work Profession

M. *Maintaining the Integrity of the Profession.*   The social worker should uphold and advance the values, ethics, knowledge, and mission of the profession.

1. The social worker should protect and enhance the dignity and integrity of the profession and should be responsible and vigorous in discussion and criticism of the profession.

2. The social worker should take action through appropriate channels against unethical conduct by any other member of the profession.

3. The social worker should act to prevent the unauthorized and unqualified practice of social work.

4. The social worker should make no misrepresentation in advertising as to qualifications, competence, service, or results to be achieved.

N. *Community Service.*   The social worker should assist the profession in making social services available to the general public.

   1. The social worker should contribute time and professional expertise to activities that promote respect for the utility, the integrity, and the competence of the social work profession.

   2. The social worker should support the formulation, development, enactment, and implementation of social policies of concern to the profession.

O. *Development of Knowledge.*   The social worker should take responsibility for identifying, developing, and fully utilizing knowledge for professional practice.

   1. The social worker should base practice upon recognized knowledge relevant to social work.

   2. The social worker should critically examine, and keep current with, emerging knowledge relevant to social work.

   3. The social worker should contribute to the knowledge base of social work and share research knowledge and practice wisdom with colleagues.

VI. The Social Worker's Ethical Responsibility to Society

P. *Promoting the General Welfare.*   The social worker should promote the general welfare of society.

   1. The social worker should act to prevent and eliminate discrimination against any person or group on the basis of race, color, sex, sexual orientation, age, religion, national origin, marital status, political belief, mental or physical handicap, or any other preference or personal characteristic, condition, or status.

   2. The social worker should act to ensure that all persons have access to the resources, services, and opportunities which they require.

   3. The social worker should act to expand choice and opportunity for all persons, with special regard for disadvantaged or oppressed groups and persons.

   4. The social worker should promote conditions that encourage respect for the diversity of cultures which constitute American society.

   5. The social worker should provide appropriate professional services in public emergencies.

   6. The social worker should advocate changes in policy and legislation to improve social conditions and to promote social justice.

   7. The social worker should encourage informed participation by the public in shaping social policies and institutions.

PART

V.

SOCIAL PROBLEMS AND SOCIAL SERVICE SYSTEMS

T he three chapters in this Part sample several of the many social problems that exist in our society today. These problems may be defined as involving social conditions in which large numbers of individuals engage in actions (or are affected by situations) that are recognized as inappropriate by a sizeable segment of the community (or its agents) and that are subsequently put on the social agenda for suitable change.

For example, large numbers of persons are in situations in which they are not able to earn enough money to keep them above the poverty line. There are many individual reasons for such circumstances, but the common problem is obtaining enough money to buy the necessities of life. The causes are seen to stem from both external and internal factors—from such social events as shut-downs of industries that leave people unemployed, or from lack of education and skills individuals need for technically advanced jobs.

The effects of poverty are widespread and are among causes of other social concerns, such as malnutrition of families, child or spousal abuse, or mental illness. Many politicians have tried to grapple with the problems of poverty—how to provide help for the poor, both as immediate relief from hunger or cold and as long-term training and support to enable them to get out of the welfare system. Popular interest in poverty waxes and wanes, but it remains on the national agenda because it affects so many people in so many different ways.

Widespread concern is apparent also for the problems of physical and mental illness, of suicide, of homelessness, and of unemployment. Other types of social problems are discussed under various headings—as aspects of fields of social work practice, or as kinds of special populations and issues. For each social problem, the same basic questions may be asked: Who is involved, with what specific problems or challenges, under what social and physical environmental conditions, and with what effects? This is another way of stating the configural perspective with regard to the largest issues facing our society. All levels of the social configuration will be involved in resolving any one issue.

OUTLINE

CHAPTER ELEVEN

Poverty and Wealth

Most of us do not know the extreme of poverty or of wealth, and yet helping professionals are frequently called to provide services for both the poor and the nonpoor, though the services differ. Governmental supports, moreover, are given to people across the economic spectrum, even when such assistance is not called by the pejorative name of welfare. This chapter introduces the complex topic of poverty and wealth through some exercises that suggest what life is like at the extremes. It contributes to an understanding of what programs are needed and how they work.

POVERTY

We come into this world totally helpless and dependent, clothed only in our "inalienable rights of life, liberty, and the pursuit of happiness." We are born equal before the law, with only our natural wits and a little help from our friends and relatives to make our way in life. But even before we leave the womb, we are different. Whom we are born to, how well we are nurtured in that uterine environment, what possible mishaps we are heir to, all these differ according to social and cultural forces over which we have little control. What happens to us afterward, unto the moment of our death—and even in the funerary arrangements—is an exploding picture of differences of every possible sort. Let us explore some of these differences among people, particularly those having to do with wealth or the lack of it, and all the things that wealth can command.

Following is an exercise that the reader can perform by drawing directly on experience in his or her own life. Following the experience vicariously through the next few pages provides only one side of the picture, however. The rest of the chapter tries to provide other perspectives—what structural factors influence poverty? Who are the poor? Where does poverty occur and why? And what has been the response of helping professionals? But first, let's put you onto center stage.

An Experience with Poverty: Budgeting

To begin with, let's pretend that you have just received a "gift" of $100. That amount represents roughly an average monthly payment that each recipient from the largest cash assistance program gets in the United States— Aid to Families with Dependent Children (AFDC). The actual amount people receive depends on the family size and other factors. For this exercise, $100 is reasonably close. The gift to you has one string attached. You must learn how to live for a month on that income. This is a lesson that millions of Americans relearn every month.

First, distinguish between *income* (money coming in currently) as contrasted with *wealth* [a person's total assets, which include such things as personal possessions (like jewelry, cameras, and hifi equipment), real estate (a condominium apartment or a house), money in the bank, any stocks or bonds, and so forth]. Another basic distinction is that of *cash income* and *in-kind or noncash transfers* (such as food stamps, Medicaid, and the like). The money that pays for the in-kind goods actually goes to the providers, for example, the grocers or doctors. A question arises as to whether, when, and how to count in-kind transfers when determining who is poor. We return to that thorny question later in the chapter.

Where shall we begin to live on $100 for a month? Do you at once begin to feel a bit of tension even thinking about this challenge? Then you have had your first "experience of poverty," a pervasive sense of pressure of simply keeping body and soul together, of surviving.

Begin with the basics of budgeting: Food, clothing, shelter, and other necessary features of life in modern America. The government assumes that one-third of the average household income is spent on food, based on findings from a 1955 consumer survey. A 1965 survey corrected this figure to 34.5 percent, but the point is that some arbitrary and absolute figure is used to determine the poverty line or threshold (Harrington, 1984, p. 82). Thus, while this figure may not be accurate, and while it does not take into account cost of living variations among regions of the country, or special conditions of people— the retired, students, or parents of handicapped children who may require costly expenditures, for example—it is used in calculating the important *poverty index*. The poverty index controls the amount of money presumed to be needed on the average to maintain a decent standard of living. Each year, the poverty line is indexed, or changed automatically, to make cost-of-living adjustments according to changes in the Consumer Price Index. In 1969, nonfood items were also included in the calculations. So this formula gets revised on occasion, as the government seeks to have it reflect current life-styles and needs.

What such remote government decisions mean to you is that you can take about $34 to the grocery store to buy foods and nonfood items for the whole month. Assuming that you have a small stock of basic supplies at home—and they have to be replenished every so often too—what are you going to buy? Like the vast majority of us, you are a rational person (most of the time), and so you know that with limited funds you have to plan carefully to get as much nutrition for your money as possible. Perhaps you remember a lesson from school, or perhaps you read somewhere about basic nutrition, so you recall that you should eat foods in four basic groups (Center for Science in the Public Interest, 1979; Brody, 1985):

1. Milk products: children, three to four servings a day; adults two servings a day.
2. Fruits and vegetables: four or more servings a day.
3. Poultry, fish, meat, and eggs: two servings a day (vegetarians must get equivalent nutrients by eating proper combinations of vegetables and grains or milk or poultry—for example, a bowl of thick minestrone soup, a bean enchilada, or a peanut butter sandwich and a glass of milk).
4. Beans, grains, and nuts: four or more servings a day

Let's go shopping to see how you will spend your $100 for this month.

Milk Products.   You have heard that milk is nature's most perfect food (courtesy of the dairy industry), so let's get some. Do not get the convenient single quart size, because the gallon size is cheaper per unit of milk. (In some grocery stores, unit pricing is provided along with the actual cost of the item, as an aid in making wise decisions. But even when unit pricing is not available, you can figure it out by dividing the price by the number of units, which gives you the price per unit. Generally, but not always, the larger volume is sold for a smaller per-unit price.) However, powdered milk is far cheaper per quart than liquid milk, and even though you may not be accustomed to the taste—mix it with some liquid milk until you get used to the change—it has all the nutrients you need. Here's a box that contains powder for 20 quarts of milk at only $6.

What? Six percent of your entire monthly income, and about 16 percent of your food budget? Can you afford to take advantage of the good economics of buying in large quantity? Probably not, so you take the next larger size, 10 quarts, for $4.25. Look, that's not fair! Half of the 20-quart size should not cost much more than $3.00 (half of the $6.00 of the 20-quart size). You contemplate writing the manufacturer to offer your complaint. But you estimate that the paper and the stamp will cost you at least 30 cents and decide maybe that might be better spent on food.

Now comes the choice among brands. You recognize several nationally advertised companies, and you see that their prices are somewhat higher than the brands you do not recognize (including the house brand, often the lowest price of all). You reach for the economilk in the dull plain wrapper, but to comfort yourself, you look at the nutritional information on the side panel and compare it with the higher priced brands. The protein, carbohydrates, sodium, and potassium, and the calories per eight-ounce glass are about the same, as are the percentages of U.S.-recommended daily allowances of vitamins and minerals. A glass of milk seems to be a rich source of these substances, so maybe there is good reason for the milk-promotion slogan, "nature's most perfect food." Enough for the milk group—no cheese, commercial yogurt, or similar foods for you today.

Fruits and Vegetables.   There they are, piles of beautiful grapes and strawberries, your very favorite. The prices are astronomic, however, and there is a boycott on grapes on behalf of striking farm laborers, so you continue to shop.

Here is a cart filled with bruised and elderly fruit at much reduced prices. Is it worth it? You recall that elderly fruit lose much of their vitamins and minerals, let alone taste, so you pass up these "bargains" in favor of the cheapest-in-season fruits. Apples are in season, and they look so nice and shiny—unfortunately, the chemical used to induce that shine may be harmful to your health. You look for locally grown fruit; presumably local growers do not have to add preservative or cosmetic chemicals. The price is $2 for 4 pounds. Some oranges are on sale, ten cents apiece. You put ten in a plastic bag and move on past the exotic fruits.

You may never have cared much for vegetables. You know you should eat some, so you look around. Carrots look good, 3 pounds for a dollar. Lettuce at 50 cents a head seems reasonable. As you dive into the pile of heads, you soon realize that not all heads are created equal. And with a little exploration, you discover that you have a head that is nearly twice as large as the first one you picked up, at the same price. Ha, you fooled the store that time. And so it goes—with onions, zucchini, broccoli, and the like. You appear to be getting a lot of good food for the money. All of a sudden, vegetables look a little better to you.

You might be inclined to pass up potatoes because you have heard they are fattening. In fact, potatoes themselves contain almost no fat. It is only the things we put on potatoes—like butter or sour cream—or how we prepare them—like frying them in saturated oils—that adds the fat. Jane Brody (1985, p. 30) points out that the potato is a nutrient bargain, giving many essential vitamins and minerals, especially the trace elements. Ten pounds for a dollar is another bargain, compared to french fries at the local greasy spoon for a dollar a serving.

Poultry, Fish, and Meat.   Proteins are an essential element needed every day. You know that a juicy red steak with fine veins of fat is both tasty and filled with proteins. But meat carries a high cost, both in money and in increases in risk of heart disease associated with cholesterol and saturated fats. This says nothing of the amount of grain needed to produce a pound of meat instead of having that grain go directly for human consumption. All fats, both saturated and unsaturated, may increase the risk of bowel and breast cancers (Center for Science in the Public Interest, 1979). Americans, on the average, eat two to four times as much protein a day than is needed by the body (Brody, 1985, p. 168). It may be wise to use smaller amounts of meats, more as condiments to accentuate the flavor of rice, pasta, or vegetable dishes. But most meats are expensive, especially to one on a limited budget. What are the alternatives?

Fortunately, there are many. Chicken or turkey is relatively inexpensive and they provide good sources of complete protein (when prepared by baking, roasting, or boiling, without skin). Various kinds of fish, including water-packed tuna, are good alternatives—cod, flounder, haddock, perch, and the like. Eggs are all right if the yokes, which are high in cholesterol, are avoided in favor of the whites.

Chicken is on sale at your local grocer. A "family package" (which includes wings, backs, and other relatively unmeaty parts, as well as some breasts and legs) are 4 pounds for $3. You recall that your mother made chicken soup from the backs and wings, covering them with water and simmering them for an hour along with a piece of celery and a touch of salt. Then, discarding the skin and bones, you have the broth plus tiny pieces of chicken for salads. With that broth, you can make all sorts of nourishing dishes by the addition of some vegetables or rice or pastas, even peanut butter (an old colonial Williamsburg favorite). It clearly takes some thoughtfulness and creativity to keep three appealing, nourishing, and inexpensive meals on the table each day.

Beans, Grains, and Nuts.   For beans, you head to the canned foods section, or to the frozen foods, and find all sorts of varieties. If you read carefully, you recognize that the price per unit of food is very high—payment for the convenience—and frequently salt or sugar, which you do not need, is one of the leading ingredients. So, we go to the dried beans and peas (legumes, to be precise), and see what is available. You may never have heard of all of the types, such as lentils, or the variety among beans. It will take practice to learn which suit you best. The recipes on the packages are a start. The price is quite low, but note that it takes time to prepare dried beans. Soaking and discarding the water helps to reduce gas produced by beans, but some—lentils, lima beans, chickpeas, and white beans—are less likely to cause these problems.

Some canned goods, such as canned tomatoes and corn, are useful to have on hand, both for the nutritional values and for availability out of season. When combined with pasta and cheese, for example, these vegetables become a source of the complete proteins that are needed by the body—vegetables alone contain only some of the needed proteins.

Other types of grains and nuts that are also very good for us include whole grained breads and cereals. Highly processed grains have most of the nutrients ground out of the flour. Relatively inexpensive foods, such as oatmeal, bulghur (cracked wheat), and whole wheat pastas that come in dozens of different shapes are good.

Peanut butter, though high in unsaturated fat, can be eaten in moderation, as can such favorites as pizza, tofu (a soy bean curd that is a favorite in the Orient for good nutritional reasons), macaroni and cheese, nuts, pancakes and white bread. It is only when you feast exclusively on sweet sticky doughnuts, rich (meaning fattening) chocolate cakes, as well as ice cream that you get into trouble both with fats and with high sugar contents. These snacks take up the room in your stomach that other, more nutritious foods would have supplied.

There are other "special sales" that you see as you go to the checkout counter, but they all seem more like sales promotions than genuine bargains. Sometimes there are "cents-off" coupons on major brands, but the reduction of price may not be as much as the original higher price, so one must watch carefully. There are other temptations awaiting, as you get ready to checkout—cigarettes, gum, racy film magazines, and the like. Since you are "addicted" to another product—food—you know you have to cut down on luxury items you may want. It's going to be a long month, you can tell.

The clerk asks whether you have any food stamps or coupons—you notice others looking at you as you answer, a silent judgment about your purchases and perhaps about you as a human being. To qualify for food stamps, one has to meet certain tests of the level of one's income—that is, one has to prove that one is poor. (This is one of the stigmatizations that occur when you are identified as poor.)

The total bill is $20.00. Your order includes perishable foods for just this week, as well as staple items that will last the whole month. By figuring what additional perishables will be needed this month, you can see how the total food bill will be at least one-third of your total monthly income. Before you leave the grocery store, consider what is not in your grocery bags: There are no cookies or crackers, no ice cream, no cheese, no candy, no liquor, wine, or beer. Also, there are no paper towels, plastic bags, laundry detergent, or contraceptives. Either you can get along without them, or you will have to get more when your current supply runs out. Generally speaking, there is not much "fat" in those grocery bags.

Clothing. Assume that you live near the grocery store, and you will walk home carrying two large bags. You suddenly realize that it is a lot farther than you recall when you were not toting the bags. The exercise may do you good, however, and you get a chance to look at the store windows for some clothes you need for the winter. The prices almost make you drop your bags—$60 to $100 for winter coats! That's out of the question, even though they do look great.

You had noticed a church rummage sale, and after you deposit your food at home, you return for a look. Ah, a very serviceable jacket on the front rack for only $5, only it is a bit small. Should you wait until a better fitting one comes along? The price is right, but there are always rummage sales somewhere, you imagine. You ponder these things. You also remember your annoyance of always getting your older sibling's hand-me-downs, and when you return to look at the bargain jacket, it is gone. That solves that problem. Somewhat discouraged, you return home.

Rent. Rent is due for the month. You know what you actually pay for rent now, but assume that you are in a rent-subsidized room. You have to pay only one-quarter of your income for rent. It is not the kind of place that inspires the imagination or the soul, but it is cheap, usually warm enough, and dry. You notice that some four-footed visitor has been nibbling on a potato that you left in the bag on the floor, so you figure out a way of suspending the bag from the door, while you go out to buy a mouse trap.

Other Necessities of Everyday Life. You still have about $40 left. It has to be spent for transportation to work or school; utilities; incidentals like soap, aspirin, toothpaste, and the like. You probably want to have some money in reserve for emergencies that involve doctors and medicine; perhaps you want to include some money for recreation, or to be able to loan something to a friend who is hard up, or to give money to charity. What about long-term matters such as insurance, savings, or the like? Not much is left for extras, things that most middle-class people think provident and essential for the good life. Especially toward the end of the month you discover things you need to buy, and sometimes the money is not there. Maybe you can borrow a few dollars from a friend to tide you over. Maybe.

There is not much to cut down on, if you are in the habit of eating. You could cut out breakfast, but that is a poor way to start the day. Lunch can be somewhat lighter, especially if you take some time for exercise, perhaps going for a long walk rather than eating that dollar serving of french fries with salt. Exercise actually gives you energy and better muscle tone, rather than taking it away, and you will sleep better as well. Dinner time is a time for relaxing, but not necessarily eating heavily. It is difficult to go to bed hungry—though it is estimated that millions of people all over the world do go to bed hungry every night. Maria de Jesus writes, "those who lie down with hunger do not have pleasant dreams."

Studies have suggested some basic life habits that are positively associated with longevity. These include eating breakfast, getting regular exercise, staying within the norms of your weight, not smoking, not drinking to excess, not eating between meals, and getting seven to eight hours of sleep each night (Belloc and Breslow, 1977). Others would note additional correlates of longevity: choose your parents wisely—long-lived parents are a good indicator of longevity in their children; be rich, so as to be able to afford good nutrition, health care, recreation, and so on. Live moderately—some aspects of the affluent life are unhealthful. (Cf. Zastrow, 1986, p. 436.) Consider how many of these characteristics the poor are likely to possess.

There is not much fun in being poor. Why would anyone want to live like this? There must be ways of getting out of the dead-end trap of being poor. Or are there?

Who Are the Poor? Where Does Poverty Exist?

Using 1987 figures, some 32,500,000 Americans were defined as poor, that is, as having an income below a defined level called the poverty line or index which is based solely on money income (Statistical Abstracts, 1989, Table 746). This is about 13.5 percent of the whole population or about one person in seven. This is probably a low estimate, as many poor people are "invisible" to census takers. They may have no permanent home, such as the migrants, or those illegally crowded into shared apartments, or as unauthorized aliens trying to keep out of sight. Yet, that percentage is far better than Franklin Delano Roosevelt's observation in 1933 that one-third of the nation was "ill-housed, ill-clad, ill-nourished." In fact, the rate of poverty has varied considerably over time. Trattner (1984) reports that about 25 percent of adults in colonial America were unemployed, and thus presumably below the poverty line at that time. Our own times have seen many fluctuations in the rate of poverty. In 1960 it was 22.2 percent of the population; by 1965 it was 17.3 and in 1970 the rate was down to 12.6. The lowest level recorded in recent times was 11.1 percent in 1973. Since that time, the rates have changed, but in general rates have risen. By 1987 the figure was 13.5 percent.

These general figures hide important differences within the standard descriptive categories used—age, race, sex, marital status, educational level, rural and urban location, and region of the country. Let us examine who are the poor within each of these categories. (But, to anticipate a discussion that occurs later in this Chapter, I will use an alternative way of figuring the poverty level by including not only money income, but also noncash benefits calculated by their market value had they been purchased, such as Medicaid. This is the way information is presented by the Bureau of the Census for the following categories.)

Poster reproduced with permission of
United Way Services, Richmond, Virginia

Poverty is a brutal way of life
for millions of Americans, and
tens of millions of citizens of
other nations. The effects of
poverty are seen in almost every
other major social problem. Poverty is a societal problem, even
though it ultimately rests on individuals, some of whom "eat
out every night."

Age.   A disproportionately high percentage of children under six years of age
are in the poverty group—22.8 percent as compared to the 13.5 percent of the
national average. Young people in general are above this national average;
19.4 percent of those 6 to 17 years old and 15.3 percent of those 18 to 24 are in
the poverty group. During the work years, the rates of poverty vary, but are
generally below the national average; 10.2 percent of those 25 to 44, and 9.1
percent of those 45 to 64 are poor. Then, the rate of poverty starts to climb
again. Persons 65 years old or older constitute 10.2 percent of the poverty
group as of 1987. It is important to note that in 1970 about 25 percent of older
persons were in the poverty group. In the interim, important social changes
have taken place that have reduced by more than half the percentage of poor
aged, a point that is notable in terms of social progress.

Race and National Origin.   The largest group of poor persons are white, simply because whites compose a large proportion of the total population. About
21,400,000 whites are poor. In proportional terms, black Americans are
overrepresented among the poor—about one in three black persons (33.1 percent) is below the poverty line. Although blacks represent about 12 percent of
the total population, they constitute about 25 percent of the poor. In numbers,
this means about 9.7 million persons. In 1987 the U.S. Census reported that

the median family income was $32,274 for whites and $18,098 for blacks. A sobering statistic is that about *half* of all black children (45.1 percent) grow up in poverty. Moreover, unemployment rates per 100 persons in the labor force differ significantly by race: unemployment for black men and women 20 years old or older was 11.3 percent and 10.4 percent respectively, compared with 4.1 percent and 4.5 percent for white men and women (February 1988). Black teenagers suffer an unemployment rate of 38.3 percent compared to 12.4 percent for white adolescents (Colburn, 1988).

Likewise, Hispanics (who may be of any race) and Native Americans are overrepresented among the poor. About 5.5 million Hispanics fall into that category. These people tend to be concentrated in several areas and states, so the problems are aggravated in those areas.

The poverty rate among Hispanics is 28.2 percent, slightly below that of blacks, whose rate is 33.1 percent; both are well above the national average of 13.5 percent and the comparable figure for whites, 10.5 percent (*Statistical Abstracts*, 1989, Table 743).

Among Native Americans, about 27 percent have incomes below the poverty level. This figure disguises the fact that poverty among these people living in certain areas, such as South Dakota, is very much higher than of people living in other areas (*Money Income and Poverty Status of Families and Persons in the United States: 1984*, 1985). Oriental Americans are underrepresented among the poor, meaning that the average income level of these Americans is higher than white Americans, a remarkable achievement given the pattern of discrimination against Oriental Americans for the past century (Chapter 17).

Gender and Marital Status.   Women comprise the largest number of poor persons, particularly minority female householders with no husbands present. As DiNitto and Dye (1987) report:

> The poverty rate for families headed by couples is 7 percent, and the poverty rate for families headed by males is 13 percent, but poverty in female-headed households is 35 percent. For families headed by white women, the rate is 27 percent; for families headed by black and Hispanic women, the rates are 52 and 53 percent respectively (p. 53).

Simon (1988) sketches the significant dimensions of this feminization of poverty. She points out that in the 1980s, 80 percent of women's jobs were in just 20 of the 420 occupations—mostly retail sales, clerical services, and light assembly work—catalogued by the U.S. Department of Labor. These are relatively poorly paying jobs, contributing to the well-known and persistent result that women earn 59 cents for every dollar men make. (This ratio has not changed much over three decades!) Simon also notes that our cultural conceptions of women as dependent on men as breadwinners—although grossly out of touch with the reality of contemporary dual wage-earning families—means that women take on major household, child rearing, and care of elders as well as employee roles, which have both physical as well as emotional costs. Women, much more than men, interrupt their careers to attend to their children, household, and elders, and so retirement benefits for women are consequently much lower. Simon goes on to note that racial discrimination and sexism exacerbate these factors.

The feminization of poverty is a grim reality in another way. A third of America's children grow up in restricting circumstances. More than half of these children grow up in families in which the father is absent. Particularly problematic is the rapid increase of adolescent parenting (among white teenagers) at the same time that black young persons are maintaining their very high levels of parenting. The likelihood of escaping poverty is poor for such persons. The prospects for their children to break out of the stunting circumstances of poverty without major social intervention is similarly pessimistic.

Education. Poverty among the less well educated is higher (28 percent among those with less than an eighth-grade education, compared with 10 percent among those who completed at least a high school education). At all educational levels, whites earn on the average between one and four thousand dollars more than do Hispanics with the same educational level, but Hispanics earn between two and five thousand dollars more than do blacks at comparable educational statuses (*Statistical Abstracts*, 1985, p. 447).

Locale and Region. Rural areas have higher percentages of people living below the poverty level, but in absolute numbers urban poverty is the larger problem. Rural poverty is more invisible to the majority of Americans while urban poverty appears more oppressive and concentrated. Poverty varies to a small degree by region of the country, with the South having the highest rate (16.2 percent), and the West and Northeast the lowest (13.1 and 13.2 percent, respectively). The Midwest has a poverty rate of 14.1 percent. There are special pockets of poverty in various regions, due to changes in economic conditions, unproductive land, or other local events. For example, Appalachia has suffered from shutdowns in the coal industry, little available farm lands, and an out-migration of young people seeking work elsewhere.

The Working Poor. Booth's 19th-century surveys of London's poor uncovered a remarkable fact: many full-time workers were still living below the poverty line. In our own day, about 35 percent of women and 18 percent of men aged 22–64 who were in the poverty group worked part of the year or part-time; 4 percent of women and 3 percent of men in that group worked full time (Rosen, Fanshel, and Lutz, 1987, p. 21). Partial work does not protect people from poverty. For some, even full-time work at minimum wages is not sufficient to keep them from being below the poverty line. Earning even small amounts of money prevents some from applying for certain kinds of public assistance, and pride inhibits others from applying even when they are eligible.

Farmers. Farmers encounter a difficult life in the face of unpredictable Nature, and perhaps an equally unpredictable socio-political environment whose laws may vary with each political administration. When farmers try to expand their holdings in inflationary times, and then try to pay off loans in recessionary times, they get caught in yet another double bind in our society. It is difficult to calculate poverty among farmers because they can produce some of their basic supplies (foods). Yet the evidence is clear—poverty is a continuing threat to the farm family. One indication is the total farm debt, which rose from $80 billion in 1974 to $214 billion in 1984. Farm income in 1983 was the lowest since the 1930s (Rosen, Fanshel, and Lutz, 1987, p. 13).

Students and People Who Would Be Students.   Few consider students poor, except the students themselves. In fact, large numbers of persons are prevented from continuing their education because of financial limitations, and many who are able to attend colleges and universities do so by working part-time. This is not in itself a terrible burden unless the work prevents students from spending the time and energy needed in their studies. Moreover, the college years are time-limited, and with a degree, graduates are presumably able to get better paying jobs (in part to be able to pay off debts accumulated in order to go to school). Other nations have scholarship programs for all those who are able to demonstrate high academic performance. What is the price individuals and the nation pay by not having the best minds prepared to achieve all they are able to achieve?

What is Poverty? Why Does It Exist?

The vicarious experience of "living" for a month on $100 may suggest what life is like for some 35 million Americans, citizens in the richest nation in history. As pointed out previously, about one person in seven in America has firsthand experience with some portions of the scenario described above. But what is poverty and why does it exist?

The question of what is poverty is not as simple as it might seem. The choice of criteria to define poverty has enormous political and financial implications, such as who can be admitted to the welfare roles as being in need of aid. One approach to the definition of poverty is to consider it as a kind of *absolute deprivation* of the basic essentials for living, such as food, clothing, and shelter (DiNitto and Dye, 1986). Thus people who do not have enough income to obtain these essentials are considered poor and become eligible for aid under certain conditions. The U.S. Social Security Administration determines the level by using the poverty index, whose formula stems from the Consumer Price Index, as described above. The poverty level varies by size of family. In 1987, the poverty level for one person was set at $5,778; for two persons, $7,397; for three persons, $9,056; and for four, it was $11,611. (*Poverty in the United States*, Table A-2, page 157, 1989.)

A controversial issue must be discussed at this point. Poor people may be able to get not only financial aid to help them approach the poverty level (a minimal level for having a decent standard of living), but they also may be able to get what are called *in-kind benefits* or *noncash transfers*, such as the value of food stamps, school lunches, subsidized student loans, public housing, Medicare and Medicaid, among other benefits. The other forms of noncash transfers, it should be noted, are likely to involve the nonpoor as well as the poor. Examples are Medicare, payments that employers make for employees for medical insurance or retirement benefits, and the expense accounts that are not officially counted as income. Likewise, there are nontaxed categories like interest paid on home mortgages, which is a deduction from income on federal tax returns of those who own homes and itemize deductions—generally, the nonpoor.

TABLE 11.1 Noncash transfers to the poor and the nonpoor

To the poor	billions ($)	To the nonpoor	billions ($)
Food stamps	9.2	Employer subsidies	83.5
School lunches	3.3	Uncollected mortgage	
Public housing	5.4	interest	32.0
Medicaid	26.2	Other government sub-	
Medicare (provided to		sidies, such as medical	
poor and nonpoor		payments to veterans	27.8
alike)	28.4		
TOTAL:	72.5	TOTAL:	143.3

Source: Smeedling, 1982

Some conservative writers, for example, Edgar Browning (1975), suggest that if these noncash transfers are recalculated as income for the poor, then poverty becomes "virtually nonexistent" since their income plus the value of the noncash transfers raises them out of the poverty level, defined as deprivations of food, clothing, and shelter. The Census Bureau defines about 12 percent of the people as being below the poverty line. Who is right?

It does make some sense to count noncash transfers for the poor as income—but only if noncash transfers for the nonpoor are also counted. As liberal commentators, such as Harrington (1984), point out, when the noncash transfers of the nonpoor are examined, it turns out that the rich get about double the amount of the subsidies of the poor. Smeedling (1982) summarizes these noncash transfers to the poor and to the nonpoor (see Table 11.1).

But even if the nonpoor get about twice as much in noncash transfers, on an absolute basis, a large number of the poor are in effect lifted above the poverty level. It must be noted that these noncash transfers go to the providers of the services consumers receive, so in strict terms, the poor themselves do not have incomes that take them above the poverty level. How one interprets these factors depends on one's value position. The facts support both conservative and liberal positions.

A *relative deprivation* approach to defining poverty tries to take into account the fact that while some persons may have income or in-kind transfers or both whose combined effects pull them above a poverty line, they are still poor (DiNitto and Dye, 1986). While you may not be starving on $100 a month, you have few luxury items. Underlying this relative deprivation is the fundamental fact of the maldistribution of income in the nation.

The highest fifth of the population owns 42.7 percent of family personal income.

The second highest owns 24.4 percent.

The third highest owns 17.1 percent.

The fourth highest owns 11.1 percent.

The lowest fifth of the population owns 4.7 percent. (If income were distributed perfectly equally, each quintile would have 20 percent.) (*Statistical Abstracts*, 1985, p. 448.)

Again, different conditions mitigate relative deprivation. Farm families grow some of their own foods and have a more modest life-style than condo dwellers on the sophisticated avenues of major metropolises. But few people are so naive that they do not realize the gross maldistribution of income when their native talents and hard work are not significantly less than that of others who earn extremely high amounts of money.

This view of poverty is clarified by Harrington's (1984) insight: Poverty is not an income level; it is a condition of life, a way of existing (p. 77). The poor are poor in every respect: cash income, noncash income, legal services, public amenities, basic human respect, life chances, longevity rates, among others. The term poverty must reflect this system of interrelated events.

There is another encompassing view of poverty, called the culture of poverty (Lewis, 1969). This represents a kind of learned helplessness concept (Seligman, 1975) applied to people who are locked into impoverished settings and who consequently are presumed to take on the mental set of indifference or apathy—since nothing they can do seems to have any effect on their life. With alienation from social bonds comes reduced self-worth and a generalized hedonic behavioral pattern, outside the law if necessary, since the threat of police power holds little sway to such persons. A corollary to this pessimistic view is that little can be done to help such people move out of this mental and cultural rut. They see no future for themselves, and so live only in the present. Whether they buy processed American cheese or brie, it doesn't matter. They will be hungry at the end of the month in any case.

Do people really live like this? The answer is, in part, yes. Those who have been on welfare for several generations probably have strong expectations of being locked into an underclass. In fact, only a small minority of people are in this underclass. Scholars distinguish between "welfare spells" (continuous periods of time in which one receives welfare) and "welfare careers" (the total time spent on welfare over one's lifetime) (*Welfare Programs for Families with Children*, 1987). Welfare spells are relatively short—about half lasting two years or less, and only 10 percent lasting as long as 10 years. However, about 40 percent of unmarried mothers who have completed welfare spells subsequently return to AFDC programs, so that the total time on welfare is much longer. About half will have welfare careers of more than four years. About a quarter of these AFDC mothers will receive benefits for 10 years or more. This is especially true of young mothers who have never worked. How do people get out of this cycle? Evidence suggests that family changes make a big difference. In 35 percent of all cases on the Panel Study of Income Dependents involving AFDC mothers (the major source of data on the duration of welfare recipiency), mothers who got married left AFDC roles. (See *Welfare Programs for Families with Children*, 1987.)

Critics of the culture of poverty concept argue that it is a blame-the-victim approach rather than one that attacks the structural and socio-economic causes. Once we accept the statement that some people are hopelessly present-oriented hedonists as the culture of poverty concept seems to suggest, then it does not make much sense to try to change the external causes of their behavior.

Defenders of the view argue that regardless of where these values of hopelessness and alienation come from, they are facts of existence that stubbornly resist change. Simply giving such persons money or some in-kind transfers that are used for hedonic purposes (such as food stamps) is not effective.

It is difficult to work with the multi-problem person or family, no question of that. Whether it is as hopeless as some defenders of the culture of poverty concept suggest is a question that requires empirical testing.

Another definition of poverty derives from a Marxist perspective. Poverty is exploitation by the wealthy (the owners of the means of production and other members of the ruling class) of the masses (who have only their own labor to exchange for wages) (DiNitto and Dye, 1986). In this view, social workers and others in the welfare system are simply aiding and abetting exploitation by making superficial adjustments in people's lives, rather than changing the basic structures of society (cf. Galper, 1974). A related interpretation uses the reasoning of an early sociologist, Durkheim, who found functional uses of existing societal entities. So, for example, crime was functional, according to Durkheim, because it focused and activated the moral conscience of a group, which strengthened that group.

In a like way, Gans (1972) noted a number of positive functions of poverty to the larger society. First, poverty generates a group of relatively unskilled workers who perform the menial, boring, dirty, and dangerous jobs that the nonpoor do not wish to do. So, while we are sorry that there are a large proportion of high school dropouts, we do not complain if they pick up our garbage. Who else would do such work?

Second, poverty functions to keep prices down because the low pay of the unskilled work force keeps the prices of consumer goods and services down. If you and I had to pay what it really should cost to dispose of garbage, there would be a lot more mulching of vegetable matter in our personal gardens.

Third, poverty provides jobs for the nonpoor who work with or against the poor. This includes social workers, police, lawyers, and administrators of public programs, to say nothing of pawn shop operators, grocery store personnel, and others who are dependent, directly or indirectly, on being paid by the poor. Almost all noncash transfers go to these others, not to the poor themselves.

Fourth, the poor are the scavengers of society. They are obliged by social circumstances to buy the cheap, shoddy products that the nonpoor—or any rational person—would prefer not to own. They are often exploited by sales techniques and devices like the extension of credit that raise the overall price of a good and may require payment after usefulness of the product has been outlived. Because the poor have few spokespersons and little political clout, they are often the ones to absorb the political and economic costs of change. For example, when budget cuts were enacted regarding the AFDC recipients in 1981, more than a half million persons were pushed below the poverty level, 325,000 of whom were children (Physician Task Force on Hunger in America, 1985, p. 147). Moreover, as Danzinger and Weinberg (1986) note, "By 1983, a family of four at the poverty line was paying more than 16 percent of its income in direct taxes, almost double the percentage paid in 1965 (p. 10)."

The Changing Face of Poverty: Challenges for Helping Professionals

As people age, one can see changes in their faces, from the smooth bright complexions of infancy and youth, to the weathered skin of the mature. So too with the face of poverty. There are changes according to how poverty is itself perceived over time. As the 1960s began poverty was invisible insofar as the federal government was concerned (Danzinger and Weinberg, 1986; Beeghley, 1983; Harrington, 1984). There were relatively few programs beyond what had been generated out of the New Deal legislative initiatives such as the limited Social Security law. In the presidential campaign of 1960, however, John F. Kennedy made poverty an issue. Born to wealthy parents, he was nevertheless stimulated by his own campaign experiences among the poor of West Virginia and by the powerful exposition about the poor in Harrington's *Other America*. Kennedy began the process by which Americans began to face up to poverty in their midst. Although he was cut down by an assassin's bullet, Kennedy's work was extended by President Lyndon Johnson.

In his first State of the Union address, Johnson proclaimed his mission to be the creation of a Great Society: "We cannot and need not wait for the gradual growth of the economy to lift this forgotten fifth of our Nation above the poverty line. . . . We know what must be done, this Nation of abundance can surely afford to do it" (Johnson, 1972, p. 15). The initial federal policy in the war on poverty involved a broad range of interventions: job training, education, health care, legal services, and community development with citizen participation. These initiatives were aimed at the structural deficiencies in society that kept the poor from working or from getting the skills needed for better jobs (Danziger, Haveman, and Plotnick, 1986). Income transfers such as direct public assistance were not initially viewed as a major aspect of the war on poverty. As pressure grew from the rising expectations of the poor and their increasingly assertive leaders, many additional programs emerged as part of the Great Society.

Heclo (1986) points out that public opinion polls in the first half of the 1960s indicated that Americans were about evenly divided about whether welfare spending should be increased or decreased. Most attributed poverty to lack of individual effort rather than to circumstances beyond the individual's control.

Several factors converged to bring about the powerful social reform: First, there was a clearer definition of the problem, ranging from Harrington's exposé to popular dramatizations, such as *West Side Story*. A second factor was political, an activist president and his liberal supporters pressing for a domestic initiative to end poverty and injustice at home, just as they took a Cold War stance abroad. The third factor involved contributions of social science and policy experts whose proposals came at an opportune moment. But, as Heclo points out, there were also some important weaknesses that soon emerged—an economic slowdown, the costly and demoralizing Vietnam War, president-centered reform, and the vulnerability of a black-dominated coalition; conservative and southern opposition to aspects of the antipoverty program and personnel also emerged. It is said that America lost only two wars, one in Vietnam, the other against poverty.

Burtless (1986) distinguishes three kinds of programs that were intended to equalize incomes and reduce poverty: (1) means-tested income transfers; (2) social insurance, and (3) human capital programs involving education and training. See Table 11.2. Let us examine each in turn from its inception to the present day.

TABLE 11.2   Selected actions in public and private sectors that contribute to social well-being*

| Actions aimed at the poor/nonpoor to obtain/maintain equality/inequality | PUBLIC SECTOR FEDERAL GOVERNMENT WELFARE PROGRAMS | Means-tested Income Transfers | |
	Social Insurance	Cash grants	In-kind benefits
EQUALITY a) actions affecting the poor on a temporary/ emergency basis		1. Aid to families with dependent children (AFDC) (p. 69) 2. Supplemental Securities Income (SSI) (p. 70)	1. Food stamps (p. 73) 2. Nutrition programs (school meals, etc.) 3. Housing assistance a) public housing (p. 79) b) rent supplements (p. 79) 4. Energy assistance (p. 80) 5. Social services as adjunct to AFDC, etc. (p. 80)
b) actions effecting a permanent structural change	1. Social Security benefits (OASDHI) 2. Medicare 3. Railroad retirement pension (p. 65)		1. Medicaid (p. 76) 2. Legal assistance (p. 81)
STATUS QUO actions serving poor and nonpoor alike, more or less			
INEQUALITY actions affecting the nonpoor proportionately to their contributions, or their prior status	1. Unemployment insurance (p. 68) 2. Veterans' medical benefits (p. 77) 3. Workmen's compensation	Veterans' income supports/ pensions	Housing assistance (e.g. Federal Housing Administration—aid for home mortgages)

*B. I. Page, 1983. (Numbers in parentheses refer to the Page book.)

PUBLIC SECTOR *(continued)*

FEDERAL GOVERNMENT *(continued)*

WELFARE PROGRAMS *(continued)*

Human Capital Programs		TAXES and other fiscal policies	PROTECTION	RECREATION and ENVIRONMENT
Education	Manpower training			
Head Start and similar programs (p. 86)	1. Job-training programs (e.g. Job Corp) (p. 82) 2. Job-creating programs (e.g. CCC; CETA—both discontinued) (p. 83)	Unemployment as affected by govt. policies has structural effects on long-term unemployment, esp. among minority youth (pp. 183–5)		
		1. Federal taxes (in combination with state and local taxes) (p. 35) 2. Inflationary policy (p. 183) 3. Economic growth	1. The military and defense establishment expenditures. 2. FBI and other law enforcement agencies	1. Museums, art galleries, etc. 2. Environmental protection (p. 127)
1. Federal scholarships (e.g. NSF, etc.) 2. Student loans		1. Excise taxes on consumable goods (regressive tax) (p. 34) 2. Tax deductions for home mortgages; charitable contributions (p. 80) 3. Tax shelters (p. 27) 4. Capital gains (p. 188) 5. Child care (dependent care) tax credit	Justice system (benefits tend to accrue in proportion to property ownership) (p. 124)	1. National Parks, etc. (use is roughly proportional to income) (p. 128) 2. Agricultural subsidies (tend to favor large farm holders) (p. 132)

TABLE 11.2   (continued)

Actions aimed at the poor/nonpoor to obtain/maintain equality/inequality	PUBLIC SECTOR (continued)		
	FEDERAL GOVERNMENT (continued)		
	COMMUNICATION and TRANSPORTATION	SCIENCE and TECHNOLOGY	OTHER
EQUALITY a) actions affecting the poor on a temporary/ emergency basis			
b) actions effecting a permanent structur- al change			1. Anti-discriminatory laws and court deci- sions in general 2. Some federal regu- latory agencies (like National Labor Re- lations Board) had income equalizing effect (p. 164)
STATUS QUO actions serving poor and nonpoor alike, more or less	1. Power (e.g. TVA and similar programs) 2. Communications (equal access)	Effects of inventions/ discoveries probably affect poor and nonpoor about equally	1. Public health (p. 125) 2. Overall net effect of regulatory agencies not clear (p. 173) 3. Postal Service (though regressive costs favor nonpoor)
INEQUALITY actions affecting the nonpoor proportion- ately to their contribu- tions, or their prior status	1. Transportation (air, rail, highway) prob- ably proportional to income for con- sumption (p. 130) 2. Energy subsidies (in proportion of in- come to use of en- ergy) (p. 126)		Some federal regulato- ry agencies (like Inter- state Commerce Com- mission, EPA) lead to outcomes that cost the poor proportionately more than nonpoor (p. 167)

PUBLIC SECTOR *(continued)*			PRIVATE SECTOR	
STATE GOVERNMENT		LOCAL GOVT		
Cash grants	In-kind benefits	In-kind benefits	Not-for-profit	For profit
General assistance (state and local payments, usually for disabled) (p. 84)	Housing subsidies (federal and state payments)		Private charities	
		Community action programs (federally sponsored) help the poor to gain access to jobs and services	Some self-help groups produce structural changes for the poor (e.g. food cooperatives)	
	1. Education (p. 83) 2. Police and justice system (tends to favor nonpoor) 3. Highways/ roads 4. Institutions to care for mentally ill or retarded (tends to favor poor) 5. Parks, museums 6. Social services	1. Education (tends to favor nonpoor) (p. 84) 2. Police/fire/ justice 3. Roads 4. Local public institutions 5. Local recreations 6. Social services 7. Housing 8. Public transportation (tends to favor poor)	1. Emergency relief (e.g. Red Cross) 2. Religion 3. Unions 4. Medical clinics 5. Schools 6. Most self-help groups 7. Ombudsmen	1. Medical services on fee basis 2. Private schools 3. Private child care 4. Some employee assistance programs (costs shared by employer and workers) 5. Private therapy
1. Non-federal workmen's compensation (tax paid by employers) 2. State taxes tend to be regressive (p. 35)		Local taxes tend to be regressive (p. 35)	Tenure/seniority	1. Wages and fringe benefits 2. Private insurance (home, car, person) 3. Quality medical/ nursing care institutions

Means-tested income transfers include programs that distribute money and other resources directly to the poor or near-poor families. The two major forms of income transfers are cash grants and in-kind transfers. Cash grants constituted the large bulk of means-tested transfers until the mid-1960s. These cash income transfers included AFDC, General Assistance, some veterans' benefits, and the Supplemental Security Income, which, in 1974, combined the separate programs for aid to the blind, the disabled, and certain elderly. All of these involved people who could prove that they were destitute; this is what the means test involves.

The in-kind transfers include food (such as food commodity distributions, subsidized school meals, and especially food stamps); housing (through public housing projects and housing subsidy programs); and medical care (primarily through the Medicaid program). Burtless notes that these in-kind transfers have continued to rise in cost from their inception, while the cash income transfers have leveled off and are decreasing slightly. About three dollars out of ten are transferred in the form of food, housing, and energy; four dollars are transferred as free medical care; and the remaining three dollars are distributed as cash (Burtless, 1986, p. 23). He suggests that this new proportion in income transfers favoring in-kind transfers reflects the voters preferences for reduction of specific deprivations—food, decent housing, and essential medical care—while being less concerned with general income poverty.

The second general type of program to address poverty issues is *social insurance* (Burtless, 1986). It includes Social Security, Medicare, and unemployment insurance, all of which expanded dramatically during the middle 1960s, although none of these programs was directed toward eliminating poverty as such. Indeed, most middle-class workers can expect to receive some social insurance benefits at some point in their lives. (The amount received by Social Security and Medicare beneficiaries far exceeds what they contributed to those programs, but eventually the differences will even out. Minority people, who have shorter average life expectancies, may literally not live long enough to receive their own contributions to Social Security. Many married women who work will not receive Social Security based on their own labors, but rather as a spouse—another inequitable feature of the system.)

Nonetheless, Burtless notes that these social insurance programs have been far more important than means-tested transfers in raising families out of poverty, especially for the elderly and the disabled. (For example, the 1959 income poverty rate of the elderly was 35 percent, compared with 22 percent for the rest of the population. By 1983 the figures were 14 percent for the elderly and 15 percent for the others. If one figures in the monetary value of the in-kind transfers such as Medicare, the poverty rate of the elderly was less than 10 percent in 1983.) However, the costs involved in social programs are very high and rose rapidly until 1983, when they leveled off. In spite of the successes of social insurance programs and the contributions of the means-tested income transfers, other groups still experience poverty. Burtless cites a Bureau of Census report (1984) indicating that one-fifth of all children under 18 and one-quarter of children under 6 live in families with money incomes below the poverty line.

The third general program to affect poverty is termed investment in education and training or, more broadly, *human capital programs* (Burtless, 1986). This reflected the optimism of the times in the efficacy of education: " . . . if children of poor families can be given skills and motivation, they will not become poor adults" (U.S. Council of Economic Advisors, 1964, p. 75). Two major categories of human capital programs can be distinguished: The educational emphasis on disadvantaged students from nursery school through college and the manpower training programs.

The human capital programs were meant to be the major emphasis of the antipoverty agenda, but in fact were the smallest of the three approaches. Burtless provides a comparison among these approaches as a percentage of the Gross National Product (GNP), the total market value of all goods and services produced by the nation for a given fiscal period (p. 40):

TYPE OF SPENDING	1960	1965	1970	1975	1980	1984
Means-tested transfers	1.1	1.2	1.9	2.9	3.0	2.8
Social insurance	2.9	3.1	4.2	6.3	6.6	7.1
Targeted educ & training	—	0.1	0.4	0.5	0.8	0.4

Burtless raises the critical question: How much poverty reduction—as distinct from the temporary amelioration of poverty—did these various expenditures buy and for whom? It is clear from the nature of the programs that means-tested income transfers were not intended to reduce poverty but merely to ameliorate it temporarily. (This might be enough for some people to "get a second wind" and pursue successfully the American Dream of achievement, but it does not work this way for most people on assistance by cash income.) Social insurance programs were not intended specifically to reduce poverty, but in fact had that effect for the elderly and the disabled, as described above. These insurance programs, though very expensive, have the support of the middle classes who are major beneficiaries.

The third type of program, targeted education and training, was supposed to change fundamental social structures and thereby permit the poor to escape their poverty. Did it work? With regard to educational programs targeted to various age groups, the evidence is mixed. Mullin and Summers (1983, p. 339) summarize their review of 42 evaluation projects and reviews, and offer the following observations: The programs have a positive, though small, effect on the achievement of disadvantaged students, but the results tend to be overstated because of upward biases in several statistical procedures commonly used. Gains appear to be greater in earlier years, but such early gains are not sustained. No given approach or program characteristic was consistently found to be effective, and there was no association between dollars spent and achievement gained.

Glazer (1986) believes Mullin and Summers understate the actual achievement. He cites some research (by Darlington, et al, 1980; Lazar, 1981) that indicates lasting effectiveness of preschool education when variables such as not being held back in grade, or not being assigned to remedial education classes, are considered outcome measures. Glazer also summarizes the impact of the Head Start program, as much on middle class parents (who more than doubled their use of preschools for their children between 1968 and 1980) as for the poor.

Head Start is the most popular of any antipoverty program. Even in the retrenchment years of the 1980s, Head Start continued to win support. Some 450,000 children were involved in 1985 at a cost of about $1 billion (Kahn and Kamerman, 1987, p. 132).

Head Start began in 1965, amid great enthusiasm and perhaps insufficient pilot testing, and grew rapidly. Richmond, Zigler, and Stipek (1975/1980) note that Head Start is actually a flexible, evolving set of programs that includes some experimental projects like Follow Through (providing nutritional and health care, social and psychological services, and special teaching assistance to children during their early years of elementary school); Parent and Child Centers (helping parents learn about the needs of their children and about supportive services available in their community); and Home Start (providing Head Start health, social, and educational services to children and parents at home, rather than at a center).

Each program, tailored to meet the needs of an individual community, had to contain six major components representing the broad goals of Head Start. They are: (1) health (each child gets a complete medical examination with follow-up treatment); (2) nutrition (Head Start centers provide at least one hot meal and one snack every day; some programs train parents how to prepare well-balanced meals at home); (3) education (including planned learning experiences and the development of self-confidence, with special reference to the needs of the ethnic groups in the community); (4) parental involvement (opportunities are created for involvement in all phases of the program); (5) social services (coordinating the needs of individual families with services provided in the community); and (6) mental health services (helping both parents and staff become aware of ways to foster the emotional and social development of the children) (Richmond, Zigler, and Stipek, 1980).

Because of the large numbers of persons involved, evaluation of the total Head Start program is difficult to obtain. The largest study, conducted in 1975, tested over 300 schools (out of more than 5,000) and involved 120,000 students. Significant gains in mathematics and reading were noted, especially in the early grades, and while these gains held over the summers, they were not sustained by the time students reached junior high (Carter, 1984; Glazer, 1986). In other research, investigators tried to tease out what the relative influences of a student's background and school learning experiences were on final achievement. At the beginning, the school learning experiences were almost as important as background. When the same students were studied three years later, the influence of the school learning experiences decreased and by the sixth grade, they exerted little influence on final achievement (Carter, 1984, p. 11).

Reports of a longitudinal study, the Perry Preschool Program in Michigan, are promising. The Perry Preschool Project is richer and more costly than the typical Head Start program, but its graduates in general show better school achievements in reading, language, and arithmetic. They show less need for special education classes; less unemployment after school; fewer arrests by age 19; and fewer births by age 19 (Kahn and Kamerman, 1987; Schweinhart and Weikart, 1986). As Kahn and Kamerman point out, not all of the gradu-

TABLE 11.3   Percentage of female-headed families, no husband present, by race and Spanish origin, 1975–1983

Year	White	Black	Spanish origin	Percentage of all families
1975	10.5	35.3	18.8	13.0
1980	11.6	40.2	19.2	14.6
1983	12.2	41.9	22.8	15.4

Source: U.S. Bureau of the Census

ates of the Perry Preschool Project turned out this well, but the outcomes are provocative for what is possible in early compensatory education.

Dropouts are another aspect of the problem. The National Center for Education Statistics (1984, Table 5.1) reports dropout rates in 1982 for high school students: The white non-Hispanic rate was 12.2 percent; the black non-Hispanic rate was 17.0; the Hispanic rate was 18.0; and the Asian American rate was 3.0. The dropout rate for the low-income group as a whole—as distinct from minority group rates—is 17.4. Glazer notes that low-income whites are not demanding educational improvements. In the main, minority groups, and particularly blacks, are seeking redress.

Burtless notes that there is consensus among manpower training experts that the main training programs have been beneficial to some people, at least in the short run. For example, the Comprehensive Employment and Training Act (CETA) programs have helped adult women, but have been less helpful or not helpful at all for adult men and teenagers. The Job Corps, dealing primarily with hard-core unemployed youth, was beneficial in various ways: First, it provided comprehensive health, basic education, and vocational services to young people; second, it raised their postprogram earnings; and third, a major social benefit has come from reductions in criminal activities during and after a person's participation in this program (Burtless, 1986, p. 38; Taggart, 1981).

Overall, Burtless points out that the census figures show some reductions in poverty. The percentage of persons below the poverty level in 1959 was 22.4 percent, as compared with 11.1 percent in 1973, and about 14.4 percent in 1984. But he notes that most of the reduction was concentrated on the elderly and the disabled, while single women with children and some other groups continued to show very high rates of poverty.

These facts have given rise to a phenomenon termed the feminization of poverty, the disproportionate representation of women living alone or with their children in the ranks of the poor. In 1982, 46 percent of all poor families—and 71 percent of all poor black families—had female heads (Wilson and Neckerman, 1986). (See Table 11.3.)

These figures on families headed by women disguise some important changes, such as the rise in the breakup of marriages; but it was the growth of out-of-wedlock births, especially in young women, that contributed to the rise of female-headed families, especially in black families. In 1980, Wilson and Neckerman note, 68 percent of births to black women aged 15–24 were outside marriage, compared with 41 percent in 1955.

WEALTH

Another Challenge for Helping Professionals

In a sense, it is difficult to put oneself into the position of a person with great wealth—what if you had $10,000 or more a month to spend on food, clothing, shelter, and other items? (Think about it—after the initial pleasure at the idea, it would require some effort to sustain a hedonic life at such a level.) It may be useful to study the wealthy in order to gain some perspective, not only about affluent people but also about the poor.

There are about 200,000 millionaires in the United States. The richest 20 percent of Americans own more than 75 percent of the wealth of the nation (Zastrow, 1990). Of the 400 richest people in America in 1985, the average net worth was $335 million. The combined net worth was $134 billion. Of these 400, 15 had assets of $1 billion or more (Rosen, Fanshel, and Lutz, 1987, p., 12). The families in the top one percent held about 19 percent of all assets and 34 percent of financial assets (Rosen, Fanshel, and Lutz, 1987, p. 13). However, Bell (1987) notes that families reporting incomes of one million dollars or more in 1981 paid taxes, on the average, at an effective rate of 17.7 percent— all this was legal because they were able to take advantage of certain tax provisions that favor the affluent. For example, home mortgage interest deductions saved the richest two percent of Americans about $7 billion in tax breaks, 25 percent of the total home mortgage interest deductions. Changes in the tax laws presumably have been aimed at closing certain loopholes, but time will tell.

As interesting as these facts and figures may be, they have little to do directly with social services. Very wealthy people will, by and large, take care of their own well-being—or pay fancy prices to have someone else try to help them do it. It does not seem likely that they will voluntarily share their $134 billion with the rest of us as a way of approaching fiscal equality. Nor is the nation likely to vote such a redistribution of wealth—since those with wealth are a close part of the ruling structures of the country. So we must figure out ways to provide social services in a society with gross inequalities of the distribution of wealth, while at the same time raising the levels of freedom and opportunity that are theoretically available to everyone in the society.

Switch our focus to another affluent group, the enormous numbers of Americans who are in the broad spectrum between the very rich and the very poor. Social work, with its historic commitment to the poor and the oppressed, has not identified its appropriate relationship with the middle-class groups, even though increasing numbers of social workers are going into private practice with middle- and upper-middle-class clients. (This shift toward private practice has produced unsettling ideological divisions in the profession, as those oriented toward the traditional poor and oppressed clientele lock horns with those oriented to new, more affluent ones.) It is obvious that even the relatively affluent middle classes have serious problems for which social services would be most appropriate—matters to do with mental health, social functioning, substance abuse, occupational concerns, social status issues, and the like. The question is: Are social workers the appropriate profession to provide these social services?

One answer is provided by the work of Kahn and Kamerman (1977; 1982; 1987), in whose many writings one major theme emerges. All persons, the poor, the middle class, yes, and even the rich, face similar challenges over the life span: Bearing children requires adequate nutrition, facilities, and services. Educating and stimulating children requires day care (especially when both parents work), public education, and extra services for the exceptional (the gifted and talented as well as the mentally and physically handicapped). Employment situations are required that provide adequate pay for workers to survive and also provide human companionship and stimulation in their lives. All persons require adequate medical and health care, as needed. Older retired persons may require services and facilities to supplement their needs at certain stages in life. All of these are ordinary and expectable challenges that every person faces. For some, like public education, American society has seen fit to provide a universal service, although it is unevenly delivered. For many others, from day care to elder care, American society has reacted with suspicion, fearing that providing such services universally to all—simply because they are inevitable challenges of human life and deserve the humanity of adequate provisions—will somehow corrupt people, make them less autonomous, less independent. One must wonder what freedom and independence there is in poverty caused by conditions beyond one's control. One must also wonder why the lessons of public education do not get applied to other social utilities, that all benefit when everyone is provided with basic human services related to ordinary developmental challenges.

Thus there is a role for social services to other than the poor and the near poor. It cannot simply be private practice with the affluent; it must also seek to offer fundamental provisions to assist everyone through the basic life challenges so that everyone can contribute to society to the fullest extent possible. What great talent and resources are lost to the nation when minority children receive inferior educations, when women are put down and kept down in inferior work positions, when discrimination prevents anyone from being free to participate in a democratic society that benefits in proportion to the fullness of participation.

SUMMARY

Being poor does not necessarily mean being unhappy; being rich does not invariably produce contentment. What income and wealth offer are the opportunities to choose among options; the more resources one has, the more options are open to one. We find incidents of child and spousal abuse among the rich as well as the poor. We encounter mental illness and substance abuse across the socio-economic continuum. We recognize universal developmental needs among all people, regardless of how much money they possess. While the traditional focus of social work is with the poor and the oppressed, we also recognize the need for preventing predictable problems and promoting desired life objectives for all people. Public social utilities that "support, strengthen, enhance the normal family" are appropriate goals for social policy and planning. In a word, social work is not for the poor alone (Kahn & Kamerman, 1977, p. 172).

OUTLINE

Health Quiz

Physical Health and Mental Health: Separate or Not?

Health and Illness: A Definition of Healthy and Nonhealthy Functioning

Physical Health and Illness
    History
    The Dimensions of the Problem
    Programs Related to Physical Health and Illness Costs
    Costs
    Social Work Functions in Physical Health Settings
    A Case Study: An Elderly Woman with a Hip Fracture

Mental Health and Illness
    The Nature and Dimensions of the Problem
    History
    Programs and Social Work Functions Related to Mental Health
      and Illness
      A Primary Prevention Program for Children of Divorce
      An Intervention Strategy for the Developmentally Disabled
        in Rural Areas
      Community Lodges as Rehabilitative Support Systems
        for Former Chronically Mentally Ill
    A Case Study: A Young Woman with Drug and Family Problems

Summary

CHAPTER TWELVE

Health and Illness—
Physical and Mental

Health is near the top of everyone's wish list. But attaining and maintaining health is not an easy business, for individuals or for the nation. This chapter examines physical health and illness separately from mental health and illness and the part social workers play in each. But from a configural perspective, we must view physical and mental health simultaneously within the larger contexts of society, culture, and the physical environment. Thus the chapter discusses the interrelatedness of physical and mental health within the configurations of human behavior.

HEALTH QUIZ

The purpose of the health quiz on the next page is to alert you about your own health status and the associated risks of various life-style practices. But it will also serve as an introduction to the collective issues of health and illness in our society, because the small actions we individually perform are cumulated into the millions by the similar actions of others.

It will be obvious that the higher the scores (ranging from 0 to 10), the more at risk one is for health or mental health problems. Research by Belloc and Breslow indicate that a person of 45 years of age who follows the first six (physical health) practices (seven if you count not eating between meals) has a life expectancy 11 years longer than a person who practices fewer than four of them. Likewise, a 70-year-old person who follows all seven of these health practices is likely to be as healthy as a 40-year-old who practices only one or two of them (Zastrow, 1986, quoting Ehrbar, 1977, p. 169; also see Heffernan, Shuttlesworth, and Ambrosino, 1988, p. 122; and *The Blue Cross and Blue Shield Guide to Staying Well*, 1982).

Thus what we do with our own lives, and what the social and physical environments contribute, for good or evil, are significant factors in physical and mental health and illness. Moreover, what we collectively do in these same matters adds up to a national bill of health—as we shall see.

1. **Do you smoke cigarettes? (Yes= 1 No=0)**
The illnesses associated with cigarette smoking include: Cancers (lung, oral cavity); cardiovascular diseases (health disease, stroke, hypertension); pregnancy and birth complications (prematurity and low birthweight, in turn related to mortality); respiratory diseases (chronic lung diseases, influenza and pneumonia). Smoking is probably the most preventable of all health risks. While fewer people are smoking today than a decade ago, the number of smokers runs into the tens of millions, and adolescent girls are increasing in number of smokers as every other age and gender category is decreasing.

2. **Do you drink to excess—to a point where alcohol interferes with your social or economic functioning? (Yes=1 No=0)**
There are a number of illness conditions associated with excessive drinking: Hypertension; chronic liver disease; diabetes; injuries from motor vehicle accidents, falls, violent injuries; mental health problems; pregnancy and birth complications such as congenital anomalies, low birth weight; and cancer of the oral cavity. In spite of this array of alcohol-related problems, about 10 percent of adults are alcohol abusers. A large number of children and youths are also alcohol abusers. In addition, family members of alcoholics are subject to mental health problems.

3. **Do you exercise regularly? (Yes=0 No=1)**
Inadequate exercise is associated with the following illness conditions: Cardiovascular diseases (heart disease, stroke, hypertension); osteoporosis; mental health problems (associated with one's body image compared with conventional or stereotypic norms); poor body tone that might result in accidental injuries. Regular exercise strengthens the heart, lowers high blood pressure, helps regulate high blood sugar, and reduces weight (body fat) as it tones the body.

4. **Do you eat properly? (Yes=0 No=1)**

5. **Do you stay within 10 percent of your proper weight? (Yes=0 No=1)**
Inadequate nutrition is associated with the following illness conditions: Cancer (breast, uterine, and colorectal); cardiovascular diseases (heart disease, stroke, and hypertension); dental and oral diseases (tooth decay and periodontal disease); mental health problems (probably associated with body image); osteoporosis; and low birthweight. Inadequate nutrition is sometimes produced by economic conditions, while at other times, it is the result of not knowing what foods to eat and not to eat—as well as knowing when not to eat (i.e., between meals). Eating too much, too little or inappropriately (as in bulimia) can be problems. Many of these reasons may act together in some persons.

6. **Do you sleep seven to eight hours a night? (Yes=0 No=1)**
Lack of sufficient sleep leads to problems in functioning mentally (such as attention level at school) and physically in the short run; cumulative lack of sleep offers potential harm to the entire physical system. Compounding sleep problems is the massive use of drugs to facilitate sleep, which are often ineffective while some are actually harmful.

7. **Are you able to manage the stresses in your life? (Yes=0 No=1)**
The mental health and health factors associated with inadequate management of stress include both mental and physical health problems, as well as interpersonal difficulties. Heart disease, attempted suicide; various forms of violence (child, spousal, and elder abuse); as well as the misuse of alcohol may be associated with inadequate control of stress. It is not the absence of stress that is sought, because its pressure may add motivation and zest to life; rather, stress is problematic when it overwhelms one's coping abilities and resources.

8. **Do you take appropriate precautions in relation to your sexual behavior? (Yes=0 No=1)**
Problems associated with inadequate precautions in this domain include unwanted pregnancies; sexually transmitted diseases, including AIDS; uterine cancer; and other problems. The sexual imperative is very powerful, but as one candid advertisement expresses it, love is grand but I'm not willing to die for it.

9. **Do you work in safe areas, using nonhazardous substances or machines? (Yes=0 No=1)**
Unsafe work conditions can give rise to major injuries and fatalities. Hazardous substances are associated with forms of cancer: lung, breast, skin; birth and pregnancy complications; respiratory diseases; and mental health problems. The scope of occupational illnesses and injuries is enormous. Deaths exceed 14,000 a year, and over two million workers are either permanently or temporarily disabled annually. Millions of other injuries go unreported (Stellman and Daum, 1973).

10. **Do you have a philosophy of life or a spiritual-social anchoring that provides direction and meaning to your life? (Yes=0 No=1)**
This is not a question of whether or not you belong to a church; it is rather the meaning you have constructed in giving direction to your life. Many use traditional religious or social groups to provide this meaning; others modify these traditions; still others strike out on their own. The hypothesis with regard to health and healthy functioning is that having such an integrated principle in one's life is itself life-promotive.

PHYSICAL HEALTH AND MENTAL HEALTH: SEPARATE OR NOT?

It is traditional in social work texts to distinguish physical health and illness from mental health and illness. This is done for the very good reason that agencies in the community are often likewise distinguished, with specialists working on problems of particular concern to them. A broken arm looks nothing like a broken heart; a strained ligament is very different from a strained relationship. The language is different. The historical background of physical and mental health are divergent. Some people assert that the philosophies or basic assumptions are also distinguishable.

The commitment of social work to a holistic or systemic perspective, such as the configural approach, means, however, that the physical and mental (and social and economic) are all components of one system and must, for maximum understanding, be viewed together as service plans are being made. This chapter, therefore, combines some considerations of health and illness for both physical and mental aspects of the person-in-society. But for other purposes, we will separate out these two ways of being healthy or ill. Two case illustrations are presented—one clearly dealing with a physical health issue (a hip fracture) and the other mental, emotional, and social dimensions (a daughter and mother conflict involving drug abuse and potentially AIDS). Please note, however: each case could have well been used to illustrate mental or physical health and illness. Indeed, the case involving a hip fracture hinges on the importance and lack of social relationships, while the daughter and mother conflict is set against a background of a fatal disease.

The question regarding the connections between the physical and the psychological has been the subject of an on-going debate for centuries. Recent versions have been couched in terms of psychosomatic illnesses, and in studies of the behavioral effects of psychological stress and disorders, as well as the psychological effects of physical illnesses. There are many health institutions, such as health maintenance organizations that provide a full continuum of services, both for physical and emotional needs. However, there are political and bureaucratic reasons for maintaining the separation between the physical and the emotional. Health care services in America in the future will have to provide the answer of whether these two major dimensions of human functioning are to be considered separate or systemic (see Pilisuk and Parks, 1986, Chapter 2; Moos and Insel, 1974).

HEALTH AND ILLNESS: A DEFINITION OF HEALTHY
AND NONHEALTHY FUNCTIONING

It is difficult to get a firm hold on the concept of health, or more broadly speaking, healthy functioning—that is, the way health is expressed in a person's life. We can more easily define illness because we can recognize physical pain or mental confusion as problems in functioning. But when it comes to health, we frequently fall back on negative definitions—the absence of illness—even though most people are healthy at least some of the time, and some experience high levels of wellness, when bodies, minds, and spirits are in fine tune and performing at near capacity levels of functioning.

In the late 1940s, the World Health Organization offered a broad definition of health as a state of complete physical, mental, and social well-being, and not merely the absence of disease or infirmity. Unfortunately, well-being was not defined so we have only a general clue as to what health means. A more recent ecological perspective on health (Germain, 1984) emphasizes the transactions regarding the well-being of the individual in question and the various psychosocial, cultural, and physical environments in which that person lives. This is a process-oriented interpretation, which makes it possible to recognize that a person may be relatively healthy on one dimension (say, the psychosocial) while not functioning fully on another (perhaps the physical dimension). Obviously, the interactions between these dimensions affect the single person of which they are conceptual pieces. Indeed, health-care professionals often use the strengths of one dimension to offset and influence problems in the other, as our case examples will illustrate. Specialists frequently work together, in part because of the complexity of the problems of human behavior, in part because each contributes something distinctive in comprehending and resolving the different dimensions of the problems facing that single individual in his or her social configuration.

Health and illness, therefore, are not the special prerogative of any one helping profession, although different specialists may take the lead in different health settings. It is interesting to note that when some "health or mental health professionals" talk about "health," they tend to spend most of their time discussing illness. This pathology orientation reflects the fact that these specialists tend to see sick people rather than healthy ones. Only recently systematic efforts have been made in trying to prevent problems before they occur and to promote the achievement of healthier states of existence. Folk wisdom has always recognized the value of prevention—"an ounce of prevention is worth a pound of cure." Now, modern health sciences, both in physical and mental health, are catching up with this enduring folk knowledge. Encouraging evidence supporting primary prevention has been forthcoming (Buckner, Trickett, and Corse, 1985; the Vermont Conferences on the Primary Prevention of Psychopathology and its resulting publications; Rosen, 1975).

Thus, in the working definition of functioning presented in Table 12.1, there will be components of both health and illness reflected in the three traditional modes of helping—prevention, treatment, and rehabilitation. This definition consists of a series of levels of functioning, together with the kinds of activities that either the persons involved or some helping professionals must engage in, so as to attain or maintain that level. This definition also suggests what classes of activities social workers might wish to perform for their clients.

This working definition is intended to begin discussions on meanings of health and illness, physical or mental. Prominent in this working definition is the idea of the continuum of functioning, with both an action component (the functional part) and a feeling or belief component. Although it is one person's health or illness, others are intrinsically involved. However, other aspects of the definition are relative to the given situation. What "capacity" means will vary by the particular organ system (such as the eye) or function (for example, mental capacity measured by an intelligence test). What is "high," "middle," or "low" for a person in question will vary individually, as when referring to a personal frame of reference ("not seeing as well as I used to"), but also

TABLE 12.1   A working definition of functioning regarding health and illness

LEVEL OF FUNCTIONING	HELPING ACTIVITIES
High level healthy functioning A person operating at or near physical and mental capacity, and feeling exhilarated with self, significant others, and one's major social roles.	*Promotive activities* Actions that motivate or support the person achieving high-level potentials, or making environmental changes for same ends.
Adequate healthy functioning A person operating in the middle of physical or mental capacity sufficient to deal with ordinary life demands, with attendant feelings of satisfaction with self, significant others, and one's major social roles.	*Protective activities* Actions that maintain or move a person into the zone of adequate functioning.
At-risk functioning A person engaging in behaviors, or living in an environment, thought to put that individual at risk for a predictable problem. (Note that the person is currently functioning adequately regarding the environment in question.) The feeling states are the same as in No. 2.	*Preventive activities* Actions that forestall predictable untoward events from occurring, either by eliminating the harmful environmental agents, or strengthening the person's resistance to the harmful agents, or both.
Unaware problematic functioning A person operating at or below adequate physical or mental ranges, but who is not aware of any felt difficulties. The same feelings as in No. 2 prevail.	*Advanced service activities* Actions that screen, detect, and treat subclinical problems through the use of technological devices.
Crisis and acute problems A person operating below adequate levels of physical and/or mental functioning who is aware of the difficulty. This awareness is expressed as unhappiness or negative feelings about self and the physical and social situation.	*Acute service activities* Actions that treat observable problems promptly (such as through standard medical practices, crisis intervention, etc.).
Chronic problem zone After the problem has been resolved as far as possible, the person is operating at or below ordinary levels of functioning. Feeling states depend on the level and degree of recovery.	*Rehabilitative services* Actions that assist the person to regain the highest levels of functioning possible, including personal or environmental protheses.
Terminal zone Eventually the person will exhaust all capacities for life functioning and the environment's ability to sustain life artificially will be exhausted; the period of time between these conditions is the terminal phase of life. Feeling states may vary from existential contentment and peacefulness to raging anger and depression.	*Palliative actions* Activities that recognize the terminal phase of a person's condition and seek to reduce pain and to promote personal contentment and fulfillment through communication with family and friends, so far as possible.

normatively, as compared to standards such as intelligence test quotients. The most important purpose for this working definition of healthy/nonhealthy functioning is to recognize that people can be on different levels for different functions. It is always possible to try to move the client to a higher level—even in terminal stages, where higher levels of mental or existential health may be attained, and actions may be taken to protect the health of the survivors.

PHYSICAL HEALTH AND ILLNESS

History

Every society throughout all of human history has needed some problem solver to address basic concerns like birth and death, illness and injury. During each era, the problem solvers practiced their craft within the ideology of their times. In ancient times, the problem solvers had to be part priest (because events were seen to be controlled by gods and spirits), part sorcerer (so as to be able to ward off the agents and objects of evil forces thought to inhabit the world), and part physician-psychologist (to help the afflicted person recover physically and psychologically).

Over time, these functions were separated out, each to go its distinctive way, although none has died out completely, particularly in the minds of the lay public. Hippocrates (?460–377 B.C.), said to be the foremost physician of antiquity, formulated important understandings about disease, as being caused by environmental influences—the airs, waters, and places in which people lived. These environmental factors could upset the basic elements of which all human beings were composed, and so proper medical guidance involved reestablishing these balances. When health problems emerged, the Hippocratic physician tried to see to it that Nature had its way again, with rest, good food, fresh air, and exercise, so that the body might heal itself. If that did not work, artificial devices might be applied to help Nature along— heat for a body that was chilled, cold for a feverish one, etc. (Sigerist, 1956).

Since the time of Hippocrates, we have obtained more facts about the workings of the body, but are no wiser about bedside manners, nor more professionally virtuous than when this master physician-teacher stated the ethical principles that still influence us today. The peoples of many countries contributed to our advances in health: Roman engineering triumphs, such as drainage sewers and aqueducts, gave these ancients better sanitation than London had up to the middle of the 19th century. Scientists from many nations discovered basic facts about human beings (Harvey, on the circulation of blood, for example) and the objects we share our world with (Pasteur, on bacteria that cause specific medical conditions, for instance). Others developed tools (van Leeuwenhoek and his microscope) and procedures (Halley and his contributions to epidemiology and life tables) that advanced the arts of medicine. We now know a considerable amount about what we ought to do so as to have a long and healthy life—recall the quiz at the beginning of this chapter—but we obviously know little about how to persuade people to perform these simple actions, given the high rates of problems they cause. Let us now turn to the contemporary scene.

The Dimensions of the Problem

Health care is enormously expensive. Who pays what? And what are we getting for the $400 billion spent on health care (1986)? Marcus (1987) summarizes the financial picture regarding health care. There are three major sources of health care funds:

1. The various levels of government, which provide 41 percent of the costs;
2. insurance companies (such as Blue Cross and Blue Shield), which pay 31 percent of the total costs; and
3. consumers, who pay 25 percent of the total amount spent on health.

The remaining three percent is derived from philanthropic organizations, industry, and private sources.

These funds are spent in different ways. Consumers pay 8 percent of the total hospital costs, but 28 percent of all physicians' fees. The government pays 53 percent of hospital costs, but only 28 percent of physicians' fees. It is important to note that most of the medical bills are not paid directly by the consumers of the services, so that financing of health care by third-party payments becomes a major public policy issue. We are all involved in the health of the nation as well as ourselves. These financial matters are very significant, constituting more than 10 percent of the Gross National Product (GNP).

Programs Related to Physical Health and Illness

The American approach to health care coverage is a piecemeal affair. The major components of health care funds are as follow:

Governmental Programs.   Medicare was started in 1966 as a federal insurance program aimed at covering hospital costs and physicians' services for the elderly (Marcus, 1987; Lum, 1987). The program was later extended to include some other categories of persons with serious illnesses (end-stage renal disease) and permanent disabilities; dependents of these people were also covered. There are two benefit programs, developed to accommodate the political philosophies extant at the time of the writing of the legislation: Part A is a hospital insurance program that pays for hospital, nursing home, and home health services. The funds for this part come from a payroll tax on employers and employees, with only a small percentage taken from general revenues. Part B is a voluntary supplemental medical insurance that covers physicians' services and other services. Most of the funding for Part B services comes from the general tax revenue, since the premiums from enrollees cover only about 22 percent of the total costs. Thus, in one program, we have a government funding of health care alongside a plan requiring individual initiative and payment. Medicare is an expensive program—costs were $58.8 billion in 1983—but a very popular one. Efforts regarding Medicare are aimed at cost containment rather than change of the total program.

Medicaid provides medical assistance to low-income people, including the aged, blind, disabled, and members of families with dependent children (Marcus, 1987; Lum, 1987). Rather than being a single national health care program like Medicare, Medicaid is administered and funded at the state level (46 percent), with matching grants from the federal government (54 percent). Thus there are 50 different programs depending on what choices states make in seeking matching funds beyond certain mandated services that all states have to provide—inpatient and outpatient hospital care; laboratory services; skilled nursing home care; and several others. The differences among states are extreme, even considering the cost of living in various parts of the country. Medicaid is the nation's financing mechanism for long-term care. It provides 45 percent of nursing home expenditures (as of 1979) (Mechanic, 1986, p. 19).

Medicaid is also expensive—$35.6 billion in 1983—but 21.5 million persons received benefits, including two-thirds who were members of families with dependent children. The aged and the disabled account for 70 percent of all Medicaid expenditures, even though they make up only 28 percent of recipients. This reflects the high cost of medical services. Other governmental programs, such as the Veterans Administration's health-care system, also serve many elderly veterans in the 172 medical centers across the nation; $7.7 billion was spent on these services in 1983. The federal government's Civilian Health and Medical Program of the Uniformed Services (CHAMPUS) also provides health-care services to active and retired military personnel and their dependents and survivors. The costs in 1983 amounted to $6.5 billion.

Private Health Programs.   Private health insurance paid $100 billion in medical benefits in 1983 (Marcus, 1987). Seventy-five percent of the civilian noninstitutional population had some form of private health insurance—as cushion against the extremely high costs of health care. Commercial insurance companies, such as Aetna and Metropolitan Life, financed $48 billion in health care benefits, while nonprofit programs, such as Blue Cross and Blue Shield, paid for $35.2 billion in health care benefits in 1983.

Direct Patient Payments.   The third major source of health care financing comes from direct patient payments, $85.2 billion in 1983 (Marcus, 1987). However, about 15 percent of the American people do not have any form of health insurance. Sixty-one percent have health insurance connected to the current employment of a family member, but that means that in times of unemployment large numbers of persons dependent on the workers are affected.

Costs

Unfortunately, costs for health services will continue to rise, especially as an increasing proportion of the population becomes elderly and in need of more extensive and expensive services. Yet, in a time of rising health care expectations, many people are demanding the "best available services," which inevitably drives costs even higher. Health providers are ordering more medical tests and procedures for patients as safeguards against being sued, another element in rising costs. The level of technological sophistication and the dazzling variety of new drugs also drives up the nation's expenditures for health care.

There are two general approaches to cost containment (Marcus, 1987). The first is a federal regulatory approach, such as the introduction of *diagnostic related groups* (DRGs), a method of reimbursing hospitals for acute-care services involving Medicare patients on a fixed-cost basis. This provides some incentive to provide the given medical service within the prescribed time period so as to avoid higher costs to the hospital if a patient is kept longer than the DRG allows, since the additional expenses are not reimbursed by the government. Critics say this method produces unwise pressures on hospital personnel to think first of saving money, second of caring for patients. Peer Review Organizations (PROs), established in 1982 under Medicare, also seek cost containment by avoiding unnecessary operations and other medical procedures.

The second approach to cost containment involves a competitive situation. For-profit health-care services are emerging that provide cheaper services than regular hospitals for selected illnesses on which a profit can be made. This leaves high-risk patients with nonprofitable conditions to public hospitals (Mechanic, 1986, p. 12). Hospitals are forced to make up the difference by being more efficient in their total operations, which critics observe may lead to a reduction in overall quality of service. For-profit corporations, like the Hospital Corporation of America, own or manage hundreds of hospitals across the country and are expanding to control medical supplies and other resources needed in health care. Corporate medicine has become big business, and complicates an already complex picture of forces increasing and decreasing the total costs of health care in America.

Social Work Functions in Physical Health Settings

There are a number of roles social workers might play in the many settings where health care is provided. First, social workers are part of the health care-team, not in providing the primary medical or nursing services, but in facilitating usable information and mediating conflicts among the clients, family, medical staff, and hospital support staff and administrators. An important part of this communication function is to clarify the several objectives that different parties to the situation may hold. Kleinman (1978) and Germain (1984) distinguish the ways in which the same medical problem may be viewed: (1) as a disease, a deviation from measurable biochemical states that requires a special technology for treatment; (2) as an illness, a feeling or experience of discomfort by the patient; and (3) as sickness, a label applied by others to a person's behavior or traits, and accepted by that person. Corresponding to these biological, psychological, and socio-cultural perspectives, respectively, are three views on helping: (1) cure of the physical disease and/or reduction of its negative effects (the physicians' perspective); (2) care for the personal discomfort of the patient and healing of the perceived illness (the patients' perspective); and (3) control of the manifestation of the client's discomfort, while also reducing the stresses on the others caused by the patient's sickness (the perspective of outsiders, friends, staff of the institution, and strangers) (cf. Goffman, 1961). Obviously, sometimes these definitions of the situation and the relevant method of helping will differ among the three perspectives. One social work function is to help resolve differences among them (see the Ogawa case in Chapter 16 as an example). The physician's scientific perspective does not always take precedence over the patient and family wishes. For example, in some ethnic minority contexts, physicians participate with native healers so as to increase patient motivation for cooperating with all the measures to regain health.

A second major function of social workers in medical settings is to provide generic social work. This may include counseling in regard to problems that may be interfering with the medical procedures. Obviously, such problems may involve the patient, but there also can be difficulties at home or at work that create stresses on top of the already stressful medical situation. In general, this person-in-environments approach is the distinctive contribution of social workers in host settings such as the hospital.

A third function of social workers in medical settings concerns the special needs of admission and discharge, including referral to other helping resources. Ordinarily, admission to a medical facility is handled in a routine administrative manner, with a physician calling in the admitting information, and the patient appearing at the correct time and supplying various kinds of financial information. But on occasion, the admission may be more complicated, either because of the special problems of the client (such as confusion or some involuntary arrangement) or of the context (such as an acting-out mental patient needing physical medicine at a hospital that is not set up to deal with psychological problems).

Discharge planning is an important part of the social workers' role at many hospitals, when the patient is reconnected with his or her family and the existing supportive networks. New resources may also be needed, and so the social worker acts to enlarge the helping network.

A fourth function of the social worker in the medical setting involves evaluation and cost/effectiveness studies. Sometimes these efforts are formally entered, as when a social worker takes part in a research study, designing the project, collecting data, interpreting the information, or writing the report. At other times, evaluation is part of the routine processes of the hospital, and serves an administrative function. With the advent of the DRGs for payment of Medicare patients, it becomes necessary for each member of the health-care team to demonstrate his or her worth in hard dollar terms.Recent studies of social workers in doctors' offices support the value of their function in the overall health-care team.

A fifth general function of social workers in health-care settings involves their contributions to administration, policy, and other activities that connect the hospital with the larger community and with political-economic structures in the society at large. Hospitals are a very visible member of a community, and they must contribute to that community in ways that will enhance their good name, especially as competition for clients gets more heated. How the hospital balances fee-paying customers with those who cannot afford to pay affects the reputation of the hospital, as well as its fiscal health. Local efforts to hold health fairs, to encourage preventive health, and to reach out sensitively to accommodate community needs in all its cultural dimensions affects the position of the hospital within this larger environment.

The settings in which all of these service functions take place are also varied. Social workers in hospitals provide many traditional services such as collecting social histories; explaining services to clients and families while interpreting their concerns to the medical staff; assisting in the financial arrangements; and discharge planning—all of which are often set within the context of DRGs. Long-term care facilities dealing with persons with chronic illnesses (such as nursing homes, homes for the aged, and congregate living situations for some physically healthy persons who may be mentally unclear) obviously involve different levels of need. But in general, the physician is less prominent, since all the medical assistance that can be rendered has already been given. Now the focus is on either specialized rehabilitation services or

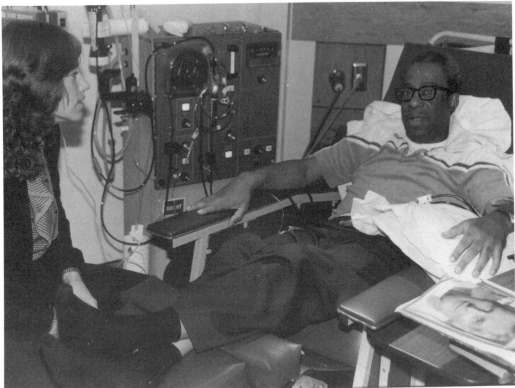

David Antebi

Health is more than medicine; it involves an entire life-style that may use, on occasion, recent powerful technologies such as the kidney dialysis machine seen in this photograph. But even when these complicated machines are used to treat the ill, it is still necessary to have social services to connect the individual to the complex health system in which we live and die.

long-term care for which the services of nurses of various degrees of training, social workers, nutritionists, occupational and physical therapists, and other allied health workers are more relevant.

There are also various community facilities organized on an outpatient basis. The health maintenance organization (HMO) is such a facility. This is a health agency offering comprehensive care to whole groups, like members of a union or a school system, on a prepaid basis; a permanent staff of salaried health-care providers is present in the facility so as to offer continuity of care, as well as preventive services, like physicals and screening exams. In this delicate balancing between medical services and health care (especially preventive care that reduces costs in the long run), the health-care team is more evenly balanced in status and power since much of the service involves education and transfer of health knowledge to the clients' home environments. Crisis centers, community mental health centers, and Mothers' and Children's Health Care Centers (like those from the old Sheppard-Towner Act of 1921) are also current examples of community facilities. Hospices for those terminally ill may also be served by social workers. The concern at the hospice is on easing the pain of dying and sustaining the person in his or her final hours so that death may come with dignity. This requires little technology but enormous compassion and understanding. Social workers may join religious counselors and lay volunteers in working at hospices (cf. Rusnack, et al, 1988).

Note in the discussion of the setting for medical care that we moved from a physical health orientation at a hospital to a mental health orientation in various community facilities, especially the hospice, another reflection of the connections between physical and mental illness and health.

A Case Study: An Elderly Woman with a Hip Fracture

One fine spring morning in a large city in Sweden, Mrs. Berg decided to look into some boxes she had stored on a high shelf in the closet. She fell and broke her hip bone, a serious matter for this 80-year-old widow who lived alone in her third-floor apartment. Although she was in pain and felt very fearful, she lay on the floor without moving because she knew her homemaker, Ola S, was due to arrive at any moment. The homemaker went to her home every day for three or four hours, not only to do light housework and to make meals, but also to take Mrs. Berg out for walks and to provide social stimulation.

Ola duly arrived and quickly arranged for the ambulance to take Mrs. Berg to the emergency department of the community hospital. Ola rode in the ambulance with Mrs. Berg, trying to keep her calm. She obviously had developed a close personal relationship with Mrs. Berg, in addition to her occupational role. At the emergency department, Mrs. Berg received attention from the attending doctor, nurse, and aides. As soon as she was made comfortable and the diagnosis was made, the staff social worker was informed of the situation. The goal was to begin coordinating services that were in place before the accident occurred with those that would be necessary during and after hospitalization. The social worker, Miss Magnusson, determined that Mrs. Berg was receiving regular home aide services from the government Home Services Department (for which she paid about $42 a month—a figure assigned on a sliding scale based on Mrs. Berg's income). She called Home Services and informed them of the situation so they could suspend services for the duration, although she requested that Ola visit Mrs. Berg several times after her hip operation, so as to have a familiar face among the hospital staff. Miss Magnusson would notify them about post-hospital plans as soon as discharge was clear.

In the days immediately following the operation, Miss Magnusson visited Mrs. Berg frequently for short intervals, trying to develop a sense of trust between them, as well as to learn more information about her wishes and resources for the post-hospital period. The social worker learned that Mrs. Berg was living on a limited pension fund from the government of about $500 a month, of which rent and utilities took more than half. She had moved to this small apartment in the same neighborhood where she had lived with her husband of 30 years, and wanted to remain in this upper-middle-class area. The cost of living was generally high, and Mrs. Berg had little money left for emergencies such as this hip fracture. Fortunately for her, the government's Insurance Office helps persons in such times of need with extra income. The social worker explained the program to Mrs. Berg, including the information that it would be necessary for her to apply for the extra aid in person. The bureaucracy in a modern welfare system is frequently very complex, and one function of the social worker is to help clients make their way through the maze of legitimate services more easily.

The nurses mentioned to the social worker that they had trouble understanding Mrs. Berg, and they wondered whether she was mentally clear. Miss Magnusson observed closely and discovered that Mrs. Berg was having troubles with her dentures. She had grown used to the discomfort and had not thought of getting them repaired, particularly since she did not have the money for the work. The social worker explained to her that another government office, the Social Office, would be able to help her out, but that she would have to apply and show financial need. This meant that she would have to assemble her financial records to show need. Mrs. Berg was worried that she would not be able to do that, but the social worker promised to work with her in filling the forms.

No one but Ola visited or called Mrs. Berg, and the social worker inquired about her family and friends. She had some distant relatives in another part of the country, but she was not particularly close to them. Nor did she have any special friends in her neighborhood. Most of her good friends had died or moved away, and as she retreated increasingly to her own apartment, she simply lost contact with people. The social worker providing this case observed that in Mrs. Berg's country old persons are not treated with much kindness except by family or close friends. And so Mrs. Berg was feeling very lonely and isolated, partly due to her infirmities and partly due to cultural conditions.

Mrs. Berg's operation went smoothly, and even though she would have to have a considerable period of time to recooperate, the medical staff knew that the longer she stayed in the hospital, the worse her mental clarity would become. So they requested discharge planning soon, to allow her return to her own apartment—along with the necessary medical and social supports. But Mrs. Berg was very fearful about returning home, and she requested the social worker to make arrangements for her to enter a Service House for the elderly, a government-sponsored high-rise living facility in which one owns his or her own apartment, but can get extra medical and social services as needed. Such accommodations are not usually sought by the elderly, who ordinarily favor homes that are usually in pleasant physical settings, even though one does not own one's own apartment.

As the social worker explored this request for supportive living arrangements, she learned that Mrs. Berg in fact has an estranged daughter living in the city, but she felt that there was no hope in getting any help from her, even in this twilight period of her life. Miss Magnusson asked whether she would like her to try to reestablish contact with her daughter. After a tearful few moments, Mrs. Berg nodded yes. And so, in the weeks that followed, Miss Magnusson located Mrs. Berg's daughter, and tried to reestablish family ties, but without much success. The daughter did visit her mother at the hospital and called occasionally after discharge, but no significant changes were made between mother and daughter.

Working in coordination with the medical staff, and the various social services agencies providing support and services for Mrs. Berg, the social worker renewed the secondary social network aiding her client, even though it proved impossible to reconstruct a primary network.

MENTAL HEALTH AND ILLNESS

The Nature and Dimensions of the Problem

Stress, which may be broadly defined as any force directed at some portion of the social system, is not bad in and of itself. It is only when people lack the personal and environmental resources to manage or control stress that a reaction occurs (Selye, 1956) and possible breakdown of the system results (Cox, 1978). It is important to recognize that when such pressures are controlled, they become part of the energy or motivation to accomplish some purpose, and thus serve a useful purpose.

Physical stress, such as that from a voluntarily endured weight-lifting machine, may contribute to the development of muscle tissue. Psychological stress, such as that from the pressure expressed in the injunction "publish or perish" may contribute to the development of scholarly activity. Pain may be involved in these gains—that is, people feel the effort going into weight lifting or writing, and these feelings may not be pleasant if they are excessive. But certain amounts of effort, relative to the history and capabilities of the person involved, may produce positive feelings, such as the pleasure of good muscle tone or the sense of accomplishment in writing a scholarly paper.

Some situations do not permit reasonable or achievable goals. The unloved child, although he or she may try very hard to be loved, may never receive that affection from a parent whose difficulties in expressing feeling may stem from other dynamics beyond the child's ability to change. The children of divorcing parents face multiple problems at home and at school, which may lead to a variety of emotional stresses—from feelings of self-blame to feelings of inadequacy to help reconcile the marriage.

Getting help in these and countless other examples of personal and interpersonal stress situations essentially involves working with someone who understands the sources of the stress and provides either help in developing individual skills or environmental supports to counterbalance those stresses, or help in adapting to the inevitable. The unloved child may be helped to find love from other suitable substitutes. The children of divorcing parents may be given the skills to accept the inevitable situation and adapt effectively to living with the consequences (Stolberg and Garrison, 1985; Stolberg, 1987).

Sometimes people in such circumstances can learn how to overcome personal and interpersonal stresses. The autobiographies of many great people are filled with such accounts of their surmounting social obstacles. But for many others, help may be needed in the form of "mental health therapy" of some type. Indeed, estimates from mental health surveys suggest that an incredible 15 to 25 percent of the American population have mental health needs that could benefit from professional services. But in fact only a small proportion of those in need have mental health services available to them or their families (cf. Albee, 1983). (By the way, this scarcity of helping professionals was one component of the pressure that legitimated BSWs as a bona fide level of service worker, rather than being minimized as a "pre-professional.") Therefore, we have to consider not only the nature, scope, and programs related to mental health treatment, but also the important new developments in primary prevention. It seeks to forestall such problems and in so doing gain benefits in economic considerations and in reduced human suffering.

History

Because mental illness, mental retardation, and other developmental disabilities are essentially invisible disorders, occurring within the genetic structure of the individual and in his or her learning experiences, there has always been much speculation about what lay behind these mental states. From the speculations of primitive peoples about evil forces or beings inhabiting the minds of the afflicted came few effective treatments and little in the way of preventive mental health. (Remember the Book of Job as an example of divine retribution, as well as the witches of Salem, described in Chapter 10.)

When the prevailing philosophy made demons the cause of mental illness, punitive methods frequently were used, literally, to beat the devil out of the afflicted, even though that person might die under such treatment. Less fatal but still punitive methods were used when the insane were put into prisons along with paupers and thieves, and were often chained as a way to obtain compliance. When a gentler common sense prevailed, more humane methods of treatment were used, as in the city of Gheel, Belgium, which has, for centuries, housed its mentally ill in the homes of the townspeople to be treated with kindness and firmness regarding responsible ways of behaving (Roosens, 1979). This is the core of what came to be called moral treatment. The success of this approach is legendary, but it has been largely ignored by the helping establishment.

The history of mental health practices are marked by several major revolutionary developments and many important landmarks. The first revolution in mental health occurred in the late 18th century in France. Philippe Pinel, the medical director of several insane asylums in Paris, took the chains off the inmates, signaling the change of a view of the insane as dangerous and untreatable to one offering the possibility of treatment—even though little was then known about personality and social dynamics that caused these disorders. At about this same time, a Quaker, William Tukes, established the York Retreat in England, using the principles of moral treatment as its basis.

Leaders in medicine in America, such as Dr. Benjamin Rush, picked up on this idea and developed moral treatment in the new nation (Armour, 1986). Contemporary evidence suggests that this system was much more successful than the punitive approach, but moral treatment broke down when the large numbers of mentally ill came out of the vast waves of immigrants in the middle to late 19th century. As McGovern (1985) notes: "Since moral treatment was essentially a system of management of the total life of the patient, it worked best with small patient populations. Its success, however, brought increasing numbers of patients, and the moral therapists continued to try to apply their principles . . . " (page 115) without adapting to the new realities.

The institutions housing the insane became increasingly ineffective, and custodial care turned to oppression. This is the situation that Dorothea Dix discovered by accident in 1840 when she volunteered to work at one such institution. Her campaigns to develop caring institutions for the mentally ill first met with enormous popular success, only to be thwarted by President

Franklin Pierce's veto of a bill that would have given federal support to assistance for the mentally ill by means of land grants. His reasoning was that the U.S. Constitution did not assign to the federal government a role in helping states set up social welfare programs, an opinion that continued to dominate thinking until the Great Depression of the 1930s. Dorothea Dix took her cause to many of the states, documenting the miserable conditions in local institutions. She received wide support, and must be credited with rousing the conscience of the nation to reduce the physical abuse directed at inmates.

The national conscience is more easily aroused than it is maintained in a state of vigilance, however. As hospital populations increased, expenditures did not keep pace, and once again these institutions became primarily storehouses of the deranged. Instead of serving their intended purpose as brief treatment sites, they held patients for long periods of time.

Another landmark event was the publication of an exposé by Clifford Beers, a Yale graduate who had been hospitalized several times for mental illness. His *A Mind that Found Itself* (1907; 1981), reported the maltreatment and the ineffectual care he received. It is still a highly readable book. Beers was suicidal, paranoid, and hyperactive, and thus was frequently physically restrained as part of his treatment. At one point, when he was in a public mental institution, he was assigned to the "Bull Pen" for his obstreperous behavior. It was a particularly miserable place—a small cell, no ventilation, no furniture, just the floor to sleep on, cold. In his view, the greatest indignity was that they stripped him of his clothes down to his underwear. It was in the Bull Pen that Beers quotes one new attendant, a young man studying to become a physician, who had treated Beers kindly at first: "When I got here," the attendant says, "if anyone had told me I would be guilty of striking patients, I would have called him crazy himself, but now I take delight in punching hell out of them" (p. 136). The institutions were not only brutal, they were also brutalizing. (Cf. Hanley, Banks, & Zimbardo, 1973.) After his release, Beers took his cause to the leading psychiatrists of the day and gained their support for his dream, a lobbying organization on behalf of the mentally ill. (That organization led to the National Committee for Mental Hygiene, which eventually became the National Association for Mental Health.)

The second of the mental health revolutions occurred in the work of Sigmund Freud. Freud provided a broad panoramic view of the territory of mental illness, along with several therapeutic methods directly linked with his theory. This systematic view of healthy and sick personalities was to sweep America in the 1920s, although Europeans took a more skeptical view. Psychiatric social workers adopted his theory because it provided a rationale for what was the cause of mental problems and what methods might be used to mitigate those causes. As difficulties with the model and especially its resistance to empirical testing became apparent, helping professionals turned to variations of the psychodynamic system or entirely new approaches that also began to provide systematic rationales concerning the dynamics of human behavior.

A less well noted event occurred about this same time in America. Behavioral theories and practices in therapy were introduced. Behavior clinics were begun in the mid-1920s to focus specifically on behavioral problems (Orme and Stuart, 1981). In the 1940s and 50s, powerful methods for dealing with anxiety-producing situations were derived from behavioral theories by Joseph Wolpe. Applications of operant models were developed in mental institutions as token economies—patients were rewarded for healthy behaviors. Non-healthy behaviors might result in the removal of tokens used for purchase of desired things or privileges (Ayllon and Azrin, 1968).

The third mental health revolution occurred in the 1960s after a major policy reconsideration took place on mental illness and health at the federal level. It was the birth of the concept of community mental health. Mental hospitals were often located in distant rural areas for cost considerations, but it was recognized that mental illness was caused in community settings, and the means for its treatment and social support should be found there as well. At the same time, landmark changes were occurring in the use of psychotropic drugs, which had the effect of reducing anxieties and depressions to manageable levels. (That they also had unpleasant side effects, especially when their dosage was not carefully balanced or when patients were irregular in taking their medicines, was not as well advertised as the immediate therapeutic effects.) Therefore, a new form of health institution, the community mental health center, would become the focus of attention. Patients at long-term hospitals could be discharged, assuming they had some support system in the community to help them adapt and to maintain their medical regimen. Large numbers of patients were discharged from mental hospitals back to their communities, but unfortunately there were not enough community mental health centers to accommodate their numbers, nor did all such centers fully adopt the spirit of the new policy. Lacking was continuity of full-spectrum service, both preventive and curative, for persons in the local catchment area. Ideals outran realities, and soon the deinstitutionalized populations were walking the streets, without any regular care or caring helpers. We are still in the age of the community mental health center; there is more to be done with this concept.

At the same time, another revolutionary development was taking place, the revolution in "societal efforts at preventing mental illness and emotional disturbance" (from the Preamble to the Task Panel on Primary Prevention, for the President's Commission on Mental Health, 1978). Primary prevention includes the prevention of predictable problems, the protection of existing states of health and healthy functioning, and the promotion of desired states of affairs. While individuals often make preventive/promotive plans for themselves or their family members, primary prevention is usually concerned with total populations, especially groups at high risk, like infants and the aged, minority peoples and those with different life-styles. Primary prevention seeks to engage and optimize the strengths of people, in contrast to preoccupation with their weaknesses or acceptance of "blame-the-victim" stereotypes.

Primary prevention takes a strong systems perspective in identifying the strengths and limitations of both involved persons and relevant social and physical environments. Its methods, therefore, involve provision of information, attitudes, or skills to persons at risk, or making modifications in environments that reduce risks to them. Primary prevention has accumulated a most encouraging track record of cost/effective successes in particular areas that have the potential of reducing the costs in money and human lives that otherwise would have been incurred (Albee, 1983). Keep your eye on this latest revolutionary development in the mental health field.

Programs and Social Work Functions Related to Mental Health and Illness

Many types of programs deal with mental health and illness, ranging from the formal mental hospitals to the sidewalk services of workers who walk along with homeless deinstitutionalized persons, talking about their concerns and needs. Note that social workers form the largest single group of mental health professionals, and frequently serve as directors of community mental health centers. Social workers may be found in traditional settings like family agencies, public social service settings, community mental health centers, or child treatment facilities, or they may provide social work services in schools, industry, the military, or prisons. They even serve in banks, on wilderness treks, at homes of the aged, or in crisis centers for persons who are victims of violence.

The types of services delivered also differ. They may range from intensive counseling to cooperation with teams of helping professionals, especially in the role of case managers, a relatively new concept that emerged with the professional legitimization of the BSW degree. A case manager coordinates the services of a variety of specialists as well as family members, making sure that the client does not "slip through the cracks" in our piecemeal welfare system. The case manager may provide some services directly, but often sees to it that the client is receiving all the needed services from different sources, and is taking whatever medications are needed on a regular basis. The point about medications is especially important for discharged mental hospital patients who need them for help in maintaining their equilibrium while living in the community.

At a macro level, social workers in the mental health area may serve as lobbyists on behalf of legislation or in support of administrative rulings that serve the interest of client groups or consumers in general. They may work with other interest groups in mass media campaigns to alert the citizenry on important issues of the day. They may serve as public consciences to businesses and unions, so as to mobilize these groups to support social change. Social workers may be active in supporting various types of civil rights actions, or work as advocates on behalf of oppressed peoples to gain their fair rights in society.

Social workers are also involved in research and evaluation projects, seeking to build knowledge or monitor practice effects, while documenting the social accountability of the profession. (In the chapters in which the history of social work and history of social welfare have been described, you will recall how important each macro-level activity has been—and continues to be.)

Social workers may be found in specific organizational settings, such as work with the developmentally disabled, work with veterans suffering from post-traumatic shock syndrome, or work, as resources, with self-help groups. They may work at college health centers, or handle hotlines (crisis centers that people-in-need may call for help at any time of the day or night, and receive on-the-spot advice and then referral for further information or assistance). In general, wherever and whenever people need assistance in personal functioning in an impersonal and sometimes oppressive world, social workers are likely to be there providing that assistance.

Many programs in mental health might be described. Here we illustrate three situations—preventive, interventive, and rehabilitative—that may give a flavor of the range of services.

A Primary Prevention Program for Children of Divorce.   The work of a psychologist and social worker team illustrate creative programming for an increasingly recognized problem, the untoward effects of divorce on children in the divided family (Stolberg and Garrison, 1985; Stolberg, 1987). Reports of cognitive, affective, behavioral, and psychophysiological problems in children of divorcing families have prompted various efforts at preventing such difficulties before they occur and leave their harmful and unhappy effects on their victims, either at home or at school. As Stolberg and Garrison (1985, p. 112) state: "Although chronic marital hostility that has already taken place cannot be undone, the child's understanding of such interactions can be modified. Similarly, environmental changes cannot be reversed. The child's perception of these events can, however, be modified and behavioral skills needed to meet the new circumstances can be provided." Their research project addressed children who were currently functioning at an adequate level (level 3 in Figure 12.1), and thus this study is a true primary prevention project. Their program was intended to enhance children's mastery of normal developmental tasks interrupted by the changes caused by the divorce. The project also sought to prevent acting-out problems, poor self-concept, and academic failure. They also tried to help the children indirectly by enhancing parents' adjustment to divorce and their parenting skills. Participants in this project were 82 mothers (mean age about 36) and their 7- to 13-year-old children; separation time ranged from 9 to 33 months. A number of instruments were used to measure changes in children and parents before and after the 12-session intervention. The sessions each dealt with specific topics ("who is at fault in this divorcing situation?") and with the modeling and rehearsal of specific cognitive-behavioral skills such as problem solving and anger control. A complex research design was used to test whether the children's support group alone or in combination with a parents' support group (or a parents' support group alone) would yield better results.

Results from the Stolberg and Garrison study, and some similar replicated results by Pedro-Carroll and Cowen (1984), show that the children's support group alone showed significant reductions in acting-out behaviors and increased competences at home and in school, as compared with the control group. When the children's support group was augmented with the parents' support group, it is interesting to note, the results were not as strong. The parents' adjustment was improved, but this did not appear to affect their children, possibly due to the characteristics of that group of participants (separated longer, holding poorer jobs, etc., than the other groups). In any case, the ultimate goal of the project was attained, to prevent untoward problems from occurring in children of divorcing parents.

An Intervention Strategy for the Developmentally Disabled in Rural Areas.   Rural social work has several distinctive features that must be understood to appreciate the issues involved in delivering services to a special type of population such as the developmentally disabled (DeWeaver and Johnson, 1983). Obviously, distances involved in large rural areas present challenges to the social worker, as do the relatively small number of persons in any one area. The life-style of rural people tends to be much more informal, more oriented to self-help groups within a tradition of rugged individualism and other traditional American values. Many minorities of different types live in rural America.

There are fewer services and a smaller tax base to support such services. And since the rural economy is often based on agriculture, forestry, or mining, there is a sense of closeness with nature that city-dwellers, locked into their overheated or over-air-conditioned environment, sometimes forget. As Johnson and Schwartz (1988) point out, the general system of social welfare that developed in the United States had largely ignored rural people; public welfare was never popular here, and the original Social Security Act excluded farmers and other self-employed persons. So doing rural social works often involves some creativity. The skills of the social work generalist are often very appropriate (Porter, et al, 1983). It should also be pointed out that rural life provides many strengths (Bachrach, 1983), such as family stability, good neighborly support systems, and tolerance for others' ways of adapting. These become points of departure in service programs.

DeWeaver and Johnson (1983) discuss the strategies of using the case manager concept for developmentally disabled persons in such rural environments. The developmentally disabled include persons who are mentally retarded (that is, whose intelligence levels permit limited degrees of adaptive behavior relative to societal demands). It also includes those who have such chronic conditions as cerebral palsy (a neurological-physical condition that prevents its victims from controlling the normal use of their limbs; there is no effect on the person's intellectual functioning) that develop before the age of 22 and that result in substantial limitations in how those afflicted are able to function in everyday life activities. It is important to note that three-quarters of the mentally retarded, who compose the lion's share of the developmentally disabled, are only mildly retarded. So they can be trained to function somewhat independently. Only about 5% are profoundly retarded, requiring constant supervision. When the mildly retarded are in school, they frequently are identified for educational reasons, which sometimes includes being put in special educational environments. However, when they leave school, they become "invisible," that is, they tend to go about their ordinary routines much like the rest of us, adapting as best we can to life's exigencies (Mercer, 1973). Recent legislation regarding the education of handicapped children requires public schools to offer instructional opportunities within the mainstream if possible, and in the least restrictive environment as possible. Moreover, social workers are involved in helping teachers and parents to develop and monitor a child's individual educational plan (IEP) to ensure that the intent of the law is carried out.

Service strategies are needed to provide social services to the developmentally disabled in rural areas. Case management, as defined in the Rehabilitation, Comprehensive Services, and Developmental Disabilities Amendment of 1978 (P.L. 95–602), consists of services to persons with developmental disabilities that will assist them to gain access to needed social, medical, educational and other services. Case managers follow along with clients and immediate relatives through continuing relationships to help them adapt to changing conditions; they also provide coordination and, often, mediation, among various service providers. The rural case manager, as described by DeWeaver and Johnson, is involved with diverse activities requiring flexibility, ingenuity, and energy. Traditional clinical social work training may not be as useful as generalist experience and training.

Among the programs required for the developmentally disabled are training centers, sheltered workshops, and activity centers. Training in skills required in rural settings may include structured farm work and chores in rural institutions (remember that many public institutions were established in rural areas). Sheltered workshops require transportation or living facilities, and are difficult for many rural areas. But activity centers can probably be connected with other rural settings, such as local Grange halls, 4-H clubs, and the like.

Community Lodges as Rehabilitative Support Systems for Former Chronically Mentally Ill.   The third illustration involves one of the most successful innovations in the mental health field, the self-governing community lodges for ex-mental patients who share living and working arrangements (Fairweather, 1980). The concept of a self-governing community of former backward patients grew out of a long series of painstaking studies by Fairweather and his colleagues, summarized in a 25-year retrospective publication (Fairweather, 1983). Recidivism for discharged mental patients has always been high, but Fairweather and his coworkers decided to figure out how to reduce it. By careful analysis of what skills discharged mental patients needed to make it in the outside world, the researchers realized that opportunities for learning many skills were not being provided to patients in institutions. They included problem-solving experiences and working and living within a supportive community.

Slowly and carefully, Fairweather and his colleagues developed a prototype community, first within and then outside the hospital grounds. They experimented with the group dynamics needed to sustain ex-mental patients in the normal world. It included finding employment for members so that some of them, at least, could do work outside that would sustain the community of fellow residents who helped out only within the lodge itself. When they were patients in chronic mental hospitals, the residents often exhibited bizarre behaviors (such as hallucinating), but they were tolerated within hospital walls. Outside, however, the lodge members had to learn when such behaviors were permissible (at the lodge) or not permissible (out on the job).

What was equally difficult was figuring out the new roles of the helping professionals who were used to guiding and directing most facets of such patients' lives. As the prototype lodge community was set up, the professionals gingerly gave many democratic rights to lodge residents, retaining the (therapeutic) veto, as needed. But with time and a growing confidence in lodge members to govern themselves as interdependent members living in the community, that veto power was rarely used and was eventually removed. The powerful motivation of being an autonomous adult, so common to us, was a precious force encouraging these lodge residents to make the best of their opportunity for freedom. Equally careful outcome studies supported

Fairweather and his colleagues' hypotheses: Measured by reduced recidivism, higher employment, and lower costs, the lodge proved its worth. Later, other lodges were set up, including many by different therapists in different parts of the country. Each reported similar results, and so was born a significant rehabilitation methodology for the long-term mentally ill. What few individual ex-patients could manage on their own, groups of patients in carefully developed living and working places could manage in everyday life.

A Case Study: A Young Woman with Drug and Family Problems

This case, which takes place in a large city in Great Britain, illustrates that mental health issues are frequently mixed together with physical health and social concerns. (The case has a superabundance of problems!) Although there are several significant problems, including the client's testing positive for AIDS, the social worker is focusing on her psychosocial development and the personal and interpersonal problems in living that result from various factors in her life. The social worker practices in the main office of a large public housing complex, one of the historical beginning points of social services in England.

Marianne looked much older than her 21 years. She nervously smoked a cigarette and fidgeted in her chair as she talked to the court-appointed social worker. Marianne had been convicted of theft—she had stolen money and property from her parents, who had reported her to the police, a very rare occurrence among the residents of the public housing project, who ordinarily put up a common front against the law. But Marianne's parents were solid middle-class people who lived in a pleasant area of town far from this vast public housing project with its sea of two- to four-story buildings with occasional high-rise buildings appearing as islands.

Marianne told her story quickly, without feeling. There was no history of multiple deprivations common among public housing residents, just self-perceived family pressures and feelings of isolation and low self-esteem. As Marianne talked, the social worker recognized that she was a bright and articulate young woman with many skills. She had been a good student and a compliant daughter until about age 15; then, suddenly, everything seemed to fall apart. She seemed to go wild. She practically dropped out of school, and took up with shady characters who were deeply involved with drugs and alcohol. Soon, she was too.

At first, her family was overwhelmed. They tried to help her, to be supportive, to find out what had gone wrong. But barriers between them and their daughter emerged—or perhaps they had always been there, but now became visible. The parents tried to encourage her with all kinds of promises to come back to their way of life, but at their wits' end, they alternated these solicitous offerings with throwing her out of the house. The family relationships quickly disintegrated. Her two younger brothers were put on tight leashes and were as hostile toward her because of these restrictions as she was toward her parents.

She left home for short periods of time, without telling her parents where she had gone. But she came back, sick and depressed. She never told her parents about her problems. There were blanks in her memory—she could not have told her parents where she had been even if she had wanted to. This frightened her into returning home, only to grow quickly argumentive and to leave again. In fact, she had moved to an apartment with some drug users and a series of boyfriends, all of whom became abusive to her. Her drug habit was becoming expensive, and she turned to prostitution to support her habit, as did others of her friends.

In the drug culture of which she was a member, there was a ritual sharing of needles for intravenous use. Unknown to her at the time—indeed, unknown to the medical community worldwide—she was exposed to the virus for AIDS. She eventually tested positive for the AIDS virus (something like 60 percent of intravenous drug users show HIV positive). She continued to be involved in the drug scene for about two years when the theft occurred that brought her to the attention of the police.

In Marianne's country, the legal procedure in drug cases is that a suspect is charged with a crime, asked how he or she pleads, and then, if convicted, is seen by a social worker appointed by the court prior to sentencing. Marianne pleaded guilty. Being obliged to see a social worker is not necessarily the royal road to successful treatment, however. After asking the court for a deferred sentence for one month while a report could be made, the social worker had to determine whether the client and her family thought there was a problem to be resolved. Being convicted of theft may not be viewed as a problem by some clients.

But Marianne was frightened. She was scared of being in custody during the several days before the trial and afterwards. She was concerned about the expense of her drug habit and her inability to support it; she had been paying as much as the equivalent of $200 a day for the drugs she required. But most significantly, her current boyfriend had written her a letter when she was in prison informing her that he had burned up all her clothes and was completely breaking off the relationship. She was alone and very fearful.

Even so, the social worker was leery of moving in too soon. She felt that the client had to have reached some level of recognition about drugs to be ready for engaging constructively in a rehabilitation program. Marianne had thought about getting off drugs before, but now the motivation was extraordinarily high. The social worker decided this was the time to act—immediately, while the motivation was at its highest, because a trough of depression might soon follow.

The court approved the month extension, and the social worker made plans with the client to enter a residential treatment program in another part of the country. She also dealt with practical matters like clothing, medication, and the like. She met with the family to assess their potential strengths for assisting their daughter's recovery. The worker discovered that Marianne's mother was a dominating woman who seemed to love her daughter genuinely, but aggressively. This gave an idea to the worker about how to proceed: taking a motherly role supporting but not dominating the daughter's growth toward maturity. The daughter was still engaged with the tasks of adolescence, even though she was 21, especially those dealing with emotional dependence. The drugs had been a crutch; Marianne seemed unable to give up her juvenile behaviors. She was uncertain of her self as a person, as a young adult.

The social worker presented Marianne with small concrete choices, as points of development toward the larger choices that would soon be forced on her. At home, her mother was trying to force Marianne to make these decisions, such as getting a job or going back to school, right away. So there was some tension between the mother and the worker. Marianne's father was very distant throughout this time period, and refused to have anything to do with the treatment. The younger brothers were, fortunately, involved with school activities and did not present any particular problems to Marianne at the time.

In addition, the social worker tried to get Marianne involved with others and in other organizations, as aids to building up her self-confidence. She would escort her to various activities and encourage her to make the many small choices that inevitably arise, such as whether to check the coats at the museum, or what to have for lunch at the café.

It is important to note that after she was picked up by the police, Marianne went off all drugs (except cigarettes) completely. Coming off drugs is not so much the problem for some addicts as is staying off. When an adolescent has no particular role in a drug-free society, when one's associates are still using drugs, when there is little in life to look forward to, it is hard to stay off the mind-dulling substances. The worker had numerous contacts with Marianne, and she tried to help Marianne emphasize her strengths while minimizing her limitations and involving her in growth-promoting activities suitable for her stage of emotional and social development.

The social worker encouraged Marianne to make healthy choices, and she found for her some supportive peer group associates that would also reinforce those healthy choices. For various reasons, the family does not yet appear to be able to provide constructive support for Marianne. (That will be a future objective for the social worker.) After all, Marianne has been a veritable outsider for several years and now appears to be moving in the right direction. But the parents (especially the mother) are impatient and want immediate conformity. Against that, the social worker has to protect the fragile development of this immature young woman. Given the complexities of this case, and the convoluted family relationships still to be untangled, the worker is cautiously optimistic at this stage of the case.

Marianne's situation reveals how complex and involved a life can become, with the mix of substance abuse and crime, family problems, and personal development crises, as well as health concerns. Almost every aspect of the configuration is implicated in this case—the person, several primary groups (family and peers), several secondary groups (the police and courts, medical facilities, welfare organizations), all set within the context of Great Britain's welfare state. The social worker deals with this complexity by addressing the presenting concerns as they emerge—first, the matter of criminal behavior; then the family problems; and finally, the several welfare and health resources that may provide a structured path to some semblance of a normal life. But with each focal concern, there is awareness of the other factors influencing matters. The manifest criminal behavior was the theft of the parents' money, even though Marianne's "social history" revealed other criminal behavior (prostitution; use of illegal drugs). The court permitted the social worker to propose a plan that would address the major causes of criminal behavior, and not simply impose some punishment in the absence of other considerations (see Chapter 12 on Justice).

The family problems concern both her relationship to her parents (and siblings), but also to her proto-families, the men she lived with—and was abused by. These matters of medical concern are related to her own immaturity and lack of skills in dealing with her friends or her own self. But in the same fashion, this immaturity is viewed by the worker as an unresolved problem between the 21 year old and her mother. Thus, to assist Marianne to begin to become a mature adult, the worker begins to present her with the types of ordinary challenges that a 12 year old might face, and thereby slowly move through the developments of the adolescent years that somehow Marianne missed.

SUMMARY

Where we as individuals fall on the continuum of healthy functioning depends on a combination of our own efforts and the influences of our social and physical environments. The configural approach helps to identify these interlocking systems of events and forces that affect us so powerfully. Helping interventions involve working with the clients' strengths and those of the environments' resources, so as to minimize or turn around individual weaknesses and social stresses.

These same principles apply to both physical and mental health and illness, but because of the tradition of separate facilities, we must understand the distinctive languages each area uses. The social work tradition of dealing with the whole individual in the totality of settings in which he or she lives means that we have to make the linkages between physical and mental health and illness in order to work more effectively and humanely with our clients.

OUTLINE

Introduction to Alienation

Suicide
A Case Study: Suicide and the Art of Living Unto Death

Homelessness

Unemployment
The Many Meanings of Employment, Unemployment,
and Underemployment
The Effects of Unemployment
Theories of Employment and Unemployment
Employment Policies and Legislation

Practice Approaches to Alienation

Summary

CHAPTER THIRTEEN

Alienation—
Studies in Suicide, Homelessness, and Joblessness

Alienation, or a sense of meaninglessness, has been viewed from many perspectives ranging from the sociological to the psychological. From a configural perspective, each of these levels or systems components may be a causal factor, and a point of intervention or prevention. Alienation may take various forms; it may have many causes, and it may produce many effects. This chapter examines three issues related to alienation among the many that could be studied: suicide, homelessness, and joblessness. We seek to understand how unemployment may cause alienation, just as we want to recognize suicide and homelessness as results of alienation. We consider how depression and suicide may be viewed as alienation from the authentic self and others in the world (Wetzel, 1984, p. 224); how the homeless may be viewed as alienated from primary and secondary groups; and how the jobless may be seen as alienated from the larger social structure and its organizations. In short, we will view the various forms of alienation within the configural perspective, both for understanding and for a basis of professional action.

INTRODUCTION TO ALIENATION

Alienation is a person's estrangement from society brought on by societal structures and forces or by natural events that take away one's ability to control the direction and nature of one's life. It is like feeling that one is a stranger in one's own home and homeland. It is generally characterized by feelings of powerlessness in the face of an all-powerful and hostile social order (particularly the economic structure) or nature, and by a sense of meaninglessness in the presence of irrelevant social norms and values. The person becomes isolated from the society, and the society loses the contributions of the alienated member.

A person is not born alienated. The person learns this relationship through his or her interactions with others, particularly when the contacts extend beyond the family. Ideally, the childhood years are filled with learning how to

Alienation is an abstract term that involves a separation of the person from his or
her society, with a concommitant sense of hopelessness and meaningless—because
it is our social involvements and commitments that provide hope and meaning.
Abstract terms such as alienation nonetheless may appear etched in the faces of
the alienated, such as this family whose home is an old school bus, but whose
community is Nowhere. (This family subsequently found other housing.)

become an effective person and a good citizen. The adolescent and adult years
involve the expression of these skills. But for reasons that may involve the entire configuration of human experience, the ideal may not occur. A person's
sense of self and his or her relationship to society may become problematic.

These problems can take various forms. For simplicity, we deal here with
three classes of ways people can attempt to cope with the forces producing alienation. First, people may become angry and aggressive at not being able to
direct their own lives or find meaning in their ordinary activities, particularly
when societal structures are changing in ways inimical to them. When this
anger is directed inward, suicide may result. When the anger is expressed out-
wardly, various forms of violence may occur, such as homicide.

Second, people may avoid the hostile social forces, either by means of psychological mechanisms, as in a retreat to mental illness, or various forms of social isolation. Social programs and policies may accidently or purposively
stimulate retreat and isolation, as appears to be happening with the new army
of the homeless.

Third, people may attempt to accommodate these inhospitable forces by
performing whatever actions are required for survival. They may passively accept welfare and its means-testing requirements or actively struggle to make it

within the terms of the society, even when the conditions are not ordinarily under the control of the individual, as with the jobless who may be seeking work.

Many philosophers, theologians, and social scientists have speculated about the nature and dynamics of alienation in general, but helping professionals have generally dealt with specific instances of this warped and warping person-society condition. In this chapter, we will look at several specific problems, each of which shares one or another aspect of the general conditions of alienation. We will look at suicide as a self-aggressive action. We will look at homelessness as a way society is avoiding the issues of deinstitutionalization and poverty. And we will look at joblessness as one form of accommodation to conditions of discrimination and changes in national and international economic structures. In each case, we will try to understand the specific kinds of person-society pressures that alienation may take.

The primary reason for considering these very different types of social problems—suicide, homelessness, joblessness—is to look for ways in which practitioners and policy makers have been successful in helping people on the hypothesis that each of the kinds of helping activities share some basic commonalities. Perhaps by being aware of successful efforts in one area, we might discover new possibilities for prevention or treatment in another.

SUICIDE

In the next hour (on the average), three people are going to kill themselves somewhere in the United States. Another 37 people will commit suicide somewhere else around the world (Moore, 1986). But for every "successful" suicide—some 30,000 people in America in 1982 intentionally took their own lives—there are more than 10 times that number who tried. In the case of adolescents the figure is higher: 25 to 50 youths attempt suicide for everyone who succeeds. (Classifying certain behaviors or the intentions behind such behaviors, like one-car accidents or overdoses of drugs, as suicide attempts is difficult, which makes any statistics on suicide somewhat uncertain.) Such occurrences place suicide among the top ten causes of death in America. Among adolescents and young adults, suicide ranks third (after accidents and homicide) as the most common cause of death (Ivanoff, 1987).

As bad as these numbers are, they must be seen in context of one more fact. The rates of suicide have been increasing steadily over the last three decades, with particularly sharp increases occurring among adolescents and blacks. As has been the case for many years, males outnumber females by three to one among those who commit suicide, although four times more women than men attempt suicide. As Ivanoff (1987, p. 739) notes, with the exception of young professional women, those who commit suicide are more likely to be unemployed or retired. Elderly persons have historically exhibited the highest rates of suicide—persons 60 years of age or older composed only 16 percent of the population, but accounted for 23 percent of those who committed suicide. However, there has been a small decline in suicides among that age group (Wass and Myers, 1982).

Suicide—the ultimate in personal alienation from the society of family, friends, co-workers, and strangers—takes place in a complex configuration of events that lead to this deadly outcome. Sociological and socio-economic factors (Durkheim, 1952; Henry and Short, 1954) suggest ways in which individuals are not integrated into the social fabric, or are torn away from it, as when one is forced to retire or is fired from a job, generating pressures that some people resolve through suicide. Other micro-sociological explanations point to interpersonal losses, ranging from broken friendships to death of spouse, as triggers for suicide.

Psychological factors of various types are employed to explain why suicide is chosen as the means to resolve pressures, rather than some other alternative behavior. Psychodynamic theories view suicide as the result of unconscious motives, the aggressive drive turned inward without corresponding defenses against it (e.g., Menninger, 1938). Cognitive theories view suicide as unsuccessful attempts to solve problems, with the subsequent feeling of hopelessness and depression (Beck, Resnik, and Lettieri, 1974; Farberow and Shneidman, 1961). Moore (1986) reports that persons with histories of serious depression are 30 times more likely to attempt suicide than is the general population. There is also a perverse element of learning present, as people who have attempted suicide previously are at very high risk to try again.

There are also what might be called physiological explanations for suicide. Cases may include persons who have terminal illnesses or who have extremely painful physical conditions, for example. Another physiological explanation involves persons who are under the influence of drugs or alcohol. Alcoholics have extremely high rates of depression and suicide. Moore (1986) reports that between 7 and 21 percent of alcoholics kill themselves, compared with about one percent of the general population. (See also O'Neill, 1986.)

No one explanation is able to account for all of the variety of reasons a given individual attempts suicide. It seems likely that physical, cognitive, emotional, and interpersonal factors interact with each other and with social structures and forces—this is the configuration of elements of which life is composed—such that the actor involved makes his or her fatal decision. Different theories guide our thinking about what factors are critical at different times. For the adolescent who does not have a long time perspective, events of the moment become powerful stimuli for impulsive acts. O'Neill (1986) reports an unfortunate occurrence of an adolescent male who ends up in jail for drunk driving and who is overwhelmed by the humiliation and hangs himself. He lacks a sense of perspective that an older person might have obtained in the course of living. The young adult may face numerous pressures, brought on by the burst of independence that having a job creates. It is exhilarating for a time until the demands become unrelenting and overwhelm the ability to cope.

For the elderly persons who may have lost a spouse, friends, and connections with distant relatives, suicide may take on a more deliberative air. Indeed, in the professional literature there is a controversial discussion of the ethics of suicide for people in life-threatening situations. They are seen to have the right to freedom of choice, even to the point of committing suicide (see Veatch, 1981). When all matters are fully considered, when a rational choice appears to be made, then "death with dignity" becomes an option for some people, it has been argued. This may take the form of refusal of extreme life-prolonging treatments, or it may involve voluntary euthanasia. It is difficult to distinguish this logical approach from other situations when the rationale is less clear, however. (Ivanoff, 1987.)

For each of these various causal factors set within the changing context of the life span, we look for different forms of prevention—the only cure of suicide is prevention (cf. Heller and Swindle, 1983; Welu, 1972; Draper and Margolis, 1976). Ivanoff (1987) points out that the United States has focused heavily on suicide prevention centers, with hot lines and other services. Unfortunately, there is little evidence that these centers actually lower national suicide rates, although the highly coordinated program of the Samaritans is reported to have reduced the suicide rate in Great Britain (Farmer and Hirsch, 1980).

Nonetheless, it is important to be aware of the warning signs of suicide, even though none alone is an accurate predictor. Moore (1986, pp. 15–17) lists the following:

1. Previous suicide attempts
2. Suicide talk
3. Making arrangements to put one's affairs in order
4. Personality or behavior change for no apparent reason
5. Clinical depression including at least four of the following that occur nearly every day for at least two weeks:
   a. change in appetite or weight
   a. change in sleeping patterns
   c. speaking and/or moving with unusual speed or slowness
   d. loss of interest or pleasure in usual activities
   e. decrease in sexual drive
   f. fatigue or loss of energy
   g. feelings of worthlessness, self-reproach, or guilt
   h. diminished ability to think or concentrate, slowed thinking, or indecisiveness
   i. thoughts of death, suicide, wishes to be dead, or suicide attempt

When such symptoms occur, time is of the essence. Since suicidal people do not believe they can be helped, even though their behaviors may be a cry for help, it is up to friends and professional helpers to reach out, talk about these feelings and behavior, and to seek help as needed. Such help frequently involves reconnecting the individual with his or her natural configuration, the family and friends, business associates, and public services that form the context of that person's life. Crisis intervention hot lines are useful for identifying services in one's community that can be called on for help. But much work is needed to reconnect the potential suicide attempter, including changing the social structures surrounding that person's life as well as helping the individual to cope with stresses.

The following case study of a person who attempted suicide and who was at high risk of doing so again is examined in some detail so that we can identify the physical, cognitive, emotional, and socio-cultural factors that were involved. It is a case of extraordinary drama, a demonstration of effective social work in stimulating the art of living even as the person approached her death. It is a case filled with surprises, not all of them stemming from the client.

A Case Study: Suicide and The Art of Living Unto Death

Mrs. Sylvia Rathbone, a tall imposing woman in her mid-50's, was admitted to the emergency department of the hospital one Friday afternoon because she had attempted to commit suicide by slashing her wrist. This story takes place in one of the large cities of Great Britain, where the law requires that a social worker contribute to the decision on the need for compulsory admission to a psychiatric hospital. In accord with the legal requirements for such cases, a social worker was called in to make a compulsory assessment, a social history of the factors presumed to have led to this dramatic act. One medical opinion was sufficient to have her admitted to a mental institution, provided the social worker's report was in agreement.

The worker, Ann Clayborn, spoke with Mrs. Rathbone for more than two hours, longer than usual due to a delay in the physician's being able to examine her after she was treated in the emergency room. Because of the long conversation, the social worker saw something positive in the woman that did not appear on the surface of events surrounding the attempted suicide. The staff physician recommended that she be admitted to the mental institution. "A clear case of mental instability," he wrote in his report. But the social worker was not convinced. She requested a second medical opinion, that of the woman's own general practitioner. Mrs. Rathbone's own doctor was Roman Catholic, as was Mrs. Rathbone, and he was angry with her for making the suicide attempt. He too recommended that she be hospitalized as an involuntary patient. Mrs. Rathbone was in tears; a state of crisis emerged.

What were the facts? Mrs. Rathbone's husband had died nearly two years ago in an automobile accident. She herself had undergone surgery for cancer about a year after that, and was informed that she was terminally ill. Her only child, a daughter, had married and lived with her family in another part of the country. And while Mrs. Rathbone was a successful businesswoman, she felt that she had nothing to live for. Moreover, she believed that her husband was there waiting for her after her death. So, rather than suffer the inevitable pain of the last stages of her cancer alone and isolated from any significant loved one, she had decided to take her own life.

These facts were corroborated by her general practitioner. Yet the social worker felt she was on the horns of a dilemma. She did not think this woman was insane to the extent that it was necessary to institutionalize her against her will; but, even though she had developed a good working relationship with her in the several hours they had talked together, she did not feel she could trust Mrs. Rathbone to be on her own. The worker wanted to emphasize the healthy portions of the client's actions and behaviors. Yet she had to face up to the unhealthy portions as well, without further impairing the healthy side. Finally, the worker said to Mrs. Rathbone: "I need you to meet me halfway in trying to help you." The client later told the worker that she heard the vote of confidence in her health from the worker, in contrast to the vote of madness from the two physicians.

They decided to ask for a *voluntary* admission to the mental hospital, thus granting what the physicians wanted while putting it into an altogether different context. The worker had to be away over the weekend, and called the hospital early Monday morning only to learn that Mrs. Rathbone had discharged herself, with the staff physician's consent, Saturday morning. In panic, the worker quickly called Mrs. Rathbone's home, and was relieved to hear her voice, albeit a very weak and quavering voice.

The worker went to Mrs. Rathbone's home immediately. She began to reinforce the observation that Mrs. Rathbone had been resourceful in this very difficult period. She had managed to keep herself alive over the weekend. The worker planned to continue to reassure her about her coping abilities, and the worker also arranged to make frequent visits and called many times between visits. The focus was on emphasizing concrete steps on how to survive despite feelings of meaninglessness.

This was difficult for many reasons. Mrs. Rathbone would sit in her living room with a bottle of brandy and jars of pills in full view. She had the access to suicide available at any moment, should she choose to use it. Moreover, as meetings between client and worker continued, the worker recognized that Mrs. Rathbone was anorexic. She was living on cottage cheese and whole wheat bread; she was losing weight rapidly. She seemed to be death-seeking. She would feel the lumps on her neck and underarms and would comment that they were getting larger. "Cancer will do me in soon," she would say.

But throughout this time, Mrs. Rathbone was always well-groomed. She was always on time for appointments, and she even took up water-color painting during this very stressful period. She obviously had strong feelings of attachment for the worker: "I baked you a cake today." And she went for her chemotherapy treatments, and later, to her outpatient appointments every three months.

Client and worker discussed the meaning of life on the edge of dying. Mrs. Rathbone became fatalistic: "God moves in mysterious ways and so be it." They discussed a book that Mrs. Rathbone had been reading whose hero also felt fatalistic, and who took to making decisions on the basis of a throw of a die. Mrs. Rathbone stressed the fatalism, but the worker emphasized that it was still by the hero's action that the decision to throw dice was made. The hero was still in charge of his life to that extent.

These elements of ambivalence in Mrs. Rathbone's life became increasingly evident: the passive giving up and dying versus the active, responsible choices for living. At one critical time, she decided to go off on a short holiday with her favorite niece and her husband. They got along well, but the niece was rather patronizing and tried to dominate Mrs. Rathbone. When the niece proposed a particular outing one day, Mrs. Rathbone decided to stay at the hotel, much to the younger woman's surprise. During her absence, Mrs. Rathbone decided to buy a magazine to pass the time, and to her amazement, the lead story was about throwing dice. She wrote a postcard to the worker telling her of this coincidence, her asserting herself just when she chose to buy a magazine that described games of chance. This incident became a turning point in Mrs. Rathbone's life, demonstrating that she was indeed able to make choices in her life, however limited.

She took increasing pleasure at making these small decisions. She delighted in making the small choices of which everyday life is composed. She was living in the moment by acting, by choosing to do what she wanted to do. These were not big decisions, just familiar ones.

She was also experiencing great pain in her back and arms, however, and she said to the social worker that this was good, as she wanted to die. She went to the outpatient clinic, and it was confirmed that indeed the cancer had started to become active again. She was in the terminal stages of her life. It was then that Mrs. Rathbone said that she was not ready to die yet.

The social worker reminded her that she still had the capacity to make many choices. The worker met more frequently with her, supporting her choices in how to live and how to die. Mrs. Rathbone decided not to receive any further treatment, just pain relief. Her doctor pressured her to continue in treatment, but she calmly and resolutely refused.

Indeed, she became much calmer and more focused in her life. She located a hospice and visited it with the worker. She like its philosophy of the relief of pain rather than the technologic efforts to sustain the life of a dying patient. With the worker's help, she arranged for a visiting nurse to help her monitor her pain relief at her own apartment. She made short visits to the hospice as an outpatient. She revised her will and put her other affairs in order without any help from others.

Then she went for another appointment at her physician, who informed her that her cancer had once again gone into remission. She called the social worker and laughed: "This could only happen to me." The touch of irony and ambivalence was still in her voice, wanting to live and to die, but recognizing that it is her choice to face living and dying. She had finally brought these two aspects of all living human beings into alignment.

The social worker had been seeing Mrs. Rathbone for more than a year, and had formed a deep and very satisfying relationship with her. Mrs. Rathbone had shown considerable resourcefulness for living in the face of dying. Both women expressed how much they cared for each other, how important each was in the life of the other. Thus it was with great disappointment to the client when the worker announced that she was going to fulfill the professional contact between them, which had always included a provision to terminate the relationship. Why? Because the worker saw that Mrs. Rathbone was resourceful, was able to make vital decisions, and was able to get the help she needed when she needed it. The worker had successfully supported Mrs. Rathbone's quest to live. She was not needed any longer merely to wait for Mrs. Rathbone's death. And there were other clients to be served. Mrs. Rathbone was angry and rejecting at the last meeting with the worker, but she never made any requests for further contacts.

Asked how she felt about this termination, the worker replied that she herself was very sad at parting. Yet she felt that professionally she had done the right thing, an affirmation of life, of self-responsibility. This was the ultimate gift that the worker could give to her client.

HOMELESSNESS

This is a study in ignorance. What we do not know about the amorphous group labeled the homeless far exceeds what we do know of them. One group of investigators estimates that there were 250,000 to 350,000 homeless persons in the United States in 1984; another places the estimate at 2.5 million (Bassuk, 1984) or 3.5 million (Hirsch, 1986).

The "popular" image of the old white male alcoholic living on Skid Row no longer fits even the sketchy facts about the large numbers of younger people, women as well as men, adolescents as well as adults, minority persons as well as majority, unemployed as well as mentally ill or substance abusers, those bereft of home as well as those bereft of hope. And perhaps most disturbing of all is the fact that there are increasing numbers of whole families among the homeless. Connell (1987, p. 792) reports estimates that about one-fifth of all homeless are composed of people in family groupings. She also distinguished between the youths who run away—usually a temporary, crisis situation, with most eventually returning home—from the throw aways—those who leave or are shoved out permanently, often after physical abuse. Numbers range from one to two million runaways, and perhaps a quarter to a half-million homeless young persons. These figures illustrate the problem of compiling accurate statistics, since these alone would equal one estimate of the total number of homeless.

The following analysis takes up the notion of paths to homelessness. There are several distinguishable though possibly overlapping avenues by which people become homeless. The first path is deinstitutionalization, another monument to the helping professions' good intentions that may have turned into a horror for thousands of individuals. With the development of tranquilizers and related medicines, it became possible to calm agitated individuals so that they would not need environmental control—so long as they took their medications and had suitable social supports.

Some 380,000 persons left mental hospitals between 1973 and 1981. The current hospital census is about 125,000. Even the chronically mentally ill, who in times past would have ended up in state institutions, were to be treated in local clinics. At the same time, the community was rediscovered as not only the source of problems for many types of psychological disturbances, but also as the source of potential healing—provided that the 2,000 community mental health centers could be built to offer discharged patients the out-patient services they needed. Unfortunately, only one-third of the needed community mental health centers were ever built. Much of their functions involved treatment rather than the preventive services originally conceived to be a major function. Changes in payment of services and from public to private practice also meant that the welfare "customer" was less likely to be able to obtain as many services as he or she once had.

In all, the deinstitutionalized came home to bare cupboards—those who ever came home. But in fact, most of the decline in the patient population of state hospitals resulted from the deaths of elderly patients who were not "replaced" by new like patients. Connell (1987) estimates that this occurred in between 20 to 40 percent of the numbers involved; moreover, many deinstitutionalized were simply transferred to nursing homes—Connell estimates this number to be 85,000. For some discharged patients, their families and friends were able to provide some home, at least temporarily. Sometimes the relatives could not take it and the former patient had to leave. For others, especially as they stopped their medical regime and as difficulties in living with others mounted, their home became the street. Some of them may be seen pushing a broken shopping cart piled with shopping bags filled with meager possessions; others are seen talking animatedly to no visible persons.

They are the disturbed and the disturbing, a point to which we shall return. (Conklin, 1985.)

Using Connell's figures, we may calculate that of the 380,000-person decrease in mental hospital censuses up to 1981, between 76,000 and 152,000 institutionalized persons died and another 85,000 went into nursing homes. This means that between 219,000 and 143,000 deinstitutionalized persons were available to enter the ranks of the homeless. In any case, however, note that the number of those who are actually homeless is estimated to be much larger, and so other sources have to be explored.

A second major path to homelessness seems to arise from the decrease in available housing of the type needed by the very poor. Building costs have been very high, and public programs have been limited or halted (cf. Talbott, 1980). The numbers of persons sharing housing space has climbed remarkably (Connell, 1987, p. 790). But it may have been changes in urban living that caused a major influx of members of the army of the homeless, as old, low-cost inner-city housing—single-room occupancies (SROs)—was destroyed to make way for "progress" in the form of downtown shopping centers, parking lots, or gentrified living quarters for wealthy yuppies. Increases in rents, stemming from urban renewal, along with decreases in support for public housing, led to decreases in low-income rentals and houses that poor persons can afford. In addition, Connell reports that the Mortgage Bankers Association has estimated that 130,000 American farmers lost their homes through foreclosure in the face of falling farm prices and rising costs. But exactly how many urban and rural persons lost their living places and eventually became part of the homeless remains unknown.

A third path to homelessness is sheer poverty. There are, as discussed in Chapter 11, many sources of poverty, from rising rates of unemployed to rising costs and expenses that may have broken those who were only marginally financially able. Medical insurance leaves many wage earners uncovered; their illnesses may plunge them into abject poverty. Changes in marriage and family arrangements have led to enormous increases in female-headed one-parent families, often with only meager resources of every kind. Battered women and their children often turn to public shelters for relief. Changes in industry that are related to world market conditions produce misery in the lives of affected individuals, as such changes did in the coal fields of Appalachia and in the steel mills of Pennsylvania. Bassuk (1984) points out that changes in eligibility for Social Security Disability Insurance instituted between 1981 and 1984 resulted in between 150,000 and 200,000 persons losing their benefits, another source of stress to the marginally financially able. There are many causes of poverty, and some victims of poverty—the exact figure is unknown—end up among the homeless.

From these various paths to homelessness, it must be clear that not all of these persons are seriously mentally disturbed, although to be torn from work, home, and other sources of social stability is hardly the prescription for good mental health. On the other hand, Connell (1987) cites surveys that indicate about half of the homeless men (in New York) are substance abusers, and a third have histories of psychiatric hospitalization.

There may also be many paths away from the problem of the homeless, but few have been well traveled and our experience is very limited. One path is simply to provide more emergency shelters for the immediate need. Connell (1987) estimates that nationally, there are about 110,000 beds in shelters, which means that on any given night, the majority of homeless do not have a homelike shelter.

Another solution involves longer-term low-cost housing. Jordan (1987) notes that as federal housing developments have retreated, local governments and private foundations and groups have entered the breach to provide housing for low-income persons. The new emphasis is on home ownership, not rental of public project apartments with the associated problems of poor maintenance and unresponsive tenants. Private, nonprofit groups are purchasing housing units, refurbishing them, and then selling them at low interest rates, with the assistance of municipal governments who provide tax breaks. Motivation to own one's own home runs higher than desire to rent the government's apartments.

Another important step on behalf of the homeless comes through the courts. A 1979 decision in New York City established the local government's responsibility to provide a bed for every person who needed one. This "right-to-shelter" lawsuit provoked local jurisdictions around the country to provide decent shelter for the homeless (Hirsch, 1986). In addition, advocates from the National Coalition for the Homeless seek legislative actions to put social supports for the homeless on a stronger foundation.

Activists for the homeless have taken other paths as well. Mitch Snyder, a nationally visible spokesperson for the homeless, runs the Community for Creative Non-Violence (Washington, D.C.). By means of dramatic social actions reminiscent of both Saul Alinsky's radical social work tactics and Mahatma Gandhi's nonviolent methods, Snyder staged near-suicidal hunger strikes, sit-ins (by the homeless), lived on the streets for four months along with many other denizens of the nation's capital, and in general has raised hell, money, and the American conscience on behalf of the homeless. (Hirsch, 1986.)

Much less well known are the efforts of the many shelters for the homeless across the country, the almshouses of our times, the quasi-community mental centers that never were built with government money but exist as expressions of charity. Particularly noteworthy is the work of the House of Ruth, a large urban shelter in Washington, D.C., because it exemplifies a strong philosophy toward homelessness not easily seen amid the more spectacular activities of other leaders in this movement. The main task of this shelter is to break out of the cycle of alienation that has surrounded the homeless. It undertakes to reestablish connections between the homeless and other portions of the community, and thereby to rebuild self-respect as well. Women go to this shelter for many different reasons, and they are brought together in smaller units on the basis of common needs, such as a section for pregnant women and women with newborns and another unit for handicapped elderly women who have been abused. Unlike most shelters that permit only very short stays, residents at the House of Ruth can stay from seven weeks to ten months. This enables the residents to be involved in counseling and training classes, both on a voluntary basis. Women move at their own pace in reestablishing ties with others and in developing skills necessary to survive in the outer world. When they are ready, in both their own eyes as well as those of their counselors, the residents move into a transitional unit where they take a job at the shelter for nominal pay ($3.50 an hour for a 40-hour work week in the late 1980s). Readiness is the key factor in reintegrating people back into the social fabric with both personal and social implications. When possible, residents are encouraged to share accommodations with other women so as to be more likely to manage in the community where expenses are very high. What is communicated is not only a quality of caring about these individuals, but a firmness of commitment to help them help themselves back into the society (Hirsch, 1986).

UNEMPLOYMENT

The unemployment rate is one of the prime indicators of the health and prosperity of the nation, although it is a politically controversial topic. There are obvious costs of unemployment in a nation, not only the economic costs of lost production, but also the social and personal costs to the unemployed persons, their families, and their communities. Some indirect or hidden costs of unemployment arise, as persons alienated from the major means of their support may react in harmful ways. Baumer and Van Horn (1985) summarize these indirect costs: "As unemployment spreads, crime, family disintegration, spouse and child abuse, and physical and mental illnesses also increase. The victims of unemployment lose more than their jobs; their health, property, and hope for the future are also at risk" (p. 1).

The Many Meanings of Employment, Unemployment, and Underemployment

To be employed is to be working for pay—what could be simpler? Yet the concept of "full employment" is crowded with contradictory meanings that reflect different political conceptions. [This brief presentation follows the analysis of Ginzberg (1983) and Baumer and Van Horn (1985).] A liberal position calls for jobs for all who seek them. Economist Russell Nixon (1973) added to this view several conditions: the jobs ought to pay a living wage, under decent conditions, and with the opportunity for advancement and fulfillment of a person's potential in that circumstance. This sounds very reasonable and desirable, but it is difficult to create large numbers of jobs that fulfill these conditions.

Other definitions of "full employment" begin to remove one or another factor from the ideal picture. For example, government actions in being an employer of last resort might be undertaken if the private sector cannot supply the quantity and quality of jobs needed, but doing so might require wages below the minimum wage, if limited funds are to be allocated equitably. A more conservative political position holds that some amount of unemployment exists naturally in the course of running a complex social system. Policies should aim at maintaining that natural level of unemployment as a pool of available labor, as a way of keeping wages down, as a tool to weaken the role of unions, and as a mechanism of social control (cf. Piven and Cloward (1971).

A more extreme conservative position holds that we should recognize a trade-off between the level of unemployment and the level of inflation because as one goes up, the other goes down. Since the level of prosperity for all is grossly indicated by the level of inflation, policy should provide for acts that increase unemployment and thereby decrease inflation. As policies such as tax cuts, favoring the wealthy and big business, stimulate increases in production, benefits for everyone will trickle down, according to one theory. For such conservative arguments, "full employment" exists when, by intentional policy and programming, a sizeable proportion of citizens who wish jobs cannot obtain them. This is indeed a strange way to use langauge, but welcome to the wonderful world of economics.

We must first define terms because official measures of unemployment and underemployment are themselves controversial. Ginzberg (1983) speaks of "official unemployment" as "the tip of an iceberg," meaning that the official jobless rates presented by the Labor Department is only a portion of the full picture. Begin with the official figures, which are the ratio of persons officially counted as unemployed by a government survey compared to the total number of persons in the labor force. In 1929 the unemployment rate was 3 percent, but by 1933 it had risen to 25 percent, and during the decade of the 1930s, it never fell below 14 percent (Ginzberg, 1983, p. 9). With the coming of World War II, the rate of unemployment fell sharply, and reached its low of 1.2 percent in 1944. After the war, to about 1970, the rates fluctuated but were in the range of 4 to 5 percent. Thereafter, the rate had a general upward trend, as indicated by the following figures: 1970 (4.9 percent); 1975 (8.5 percent); 1980 (7.1 percent); 1985 (7.2 percent). The year 1982 saw the highest rate, 9.3 percent, including a rate of 10.8 percent during the last two months of that year. (Rosen, Fanshel, and Lutz, 1987, p. 30; Swardson, 1987, p. A1, A11).

Percentages hide the human dimension. So be aware that in 1985, 8.3 million persons were unemployed according to official statistics. (The most recent figures available at the time of writing show a 5 percent unemployment rate in July 1987, which translates into 7.2 million unemployed persons out of nearly 120 million workers (Swardson, 1987, p. A11).) Moreover, as Ginzberg (1983, p. 91) points out, the annual unemployment figure represents an average number of unemployed, but in fact two to three times that number of individuals were jobless at one time or another during that year.

Below the tip of that iceberg are other persons who are not fully employed. We use Ginzberg's data (1983) here. First, there is a group of persons (4.7 million) who wanted full-time jobs, but could only obtain part-time work and were thus counted as employed. Second, there is another group of persons (1.1 million) who wanted jobs but were so discouraged about employment prospects that they had stopped looking for work and so were not included among the unemployed (defined as persons who had sought work in the past four weeks). Third, Ginzberg speculates that there might be millions of other adults (such as housewives, retirees, students, and the ill and disabled) outside the civilian labor force who would probably take jobs if they were available (p. 39). Fourth, institutionalized persons are not included in the labor force statistics at all, nor are persons in the armed forces counted in the civilian labor force. Fifth, people, minorities especially, who are kept out of the labor force because of discrimination and other structural reasons may turn to crime or

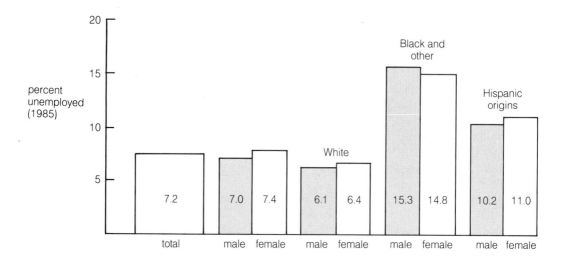

FIGURE 13.1   **Percent unemployment by gender, race, and persons of Hispanic origins.** (*Source*: **Adapted from Rosen, Fanshel, and Lutz, 1987, p. 311**)

hustling as an expression of their alienation from a society that in effect does not allow them legitimate access to earning a living. Overall, it is arguable that there are at least twice as many "unemployed" as the official figures present. Gross (1980) suggests that the number of persons not working for pay but willing and able to work is about three times the official unemployment rate.

The unemployment rate may be further broken down by sex, race, and ethnic category. For unemployment rates by gender, race, and Hispanic origins, reported by Rosen, Fanshel, and Lutz (1987), see Figure 13.1.

The same editors also report the rates of unemployment (July 1985) for teenagers (white teenagers, 16.3 percent; black teenagers 41.3 percent); women heads of households (10.2 percent); farm workers (14.3 percent), and construction workers (13.4 percent)—when the overall unemployment rate was 7.2 percent. Total figures hide some important differences within segments of society.

Baumer and Van Horn (1985) point out that blue-collar workers have an unemployment rate nearly three times that of white-collar workers, and that different states vary greatly in their rates (for example, West Virginia has the highest jobless rate in 1984 at nearly 16 percent, while New Hampshire had the lowest at 4.3 percent). The authors call attention to the distinction between cyclic unemployment (temporary changes in demand for workers, including seasonal variations) and structural unemployment (due to prolonged barriers to employment, such as lack of skill or education, or because the jobs themselves no longer exist after the demise of an industry itself). Structural unemployment is also produced by factors related to discrimination based on race, gender, disability, age, and sexual preference. The importance of the distinction between cyclic and structural unemployment becomes clear as we examine some of the federal policies and legislation for the jobless. Briar (1987) notes a third type of unemployment (frictional) made up of workers who are changing jobs at the time when the monthly government survey was made.

Ginzberg (1983) notes that there are yet other areas of unemployment problems, but that too little information exists to describe them fully. These include unemployment among Native Americans (the highest incidence of unemployment in the nation); Hispanics; displaced homemakers (older women who enter or reenter the job market after a long absence); welfare mothers and single women heads of households; the disabled; and some Vietnam era veterans. Fineman (1983) calls attention to the problems of the white collar unemployed, professionals or managers who lose their jobs as budgets are cut or rollbacks experienced in an industry or business and are not able to find work.

Underemployment is another aspect of work-related problems. In a general sense, underemployment occurs when a person is working at a job that is not commensurate with his or her education, skills, or capacities. This is very difficult to prove because it is hard to know what a person's capacities are and what a specific job demands of a worker. Presumably, one can distinguish between cyclic and structural underemployment. When a "season" is over, the worker may take a temporary job until the main work cycle returns. For example, a school teacher may take a job as a night watch during the summer. Structural underemployment is more serious; it occurs when people are locked into dead-end jobs that offer little opportunity to move up to a managerial level. Part of the problem is that someone must do the scut work that goes into running a complex society. In utopian literature (such as *Walden II* by B. F. Skinner), people who volunteer to do the undesirable but necessary work of the commune earn more labor credits than workers in the more desired high-status jobs. The point is that it is possible to compensate people who do the work below their capacities, although this does not solve the problem.

The other side of the coin is that major problems exist for people who may be working full or part-time. As discussed in Chapter 11, about 35 percent of women and 18 percent of men aged 22–64 who were defined as being in the poverty group worked part of the year or part-time, while 4 percent of women and 3 percent of men defined as having incomes below the poverty line worked full time (Rosen, Fanshel, and Lutz, 1987, p. 21). Current laws impose a difficult choice for some elderly who either have to stop working or face a reduction in their welfare benefits.

The Effects of Unemployment

The initial effect of unemployment is lost productivity. When workers are not working, goods and services are not produced. Ginzberg (1983) cites a 1975 Senate Budget Committee report that estimated that the recession of that year cost the nation $200 billion in lost production. Moreover, unemployed workers pay less in taxes (as do companies that earn lower profits). As unemployment rises, governments spend more on unemployment compensation and food stamps and to a lesser extent on welfare, Medicaid, and other social programs. All this means that with every percentage-point rise in the jobless rate, there is another $25 to $29 billion increase in the federal deficit (Ginzberg, 1983, p. 88).

Unemployment insurance is a vital and stable part of the American welfare scene; Baumer and Van Horn (1985) call it the principal legacy of the Depression-era policies. However, in recent years, only about one-half of the unemployed actually collected the insurance, and the amount they received comes to less than one-half of the workers' before-tax average weekly income (Ginzberg, 1983, p. 90–91). There is a maximum length of coverage (typically 26 weeks), and most workers find jobs before that time, although about two-fifths of them exhaust their unemployment benefits and have to go on welfare; most of these workers lose their job-related health insurance at a time when they and their families are most vulnerable to many stresses. Other fringe benefits may also be lost, such as retirement income (Social Security rates reflect earned income, not unemployment benefits). (See also Jones, 1987.)

Brenner (1973) estimated the human costs associated with changes in unemployment. With a sustained one percentage point increase in the unemployment rate in the United States, there was an association five years later in (1) a 1.9 percent increase in total mortality and mortality from cardiovascular-renal diseases (20,240 deaths) and from cirrhosis of the liver (495 deaths); (2) a 4.1 percent increase in suicides (920 deaths); (3) a 3.4 percent increase in state-hospital admissions (4,227 admissions); and (4) a 5.7 percent increase in homicides (648 homicides). The initial stress of losing a job may be seen in various kinds of effects, ranging from apathy, demoralization, humiliation, and hopeless despair, to stimulation to start a new career or take a new look at how one has been leading one's life (cf. Fineman, 1983). But the Brenner data suggest that the negative effects may build up over time for some people, with deadly outcomes (see also Kasl, Gore, and Cobb, 1975).

Briar (1987) points out further personalized dimensions of joblessness. Frequently, in American society, one's identity is bound up with one's work. Failure to find work by a teenager, particularly a minority teenager, for example, can have a broad effect on his or her developing personality. Added to this, if the parents and relatives of the teenager also are not employed, the milieu creates a hopelessness that breeds high degrees of alienation from society. Alternatives, in drugs and crime, may provide temporary release from pressures of the situation. Briar cites a 1980 U.S. Department of Justice report that up to 70 percent of jail inmates may be unemployed at the time of their arrest and that recidivism may also be attributable to the lack of a job after parole or release from prison (p. 783). Interpersonal effects of joblessness have been reported as well. Briar (1987) notes that impaired functioning in the family may be produced by the unemployed person's feelings of self-blame, which may lead to defensive actions that attack his or her support group, the family. This, in turn, may be linked to infant mortality, child abuse, spouse abuse, divorce, and parent-child conflict, among other associated outcomes. The configuration of effects of so central an event as unemployment is broadly felt.

Theories of Employment and Unemployment

If the effects of unemployment on millions of people, to say nothing of the larger society, are so horrendous, then why doesn't someone do something about it? In fact, many things have been done about the issue of unemployment and underemployment, some with remarkable success, others with dismal failure. Because the larger national and international contexts continue to change, however, so do the activities undertaken to resolve the unemployment problem. It is important to note that unemployment of large numbers of urban workers as well as rural workers has been a problem for several hundred years. We did not discover unemployment just yesterday.

Why is there unemployment? There are many complex and interrelated factors such as changes in economic activity, long-term changes in the size and composition of the labor force, technological changes, international events and multinational business arrangements, the price of energy, and governmental policies and politics, among others (Baumer and Van Horn, 1985). It is the task of theories to sort out these ingredients and present some coherent view of how they interact and what can be done, if anything, to harness them to serve human needs. There are many theories, especially those that stress economic factors—sometimes to the exclusion of social factors. We will follow Ginzberg's (1983) analysis in the following discussion.

One position favored by conservative economist Milton Friedman holds that there is some natural level of structural and cyclical unemployment that represents a balancing weight against inflation. The percentage of unemployed considered "natural" has changed over time, from 4 percent to 7 percent or more, to fit the then-existing unemployment level. This led to the paradox of statements that x percent of unemployment constituted full employment.

A nation must have unemployment of this natural level, it is argued, in order to offset inflation. This theory views unemployment as inversely related to inflation—as one goes up, the other goes down. The reasoning is complex, but briefly put, prices of goods are determined by wage costs; when unemployment is low, wages rise because of the competition among workers for scarce jobs. Higher wages lead to inflation (when there is more money and credit relative to the available goods, prices rise). Some presidential administrations have viewed increased unemployment as a necessary interim step toward reduced inflation, even though it creates stress to millions of workers in the trade-off. "Safety nets" of unemployment insurance and other welfare provisions were intended to see the jobless through a temporary period of unemployment. As the economy picked up steam (in part because of low inflation rates), it would generate substantial job opportunities for the unemployed workers, according to this argument. Unfortunately, things did not work out that way. We had a condition in which both inflation and unemployment were high ("stagflation"), contrary to the theory.

Conservative economists blamed new structural features of the labor force (the entrance of women and youth into the labor market) for stagflation, ignoring ominous other signs such as the growth of multinational organizations, large peacetime military expenditures, and the increasing concentration of American industry, which raised prices when firms lacked competition. (To clarify the point about military expenditures: When we spend money for military goods and services, we do not satisfy general consumer needs. Additional goods and services must be created at higher costs because fewer resources are left.) One study cited by Ginzberg (1983) showed that every time the military budget rose by $1 billion, it meant a loss of 11,600 jobs from the national economy (p. 27).

Another theory, called the "trickle-down approach," was introduced when President Ronald Reagan took office. The idea was to provide tax cuts heavily in favor of the wealthy and to corporations who, thus stimulated with new capital, would become more productive. This productivity would add to government revenue, and would thus reduce inflation, unemployment, and the budget deficit. The philosophy was that when the waters of productivity rise (through government's favoring the rich to be more productive), everyone's boat would rise with it. And so Reagan did not support measures to reduce unemployment directly. Such unemployment has the effect of controlling workers, weakening unions, and holding down wages, critics charge.

Employment Policies and Legislation

Unemployment rates are something that no politician of either political party can ignore, and so there have been grand proposals favoring full employment (variously defined, as discussed above). It is worth examining some of these policies and enacted legislation to see how a philosophical conception gets embodied in law. The Humphrey-Hawkins Full Employment and Balanced Growth Act of 1978 was an attempt to embody the liberal view of full employment as a law, but in fact, as Ginzberg (1983) relates, it was a bill that embodied more the political and practical compromises of that time.

The initial version of the bill (1974) spoke of the government's creating jobs to employ everyone who wanted one, if its economic policies acting on the private sector could not do the job. Later versions came out at the time of a serious recession when large numbers of persons had suddenly become unemployed. The emphasis first involved grand-scale social planning for national priorities such as adequate housing, health care, universal education, mass transit, conservation of natural resources, and the elimination of poverty within ten years. Then it retreated from the idea that the government should be the employer of last resort (creating jobs for the poor). Emphasis shifted toward accepting the notion of a four percent jobless rate for adults as an interim way of reducing the growing inflation. The final version of the Act passed in 1978 retained a portion of the original dream of full employment, but emphasized the creation of jobs in the private sector *by* the private sector, aided as needed by the government. The role of government as employer of last resort was more circumscribed, and even then, the law was never used by any president, Republican or Democrat. Massive grass roots support for full employment as a guiding concept for the nation never emerged.

In place of that general guiding philosophy came a series of specific laws aimed at emergencies such as high rates of unemployment. Generally speaking, the legislation focused on giving temporary relief in various forms to the unemployed (cyclic or structural unemployed, or displaced workers) or on providing training or creating jobs (dealing with structural unemployment problems, often with disadvantaged persons). Many innovations were introduced, such as giving tax credits to businesses that hired and trained the disadvantaged unemployed. The government also aided some unemployed to relocate, gave temporary jobs to others, and created some public works projects reminiscent of the 1930s.

All of these unemployment-related laws provided enormous amounts of money for remediation of problems or the promotion of cures. (In 1983, 5 million unemployed workers received benefits totaling more than $33 billion.) But the difficulties still remain and millions of person are not integrated into the labor force effectively or humanely. Personalized services, such as job-retraining programs, provision of basic educational skills in order to profit from job retraining, and the like, may have helped in individual cases, but jobs—real jobs, with liveable wages, decent conditions, and opportunities for growth—have to be available.

PRACTICE APPROACHES TO ALIENATION

This chapter assumes that there are some common themes of alienation present in suicide rates, homelessness, and the effects of unemployment. We also assume as a practice hypothesis that there are some common modes of service that reduce or eliminate alienation, regardless of its form.

Following a configural perspective, consider at least three levels of actions that are required simultaneously. First, the macro-social level needs to have changes made in the structures and forces that cause the conditions whereby some numbers of individuals are alienated and made to feel isolated from the community of others. For example, with unemployment, some changes must be made in the society so that jobs are available for those who want to work, or some suitable support system must be in place if people are not able to work or are not needed. This is often quite difficult because there are many steps of causation between macro-social structures and the problems experienced by the individual. To continue the employment example, it is difficult to know whether creating jobs or creating training for jobs or both is more effective in changing the unemployment situation in the long run. On the other hand, it may be necessary to make social changes so that adult education and equivalent experiences become subsidized and socially valued—through adult scholarships and citizen sabbaticals—for certain classes of citizens who are no longer needed for contributing to the productivity of the nation. These could be life fulfilling and dignified activities, even though they do not necessarily add to the Gross National Product. The form of support would not be a "dole," but it would be a benefit for having served in society to the extent possible. Later, at the requisite age, such persons would also retire into the Social Security system.

Creative thinking is necessary in a society in which not everyone will be filling paying productive jobs, if we are to avoid the social waste of frustrated and alienated lives. A humane and democratic society will provide some means of support for these people. A creative society will turn this type of welfare into an enhancing situation for both the individual and society. The number of variables needed to study these macro-social changes are many and complex. We have many theories to suggest the possible paths, however, and predictions derived from the theories might tell us whether or not we are on the right path.

Second, the mezzo-social structures and forces that act as filters or buffers between the individual and the larger society have to be changed so that they are able to do their task more effectively and humanely. To continue the employment example, workers have networks of friends who provide a variety of social and personal supports. In times of unemployment, those natural networks may be called upon to provide additional kinds of supports—perhaps at a time when members of those groups are equally stressed (as members of the same factory that has closed its doors, for example). Even close-knit families eventually feel the pressures of restrictions on finances and the emotional stresses that affect the unemployed worker. In general, the helping professions must find ways of assisting natural helping systems to continue their supportive tasks. When these natural helping networks are themselves under stress, then helping professionals must find ways of supporting them or providing artificial helping networks.

Third, the micro-level involves individuals who have an assortment of strengths and limitations relevant to the mezzo and macro stresses and resources. The challenge of helping is to improve the goodness of fit of the individual's coping and mastery skills with the stresses and opportunities of everyday life. This is not to take a completely individualistic approach to social services. We recognize that primary and secondary group structures may have to be changed for the sake of this client and comparable others as well. But from a configural perspective, social services must be directed toward helping clients to learn to accommodate effectively to the changing social conditions as well. The individual's changes may in fact influence changes in the social structures, as when a person asks assertively for fair rights in a work situation, and new rules are instituted so as to provide all such workers with equivalent privileges.

As in traditional social work, clients need to be connected with existing resources, referred to other agencies dealing in specialized services, and in general counseled to find ways to help themselves. A configural perspective notes that these transactions have synergistic effects, each stimulating the others. Thus the social worker enters the overall system to find the most opportune points of change, which will then affect the next most modifiable elements of the configuration.

This is one approach for dealing with one kind of alienation, but who is to tackle all of these things? It is sometimes suggested that an individual worker should be involved at micro, mezzo, and macro levels, and where this is possible, it would be ideal. But it seems more practical that social workers and other helping professionals will have to move one day to working in teams , some of whom specialize at the macro level, others at the mezzo and micro levels, but with such closeness of contact that each knows what the others are doing. Indeed, it would be necessary for the micro worker to know that jobs are being made available through the macro worker's efforts, so as to be able to get the client to the available job; when both knew that helping networks were in place, that would sustain the individual in making and keeping contact with that new job situation. The network might appear at the new job setting, or it might involve training existing networks to be more adaptive under the new conditions of pressures on its members. Thus the configuration of components and events in the clients' lives should be matched by the configuration of professional efforts.

SUMMARY

This chapter has described several forms of alienation as examples of a general phenomenon of social unconnectedness. Suicide is the ultimate separation of self from others; homelessness tears apart the nurturing structure of the family and neighborhood; joblessness removes the flow of financial support and the derived social status. What is centrally important to the helping professional about all forms of alienation, however, is that it is a painful state for the persons involved. The pain may be expressed in different forms.

Those who are not directly affected by alienated persons also suffer pain in various degrees—the survivors of the suicide, the observers who pass by people sleeping over heating grates in the city streets, and the friends and neighbors of people who cannot find jobs. Alienation represents the flip side of a basic aspect of society, that people need people to be human. A society needs as many of its citizens as possible to be productive contributors; the loss of one person is a loss to us all.

Therefore, it makes practical and ethical sense to face the issues of alienation, both to prevent problems so far as possible and to intervene when problems occur. This chapter has described the scope of the problem and has indicated some approaches for dealing with it. It clearly can only be a beginning statement.

PART

VI.

FIELDS
OF
PRACTICE

Even though social workers are trained to use a general problem-solving model across a wide array of situations, they too have to specialize to some degree. No one can be everything to everyone. Because of pressures to concentrate one's attention on certain kinds of problems (such as substance abuse) or with certain types of clientele (such as senior citizens) or in certain work sites (such as at the place of employment), fields of practice have emerged. The label field of practice refers to certain kinds of commonalities—of problem, client, or setting—in which the general methods are sharpened to fit specific circumstances. Thus the term helps to orient the worker to the particular ways in which the human condition is expressed in a given "field of practice."

Fields of practice in social work emerged as part of the history of the profession. It was not easy to give up professional turf so hard won, but eventually the specialized groups such as medical social workers and family social workers merged together into general associations of social workers. They recognized the strength of the common core of expertise each group showed. The realities of practice are, however, that we have to learn the special features of whatever field of practice we enter. Thus the continuing paradox of having both general problem-solving skills and specific expertise remains. The resolution of the paradox lies in the common core of training and values that represents the heart of this helping profession.

The following list identifies the commonly recognized fields of practice:

Public Welfare (or Public Assistance)
Child Welfare
Social Work with the Family
Criminal Justice System
Medical Social Work (including
   Public Health; Rehabilitation;
   and Developmental Disabilities)
Psychiatric Social Work
Social Work in the Schools

Social Work at the Work Place
   (Occupational Social Work)
Group Services
Community Planning and
   Administration
Substance Abuse
Social Work in Rural Settings
Gerontological Social Work

OUTLINE

Introduction to Child and Family Welfare

Spheres of Defense and Enhancement of Well-Being

Services
  Supportive Services
  Supplementary Services
  Substitute Care Services

Summary

CHAPTER FOURTEEN

Child and Family Welfare

Social work is the primary helping profession in the field of practice of child and family welfare, which involves the delicate balance of psychological and social factors of persons in their natural environments—or in specially arranged ones—that facilitate growth and development. This field of practice includes many forms of helping—protective services for abused and neglected children, homemaker services for families burdened by illness of a primary care giver, day-care services, foster care, family-life education, to name but a few. This variety of programs makes it difficult to describe the field of practice, and so we again make use of the configural model to indicate the social categories of family and child services. The primary groups, secondary groups, and socio-cultural environments are here viewed as spheres of defense against the many hazards of ordinary life—these are treatment and rehabilitative services. The same social categories may be spheres of enhancement for individuals and families to attain a quality of life beyond what they currently have—these are preventive/promotive services. For both preventive and interventive services, there are forms of supportive, supplemental, and substitutive services (Kadushin, 1980) by which family and friends, educational and health institutions, and social agencies seek to provide for the well-being of children and families.

INTRODUCTION TO CHILD AND FAMILY WELFARE

Child and family welfare is probably the oldest helping activity. Recall the Biblical exhortations that urged the ancients to provide charity to those in need. It is also the first identifiable field of practice in social work. From the beginnings to the present day, social work has been the primary profession responsible for the broad and diffuse collection of activities that go under the label "child and family welfare." These include protective services for abused and neglected children, aid for unwed mothers, homemaker services to sustain families through difficult periods of time, day care, foster family services, adoption, and the various institutional and residential treatment centers.

We begin with a drama, unfortunately a real life story of the first "case" in this field of practice. New York City was the scene of the action; the year was 1875. Neighbors, and then city authorities, stood by powerless to interfere with the ways in which one family was "disciplining" a young daughter, "Mary Ellen." Her parents were beating her severely. No laws set the limits on child rearing by parents, no ordinances restricted corporeal punishment of children. Someone thought to prosecute the parents under the only existing protective legislation of the time, that regarding cruelty to animals. Thus, with the cooperation of the Society for the Prevention of Cruelty to Animals, a small, undernourished and physically abused human animal was removed from her parents. Later photographs suggest she was aided to develop into a healthy adult. This case led to the enactment of a growing series of laws that protected children from harm and neglect. It also provided children with the wherewithal to grow and develop in a healthy manner.

There is an important point to learn from this case study. Notice that multiple services were provided—removal from harm, regaining health, and providing assistance to find opportunities to make something meaningful of her life. More generally stated, child and family development frequently makes use of preventive/promotive, treatment, and rehabilitation services, even within one case situation.

The research program of Klein, Alexander, and Parsons (1977) presents a good example of a multiple service perspective. They designed a model family service program in which there was treatment (interventive work with a delinquent youth, so as to reduce recidivism); rehabilitation (efforts to help the family start talking together again after the trauma of the son's delinquency tore them apart. They did so by trying to achieve a more effective mode of communication among members that would make them comparable to families with nondelinquent adolescents); and primary prevention (promoting effective problem solving skills in the younger siblings of the delinquents, so as to prevent them from following in the anti-social tracks of their older brothers). Empirical results suggest that the demonstration projects were successful on all three counts. The importance of this model for the present discussion is that this multiple perspective in professional helping can be embodied in about every service area, given appropriate imagination.

It is easy to assert this ideal—that all cases should be provided preventive/promotive, treatment, and rehabilitation services as far as possible—but it is more difficult to put into practice. There are more than enough people currently hurting in one fashion or another to keep every professional helper busy all of the time. But it should be obvious by now that if we do not devote some time and energy to preventing predictable problems by dealing with the causes and conditions of the problems, we will never come to the end of that seemingly endless line of persons who are the victims. We may treat one person today and tomorrow another one or two will take that person's place. Treating victims one by one will never resolve any social problem (Albee, 1983).

In configural terms, we must approach every problem we encounter with an orientation toward dealing with personal, primary, and secondary groups and with socio-cultural contextual factors in this time and place. Whether we begin social work service with an individual, with a group of persons with like problems, or from an administrative or policy position regarding the broad class of individuals affected by identifiable social conditions, we have to take into consideration the several components of the human configuration. Let's try a case example.

Elaine, a social work student, is interning at a women's shelter. She meets a black teenager, Ann, who is conspicuously pregnant, and they discuss the course of her pregnancy and her future plans. During this time, the social worker notices that Ann has been smoking continually, and so in the course of their conversation, the student mentions that heavy smoking during pregnancy is known to increase chances of unhealthy outcomes for the baby (prematurity, low birth weight, etc.). In addition to helping Ann find a permanent place to live, Elaine offers to assist her to find an "end-smoking" group (see Searight and Handal, 1986; Schinke and Gilchrist, 1984).

Rather than end this case illustration at this point, let's continue the configural implications. Suppose there are several pregnant women at the shelter who smoke heavily. It might be an obvious idea to get the group of young women to an end-smoking clinic. That would help the small number of women at the shelter who share the same problem. Yet there are other possibilities for action. Suppose you knew about the recent studies by the federal Office on Smoking and Health that calculated that Americans who died of smoking-related causes before the age of 65 lost a total of 949,924 years of potential life in 1984 (Okie, 1987, p. A23). The deaths of more than 320,000 persons who died in 1984 could be attributed to smoking, the chief preventable cause of death in the United States. Men have mortality rates twice that of women; blacks have a 20 percent greater mortality than do whites. While fewer people in general are smoking than were a decade ago, adolescent females, as noted earlier in this book, have been starting to smoke in increasing numbers. They now smoke in larger proportions than adolescent boys. Thus the larger practice question is whether or not to expend some effort at publicizing the dangers of smoking to young women in general through mass media and possibly legislative actions. As you see the young pregnant teenager before you at the women's shelter, you can as well see the thousands of others with the same problem now, the tens of thousands of young girls who may follow in their footsteps, and the many thousands of others needing rehabilitative services because of smoking-related problems.

As Charles Horton Cooley, an American sociologist, said more than a half-century ago, a person is like a coin with an individual side and a collective side. The individual sits before you at the women's shelter; the flip side of the coin is that she is one of thousands of persons having a common problem for which there are ways to seek effective solutions for all. The configural update of Cooley's analogy is that each person has an individual aspect, a primary, and a secondary group aspect, and a socio-cultural aspect, all of which must be taken into consideration for an effective service program. We treat this individual and seek to prevent like problems for others in her same risky situation. It is not easy, but the alternative is an endless line of persons repeating the same preventable problem.

Child and family welfare consists of a vast assortment of services that are

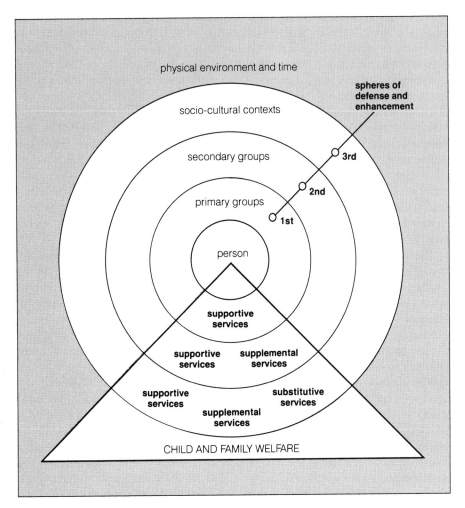

physical environment and time

socio-cultural contexts

spheres of
defense and
enhancement

secondary groups

3rd

2nd

primary groups

1st

person

supportive
services

supportive
services

supplemental
services

supportive
services

substitutive
services

supplemental
services

CHILD AND FAMILY WELFARE

FIGURE 14.1   The configural model with the child and family welfare system super-imposed

aimed at particular needs at certain points in the lives of the people involved. To help get some grasp on the whole of this welfare system, we will use the configural approach as the frame of reference on which to impose the child and family welfare system. Figure 14.1 represents the familiar configural model: The individual is surrounded by primary and secondary groups, within the socio-cultural and physical environmental contexts over time. But, on top of that configuration, is superimposed the child and family welfare system, a triangle touching the individual, but with specified kinds of services at the primary and secondary group levels and in the socio-cultural context. These services—the supportive, supplemental, and substitutive—are described in this chapter, and are progressively added to the social configuration, as seen in the lower half of Figure 14.1: Support is given by primary groups; support and supplementation is provided by secondary organizations; support, supplementation, and substitutive services are offered by society—indeed, only society can assume the power to step in and create substitute family situations. The sum of these three classes of supports, provided by public and private agencies and natural helping networks, represents child and family welfare.

We supplement our usual terminology when referring to primary and secondary groups and the socio-cultural context because what is important in child and family welfare is that these groups and contexts serve as spheres of defense and enhancement. Defense refers to aid provided to persons and groups in need of treatment or rehabilitation. Enhancement refers to aid provided to persons and groups whose currently problem-free lives may be improved with appropriate preventive/promotive services. This chapter discusses both the traditional treatment services in child and family welfare and the newer preventive/promotive services.

SPHERES OF DEFENSE AND ENHANCEMENT OF WELL-BEING

In your own life experience, you are aware of the many things required to aid your developing personal well-being, like being fed, clothed, housed, amused, educated, and the like. And when you think about it, you also recognize the various people involved in all these activities—your parents, siblings, relatives and friends, teachers, employers, and so forth. Most of us probably are not often aware of the other less visible services provided, for example, by the police, the telephone repair service, governmental structures, and market place forces, among others, all aimed at trying to keep the environment stable enough for you to achieve and enjoy your well-being.

What we take for granted in going through our lives may be a continuing problem or challenge for others. If we assume that the functions of providing food, clothing, and shelter are taken care of by the father, while the mother stays home and tends the children, we are talking about a family configuration that is typical of only 5 percent of Americans today. It is typical that the mother now works out of the home for pay, and consequently there are large numbers of latchkey children returning from school to find both parents out of the house, working. Another increasingly common pattern is the one-parent household (usually with the woman as head of that household); this is especially common in minority families; about 50 percent of minority children are growing up in female-headed, single-parent households. The single parent has to attend to all the functions that the husband-wife family did with two adults. It is not impossible to do, but it obviously puts the single parent under more pressure with possibly fewer resources than the two-parent family, unless other arrangements provide some help. For example, help from the extended family members may complete some functions that the second partner ordinarily performs. When the extended family or friends perform these functions, it puts them at risk for overextending what they can do for their own families. In the traditional two-parent family, it is also possible that illness, absence, or whatever may cause some family functions to go uncompleted, unless extended family and friends pitch in on a short-term basis (cf. Edmondson, Holman, & Morrell, 1984).

All well and good for those families who can make suitable accommodations on their own for themselves and their children. One way or another, however, the basic functions of life must be fulfilled, and if the immediate individuals cannot perform them, and if family and friends are not willing or able to help with the burden, then some outside agent is needed. Think of these agents as representing spheres of defense. The person himself or herself is at the center of this discussion. Many of the basic tasks of life are adequately performed by the involved person; some are not, including tasks that may be essential to survival, especially for young children and older adults. But to be interdependent on others is a defining characteristic of persons in modern societies. So, let us examine the nature of these dependencies.

Intrinsic to meeting the expectable challenges of everyday life is the system of primary groups, families, close friends, and relatives in particular. Intimate and diffuse relations among these persons mean that helping occurs back and forth (Hanlon, 1982), unless there are tensions that change the meaning of primary group to something less than intimate and supportive. Primary groups are the first line of defense in seeking and maintaining well-being. They provide the first requisite of welfare: support—activities that enable the individual and his/her family to achieve some basic standard beyond what they can attain on their own (cf. Kadushin, 1980). A parent may be working at minimum wage, for example, and it may be insufficient to provide an adequate diet for the large family. Supportive aid would add to the already existing efforts of the parent—perhaps the extended family would share meals or give gifts of money.

Another example of support among primary group members would be a family in which the existing methods of discipline do not seem to be having their desired effect. Friends or relatives might offer advice or possibly respite services (taking the children off the hands of the overworked parent for a short time). In general, natural helping networks provide support so that individuals can continue to function according to the norms of the society. They may also provide the encouragement and stimulus so that individuals and families are enhanced to attain higher standards of living and quality of life. Without the countless ways these natural helping networks supply aid, the formal social welfare structures of society would be overwhelmed (Pilisuk and Parks, 1986).

The second sphere of defense and enhancement involves secondary groups, whose contacts with a given individual are on a specialized and usually task-focused basis. For example, school teachers are employed to educate children about the formal tools needed for living in complex society, such as reading, writing, and arithmetic. The clergy provide spiritual and moral guidance for parishioners. Home aides may come into the home on a temporary basis to help out when a parent is disabled. Counselors might see the family in order to recommend better methods of child rearing (as in the Rogers case in Chapter 6). In general, these people of the second sphere are nonfamily members, trained in specific skills to provide short-term or part-time helping (broadly interpreted) in normal environments like the home or the school.

Note that the kinds of service provided by people in this second sphere may include support, but may also extend beyond support of normal functioning of the family. Services may involve a second major type: supplementation (Kadushin, 1980). These services involve actions that supplement

Alan Carey/The Image Works, Inc.

Child and family welfare comes from many sources, some from federal and state welfare programs, some from private agencies; perhaps the greatest share comes from nonprofessional individuals—people helping people. Helping may take the form of resolving problems, but it may take preventive forms—as pictured here, a family-life education meeting of mothers discussing effective child rearing.

parental functions in order to maintain ordinary family operations and the growth and development of the children. Typically, supplemental services are extended to families who are overloaded with problems and challenges and who are not functioning effectively as a result. (Support functions, in contrast with supplementation, are aimed at essentially healthy families with insufficient resources, not at families with problems of dysfunction that may express themselves as having insufficient resources among other ways.)

In addition, some of the services of the second sphere involve enhancement of family functioning. Special classes at school for the gifted and talented, Head Start programs for preschoolers, family-life education classes for adults, job training skill classes for adolescents—all involve short-term task-specific relationships that enhance the participants' ability to achieve desired goals. They supplement what families cannot do, not because they are dysfunctional, but because they lack the knowledge or skills to achieve them.

The third sphere of defense and enhancement involves the socio-cultural context, particularly the power of the state to ensure the growth and development of its citizens, especially the youngest. This sphere is called into action when power is necessary to enforce investigations of possibly illegal behavior (such as the abuse or neglect of children). Frequently, the state is involved in long-term and sustained assistance to families when the extended families, charities, or private agencies cannot do the job alone. Moreover, some of the efforts by representatives of society involve use of institutions or non-ordinary environments. Care may be provided by trained (or nontrained) attendants to meet persisting needs. The original family would have to be in a very dysfunctional state for such institutional or unusual changes to occur. This may require permanent changes, as when a child is adopted into a new family with all the rights and responsibilities thereto for both adoptive parents and child.

SERVICES

As indicated in Figure 14.1, there are three broad types of welfare services at this socio-cultural level: Supportive and supplementary services may be provided by governmental agencies, but the third major welfare service—substitutive care—is largely part of the domain of the state and its representatives. The remainder of this chapter outlines the various supportive, supplementary, and substitutive care services at the second and third spheres of defense and enhancement. What is important to recognize is that the path to personal well-being involves simultaneously the several spheres of social life, where the innermost spheres are activated first, followed by the outer spheres as needed. The broad classes of services—support, supplementation, and substitutive care—are sequentially provided as the need warrants. Much of the literature in family and child welfare emphasizes services directed at problems (Wilensky and Lebeaux, 1965; Kadushin, 1980). Others amplify this picture by pointing out the many ways people receive enhancing services, even in the absence of problems (Kahn and Kamerman, 1982; Bloom, 1981). There are universal needs that all children and families have, and society should provide these as a matter of course like any utility (such as public education). To do less demeans the individual, and if some do not obtain these required goods and services, then not only do they suffer but society is itself the loser in the long run (cf. Kahn and Kamerman, 1976; 1977; Kamerman and Kahn, 1978).

Supportive Services

This section summarizes some of the kinds of supportive services individuals and families receive, either from their own efforts or from those from their extended family and friends, as well as those from specialists in educational institutions (like schools and religious centers), in health and mental health institutions (including social agencies as well as various types of hospitals and clinics), and in institutions of social control (such as detention centers, prisons, and certain types of social agencies like those dealing with abused children). The configural perspective views all individuals and families having ordinary developmental needs, while some have extraordinary needs arising from socio-economic conditions or personal factors or combinations of such factors.

The spheres of defense and enhancement simply describe the sequence of actions, starting at the center with the self-help of the involved persons, and then proceeding through the second and third spheres, as needed to obtain aid for various types of needs and opportunities. A more realistic view of this configuration of events recognizes that the three spheres are at work simultaneously, even when the individual or family does not signal a given need. For example, society provides schools that not only educate children but influence the lives of all family members because of the school week and school year. Likewise, society's laws and the subculture's mores set expectations and limits on parents' actions toward their children. When certain problems emerge, however, the progression of events moves in sequence through the second and third spheres of defense and enhancement. These are the focus of child and family welfare services in the narrow sense of a field of practice.

We begin our consideration of supportive services in the first sphere of defense and enhancement. By sheer volume, this is undoubtedly where most of the child welfare originates. Parents generally provide basic nurturance for their children, as far as they are able. Friends and relatives may take over on occasion to give parents some respite. Family vacations may revitalize the members; naturally existing support groups may provide other resources that make the tasks of parenting easier or more enjoyable. Collins and Pancoast (1976) provide guidance to helping professionals on how to facilitate these natural helping systems, which both help friends in need and also enhance those who have opportunities for growth and development (cf. Gottlieb, 1982).

Notice that the helping at the first sphere is essentially personal and private, augmented on occasion by social workers who try to facilitate these naturally existing networks.

In this first sphere of defense and enhancement are self-help groups, a special form of support. Participants are lay people who come together, often in intense interpersonal situations, to offer each other support and assistance in dealing with common problems (Pilisuk, Parks, Kelly, and Turner, 1982). The groups may be preventive/promotive in orientation, such as single-parent groups, or they may serve treatment and rehabilitation objectives, such as Alcoholics Anonymous or parallel groups for spouses (Al-Anon) and children of alcoholics (Alateens). Frequently self-help groups are started by the members themselves, or sometimes helping professionals get the groups going. Recreation groups, such as summertime day camps or extended service camps, may not only provide stimulation for children (Young and Adams, 1984), but also respite for parents (Valentine and Andreas, 1984). Hot lines that make crisis interventions and support services available at all hours of the day or night may also provide treatment or preventive services.

For some, this first sphere of defense provides to be insufficient— because of an absence of a parent; because of a deficit in the person that renders a parent unable to perform a function, or who performs it poorly as a result of personal limitations; or because the scope of the child's problem overwhelms the parents' resources (Kadushin, 1987). Or it may be that support to families within the home setting is not sufficient. In any case, agents of the second sphere (or, occasionally, the third sphere) may enter the scene.

The second sphere provides normative supports. Schools teach children; hospitals treat illnesses; churches provide moral instruction. In a sense, each of these support what a family could do for its members in their own homes, but in a complex society, specialists provide these services more effectively than most parents can for their own children. Such supportive services aid parents in nurturing their children, even though these services take the youngsters away from the home for part of the time. The home remains central in the children's lives; parents are viewed as effective people needing support for specialized services.

In the United States, the third sphere provides emergency supports for unusual and temporary needs. This reflects a *residual* perspective that Wilensky and Lebeaux (1965) described as a view of governmental services that presumes that ordinarily the market place and the family will be adequate to supply all of the children's needs, but in times of emergency, families may need temporary assistance until the market and/or the family recover their economic balance. The contrasting view of government sees social services like day care, job training, homemaker services as types of *social utilities*, reflecting common human needs whose fulfillment is the basis of societal stability and growth. Provision of these social utilities should be universal, without stigma, and for the betterment of all. The institution of public education in the United States would be a parallel example of an existing social utility. Other countries, such as Great Britain and the Scandinavian nations, provide other social utilities universally for their citizens, so it should be noted that the third sphere of defense and enhancement need not be organized only in the residual way.

Some specific services of this third sphere of defense and enhancement include various forms of counseling and mental health services for children and parents, provided on an out-patient basis. Generally, identified problems emerge that resist solution at home, and sometimes the people involved eventually seek professional help after advice from others fails to resolve the problem. Family service agencies frequently employ a variety of individual and/or family practice methods (as in the Rogers case, in Chapter 6). Child guidance clinics tend to deal with more seriously disturbed children, or those involved in delinquencies when the power of the state is employed to require counseling services. The objectives in all such cases are to enable the family, both children and parents, to deal more effectively and responsibly with their respective challenges. The solutions generally involve the family members who make changes in their own behaviors and in their responses to other family members in the home setting.

Another example of a supportive social service at the level of the third sphere of defense and enhancement is that given to unmarried mothers and their children born out of wedlock. America has long held negative attitudes toward illegitimacy—think of Hawthorne's novel *The Scarlet Letter*—in part stemming from religious values favoring monogamy. But Kadushin (1980) notes some secular reasons for this antipathy. It was better economically and familially for husbands to deny their illegitimate offspring, and wives agreed, in order to keep inheritance claims for the legitimate children. In any case, the illegitimate child has received few protections and little compassion from society until comparatively recently. The change of labels tells all: from bastard to love child or out-of-wedlock child. A child may be legitimated now by the marriage of the parents, by petition to the court if the parents are not married, or by the father's acknowledgment of paternity (Kadushin, 1980). Birth records are changed accordingly, and in the case of acknowledged paternity, the father is required to support the child. The mother is acknowledged as guardian of the child and has the right of custody and control of the child.

There is a disproportionate number of illegitimate births among nonwhites, although in recent years, there has been a reduction in the differences among the races as sexual activity, contraception, and related activities are becoming more nearly equalized. In 1982 the rate of nonwhites (73.9 births to unmarried women per 1,000 unmarried women) was three times greater than that of white women (18.8 births per 1,000 unmarried women), and the scope of the situation is very large—involving some 715,000 unmarried women (Rosen, Fanshel, and Lutz, 1987, p. 6). The acceptance of illegitimate children into their subculture also differs; the black subculture is more accepting than others.

Unmarried pregnant women require a range of services, from support of the pregnancy itself, to counseling services regarding decisions on educational and vocational plans, abortion, marriage, adoption (a rarely chosen option these days), or whatever is needed. Modern maternity homes (like the Florence Critterton Homes) have changed from places to conceal a pregnancy to multi-service centers that provide the wide variety of services, including housing, medical, financial assistance, and basic parenting skills frequently needed by the women. Kadushin (1980) notes that services are increasingly being given to mother, father, and child, rather than to the mother alone.

Note that pregnancy is not, in itself, an illness. It may be socially problematic, but the individuals involved are usually healthy, so that services offered to them would come under the heading of preventive or promotive services. Likewise, in family-life education settings, healthy and well-functioning individuals come to an agency to deal effectively with a recognizable challenge facing them, such as normal developmental issues. For example, young parents may want to discuss child-rearing practices such as methods of discipline, toilet training, and how and when to discuss human sexuality with their children (Lamberts, Cudaback, & Claesgens, 1985). Such discussions help to forestall problematic behaviors such as harsh methods of discipline or premature pressures for toilet training in favor of approaches that are more conducive to healthy growth and development. In general, family-life education programs offer the opportunity to address issues of personal growth and improvement of one's quality of life (Patrick and Minish, 1985), as well as to adjust to some chronic conditions like living with a person with Alzheimer's disease. Sensitivity training groups or group counseling may also be useful to help individuals and family members learn how they come across to others and thereby learn to become more sensitive and effective communicators.

Supplementary Services

The second major type of services offered to children and their families involves actions that supplement parental functions. They help maintain ordinary family operations and the growth and development of the children (Kadushin, 1980). This means that some outside agent enters the family system for a short or extended period of time to perform some function or functions that one of the parents would ordinarily have performed. Three main subdivisions in this type of service are income or in-kind supplemental programs; homemaker services; and day-care services. The treatment/ rehabilitation services will again be distinguished from the preventive/ promotive ones.

Supplemental service coming from this sphere of defense and enhancement include income and in-kind supplemental programs (such as forms of social insurance like OASDHI, or means-tested income transfers like cash grants from AFDC, and vouchers for food stamps, as well as in-kind public assistance such as school meals, public housing assistance, and medicaid), and these have already been discussed in Chapter 11. Kadushin (1980) describes them as child and family welfare services in the sense that these programs provide income or in-kind benefits in place of, or as supplements to, inadequate levels currently provided by, the parents.

Another service at the third sphere of defense and enhancement involves agency homemaker programs, which may be called home aides, home health aides, or homemakers. When these programs first began, they involved the provision of ordinary housekeeping and child-care services to families as a result of temporary absence or inability of parents (especially mothers) to perform these functions. In 1903 they were called "visiting housewives" (Kadushin, 1980, p. 235). Changes were made in the level of training of these workers so that they became what is known as paraprofessionals, persons who receive short, intensive but focused training on direct-service methods. Homemakers later came to provide the kinds of medical services that might have been provided by a family member, as well as psychological services in comforting persons in distress. Sometimes, homemakers are used to train parents in effective childrearing and housekeeping activities. Programs differ as to the degree of professional supervision involved. Teams of helping professionals may be used to combine housekeeping with nursing, social work, or medical services. Homemakers may work under public or private auspices, in health or welfare settings. Effective use of home aides with the elderly has also been reported (Nielson, et al., 1972). But the predominant use of homemakers has been to supplement a parental function so as to prevent placement of children and the breakdown of the family facing some personal crisis. (See Kadushin, 1980, pp. 255-7.)

It should be noted that the United States has only a small number of these workers (29 per 100,000 population in 1976) compared with Sweden (923 per 100,000 population) and with other European countries. This reflects the ideological differences between two assumptions: one is that society must share in the responsibilities of child care for both personal and collective goods, another that raising children is strictly a parental responsibility. Cutbacks in government funding of homemakers reduced the number of public agency programs in the United States in the late 1980s. There has been an increase in homemaker programs on a fee-for-service basis, although monitoring quality of such services that lack agency oversight is difficult. A National Council of Homemaker–Home Health Aide Service was attempting to set standards to provide some quality control, but some critics are not optimistic about achieving that.

Day-care services can be conceived as stemming from the first, second, or third spheres of defense and enhancement. Informal neighborly sharing of baby sitting is a function of primary groups; more formal day-care arrangements in schools (for unwed teenage mothers, for example, or college students) is a function of normative secondary organizations. We will concentrate on day care as a social agency function in the third sphere because of the potential scope of such programs and the possible source of government funding to pay for these services.

The provision of informal services to care for children is ancient, but formal services by trained helpers is quite recent in history. At times of social need, such as during and after the Civil War, which required women to work in factories or which left them widowed, formal day-care services emerged. In World War II, the 1942 Lanham Act involved the federal government in providing 50 percent matching grants to local communities to set up day-care centers for working mothers for the duration of the war. In 1976 a Dependent Care Tax Credit was established—families could claim a tax credit on a sliding scale basis for child care expenses, the lower the income, the larger the tax credit. By 1982 some 5 million families had claimed this tax credit, but they were mainly from middle- and upper-income tax brackets; a single mother on AFDC is not in an economic position to apply for the tax credit.

With the large increase in the numbers of mothers who are working outside the home, particularly those with very young children, we are facing a reality that requires a supplementary service to care for children in such ways that will aid their growth and development. Indeed, it is an economic necessity to large numbers of working parents. More than half of the mothers in the United States are in the labor force. The figures for 1985 showed that 49.5 percent of mothers with children under 3, 53.5 percent of mothers with children under 6, and 69.9 percent of mothers with children 6 to 17 years (none younger) were working (Bergmann, 1986, p. 25).

But once having determined to set up day-care facilities, we encounter a number of dilemmas. For example, many mothers who go to work earn relatively low wages, and if they have to pay a large amount for day care, taking a job may become self-defeating. Two major variables—the staff/child ratio and wages of that caretaker (as indicator of level of professional training)—determine the bulk of the costs. The quality of day-care services is inversely related to low child/caretaker ratios and directly with wages paid to the caretaker (Ruopp and Travers, 1982, p.87). Thus the costs of using day care can be a great burden for low-income and even middle-income families (Hofferth and Phillips, 1987).

Rutter's review (1982) of the research on quality day care shows that children's emotional bonds with their parents are not disrupted, that parents are still preferred by the child, and that social and emotional problems are not frequently caused by such arrangements. Day care, Rutter notes, is not without risky effects. Day-care influences a child's social behavior in ways that may be either helpful or harmful. Rutter's point, however, is that fears stemming from early studies of the detrimental effects of residential care on children that were generalized to day care are not well founded. More research is needed, but quality day care can be a positive experience for large proportions of children. The emphasis is on quality. (See Jones and Prescott, 1982.) For example, a five-year follow-up study of the participants in the Yale Child Welfare Research Program (Trickett, Apfel, Rosenbaum, and Zigler, 1982; see also Rescorla, Provence, and Naylor, 1982) suggests that a comprehensive program focused on the whole child, especially with a close involvement of parents (Bronfenbrenner, 1974), can be very beneficial for economically disadvantaged children.

Nelson (1982) notes that there have been long-standing regulations to govern federally-funded day-care centers, but they have never been enforced. Studies of children from low-income families indicate that 39 percent have had no medical care, 50 percent have had no dental care in the 12 months prior to beginning Head Start programs, and only 19 percent have had the appropriate and up-to-date immunizations. Such children are more likely to live in deteriorated and overcrowded housing, with inadequate plumbing that contributes to the spread of disease and infection (Richmond and Janis, 1982, pp. 447-8). Moore (1982) points out that poor black families, whose children constitute a disproportionate (44 percent) portion of nonprofit, federally-funded day-care centers, are especially hard hit by retrenchments. In spite of these enormous needs, preventive health, nutrition, and accident prevention programs are not being implemented fully in many day care settings.

Thus, as Zigler and Gordon (1982) note, the expanded use of quality day care in America has produced some important gains, but there is much day care that is not of a high quality, and there are many gaps in the availability of any day-care service. The importance that day care is assuming in the United States is, unfortunately, not being matched by careful longitudinal study of the range of effects of these services. Much more study is needed about the nature of quality day care and ways to provide it for large numbers of families.

Supplemental services, like supportive services, have the potential for preventive/promotive as well as treatment and rehabilitation outcomes. Day care, in particular, offers great potential for promoting growth and development under certain circumstances. For example, research by McCartney, Scarr, Phillips, Grajek, and Schwarz (1982) suggest that high-quality day-care centers affect positively the development of language and of social behavior of children in them, when there is a high level of adult-child interaction. Without this high level of verbal interaction, children scored higher in maladjustment, even though the facility itself was of high quality (cf. McV. Hunt, 1982; Barth, 1986).

Substitute Care Services

Substitute care services are those that replace all parental or guardian functions, either temporarily or permanently. Obviously, such drastic measures are used only when other supportive or supplementary services cannot provide the care needed for appropriate growth and development. These services require the power and legitimacy of the state, and thus represent actions at the third sphere. The child has to make major changes—in living place, possibly in school setting, and likely in friendships and in the kind of authority represented by those who are acting toward them in a parenting capacity. Parent substitutes might receive supportive or supplemental services; foster parents, for example, sometimes receive payments, to help underwrite the costs of raising the foster child.

There are degrees of substitute care, from that involved in foster families and institutions in which legal custody of the child is required, to adoption, in which legal guardianship is changed. When an agency gains legal custody over a child, it may place the child in a foster family setting, but the biological family still retains legal control, for example, in being required to consent to surgery for the child, or enlistment in the military, or consent to marry (Kadushin, 1980, p. 313). It is possible for the child under legal custody of an agency to be returned to his or her natural parents, should the initial conditions change for the better. But when legal guardianship is changed, the legal status is permanent.

Foster Care Services.   When a family cannot, will not, or is not allowed to care for its children, either on a short- or long-term basis, then one alternative is foster care. This service involves a child being placed in a living situation with another family. Foster care should be distinguished from the informal placement of a child with relatives when parents were not able to care for him or her. Neither an agency nor the state had anything to do with monitoring such a relocation. Also, distinguish foster family care from adoption, in which a child is legally incorporated into the new family as a permanent member. Agencies make careful assessments and arrangements for foster family placement because of the importance of such a permanent relocation. About three-quarters of children are in foster care by court order (Stein, 1987).

AFDC provides federal funds for foster placement (as does SSI for children with special needs). About a quarter of a million children were involved in foster care in 1983, down considerably from the half-million in 1977. This change is probably due to more emphasis being placed on the provision of services to children in their own homes or in permanent home situations. The median age of children in foster care is rising, from 10.8 in 1977 to 12.6 in 1983. Males slightly outnumber females, and more whites than blacks are involved in foster living (Stein, 1987).

Group Living.   Group home care or congregate living situations provide a protective setting for young persons, usually adolescents or young adults, with less control by adults (as occurs with foster parents or institutional staffs), but with some family-like supports. As such, it also provides some training in independent living. Usually a referral is made by an agency worker on behalf of a youth unable to deal with close authority but not in need of total control. The youths live in a residential setting run by a house parent or counselor. Sometimes, the youths help formulate rules of the house, and they may be involved in doing chores. In France, this type of living arrangement is also used as a transition device for young people who come to an urban area with no family ties (Kahn and Kamerman, 1977).

Institutions.   Each type of institution described below has its own distinctive focus, but in general, institutions are relatively large-scale organizations that are supposed to deal with an enduring common problem in a cost-effective and humane way. Thus a large physical plant may be built that houses many clients who are sent from a large catchment area to be served by specialists and supportive staff. Kadushin (1980) lists the following types of institutions for children (p. 583):

1. For normal but dependent children (like orphanages)
2. For physically handicapped children (such as the separate facilities for the blind, deaf, and others)
3. For mentally handicapped children (the mentally retarded; the mentally defective)
4. For emotionally disturbed children (these children are usually placed in residential treatment centers)
5. For socially disturbing children (these children are often adjudicated delinquents, and are placed in what are called training schools).

Available figures (as of 1976) indicate that there are about 40,000 children living in orphanages; another 17,700 in residential treatment centers of emotionally disturbed; and about 100,000 in institutions for the physically, mentally, and emotionally disturbed (Greene, 1986, p. 107).

Because institutionalization is the most extreme form of substitution, it must be justified by the severity of the need, as well as by the particular specializations and resources that the institution offers. Often the staffs of institutions are highly specialized in their training. Nonetheless, the institutional environment may have negative effects on the children involved. So judgment of what constitutes the best interests of the children and the families involved is difficult. Even if an individual is placed within a total institution, it must never be forgotten that that person still lives within a social configuration that involves natural or substitute parents, relatives, friends, peer groups, natural helping networks (and possibly antagonistic groups and individuals), subcultures, and, indeed, the entire spectrum of the real world of social systems that influence human growth and development. Such influences may be more tightly structured or more invisible within an institution, which means that helping professionals have to nurture their constructive functioning more than in a typical community environment.

Adoption.   Adoption is a legal proceedure through which persons not related by birth are formally joined in parent-child relationships, with all the rights and responsibilities thereto. This involves a legal severing of the relationship between biological parents and child and a social joining process between the adoptive parents and child. Adoption is made concrete by legal agreements, after a trial period of about six months. The emphasis is on the child's needs— finding a family for the child—and not on the family's (Cole, 1987, p. 68).

There are two eligibility procedures. If a child is without parents or personal guardians, then he or she may be available for adoption into a permanent home, which is considered preferable to temporary family arrangements. The would-be adoptive parents are screened and studied for suitability as adoptive parents. Factors such as physical and emotional health, age, motivation, financial status, and marital status are considered. Recently, especially for hard-to-place youngsters, single persons have been considered as adoptive-parent candidates. The point is to make a good match between the characteristics of the adoptive parents and the child to be adopted.

About eight out of ten nonrelative adoptions go through agencies. There is a black market in adoptions, in which the intermediaries charge large fees, with more concern for profits than for effective matches between child and adoptive parents. International adoptions have increased, partly as a humanitarian concern in the aftermath of the war in Vietnam.

Data are hard to obtain about adoptions. The most recent reliable data suggest that over 60 percent of children adopted in 1975 were related to the adoptive parent, such as in the case of stepparents. Most children (according to 1975 data) are problem-free, white infants and preschool children. Impressions after that date suggest a continual decline in the numbers of available white infants, and a corresponding rise in intercountry adoptions. Data from 1984 suggest that of the 50,000 children awaiting adoption, there are more likely to be minority children, those with severe handicaps, and older children (11 and up). The figures show the changing patterns among children available for adoption. Black children are not placed as readily as white children, even though black families adopt at a rate more than four times as great as white or Hispanic families (Cole, 1987).

Protective services for abused, neglected, or exploited children represent another major category of child welfare services. It is difficult to categorize protective services; sometimes they are supportive, supplemental, or substitutive. Difficult ethical issues arise, however, such as when the parents' rights to raise and discipline their children exceed the limits of society's tolerance. The state has an obligation to defend the civil liberties of adult parents and the rights of their dependent children.

States have delegated legal authority to protective service agencies to investigate all charges of abuse and to intervene as necessary. Parents have the corresponding rights to defend their actions, if they choose to use them. Note that this power includes investigations of potential problems—thus there is a preventive component to these services (cf. Goldstein, Freud, and Solnit, 1973; 1979). Once a protective agency has begun an investigation, it cannot withdraw until it is sure that the child is no longer in danger. If the parents refuse to cooperate, the protective worker can obtain further legal sanction (by filing a petition at the court regarding likely cause of danger to the child). Once such a petition is granted, the agency has available to it police power to force parental cooperation, should that be necessary.

Kadushin (1980) lists the kinds of situations that are involved in most child protective work. They include physical abuse of the child; malnourishment (including "failure to thrive" at normal rates of growth and development); having inappropriate clothing, sleeping arrangements, medical care, or shelter; failure to attend school regularly; being overworked or exploited; exposure to unwholesome or demoralizing circumstances; or sexual abuse. These situations generally involve an act on the part of the parent or caretaker, whereas neglect, which may take some of the same forms as abuse, usually results from the omission of necessary actions on the part of the adult.

One difficult aspect of substitutive services is that the child gets moved to some new setting with new caretakers and bears the burdens of the situation, both those that created the problem and those that represent the solution.

Thus we are likely to find the need for mixing supportive and supplemental services combined with the substitute care function. In general, most substitutive services come from the socio-cultural sector, and have at base the power of the state to decide ultimately wherein the child's welfare lies.

SUMMARY

Three hundred years ago, a ten-year-old orphan might have been indentured (forced to be a servant or apprentice in the home of a craftsman until his or her majority). This was viewed as a humane and practical way to help the child live with a family, as well as to produce new workers where labor was scarce. Sometimes poor families were forced by circumstance to sell their children for indentured servants, however, so this system was not the answer (Datta, 1977). Two hundred years ago, the same orphan might have ended up in an almshouse (the local poorhouse). The first such almshouse was established in New York in 1657. By 1790 almost all municipalities had such institutions. Soon the mistake of mixing children with adults, the dependent with the criminal, the well with the sick, was seen to be malproductive, and so this system was not the answer.

One hundred and fifty years ago the same orphan might have found his or her way to one of the orphanages that was just opening up in the United States. The first public orphanage was opened in 1790 in South Carolina. The other states followed suit by the middle of the next century and were just in time to discover that orphanages could be very unpleasant and harmful places for the children—so that was not the answer.

About one hundred years ago, such an orphan might have been "rescued" off the streets of New York and sent west to a "good home" in a healthy rural area, in contrast to the dangerous metropolitan areas. The Reverend Charles Loring Brace, Director of the New York Children's Aid Society, placed about 100,000 children in free foster homes out west. Unfortunately, the families who received those children were not carefully checked and the possibilities of exploitation appeared. Criticism arose from Catholics (from whom the city children were largely drawn) since placements were made with Protestants in the west, so this was not the answer either.

Likewise, adoption might have been another option for the 10-year-old. Adoption was a relatively recent invention. The first state statute on child adoption was passed in 1851; by 1929, every state had such laws. Again, this might lead to abuses, such as the parents' selling children into adoption. Even though controls were later enacted (such as the 1917 Minnesota law that required detailed investigation of the adoptive home), this was not the answer.

About 75 years ago, our orphan might have been placed in one of the newly subsidized foster care homes in his or her own city. The 1909 White House Conference on Children declared that a carefully selected foster home is, for the normal child, the best substitute for a natural home. Foster family placements became the responsibility of social welfare agencies, rather than private charities. Children were no longer supposed to work to repay the costs to society for their upbringing, as had been assumed by earlier child welfare schemes. Now the state paid foster families. However, there are not enough foster families to go around, and such families are not necessarily free of problems themselves. They require some training and support during their time of providing foster services.

The point of this historical sketch of child welfare services provided to one type of client is that each innovation was developed as the best answer to the problem, but soon it was seen to contain some important flaws. So the search for ways of providing effective and humane child welfare services goes on. Perhaps in the next 50 years, we might see services aimed at preventing the events that orphaned the child, while promoting the well-being of both child and parents. The only thing permanent is change. One can be fully certain that a "perfect" solution will need changing.

Finally, it should be clear that my classifications (adapted from the work of major scholars in this field) are arbitrary. Supportive, supplemental, and substitutive services may sometimes blur into one another. The first, second, and third spheres of defense and enhancement also change in certain contexts. As a general overview of this large and heterogeneous cluster of services, however, this chapter may serve as an initial guide.

OUTLINE

CHAPTER FIFTEEN

Criminal Justice

This chapter contains a running description of the author's ride in a police patrol car, some court room visits, and some volunteer work in a local juvenile house arrest program. It provides that background as part of an introduction to the criminal justice system composed of the police, the courts, and a network of corrective and rehabilitative institutions and procedures. The complex steps in the criminal justice process are described, both in theory (following the federal model) and in practice (based on an empirical study of the attrition that occurs along the way to justice). The chapter concludes with a discussion of the juvenile justice system.

INTRODUCTION TO THE CRIMINAL JUSTICE SYSTEM AS A FIELD OF PRACTICE

Social workers practice their craft alongside criminal justice officers who have primary control over the clients in this field of practice, their legal authority derived directly from the powers of the state. Social workers are part of a secondary discipline in this context and are said to work in a *host setting*. But even as members of a secondary discipline, social workers may be involved in a wide range of practices:

- Social workers may take part in primary prevention projects to divert youths from making behavioral choices that could lead to crimes and criminal careers.
- Social workers may serve in consultative functions to the police, especially on calls involving marital conflicts or in personal-violence situations.
- Social workers may serve the courts in providing background information vital in aiding judges and juries in the sentencing process.
- Social workers may serve in probation or in parole contexts.
- Social workers may work in prison rehabilitation programs.

In all of these situations, there are criminal justice officers to whom society has assigned the authority to have control over individuals who threaten society or break its laws. Social workers work with those criminal justice officers, whose guiding value—controlling behaviors that threaten society—is quite different from traditional social work values, with its emphasis on client self-determination. Living with these value differences is not always easy. Moreover, the clients are not usually voluntary, which adds another dimension to the challenge of gaining rapport and providing services that help the client to help him or herself.

Yet, as in any field of practice in which social work skills are not the primary mechanism of service, it is still possible to use or to adapt traditional social work skills in the service of these clients. Specialized texts present these adaptations; this chapter presents an overview to the field of criminal justice itself.

4:30 P.M.

Having been given permission to ride in a patrol car by the chief of police, I am introduced to Officer A and join him on his evening patrol duty for an opportunity to see law enforcement and the ensuring of public safety at the front line of the justice system. As I will describe throughout this chapter, I in fact saw a good deal more.

EVOLUTION OF THE CRIMINAL JUSTICE SYSTEM

The justice system in America is composed of three major parts: the police, the courts, and the network of educational (preventive) and corrective institutions (for the detention and/or rehabilitation of offenders). In theory, the police spread throughout the community so as to prevent crime, promote law enforcement, ensure public safety, and provide emergency services for a wide variety of matters on a 24-hour-a-day, seven-day-a-week schedule. Likewise, in theory, the criminal courts respond to cases brought to them by applying laws to specific circumstances and reaching decisions fair to both the violator and the victim in criminal cases. (Civil hearings involve disputes between individuals or organizations over their respective rights and obligations.) Continuing in theory, the corrective institutions seek to carry out the judicial decision, balancing retribution for a wrong-doing with rehabilitation of the offender so that he or she will be able to return to society as a citizen in good standing. This chapter discusses the theory and the reality about the justice system in America.

To get some perspective about where we are now, it is necessary to observe some of the major features of the evolution of the justice system. In the colonial period there was no formal justice system as we now understand the term. There were no police, let alone police academies or police unions; no prisons, and certainly none that separated criminals from the mentally ill or the transient, or the young from the old; no juvenile courts, and no probation or parole as such. There was no plea bargaining (admitting guilt to a lesser offense and accepting official punishment to escape prosecution of a more seri-

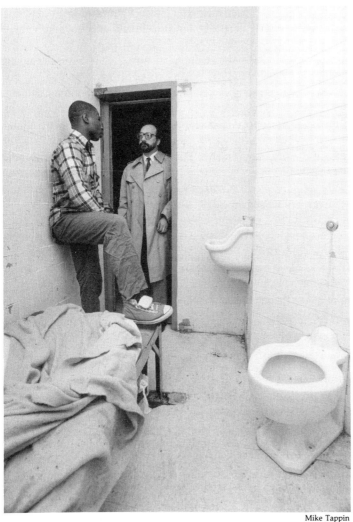

Mike Tappin

Here a social worker visits a young man in his jail cell. Crime does not pay, the idealists say. But in fact crime is big business, both in the scope and depth of people trying their luck at it (or being forced by circumstances to go into crime, depending on your views of causality) and those whose work concerns maintaining the justice system. The only group for whom crime does not pay at all are the victims of crimes; restitution, where it exists, rarely suffices.

ous one). There were no indeterminate sentencings that awaited signs of growth in prisoners before they were returned to society. There were no federal police, no social workers in the justice system, and nothing was done to prevent crime as such.

There were laws, but you might not recognize some of them. They included blasphemy (offenses presumed to be against God), which merited the death penalty in most colonies. Crime and sin were virtually synonymous in that religion-centered society (Walker, 1980). A 1650 Connecticut law stipulated that any 16-year old who cursed or hit his or her parents could be put to death. Walker (1980, p. 17) notes that offenders of the early 17th century could be placed in a lifetime of servitude, but that sentence was exclusively reserved for Indians captured in wars or for nonwhites, an early indication of the racist orientation in that system of justice.

There were juries, but they were unlike contemporary juries, since they ruled on both the facts of the case and the law itself. You might recognize the stocks or pillary as punitive devices. You might be more squeemish in front of the place where they whipped or branded certain offenders; all of these "dramatizations of evil" were intended to bring the community closer together.

The county sheriffs were probably as popular then as they were in Robin Hood's time. They not only enforced the law by responding to problems, but spent most of their time collecting taxes and handling much of the legal business of the county. The courts in colonial times served legislative and executive, as well as judicial, functions for the small-scale and diffuse social structures of the time. Justices of the peace were present (as they had been in English law for hundreds of years before), but they were political appointees and the justices were often untrained. On the other hand, there was no organized crime, no ghetto riots, no drug culture—although tobacco, perhaps the Indians' ultimate revenge, soon emerged.

All of these structural changes were to come, not easily, not without considerable struggle and hardship. The Amendments to the Constitution were an important step toward defining the concept of individual freedom and liberty, even though it took two centuries to refine this ideal in workable terms, with many discouraging setbacks along the way. These setbacks, threats to individual liberties, are ever present, which justifies the axiom that eternal vigilance is the price of freedom.

Beccaria: A Philosophical Basis for Criminal Justice

What led to the extensive system of justice that emphasizes the equality of all people before the law? Probably many factors were involved, such as the Enlightenment that sought rational ways to achieve democratic goals. One of the most significant influences on criminal justice during this time was the publication of an essay, on *Crimes and Punishment*, by Cesare Bonesana, Marquis of Beccaria (Italy), in 1764. (He is known in the professional literature as Beccaria.) The brief summary and excerpts that follow suggest why this essay stirred such universal excitement.

Beccaria begins with a statement of the purpose of an enlightened government: "The greatest happiness shared by the greatest number" (Beccaria, 1963, p. 8). (Jeremy Bentham read Beccaria and developed this idea into his philosophy of utilitarianism.) Laws are, or ought to be, "compacts of free men" (p. 8) who have united to form a society so as to attain these greatest goods. (This is another statement of the social contract theory that Hobbes, Rousseau, and others had developed earlier, whereby independent men were said to have given up part of their liberties to a sovereign in return for a peaceful society.)

But instead, Beccaria notes, laws have been, for the most part, tools of the passions of some, or have arisen to meet temporary needs. Laws relating to crime and punishment need to be logically reconsidered in light of the greatest happiness principle. Beccaria begins by noting that "punishments that exceed what is necessary for protection of the deposit of public security are by their very nature unjust" (p. 13).

One important consequence of Beccaria's rational approach is that "only the law can decree punishments for crimes" (p. 13). Laws should not be proclaimed by judges who wish, out of zeal or concern for the public good, to change the rules that legitimate authorities had written as part of the social contract. Rather, "for every crime that comes before him, a judge is required to complete a perfect syllogism in which the major premise must be the general law; the minor, the action that conforms or does not conform to the law; and the conclusion, acquittal or punishment" (p. 15).

Beccaria formulates a number of hypotheses throughout this work. They include: The greater the number of persons who can understand the law directly, the lower the frequency of crimes from these people, because " . . . ignorance and uncertainty of punishment add much to the eloquence of the passions" (p. 17). He also hypotheses that "the more promptly and the more closely punishment follows upon the commission of a crime, the more just and useful will it be" (p. 55). Likewise, he suggests that "the certainty of a punishment, even if it be moderate, will always make a stronger impression than the fear of another which is more terrible but combined with the hope of impunity" (p. 58) (that is, the possibility of escaping detection). Beccaria later applies this point in denying the usefulness of the death penalty, except in cases of treason.

Beccaria develops a systematic view of dealing with crime: "The strictness of confinement (i.e., pre-trial detention) should be no more than is necessary to prevent [the accused person] from taking flight or from concealing the proofs of his crimes. The trial itself should be completed in the briefest possible time" (p. 56). Regarding crimes, Beccaria sees the real meaning in "the harm done to society," and not in the intentions of the criminal because people's intentions are constantly in flux, and laws based on such intentions would have to be individualized for each citizen and for each crime (pp. 64-65). Such crimes differ in the seriousness of their harm on society, and therefore, punishment should fit the crime, that is, the category of seriousness to society, not the criminal. His own summary statement deserves careful consideration:

> In order for punishment not to be, in every instance, an act of violence of one or of many against a private citizen, it must be essentially public, prompt, necessary, the very least possible in the given circumstances, proportionate to the crimes, dictated by the laws (p. 99).

Beccaria gives most of his attention to crime and punishment, but leaves to the end his strongest point: "It is better to prevent crimes than to punish them. This is the ultimate end of every good legislation, which, to use the general terms for assessing the good and evils of life, is the art of leading men to the greatest possible happiness or to the least possible unhappiness" (p. 93). And how are we to prevent crime? "See to it that the laws are clear and simple and that the entire force of a nation is united in their defense. . . . See to it that enlightenment accompanies liberty. . . . Reward virtue. . . . Finally, the surest but most difficult way to prevent crimes is by perfecting education. . ." (pp. 94-98).

Beccaria recognizes that it is impossible to prevent all crimes. They increase "according to a ratio compounded of population and the crossing of particular interests, which cannot be directed with geometric precision to the public utility. For mathematical exactitude, we must substitute, in the arithmetic of politics, the calculation of probabilities" (p. 63). This is as clear a statement of the complexities of the social sciences as any that has ever been described. Although written more than 200 years ago, it still sounds as clear and vibrant as when it first appeared. It quickly influenced almost all of European criminal justice systems to greater or lesser degrees—except England, where the criminal code of that time began to grow worse, not more rational.

6:45 P.M.

Officer A receives a communiqué on his car radio to join two other officers to pick up a man by court order so that he can be taken to the state mental hospital for psychiatric observation. He has threatened to harm his ex-wife. A Vietnam veteran armed with a hunting rifle, he is considered dangerous. The three police officers meet at some distance from his apartment to map strategy. One goes behind the apartment house. Another stands with rifle at some distance from the front door while Officer A goes to the door and rings the bell. After a short conversation, the man permits the officers to enter his home and take him, hand-cuffed, to the hospital. He shakes their hands as they leave him, thanking them for being gentle. I am impressed at the amount of raw courage it takes to perform these ordinary assignments.

THE POLICE

The 19th century was a time of rapid change in America. Many innovations, borne out of necessity, were to become basic elements in the modern justice system. For example, night watchmen had long been employed to keep an eye on someone's property. As the population expanded and diversified, people in power saw the need to have day watchmen, the beginnings of the modern police. The model of the English "bobby" (named after Sir Robert Peel, the founder of the London police) was militaristic, with uniform, night stick and all. This led to the situations in which the local police officer was providing "street-curb" justice, interpreting the law on the spot, occasionally with the aid of his night stick. Enter police brutality. Initially, the police were chosen by local political leaders, which led in some cases to problems of graft and corruption. (See, for example, Lincoln Steffens, *The Shame of the Cities*, 1957.)

Reform was long overdue when it arrived in the early 20th century. The police became professionalized and were removed (somewhat) from local partisan politics. Leaders among the police, moreover, recognized their role in personal and social reform. For example, August Vollmer, head of the Berkeley, California, police from 1905 to 1932, called for police work to prevent crime as well as to prosecute lawbreakers. For police officers, this meant going into schools to work with high-risk youth identified by teachers. That innovation brought about others. They included appointing women police officers, creation of specialized police units, and early attempts to divert youth from the criminal cycle (Walker, 1980).

In our own day, experiments with the social work-like functions of the police have been extended to include specialized training in handling family conflicts, or having social workers ride with the police to the scene of marital disputes (Bard, 1970). (Police suffer more injuries in handling marital disputes than in any other setting.) Other social work-like functions may be called upon in cases of victimization—rape victims or child, spousal, or elder abuse, for example. Whether police officers should learn more of the skills of social workers, or social workers should more often work with, or even become, police officers, is a question not yet decided. But the need for such skills in police work is clear.

> **7:20 P.M.**
> *We are driving through some back roads, past scraggly corn fields, and wild underbrush. There are some small scattered houses and shacks—rural slums that city dwellers rarely see. In front of one house are several old cars, and around and on top of the cars sit a bunch of youths and some older men. I can see their eyes following the police car as we approach. Officer A slows down, rolls down his window, and gives them a friendly wave. They smile and wave back. Officer A rolls up his window and drives on. "They're a nice bunch of guys," he says in passing.*

THE COURTS

The most dramatic aspect of the courts, namely trials, are in fact the least common aspect of judicial services. Most convictions are obtained through plea bargaining between the prosecuting attorney (representing the state) and the defense attorney (representing the client). The judge is not legally bound to accept their negotiations, but usually does so in the name of expediency and cost savings (trials are very expensive for all concerned). But courts play a critical role in the criminal justice system. Their primary role is to interpret and apply the law to situations with justice and fairness to all concerned.

What is law? The English Common Law, from which much of our own laws are derived, comes from age-old rule-making agents such as church laws or the judicial precedents established in various local settings in attempts to resolve disputes peaceably. These local customs and procedures become codified to form a body of formal rules reflecting the norms of the society at that time. New decisions would amplify or modify the common law, but rarely would they make major changes in it.

New judicial structures evolved, as part of the system of checks and balances worked out in the American Constitution and its Amendments, which contain the broadest principles of law. From these flow the particular laws or statutes generated by authorized legislative bodies. When cases are brought before the courts, these bodies interpret whether or not the statutes conform to the letter and spirit of the Constitution and other laws that follow from it. They also interpret whether or not administrative regulations that direct particular role holders to perform certain actions are legal.

Statutes (from federal or state legislative bodies) and ordinances (from counties or communities) are categorized into codes that represent the current body of law for a given jurisdiction. Each jurisdiction interprets its own laws, but should one party to a case disagree with the local decision, that party may appeal the case to higher courts and, ultimately, to the Supreme Court, the highest court in the land. Typically, each state has some form of the three-layered court system like the federal courts: a supreme court, courts of appeal (appellate courts), and district trial courts. Depending on the size of the community, there may be other divisions at the trial level, such as traffic courts, family courts, and the like.

Crimes are divided into categories. Felonies are the more serious crimes, such as the violent crimes of murder, assault, rape, armed robbery; the nonviolent crimes include theft and burglary, forgery, and the so-called victimless crimes, like gambling and prostitution. Felonies are punishable by jail sentences of a year or more or large fines or both. Misdemeanors comprise the category of lesser offenses, like traffic violations; these are subject to fines and short jail sentences.

One of the enduring value conflicts in criminal justice involves the question of law and order versus freedom from excessive interference in one's personal activities. Both are important to a democratic society; it is how they are balanced that is the critical issue. A series of U.S. Supreme Court decisions in the 1960s and 1970s combined to increase the rights of individuals in relationship to the police and the courts. The accused had to be informed of their right to remain silent and warned that their statements might be used as evidence against them, and they had to be told that they had the right to receive an attorney's counsel when criminal charges were being made, at public expense if necessary (the Miranda rule). The decision of *Mapp* v. *Ohio* (1961) recognized the rights of individuals in all states and municipalities: it was held that the Amendments to the federal Constitution applied to other jurisdictions.

These and other aspects of due process procedures in the criminal justice system are a page out of Beccaria's book: Definite limits and guidelines are set up on how governments shall investigate offenses and conduct trials, given the fundamental premise that a person is innocent until proven guilty. There are still questions on whether we have reached the limits of due process, as it appears that receiving justice depends on one's social characteristics as well as one's criminal acts. For example, the issue of posting bond as a guarantee that one would appear in court was class-linked and affected the poor more heavily than the rich. The poor were more often kept in jail since they could not afford to post bond. Research by the Vera Foundation in the 1960s showed that people could be trusted to appear on their own word, without the imposition of bail bond. Now, except for major offenses, people are usually released on their own recognizance to await trial.

NETWORK OF CORRECTIVE AND REHABILITATIVE INSTITUTIONS

Many sources led to change in the array of institutions of detention, correction, and rehabilitation. The English reformer John Howard made a scathing attack on the state of the prisons of his day (1777). Yet, more important was his suggestion that we not only had to restrain criminals in prisons, but we also had to help them to be constructive citizens by teaching them a useful trade. This reflected Enlightenment views that criminals could be reclaimed to society by rational means.

About a decade later, Pennsylvania led the colonies with a new criminal code that combined punishment and rehabilitation. It led to the establishment of the first state prison, the Walnut Street Jail in Philadelphia, since public "dramatizations of evil" did not seem to be improving the moral fiber of the community. Thus began the long series of experiments to balance punishment and rehabilitation, in and out of institutional settings, that continue to our day.

The design and location of prisons also changed over time. Jails in large cities were often dreary, overcrowded, unsafe, stacks of barred cages, with little to do and nowhere to go—the Tombs, a New York City jail, is well-named. Prisons, often built in rural areas, were equally bleak and far from the homes and families of the prisoners as well, thus increasing the problems of maintaining linkages with family and friends.

Prisons—variously described as "(1) cafeterias of remediation efforts, (2) hotbeds of violence, (3) schools of crime, (4) concentration camps for the disadvantaged, and (5) repositories of revolutionaries" (Toch, 1977, p. 6)—are in fact complex institutions that seek to perform possibly contradictory functions for a society holding differing views on the ultimate purpose of these facilities. It is useful to consider the current—indeed, perennial—controversies if we are to understand how prisons fit into the larger criminal justice system.

First, some numbers: There were more than a half-million adults (528,945) in prisons and jails in 1986, as reported by the U.S. Justice Department. Included were 44,330 persons in federal prisons, about 8 percent of the total. There were 25,192 female inmates, about 5 percent of the prison population. Another 75,000 youths are held in special juvenile facilities (Sherman and Hawkins, 1981). In 1986 most adult inmates (51.7 percent were white, 45.3 percent were black, 1 percent Native American, and the remainder, from other ethnic groups. Relative to their proportion in the total population, blacks are overrepresented in the prison population.

These figures disguise an important phenomenon: about six million adult jail admissions of various lengths of time are recorded in a single year. Another one million juveniles are detained for short periods of time during a single year (Sherman and Hawkins, 1981, p. 1). Clearly, prisons, jails, and juvenile facilities are a big business, one that most people would prefer to forget.

Prisons are costly too. About $40 billion was spent on correctional services in the 1970s (Sherman and Hawkins, 1981). One new maximum security cell costs between $30,000 and $60,000, while it costs another $7,000 to $10,000 for annual maintenance of an inmate in that cell. And when indirect costs, such as lost income from not working, are included, a figure of $50,000 a year over a ten-year sentence has been estimated (Sherman and Hawkins, 1981, p. 2). If imprisonment is viewed as an end-stage of services to people convicted of crimes, then it seems perfidious not to invest equivalent funds in research and services related to crime prevention.

As in many other social issues, there is a continuum of opinions on what should be done. The liberal position usually suggests preventive proposals that involve social and educational programs whose effect is to be felt in the long run. The conservative position usually suggests punishment programs for the current offenders, more prisons, and larger police forces. That position seldom takes into account the past lack of correlation between retribution and decreases in crime rates, and it does not give sufficient weight to what actually happens. Most prisoners are eventually released, whether or not they have received aid in becoming good citizens.

Prisons are heavily influenced by fads and crises emerging from singular violent incidents, for they are part of a criminal justice system that is often politicized. "Despite a rash of ostensibly tough laws regarding sentencing, the actual time served in prison has not lengthened substantially even in those jurisdictions where politicians have made capital on their hard-nosed approaches" (Sherman and Hawkins, 1981, p. 3).

Efforts were periodically made to provide some meaningful activities for prisoners, including involving them in paid labor (which was often opposed by unions) and offering opportunities for education and for religious and artistic expression. These were and continue to be secondary, however, to the major functions of prisons, as holding places for undesirable persons.

Prisons have been given little attention from the public. At various times, reformers attempted to break down the large prisons into smaller units, particularly when only minimum security was needed. Cottages were built for youthful offenders, in an attempt to humanize the experience. Other experiments were tried, such as Bentham's Panopticon—a circular arrangement of prison cells that could be watched by a central administrative unit—and vice versa. In spite of the various designs and locations, prisons tended to be total and oppressive institutions, out of the sight of the good citizens and out of mind, in spite of the best efforts of a continuing series of reformers.

Some of the more important innovations had to do with diverting people from entering such institutions, or getting them out as soon as possible. Probation was a vitally important addition to criminal justice workings. It involved suspending the sentence of a convicted offender subject to his or her obeying various requirements such as being under the supervision of a probation officer, limiting contact with "bad influences," and holding a steady job. Parole was another important dimension in the changing picture of criminal justice. By receiving conditional releases from prison based on "good behavior" and other predictive factors, the offender was enabled to return to the community to resume a normal life, subject to various requirements; they include seeing a parole officer regularly, keeping out of trouble with the law, and the like. It is important to note that about three-quarters of all offenders are on probation or parole; thus these programs represent our dominant approach to corrections (Johnson, 1986, p. 255).

Community-based corrections includes a number of types of programs that house offenders in nonprison settings so as to minimize the stress that prison life itself creates, which in turn acts as an impediment to their rehabilitation. This is an important point, given the increasing rates of crimes and the general fearful public reaction to it. However, since 95 percent of imprisoned offenders will be back in the community sooner or later, whatever the form of incarceration, it had better be done in such a way as to optimize chances for their civil behavior.

Other programs include diversion of first-time offenders away from the correctional institution (to prevent stigmatizing or traumatizing them, and thus making it harder to change them into useful citizens). Diversion may take place from the moment a police officer chooses to lecture a person rather than arrest him or her; or it may take place more officially, at other points during the adjudication process. Recently, plans for restitution have been used whereby the offender restores, so far as possible, the losses of the victim, or performs public services as repayment to society. Seeing what damage they have caused, and helping to repair it, appears to be an important and rehabilitating lesson for some offenders.

Other opportunities include combinations of confinement and freedom, as in work-release programs. These are useful because the offender who is restricted in everyday activities as retribution for the crime can continue at the same time to earn money for his or her family. It is possible to use one or another of these alternatives, individualized to fit the circumstances of the offender and the prediction of what controls and freedoms would be most helpful in the resocialization process.

8:10 P.M.

While driving past the state mental hospital, Officer A swerves to avoid hitting three men walking across the highway with beer bottles in their hands. He turns his police car around and drives toward the men, who have tossed the bottles into the woods. (It is illegal to drink in public in this community.) He steps out of the car and orders the three to stay where they are—some 15 to 20 feet away. He asks what their names are and radios this in. One man argues with the policeman and starts to walk toward him. Officer A orders him to stop and stay where he is; he then calls the state hospital on his radio to see if these men are patients. They are. Within minutes, two more police cars pull up, plus a police car from the hospital. The men are loaded into the hospital car and they are driven off. This maneuver is a matter of jurisdiction. Strictly speaking, Officer A could make an arrest, but because they are so close to the hospital grounds, he thought it would be better to let the hospital staff handle this violation of rules.

CRIMINAL JUSTICE PROCESS: IN THEORY

A complex process has been established in society's attempt to protect the innocent and to prosecute those accused of crimes. Social workers as well as all citizens should have a clear sense of the steps in the process. The following overview of the federal criminal justice process is presented with the recognition that each state and jurisdiction may have some variations from this general process. Practitioners must learn the specific formal paths by which accused persons are taken through this adjudication process in their own localities. In addition, there are informal aspects of justice, such as the quality of one's defense attorney, or the orientation of the judge, or the political aspirations of the prosecuting attorney. Each of these factors, when relevant, powerfully affects the formal structure of justice. For further details, see Alpert (1985); for a discussion of the flow of events in juvenile justice proceedings, see Pappenfort and Young (1980).

The configural context for any given action, such as a criminal behavior, involves personal factors interacting with relevant primary groups, secondary groups, and cultures, in a physical environment at a given time in history. Many theories have been put forward to explain causes of criminal behavior. They include the physiological explanation (the "born criminal" of the 19th-century writer Lombroso, or the more recent sociobiology version), the psychological (such as the psychodynamic interpretation of uncontrolled Id impulses), or the socio-cultural (such as Sutherland's theory of differential association, in which one learns criminal behaviors from one's primary associates). The social work perspective of the person-in-the-environment requires consideration of several of these dimensions. (See Johnson, Bird, & Little, 1979.)

Steps in the Adjudication Process

1. The first step of the justice process is the *committing of an act that is criminal* according to legal codes of the given community and time. Ignorance of the law is no excuse; it is the behavior that counts.

2. *Gatekeepers* (members of the public or the police themselves) bring notice of criminal acts to police attention.

3. There is an *investigation* by the police. Certain options are available, depending on their findings: (a) An arrest may be made; (b) further investigations may be called for; (c) the investigation may lead to the case being dropped; (d) the jurisdiction for handling a case may be switched to a more appropriate place (either federal or state/local); or (e) as part of the next step, a warrant for the arrest of a known suspect may be issued.

4. An *arrest* is made. Either the suspect is taken directly into custody if observed in a criminal act (or if there is reasonable certainty thereof), or a complaint is filed by the arresting officer and a warrant for the arrest is issued by the state, based on probable cause. When the suspect is found, he or she is then taken into custody. The arresting officer is required to inform the accused of his or her rights, including having legal counsel, and being informed that what is said may be used as evidence against him or her.

5. The *booking*. Once in custody, the accused person's name, address, place of the crime, nature of the charge and related information is entered in the police log, along with fingerprints and photographs. This is supposed to take place in a short time so that the accused can be taken to a judicial officer to be formally charged.

6. The *charge*. The state's judicial officer (usually the prosecuting attorney or an assistant) must decide whether or not to make the formal complaint—a charge that the accused has committed a specific offense defined in the criminal codes—based on adequate evidence and in the best interest of the community. Options include: (a) continue the adjudication process; (b) reduce the

charges; (c) accept a guilty plea from the accused; (d) drop the case for lack of sufficient evidence or reliable witnesses. If a charge is made, then other options occur: (e) the accused may be released on his or her own recognizance (ROR), or (f) bail may be set (intended to ensure the person will show up at trial), or (g) the accused may be held in jail if he or she cannot post bail, or if the prosecutor refuses to permit bail because of the nature of the case or the known reputation of the accused.

7. *Court-determined probable cause.* This may be determined in one of two ways, depending on local rules: either by a *grand jury* or by what is called *information* (a document of charges formally filed by the prosecutor to the court). If the grand jury decides that there is *probable cause* (not guilt), or if the court accepts the information presented by the prosecutor, then the case proceeds to arraignment for trial.

8. *Arraignment* in the court of original jurisdiction. An arraignment means that the defendant is appraised of the formal charges against him or her and about matters to do with the trial. There are options at this point: (a) plea bargaining may take place between the defense attorney and the prosecuting attorney or (b) the parties may proceed to a trial.

9. *Adjudication.* After some possible pretrial motions are settled (e.g., to have the charge changed or the jurisdiction moved), the trial itself is held, either before a jury or, in nonjury trials, before a judge.

10. *Pre-sentence investigation.* Assuming that the defendant is found guilty but before the sentence is pronounced, an investigation is made as to the circumstances of the defendant that is to help the judge or jury decide what sentence would best serve the purposes of justice in regard to the defendant as well as of the community.

11. *Disposition.* The judge or jury sets the sentence. Options include: (a) a fine and/or restitution to the victim (or more likely, to the community at large); (b) probation and/or community services; (c) incarceration at an appropriate correctional facility; and (d) capital punishment, in 38 states where it is permitted for certain crimes. Sutherland and Cressey (1970) have estimated that about three-quarters of all judicial penalties take the form of fines, which offer the advantage of being a punishment adjustable to the scope of the crime and require little administrative machinery (especially in comparison with imprisonment or probation), while providing some funds for the state. Zastrow (1986) notes that fines discriminate against the poor, for whom a given dollar fine represents a larger share of their available wealth than it does for a middle-class person. He describes a Swedish plan that reduces the discrimination by assigning fines in units of whatever amount of pay per day a person receives.

12. *Supervision of the sentence.* Supervision can be done by the court through its probation officers in accordance with the restrictions set by the judge on the probationer. Or supervision may be carried out at the correctional institution.

13. *Release* from an incarceration may occur through *parole* (under the jurisdiction of a parole board completely separate from the court), or by having served one's time. Some inmates are conditionally released before the end of their sentences to a halfway house, a type of correctional facility in the community that helps to aid their reintegration back to society.

This process is intended to be largely rehabilitative, an attempt to put back the social pieces after a crime has occurred and the offender apprehended and tried. After the inmate has been released, he or she is in principle back at the beginning of the process. Should the person commit another crime and go through another adjudication process, this would constitute recidivism, which represents a failure of the criminal justice process to affect the offender in a constructive way.

9:05 P.M.

A call comes to Officer A in code: Go to a particular address for a certain type of problem. Officer A turns the car around and proceeds rapidly to the destination, while translating the code as being a marital dispute that threatens to become violent. Mr. and Mrs. B live in a cluttered house trailer at the end of a washed-out dirt road on the outskirts of town. Officer C has arrived first and is attempting to separate the couple. Mrs. B claims that her husband burned her with his cigarette; Mr. B denies this and says that it was just an ash that fell on her. Also, he shouts angrily that the police should get out of his house. Officer C calmly explains that this is an official call and that they cannot leave until they are certain no one is going to get hurt. The B's three-year-old daughter stands in the middle of the room, thumb in mouth, looking first at her parents, then at the police, and then at the TV, which is on at top volume.

Mr. B is directed to sit on the couch and calm down. He does so, complaining about the intrusion into his home. Meanwhile, Mrs. B is going about the room picking up clothing and stuffing them hurriedly into a clothes basket, preparatory to leaving with the child. Officer A tries to talk with her, but she is alternately crying and yelling at her husband. Finally, she picks up her purse and the child in one arm and the basket in the other, pushes out the front door, and drives off in a shiny new pickup truck.

Back in the police car, Officer A sighs out of frustration for not being able to make any headway with the couple, even though violence has been averted.

CRIMINAL JUSTICE PROCESS: IN PRACTICE

The *theoretical* process of criminal justice has been described—the steps by which persons who actually commit acts that are illegal are identified, brought into the criminal justice system, and brought to some resolution. Now it is time to look at the *realities* of that process. The fine analytic work of Hans Zeisel (1982), who has clarified some of its major features, deserves careful consideration, particularly because of his controversial conclusion: "law enforcement by itself is relatively powerless to control crime" (p. 5).

Zeisel's study was conceived in 1972 to test the assertion by the New York City police commissioner (Patrick V. Murphy) that, while many components of the justice system were not working as effectively as they might, the courts, in particular, were neglecting to punish guilty offenders. As evidence, Murphy pointed out that of 136 felony charges for criminal possession of handguns, not one was convicted of the original felony charge; only 53 were imprisoned on some other charge, and then only for an average of one month.

Zeisel used two data sets for his analysis. The first was a probability sample of 1,888 felony arrests (out of 102,000 made in 1971 by police in New York City, excepting Staten Island) in which records were studied for the disposition of these cases. A second probability study of 369 defendants of felony charges (1973) involved the same search of records plus interviews with the major justice participants in each case (the arresting officer, the prosecutor, the defense counsel, and the judge—but not the offender). Because New York City seems so exceptional in so many ways, Zeisel compared relevant crime statistics with other American cities as well as with some foreign countries. It turns out that New York City is not very different and that what we may be seeing is how criminal justice is processed in western nations in general. The magnitude of the American crime situation may be unique, however. Comparing New York City with London and Tokyo (cities of comparable size), for example, the following emerges:

	London (1975)	Tokyo (1973)	New York City (1973)
Homicides	110	196	1,680
Robberies	2,680	361	72,750

America is simply a more violent nation, as measured by these crimes.

But the most striking findings from Zeisel's study are the discussions of the "attrition of law enforcement." In his analysis, he traces the index felonies—those found in the federal uniform crime reports (homicide, rape, aggravated assault, robbery, burglary, auto theft, and other grand larceny)—from the time an illegal event was committed to the time a person was sentenced to prison (p. 18). The process of attrition is dramatic. Of 1,000 felonies committed:

540 are reported to the police, of which
 65 arrests are made, from which
 36 are convicted, with
 17 of these sentenced to custody, of which
  3 receive prison sentences over one year.

It looks as if Police Commissioner Murphy's accusation against the courts was valid, but Zeisel examines the process more closely. First, the number of felonies committed is actually an estimate based on a victimization survey, not specific felonies reported to the police. This survey was conducted by the Law Enforcement Assistance Administration in 1975. It involved a probability sample of potential victims—individuals, households, businesses, and institutions—regarding the crimes they had experienced in the preceding year, whether or not they were reported to the police. Based on these figures, Zeisel projected the numbers of actual felonies to be about double the reported ones (46 percent unreported to 54 percent reported, pp. 94-95). For example, about 73 percent of auto thefts are reported, probably because insurance is involved, while only 41 percent of aggravated assaults are reported, perhaps out of fear of reprisal. Thus the first point to be made is that the public is involved in a major way in the first-step attrition, in not reporting crimes to the police for one reason or another.

The next step, from reports to the police to arrests, involves another large attrition (from 540 events reported to the police to 65 arrests of persons—who may have been involved in multiple events). This represents an arrest rate of about 12 percent. When nonindex felonies are included (such as narcotics crimes), the arrest rate rises to 20 percent. Why is it that only about one in five felons is arrested? Zeisel reports that arrests are higher for the violent personal crimes (homicide, assault, and rape—about 47 percent arrested including 78 percent on homicides and 41 percent on rapes), while it is lower for nonviolent property crimes (about 8 percent arrested). Daniel Glaser (1975, pp. 79-80) calculated that although a robber has only a 1 in 5 chance of being arrested for any one offense, the probabilities are 9 in 10 of being arrested at least once if he or she commits 10 robberies. Hollywood detective images to the contrary, most police arrests come from police being on the scene at the time of the crime or being called very soon thereafter—about 56 percent of the total number of arrests. (Another quarter of arrests are due to the suspect being identified by the victim who knew him or her, p. 32).

Attrition also occurs when cases of arrested persons are dismissed when at the criminal court, some 44 percent of the total arrested. Why should this occur? Part of the answer lies in the structure of the American criminal justice system whose components have different standards of operation. Zeisel points out, for example, that the amount of evidence sufficient for arrest is different from the amount of evidence required for conviction (p. 109). Cases are dismissed for various evidentiary considerations, such as the complaining witness withdrawing the complaint. Zeisel presents many examples, such as the grandfather who returns home to find his son and grandson ransacking his apartment. In outrage he has them arrested, but he does not show up at the hearing to press charges.

Of defendants convicted in the criminal courts, 98 percent were the result of a guilty plea; only two percent are tried, of which about one percent are convicted. Most of these guilty pleas are preceded by some bargaining with the prosecutor, a unique American institution. The general public and especially the victim find it difficult to accept this mix of justice and bargaining. The Supreme Court has declared plea bargaining "necessary, beneficial, and legal" (p. 127), however. The rationale made for such bargaining is that it speeds the justice process and reduces costs (trials are very expensive for everyone). Two kinds of bargaining can occur: reductions in the crime charges or reductions in the expected sentences. In 60 percent of the cases, Zeisel notes, the evidence supporting the arrest deteriorated after arrest but before trial. When that occurred, there was an average of 2.8 crime-class reductions as a result of plea bargaining—that is, the defendant's class of crimes was dropped to a less serious class in exchange for a guilty plea (there were nine such crime classes in New York at that time). Where no deterioration of evidence occurred, the reduction was 1.6 crime classes. Regarding reduction of sentences, it turns out that those who plead guilty receive lower sentences than those who do not, raising some ethical issues about the structure of justice. (Indeed, a defendant may legally offer a guilty plea along with a protestation of innocence, p. 39.)

The bail system represents another sticky issue in the American criminal justice system. Only one-third of all persons arrested on felony charges are kept in pretrial detention—most of them because they cannot afford bail fees. Zeisel reviews the important studies by the Vera Institute of Justice which show that bails had been set too high for too many people who would appear in court anyway and many of whom could be exonerated. Those studies helped judges to release more defendants on bail—bail-jumping rates have not changed since the easing occurred.

For these and many other reasons, Zeisel looks ultimately beyond law enforcement in the criminal justice system, to prevention:

> The power of law enforcement is limited not only because its reach is small but also because it comes too late. It is late in two respects: it acts only after the event, and it confronts the lawbreaker at a point in his life when it is usually too late to change course. That is why law enforcement alone can never solve the crime problem. . . . Crime, as we saw, begins early in life, and we must make a radical effort to reach these youngsters early in life before their life-style is formed (Zeisel, 1982, pp. 84, 86).

So, once again, when faced with a persistent social problem, a profound student of the issue has suggested primary prevention as society's ultimate and necessary course of action.

> **11:35 P.M.**
>
> *Officer A has just driven up to the sixth all-night fast food store. I didn't realize this small town had so many. He observed the store from a distance for a few minutes; everything is very visible inside. We see two customers, one at the counter, the other in the food section. The clerk is talking with one customer as the second person brings some goods to the counter. The customers pay their bills and leave. Officer A gets a wave from the clerk who notices him, and he waves back and drives off. While driving onto the highway, Officer A suddenly puts on a burst of speed, makes a quick turn, and turns on his siren briefly. He then follows a truck onto a side road. Everything happened so quickly that I didn't realize what was going on. The policeman stopped twenty feet behind the truck and put his spot light on, blinding the driver who was getting out and making his way toward the police car. Officer A ordered him (by loud speaker) to go back to his truck, while he checked the license with headquarters. Satisfied with the report, he got out, talked with the driver for a few minutes, and then returned. The driver had not stopped at a stop sign when crossing the double highway. He got a ticket.*

RACE AND GENDER IN CRIMINAL JUSTICE

One of the explosive questions in the criminal justice arena involves the relationship of race—and racism—in the commission of crimes and in arrests and punishment. The facts are clear. Zeisel's (1982) study showed that about 9 out of 10 persons arrested for a felony were male, nearly 8 out of 10 were under 30 years of age, and three-quarters belonged to ethnic minorities. The immediate inference is that ethnic minorities typically are poor and, therefore, rates of felonies should be related to poverty or low educational levels. However, Silberman (1978) notes that New York's Puerto Rican population is more poor on the average than its blacks; Puerto Rican New Yorkers also have had less education than blacks and hold a higher proportion of menial jobs. Nonetheless, the rates of crime committed by members of those ethnic groups are very different. Zeisel notes that 53 percent of the arrested felons in his study were black, 23 percent Hispanic, and 24 percent white. Silberman (p. 120) reports that blacks commit violent crimes three times more often than do Puerto Ricans, and robberies more than four times as frequently, a pattern that is repeated in other American cities as well. Why should this be the case?

Silberman (1978) offers a grim historical analysis, reflecting on the violence that has been part of the black American's life before and after slavery. He writes:

> To understand black crime, in short, is not to condone it. Understanding is essential; unless we comprehend the reasons why black adolescents and young men commit so many acts of criminal violence, we are not likely to find effective remedies. But to excuse violence because black offenders are the victims of poverty and discrimination is racism of the most virulent sort; it is to continue to treat black people as if they were children incapable of making moral decisions or of assuming responsibility for their own actions and choices. "There is no surer expression of superiority than to treat people primarily as victims," the *Washington Post* columnist William Raspberry has written. "There is no more crippling an attitude than to think of yourself primarily as a victim." For "victimism," as Raspberry calls it, teaches black children "to see themselves not as intelligent beings with the capacity to shape their own destinies but as victims of a racism they can't do anything about. . . . (p. 162)."

James Q. Wilson (1975) has argued that attempts to reduce poverty or discrimination have not produced any reductions in crime, in particular, street crime. He points to the 1960s when major social change programs were instituted to reduce poverty and discrimination—and yet crime rates reached new heights. "Creating a war on (poverty) means we create an army of social workers or poverty fighters or crime fighters and pretty soon the maintenance of that army turns out to be more important than winning the war" (Wilson, 1977, p. 44). His solution is to send more convicted felons to prison and to build more prisons if necessary.

It has been well-documented, however, that when an immigrant ethnic group moves from the lower to the middle class, involvement in street crimes drop (Silberman, 1978) as do rates of mental illness (Albee, 1983). Among blacks, many gains in civil rights were made during the 1960s, even though unemployment rates were high. Whether the war on poverty was won or lost, or even fully waged, is a debatable question. We clearly do not have the best answers to deal with crime (or poverty or many other persisting social problems), although we must continue to seek optimal answers. The complex set of social forces interacting with the personal experiences of individual minority group members makes it difficult to understand, let alone change, these patterns of behavior.

Women's roles in the criminal justice system are poorly understood by the public, and are complicated by stereotyped views held by professionals. Clarice Feinman's (1980) book, *Women in the Criminal Justice System*, provides a remarkable review of the literature of women as criminals, corrections officers, police officers, lawyers, and judges. The first policewoman was Alice Stebbins Wells, a social worker who dealt with women and children in trouble with the law. She believed that having police powers would make her more effective than working through a charity agency. She received her appointment to the police in 1910 by a mayoral act and proceeded to formulate a policy of engaging in crime prevention as well as protective work with women and children. This view was common along policewomen until the 1960s. She met with much hostility in her new role, but she and later policewomen won respect by effective work.

Many forms of discrimination were present, however. "Quotas were set on their presence on police forces and restrictions on advancement—it took court cases to change this. Women officers also suffered various kinds of harassment, sexual and otherwise. But performance studies, such as one done by the Vera Institute of Justice in New York City, demonstrated that women performed as well as men (p. 80), and were likely to treat women victims and offenders more sympathetically than men (p. 81). While the future for policewomen seems encouraging, there is a call for women to work with women victims and offenders, just as minority policemen are often asked (and often want) to work in minority communities. These very strengths may serve to limit advancement opportunities for policewomen.

JUVENILE JUSTICE SYSTEM

The pendulum swings toward harshness or toward leniency in dealing with crime are most clearly seen in the juvenile justice system. From the earliest colonial days to the beginnings of the Republic, juveniles were essentially chattel or property of their parents. Parents had some obligation to support and educate their children, but their primary obligation seems to have been religious—to break the willfulness of youth for the sake of their eternal salvation. The 19th century saw two contradictory tendencies emerge. One involved the establishment of institutions for juveniles (such as houses of refuge) required either by their own anti-social deeds or by the lack of family willing and able to care for them. The other tendency was a noninstitutional "child-saving" in the form of removing homeless children from "dangerous" conditions of the big city and sending them to farm families in the west to live and to work. The latter activity, sponsored by the Children's Aid Society of New York, founded in 1853 by Charles Loring Brace, was very controversial, especially because there was little inspection to ensure good living conditions for the children. (See Charles Loring Brace, *The Dangerous Classes of New York and Twenty Years' Work Among Them, 1872.*)

The pendulum swung again at the beginning of the 20th century when the first juvenile court was established in Chicago, signifying a legal tool for social reform. Most of the other states followed within two decades. From the beginning, juvenile courts were proclaimed to involve treatment and rehabilitation rather than punishment. One prominent juvenile judge in 1909 said that the goal of the court was "not so much to punish as to reform, not to degrade but to uplift, not to crush but to develop, not to make him [the delinquent] a criminal but a worthy citizen" (quoted in Silberman, 1978, p. 310). To accomplish this, judges of the juvenile court took the position that they were acting in the role of a wise parent. As such, they did not need to observe the formal due processes adults had to protect their liberties, since the judges were on the side of the juvenile. It meant, further, that offenses could come to the attention of the juvenile court that would not be crimes if committed by adults; these are the *status offenses*, including incorrigibility, truancy, and running away from home—as well as all the other adult crimes.

A whole new vocabulary is needed to differentiate adult courts from the juvenile ones that operate in the "child's best interests." Juveniles (generally, persons under 17 years of age, but this varies by state) are said to be *taken into custody* or *referred to the juvenile court*; they are not arrested as such. (Juveniles under the age of 17 may be tried in adult courts for serious felonies.) Unlike adults, juveniles may not obtain bail. If they are not screened out at an intake process, they then go into a pretrial detention. At the court, a *petition* is filed on their behalf. It states the reasons for their appearance at the court and is used in place of the formal charge for an adult criminal. A private hearing without a jury is held during which the young person can make an admission of guilt (rather than pleading guilty in an adult court). Or the case may be presented with a prosecutor, but without a defense counsel (this was changed in an all-important Supreme Court decision, *In re Gault*, to be discussed below); the judge was to act on behalf of the youth. If the judge makes a finding of delinquency, the youth may be subjected to several possible dispositions: He or she might be placed in some formal or secure institution (such as a detention center); in an out-of-the-home placement in a nonsecure setting (such as a foster home); on probation (the youth continues to live at home but is supervised in his or her community activities and might receive counseling); or a lecture might be administered by the judge before the child is sent home under the control of the parents (cf. Pappenfort and Young, 1980).

Remember that many reformers (including Jane Addams and other prominent social workers) labored mightily to change the harsh 19th-century criminal justice system in which adults and juveniles went through the same court proceedings and were often imprisoned in the same jails. In spite of the treatment orientation stated in the juvenile court's philosophy, however, many abuses occurred. For example, status offenses were treated more punitively than were burglaries or other delinquent acts. How can we account for this anomaly? Silberman (1978, p. 336) cites a former president of the National Council of Juvenile Court Judges to the effect that juvenile judges look for the meaning of what the child has done and what the child is likely to do in the future rather than the current offending behavior. But such predictions have little accuracy, leading to idiosyncratic handling of cases. Juvenile detention centers have as unsavory but well-earned a reputation for violence and sexual abuse as do adult prisons. As Justice Fortas noted in the *Gault* decision, the child receives the worst of both worlds: he gets neither the protections accorded to adults nor the solicitous care and treatment children were supposed to be receiving.

Starting in 1967, much of this changed. A Supreme Court decision, *In re Gault* (1967) (387 U.S. 1), overturned the basic philosophy of the juvenile court. Young people, as well as adults, must be protected by the due process clauses of the Fifth and Fourteenth Amendments. This means that all persons accused of crimes have a right to adequate notice of the charges against them; to the assistance of legal counsel and advice; to confront and cross-examine witnesses; and to protection from the use of forced confessions (Castelle, 1987, p. 17). Juveniles could not be institutionalized or otherwise punished arbitrarily.

Further court decisions and laws were needed to clarify the due process rights for juveniles and to reform the juvenile court itself. The important Juvenile Justice and Delinquency Prevention Act of 1974, for example, provided financial incentives for states not to incarcerate status offenders; new alternative service programs were to be offered, so as to divert youths away from the criminal justice system. (Already-incarcerated status offenders were to be released from correctional institutions as well.) Hawkins and Doueck (1987) describe the community-based services that emerged from this federal initiative, such as youth service bureaus, group or foster homes, halfway houses, and adolescent units in psychiatric hospitals—seeking the least restrictive setting in which to help young persons continue to remain in their ordinary community as much as possible while receiving services.

> One evening, just past the dinner hour, I telephoned a young man whom I have never met. (This happens each day at random times.) The conversation is short. I simply ask how his day has been—"well, not so good." Why?—"had an argument with my girlfriend. But I sort of got it straightened out." I make note on a log sheet of the time of the random call and a brief notation of its substance as part of a court-designed home monitoring system for youths placed under house arrest rather than in detention centers. Such youths agree to certain rules; one is being only at school or home or work at specified times. Random phone calls confirm whether they are living up to their agreement while awaiting their hearing. This arrangement allows them to remain out of an institution—and, indeed, supports the parental controls over their children. It is cheap (using volunteers as callers) and effective (few violate these house arrest contracts).

Stehno (1987) describes the parameters of the juvenile court world. Of the 1,348,000 cases handled by juvenile courts (1981), 661,900 were characterized as property crimes, 248,300 were status offenses, 206,000 were offenses against the public order, 159,000 involved crimes against people, and 72,800 were violations of drug laws. (Also 185,200 child dependency cases were handled by the juvenile courts.) Of these cases, about half were resolved without a formal petition of delinquency being written. Of those who were formally adjudicated by the juvenile courts, Stehno notes that half were placed on probation, while a fifth were sent to some form of institution. She notes that nearly 72,000 juveniles are likely to be in a secure institution on a typical day

(1981), while four times that number will be on probation or parole (the after-care services given to youths who had been incarcerated).

Pappenfort and Young (1980) conducted a study of the use of secure detentions for juveniles—that is, the incarceration of juveniles waiting for a hearing before a juvenile court—and the various residential and nonresidential alternatives to such detention. They found that detention for juveniles was overused and inconsistently applied among different jurisdictions and that there was a lack of appropriate alternatives for juveniles who needed supportive supervision, but did not need detention as such. Jails continue to be used as detention centers, especially in rural areas. (Also see Cronk, Jankovic, and Green, 1982.) The 1974 Juvenile Justice and Delinquency Prevention Act sets among its major goals the reduction in the use of secure detention and the provision of alternatives to detention. Pappenfort and Young visited 14 such alternative programs. Some of the conclusions they reached are reported here.

The residential and nonresidential program formats appear about equally able to keep assigned youths trouble-free—that is, committing no new offenses and not running away. This is not to say that any group of delinquents can be placed successfully in any type of program, nor that alternatives to detention are always successful. But well-conceived nonsecure residential programs can retain youths who have run away from home, at least temporarily. Such alternative programs require the close cooperation of other social agencies in the community. Home detention programs have been successful with delinquents and with some status offenders, although care has to be taken with those whose conflicts are with their own families. Secure detention was essential for a small proportion of alleged delinquents who appear to constitute a danger to others (pp. 90-92).

Pappenfort and Young provide brief descriptions of the alternative programs. One example is Attention Homes, a concept that originated in Boulder, Colorado. "The term attention, as distinct from detention, signifies an environment which accentuates the positive aspects of community interaction with young offenders" (p. 73). These include enough structure for the necessary control of the juvenile, but in a homelike atmosphere where the youngsters can be given individual attention. When the youths arrive (usually referred by a juvenile court officer and formally accepted by the houseparent), they are restricted to the house for three days and spend time talking to houseparents about the problems that brought him to the Home. They earn more free time off the premises by cooperation at the Home, and later continue to attend school or work in a county-sponsored program. College-student volunteers organize evening and weekend activities with the youths, and the houseparents meet weekly with the juvenile court judge and probation staff to discuss progress for each youth in residence (p. 75). Pappenfort and Young find the Attention Home format very adaptable to the needs of less populated jurisdictions where separate programs for special groups may not be feasible (p. 91).

Rowdy behavior of adolescents is a common theme, from Augustine's *Confessions* to the latest Sunday supplement, and has worried adults (especially parents) from time immemorial. Ages-old folk wisdom and the most current scientific pronouncements agree that prevention is far better than cure (treatment or rehabilitation). And so it should come as no surprise that many preventive programs have been instituted. What might be surprising is the information that practitioners have continued to use a wide array of programs and approaches that have been almost *completely unsuccessful* in yielding positive results.

A monograph by Johnson, Bird, and Little (1979) documents the empirical basis of different theoretical approaches or practice methods related to preventing juvenile delinquency. Briefly summarized, they offer five categories:

I. Category of rejected approaches (i.e., those lacking defensible theoretical and empirical bases): Included would be theories on the biological bases of delinquent behavior; personality differences distinguishing delinquent and nondelinquent youths; programs focusing on individual characteristics of delinquents such as individual psychotherapy, group counseling programs, and academic educational programs; and theories that emphasize environmental deprivations (e.g., broken homes or minority status).

II. Category of empirically rejected programs: Included here are behavior modification programs which have not been designed to be generalized beyond the treatment setting; wilderness program; family therapy; recreational programs; employment training programs that lack real employment possibilities; and the detached worker projects.

III. Category of programs of questionable merit based on evidence to date: Includes the use of teacher ratings to identify predelinquents; or programs focusing on parents of infants.

IV. Category of programs that offer limited benefits at substantial costs: Includes program instructing parents to use social learning theory to reduce troublesome behaviors in pre-puberty children.

V. Category of programs promising broad and lasting benefits at moderate costs: These include programs that change policies of organizations involving youth, such as modifying ability groupings in schools to reduce inappropriate labeling and to increase opportunities for more youth to have successful experiences that demonstrate their usefulness and competence.

A recent contribution to the community-based efforts in delinquency prevention is the interesting work of Feldman, Caplinger, and Wodarski (1983). This study involved combining antisocial youths with prosocial peers in youth-center activity groups led by experienced and inexperienced leaders using either behavioral, traditional group-work methods, or a minimal treatment method. Over a three-year period, some 1,000 youngsters were involved in this complex project that involved multiple objective measures; clearly, this is a research and demonstration project that requires careful study. The findings can be summarized briefly, for present purposes: The mixed groups yielded favorable outcomes for the antisocial youths with few adverse consequences for the prosocial ones; experienced leaders were more effective than inexperienced ones; and the behavioral group methods were somewhat more fruitful than the traditional or minimal methods. The details of the interrelationships—that is, what group dynamics were operating in these mixture of prosocial and antisocial youth—provide important hints for further study. Moreover, the authors indicate that not only were the results largely positive, but that the costs were relatively low, thus indicating that group work methods provide a cost-effective tool in dealing with the prevention of delinquency in the community setting.

> **MIDNIGHT:**
> *After filling the tank with gas from the municipal station, Officer A drives back to police headquarters. He has several hours of reports to complete—he is the officer in charge this night. I take my leave with thanks for the interesting experiences, and he says, "Oh, it was a quiet night."*

Let's look more closely at how one helping professional works with clients within the juvenile justice system. Notice both the typical social history material and the special format required by the justice system. This blend of social work and host agency procedures is typical in any field of practice in which two or more professions work together.

A Case Study: Laurie's Conflictive World

Laurie McAdams is a 13-year-old girl going on 25. She is attractive, petite, and bright, but she is also a very mixed-up teenager. Laurie's story, as revealed in case records of a juvenile court, is illustrative of several points: first, how juveniles enter the justice system; second, what happens to them and their family and friends during this process; and third, what part counselors play in assisting the court to provide justice with humaneness.

One spring night, Laurie was talking on the telephone to a friend. The conversation went on and on, and eventually her mother asked her to get off the phone so she could use it. Slowly and reluctantly Laurie relinquished the phone, but her mother did not make any calls. This led to an argument like those mother and daughter frequently had, but this one escalated. Laurie struck her mother with a tennis racket. The next day the mother was at the juvenile court, once again asking for help in dealing with her daughter whom she felt was beyond her control. On this occasion, the mother charged the daughter with assault.

Della McAdams, the mother, had asked for assistance on several earlier occasions. Each time the court responded by arranging for counseling, which seems to help—for the time being. On this occasion, the court found the juvenile "not innocent," and placed her under house arrest, which meant that she was obliged to be either at school or at home and under her mother's orders—or else she would be subject to placement in a detention center.

Laurie was insolent at the court hearing. She was defiant of the judge and all the other adults now in her life. Moreover, she looked slovenly, dressing in a manner more like a streetwalker than a junior high school student. (In fact, soon she was breaking the house arrest contract by skipping school and staying out late—and even away from home for several days at a time, presumably with the older men that she was seeing at that time.) The Judge ordered a home evaluation and a social history as part of the proceedings. The following is a brief (disguised) summary of the social history, prepared by the court service unit counselor after a long and careful conversation with both mother and daughter. The basic details are listed briefly in the following Fact Sheet.

SOCIAL HISTORY FACT SHEET

JUVENILE COURT OF X DISTRICT   COURT DATE: 7/5/88   COUNSELOR: Mrs. Carswell

NAME: Laurie McAdams   DATE OF BIRTH: 7/11/75   SSN 123456789   RACE: white
HAIR COLOR: brown   EYE COLOR: blue   ADDRESS: 123 Trouble Lane
CUSTODY IS HELD BY: mother   CHILD LIVES WITH: mother   CURRENTLY IN DETENTION: yes
DATE PLACED: 7/10/88   OFFENSE: assault   PRIOR OFFENSES: none   PREVIOUS TREATMENT
BY COURT UNIT: none   OTHER AGENCIES INVOLVED: Welfare Dept. (food stamps; subsidized apt.)

HEALTH INFORMATION

GENERAL HEALTH: good   PHYSICAL HANDICAPS: none   PAST HEALTH PROBLEMS: asthma (controlled)
PRESENT HEALTH PROBLEMS: nothing significant

SCHOOL INFORMATION

SCHOOL: East Junior High   GRADE: 7th   CHILD'S ATTITUDE TOWARD SCHOOL: likes school
PARENT'S ATTITUDE TOWARD SCHOOL: generally satisfied   BEHAVIOR REPORTED BY SCHOOL STAFF:
good student but absent too often   CURRENT GRADES: above average in every subject
ATTENDANCE: poor; absent 1-2 days a week in spring semester but kept up grades in spite of this
EDUCATIONAL HANDICAP: none

BEHAVIORAL INFORMATION

OVERALL BEHAVIOR PATTERN: bratty, uncooperative   RELATIONSHIP TO PEERS: poor; associates
with older teenagers   ATTITUDES TOWARD AUTHORITY: defiant, manipulative
MENTAL HEALTH: normal

EMPLOYMENT INFORMATION

EMPLOYMENT STATUS: not working

INFORMATION ON MOTHER

NAME: Della McAdams   AGE: 40   ADDRESS: 123 Trouble Lane   MARITAL STATUS: widowed
EDUCATIONAL LEVEL: high school   EMPLOYMENT STATUS: working   EMPLOYER: fast food deli
OCCUPATION: waitress   MONTHLY INCOME: $145 from job and $202 from Social Security=$347
COURT RECORD: yes   MOST SERIOUS OFFENSE: assaulted neighbor

INFORMATION ON FATHER

NAME: Frederick McAdams   AGE: deceased   EDUCATIONAL STATUS: high school
OCCUPATION: was auto mechanic   MONTHLY INCOME: wife receives his Social Security--$202 mo.
COURT RECORD: yes   MOST SERIOUS OFFENSE: DWI

FAMILY INFORMATION

NUMBER OF BROTHERS: 1   NUMBER OF SISTERS: 0   PEOPLE LIVING IN HOME: 3
RELATIONSHIP BETWEEN FATHER AND MOTHER: mother reports it to have been good, but with tensions,
especially over his indulgent behavior toward children
RELATIONSHIP BETWEEN FATHER AND CLIENT: Mother reports very warm relationship; Laurie deeply
affected by her father's death two years ago

(continued on back)

SOCIAL HISTORY FACT SHEET (continued from other side)

RELATIONSHIP BETWEEN MOTHER AND CHILD:_____conflictful_____

RELATIONSHIP BETWEEN CLIENT AND SIBLING:__good (brother is about six years younger than Laurie)

PARENTAL NURTURANCE OF CHILD:__highly inconsistent; over-protective one minute and hostile/cold

___the next; parenting skills very limited_____

PARENTAL CONTROL OF CHILD:_____nonexistent_____

PARENT'S VIEW OF CHILD'S BEHAVIOR AT HOME:__out of control, even with house arrest_____

PARENT'S ESTIMATE WHEN PROBLEM BEHAVIOR BEGAN:__after Mr. McAdams died of emphysema at age 48

SIGNIFICANT FAMILY OCCURRENCES DURING PAST YEAR:__some recurrence of Mrs. McAdams mental prob-

__lems; she had been institutionalized for depression when Laurie was an infant_____

FUNCTIONING STRUCTURE OF FAMILY:__disorganized_____

FAMILY INCOME:__$347 per month (not including housing subsidy and food stamps)_____

HOME AND NEIGHBORHOOD INFORMATION

SIZE OF HOME:__2 bedroom, 1 bath____TYPE OF STRUCTURE:__single family_____

CONDITION OF HOME:__fair_____TYPE OF NEIGHBORHOOD:__lower income_____

FAMILY'S VIEW OF NEIGHBORHOOD'S IMPACT ON CHILD:__positive_____

COUNSELOR'S VIEW OF ITS IMPACT ON CHILD:__neutral_____HOME OWNERSHIP:__rental____

COUNSELOR'S COMMENTS (date 7/1/88):

Review: Laurie was brought to the Court's attention because of her assault on her mother, the culmination of a long and difficult relationship ever since her father died about two years ago. Laurie's early sexual maturity led her to associate with older men, against her mother's wishes. She has been increasingly estranged from her mother, and while she has done well in school grades, she has also been absent frequently.

Mrs. McAdams has had a difficult life. Orphaned at an early age, she spent almost all of her childhood and adolescence in institutions. She met her husband-to-be on a blind date and married him within the month, thus escaping the orphanage. But her depression, especially after Laurie's birth, led to another institutionalization at the state mental hospital. Her mental stability has been somewhat precarious much of her adult life, but she has held her current job (waitress) for the past six years. Her husband was generally supportive of her, but had a sharp tongue and frequently put her down with references to her past mental illness. (She reports that the daughter now does the same thing, almost using the same words as her late husband.)

Because of Mrs. McAdams' own personal problems and her limitations as a parent--she has her hands full with her younger son and her work schedule--we recommend the Court consider foster family placement for Laurie for six months, with her status to be reviewed regularly thereafter for whether she has gained sufficient self-control to return to her mother--as well as whether her mother is less mentally frail and has learned some parenting skills. (Mother will be invited to join a parenting group, and possibly counseling as well.) We recommend a firm but loving foster family; Laurie needs clear limits and higher expectations set in order to make better use of her schooling and talents.

ADDITIONAL COMMENTS (date 10/5/88)

The Court agreed with the counselor's recommendation. A suitable foster family was located and Laurie has been doing very well. She is dressing more neatly and in a fashion appropriate to her age. Laurie is also socializing more with peers in her class at school. She visits her mother on some weekends, but is well ensconced with the new family. Her school attendance has improved and her defiance of authorities has been toned down. It is not clear whether it is in Laurie's best interests to be returned to her mother, or whether she should remain longer with this effective foster family. The mother has refused counseling and did not attend the parenting classes; the Court counselor has given her some informal counseling because she felt Mrs. McAdams was growing increasingly depressed at the course of events and was not able to cope with the situation. Regular reports will be made to the Court concerning progress in this case.

SUMMARY

Where do we stand with regard to the criminal justice system? The great emphasis in criminal justice has been on dealing with persons who have already committed crimes in a mixed-motive attempt to both punish and rehabilitate them. Centuries of results suggest that we have yet to perfect an after-the-crime approach that reduces rates of crimes or recidivism.

Relatively recently, many efforts have been directed in a preventive direction, such as diverting youths showing signs of antisocial behavior into more constructive pursuits, or in promoting alternatives to illegal or harmful activities. However, the low success rate in preventing juvenile delinquency has been discouraging, in spite of occasional successes (cf. Johnson, Bird, and Little, 1979).

One has to view criminal justice within the American tradition and history—a tradition of independence required in rugged frontier life and of criminal punishment meted out by vigilantes; the glorification of violence through the mass media; permissiveness regarding private purchase of assault guns and other violent weapons; the entrenchment of sophisticated mobsters, extensive networks of white collar criminals and the toleration of petty theft at early ages; the apparent double standard of justice, one for the rich, the other for the poor; and the legal status of corporal punishment in schools and harsh child discipline methods used by many parents. Finally, America's rates of violence and criminal behavior are among the highest in the world. It is hard to practice criminal justice in such a context.

In spite of these difficulties and frustrations, criminal justice has attracted a large number of dedicated workers in every aspect of its administration—men and women in blue on the front of lines of violence; jurists balancing protection of society and the rights of each citizen; corrections officers attempting to aid the inevitable transition of the vast majority of law breakers back to a citizen status in the community. For other workers in criminal justice, it may be simply a job, and, at its worst, some in authority may use their status in harmful ways. But at every point in criminal justice—except perhaps in the primary prevention efforts—we are dealing with difficult-to-work-with people or situations that make life difficult for such people. It is not an easy career, although it can be rewarding when one can observe constructive outcomes.

Clearly, in spite of perhaps the most extensive theoretical bases in the applied social sciences, and possibly the most elaborate empirical findings available, the criminal justice field of practice is still in need of fresh ideas and hardy workers. Social work, with its systemic perspective of person-in-the-environment, represents an excellent beginning point for entrance into this field of practice.

OUTLINE

CHAPTER SIXTEEN

Occupational Social Work—
A New/Old Field of Practice

Work is such a central part of everyday life that we tend to take it for granted—until some crisis emerges such as becoming unemployed or encountering difficulties on the job because of drinking or marital problems. Relief may be in sight as a new field of practice, occupational social work, enters the marketplace to help both to prevent problems and to help treat those that have emerged. Occupational social work developed from a long history of concerns about the workplace, from the 19th-century welfare capitalism (where businesses and industries performed some of the same welfare functions that government does today) to the most recent employee mental wellness programs. This chapter focuses on the current major expression of occupational social work—Employee Assistance Programs (EAP).

LIFE AND DEATH OF A SALESMAN AND THE ORGANIZATION

It is presumptuous to suggest that some Great Therapist could ever talk away the even Greater Existential Dilemmas that playwriters have presented to us. A *New Yorker* cartoon depicts a death scene from *Othello* or some such tragedy. Two members of the audience are talking in the balcony. They suggest that all of this could have been prevented if only the king and queen had consulted a therapist in Act 1!

Presumptuous or not, it is also true that real life situations are every bit as complex and messy as those dramatists so grandly stage. Consider Arthur Miller's American classic, *Death of a Salesman* (1949/1967). This is the story of Everyman, American working-class version. Willy Loman has been a salesman for the same firm for 36 years. Never a brilliant success, he had his occasional bright spots. Willy believes that salesmanship is a matter of projecting one's personality, of "riding on a smile and a shoeshine" (p. 138) and lives his life and dreams to match. As Willy gets older and less successful, his boss (the son of the original owner of the firm) has reassigned Willy to less fruitful territories with inevitable results. Finally, the young manager fires Willy because it is no longer profitable to retain him on the payroll.

The play opens as Willy is coming home to his family, a man with his dreams dashed and his spirit crushed. His two sons have come home as well. Biff, the older son, 34 years old, has recently returned from the west, where he has been a farmhand for the past decade. Happy, his 32-year old brother, is employed in a minor managerial capacity in town and spends his free time as a Don Juan. As teenagers, both boys idolized their father, whose flashy words spurred them on to believe great things about themselves. Willy's faithful and supportive wife, Linda, is always mending silk stockings (a subtle mark of at-the-edge-of-1930s poverty).

Willy idolizes his teenage sons for what they can achieve as much as they worship him. As youths, both sons (and especially Biff) engaged in small thefts, with the covert encouragement of their father. "I gave them hell (for stealing some lumber Willy used to repair his house) understand. But I got a couple of fearless characters there," Willy tells his friend, Charley, who replies that the jails are filled with fearless characters.

Biff is the symbol of Achievement Unfulfilled. Star football player at high school, he fails a math class in his senior year and never took the scholarship he had to the university. The reason, we later learn, is at the heart of the play: Biff paid a surprise visit to his father to inform his hero of his failure in math and to ask his help to "talk" to the teacher (talk away the problem). But Biff was profoundly shocked to find Willy had been unfaithful to his wife. There was a woman in a black slip in his hotel room, someone to whom Willy had been giving silk stockings. All that is buried in the past, and comes to the surface in bits and pieces as the play proceeds.

Lack of achievement has not stopped Willy from bragging about his sons to an old friend, Charley. But Charley's son, Bernard, once a young admirer of Biff's at school, went to college and to law school, and is at this moment on his way to argue a case before the Supreme Court. Bernard did not even mention it to Willy, who is stunned as Charley tells him: "He (Bernard) don't have to [talk about his achievements]—he's gonna do it" (p. 95).

Willy's family has also shared that great American Dream, as filtered through the lens of the traveling salesman. It is a family life of bravado and deception, dazzle without intimacy. Linda comprehends some of Willy's misery. His eventual suicide comes as no surprise to her.

Each of the sons reacts to the growing crisis in a different way. Happy, the younger son, understands nothing of his father's life or death; he holds a belief in the same allusive dream. Biff, returning after years of absence, tries to please his father once more by getting financial backing from a former employer (from whom he had stolen some basketballs) in order to float an idea Happy has for making a pile of money in Florida. But the bubble bursts, and Biff comes closer to the reality of his life and that of his family than he has ever come. "I am not a leader of men, Willy, and neither are you," Biff explodes at his father. "I'm [worth] one dollar an hour, Willy! I tried seven states and couldn't raise it." But truthful communication at this late hour is too painful for Willy, who replies to Biff: "you vengeful, spiteful mutt!" (p. 132).

On the day of the suicide, Willy has just made the last mortgage payment on the house. That evening he had gone out into the garden in the dark to scratch around, desperately trying to plant seeds.

If only Willy and his family had seen a therapist in Act 1. . ., we would not be as rich in the insight that his fictional life and death provides. But suicide is real; it is a serious problem for elderly men, and recently, for increasing numbers of adolescents, and for young black adults. Unfulfilled family life, marital problems, uncompleted schooling, unfocused career plans, and so forth, are also serious problems—both to the individuals involved and to the rest of us. We are all members of one society, and the unproductivity and unhappiness of one part eventually has repercussions on all the other parts of the system.

It can be said that Willy showed signs of considerable strength. He continues to plug away as a traveling salesman, even as he is given poorer sales territories. Other persons in similar stressful circumstances might have succumbed to alcohol or other substances that deaden the hurt. Myers (1985) notes that 20 percent of employees in the United States have personal problems that cause job performance deficiencies in attendance, conduct, productivity, work quality, and safety. He further notes that troubled employees cause as much as 75 percent of all job-performance problems, are a major source of internal occupational crimes, and require excessive amounts of expensive health benefits and paid sick days. The story of Willy Loman is played out every day on the stages of businesses and industries across the country, with theme and variation.

This chapter introduces a new product in the therapeutic marketplace, called occupational social work. (As we will see, it is actually an old approach to helping with some new improved ingredients that one hopes will make it more effective.) Occupational social work involves helping, but not therapy in

Work not only creates products or services, but it also structures our lives and shapes the kinds of people we become and the kinds of lives we lead. The helping professions realize that physical and mental health problems for individual workers and their families may emerge in the office or the factory. Some businesses, unions, and agencies have formed employee assistance programs to help workers and their families; these have become a new field of practice for social workers.

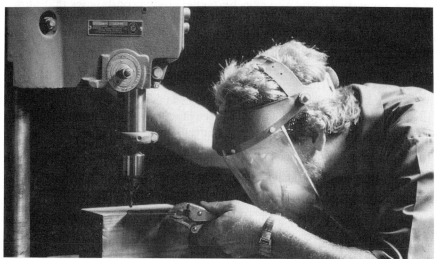

Courtesy Virginia Commonwealth University

the conventional sense. Instead, occupational social work takes into consideration employees like Willy and his family, as well as the employing business or industry, before as well as during life crises and occupational problems. In the play, we can see Willy and the series of life circumstances, some of his own making, others reflecting changes in the occupational world and society—the whole of which represents the full configuration of problems. Ordinary therapy is far removed from most of these circumstances—the grind of always being on the road, the noise and the heat of the factory, the computerized monotony of the white collar worker—but because many of life's problems and potentials originate in, or are expressed through, the opportunities of the workplace, it is a logical place to begin helping. So it is that we encounter a field of practice, occupational social work.

SCOPE OF THE PROBLEMS AND POTENTIALS OF OCCUPATIONAL SOCIAL WORK

It is very difficult to provide exact figures for the scope and depth of occupational problems, such as alcoholism or drug abuse.* Scanlon (1986) offers estimates in the range of $15 to $20 billion annually for each, a total of between $30 and $40 billion in productivity losses, lives lost, futures forfeited, and unnecessary accidents (p. 2). These figures do not include the impact of the problem on the lives of those most closely associated with substance abuse. He also reports a recent study that indicates that women account for one-third of all cocaine users who need treatment (pp. 3,7). Problems at the workplace appear to be an equal opportunity experience.

Masi (1982) reports studies which show that about 10 percent of the average work force are active alcoholics, 2 to 3 percent are drug addicts with either legal or illegal drugs, and 6 to 7 percent are emotionally ill. These people perform at about 75 percent of their capacities (p. xiv). Masi (1984) later notes that mental and physical illness attributable to occupational stress is estimated to cost business and industry about $20 billion a year in the white collar area alone (p. 2). She also cites two other studies: one shows that illness caused by poor nutrition costs employers $30 million annually; the other estimates that the cost of cigarette smoking to the country (in 1976) was $27.5 billion, of which $19 billion was attributable to lost productivity (p. 134). Altogether, these cost figures total something like $70 to $80 billion in largely preventable losses. That is enough to make the most tough-minded business person sit up and take notice.

Myers (1985) expands the list of causes of employee deficiencies; in addition to substance abuse (alcoholism and drug abuse), he includes family and

---

*The term "user" refers here to someone who uses a substance; in this sense, some 70 percent of Americans are users of alcoholic beverages on occasion. A "problem user" is one whose use is problematic on a given occasion to himself or others; the sense of the term is that the problem occurs rarely and without any clear pattern. An "abuser" is one whose use is problematic on a consistent or repeated basis. Technical and legal definitions of substance abusers are complicated and sometimes inconsistent, as when different state laws define driving under the influence of alcohol by different percentages of blood alcohol elevations.

marital problems, legal difficulties, personal financial problems, stress, and compulsive gambling.

Vaught, Hoy, and Buchanan (1985) provide an overview of the broad area of employee development. Many factors have required rethinking about how to make work meaningful by involving the worker in his or her job. Factors include lagging productivity, increased international competition, technological change, legal pressures to employ more minorities and women, and, in particular, the well-studied phenomenon of worker dissatisfaction. For each factor, the question is how to increase worker satisfaction and productivity. This critical point is made in Herzberg's subtitle to his book (1982), *The Managerial Choice: To Be Efficient and To Be Human.*

A cost-effectiveness-conscious business world has rapidly awakened to the usefulness of programs that deal with problems at the work site. Scanlon (1986) notes that in 1959 there were 50 occupational alcoholism programs in place; by 1973, there were about 500 such programs; and by the later 1980s, the number was over 8,000 (p. 22). The various types of occupational services is a "growth industry" for helping professionals, if only they would recognize the import of these national trends. Cost-effectiveness studies of companies that use employee assistance programs are generally encouraging. Scanlon (1986, p. 99) cites such cases as General Motors, which had a 72 percent reduction in the dollar amount paid for accidents and sickness disability benefits as a result of its EAP program, a $3 benefit for each $1 of cost (see also Lawton, 1985; Skidmore, et al., 1974).

Occupational social work (OSW) is probably the most recent field of social work practice. OSW refers to an array of practices that originate in order to serve clients who are employees of some organization and who face some problem (e.g., alcoholism, marital difficulties) or potential (e.g., reduced risk of heart disease, more fulfilling family life) that may affect the worker and his or her family and friends. Such problems or potentials, moreover, affect both the organization (e.g., productivity, community image as a responsible employer) and the individuals (e.g., worker morale, family life satisfaction). Because conceptualization, research, and practice in this area are relatively recent, there is little agreement as to practice definitions or parameters of OSW, its evolutionary development, or its appropriate value posture. We will rely heavily on several recent books in this discussion, particularly the excellent work of Googins and Godfrey (1987), Masi (1984, 1982), and Shain and Groeneveld (1980). Myers (1985) is especially useful for its separate analyses of chemical dependence counseling (Lawton, 1985); others concern counseling employees with legal problems (Rasnic, 1985); family and marriage problems (Brown, 1985); family financial problems (Bagarozzi and Bagarozzi, 1985); pathological gambling problems (Myers, 1985); and the preventive management of stress (Quick, et al., 1985).

Traditional social work has provided services directed at individual problems mentioned above (except such issues as productivity and corporate image building), but it is the context of dealing with these problems and potentials as a whole that constitutes this new field of practice. As with medical or school social work, the social worker in an occupational setting is a visitor at a host agency, and thus is obliged to follow the general rules of the involved organizations—the business itself and possibly a union, if present. But business, unlike public schools or community hospitals, seeks to make a profit by producing a saleable product or service within a competitive marketplace. Such a capitalistic orientation has been foreign to the main stream of social work since its inception in charitable and voluntary organizations; however, the vigorous and controversial activities of private social work practice is certainly entrepreneurial. The conservative national political climate, starting with President Nixon and extending through terms of Presidents Ford, Reagan, and Bush, supported reduced federal and state funding of social work programs. That, in turn, required such programs to seek support from new sources—including the business world.

Social work has had a love/hate relationship with the business world, while business has only recently found much lovable about social workers. The next several decades will likely see the continuing growth of OSW, many new experimental forms of practice, and a host of new structural relationships between business and the helping professions—and continuing controversy as both partners sort out the practical aspects of this marriage of convenience.

WHY THE OCCUPATIONAL WORLD NEEDS HUMAN SERVICES FOR ITS EMPLOYEES: AN HISTORICAL OVERVIEW

The reasons for the recent emergence of occupational social work are many, and they require an historical context in order to appreciate the current state of affairs and possible future developments. (See Masi, 1982; Googins and Godfrey, 1987). Consider a business—any business organization within a capitalistic state: It requires some organization of people working together to generate a product or service by changing raw materials (either physical objects or ideas) into new and usable forms, and then marketing these within a competitive environment to potential buyers for a profit, and thus continue the operation. As businesses develop, so too do the organizational structures among the cooperating individuals involved. Herein lies the drama of the workplace.

The industrial revolution involved the development of machines within factory settings, and required large numbers of operators who lived nearby. This, in turn, spawned large urban areas made up of former rural peasants. Old relationships, such as those between master and apprentice, dissolved in the new social structures. No longer, for example, did the foreman in the factory have responsibilities to educate his many youthful employees, as did the master to his apprentice. Overall, it was an owner-dominated situation. They set the (low) standards of wages and the (poor) work conditions, while ignoring any community responsibilities. The goal was to make as much profit as possible. They established these conditions under religious and philosophical banners that justified their actions—laissez-faire capitalism combined with the Protestant Ethic and, later, social darwinism.

Soon there were many voices of complaint. They ranged from the laborers themselves as expressed in strikes and in the formation of unions to social commentators and reformers including some from within the business community itself, such as Robert Owen. The 19th century, however, was essentially dominated by powerful business interests while worker misery escalated—as Karl Marx, William Booth, Jane Addams, and many others documented.

The post-Civil War era saw some important developments of programs sponsored by business—there was almost no governmental aid to workers until early in the 20th century. It is critical to understand these business-supported social services because we are currently expanding on some of them and because the ethical issues they raised are still with us. Jane Addams bears some responsibility for promoting business-oriented social service, in some cases at the expense of the development of unions. Her responsibility is not well known, but the direction set has left a residual of ill-will that has required years of effort to undo. (See Googins and Godfrey, 1987).

The history of occupational social work may be conveniently summarized under seven headings (following the work of Googins and Godfrey, 1987; Masi, 1984; and others). These events often transpired concurrently, with phases of blossoming and withering.

1. *Welfare Capitalism and "Social Secretaries."* In 1887 the H. J. Heinz Company of Pittsburgh hired Mrs. Aggie Dunn as "social secretary," the first welfare worker in the business world. She hired, counseled, and in general watched over the well-being of the large number of young women employees who worked in the factories. The role of social secretary was only one aspect of the many programs American businesses created in the late 19th century to ensure healthy and productive workers; the emphasis was clearly on maintaining the workers as productive cogs in the business system.

Like the successful utopian conditions Robert Owen established several generations earlier in Scotland, the American form of early welfare capitalism included building houses for workers; schools for their children; and church and recreation centers for the family. Competitive businesses also established medical care, pensions and retirement systems for their workers, and they attacked the alcoholism prevalent in that era. All of those welfare-like services were provided without government aid and under the aegis of economic paternalism. As Robert Owen had done, services were handed from the top down, often without choice by the workers. In providing such business-sponsored services, moreover, early businessmen could deflect the development of the fledgling unions. (This is what Jane Addams supported in several instances.)

2. *The Rise of Unions.* Unions did emerge, however, after some ineffective starts. Unions of specific craftsmen had existed for centuries in the form of guilds and, later, benevolent associations that aided members at critical lifetime junctures such as funerals. With the rise of industrialism, new forms of association were needed, particularly to counterbalance the enormous force that employers could bring to bear on individual employees. The history of unions is a cyclic affair. Great celebrations on unity are mixed with some depressing dissolutions attributable to the forces of management and governmental opposition and occasionally to the incompetence of union leaders themselves. There were also trends ranging from the special craft unions (AFL) to the general unions (CIO) and from anti-union legislation and court decisions to pro-union legislation and supporting judicial actions. Each step of these changes required great efforts by the involved parties to bring about movement—or to oppose it.

Googins and Godfrey (1987) note that at no time in American history was more than 30 percent of the work force unionized. The 1982-83 *Statistical Abstracts* reports that the median weekly earning of unionized men exceeded nonunion members, $318 to $249; the median weekly earnings of unionized women also exceeded nonunion members, but the rates were much lower, $191 to $129, respectively (Table 673). Specific union actions on behalf of their members' wages, working conditions, job security, health benefits, and pensions have had repercussions across the entire occupational scene, although not to the same extent as in unionized settings.

The major turning point in contemporary labor/management relations came in the 1930s as the basic legal mechanisms for collective representation and bargaining were set. Later legislation set some limits, but the overall balance seems to be holding, with shifting setbacks or advances, depending on the particular political leadership of the time.

3. *The Replacement of Social Secretaries by Personnel Departments and the Beginning of the Demise of Welfare Capitalism.* The paternalistic system of welfare capitalism is perhaps most vividly illustrated by the "company towns," in which the business organization owned everything, sold everything, and ultimately became creditor to every one in the small mining or milltowns. A folk song refrain, "I owe my soul to the company store," captures the irony and pathos of being dependent on the business for both salary to pay for foods and services, and the foods and services themselves. Unions began to resist such paternalistic efforts as being a cover for rampant exploitation of workers. Eventually, the hiring and welfare functions of social secretaries were taken over by personnel departments who dealt with employees in a less paternalistic manner about wages and benefits, as well as rights and responsibilities of workers. As equipment and operations became more sophisticated, the required level of education and training of workers rose, and so more skill in recruitment and training were needed. These signaled the beginnings of great shifts in the relationship of labor and management.

4. *Changing Political-Economic Conditions: The Rise of Fringe Benefits as a Second System of Remuneration.* Cycles of economic prosperity and depression, as well as periods of peace and war, mark American history. When such combinations of events occurred to produce shortages in trained laborers, businesses would offer additional nonfinancial benefits (like use of the company car for personal use) or indirect financial benefits (such as paying for the employee's health insurance) on top of the direct financial returns. When there was a wage and price freeze in World War II, the only way employers could attract and hold valuable workers was through an elaborated fringe benefit package. Because of the conditions of modern life (such as expensive health costs), it is necessary for a prospective employee to consider carefully both the financial and nonfinancial packages of benefits.

Some commentators note that fringe benefits have become so large— approximately 25 percent of the wage dollar (Herzberg, 1982, p. 56)—and burdensome to the companies that they are unrecognized threats to the economic health of the firms. One large firm discovered, for example, that it was spending more for health benefits than on raw materials to produce its wares. Masi (1984) reports that in 1983, U.S. companies paid $77 billion in health insurance premiums—that is more than those companies paid in dividends.

From the perspective of social well-being, this means that business and industry are deeply involved in providing services and benefits for their employees as well as earning profits for their investors. Recent negotiations on contracts have seen cutbacks on fringe benefits so that, it is argued, the firm can remain competitive. More modifications in fringe benefit packages may be expected.

Be that as it may, fringe benefits constitute a significant portion of the individual's social well-being, a part of the welfare-and-well-being-system not covered by federal or state governments. Both aspects of organizational functioning, wages and benefits, are important to recognize. One part is not "good" while the other is "bad." This is simply a choice that America has made—some would say, stumbled into—on how to provide social well-being for its citizens. As changes are made in fringe benefits, an obvious question arises: what part of the social system is covering these diminishing services and benefits for the worker and his or her family's health, education, pensions, and the like? Likewise, a fundamental question emerges as to the optimal level of benefits and services needed by workers and their families to achieve the triple goals of organizational productivity, individual well-being, and national enhancement?

5. *The Beginnings of Problem-Specific Programs within Businesses: The Example of Occupational Alcoholism Programs (OAP).* Business people have long been aware that the health and healthy functioning of their workers are critical to successful production or services. An historic problem, alcohol abuse has been present in American society from its beginnings. Hard-drinking and independent people were corralled in urban areas by the pressures from industrialization, and were required to follow rigid work schedules that were antithetical to their cultures and previous experiences. This produced problems for employers as well as the workers' families. Early employer efforts were often a mix of moralism and economic pragmatics: Shape up or be fired.

As companies became more sophisticated by employing doctors and nurses to examine workers for disability benefits, a new stage was begun in assessing alcoholism and treating it. But the company doctor was often suspect by workers, and so, in the 1940s, the first occupational alcoholism programs (OAPs) were formed with the specific purpose of reducing the sizable losses (in absenteeism, turnover, illness benefits, and internal crimes) caused by alcoholism. The OAPs used job performance as one criterion by which symptoms of a worker's alcohol problem could be recognized by his or her immediate supervisor. But usually front-line supervisors were involved in diagnosing employees, so higher-level staff were rarely identified (Masi, 1984, p. 8).

Generally, a "constructive confrontation" (Roman and Trice, 1972) or a "tough love" approach was used to make employees face the drinking and work-related problems, while at the same time showing concern for their well-being and offering them the opportunity to get help, for example, from Alcoholics Anonymous (AA). AA had gained prominence by the 1940s as an effective support group that advocated the method of controlling a person's alcoholism by total abstinence through its members' support and group pressure. In addition, the powerful leverage of the job was seen as important in making an impact on the addiction, when other factors, including family and self-esteem, seemed unable to lead to control of the problem.

Alcoholism was always complicated by related personal difficulties. Occupational alcoholism programs tended to be evangelistic, which alienated business people. At this same time period (the 1950s), a disease model of alcoholism emerged that viewed the alcoholic as a person with a physical disease over which he or she had no control, and thus was not responsible for the resulting problems. As a disease, alcoholism was worthy of treatment, not abuse. Masi (1984) recognizes the confusion this definition generated. How is one to confront a person constructively about a physical disease over which he or she has no control? Eventually, a view emerged that saw alcoholism as a predisposition to a disease or as a psychological addiction that can cause a physical disease, in which case intervention and threat of job loss is justified through personnel actions, not medical treatment as such. This view led to a new approach, the employee assistance programs.

6. *The Beginnings of Broad-Spectrum Programs in Business and Industry: The Employee Assistance Program (EAP), or the Employee Counseling Services (ECS).* In 1971 the National Institute on Alcoholism and Alcohol Abuse (NIAAA) was established to encourage innovative approaches to alcoholism. While emphasizing the use of the job performance criterion (from the OAP), NIAAA sought to deal with a broader array of behavioral problems through a mechanism called employee assistance programs (EAP), or employee counseling services (ECS). It connected the individual workers and their problems (including their family-related problems outside the work place) with relevant organizational social services. A case example is presented below.

7. *A Second-Generation, Broad-spectrum Program in Business and Industry: The Employee Mental Wellness Program (EMWP), or Health Promotion Programs (HPP).* Even though the EAPs took a broader approach to problems than the alcoholism-focused OAPs, they were still largely focused on problems, including the prevention of problems. In the early 1980s, a different orientation was introduced that emphasizes the mental health of employees, rather than physical health or emotional distress exclusively. This came at a time when promotion of wellness was beginning to be seen as involving a distinctive set of primary prevention activities (see Bond and Joffe, 1983). The holistic health movement had its beginnings at about this time as well. In Canada, Jake Epp, the Minister of National Health and Welfare, proposed a framework for health promotion, *Achieving Health for All* (1986). Thus the promotion of positive health, rather than the mere removal of problematic stressors, was being discussed at many levels of society.

It might be instructive to review the *Blue Cross and Blue Shield Guide to Staying Well* (1982), directed to federal employees and their families, to see what ingredients are present in wellness programs. Wellness is viewed as a combination of physical fitness and sound mental health. A healthful life-style, including sound mental and physical health at the workplace, is the critical objective of this approach. There are four key ingredients to the program: nutrition, exercise, a healthy life-style, and management of stress. Getting the right quantity and quality of nutrition and exercise, combined with a healthful style of living one's life, including the management of inevitable stress, is a prescription not merely to reduce medical costs (relevant to Blue Cross and Blue Shield), but more positively, to promote health and healthy functioning even in the stress-filled workplace. A corollary benefit is the positive state of mind or the quality of life that accrues to one who actively works to stay well. Masi (1984) characterizes the differences between EAPs and HPPs: The HPPs are strictly voluntary, and deal with all employees (sometimes in groups) who are viewed as healthy; EAPs use the threat of job loss to force changes on specific employees (individually) who are seen to have declining job performance. Naditch (1985) documents some encouraging effectiveness data on an industry-based wellness program. [See also Rasnic (1985, p. 40) on quality of work-life projects that emphasize greater degrees of democracy in the workplace, more worker control, and more joint labor-management solutions to problems. Myers and Reynolds (1985) describe leisure life-style developments that involve active counseling of employees to engage in healthier recreational pursuits. O'Donnell and Ainsworth (1984) offer a comprehensive review of health promotion programs in the workplace, especially emphasizing nutrition, exercise, and stress management.]

Thus contemporary occupational social services may include some remnants of older orientations—paternalistic welfare capitalism, union benevolent associations, and traditional personnel departments. At the same time they may involve more recent changes—the fringe benefit system, focused problem-solving efforts like OAP, or various types of broad-spectrum activities, like the EAPs and the mental wellness programs. This diversity of elements, coexisting and continuously changing, makes OSW an exciting if frustrating object of study and a field of practice. Many experiments have been tried, as this historical overview suggests, but many other possibilities remain if we are to attain the multidimensional goals of social well-being—for the worker and his or her family, along with efficient production in the business or industry and quality living in a healthful community.

COMPONENTS OF THE OCCUPATIONAL WELFARE SYSTEM

Broadly conceived, there are three components of the contribution an industry or business makes to a worker's social well-being:

1. The *basic salary or wages*, which are not welfare in the narrow sense of the term, but are basic for attaining social well-being. The specific business or industry pays the salary or wages. However, as an historical note, various forms of governmental support such as negative income tax and family assistance plans have been suggested to make up the difference between a worker's wages and the poverty line. Booth's studies of London's working poor in the late 19th century shocked the Victorian world because they documented that full-time working people were still living below a subsistence level. Later research, to this present day, shows similar results (Harrington, 1986).

2. The second component to the contribution of industry or business to the worker's social well-being involves certain *central services and benefits*—those relevant to any business or industry, such as current concerns for the worker's healthy functioning on the job and his or her freedom from accidents, as well as ensuring against future inevitabilities such as retirement or job loss. These central benefits and services are paid for by some combination of the employer, the worker, and the

government. For example, sometimes the employer pays for the entire health coverage of workers through a group Blue Cross and Blue Shield plan that may vary from a comprehensive to more limited coverage. In other situations, the workers may be required to contribute to this health plan. Another example would be governmental workmen's compensation (for support due to injury on the job) or some provisions of the Social Security Act (related to work-caused disability). (See also Googins and Godfrey, 1987, p. 33.)

3. The third ingredient of the contribution of business or industry to workers' social well-being involves certain *supplemental services and benefits* that often reflect the particular history and choices of a given organization (cf. Googins and Godfrey, 1987, p. 34). Supplemental services and benefits include, but are not limited to, the following:

   a) Expanded health benefits such as annual physicals that serve preventive purposes, dental insurance, or visual or hearing aids
   b) Child care at the workplace or at outside contracted services
   c) Employee profit sharing
   d) Educational scholarships or loans to the children of employees
   e) Time off and/or tuition remittance for employees who pursue their own further education
   f) Employee and family services, such as those dealing with substance abuse, mental health, and marital functioning, legal and financial problems, and preretirement counseling
   g) Credit unions, buying clubs, and recreation programs including on-site exercise areas
   h) Supplemental unemployment income for laid-off workers (union-sponsored program).

These supplemental services may be paid for by some contribution of employer, union, and employee contributions. It is important to note that there is no common supplement program. Each industry and business formulates and negotiates its own program with employees and their union representatives, when present. The very unevenness of these benefits and services reflects another facet of the American way of competition.

OCCUPATIONAL SOCIAL WORK: SPECIFIC FUNCTIONS AND ACTIVITIES

What do occupational social workers do? Given the broad range of components in the occupational social welfare system, social workers and other helping professions may be involved with a diversity of specific activities. Googins and Godfrey (1987, pp. 5-10) offer one enumeration, which is adapted here:

1. *Counseling Services.* This category includes individual and group counseling, referral and follow-up, outreach, and crisis intervention. Counseling has often been focused on single issues, such as alcohol or drug abuse, but even so, it provides an initial means of entering an organiza-

tional setting so that relationships can be formed as the basis of offering other services, as needed (Ozawa, 1980).

2. *Program Development.* Individual concerns may be recognized as common to a whole group of employees, as possible problems that need to be resolved or challenges met. Group-focused or company-wide programs may be developed in prevention or treatment of substance abuse, stress management, general health and mental health promotion, as well as concerns like family problems, retirement counseling, and the like.

3. *Consultation to Management and/or Unions.* This category includes assessment of employee needs and concerns, analysis of the organizational dynamics and relevant group dynamics, and policy input. Important subcategories are:

    a) Affirmative action policy and programs, including recruitment, internal policy formation, and advocacy on behalf of individuals and categories of individuals.

    b) Community relations, including policies and programs reviewed with regard to their impact in socio-cultural, legal, and ethical implications, as well as with the more direct economic and technical implications.

    c) Policies and programs involving corporate social responsibility, so that the business or industry participates in the responsible development of its community. This would include working with others regarding appropriate housing, schools, and general economic growth.

4. *Research on Employee-Corporation-Community Problems.* This includes analysis of the users of OSW services and the cost/effectiveness analysis regarding its use, both in the treatment of problems and in the prevention of predictable problems and the promotion of desired end states.

5. *Training and Education.* This category includes training sessions given to employees and management on various topics such as substance abuse and stress awareness, but also on general topics like communication within a corporate context.

Now, consider the following case study that presents one form that employee assistance programs may take.

A Case Study: A Woman's Work is Never Done . . .

Mrs. Claudia Clayton, a petite blonde in her early 30s, had been working with the Business Form Company for the past four years. She advanced from a secretarial job to an assistant to the branch manager. Her work included many clerical functions along with some administrative duties, and she enjoyed the work. Her salary, about $800 a month, was a significant contribution to the family income. Her husband, John, a computer salesman, worked on a combined salary plus commission basis, and earned between $800 and $1100 a month. Jenifer, their three-year-old daughter, was at day care, and

Phillip, their seven-year-old, was in the first grade at the nearby school. Phillip came home with the neighbor's son, and played next door until either Claudia or John came home. The Claytons paid the neighbors a small amount for this service, but it was primarily a matter of mutual support, since John helped them with their computer. All appeared to be going along well, until Claudia's supervisor, Ted Applemann, began to notice some changes.

Claudia appeared to be distracted at the job, as if her mind was miles away from the discussions of business forms and contracts. Also, the supervisor noticed that she came in late rather frequently, which meant that contracts sometimes were not finished when needed. Ted was getting annoyed about this because his boss was making some harsh comments about the management of Ted's branch. But Ted did not say anything to Claudia.

This went on for several weeks until a big contract was almost lost because Claudia did not follow through on some important details. She seemed to be making many personal telephone calls when she should have been attending to business. Ted managed to salvage the contract but he was angry. He managed to cool down before he called Claudia into his office. He expressed concern over the specific contract problem but he also mentioned what he saw as a pattern of problems.

Claudia was very defensive. She said only that she was having a difficult time, personally, but that it was temporary and she was getting on top of the situation. Claudia was very upset about this session. She began to cry, and this made Ted feel very uncomfortable. So Ted backed off, and nothing more was said for the next week or two, but nothing changed. Claudia continued to come in late, erratically, and Ted continued to feel that she was too distracted to be doing what she had to do. Ted had to work on her assignments as well as his own, and he was becoming increasingly frustrated.

Then a major crisis occurred. A large contract was being prepared, which required some reports that Ted was responsible for. He assigned Claudia to do the drafts, as she had been doing for some time. But this time, the drafts were late and in haste, and Ted sent them forward without carefully reviewing them. They were in error, and Ted's boss, the general manager, caught the error just before they went to the outside firm. The general manager was very hard on Ted and accused him of sloppy workmanship. Ted responded that it was partly Claudia's fault, although he recognized that he should have checked the reports thoroughly before forwarding them. The boss listened carefully, and then suggested that Ted handle this situation by going through the firm's employee assistance staff.

In retrospect, Ted kicked himself for not having noticed and acted on these job performance problems much earlier. The firm had had a supervisory workshop on EAP at the beginning of the year, but he had not connected the particular situation to the abstract rules and procedures that the EAP staff officer had recommended. Yet it fit perfectly: a good employee suddenly showing a decline in job performance for no obvious reason. The training session had stressed that the EAP was not to replace ordinary disciplinary action, but was to supplement it. And it was not to be personal counseling, which made Ted breathe a sigh of relief since he was uncomfortable about getting into personal matters with employees. Supervisors were advised to document the situation carefully and objectively, so that the job performance problems would be indisputable. Ted's records were not too good, but he reconstructed them from diaries and other memos. The EAP officer explained the general procedure to the supervisors: First, after noticing and documenting the job performance problem, the supervisor was to discuss the matter privately with the employee, and point to the job-related facts only. He was to ask that these matters be corrected. An employee could voluntarily see the EAP officer on his/her own. If the performance did not improve, the supervisor had several choices: either to call the EAP officer to get advice on whether the facts constituted a problem or not, and then have the EAP officer carry on the counseling process; or the supervisor could talk with the employee directly (on job performance only, not personal matters). Since Ted had already discussed Claudia's job performance with her earlier (without apparent effect), he chose to go the EAP route.

Terry Andrews was the EAP counselor serving the Business Form Company as well as several other firms in a consortium of small business. His function was to receive referrals from the supervisors, who were to inform the employee of the job-related problems and their request that the worker visit the EAP officer voluntarily as a way to resolve the problem in a confidential and personalized manner. These points are important to emphasize: While the business would know that Claudia was referred to the EAP counselor, and that the counselor would report whether or not Claudia did in fact come for a voluntary consultation, no other details were to be transmitted to the company. If the worker did not show up at the EAP office, then the company would be so informed, and if the job performance did not improve, then ordinary company disciplinary actions would be taken. (Claudia could have been fired.)

Ted did in fact have this difficult conversation with Claudia, and she was predictably upset. But he was firm. He gave Claudia the EAP counselor's phone number and said it was entirely up to her, but that her job performance had to change. He also stressed that he was going through this procedure out of respect for her, that she had been a valued employee, and that he wanted to help her through this difficult period. But, objectively speaking, her job was in jeopardy.

Claudia was most upset, but she decided to call the EAP counselor, who went over the procedure with her. He particularly emphasized the confidentiality aspect. She set up an appointment with Terry Andrews and saw him at his office shortly thereafter on a warm summer evening, a time that did not interfere with her work schedule. Terry conducted a standard social history, trying to assess what problems were present as well as what strengths Claudia possessed. She admitted to having some financial problems—John was having a slump in his sales. This meant that they had to cut back on the child-care arrangements. She now had to take her child to a new place across the city, and that often resulted in her being late because of unpredictable traffic patterns. Terry listened to this, and noted how superficial it seemed. He wondered whether that was the whole story and asked about the marriage. Claudia was very defensive and would say nothing. He asked about her drinking habits quite directly, and she said that she did not drink at all. John did, and maybe because of his job situation, he might have been drinking more than usual. But that was all she would say.

After she left, Terry pondered over why she was wearing a long-sleeved dress on such a warm evening. When she returned for the second interview, she wore a long-sleeved blouse. He asked directly about spousal abuse. This shocked Claudia, and she broke down into tears. Yes, her husband has been under great pressure. He used to take the younger child to day care, but now he made her do it (and thus be late for work). Yes, he has been shoving her around lately, and has been argumentative. He knocked her down recently, and that resulted in some bruises on her arm, which is why she wore the long-sleeved dresses, but he apologized profusely. This scared her and she lost her temper too. There were more fights. She does not know how to handle the situation. She "lost her cool" with her seven-year-old last week and hit him. Now she is very frightened.

The EAP officer helped Claudia to put words to her feelings, and helped to identify some alternatives she might choose to pursue. But he did not conduct these services directly. Instead, Terry referred Claudia to a therapist specializing in spousal abuse and encouraged her to go. There was no charge for Claudia's visit to the firm's EAP officer, but she would have to pay half the expenses of the specialist—the firm's company health insurance would pay the other half. Claudia decided to go, and the specialist, Janet Ramey, continued to explore a variety of problems with Claudia and her husband.

In the meanwhile, Claudia's supervisor, Ted, called the EAP officer to inquire how matters were proceeding. Claudia was still coming in late, and he had not noticed any improvements after several weeks of counseling. Terry, the EAP officer, was caught in the middle, trying to explain the general counseling process to the supervisor in an effort to gain more time for the treatment to have an effect, while also clarifying the realities of the situation to Claudia and her abuse counselor that the job performance had to be improved soon. Terry also asked Claudia how she was getting along with the abuse counselor, did she feel it was helpful or not? (The EAP officer in this situation was the middleman among the employee, the employer, and the counselor.)

Janet Ramey, the abuse counselor, was working with Claudia's husband, John, to help him learn how to handle the stress he was under (see Quick, Kertesz, Nelson and Quick, 1985). She could not change that stress, but she could show him how to deal with it more effectively, and put less pressure on Claudia and the family. John's response reduced the tensions in the family quite successfully, so that Claudia's early thoughts of separation or divorce did not go far. Her supervisor was somewhat understanding, and fortunately his boss reinforced the point that treatment did not necessarily mean instantaneous success. After some shaky periods, Claudia got back to a workable routine. She seemed to get more energy merely from having someone to talk to about the problems. It was good to hear her laughing once again at the office.

SUMMARY

Professional helping is not confined to narrow boundaries. Problems or potentials that emerge in one sector of the human configuration quickly affect other sectors. Social work agencies often emerged to deal with specific problems, which was important to do. But problems did not stop at the doors of a given agency, even if services did stop there. And so some problems went unresolved.

At first glance, it might seem that the workplace is a strange place to provide professional help. In fact, as this chapter has noted, important forms of social and personal services were being provided to workers in the 19th century, and have only recently been rediscovered, as it were, in the form of new major movements, such as employee assistance programs and wellness programs. When we think of the critical social institutions—family, work, school—we can see that problems and potentials can emerge that sometimes are beyond the ability or the resources of their members to resolve. Hence the need for social services. But as this chapter emphasizes, problems and potentials belong to the whole configuration of life, and forms of social services need to be able to reflect this configuration both in their thinking and in action. This may be the special importance of occupational social work to the 1990s.

PART

VII.

SPECIAL POPULATIONS AND ISSUES

Social workers must be concerned with several major issues regardless of their field of practice. These issues have involved the most explosive social questions of our times, the role of ethnicity, gender, and age in the ordinary configurations of a person's life. The social history of the 20th century may well be recognized for the major advances in civil rights for these special populations of persons. Or it may be noted for civil rights unfulfilled, depending on how the last decade of the century turns out. And how this century turns out may be significantly influenced by social work efforts.

Being on the edge of historical change is rarely comfortable for anyone. We must understand both the history and the current manifestations of change, and what part a sensitive social worker may play in these events. Chapters 17 and 18 address these sensitivity issues in ethnicity and culture and in gender and age.

Chapter 19 introduces some of the many faces of violence in our age—the omnipresent potential of a nuclear war, the post-traumatic stress disorders among those who fought in wars past, and the local forms of violence such as child abuse and rape. In each of these, social workers may be able to make contributions, not just to the treatment and rehabilitation of the effects of violence, but also to their prevention.

Chapter 20 explores other aspects of human behavior that have given rise to several critical epidemics of our age—unwanted adolescent pregnancy, overpopulation and the threats to exhaustible resources, and AIDS. Each of these issues contains extremely dangerous implications for the persons involved and for the rest of us who share this tiny spaceship, Earth. The social work perspective is once again emphasized: What can we do to prevent these problems as well as to treat their present victims?

OUTLINE

Introduction to Minorities as Special Populations

Historical Overview
  Blacks in America
  Native Americans
  Hispanics
  Asian Americans

Social Work Practice with Minority Peoples

The Oncology (Cancer) Ward: Use of Culturally-Sensitive Social Work

Summary

CHAPTER SEVENTEEN

Ethnicity and Culturally-Sensitive Social Work

This chapter emphasizes awareness of, and sensitivity to, the culturally distinctive groups of people in America. The configural frame of reference calls attention to the strengths as well as the limitations of people and the environments in which they live. This chapter describes the experiences of four minority groups—blacks, Native Americans, Hispanics, and Oriental Americans—over the past 300 years, as background for understanding their lives today. Social workers must understand the distinctive cultural facts about their clients if they are to be effective and humane. This information, ever growing and changing, must be combined with a problem-solving perspective to produce an "ethnically competent social work" (Green, 1982).

INTRODUCTION TO MINORITIES AS SPECIAL POPULATIONS

The generic problem-solving process is supposed to be applicable to all people. So, why do we have a chapter on minority people—those who differ either in number or characteristics from the majority of a population and who tend to receive differential treatment from that majority? As a profession, social work has long championed the rights of all citizens, individually and as classes of individuals. Because of blatant and subtle inequalities among citizens—often in spite of laws to the contrary—we must, therefore, continually be aware of differential treatment and services, particularly when they operate to the detriment of specific groups.

As travelers to foreign countries know, everyone is in the minority in some contexts. The pleasures of travel are mixed with the stresses of being in the minority. It is more stressful to be a minority in one's own land, to be disliked for impersonal and irrational reasons, and to face hostility, if not life-threatening, discrimination. We naturally turn to people like ourselves as protectors and nurturers, even though they may be relatively powerless in the face of a holocaust. This is a universal experience that begins with our family of origin, and later extends to our neighborhood and to our subcultural groups, and eventually includes our state or nation.

To the Europeans escaping from religious and political oppression, America became a land of opportunity to develop communities as they saw fit. However, many of these new communities were as intolerant to different points of view as were the European communities from which they sought to escape. Given the persistence of prejudice and discrimination, these communities on the edge of a continent were fortunate. They were able to cooperate in the formation of a society that attempted to ensure that each group could practice its own life-style and values as long as it did not interfere with the life pursuits of others.

Some commentators have described America as a *melting pot,* where different peoples came together to live and to prosper in peace and harmony. In fact, this never happened. Some cultural groups did arrive and were so thoroughly "melted down" that their distinctive cultural characteristics are hard to see in an apparently homogeneous society—such as the Irish Americans, most of whose "cultural" expressions are in fact American inventions. But most cultural groups retained—or tried to retain—their culturally distinct identity. Some groups were "aided" by a hostile environment that did not allow them to forget their differences; however, this may have been a cultural blessing in disguise, although the living of it may not have been easy.

A more recent designation of American society as *pluralistic* suggests that minority and ethnic groups can remain distinct but still get along in harmony with other groups because they all owe allegiance to higher sets of values and laws. The dual-perspective pluralism suggests some important implications: A person who is fully involved in his or her minority group can gain pride of membership and support from its language, foods, and customs and at the same time can function as a full citizen of the entire nation. Critics of this "separate but equal" approach for a member of a minority group point out that invidious distinctions can still be made and can be used as justification for public policy—a form of blaming the victim because "they" are different from "us" (Ryan, 1976; Green, 1982).

Green (1982) has developed a transactional approach to ethnicity. It focuses on the character of the relations between ethnic individuals and the representatives of the larger society (the helping professionals) in the help-seeking process. It recognizes that a problem is both personal and social and that helping involves the client's communications about the problem as well as the community's and culture's resources for resolving it. He and his colleagues describe the four largest minority groups, covering their distinctive backgrounds and ethnically sensitive approaches to helping.

Lum (1986) has developed a different framework for social work practice with ethnic minorities. It includes five stages of the practice process (a version of the problem-solving stages), each of which details some worker, some client, and some joint worker-client tasks. For example, at the initial contact stage of practice, workers must be concerned with understanding the community and the service system as well as relating to the client in a warm, empathic, and genuine mode of communication. At this same stage, the clients have to face their own resistance to communication. They must also take into account their personal, familial, and ethnic community background. Together worker and client must begin to nurture the growth process that will go on between them as they begin to understand the client's problems and feelings related to them. Lum describes in detail the succeeding stages of problem identification, assessment, intervention, and termination from the three perspectives of the worker, the client, and their shared tasks.

The configural view on social work practice with minority persons and groups has a different conceptual base, although it shares with Green and Lum many of the practice suggestions, while adding others. Recall that the configuration portrays an individual embedded in various systems—primary groups and secondary groups, as well as socio-cultural and physical environments and time. Each of these ingredients is conceptually as important as every other one, and one's position vis-à-vis this configuration determines whether one begins with the individual or the groups or whatever. The strongest implication of the configural model is that the entire system of ingredients must be accounted for in one's practice, even though at any one time not all elements may be active.

That individual aspect of the configuration changes as the client changes. But note that what is a cultural group or secondary or primary group for that individual is composed of other individuals for whom the same analysis can be made. Depending on who is communicating with whom, everyone serves as some other person's social world. We are at once the same in the sense that all share a common world and humanity. Beyond this basic biological and ecological universality, we are similar to specific others with whom we share certain accidents of a history of heredity and learning. And beyond this, we are unique as our life experiences are unique. We are, in this view, ecologically equal, socially separable, and personally unique. Depending on which accent of this equation we choose to emphasize, we can view the world as a melting pot, a pluralistic society, or a never-to-match aggregate. But in the configural view, each of these partial views is limited. We are, at once, equal, separate, and unique.

This multiple aspect view of social relations suggests that we can communicate at various levels as needed. We may begin to meet the person who is to become our client by expressions of commonality, what we share as persons of goodwill and humanity. But even within this meeting of worker and client as human beings the recognition arises that there are differences between them. Some differences may interfere with the work at hand (problem solving); others may facilitate it (each having special information needed jointly to solve the problem). We begin to face these differences within the context of the shared commonalities.

Green and Lum have identified many ethnic and cultural differences that can be barriers to effective helping. They have placed too little emphasis on the differences that can be productive, however, such as being specialists on information, feelings, and actions needed to solve the problem. These differences should be viewed as complementary and used as such. The worker must believe that he or she has useful information or methods; clients must be encouraged to recognize their strengths and resources. Otherwise, the contact may not be worthwhile. (See also Devore and Schlesinger, 1987.)

But any worker information or method is worth nothing if it cannot be put into practice, and that requires adaptation to the client's configural context.

The client has already come in demonstrating the negative impact of several portions of the configuration, and probably would be able to document others such as discrimination and exclusion if given the opportunity. Not every personal or small group problem is related to cultural problems, even though it is likely to be aggravated by them. More to the point, cultural differences between worker and client may be a difficulty worth exploring. The configural approach bids us remain open to each of the possible influencing factors, then weighing what systems of forces are active in a particular case. We try to identify the "centers of gravity" for each relevant part of the configuration, and determine how these centers are interrelated.

The configural model notes that there are positive and negative forces acting on a given client from the several systems involved. There will be discussions of the problematic forces as part of the identification of the perceived difficulty. But workers must make a determined effort to locate strengths of person and environments because these are ultimately the tools of change. Discovery of what a strength is depends in part on the client's defining it, and the worker must be sensitive enough to use it wisely. The worker must also push further in exploring strengths (from hints from the literature, experience, or colleagues). This difference between worker and client is an aspect that has to be extended to, but not forced onto, the client. Any new ideas have to be considered by the client within familiar (cultural) contexts. We thus come to recognize our differences, both as to culture and as to our special roles in society. These may be seen not as barriers but as making use of differences in learning together how to solve problems. A heterogeneity of ideas is useful, while a proclamation of superiority of ideas or methods is not—that is, differences by class or culture are still framed within the larger context of commonality. One view of the problem is not necessarily better or worse than another. The common task is to explore how these differences may be used together to resolve the problem.

HISTORICAL OVERVIEW

A long perspective of history recognizes that all Americans, including Native Americans, were initially immigrants. Throughout American history, different peoples were the immigrants relative to others who proceeded them and received them with varying degrees of enthusiasm and friendship. It is critical to understand this history as the background to the reception you as an individual worker may receive from a client with one or another cultural background. If you are a young black woman assigned to help an older white male from some Eastern European cultural background, for example, you may sense some tensions. They may arise not only from your client who has to confront your differences from him on top of the already difficult burden of facing his problems, but also from you, in the kinds of feelings you detect in yourself in spite of your intellectual pledge to help all persons regardless of origin and culture. It is not a question of whether, but when, we will confront people who are different from ourselves. To that end, some conceptual guidelines may be helpful, in addition to the cultural self-analysis we must all undertake as we reconstruct our personal history.

Blacks in America

The history of Africans may well go back to the beginnings of human history (see Rensberger, 1987). For African Americans, however, the story begins in 1502 when the first of some ten million Africans were enslaved and brought to the Americas. Of this number, about 400,000 were taken to the United States as agricultural workers and miners. African nations were too weak to stop the slave trade, and European nations were involved in the profitable traffic as well. Black Africans were often involved in capturing fellow Africans for sale into slavery. All of these factors are interesting commentaries on the state of ethics in the 16th century.

Slavery was primarily a socio-economic arrangement that served as a means of profit for the Southern plantation economy; it did not fit into the economic system of the North, even though ship captains from Boston were involved in the slave traffic. Men, women, and children worked in the fields, or were rented from plantations during slack seasons as construction workers and skilled workers, and so added to their economic value. Others served in the masters' homes, thus creating a slave status hierarchy.

Analyses of early records suggest that blacks were better fed, less crowded, and healthier than white urban industrial workers at the time. Blacks also had lower mortality rates than slaves in South America and the Caribbean Islands. However, families of slaves were broken up to suit the owners' economic plans, while in Catholic Brazil, black families were maintained as a unit (Leigh and Green, 1982). Generally speaking, Southern planters considered slaves as property and it suited their interests to protect the commercial value of the slaves, whatever degree of altruism or brutality motivated individual slave holders. (See, for example, Gerda Lerner's documentary history, *Black Women in White America*, 1972.)

The moral dimension of slavery in a free society was debated from the beginning of the Republic, but a decision was postponed to gain a minimal national unity. The religious revival that occurred in the mid-1700s in the North sent evangelical ministers to blacks as well as whites, and many black churches emerged. They gave vent to religious feelings and were training grounds for black leadership. The call for freeing the slaves was taken up early in the 1800s, particularly by women. It was one of the continuing and mounting pressures that merged together as causes of the Civil War. During this pre-1860s period, the slave subculture evolved, blending the diverse African roots and the American experiences. Slaves were purposively kept uneducated and dependent on owners for food, clothing, and shelter; they were used almost entirely for manual labor. Yet about 11 percent of the blacks emerged from slavery into a class of free men before the Civil War. They dominated the building trades, barbering, and several other manual occupations. Descendants of this group and African Americans who were able to acquire land or an occupation after the war made up the bulk of persons who first attended college and who took various leadership positions.

The Civil War and the immediate postwar Reconstruction Period were times of rapid social change. About four million slaves were freed, but programs for their entrance into the dominant society were thwarted immediately. The Freedmen's Bureau struggled for the several years of its existence to aid dispossessed blacks and whites, and particularly, to build schools for blacks. But the nation was beginning to change from an agrarian to an industrial society, with corresponding changes in demands for farm and industrial workers. Blacks did not migrate north or west in large numbers to enter the new labor markets in part because of strict vagrancy laws that virtually kept freed blacks from moving. Nor did the plans to redistribute plantation farm lands come to fruition—"forty acres and a mule."

Instead, freed blacks became competitors with white laborers, and racial strife developed. Southern capitalists allied themselves with white labor by employing whites in the new cotton mills, while blacks were consigned to agricultural or domestic and personal service jobs. A racial caste system replaced slavery. Generations of dependency on owners made freed blacks ineffective managers of their own styles of consumption, leading to waste and improvidence, and to vulnerability to cheating by white storekeepers and employers.

Blacks largely remained in the South and were denied access to education, the trades, and political and social participation. "Jim Crow" legislation reinforced these restrictive social mores. From 1890 to 1910, blacks were barred from voting in every southern state by means of state constitutional amendments (Brieland, Costin, and Atherton, 1985, p. 196). Social indicators showed serious declines for blacks during this period; life expectancy dropped and morbidity increased. The rise of racist organizations (like the Ku Klux Klan) began lynchings, beatings, and other terroristic activities directed toward repressing black resistance.

Before the Civil War Southern states had passed laws that prohibited teaching slaves to read and write, yet in the 50 years following, literacy went from about zero to nearly 75 percent. School construction in the South was slow; it was funded mainly by private philanthropy. White missionary teachers worked under difficult conditions of Southern hostility and students lacking in educational preparation, but they slowly succeeded in building the foundations for the next generations.

By the turn of the 20th century, African Americans held jobs mainly in preindustrial types of occupations, and thus lost ground to other immigrant groups who were entering the growing industrial sector. A class of black professionals emerged to serve blacks in segregated facilities, supposedly "separate but equal." Black artists and craftspersons emerged in the Harlem Renaissance, which enriched the entire culture (see, for example, Rampersad, 1986; 1988). However, black entrepreneurs remained at the level of small businesses that served the local community without bringing new wealth into it.

As the labor movement grew stronger, plant owners in the North imported Southern blacks as strikebreakers, thus alienating blacks from the labor movement. Race riots in the North broke out, but eventually a kind of accommodation was reached, as white workers rose in the labor hierarchy, leaving the less desirable jobs for blacks who were beginning to enter the industrial sector. The Great Depression of the 1930s proved particularly difficult for blacks— "last hired, first fired"—although the labor market opened up enormously during World War II.

After 1945, there were many major social changes. Regional and urban-rural relocations moved huge numbers of blacks out of the South and into the

20th century. Unfortunately, the uprooting led to new experiences with many social pathologies—crime, alcoholism, mental illness. The new postindustrial era was emerging just as blacks were beginning to take hold in the industrial sector. Available educational facilities were deficient and segregated for most blacks, even after the 1954 *Brown* v. *Board of Education* decision of the United States Supreme Court that struck down segregated education. Many social analyses during this time stressed apparent deficits in black families and black communities, indeed in all of black culture. The analyses were intended to explain those social problems; for example, the Moynihan report (1965) described the black family as a "tangle of pathology."

Critics of deficit-oriented interpretations pointed out that black families were different from white families (Martin and Martin, 1978) and showed many strengths such as strong kinship bonds, a strong work orientation, flexibility in family roles, strong achievement orientations in work and school, and a strong religious commitment (Hill, 1971). From a configural perspective, it is probable that black individuals and families, like all people everywhere, will exhibit both deficits and assets. The more important question is whether personal and family strengths and other socio-cultural resources are available in sufficient amounts to reverse the historical cumulation of social problems among individuals and groups, whatever their origin. Leigh and Green (1982) offer a good overview of how the new understanding of the black community and culture can be used to make social work services more effective and humane. However, there is increasing concern about the emergence of a permanent underclass—people who are locked into poverty and misery by a combination of social, structural, and personal attributes.

Native Americans

It is typical of white ethnocentrism to assert that Columbus "discovered" America in 1492, yet some two to three million American Indians were already there when he arrived (Miller, 1982). With gross denial of justice, many white settlers pushed Native Americans out of their lands because the European monarchs had "granted" the lands to the pioneers. (Exceptions included William Penn's Quaker groups, who paid the Native Americans for their land.) Europeans were fearful of the "savages" and could not comprehend their lack of competitiveness, nor did they appreciate the native peoples' communal and ecological concept of land. It stood in stark contrast to the Europeans' exploitive approach to the land and all living on it. Yet most initial contacts with the Native Americans were cooperative and peaceful.

No immigrant group—British, Dutch, French, Spanish, or later Americans—wielded a predominance of power. Indians held the balance and thus received benevolent treatment. The Northwest Ordinance of 1787 stressed just, humane, and peaceful goals with the Indians. However, continuing growth of settlements and westward expansion soon provoked conflicts over land. Explorers opened the way to trappers and traders, who were succeeded by frontiersmen and military forts to protect the way for settlers (George Washington's idea). Farmers and cattlemen arrived later.

Native Americans were attacked by a more subtle weapon, however. Their ranks were decimated by the epidemics introduced unwittingly by Europeans.

Alcohol was introduced to Indians, for whom it has become a very grave problem, possibly in part because of genetic susceptibility. Wanton destruction of Native American foods, such as the buffalo, and innumerable wars, broken treaties, and legalized breakup of Indian homelands and families nearly wiped out the population, which decreased to about 200,000 by 1919 (Miller, 1982).

The benevolent policies of the 18th century gave way to unilateral expropriation of Indian lands through various legal devices or fictions. For example, the Indian Removal Act of 1830 granted President Andrew Jackson power to remove tribes of the eastern United States to the west of the Mississippi—these events have been called "the trail of tears." The Homestead Act of 1862 opened up white settlements in Iowa, Kansas, and Nebraska areas—the homelands of other Indians. By 1871, the federal government decided that the Indians did not constitute nations so that no further treaties were to be made. Instead, the General Allotment Act of 1887 (known as the Dawes Act) ushered in a new era. Indian families were allotted 160 acres held in trust for them for 25 years, but with "surplus" Indian lands to be sold by the United States. Over the next 45 years, about three-quarters of Indian lands passed to white owners. The intention of the Dawes Act was to have reservation Indians emulate white settlers; they were to become farmers of their own private property and accumulate capital in order to "get ahead"—expectations contrary to Indian culture. The Dawes Act also suppressed Indian religion and created Indian boarding schools, often at great distances from the reservations. These measures contributed to the erosion of Indian culture and their community and to many forms of social and personal pathology.

The injustice of such provisions were soon understood and efforts to redress them followed, but it was not until almost a half-century later that the Indian Reorganization Act of 1934 attempted to salvage what was left of Indian culture in America. The 1934 Act included a return to tribal management of reservation lands, creation of local schools, and encouragement of tribal practices (religious and artistic). In 1946 the federal government removed its immunity from legal suits charging mismanagement of Indian lands under the Dawes Act. It thus opened the door for various lawsuits and for reparations to Native American groups.

The change came barely in time. Among other problems, the health of Native Americans is far below national norms, even though efforts by the Public Health Service and Native self-help groups have improved conditions. Yet new threats face Native Americans as they have adopted white ways—heart attacks, cancer, and alcoholism, among others. About one-third to one-half of all Indians live in urban areas, and many of them face stresses of relocation and lack of supportive networks. Educational levels of Native Americans are about five years lower than the national average (Miller, 1982), while crime rates and indices of mental health among urban Indians are bleak. Unemployment is higher for Indians than for any other group. Difficulties are many.

Miller's (1982) study of Indian cultural traits provides important background for social work practice with Native Americans. The following statements are hypotheses she derived from the literature, and which she attempted to substantiate. Many difficulties, in language and cultural barriers, prohibited her from providing clear evidence for or against these statements; therefore, consider them still hypotheses in need of further testing.

There appears to be a general attitude of suspicion and distrust of white professionals and institutions. Indians appear to be generally passive and will avoid or withdraw from situations that may require assertive or aggressive action. Indians tend to be shy with strangers and often speak little, especially about personal problems. Indians hold a fatalistic view of life; major human events are not under their control. They take a short-term orientation to planning. Their orientation to time is not tied to clocks; immediate social claims may take precedence over appointments.

Indians show great respect for the individual. This is manifested in not controlling or disciplining children or forcing them into choices. They have strong family and extended family relationships, which are primary obligations. Indians do not wish to interfere in the lives of others, and they find direct advice and suggestions as inappropriate attempts to control the behavior of others. (See Miller, 1982.)

Hispanics

The special population discussed here comprises several different streams of people—Mexican Americans, Cuban Americans, Puerto Ricans, and Spanish-surnamed peoples from South and Central America, as well as people from Spain. Often there is some mixture of Native Americans and blacks as well. Precise classification is difficult. The name Hispanics or Chicanos is used interchangeably in this book to describe these different peoples who share some basic characteristics including language, religion, and cultural influences on family and daily life. Yet there are significant differences that have to be recognized for ethnically-sensitive practice.

The Hispanics, as a whole, are the only special population added to the American peoples through war with foreign nations—in this case, Mexico and Spain. (Native Americans were brought into citizenship through internal wars, although technically they too were foreign nations before 1871.) The new American nation was very expansionist and tried to "fill in" the map to connect east and west coasts, their own perceived Manifest Destiny. Early presidents, beginning with John Quincy Adams, tried to purchase Texas from Mexico, without success. In 1835 Texas seceded from Mexico and was annexed by the United States in 1845 as a gross expansionist move; that led to a war in 1846 that produced lingering bad memories on both sides long after its conclusion—"Remember the Alamo!" The war ended with the Treaty of Guadalupe Hidalgo (1848), under which Mexico ceded not only Texas but also its California, Arizona, and New Mexico holdings for $50 million and the cancellation of its debt to the United States (about $2 million)—including all former Mexican citizens who became American citizens whose land, religion, and cultural expression were to be protected by provisions of the treaty (de Valdez and Gellegos, 1982).

In a blatant series of illegal and unjust acts, however, the Anglo-Americans ignored the treaty guarantees and succeeded in forcing the Mexican Americans off their own land (by manipulating tax assessments for the Hispanics, who were forced by high assessments to sell their land; then, when Anglos bought the land at auction, the taxes were reduced to low rates). In other ways, as well, the Hispanics were treated as the enemy, their culture and language being subjected to assault. Protests by Mexican Americans were sharply repressed as the work of "bandits" from the point of view of Anglos. Protestors were seen as cultural heroes by the Hispanics.

Nonetheless, there were large migrations of Mexicans to the United States in search of better wages, as the Mexican economy was in difficult straits during the first few decades of the 20th century. They entered both legally and as unauthorized aliens smuggled across the Rio Grande River by labor contractors who profited by the exploited cheap Mexican labor. Attempts to restrict the flow of illegal immigration began in 1917, but they were subverted by the agribusiness interests and local government leaders when labor was needed. When it was not—during the Great Depression of the 1930s—Mexicans and sometimes Mexican Americans were indiscriminately deported back to Mexico to avoid aiding them with public assistance (de Valdez and Gallegos, 1982).

Deportations were a continual threat for Hispanics, and when they attempted to form unions or other organizations to protect their civil rights and to improve wages and to better the terrible working conditions, their leaders were labeled as radicals and deported. Hispanics were ignored by Anglo labor unions, and were organized by Communist labor leaders in the ensuing vacuum, which added to the difficulties when "Red scares" haunted America. The struggle of Hispanic farm workers continues to this day, with leaders such as Cesar Chavez directing national boycotts of the products (such as grapes) of agribusiness that does not provide living wages and decent and safe working conditions for farm labor.

The Roman Catholic Church has played a mixed role in the history of Hispanics in America. It has been of vital importance in the rituals of life and death, and its values and morals have influenced family structure and behavior. Sex is exclusively limited to married couples for the purpose of procreating, for example. In practice, however, the culture allowed what amounted to a double standard. The sexual freedom of men was condoned, if not encouraged, as part of the Hispanic macho culture. The Church's stance against birth control and abortion has resulted in large families for Hispanics, which produces both personal as well as economic problems for them. Yet family (including the extended family and some aspects of the barrio community) is the central value in Hispanic life and permeates individual behavior among those who hold traditional values (cf. Gibson, 1985).

The Church, however, did not help to unify the Hispanics as it did for other ethnic immigrant groups; nor did it speak out against injustices Hispanics were subjected to for more than one hundred years. Moreover, advanced education does not receive the general esteem in Hispanic as it does, say, in Chinese culture; consequently, Hispanics on the average achieve educational accomplishments lower than national norms.

An important event took place in 1943. During the Zoot Suit Riots in Los Angeles, when U.S. servicemen attacked Hispanic civilians who were wearing exaggerated clothing faddish for that time, law enforcement officials did nothing to protect the Hispanics from the beatings. The Mexican government sent an official complaint, to which the U.S. government replied that it was an internal matter. Out of that unfortunate happening came the recognition of citizenship for Americans of Mexican descent. Other social changes brought on by the war and a developing technology included the shift from agriculture to industrial and service employment. Hispanics began to go to the urban areas in large numbers and became a significant political force. (Indeed, Hispanics are the fastest growing minority in the United States, and projections suggest that by the beginning of the 21st century, they will be the largest minority in the country.) (de Valdez and Gallegos, 1982.)

Federal legislation in the latter 1980s continued the country's attempt to deal with undocumented aliens by providing amnesty and citizenship for people who entered and lived in the United States before 1980 and setting fines for organizations who knowingly employ illegal aliens. Whether the law would reduce the gross injustices sustained by Hispanics in the past remains to be seen.

Hispanics, who are at high risk for many social and personal problems, have been distrustful of Anglo health, education, and welfare services and have underutilized those few that exist. They often prefer their own mutual aid organizations or the extended family. A shorter expected life span reduces the probability of Hispanics' benefiting from the Social Security program, while poor educational opportunities and services limits Hispanics from obtaining quality work (cf. Ozawa, 1986). Bilingual education is a controversial topic for where there are no definitive answers (cf. Fradd, 1982).

Subgroups among the Hispanics have special concerns. For example, Cuban Americans have entered the country recently in large numbers in the wake of political difficulties in their homeland. They settled largely in Florida and overwhelmed that state's resources to help acculturate them and provide them with emergency services. However, an Hispanic mayor was recently elected in Miami, reflecting the growth of political power of this group. There are several important political organizations among Hispanics—such as La Raza Unida Party of Texas, or the Mexican American Political Association of California—that are seeking to put their problems and potentials on the national and state agendas.

Puerto Ricans, being American citizens, can freely migrate to the mainland. They tend to move to New York City, long host to immigrant peoples, or to cities along the East coast or in Florida. Typically, Puerto Rican migrants are poor, less-well-educated workers who plan to stay only long enough to make some money. In fact, they often are submerged in the welfare system without becoming assimilated into Anglo culture.

Asian Americans

The ancient culture of China had little contact with Europe or America until the 19th century. When the Chinese went to the western United States, they arrived as immigrant laborers. These men (very few women were present) were peasants who came from several very poor districts in southern China, and they transferred their tightly woven network of clan, village, and dialect groupings to the new land. The majority arrived between the time of the Gold Rush (1848) and the difficult construction of the transcontinental railroad (1869). The men built mines and farmed, working in groups by contract. The early Chinese sojourners intended to work for a short time and then return home with their savings. Many were able to return, but a large number were prevented from doing so because of legal, social, and economic impediments. One source of the problem, as described by Hraba (1979), was the fact that contracted group laborers often worked for lower wages than other Americans, earning their wrath while being exploited by their employers.

After the Civil War, when jobs were scarce in the eastern United States and a depression gripped the country, many veterans migrated west and forced Orientals out of mining jobs by a mixture of discriminatory taxation, illegal ordinances prohibiting Chinese from working in certain areas, and mob violence (Hraba, 1979). Forced out of one type of job, the Chinese (as well as Japanese) found other forms of service and manufacturing work—at the lowest rung on the labor hierarchy.

By 1882 the first Chinese Exclusion Act was passed. Supposedly a temporary measure to correct for the surplus of labor, it later was made a permanent part of American immigration policy. These laws required Chinese to carry identification cards, as is now done in South Africa by native workers. However, the laws also left many Orientals stranded in the country, unable to form families. In 1890 there were 27 Chinese men for every Chinese woman in America. The national laws, local ordinances, and cultural mores of the time so discriminated against Orientals that they were put into an enormous double bind. Not able to work or protect themselves against white violence, they were not able to buy passage to leave America. Later, some loopholes in the exclusionary laws permitted "picture brides" (arranged marriages) for some Oriental residents (Irons, 1983, p. 11). Those loopholes were eventually removed.

Under those extremely difficult conditions, the Chinese evolved what Hraba (1979) calls a middleman minority. They concentrated in certain occupations offering services between producers and consumers (such as hand laundries, restaurants, and import stores) and took residence in certain geographical locations (Chinatowns) for protection. They maintained their own cultural social structure that provided welfare and mutual aid. The social structure also permitted the formation of opium dens and other forms of vice. The result was to produce an isolated subculture, but one in which there was enough contact with the dominant culture to bring in capital, with enough community control to use that capital for development. For example, the Chinese used rotating credit associations in which each member in turn would use the pooled money for investment purposes, and then pay back the money with interest so that another person could have a chance. Oriental culture makes such a strong demand on personal honor that few ever defaulted. The culturally isolated economy exploited Chinese laborers as much as they had ever been exploited, but a kind of cultural solidarity prevailed and exploitation was largely hidden from view at a time when general labor practices were deplorable.

Overall, the Oriental subcultures were so isolated from dominant American society that it was not until World War II that major changes took place. Great ethnic pride and a strong system of cultural rules included filial piety (deference to persons in authority such as parents, as well as honoring ancestors) and the pressure to honor one's family name (to save "face" or the good public status of one's family). The Chinese exhibited self-control in the sense of silent and inconspicuous obedience to rules and role holders (from the Confucian philosophy) and also in the inhibition of strong feelings. Reciprocity or mutual aid to members of one's kin or clan was another characteristic.

As second generations of Chinese were born and raised within this internally-controlled culture, however, they became Americans by virtue of birth. The value of education was a part of the ancient Chinese tradition. The children were sent to school and to college and ended up in professional and technological fields. It is interesting to note that before 1930, the IQ test scores of Chinese children were below national norms, but by 1930 they were at or above the norm, and have remained there ever since (Sowell, 1981, p. 147).

World War II forced America into cooperation with China against Japan. This had enormous implications for Oriental Americans. Anti-Chinese prejudice decreased, and anti-Japanese sentiment was the basis of the internment of more than 110,000 Japanese-American citizens for the duration of the war. Irons (1983) tells the gripping story of the internment, called the greatest deprivation of civil liberties in America since slavery. At the end of the war, these citizens returned to their home areas and tried to pick up the pieces—they had been forced to sell their property and businesses at a fraction of the true value. By hard work, the former internees managed to regain their economic momentum and to develop their economic and educational status further.

By 1970 more than a quarter of all employed Chinese Americans were in professional and technical fields, a proportion more than double that of the country at large. The average income of Chinese Americans (and Japanese Americans) is well above the national average and reflects both their educational attainments and their occupations. This is not to say that all Oriental Americans shared equally in development; there are stubborn pockets of poverty and illiteracy. Dominant culture welfare facilities have not been effective in providing services, perhaps because of hard-dying beliefs of prejudice against Oriental people, or possibly because of language and culture problems. Local communal services are still an important part of Oriental culture in America.

It is interesting to note that comparatively recent Oriental immigrants, from Vietnam and other countries, have likewise overcome many difficult cultural problems in America, and have succeeded on American terms. Green (1982) discusses the conflicts between Vietnamese and American cultures, and presents Ishisaka and his colleagues' (1977) approach to culturally-sensitive work in this area. (See also Lum, 1986; Devore and Schlesinger, 1987; and Chapter 24 of this book.)

SOCIAL WORK PRACTICE WITH MINORITY PEOPLES

The first step in the generic problem-solving approach (described in Chapters 2, 6, and 7) is to identify the configural system that composes the client's life space, especially those portions that are problematic and those that are supportive. This directive is especially important when a worker is dealing with a person (or group) of another race because a potential difficulty may emerge whereby the worker, however well-intentioned, may become part of the prob-

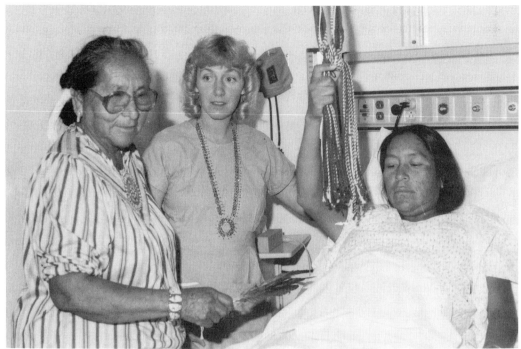

Courtesy Debra Goldstein

This photograph depicts ethnically and culturally sensitive work with a client. A Native American woman is in the birthing room of the Public Health Service Hospital in Chinle, Arizona; she is holding onto the traditional Navajo sash belt during her labor. A Navajo medicine woman is participating with a "western" health care provider who is wearing some Navajo artifacts. Every client possesses his or her cultural background, and every practitioner should be sensitive to work with, rather than against, that culture in solving client problems or helping to achieve client potentials.

lem. For example, if a black person identifies white people as oppressors, then having a white social worker would likely make this client uneasy. Likewise, if a white client who is prejudiced against Spanish-speaking peoples has an Hispanic social worker, this imposes strong if silent barriers to their effective communication. Methods to open up such problems and to overcome them have been discussed earlier (Chapter 7).

This chapter presents a full case example in which cultural differences play an important part in the treatment of a client in a hospital setting. Any intercultural transaction has the potential for activating stereotypes on the part of both client and worker, as well as collateral staff and family. Such stereotypes interfere with the helping process, and might entirely destroy it.

In examining sensitivity in intercultural transactions, we must recognize that it is the worker's responsibility for addressing these issues and for taking steps to overcome them. Some degree of cooperation must be solicited from the client; otherwise, the helping process will eventually break off, leaving both worker and client frustrated—and the stereotype reinforced, that "it is impossible to work with X-type people." Intercultural differences are a double-edged sword. Learning how to face them and use them may provide ethnically-sensitive workers with new tools to bring about desired changes.

From the configural perspective, one that views cultural background as the context in which the person and primary and secondary groups are embedded, workers are urged to make use of the context to attain desired objectives, and neutralize cultural differences that interfere with progress. Too often only the latter point is stressed. There are, of course, many such factors that might interfere with professional helping. But all cultures seek to benefit their members toward living a fulfilling life (according to its values). Thus the center of gravity of a culture, so far as a specific member of that culture is concerned, involves the promotion of desired ultimate goals. To attain these, intermediate objectives have to be attained, and may include those that are part of the helping professional's efforts. Thus, by linking a specific practice objective with the larger cultural goal, the worker has a potentially powerful ally in health and healthy functioning. Watch for these cultural factors in the following case. Although it may seem exotic, foreign, or unusual, remember that everyone has a subculture and that such cultural backgrounds are a part of every practice situation. (See also the case of a refugee family in Chapter 24.)

THE ONCOLOGY (CANCER) WARD: USE OF CULTURALLY-SENSITIVE SOCIAL WORK

There is a flurry of activity in front of the nurses' station on the eighth floor of Western State Hospital. Patients, friends, and relatives are clustered about, talking animatedly but pleasantly. Sounds of joking and laughter can be heard. But this is clearly a medical ward. Plastic holders adorn each doorway where patients' charts and records can be placed. Intravenous stands are lined up unobtrusively against the pastel-colored walls, but they are there. Trays of medications are being prepared and delivered. The loud speaker calls repeatedly for Doctor Such and Such. All this lively activity is not what one might expect in the oncology ward—the cancer ward.

Scenes of Solzhenitsyn's dramatic novel *Cancer Ward* float before the mind's eye. Pavel Nikolayevich Rusanov, the doubtful hero of the novel, first enters Ward 13 (symbol!) only to observe a different scene:

> . . . One Russian youth, thin as a rail but with a great bloated stomach, lay there in an unbuttoned coat which dangled to the floor, taking up a whole bench to himself. He screamed incessantly with pain. His screams deafened Pavel Nikolayevich and hurt him so much that it seemed the boy was screaming not with his own pain but with Rusanov's. . . .

Pain is deadly real, but it is expressed in different ways.

The doors to most of the rooms are wide open. Two beds (with a separating screen), assorted chairs, and night stands complete the furniture of the room. The window looks out over a busy highway and, beyond, a cemetery (symbol?). Some doors are closed, and display warning signs that say that anyone who enters must be dressed in a hospital gown and wear a mask to prevent contamination of the frail occupant, a reminder that this is a dangerous business, in spite of the friendly, cheery banter at the front desk.

I do not have to tell you that the banter is in English. We might assume this, but it need not be so, and no English flows from room 4-D-5. Behind the closed door is a 35-year-old Japanese woman who has a form of bone marrow cancer.

Mrs. Ogawa was flown in from her home in Tokyo to receive special medical services from this hospital, on recommendation of her physician. At home she left her 55-year-old husband, a wealthy industrialist, and their children, two sons, ages 11 and 14. With her came a twin sister, Mrs. Obi, and the youngest sister in the family, Mrs. Nasome. It was not by chance that these two came with Mrs. Ogawa, even though they had to leave their own families behind. The twin sister was needed as the donor of bone marrow cells that are to be used in a delicate replacement process after Mrs. Ogawa's diseased cells are destroyed. Also, should any need for blood transfusions arise during the days following the operation, Mrs. Obi's blood would be needed as the best match to the patient's blood. Helping to save her twin sister's life was the major reason for Mrs. Obi's journey half way around the world.

The youngest sister, Mrs. Nasome, was called upon to join the others in this crisis journey because she alone among the members of the extended family spoke English fluently. There would be many occasions when Mrs. Nasome would be called upon to translate from the patient to the staff and from the staff to the patient. Mrs. Nasome, as translator, was at a critical place in the communication circuit.

The social worker assigned to this case was a Japanese-American who spoke only a few words of Japanese, although she did understand the culture. As she walked to Mrs. Ogawa's room, the worker mused over the difficulties Mrs. Ogawa must feel, in a country very foreign to her in language and customs, where her only link to sustenance was by means of her younger sister, and during a time when she must be worried about her potentially fatal disease, let alone her state of weakness and pain. The worker knocked and entered the room, and the younger sister, Mrs. Nasome, rose and bowed slightly, and greeted her—in Japanese. She returned the greeting, using her limited vocabulary, and then spoke to the patient, who was lying in bed dressed in a silk dressing gown. The worker spoke to her in English. She introduced herself as Miss Koizumi, explaining her role at the hospital (social worker in the oncology unit), and offering to be of service in whatever way she could. Mrs. Ogawa smiled wanely after this recitation, and turned to Mrs. Nasome, who translated the worker's comments into Japanese. Miss Koizumi could not follow what Mrs. Nasome was saying, but Mrs. Ogawa nodded and smiled again at her.

It was difficult for the worker to communicate this way. She tried not only to say something, but to say it in a particular way that would communicate her concern, her respect, and her understanding. But she was never certain how much of these—basic aspects of interviewing—were being transmitted along with her words. It was difficult for Mrs. Ogawa because she did not seem to be concentrating during this long process. Maybe it was the pain, or the fatigue, or something else. It was difficult for the translator, too. She was clearly working hard to translate as accurately as she could; she felt a grave responsibility. But there were so many things to translate, some strange, some difficult to put into her native language. Fatigue soon showed, so Miss Koizumi cut short the visit.

Over the next few days, Mrs. Ogawa was prepared for the treatment, which was both difficult and dangerous. Lethal doses of chemotherapy and radiation were applied while the twin sister waited. Then, when the patient's condition was stabilized, healthy bone marrow was extracted from the pelvic bone of the twin to replace the bone marrow in the patient. (Bone marrow regenerates itself regularly in healthy people.)

A period of 10 to 14 days is needed to determine the success of this replacement procedure. All during this time, the patient is essentially under constant medical care and is carefully isolated. The social worker, however, kept in constant contact with the younger sister so as to aid in interpreting what the staff was saying about the patient's condition. The twin sister and the younger sister were on call all of the time, either at the hospital or at their nearby hotel.

Time passed slowly for these foreign visitors and was relieved only by letters and calls from home. But these messages were bittersweet, as the husbands urged their wives to return as soon as possible. As the days turned into weeks, the pressures began to mount, especially on Mrs. Obi, the twin sister. Mr. Obi was a man who held strict ideas about family relationships, and while he recognized the need to have his wife provide bone marrow and blood for her twin, he also stated that his wife's rightful place was at home with him and her family. This was a powerful call, based on the strong traditions of the place of the family in Japanese culture, and the duties of the wife in that family.

The critical time came, and the tests showed that the replacement of bone marrow cells was successful, although Mrs. Ogawa was not as strong as would be hoped. However, the exercise program now began. Again, through the omnipresent translator, the staff explained to Mrs. Ogawa that she must use careful oral hygiene and must begin to move about in her room to prevent infection and pneumonia. Problems over this new regimen soon arose. The patient refused to comply. In Japan, a sick person is almost fully cared for by a relative. One would never do these sorts of things for oneself. Moreover, at Western State Hospital, the medical staff was imbued with the philosophy that informing the patient of what they were going to do and why was very important (to reduce stress and to further cooperation for improvement). In Japan, patients are told far less of these details. And so the medical staff was frustrated. They could not speak directly to their patient, and the patient at times refused to cooperate in her own best interests. Moreover, Mrs. Nasome refused to translate large portions of their instructions, saying that the patient would not want to know them. It would be stressful.

The social worker was placed in the middle of these frustrated people—patient, relatives, and staff. She tried to be sensitive to what she knew of Japanese culture, particularly in regard to the way illness and sickness are viewed traditionally. She patiently listened to all sides and explained what was in the minds of the others. Slowly, the worker developed ways of having each side accommodate the other to some degree. Eventually it paid off, and Mrs. Ogawa was showing signs of improvement.

Then an even greater threat to the treatment arose. Mrs. Obi's husband ordered her to come home. The operation was a success (in his view) and there was no reason for her to stay any longer. However, the medical staff was strongly against the twin sister's leaving, as the risk of infection was still great, as was the need for her to be present should a blood transfusion be needed. The American doctor told Mrs. Obi, by means of Mrs. Nasome, that to leave now would be to risk the life of her sister.

The social worker began to recognize something else. The translator, being the youngest sister in the family, had little status or power over her older sisters, and so her translated messages did not seem to carry weight in their deliberations. This recognition of the gravity of the situation and her powerlessness to influence events drove Mrs. Nasome to tears on many occasions, and she showed signs of being depressed. Miss Koizumi had another crisis on her hands, but she gave the translator immediate counseling, and provided support and showed empathy for her. Yet the worker also confronted her with the reality of the situation. Miss Koizumi thought Mrs. Nasome was burned out as translator, not because of the work, but because she was always retranslating everything to what she thought people wanted to hear. For her sisters, she made medical orders fit more into Japanese views on care giving. For the staff, she censored portions of the patient's expression of pain, since this was only for family to hear. She was aware that she was changing messages, but what could she do?

The social worker recognized the complexity of the crisis, both medical and cultural, and suggested calling the older brother in Japan for another perspective on what to do. Mrs. Obi's husband was putting on more pressure, and Mrs. Nasome was getting more and more depressed.

In Japanese culture, when a father is deceased the eldest son represents another major force within the extended family. He has a status different from the husband in one family, because he is the leading member (eldest brother) of portions of several families. The social worker carefully prepared Mrs. Nasome to explain what the situation was, and what the options were. After some consideration, the eldest brother came down strongly on the side of the twin's staying with her sister as long as needed, in spite of what her husband demanded. This provided them with enough leverage to make the decision to stay. A sigh of relief spread throughout the staff.

During the next few weeks, the patient progressed steadily. She was discharged to return to her home in Japan, accompanied by her sisters as before. She wore a beautiful silk kimono to the airport. The three sisters were very quiet as they left the ward, but once they were outside, they began to banter happily.

SUMMARY

This brief overview to our ethnic and cultural diversity is intended both to provide you with background that will be helpful in practice situations and with a sharpened sensitivity to differences. We are all different, there is no question about that. But we also share important similarities that are sometimes more important than our differences. For example, people who have similar educational and economic backgrounds, even when they may have different skin colors or worship their God in different voices, may be more "alike"—that is, they share similar values and can communicate more easily—than those who lack this similar educational and economic background. What makes this similarity or difference is the configuration of experiences that define differences as important or unimportant.

Public schools offer the opportunity of various kinds of social and cultural mixing in contexts that enable young children to play with other children rather than avoiding the stereotypical children of their parents' imagination. But the playground is only one aspect of the human configuration, and children may learn about differences—and to devalue differences—through many sources.

Thus ethnicity and cultural differences remain a perennial concern for the helping professions, both in a personal way—Am I relatively free of stereotypes and biases?—and as an institution—Are we providing fair and equitable services for all people? This chapter has provided a point of departure for personal and professional considerations.

OUTLINE

A Brief History of The Women's Movement
in the United States

  Act 1
  Intermission
  Act 2
    Women at Work
    The Civil Rights Movement
    The Sexual Revolution
    The Critical Mass of Educated and Activist Women

Feminist Social Work: Auditions for Act 3

Aging and Age-Sensitive Social Work

Summary

CHAPTER EIGHTEEN

Gender-Sensitive and Age-Sensitive Social Work

We are all actors—men or women, young or old—in some of the great dramas of our times. They include the evolutionary developments toward fairness and equality concerning gender and aging. This chapter gives some historical background and reviews the current status of these struggles. Social workers should be acquainted with the hopes and aspirations of the leaders in these social movements. There are some obvious points of overlap between gender and age issues, but there are many differences as well. Beyond these historical reviews are the day-to-day concerns for sensitive and effective practice with women (and men), and with the elderly (and those who are not yet elderly).

A BRIEF HISTORY OF THE WOMEN'S MOVEMENT IN THE UNITED STATES

Act 1

The mass movement seeking equality for women in a male-dominated society began in the early 19th century, prophetically, as American women expressed their concern for others, particularly for the slaves. When the American Anti-Slavery Society was founded in Philadelphia in 1833, one of the speakers was Lucretia Mott, a Quaker minister who became an active abolitionist and leader of the women's movement. However, women were not permitted to sign any documents emanating from that founding. And so a paradox was born: A reform movement that sought freedom, justice, and other civil rights for 3 million slaves, but not for 17 million women.

As a consequence, women leaders like Mott set up organizations to focus their efforts. Here is an excerpt from the Constitution of the Philadelphia Female Anti-Slavery Society of 1833. (This, and the following excerpts, are taken from Papachristou's informative book, *Women Together: A History in Documents of the Women's Movement in the United States*, 1976.):

Whereas more than two million of our fellow countrymen, of these United States, are held in abject bondage; and whereas, we believe that slavery and prejudice against color are contrary to the laws of God, and to the principles of our far-famed Declaration of Independence, and recognizing the right of the slave to immediate emancipation, we deem it our duty to manifest our abhorrence of the flagrant injustice and deep sin of slavery, by united and vigorous exertions for its speedy removal, and for the restoration of the people of color to their inalienable rights. For these purposes, we, the undersigned, agree to associate ourselves under the name of "THE PHILADELPHIA FEMALE ANTI-SLAVERY SOCIETY."

Closer to home was another mass movement in which women participated in the middle 19th century, the temperance movement. This was not simply a matter of genteel Christian morality bursting into saloons and breaking up the places. It directly reflected women's powerless position in society because women were almost totally dependent on men (husbands, fathers) to provide the family income, to be legally responsible for their property, and to be protector against violence. So, when a husband used up his earnings on liquor, sold family property to get more money, and abused his wife and children, there were few legal recourses that the wife could take. She and the children were the victims of intemperance. It was more acceptable for the average woman to be a part—strictly, just an auxiliary member—of temperance societies that were frequently led by clergymen, as contrasted with abolitionist societies, but in both experiences, women began to recognize their inferior status in American society. Here is one account, from a newspaper in a small town in Ohio, 1873:

> . . . The (prayer) meeting Thursday evening (December 25, 1873) was one of deep interest and feeling. (An appeal to saloon owners to stop selling intoxicating drinks that have "desolated homes, blasted hopes, ruined lives, widowed hearts" was adopted. Then) Down the central aisle of the church marched those women ("forty of our best women in the community") to their work . . . to appeal face to face in their various places of business, to those men who are at work selling liquor. Thirteen places in all were visited . . . Into the front door, filling the front room and back rooms too. Prayer, followed by Bible arguments in answer to the excuses of men. Down into the cellar, everywhere they go with the same eloquent plea. . . . (Sometimes they were successful, and rolled out big barrels of whiskey onto the streets.) An ax was placed in the hands of the women who suffered most, and swinging through the air came down with ringing blows, bursting the heads (barrels) and flooding the gutters of the street . . . (Papachristou, 1976).

The spirit of reform in America spread to women's rights. Lecturers traveled widely—these were the mass media personalities of the mid-1800s—and frequently shocked their local audiences with discussion of abolition, the rights of women, and other hot topics including attacks on religion, sexual restrictions, and dress codes. This was the era when Amelia Bloomer, an effective temperance worker, editor of a women's journal called the *Lily*, and women's rights worker, invented the pantaloons and loosely fitting tunic that permitted women much more freedom of movement than did the long skirts, starched slips, and tightly-laced corsets of the fashionable 1850s. While feminists enjoyed this degree of freedom, the criticism was too great, and even stout-hearted feminists dropped this creative idea in favor of more central issues in women's rights.

Improvements in transportation and commercial printing permitted the publication and distribution of national magazines and newsletters that influenced large numbers of persons. The first issue of the *Lily* offered this statement:

> It is WOMAN that speaks through the LILY. It is upon an important subject, too, that she comes before the public to be heard. Intemperance is the great foe to her peace and happiness. It is that, after all, which has made her home desolate, and beggared her offspring. It is that above all, which has filled to the brim the cup of her sorrows, and sent her mourning to the grave. Surely she has a right to wield the pen for its suppression. Surely she may, without throwing aside the modest retirement, which so much becomes her sex, use her influence to lead her fellow mortals away from the destroyer's path. It is this which she proposes to do in the columns of LILY. . . (1853) (Papachristou, 1976).

On July 19th and 20th, 1848, about three hundred people (including 250 women) attended the first Women's Rights Convention held in Seneca Falls, New York. Five women arranged the meeting—Lucretia Mott, Elizabeth Cady Stanton, Martha C. Wright, Jane Hunt, and Mary Ann McClintock—whose purpose was to discuss "the social, civil, and religious conditions and rights of women." (Papachristou, 1976, p. 23.) They produced a sharp stinging document called the Declaration of Sentiments. Here are a few excerpts from it:

> We hold these truths to be self-evident: that all men and women are created equal; that they are endowed by their Creator with certain inalienable rights; that among these are life, liberty, and the pursuit of happiness; that to secure these rights governments are instituted, deriving their just powers from the consent of the governed. . . .
>
> The history of mankind is a history of repeated injuries and usurpations on the part of man toward woman, having in direct object the establishment of an absolute tyranny over her. To prove this, let the facts be submitted to a candid world.
>
> He has never permitted her to exercise her inalienable right to the elective franchise.
>
> He has compelled her to submit to laws, in the formation of which she has no voice. . . .
>
> He has made her, if married, in the eye of the law, civilly dead.
>
> He has taken from her all right in property, even to the wages she earns. . . .
>
> He has monopolized nearly all the profitable employments, and from those she is permitted to follow, she receives but a scanty remuneration. . . .
>
> He has denied her the facilities for obtaining a thorough education, all colleges being closed against her. . . .
>
> He has endeavored, in every way that he could, to destroy her confidence in her own powers, to lessen her self-respect, and to make her willing to lead a dependent and abject life.
>
> Now, in view of this entire disfranchisement of one-half of the people of this country, their social and religious degradation—in view of the unjust laws above mentioned, and because women do feel themselves aggrieved, oppressed, and fraudulently deprived of their most sacred rights, we insist that they have immediate admission to all the rights and privileges which belong to them as citizens of the United States (Papachristou, 1976).

The resolutions adopted at that Seneca Falls convention set the platform for women's rights for the next century and to our own day. They called for an end to the laws and customs that made women inferior to, and dependent on, men in matters political, legal, economic, educational, familial, and social rights in general. For this, as for later conventions and presentations across the country, the early feminists were showered with angry verbal abuse. This excerpt from the *New York Herald*, Sept. 7, 1853, is typical:

> The assemblage of rampant women which convened at the Tabernacle yesterday was an interesting phase in the comic history of the nineteenth century.
>
> We saw, in broad daylight, in a public hall in the city of New York, a gathering of unsexed women—unsexed in mind all of them, and many in habiliments—publicly propounding the doctrine that they should be allowed to step out of their appropriate sphere, and mingle in the busy walks of every-day life, to the neglect of those duties which both human and divine law have assigned to them. We do not stop to argue against so ridiculous a set of ideas. We will only inquire who are to perform those duties which we and our fathers before us have imagined belonged solely to women. Is the world to be depopulated? Are there to be no more children? . . .
>
> It is almost needless for us to say that these women are entirely devoid of personal attraction. They are generally thin maiden ladies, or women who perhaps have been disappointed in the endeavors to appropriate the breeches and the rights of their unlucky lords; . . . (Papachristou, 1976, p. 45).

With the coming of the Civil War, feminists put away their resolutions in order to volunteer in large numbers for the war effort. They were expected to return to their prewar occupations and status, and did so, except in the field of nursing. As Baxandall, Gordon, and Reverby (1976) point out, "Wherever women are needed economically it is quickly decided that they are biologically or even spiritually destined (for these jobs, such as nurses during the Civil War, or as clerical workers three decades later)" (p. 75).

With each proposed Amendment to the U.S. Constitution, including the 14th (providing that blacks were now to be counted as whole persons rather than the three-fifths of the original document), and the 15th (adding black males to the roster of voters), the feminists tried to include women among those granted civil rights—but to no avail. Challenges through the courts were no more successful. As one ruling from the Supreme Court of the United States noted (*Bradwell v. Illinois*, 1869):

> . . . the civil law, as well as nature herself, has always recognized a wide difference in the respective spheres and destinies of man and woman. Man is, or should be, woman's protector and defender. The natural and proper timidity and delicacy which belongs to the female sex evidently unfits it for many of the occupations of civil life. The constitution of the family organization, which is founded on divine ordinance, as well as in the nature of things, indicates the domestic sphere as that which properly belongs to the domain and functions of womanhood . . . (Papachristou, 1976, p. 105).

Many supporters in the abolitionist and temperance struggle refused to cooperate on women's rights. Differences in opinion on how to advance women's rights, as well as an adultery scandal among some central members of the group, produced schisms in the movement. The division effectively stopped the movement until several decades later. Personal animosities were forgotten as a new (combined) women's organization emerged, the National American Woman Suffrage Association (1890). But what was more important was the association with a much larger group, the National Woman's Christian Temperance Union (NWCTU), which had already supported the vote for women in 1881. Now large numbers of women (and men) from all over the country were united in a cause that led them to various forms of public demonstration, and political maneuverings—educational experiences for future feminist work as well.

The battle to obtain higher education was not easy. Mary Lyon had founded Mount Holyoke Female Seminary in 1837, the first independent (but all female) institution of higher education in America. A few public institutions admitted women, among them the University of Michigan, but by and large institutions of higher education were closed to women in the 19th century.

In a fascinating book on the intellectual roots of feminism, Rosenberg (1982) begins with Dr. Edward Clarke, of Harvard Medical School, who wrote some influential books—*Sex in Education, or, a Fair Chance for the Girls* (1873) and *The Building of a Brain* (1874). His thesis, based on the best scientific information of his day, was that the sexual divergence (men being socially superior to women) reflected an evolutionary process. For example, men's brains weigh one-tenth more than women's, from which was inferred that by natural selection men's brains developed higher levels of capability for complex reasoning than was possible for women. (See also, Gould, 1981.) On the other hand, having less brain, "woman" was supposed to be closer to the instinctive or emotional side of life. From this type of reasoning emerges the social diversity whereby men are better at complex reasoning and abstractions, while women are better at intuitive, emotional feelings. Rosenberg quotes Dr. Clarke: "Differentiation is Nature's method of ascent. We should cultivate the difference of the sexes, not try to hide or abolish it" (p. 9).

Dr. Clarke's ideas influenced many people about opening universities to women. His crucial point was that not only would higher education impose a severe strain on women's (weaker) minds, but it would also do serious damage to their bodies, particularly their reproductive capacities. His advice to women who did go for higher education: study one-third less than young men, and not at all during menstruation (Rosenberg, p. 10). Rosenberg goes on to report that many women and men disputed these views on sexual diversity, and did empirical research to support their position that while men were on the average stronger than women, both appeared quite able to pick up books and study them successfully.

At the same time early feminists were asserting the equality of the sexes, it should be pointed out, other reformers were seeking special protective legislation (as in labor laws prohibiting excessive hours for women and children) because of women's weaknesses. The bases of the arguments are different—physical versus mental attributes—but this kind of apparent dilemma has continued to plague reformers to this day.

By the beginning of the 20th century, America had undergone many significant changes, from industrialization and urbanization to rapid developments in transportation and communication. Women were obtaining higher education in greater numbers and entrance to the professions, albeit very slowly. Women overcame their social isolation and became more sophisticated actors in their own drama as a result of experience in many new national organizations, ranging from the Grange (affecting rural Americans) to the DAR (Daughters of the American Revolution, founded in 1891), the National Association of Colored Women and the National Council of Jewish Women (both founded in 1896), and the YWCA (Young Women's Christian Association (founded in 1905). Likewise, there were many local organizations and clubs whose manifest purposes may have been social and charitable, but whose deeper role was to bring women together for common causes.

As an example of the purposes of these early associations, here is an excerpt from a YWCA resolution, from the year 1911:

> Inasmuch as the utterly inadequate wages paid to thousands of young women throughout the country often hamper the work of the Association (YWCA) as a great preventive agency, and as the white slave traffic is admitted to be closely related to lack of living wage, the Association recognizes its responsibility as an influential unit in the body of Christian public opinion, and accordingly it is recommended:
>   a) (educating the public regarding the need for a minimum living wage compatible with physical health). . . .
>   c) (promoting legislation to regulate hours and wages)
>   d) (improving industrial conditions of the working girl). . . (Papachristou, 1976).

All of these goal statements by the various groups foreshadow features of a future social work profession. The means will often be quite different, but the ends appear to have been clearly articulated for many years before the coming of professional social work.

While a large number of women were associated in various ways with these mainstream organizations and clubs, a few women were striking out on paths that challenged more basic social and economic relationships of women to society. Through their writings and their lives, women such as Emma Goldman, Margaret Sanger, and Jane Addams began to seek some fundamental changes in American society (and world society as well).

Margaret Sanger began her formal quest for birth control with an announcement printed in English, Yiddish, and Italian:

> MOTHERS
> Can you afford to have large families?
> Do you want any more children?
> If not, why do you have them?
> DO NOT KILL. DO NOT TAKE LIFE, BUT PREVENT.
> Safe, harmless information can be obtained from trained nurses.
> 46 AMBOY STREET
> Near Pitkin Avenue—Brooklyn
> Tell your friends and neighbors. All mothers welcome. A registration fee of 10 cents entitles any mother to this information (Sanger, 1971).

This was in the year 1916, and soon hundreds of poor women crowded through the two tiny rooms to obtain information on condoms and douches—including a policewoman in disguise. Dispensing information about contraceptives was illegal. (Sanger was sentenced to 30 days in the workhouse for that offense.) She continued the struggle and six years later she organized the American Birth Control League. Its principles are similar to those of comparable organizations operating today:

> The complex problems now confronting America as a result of the practice of reck-
> less procreation are fast threatening to grow beyond human control. . . . We wit-
> ness the appalling waste of women's health and women's lives by too frequent
> pregnancies. . . . We hold that children should be 1) conceived in love; 2) born of
> the mother's conscious desire; and 3) only begotten under conditions which ren-
> der possible the heritage of health. Therefore, we hold that every woman must
> possess the power and freedom to prevent conception except when these condi-
> tions can be satisfied. (Principles and Aims of the American Birth Control League,
> 1921.) (Papachristou, 1976.)

Legal battles followed. Slowly, changes occurred, such as the break in 1936 in
the Comstock laws (prohibiting the mailing of obscene mail—including information on contraception); the 1936 change permitted physicians to receive
contraceptive information through the mails. The tide in favor of birth control
was rising. The movement took different directions, from birth control to
planned parenthood and the larger issues surrounding human sexuality. In
our own day, we continue to witness opposition to family planning clinics,
particularly when abortion is one of the services discussed or provided.
Margaret Sanger's quest is not yet won.

The National Consumers' League (NCL) was formed in 1899 with the intention of educating consumers, primarily middle-class women who in most
families were seen to hold the purse strings for purchases of food, clothing,
and household goods. If they could be informed about the sweatshop conditions under which most of these items were produced, such women might
pressure the government for reform. Florence Kelley, president of the NCL,
described the situation this way:

> We have, in this country, two million children under the age of sixteen years who
> are earning their bread. They vary in age from six and seven (in the cotton mills of
> Georgia) and eight, nine, and ten years (in the coal-breakers of Pennsylvania), to
> fourteen, fifteen, and sixteen in more enlightened states. . . . Tonight while we
> sleep, several thousand little girls will be working in textile mills, all the night
> through, in the deafening noise of the spindles and the looms spinning and weav-
> ing cotton and woolen, silks, and ribbons for us to buy. . . . The children make our
> shoes in the shoe factories; they knit our stockings, our knitted underwear in the
> knitting factories. . . . Children braid straw for our hats. . . . They stamp buckles
> and metal ornaments of all kinds, as well as pins and hat-pins. Under the sweating
> system, tiny children make artificial flowers and neckwear for us to buy. . . .
>
> What can we do to free our consciences? . . . We can enlist the workingmen on
> behalf of our enfranchisement just in proportion as we strive with them to free the
> children. No labor organization in this country ever fails to respond to an appeal
> for help in the freeing of the children (Papachristou, 1976, p. 176).

When the daughter of Elizabeth Cady Stanton took the lead in a new style
of suffragette, a second generation of feminists emerged. Harriot Stanton
Blatch had observed the more active, politicized British suffragettes, and
brought some of their methods to America, especially by including working-
class women. Large numbers of persons joined the movement, not only in suffragette groups, but through churches, labor unions, and political parties in
some states. There were successful attempts to put woman suffrage on the
ballot, but there were even more failures.

As World War I loomed on the horizon, some suffragettes took a sharper line of attack, using the public demonstrations, picketing, and effigy burnings. The proposed Amendment to give the vote to women was slowly working its way though the states, but President Wilson had not given his support. Pickets, including some prominent women, walked around the White House, attacking President Wilson for his indecisiveness on the issue. The level of anger and frustration on both sides increased. Police eventually arrested 218 of the women, threw 97 of them in jail (literally "threw" them, according to personal accounts), and kept them there, some for days, some for weeks, and others for months. One leader, Alice Paul, was force-fed. All these arrests were later invalidated by the courts.

The brutality produced a reaction to a shocked nation, but something else was going on that was even more important for women's suffrage. Carrie Chapman Catt became head of the National American Woman Suffrage Association, and distanced her organization from the more radical members of the feminists. Working behind the scenes to cement relations with the Wilson government, she also set out a national strategy for women's suffrage. It called for mobilization of a political force in each state, which would then move on the federal government to pass the Amendment, after which it would have to be ratified by three-quarters of the states.

Although the war had begun, the women's issue continued to gain momentum. Eventually, even President Wilson gave his backing to the congressional Amendment: "I regard the concurrence of the Senate in the constitutional amendment proposing the extension of the suffrage to women as vitally essential to the successful prosecution of the great war of humanity in which we are engaged" (Wilson, Jan. 10, 1918) (Papachristou, 1976, p. 187). Shortly thereafter, on June 4, 1919, Congress finally approved the 19th Amendment, and by August 26, 1920, it was ratified by the necessary majority of states. Thus women finally gained the right to vote, a privilege that certain men had since the founding of the nation.

Intermission

At the conclusion of World War I, a great conservative wave swept the country, swamping the social reform movement. Settlement houses, having been burned by the activities of some of their pacificist leaders (such as Jane Addams, who was to win a Nobel Prize for Peace in 1931), essentially moved toward safe recreational activities. Their traditional clientele began to move up in the social world and away from the ethnic inner city slums, as new occupants moved in to take their places. Social work at large swallowed the psychoanalytic model whole, and turned into psychiatric case work, even during much of the Great Depression. While it was obvious to almost everyone that the socio-economic conditions were the primary cause for the widespread social distress that left "one-third of the nation ill-housed, ill-clad, ill-nourished," social workers spent much of their energies debating fine points of a theoretical controversy current at the time. The School of Social Work in Richmond, Virginia, for example, added courses in advanced psychiatric social work during the early 30's, and finally in 1936, offered an elective course on Government Reorganization and the Depression (which was housed in the Department of Government).

This is not to say that social workers were not making contributions to deal with the Depression. Indeed, Harry Hopkins, a social worker, was President Roosevelt's chief architect for the program of social reforms that grappled with both the immediate crisis and the long-term solutions. His programs for temporary job creation led to enduring products (buildings, roads, public recreation areas, national parks, among others) that benefited society and provided models for future generations. Frances Perkins, another social worker, was Secretary of Labor in the Roosevelt cabinet and played a critical role in the development of the Social Security Act, cornerstone of American social welfare policy. Generally speaking, however, the period between the world wars was a "seedtime for reform" (Chambers, 1963) during which ideas were germinating off-stage.

Act 2

What accounts for the recrudescence of feminist activities during the 1960s and 1970s? While we may be still too close to these events to judge fully, several factors seem to be relevant: (1) Women's entrance into the labor market in large numbers; (2) the Civil Rights Movement as model and training ground for Women's Rights; (3) the sexual revolution with its changes in mores and the technology for contraceptive control; and (4) a critical mass of educated women leaders (including some who were self-educated).

Women at Work.   A veritable revolution was quietly taking place in the post-World War II era, as white women began to enter the labor force in large numbers—black women had long been working out of necessity. About 45 percent of all workers are women (including 52 percent of all married women and 50 percent of all mothers whose youngest child is less than 6 years old). By the year 2000, more than half of the labor force, it is estimated, will be women (Akabas, 1988). The reasons are largely economic; it takes two paychecks for many families to afford a reasonable standard of living. No longer does the stereotype hold that women are working for "pin money"; they do serious work for needed cash.

The structure of society prevented women from entering the more lucrative occupations and professions, however. About three-quarters of all women work in clerical or office work, and the average female worker working full-time year around earns about 60 percent of what the average male worker earns. Women are moving into "men's occupations," but the progress is mixed. For example, in 1970, women accounted for 1.4 percent of the military services; by 1975, the figure had increased to 4.6, and it rose to 8.4 percent in 1980. By law and policy, however, women are not permitted in combat assignments. They were first admitted to the armed forces (officially) in 1901, but many thousands had served in civilian status in all the previous wars. A few, like Molly Pitcher (Mary Ludwig Hays McCauley), were made noncommissioned officers by General Washington, after distinguished combat performances. Although 265,000 women served in the military in World War II, three decades passed before the service academies admitted women, by an Act of Congress, in 1976.

For newer occupations (like specialists in computer technology and science), the ratios of women's salaries to men's are more nearly equal. Yet for the rank and file of U.S. workers across the nation, regardless of level of education, the 60 percent figure has held relatively constant since at least 1955, give or take one or two points in either direction. Breaking this down further, Bergmann (1986) reports that in 1985, white females earned 67 percent of what white males earn; black females earned 60 and black males 75 percent. Even in the same type of job, there are often great disparities. Bergmann provides data on 25 occupations; for secretarial jobs, for example, women's average weekly salary in 1985 was $278 while men got $365; bus drivers—women $257, men $404; bakers—women $202, men $301 (p. 121). Such disparities are increasingly the object of affirmative action challenges. The point is well made that the inequities prevail.

Along with recent entry into the labor force comes the small percentage of women in top management positions and all that these entail. *Business Week* (November 24, 1975, p. 58; June 5, 1978, p. 99) reported that women totaled 15 percent of entry-level management, 5 percent of middle management, and only one percent of top management. Harvard did not even accept women in its MBA program until 1963. It will take a long time for women to develop the skills and the networks of contacts to become a large proportion of top management.

The Civil Rights Movement. The 1960s witnessed an amazing series of events. An oppressed group (African Americans) rose up, relied principally on nonviolent means to force the majority to change institutional discrimination (that which is structurally created to discriminate against certain classes of people, regardless of individual qualities), and succeeded in establishing itself as a force to be contended with. Many of the objectives still remain to be attained, but, along the way, this oppressed minority developed a keen sense of black pride. Their self-esteem is based in part on raised consciousness of their strengths and the sources of their limitations. Each step of the way toward full civil rights was won with difficulty, often in the face of violent opposition; advance was occasionally paid for by a life. (See, for example, the moving story [and the motion picture "Mississippi Burning"] about the 1964 murders of three young civil rights workers—James Chaney, Andrew Goodman, and Michael Schwerner—in the small town of Philadelphia, Mississippi, a town whose name means "brotherly love") (Hendrickson, 1984). But visible changes were made, and the many participants in those battles learned the lessons that the suffragettes knew many decades before.

With these models and experiences from the Civil Rights Movement clearly in mind, other groups, including women's groups, began to form and use similar tactics. Some of the action groups used more restrained, nonviolent means, others tended to rely more on confrontation. (The National Association of Social Workers reflects a typical pattern—an activist subgroup is outnumbered by a much larger group of concerned but nonactive members.)

The Sexual Revolution. The advent of effective contraceptive devices, especially the pill, over which women had full control, meant a whole new ball game of human sexuality. The old double standard—men, that is, "real men," are sexually active, while women, that is, "good women," are not—gave way to increased participation by women who could control their own fate concerning the birth of children. The Guttmacher Institute (1980) findings on sexuality indicate rapid growth in sexual activity by increasingly younger women during the 1970s. Eight out of ten men, and seven out of ten women, have been sexually active by age 19—that is, some 12 million young people. Nearly half of 15- to 17-year-old males and one-third of same-age females have had intercourse. While the proportion of black teenagers who are sexually active still exceeds those of whites, whites have shown the largest increase in sexual activity in the 1970s.

The inevitable results have occurred. There were over 1.1 million pregnancies among teenagers in 1978; some 434,000 ended in abortion, and 454,000 led to births, of which 362,000 were out of wedlock. The rest ended in miscarriages. Half of the premarital pregnancies occurred within six months of their first intercourse. Teens are using contraceptive methods, but mostly the least effective ones (withdrawal), while use of the most effective ones (the pill and intrauterine devices) declined. The title of a Guttmacher Institute publication (1981) tells the main story: *Teenage Pregnancy: The Problem That Hasn't Gone Away.*

Unwanted teenage pregnancy, as well as a host of related problems for women, have become a major challenge for the helping professions and for self-help groups as well. An inexpensive paperback, *Our Bodies, Ourselves* (1971; 1979), brought basic information on many aspects of sexuality, love (homosexual as well as heterosexual), family, and aging to thousands of women within and outside the United States. Openness about expression of sexuality and feelings of love and attachment are clearly promoted in such books. But there is also an underlying theme of being one's own person, of being in control of one's sexual expressions as well.

The Critical Mass of Educated and Activist Women.   Throughout history there have always been intelligent, thoughtful, and active women. But the 1960s and 70s saw emerge some excellent leaders of the women's movement, from Betty Friedan, Simone de Beauvoir, Gloria Steinem, Jessie Bernard, Margaret Mead, Eleanor Holmes Norton, and for negative reasons, Phyllis Schlafley, to name only a few of the people who crystallized opinions and actions across a broad spectrum of society.

Friedan's book on the *Feminine Mystique* (1963) piqued intense interest because she named a malaise that many women felt but could not verbalize. Women's consciousness raising groups formed to expand this new-found self-knowledge, which became shared knowledge. New or adapted techniques helped them express their insistence on fair rights for women, not necessarily aggressively, nor any longer passively, but with firm assertiveness (Bloom, et al, 1975).

Research information began to accumulate. Jessie Bernard reported (1972) that married women had worse rates of mental health than did single women, or married men. She writes that ". . . unmarried women are spectacularly better off so far as psychological distress symptoms are concerned, suggesting that women start out with an initial advantage which marriage reverses" (p. 35). She explains that "housework is a dead-end job; there is no chance of promotion" (p. 48). Though most women do marry, a large proportion of them experience what she calls the "housewife syndrome" (mental and emotional illnesses).

Research by Carol Gilligan (1982) begins the process of questioning science itself as an accurate tool for understanding gender-related problems. (See Hotelling and Forrest, 1985). For example, she challenges Lawrence Kohlberg's model of moral judgment that describes three levels of sophistication. A premoral level involves moral judgments made in accordance with avoiding punishment and obtaining rewards. A conventional level involves judgments made in order to maintain the approval of others and to avoid disapproval. A postconventional moral level involves complex rational decisions, including ultimately acting on the basis of one's own conscience interpreting universal moral principles. Using a test of his own devising, Kohlberg found that males score higher on this scale than do women. Gilligan counters that what may be an ultimate value for males—abstract universal principles—may not be ultimate for females, for whom relatedness—responsibility and caring—may be prior. So Kohlberg's test may have this gender bias built in. Indeed, much of social science may be biased in similar subtle ways (Keller, 1985).

FEMINIST SOCIAL WORK: AUDITIONS FOR ACT 3

Gender is a biological given; we are born male or female based on genetic composition. Sexual identity is learned; we are taught to behave in accordance with many sets of social and cultural rules, including those for how men and women are expected to act in general. Sexual preference, that is, whether we are sexually more responsive to members of the opposite or same sex, is less clearly biological or learned. Theories abound but certainty eludes us (cf. Bell, 1982).

Feminist theory mainly concerns sexual role identity: what general expectations for how men and women are to act and to be (that is, their basic personality dimensions) are present in the culture and society? Which do men and women accept and internalize as "natural"? In western culture, women in particular have been defined in ways that are frequently negative (for example, passive, dependent, and overly emotional). These cultural definitions lead to events that are detrimental to their mental and physical health (cf. Bernard, 1972).

There is ample evidence of inequality and injustice associated simply for being a woman in this society at this time. Why should this be? There are many theories (see Chafetz, 1988, for an excellent overview). A common theme running through feminist theory is that part of every problem stems from socio-cultural factors—institutional sexism, in effect—regardless of the particular events in a given case. If this is so, it provides a strong suggestion about how social workers should be conducting their practice.

To illustrate the point, consider here a variation of the theory of learned helplessness (Seligman, 1975), which stresses the social and cultural restrictions on individuals. The original study involved animals who were physically restrained and subjected to punishing conditions from which they could not escape. The animals learned to be helpless, to accept punishment without struggle—even when they were released from restraint! After the animals were so conditioned, the experimenters tried to reverse this condition of learned helplessness. They discovered that it took extreme efforts to get the animals to move out of harmful situations—so powerful was the effect of repeated exposures to uncontrollable events.

Consider further a theory of socio-cultural learned helplessness, in which women as a group are restrained by means of social rules and structures, and subjected to learning conditions that are so pervasive that there is almost no escape. Women are not physically restrained and subjected to punishing conditions like the experimental animals—unless you consider the cultural requirement to wear uncomfortable clothes, high-heel shoes, heavy earrings and other paraphernalia as social restraints that punish the victim. Rather, there are tender traps set that define girls as filled with sugar and spice and everything nice—so don't get dirty playing in the mud with your brother, who is filled with unmentionable stuff. The way adults—even educated, liberal-minded folks—play with children, socialize them, discipline them, and model expectations for them contributes to sexual stereotyping of the way girls are supposed to act and to be.

The effect of all this life-long learning is that both men and women incorporate these sex role identities in their general expectations for everyday life functioning. More important, people plan their future behavior in compliance with such expectations. So, for example, although girls are equally or more able in math in grade school than boys, at the junior-high and high-school level, girls have tended to remove themselves from advanced math classes, and thus have reduced their options for certain college courses and life careers (Tobias, 1978). There is no reason for this change other than socio-cultural expectations that girls cannot learn tough math. Teachers, students, and parents have all held these stereotypes.

At the same time, these same cultural stereotypes have appeared to direct women into fields and careers in which their presumed superiority in helping others, in being more sensitive and more caring, can be usefully applied. Examples include nursing (not medicine), education (not research), social work (not psychiatry), and the like. In fact, some women are very sensitive, caring, and warm, and these helping professions among others are well served by having such persons as members. But some men are also sensitive, caring, and warm; indeed, it is possible to be sensitive, caring, and warm, and also be highly capable in math, facile with high-tech tools, and analytic.

The term *androgynous* (Bem, 1978) describes an individual with both the so-called masculine and feminine characteristics, a person who is able to use these as a given situation calls for one or the other. A person may be sensitive and caring with a client in crisis, but be able to make tough decisions and enforce rules with the same client. That helping person needs androgynous skills and abilities. Recent research tends to show that the person having more masculine skills is more "successful" than a balanced androgynous person, reflecting once again the dominant rewarding structures of this society.

There are cases in society in which the model of social learned helplessness seems to be an apt description. For example, in spousal abuse cases, we often wonder why the woman stayed with a husband who had been abusing her, possibly for years. One explanation is that she may have felt that she was locked in: perhaps she had no job skills, a limited education, no money of her own. She may have had to move to a new setting to follow the husband's job, thus losing supportive ties. She may have children that she feels obliged to care for and protect, and she may feel guilty and responsible for not doing whatever it is that she has not done to win her husband's satisfaction—objective reality to the contrary notwithstanding. These are difficult bonds to break—bonds of her own construction, given the training received and continually reinforced in countless ways in her everyday world.

Given this perspective on feminist theory, it is possible to generate some strategies that might help to break out of this bind. First, the person has to be aware of the bind she or he is in. Given the pervasiveness of the learned helplessness, and all of the support given to "women's role in the home," this may be a very difficult first step. There are many reinforcing factors for being a traditional woman, such as being able to devote much time to raising children, being able to create domestic arts, being relatively free of timed duties and being without direct supervisors. Many women and men find this traditional sex role structure with its division of labor very satisfying for them; it is not our right to impose another value system on them. However, what feminists are calling for is an open awareness of options women and men have for being and doing, that is, for developing their personalities according to their own sense of self-fulfillment without artificial constraints, and for taking those actions (including careers and family functions) that please them intrinsically as well as serving extrinsic values. And to create a situation where this open awareness exists to make life choices, we have to develop situations that do not stereotype people from the very start of their lives.

One method or strategy toward attainment of feminist-valued objectives of freedom of choice of being and doing is assertiveness training. This method derives from work by Wolpe with certain mentally disturbed persons, but has been broadened and expanded for use with "normal" persons (cf. Bloom, et al, 1975). Assertiveness is to be clearly distinguished from aggressiveness and passivity. Aggressiveness is behavior that seeks one's objectives at the expense of others, or disregards their rights. Passivity is behavior that gives up seeking one's fair rights, and makes few demands on others in the pursuit of their objectives. (Some forms of passivity, such as artificial helplessness, in effect make demands of others based on guilt rather than mutuality or fairness.) Assertiveness involves behaviors in which a person seeks to fulfill his or her fair rights without harming others in the pursuit of their rights. Assertiveness implies the freedom of choice to work on behalf of oneself as well as to work for others' benefit when one chooses to do so. Assertiveness is standing up for one's rights, civil, legal, and ordinary, in all contexts—home, work, school, and play.

After becoming aware of one's fair rights—frequently in a context with other people who are in the same status—one can learn the skills and attitudes that will enable one to assert, to put forth one's ideas and wishes in a fair and open way, not threatening or harming of others, but with a firmness and persistence to attain the objective. "I" statements are frequently used, as these are less threatening or blaming than "You" statements. Practice in calm, cool, and collected delivery of the facts and wishes (do your homework!) helps women to break out of the cultural learned helplessness without going to the other extreme of aggressiveness. In a rational society, assertive requests based on solid reasons are frequently honored, and so there is a self-reinforcing experience in being assertive.

Group support and practice are important, which leads to another point that frequently assertive action might be a "we" phenomenon, such as when we want to change work conditions at the office. Some practice may offend me, but if I also know that it offends others, and we can collectively work together to make our reasonable request known—and to stick together as we assert our collective fair rights—then the power of the group is employed.

Yet another level of feminist action involves empowerment (B. Solomon, 1976). This strategy involves large-scale collective awareness, organization, and action on the part of many individuals, no one of whom might be able to perform such actions on his or her own. Legal actions, and general legislative procedures, address the contention of feminists that social structures are often involved in stereotyping and putting down women or others. Therefore, configurations of actions at every level of society may be necessary to address the problems identified by feminist criticism.

The main point this consideration raises for any helping professional, male or female, working with a female client individually or in a family or group setting, is to determine how much of the problems are caused by these pervasive socio-cultural factors of sexism, and how much are caused by the particular events in the given case. It is likely that to a greater or lesser extent, the problems and the way we as helping professionals view these problems will be colored by our pervasive sexist culture. We may think ourselves liberated—and perhaps some may be—but liberation is not a static state, it is a frame of mind continually to be won and to be exercised. (See the whole issue of the *Journal of Primary Prevention,* "Primary Prevention and Women's Concerns," 1988, 9:1 & 2; also, Van Den Bergh and Cooper, 1987; Pilalis and Anderson, 1986.)

AGING AND AGE-SENSITIVE SOCIAL WORK

The age of an individual becomes a special concern for helping professionals, particularly when a person is unable to care for himself or herself and lacks others willing and able to do so. This may occur in the physical and psychosocial immaturity of infancy and early childhood (and into adolescence to some extent), as well as in the older years when physical and psychosocial decrements may emerge. Chapter 14, on Child and Family Welfare, discussed the special needs of young children and their parents; this section considers the older population.

The demographic picture of older Americans provides the context for a discussion of professional helping. Many of the policies and service programs that affect individuals are based on numbers and the vulnerable people represented by the numbers. There were about 30 million persons 65 years or older in the United States in the late 1980s. They accounted for 12 percent of the total population—one in every eight persons. This age group was increasing

David Antebi

What is your response to the person pictured in this scene? Some students have replied with sympathy for the unfortunate circumstances portrayed; others have mentioned their revulsion at this kind of life, and the personal or social events that have led to it. Few mention what might be the most salient feature of this scene, that it depicts an elderly woman. Whatever else may be happening in a situation, we must always recognize the importance of gender and age as essential elements of sensitive social work practice.

more rapidly than the under-65 population, which means that by the year 2030 (when the "baby boomers" will have reached 65), about 21 percent of the population will be "older." The comparable figure in 1900 was 4 percent.

This is a highly significant change in the demographic profile. Consider what changes in everyday life events would have to occur to accommodate a situation in which one person in five was over 65: Who will be working to produce the goods and services some 300 million people will need (cf. Ozawa, 1986)? What changes in entertainment and life-styles will be popular? Who will get the increasingly scarce resources—the elderly or the very young? Who will make the decisions affecting the life and death of persons in a society that has a highly sophisticated medical technology? Some important and difficult changes will face society.

Moreover, people are living longer than they did at the turn of the 20th century. Life expectancy—that is, the number of years a given group or age cohort is expected to live on the average—was about 49 years in 1900; it is now nearly 75 years. These changes in life expectancy were due primarily to reductions in death rates for children and young adults, not because the fountain of youth for older persons had been discovered. Life expectancy differs dramatically, depending on the sex, race, and other demographic characteristics.

Women live longer than men. In 1986 there were 147 older women for every 100 men. In raw numbers, that is 17.4 million older women and 11.8 million older men. This disproportionate sex ratio grows more disparate with age. In the 65–69 year age group, the ratio is 121/100 (women to men); for the 85 and over group, the ratio is 253/100. Why? Evidence points to several major factors: Earlier in this century, it was culturally accepted that men should smoke, but not women; this one factor accounts for a large proportion of the survival differences (Grannis, 1970). In addition, the kinds of life and work stresses related to proneness to cardiovascular diseases also "favored" men (Waldron, 1976)—at least until recently. But women have "come a long way, baby," in the delights of smoking and working at high stress/low mobility jobs, so perhaps these trends may be reduced over time.

The differential life expectancy has a number of repercussions. For one, there were five times as many widows as widowers in 1986; indeed, half of all older women were widows. Many widows and widowers were living alone—another potential source of problems such as loneliness and poor nutritional habits. Older men were twice as likely to be married as were older women in 1986 (77 percent of men compared with 40 percent of women). More older men (83 percent) live in family settings, while only 57 percent of women do. The proportions living in family settings decreases with age.

Some 14 percent of older persons (18 percent of women and 7 percent of men) were not living with a spouse, but were living with their children or other relatives. Another 2 percent or 3 percent were living with nonrelatives.

Only about 5 percent of older persons are institutionalized—in spite of the stereotypes to the contrary. About an equal percentage of the elderly probably would be in institutions or group homes were it not for the efforts of family and friends and paid helpers to maintain them in the community (cf. Nielsen, et al, 1972). Institutions tend to be used by the very old. At ages 65 to 74, only one percent of persons are institutionalized. Percentages increase with advancing age: 6 percent for persons 75–84, and 22 percent for persons 85 years and older.

On the other hand, when older persons live longer, it also means that they are likely to have adult children to provide some help. About 80 percent of older persons have living children, and of these, two-thirds live within 30 minutes of that child. Over 60 percent had at least weekly visits, and three-quarters talked on the phone with their children at least weekly. So the connection between the generations continues. That connection may supply support and affection; it can also be the source of tensions as the needs and resources of the members of the extended family are stretched and pulled in different directions.

Growing old in America is also affected by the person's race and ethnicity. About 90 percent of persons 65 and over in 1986 were white; 8 percent were black; and 2 percent were other races (Asian and Pacific Island Americans, Native Americans, Eskimo, and Aleut). About 3 percent were Hispanic—who may be of any race. In general, persons of minority race and ethnic background have fewer older persons proportional to their numbers in the population, which probably reflects the cumulative stresses such persons face during their lives—poverty, discrimination, less access to helpful and healthy resources.

As mentioned in other chapters, there have been many changes in the economic status of the elderly in the U.S. with the passage of the Social Security Act and its subsequent amendments. However, in 1986, about 12.4 percent of persons 65 years and over were below the poverty line, with another 8 percent classified as "near poor," that is, having an income between the poverty line and 125 percent of that level—still a small amount of money on which to survive. Thus over one-fifth of the older population was poor or near-poor in 1986 (*A Profile of Older Americans,* 1987). (We must still keep in mind that this proportion of poor aged would constitute a considerable improvement compared with the pre-Social Security and pre-Medicare eras.) About one-third of older blacks were poor, compared with 23 percent of elderly Hispanics and 11 percent of older whites. Older women had a higher rate of poverty than men, 15 to 8 percent in 1986.

Health and illness are important concerns to everyone, but they have a particular meaning to older persons. The elderly tend to rate their health as fair to poor more often than do the non-elderly; in 1986 the ratio was 30 to 8 percent (*A Profile of Older Americans,* 1987). Most older persons have at least one chronic condition, and many have multiple problems, such as arthritis and orthopedic problems, hearing impairments and visual problems, as well as heart disease and hypertension. Most of these are conditions to which some degree of adaptation is possible, and most older persons adapt their lives to take such chronic problems in stride. The point is that we must not mistake having a chronic problem—do you wear glasses, for example?—with being at death's door.

At the same time, older persons are disproportionately represented in making more visits to doctors, going to hospitals more often, and staying longer than younger persons. They also account for a larger portion of the medical bills paid in the nation (Medicare and Medicaid pay for about two-thirds). These various health conditions reflect the facts of nature: as we age, our physical equipment begins to wear out and need repair. We should understand that between individuals and within any one person, this wearing out may happen at differential rates: we may have a 30-year-old heart, a 40-year-old liver, and a 50-year-old set of lungs—depending on our life-long health practices and our genetic inheritance.

The elderly of today are better educated than older persons of earlier generations. In 1970 the median level of education was 8.7 years, whereas in 1986, it was 11.8 years. The percentage of those completing high school rose from 28 to 49 percent during the same period of time. And 10 percent of the elderly in 1986 had completed four or more years of college, an enormous change from previous generations (*A Profile of Older Americans,* 1987).

This suggests that the life-style of today's elderly will be different from earlier generations of older persons. As Social Security and other retirement planning options emerged, older persons have decreased their participation in the workforce. However, about 3 million older Americans were in the labor force in 1986, about 2.6 percent of the total labor force. More than half were employed part-time. A significant proportion of older workers, especially men, were self-employed (25 percent of older workers compared with 8 percent of younger workers in 1986).

Older persons, especially the "young old"—persons aged 65 to 74, are much involved in recreational and leisure-time activities, often taking great pleasure in their freedom from the workaday routines. But studies find that older persons still obtain greater satisfactions in work than in leisure pursuits. This reflects a continuing work ethic that bestows value to a person in direct relationship to his or her productive contributions to society. This becomes one of the challenges of helping professionals, to enable the elderly to find meaning in new ways—for example, through further education and cultural stimulation, through enjoyment of friends and family, in which each contributes to the mental health of others, and through discovery of new dimensions within themselves and within the spiritual and philosophical worlds (cf. Erikson, 1950; Hendricks and Hendricks, 1977; Blau, 1973; and Greene, 1986). Older persons are also becoming more involved in political and social activities through such action and service groups as the Grey Panthers and VISTA.

And not a moment too soon, for there are problems facing all of us, if we live long enough. Robert Butler (1975) has given the name "ageism" to this general phenomenon, a negative stereotyping and concomitant actions as pervasive as sexism and racism (Palmore and Manton, 1973). Part of this stereotyping includes various myths of aging, that chronological age is necessarily linked with lower functional and intellectual capacities; that to be old is to be unproductive, disengaged from society, senile, and asexual. Perhaps worst of all is the stereotype that to be old means having a beautiful serene life. Each of these myths is a distorted view of the facts (see Lugo and Hersey, 1979).

People who perhaps most buy into these aging myths are helping professionals! The reason may be that they tend to see the more sick and disabled elderly and generalize inappropriately. In any event, older persons represent an enormous range of personalities, talents, resources, limitations, and stresses. The configural perspective is helpful in guiding social workers in their dealings with the elderly because older persons are often closely linked with long-standing support groups and associations that may be activated in times of need. Moreover, the older age group has received special attention through governmental health and welfare programs, and they represent important support systems that have to be implemented through prescribed and detailed bureaucratic procedures. Thus a helping professional who seeks to promote meaningful life opportunities has to be concerned not only with a given older person, but also the family and friends, the religious and volunteer associations, and many governmental programs that impinge on an individual (Green, Parham, Kleff, and Pilisuk, 1980; Greene, 1986).

One topic arises that, while not unique to older persons, concerns their inevitable fate if they live long enough into old age—and that is dying and death. Kastenbaum (1986) has written some remarkable documents summarizing our attitudes and actions in the face of dying and death, the social organizations that have grown up around these important life events, and how professionals help—or hinder—these life transitions for all concerned, the dying person and his or her family and friends.

It is not easy to look into the sun or at our own mortality, as de La Rochefoucauld observed. (See, in Chapter 13, the case of the elderly lady who attempted suicide.) Yet, as helping professionals, we will inevitably be faced with clients (as well as friends, family, and ourselves) in living and dying situations. It is necessary to get our own feelings and beliefs under control before we are able to help others effectively. In modern society, death is often denied, disguised, and denigrated by removing the dying from family and friends to sterile hospitals. Doing so provides little opportunity to confront our feelings and ideas about living and dying. Work with the aged provides some rare opportunities to recognize how those near to their deaths face dying with a range of reactions, from equanimity to existential dread. Empathy with the elderly, the sick, or the dying provides experience that may not only benefit us professionally in understanding our clients but may also benefit us personally in contributing to our own ability to deal with living and dying in our daily lives.

It might be useful to introduce a term, the new dying, to describe those who face their coming death with the desire and skill to be in control, rather than as a victim of fate. That people in general can do this reflects sociocultural conditions more open to such self-control over ultimate states. The "living will" movement is one instance of this: a person who is mentally healthy indicates his or her wishes to family, physician, and health-care institution regarding events leading to death. While not legally binding, it does have a moral force that in these times of remarkable changes in medical ethics regarding life and death issues is likely to be increasingly influential in such situations (Veatch, 1981.) Here is the text of the living will (Kastenbaum, 1986, p. 2):

> To my family, my physician, my lawyer, my clergyman
>
> To any medical facility in whose care I happen to be
>
> To any individual who may become responsible for my health, welfare, or affairs
>
> Death is as much as reality as birth, growth, maturity and old age—it is the one certainty of life. If the time comes when I, ..., can no longer take part in decisions for my own future, let this statement stand as an expression of my wishes while I am still of sound mind.
>
> If the situation should arise in which there is no reasonable expectation of my recovery from physical or mental disability, I request that I be allowed to die and not be kept alive by artificial means or "heroic measures." I do not fear death itself as much as the indignities of deterioration, dependence, and hopeless pain. I therefore ask that medication be mercifully administered to me to alleviate suffering even though this may hasten the moment of my death.
>
> This request is made after careful consideration. I hope you who care for me will feel morally bound to follow its mandate. I recognize that this appears to place a heavy responsibility on you, but it is with the intention of relieving you of such responsibility and of placing it on myself in accordance with my strong conviction that this statement is made.
>
> signed...................
>
> date............ Witness............. Witness.................
>
> Copies of this request have been given to ....

SUMMARY

"Few people know how to be old," quipped de La Rouchfoucauld. In this age of a rapidly changing society, who is to teach us how to be old—or young? How to be a woman—or a man? This chapter has tried to supply some sense of history about what these terms have meant. Knowing where we have been may make it easier to understand where we are now and where we might be headed.

This chapter has paid special attention to women and the aged because these two special groups—constituting the majority of people in our society! —are in fact subject to various forms of prejudice and discrimination. Each is perceived as relatively powerless, and, indeed, they are encouraged, if not forced, into low-status positions ("housewife," "pensioner").

Yes, someone must raise the children, and yes, some people must eventually retire because of infirmities. Others may choose to do so, drawing on resources earned over a long and productive work life. But how and when these events occur is presently fairly arbitrary. Women are extolled as "natural" housetenders and child raisers, while we "naturally" think about people retiring at age 65. But neither of these is natural or inevitable. Each has its history extending back into distant times.

Social work is not in the business of making cultural values—but it is in the business of helping people choose their own life-styles within the limits of the law and social mores. When these laws and mores are themselves unacceptable to the value base of social work, then helping professionals and other citizens fight to change laws and to become the "conscience" of the nation.

It is important to view changes in social responses to gender in connection with the responses to the elderly. We now recognize that some of the problems women experience are not self-caused per se, but are in part the result of being forced into socio-cultural positions that create stress for them. Thus feminists have been quite successful in raising the consciousness of women (and men), and have worked to empower them to make appropriate changes.

Perhaps the same insights can be applied to the aged—that some of their "problems" are in fact the result of socio-cultural stresses, and that professional helping may one day focus on raising older persons' consciousness of their victim status, and help empower them to obtain their fair rights and resources to live their lives fully, even as older citizens.

OUTLINE

War and Peace: Violence in a Nuclear Age

The Causes of Violence

Child Abuse: Violence in the Family
    Helping the Abused Child and the Abusing Adult

Rape

Post-Traumatic Stress Disorders: The Violence After Violence

Summary

CHAPTER NINETEEN

The Many Faces of Violence—
War, Child Abuse, Rape, and Post-Traumatic Stress Disorders

Violence is difficult to deal with, regardless of the many faces it wears: hostile actions that take place in secret within the family; sexual assault, whether it takes place on a date or between strangers; violent crimes; armed conflicts, especially in the form of international wars. Violence is the ultimate insult to a rational view of human nature, to the spirit of brotherly love, and to the desire for peace that all sane persons everywhere and every time share. The burning images of millions of Nazi murders in the Holocaust are indelibly etched in human memory.

Yet violence is a fact of life, and the helping professionals have a part to play in its prevention, and in the treatment and rehabilitation of its victims—and its perpetrators. This chapter examines several forms of violence (or the effects of violence) as representative of the whole: war, child abuse, rape, and post-traumatic stress disorders that some Vietnam veterans are experiencing.

WAR AND PEACE: VIOLENCE IN A NUCLEAR AGE

Albert Einstein
Old Grove Rd.
Nassau Point
Peconic, Long Island
August 2nd, 1939

F. D. Roosevelt
President of the United States
White House
Washington, D. C.

Sir:
    . . . In the course of the last four months, it has been made probable—through the work of Joliot in France as well as Fermi and Szilard in America—that it may become possible to set up a nuclear chain reaction in a large mass of uranium by which vast amounts of power and large quantities of new radium-like elements would be generated. . . . This new phenomenon would also lead to the construction of bombs. . . (Gregory, 1986, pp. 39–40).

So began the Manhattan Project. A top-secret effort in the development of the atomic bomb, it involved hundreds of scientists and workers in several sites around the country. Einstein informed the President that Nazi Germany had already begun their efforts to build the bomb. Niels Bohr, an eminent Danish physicist, wrote President Roosevelt in July 1944, a year before the bomb was actually built, and warned him of the implications regarding the control over nuclear weapons: "Unless," he wrote,

> . . . some agreement about the control of the use of the new active materials can be obtained in due time, any temporary advantage (in the war effort), however great, may be outweighed by the perpetual menace to human security (Gregory, 1986, p. 41).

By a half-century later, both prophecies were fulfilled.

"Except for fools and madmen, everyone knows that nuclear war would be an unprecedented human catastrophe," writes Carl Sagan (1983) in "The Nuclear Winter," his often-reproduced essay. The spectre of nuclear war is indeed the major public health concern of our age (Siefert, 1987), the ultimate social problem. Look at your watch now, and note the time because it takes thirty minutes for a land-based intercontinental ballistics missile (ICBM) to reach your door from its launch somewhere in Russia or elsewhere. Sagan goes on to quote a World health Organization report that concludes that a global thermonuclear war would likely kill 1.1 billion people outright, with another 1.1 billion people suffering serious injuries and radiation sickness for which medical help would not be available. Thus, in the matter of an instant in human history, almost half the population of the world would be extinguished. But, as Sagan notes, the real situation would be much worse than this fiery analysis. The great amounts of dust or smoke stirred up by a global war would blot out sunlight for weeks, so as to drop temperatures to minus 25 degrees Celsius (minus 13 degrees Fahrenheit), even in the summer, destroying all crops and animal life, at least in the Northern Hemisphere. Most of the human survivors, he adds, would starve.

Many people find these projections so horrifying that they deny them entirely, or look for exceptions, or simply fall back on the faith that such a thing could never occur. Yet practically every competent scientist from all sides of the political spectrum, here and abroad, agrees with the general thesis of the nuclear winter, whatever their differences in ways of dealing with the threat. The issues that this projected scenario present to us are, first, to face these threats to world health and survival and, second, to understand enough of the background so as to take appropriate actions as individuals, as helping professionals, and as citizens to reduce the threat.

What are the facts concerning a nuclear war? On July 16, 1945, the first atomic device was exploded at Alamogordo, New Mexico, with the force equivalent to 15,000 tons of TNT. The war against Nazi Germany was nearing its end, but the prospects for the continuing war against Japan were chilling— 500,000 lives might be lost in the Allies' campaign to recapture all the Pacific islands from the Japanese (Forsberg, 1982). So, on August 6, 1945, at 8:16 in the morning, an atomic bomb was dropped on the city of Hiroshima (Bernstein, 1983). For all practical purposes, at that moment the city ceased to exist (Jonathan Schell, 1982). About 100,000 people died instantaneously;

others lingered for days or weeks or months; some survived, told their story, and rebuilt their city. A second bomb was dropped on Nagasaki several days later. Then, on August 14, 1945, the Japanese surrendered unconditionally, ending World War II.

The atomic bombs dropped in Japan were relatively small compared to the nuclear devices developed since that time. There are estimated to be about 50,000 nuclear weapons of varying degrees of explosive power (Stockholm International Peace Research Institute, 1982). The total strength of the present nuclear arsenals is greater than 1 million Hiroshima bombs; this is equivalent to more than three tons of TNT for every man, woman, and child on earth, to say nothing about the long-term effects of radioactive fallout and the dust or smoke screen (United Nations Secretary General, 1980). Under this overkill situation, the two major powers (the United States and the Soviet Union) each have the capacity to destroy each other many times over.

Yet vast sums of money are spent by both nations to continue developing new atomic devices and upgrading old ones. A small portion of explorations in the nuclear field have produced great advances in health-related tools and other procedures, but the giant's share of the money has gone to military or potential military uses. And when large amounts of tax dollars go to the military, those funds cannot go for other uses, such as health, education, or welfare, broadly conceived. Thus it appears that we are locked into a world dominated by nuclear weapons, where the prospect of mass annihilation has taken priority over the dream of life, liberty, and the pursuit of happiness.

While the superpowers have a "hot line" to each other's capitals, the world has witnessed such visible accidents as those at the Three Mile Island nuclear reactor in Pennsylvania and more recently at Chernobyl, in the Soviet Union; their effects were felt by peoples in many nations. There have been many less visible accidents as well. The Secretary General of the United Nations wrote a sentiment common to many around the world: ". . . there is a growing concern that control (of nuclear weapons) may some day fail, under the influence of, for example, a false message or a misunderstood command, and that nuclear war is thus triggered inadvertently" (in Gregory, 1986, p. 24). Those who have seen the movie Doctor Strangelove will know the feeling.

Soon after World War II, a Cold War developed between the Communist and Western powers. The United States' monopoly on nuclear weapons from 1945 was short-lived. By 1960 the Soviet Union had acquired the bomb and had developed effective means for delivery. The United States policy at that time was termed "massive retaliation," the deterring of use of conventional weapons by the Soviets through the threat to destroy their major cities (Forsberg, 1982). However, the United States had a lead in first-strike capacity (that is, to destroy an enemy in an initial strike), the development of tactical nuclear weapons, and a second-strike capacity (that is, a destructive force available to attack an enemy, even if the nation sustained a prior nuclear attack). Between 1965 and the late 1970s, the Soviet Union built a nuclear force that gave it both a first- and second-strike capacity, so that in effect a nuclear parity had been achieved. Since that time, each side has attempted to build a better bomb and delivery system—while other nations of the world have also developed nuclear capacity—England, France, China, and possibly others (Forsberg, 1982, pp. 74–78).

American doctrine that supplemented the position of massive retaliation was called "Graduated Deterrence": relatively large attacks on U.S. allies would be met with nuclear strikes in specific locations as needed. This reflected the view of the possibility of limited nuclear wars that presumably would not escalate into global nuclear conflicts. A policy of "flexible response" called for nuclear and conventional weapons to be used in combination to deter an enemy's use of equivalent forces. Many doubted whether such a position was realistic.

Meanwhile, the equality in delivery of destruction has been raised to new heights with the more rapid, more accurate, second-generation weapons such as the multiple independently targetable reentry vehicle systems (MIRVs). This, in turn, provides for even less time for human response to a false or true attack, which leaves the nuclear combat situation much less stable than before. We now live under the conditions described as "mutually assured destruction"—since each side possesses the capacity to assure nearly total destruction of the other, each will be deterred from launching a nuclear war. But the conditions are increasingly less stable as new technological advances take place.

President Reagan's call for a "Strategic Defense Initiative"—a proposal that was immediately labeled "Star Wars"—began a new round of efforts to deter aggression because "a nuclear war cannot be won and must never be fought." (White House Paper: "The President's Strategic Defense Initiative," 1985.) New technology will be sought to provide a layered defense against attacking missiles during each phase of their flight—from shortly after take-off, during the boost phase, during the ballistic trajectory phase, when they travel in space for "tens of minutes," and finally, as the missiles descend. The Soviets possessed the only existing anti-ballistic missile system (around Moscow) in the late 1980s and have been engaged in research in this area for many years.

Critics point out that it would be impossible to prevent every missile from reaching its destination, and even if only a small number get through, the result would be terrible destruction. Moreover, such technology could be used in an offensive way as well as for defense, thus spurring yet another highly expensive round of a nuclear arms race. (See Bundy, Kennan, McNamara, and Smith, 1984/1985.)

At the same time, the Federal Emergency Management Agency promoted population shelters in case of nuclear attack: "Entry into shelter should be orderly and rapid, with shelterees placed in the safest areas. The basement area and center core of the building are the best shelter spaces . . . (Shelter Management Handbook, 1984)." A number of governors refused to cooperate with federal directives in planning for the evacuation of large numbers of people from crowded urban areas because of the impossibility of the requested "orderly and rapid" movement under ordinary traffic conditions, let alone during a nuclear emergency. Moreover, having such civil defense procedures in place might give a false sense of security to the population at large. (See also Zuckerman, 1984.)

There are many implications for the helping professions. They include specific actions to be taken to prevent nuclear war and health-related functions (Siefert, 1987). This section is simply an introduction to the topic of war and peace and lists some of the steps we as individuals may take to engage, with millions of others, in the ultimate social problem of our times. First, any action with regard to some system usually must be taken at the same level as the system in question. So, if we are to influence international affairs, we must work through organizations that address such concerns. There are, for example, organizations such as the International Physicians for the Prevention of Nuclear War, which was the recipient of the 1985 Nobel Peace Prize. (The American affiliate is called Physicians for Social Responsibility, 1601 Connecticut Avenue N.W., Washington, D.C. 20009.)

A citizen's group called Beyond War calls for a new way of thinking about the world, directed toward making it a place where war is obsolete (because of its potential for total destruction), where people are ecologically interrelated and interdependent, and where we must begin to see ourselves, though diverse, as essentially one people able to cooperate to build a world beyond war (see Gregory, 1986, pp. 316–319). Jonathan Schell (1982) calls for a world government as the way to facilitate that cooperation. Ruth Leger Sivard (1983), among others, suggests strengthening international social conditions that otherwise cause problems; building a civilian-based defense system through massive nonviolence by an entire population; using the already existing machinery of the International Court of Justice and the United Nations International Peacekeeping forces as needed to enhance security. She suggests various other ways of reducing the military machine, as have many others.

At the national level, there are many organizations that are seeking one version or another of ways to prevent nuclear war. For example, SANE (Committee for a Sane Nuclear Policy) has been active in opposing nuclear bomb testing and many other aspects of nuclear policy of national governments. SANE merged with the Nuclear Weapons Freeze movement, which campaigned in Congressional districts against nuclear weapon testing and development. The National Association of Social Workers has taken a stand with other organizations in efforts to reduce military spending and to promote nonviolent methods for resolving international conflicts (Siefert, 1987). Politically conservative groups, such as the High Frontier, are active in behalf of an aggressive nuclear policy on the grounds that a good offensive potential is the best defense.

At the individual level, we have an obligation to understand the issues and to join in support of those who express our views most effectively, through the vote and through communications with our representatives. We have the obligation to discuss these issues, however difficult that may be, so that others will come to understand the problems and challenges that cloud their lives. This is an obligation not only to our countries, our children, and ourselves but also for the human species. Check your watch. Has the half-hour passed?

THE CAUSES OF VIOLENCE

Montague (1976) notes that in the 5,600 years of recorded history, there have been about 14,600 wars, or something like three wars a year on the average. Liebert and Schwartzberg (1977) estimate that the average child of 16 years has seen more than 13,000 murders on TV, whether in cartoons or on sitcoms. And every 24 seconds, on the average, a violent crime occurs somewhere in the United States (U.S. Department of Justice, 1981), making the United States the leader among Western nations in the numbers of murders and other violent crimes committed each year (Star, 1987, p. 463). No one has calculated how many periods of peace between adjacent peoples have occurred, nor how many acts of loving kindness have been portrayed on television or in person. But we might suspect that the numbers would be even larger than those for war or TV murder. While this chapter focuses on violence, please also keep the perspective of nonviolent, constructive behavior in the picture.

Violence attracts attention, both of scientists who study it and try to figure out ways to control it and of lay people, most of whom try to avoid it. A sizable minority seem to court it in one fashion or another. In fact, we do not even have a common word for nonviolence, as we do for violence. (Peaceful, tranquil, quiet, calm, pacific, serenity all have distinctive meanings different from nonviolent.) Yet, in folkways and in written constitutions, almost all peoples have expressed the desire to live in peace and freedom, without interpersonal violence. On the other hand, who among us has not lashed out (violently) in anger or frustration over some event at some time in our lives? Or who has wanted to do so?

Violence seems so common that we must ask what are its causes. The biologically-oriented theorists often find violence to be an innate characteristic of the human being; for example, Sigmund Freud labeled one of his two instincts for violence (the aggression or death instinct). Others with a more sociological perspective, such as Jean-Jacques Rousseau, see nonviolence as the natural condition of people who get corrupted by society in various ways. In between are theorists, such as Bandura (1977), who recognize that the normal physical activity can become modified by experience to become learned violent behavior. [From the same perspective, Mussen and Eisenberg-Berg (1977) summarize the literature on the learning of pro-social or altruistic behavior.] The majority of research supports this social learning explanation, at least on the interpersonal level. It is more difficult to determine what forces are operating at the international level.

Violence is a complex term because it requires consideration not only of the behavioral outcome, but also the intention of the actor: A bone-crunching tackle may not be violence if the football player intended only a clean takedown, while a tiny harmless swat by an angry child may indeed constitute violence (Aronson, 1984). However, whether collective behavior is to be labeled violent or not, depending both on the external effects plus the internal intentions of principal actors, is another question. If the President of the United States or the Head of the Soviet Union called the other on the hotline to inform his counterpart that some intercontinental ballistic missiles had been launched by accident and were now headed toward the other's capital—but since it was an accident that could not be undone, would you please forgive us and not start a war?—one wonders whether that collective act would be considered grounds for a violent response or not.

Since aggressive behavior seems to be learned, we can look around us to find all sorts of aggressive models. They include the murderers on television, in cartoons and fictional stories and also in documentaries of real life. We also observe parents who use physical punishment as the chief mode of discipline and peers who, lacking other social skills, substitute power ploys. Then there are the legitimated users of aggression, sports figures, police, the military. And, broadly speaking, there is one other vast setting for learning legal forms of violence—the business world with its competition (conflict according to rules whereby two or more parties seek to win the hearts, minds, or money of third parties).

There are many opportunities to learn forms of violence—but there are many opportunities to learn forms of nonviolence, though nonviolence may not have such dramatic forums. Unfortunately, there is little research on how people integrate these great lessons of life. People nevertheless appear to be able to discern when it is appropriate to use one approach or the other.

One ancient theory suggested that if people could only express their aggressive or violent feelings, this would diffuse their emotions and act as a catharsis. So Aristotle proposed that drama acted as a catharsis for viewers. Modern theorists have suggested that intense physical activity removes our violent feelings—or even that watching competitive games acts as a cathartic for the spectators. Alas, for the millions of Sunday football viewers, the opposite seems to be the case; watching an aggressively fought game in which one team beats the other—note the very language by which we describe these common activities—temporarily *increases* aggressiveness (Russell, 1981).

Eron (1982) summarizes two decades of research on TV violence and the aggression in children. He notes that not only does aggression occur in the presence of the continual observation of television violence, but aggressive children tend to watch more and more violent television. Likewise, aggression is associated with low achievement; children who are not successful in school watch more television than do their more successful peers, according to Eron. In summarizing the literature on aggression, Aronson (1984) notes that violence tends to breed more violence. This unhappy finding seems to be played out on many arenas, including the violence we are now beginning to uncover that occurs in the privacy of homes (child abuse and neglect; spousal abuse; elder abuse) and in other secret or unexpected places (rape, muggings, murders, and even suicide).

CHILD ABUSE: VIOLENCE IN THE FAMILY

Let us examine the problem of child abuse as representative of violence near to home. First, recognize that it is difficult to define child abuse, even though every state in the Union has had mandatory reporting of child maltreatment since the late 1960s. Visible physical injuries to children may be accidental, or they may be intentionally caused. Injuries inflicted during temporary states (drunkenness, mental instability) are equally difficult to relate to abuse or accident. Nonvisible physical injuries or emotional injuries are two other difficult topics that call for specialized diagnosis and treatment. Failure to thrive according to normal developmental curves is yet another possible type of child abuse, although while having norms for comparison, it is still a judgment call for trained professionals. Discipline that parents and guardians use with their own children, which is sanctioned by law, may include physical punishment. Even corporal punishment by school authorities is legal, according to a decision by the United States Supreme Court.

Bob Kalman/The Image Works, Inc.

The United States is one of the few advanced societies that still permits corporal punishment of children. We are paying for this freedom as the line between appropriate parental disciplining and child abuse grows ever more indistinct. There are many forms of violence in the world: physical violence, mental violence, emotional violence, sexual violence. This chapter explores some of its many faces.

Given the difficulty in defining the phenomenon of child abuse—including physical and emotional abuse, sexual abuse, but not including the various forms of child neglect—there should be little surprise at the difficulties of identifying the incidence (the number of new cases per unit of time, such as a year). Some put the figure at roughly 200,000 to one half-million cases (Light, 1973). The National Center on Child Abuse and Neglect's (1981) estimate of about 650,000 contrasts with the American Humane Association's annual nationwide reports of over 900,000 for 1982 (Russell and Trainor, 1984). Others place the figure at over two million victims annually (Gelles, 1980). Buried in these horrendous numbers are children who are victims of incest—estimates range from 100,000 to 250,000 cases a year (Johnson and Schwartz, 1988, p. 152); runaways or "pushouts" (some two million children run away from home—or are in effect pushed out by their parents; half of the children have been physically or sexually abused by parents, relatives, or other adults (Oldenburg, 1988). For a brief overview of these figures, see Kinard (1987).

Regardless of the exact figures—and they will likely never be known because of the strong tendency to hide intrafamily problems like abuse—we do know a considerable amount about correlates of child abuse. This information can be organized from a configural perspective. Characteristics that are associated with child abuse—but that do not necessarily identify abusive situations—include the following:

The Individual. It is commonly believed that abusers may themselves have experienced abuse or neglect in their own lives, although the evidence for this is weak (Jayaratne, 1977). Probably the majority of abusing parents were not abused when they were children, and some who were abused do not abuse their own children. It is unwise to present this intergenerational link as a fact, which it is not, because we do not want to create a self-fulfilling prophecy for those burdened with their own private memories of their childhood abuse. There is clearer evidence that abusers tend to be unable to tolerate frustration or delays in gratification. And they may react impulsively or angrily to provocations. They may be immature adults, with a low sense of self-esteem. The majority of abusers are the parents of the abused child. Mothers are more likely to be abusers than fathers (on the order of 60:40), but mothers probably spend much more time with the children than do fathers. Abusers tend to be adults, but even older siblings or teenage baby-sitters may be involved.

The victims tend to have some characteristics that provoke the abusers. The children may be difficult to raise because of their demands that seem excessive to the abusers. These tasks may include ordinary duties like feeding and cleaning, but the children may also be unusually problematic such as inconsolable criers or have chronic conditions that are difficult to manage. There is about equal abuse of male and female children, although the highest incidence for males comes between the ages of 3 and 5, while abuse of females increases with age (Kinard, 1987).

The Family Group. A disproportionate number of child-abusing parents are from single-parent, female-headed households, or from nonwhite families. (Considerations of social pressures, to be discussed shortly, may account for these findings.) Parents who abuse are often weak on coping skills and effective child rearing methods. They may hold unrealistic expectations of what a child can do at a given age. When two parents are present, there may be family conflicts of other sorts (again, see below, regarding socio-economic factors), for which children may be scapegoats. Abusive families tend to be socially isolated and lack supporting networks from which they can get some relief from their perceived pressures. There is little evidence that abusive adults are mentally ill and act abusively because of such illness.

Social Factors (secondary group characteristics). The typical abusive family has a low income and thus is subject to economic pressures. This may reflect the incidence of reported cases, as contrasted with actual cases. (However, many families in the low income group do not engage in child abuse.) Abuse families also tend to have low levels of education, and they may not be aware of the community resources available to them or how to use them effectively. Other social correlates that may be related to the stresses that may cumulate and take the form of child abuse include unemployment, stressful living conditions (including poor housing), and adolescent parenthood.

Cultural Factors. The cultural acceptance of violence in its many guises may be a factor in child abuse as well. Special conditions, such as extreme religious practices—total obedience by a very young child, for example—may occasionally be involved.

Physical Environment. Some of the previously described factors sometimes associated with child abuse may have a physical dimension, such as poor housing, social isolation, and depressing and unsupportive conditions surrounding a poor family. But what is usually recognized in the abusive context is some critical event that takes place at a given time that sets off the other factors—the characteristics of the potential abuser, the idiosyncratic behaviors of the child, the lack of social and cultural supports—into an actual abuse situation.

Thus child abuse may be viewed as a configural event. Typically, a set of forces operates on an adult who has personal limitations and is under considerable social and cultural pressures and who interacts with a child with some provocative characteristics. Some triggering incident, moreover, sets off the act of violence. This broad description of child abuse as a configural event suggests some ways to prevent the problem as well as to treat it and to rehabilitate the family to the degree possible.

Prevention may involve any actions that reduce the acceptableness of violence in our culture. The American Medical Association took a stand against boxing because of the high incidence of serious head injuries. Discussions of child-rearing techniques stress alternatives to simple punishment. The very openness of the culture permits discussion of the past abuse of adults and the formation of support groups that may be able to head crises off before they occur. Efforts to reduce poverty will likewise reduce stresses on people that cumulate and may be expressed as abuse. (We know, for example, that when mass unemployment comes suddenly to a community, there will soon be a rise in various forms of disturbed behavior, including child abuse.) There are also some programs to identify high risk parents at birthing centers that hold some promise for preventive work, but more research is needed. Promotive activities, such as instigating parent-child bonding by arranging close awareness of the newborn, also holds promise.

Helping the Abused Child and the Abusing Adult

Violence in the family is not new, but over the course of American history, we have gone from lacking any laws to protect children from abuse and neglect to institutional solutions (removal of such children and placing them in institutions). Society has also tried a rehabilitation approach (protecting the child by rehabilitating the parents and maintaining the natural home as the best place to raise a child), and has combined preventive efforts along with a continuum of services as needed. These services seek to support the natural family by removing stresses, supplying training and resources, while at the same time keeping a watchful eye over the child who is maintained in his or her natural environment. However, if this does not appear to be working, then substitute services can be provided (such as foster families, group homes, or residential institutions).

The 1974 Child Abuse and Treatment Act provided for funding of state programs to help abused children. In addition, it also established a National Center for Child Abuse, which has acted as a clearinghouse and stimulus for research on the nature of child abuse and neglect. It also offered effective methods of treatment. Specialized journals and a computerized database have further helped to keep researchers and practitioners abreast of current efforts.

New approaches to helping the abusing adult are appearing, such as Gondolf's (1987) model of successive stages of moral development (adapted from Kohlberg), in which different interventions are suited to each different stage. Research on the effectiveness of this model is needed.

RAPE

Rape, according to one legal definition, is:

> The perpetration of an act of sexual intercourse with a female, not one's wife, against her will and consent, whether her will is overcome by force or fear resulting from the threat of force, or by drugs or intoxicants; or when, because of mental deficiency, she is incapable of exercising rational judgment; or when she is below an arbitrary "age of consent" (quoted in Brownmiller, 1975, p. 412).

Brownmiller's *Against Our Will: Men, Women, and Rape* (1975) is an extraordinary history of rape: By anatomical fiat, the human male was a natural predator and the human female his natural prey. The earliest records of war also report rapes, just as do the most recent records of war. The male dominant social order viewed sex as part of the property rights of men coming to them through marriage; women had few civil rights throughout history. Slavery had many grim inhumane aspects; rape was one of them. Single-sex environments, such as prisons, also provide the ground for rape—homosexual rape.

Brownmiller and many others view rape not simply as a sexual invasion of the body by force, but a deliberate degradation of the victim physically, emotionally, and socially (p. 422). Rape is not a crime of irrational, impulsive, uncontrollable lust, but a deliberate, hostile, and violent act of degradation designed to intimidate and inspire fear in the victim. Rape is an act of violence and power perpetrated through the use of sexual and other means. Brownmiller points out that rape is gender-free (males as well as females may be victims—however, women are the predominant objects of this attack); it is also non-activity specific (that is, there are more ways to rape than use of the penis in a vagina). She and others (such as Millett, 1970) have argued for a broader interpretation of sexual activities as social or political acts.

Estrich (1987) follows Kalven and Zeisel (1966) in distinguishing aggravated rape from simple rape. Aggravated rape includes cases with clear and explicit violence, multiple assailants, or the fact of there being no prior relationship between the victim and the stranger-aggressor. Simple rape includes cases in which none of these aggravating circumstances is present. Kalven and Zeisel pointed out from their research that jury convictions were nearly four times greater in aggravated rape than in simple rape cases. Estrich interprets this to reflect some cultural stereotypes of the woman who must have been enticing the man in some way, must have been cooperating to some extent, and must have been enjoying the act even while denying it. Thus, in date rape or acquaintance rape, when the parties have known each other, it often fell to the woman to prove her innocence rather than to prove the guilt of the man. This "blame the victim" orientation accounts for the massive underreporting of rape cases even today.

Aggravated rape is relatively rare, whereas simple rape—cases in which a woman is forced to have sex without consent by only one man whom she knows and who does not beat her or attack her with a weapon—is much more common (Estrich, 1987). The Uniform Crime Reports for 1984 showed that 69 of every 100,000 females were reported the victims of forcible rape. Victimization surveys further indicate that the number of forcible rapes is nearly twice as high as official records describe. Rape is reported to the police at a relatively high rate or, at least, aggravated rape is (see also Rowland, 1985).

Brownmiller (1975) estimated that only one in five rapes is ever reported (p. 190). Moreover, statutory rapes (occurring with under-adult-age females) were not included in the official statistics. In addition, about half of the offenders are apprehended, and although three-quarters are prosecuted, more than one-half are acquitted (p. 190). So, all things considered, Brownmiller estimated that the incidence of rape exceeds a quarter-million a year (as of 1973). The number of arrests for forcible rape is about 30,000 a year.

Women (and men) have been active in the movement against rape, a seeking to "take back the night," to regain the safety and humanity that all people deserve as members of society. Toomey (1987) describes the early 1970s and the emergence of Rape Crisis Centers, which used hotlines (telephone call-ins that provided information, support, and protection). This later expanded to assistance in accompanying the women through the stressful emergency room care and police interrogations that were not always friendly. During the regular prosecution of the case, the victim's former sexual activities were often drawn into consideration as a factor relevant to the rape incident (p. 570). Next steps often involved community awareness efforts to generate collective support for changes of norms, laws, and practices related to rape. (For example, methods were created to increase the sensitivity of medical personnel who worked with rape victims in the emergency room, while preserving evidence needed for criminal prosecution.) (See also Brown and Ziefert, 1988.)

Estrich (1987) argued that all forms of forced sex should be considered a crime, even where there is no weapon or beating involved. It is rape any time a woman says no or submits to sexual activities only in response to threats or lies that would be illegal if the object were money rather than sex (p. 103).

Rowland (1985) presents several long case studies of the prosecution of rapists in court. Her approach as prosecuting attorney was to inform the jury about the rape trauma syndrome, one form of post-traumatic stress disorder in which an initial phase of psychological disorganization and fear is followed by a gradual reorganization, mixed with reminders of the traumatic event that set off new fear reactions (pp. 333–344). The effects of violence live long after the event itself. The victim is revictimized. A configuration of many helping efforts is needed to overcome these stress disorders.

POST-TRAUMATIC STRESS DISORDERS: THE VIOLENCE AFTER VIOLENCE

To paraphrase Tolstoy, good wars are all alike; bad wars are different. The Vietnam War, by all accounts, was different, very different. It was a guerrilla war, with few fixed battle zones and few safe areas. It was fought with napalm and Agent Orange, and employed search and destroy tactics with helicopters—new terms, albeit for old ideas—as well as massive air attacks. It was a war fought with television recording events that were transmitted half way around the world, in all their gory details. For some, it was a popular war, an ideological showdown where Truth and Goodness (our side) would triumph over Evil (theirs). It was also an unpopular war, where at first small numbers, then increasingly larger numbers of people became outraged about the immorality of the war itself, let alone the conduct of both sides. It was called an "air-conditioned war," referring to the juxtaposition of brief periods of intense fighting, and the relaxed, often luxurious existence in the major cities of South Vietnam (Bourne, p. vii, in Figley, 1978).

But what was unique about that war was the way it was conducted by the Americans. Trying to learn from the psychiatric traumas that occurred in earlier wars, the military made decisions to limit the tour of duty to a fixed one year, so that the soldiers might have hope of leaving the battlefield other than by death or injury. Men were rotated on an individual basis, thus changing the kind of emotional support they had from buddies who had gone through difficult conditions together. Another unusual feature of the Vietnam War was the extensive use of drugs by American troops. Heroin became widely available in 1970 (Nance, et al., in Figley, 1978), and large proportions of the troops were using some form of drugs.

The Vietnam War was the longest and costliest American war; 56,000 Americans died in Vietnam from 1961 to 1973. Three million Americans (men and women) were involved in the Southeast Asian theatre. Most of them returned to civilian life, but not to the praise and community adoration that had accompanied returning soldiers in previous wars. It was a war—and warriors—that the nation wanted to forget.

But the war has not ended for many. Studies suggest that as many as 500,000 combat veterans suffered from stress disorders (Green, et al., 1985). Parson (in Figley, 1985) notes that black and Chicano veterans suffered significantly more readjustment problems than did white veterans, possibly because of a strong identification with Vietnamese civilians, and because they had been subject to stress themselves throughout their lives.

The post-traumatic stress disorder (PTSD) was officially recognized as a clinical entity in 1980 (DSM-III). The central features of the PTSD are that survivors reexperience portions of the traumatic experience in dreams or distressing and intrusive waking images, alternating with feeling psychically numb, a loss of normal affect, and low involvement in work and interpersonal relationships. These states of reexperiencing the trauma and the emotional constrictedness may coexist or alternate in cycles of predominance (Green et al., in Figley 1985). Secondary symptoms may include hyperalertness, depressive symptoms, memory impairment, survivor guilt, explosiveness, loss of capacity for intimacy, and avoidance of stimuli associated with the trauma (Green, et al., in Figley, 1985).

Haley (in Figley, 1978, p. 263) provides a case illustration that seems to sum up the profound contradictions of the Vietnam War for both the Vietnamese and the American soldiers:

> One veteran had warned his close friend, the squad medic, not to go near a crying baby lying in a village road until they had checked the area. In his haste to help the child, the medic raced forward and "was blown to bits" along with the child, who had been booby-trapped. The veteran came into treatment three years later, after a period of good adjustment, because he was made fearful and anxious by his eight-month-old daughter's crying. He had been unable to pick her up or hold her since her birth despite his conscious wish to "be a good father."

Scurfield (in Figley, 1985) notes that trauma is the primary cause of PTSD, but that professional helpers have to understand the pre-trauma, trauma, and post-trauma conditions to be effective in assessing and treating this problem. He offers five principles in treating PTSD: First, establish a therapeutic trust relationship, a difficult task for the PTSD victim, who may project his or her anger on the helping person. Second, the survivor must be educated about the recovery process—that trauma can lead to post-trauma symptoms in almost anyone, and that it is normal to reexperience the trauma and feel numbed by it, even years after the event. It is also normal to feel a loss of control (rage, crying, etc.) as one begins to work through the experiences. PTSD definitely responds to treatment, but it can never be totally eliminated from memory. One learns to control these memories, and perhaps comes to find meaning in life because of them (pp. 242–243).

Third, stress management is needed to deal with the core conditions of reexperiencing the traumatic memories or related symptoms. Old and new coping skills are developed for this purpose. Fourth, Scurfield suggests that the central purpose of therapy for stress disorders is to facilitate the eventual full reexperiencing of the trauma in the present, and with it, the extreme feelings of grief, rage, and anger, even at the death of a friend or at oneself for one's role in the death.

The fifth step is to integrate all of these reexperiences, the negative as well as the positive, with the survivor's sense of who he or she was before, during, and after the trauma. One has to accept responsibility for one's actions at that time, yet should recognize what was beyond one's control. It also includes recognition of one's feelings of guilt and one's attempts to offer some penance for them. And finally, this phase involves recognizing the positives that can arise from the catastrophic, such as advances in one's struggle to find meaning, to rise above the trivial pursuits of everyday life, and to recognize the intense bonds one had with the dead friends so that one can grieve at their loss and reexperience intimate bonds with others anew (Scurfield, in Figley, 1985).

In these ways the violence after violence can come to a partial end.

SUMMARY

Violence is inevitably a configural event, persons and groups squaring off against other persons and their groups in socio-cultural contexts at different times and places in history. The causes of violence are not innate. We do not have to make war, abuse children, rape the weak. That we do these things reflects the violent possibilities inherent in personal, interpersonal, and socio-cultural structures. Most people do not make war, or violate the bodies and minds of others. We need to know much more about how people become moral, law-abiding citizens, cooperative members of a world society.

Violence harms the victim, but it changes the aggressor in ways less clear. To violate another is to become less human, less a part of the moral community. To bear the burden of being a victim makes one forever suspicious, always fearful, under similar circumstances.

Helping professionals can play many roles in reducing violence and treating its victims—and aggressors. The discussion of the PTSD treatment is a microcosm of the kinds of services given to persons in connection with their life configuration—their pre-trauma personality and coping style; the way they experienced the trauma; and the events that occurred thereafter. Violence emerges through forces in the social configuration. Its treatment and prevention likewise require dealing with that configuration.

OUTLINE

Love and Sexuality: Why Are We the Way We Are?

Unwanted Adolescent Pregnancy: A Continuing Epidemic
   Cognitive Factors
   Affective Factors
   Behavioral, Interpersonal, and Social Factors

Overpopulation and the Problem of Natural Thresholds

AIDS: The New Epidemic
   The Actors
   The Stage
   The Drama
   The Script: What Can We Do To Prevent AIDS?

Summary

CHAPTER TWENTY

Human Sexuality, Overpopulation, and AIDS

Why do social workers need to know about human sexuality, aside from personal reasons and perpetuation of the species? Most workers will deal with clients who have problems or opportunities related to sexual behavior. Because of the highly charged nature of this topic, social workers must be knowledgeable and comfortable about discussing this central aspect of human behavior. Whether in the form of illegal behaviors—such as rape, child sexual abuse, or pedophilia—or as behaviors that run counter to dominant social mores—like homosexuality, prostitution, or premarital sexual intercourse—or even as typical marital problems—such as premature ejaculation, painful intercourse, or routinized boredom—aspects of sexuality abound. The focus of this chapter is on three particular problems: the issue of unwanted teenage pregnancy, overpopulation, and AIDS. Each is an epidemic of sorts that has dangerous implications for all humankind.

LOVE AND SEXUALITY: WHY ARE WE THE WAY WE ARE?

What is love? Many a late evening discussion has considered this topic from various angles, in the manner of Plato's famous Symposium, in which Socrates and his associates discuss numerous alternatives. My favorite is the tale by Aristophanes, whose theory of love is echoed in the writings of many others, including Jung (but Aristophanes is infinitely more humorous). According to Plato's Aristophanes, the original nature of humankind was round, with four hands and four feet, and "privy members" to match. But such persons were obstreperous, and the gods decided to reduce their strength by cutting them in half, with two hands, two feet, and "privy members" to match, although eventually these "parts of generation" were turned around so that by the "mutual embraces of man and woman they might breed, and the race might continue." (Plato, 1965.) The divine division left men and women looking for their other half, with love being that condition in which people have located the perfect fit, a wholeness or singleness of being in which the lovers are melted into one. By the way, Aristophanes uses this theory to account for homosexual as well as heterosexual matches. It depends on whether the original division included, for example, a portion of "the woman" (the feminine aspect of the original being) in women—if so, these women will seek other women as lovers. Aristophanes adds a warning about the continuing obstreperousness of humans. The gods may strike again, leaving people once more split and able only to hop around on one leg. So be careful.

Bell (1982) and his colleagues explored *Sexual Preference: Its Development in Men and Women* (1981) as well as *Homosexualities: A Study of Diversity Among Men and Women* (1978), as part of the continuing studies from the Kinsey Institute. Bell writes: "Falling in love, as distinguished from the phenomenon of friendship, can be viewed as the anticipation of self-completion through merger with the love object" (p. 264). Shades of Aristophanes! But this definition permits him to speculate on the developments of sexual preference, both heterosexual and homosexual. Admittedly going beyond his data, Bell offers the following explanation that best fits the existing information.

Beginning with hormonal events in utero that largely shape the person's propensity to conform or deviate from stereotyped conceptions of what it means to be a boy or a girl, the individual then is influenced by familial experiences such as those that do or do not promote his or her gender conforming behaviors. The outcome of these family experiences, as being like or different from others of one's gender, then gets reflected in the child's peer relationships. For example, the boy who associates almost exclusively with other boys has, according to Bell, exhausted his fascination with males and holds a realistic assessment of them. (If there should be sexual contact between two such boys, it is likely to be simply curious exploration, without strong romantic feelings.)

For a smaller number of persons, there is another pattern of developmental experiences, a greater familiarity with members of the other gender, which makes these opposites less fascinating as adolescence approaches with its resurgence of hormonal urges. Now, the same-sexed persons become objects of fascination. As Bell expresses this from his research interviews: ". . . when they (the interviewees) were asked what they most preferred in their prospective sexual partners, the largest number of homosexual males said they found distinctly masculine characteristics most desirable, while the lesbians were most apt to seek feminine characteristics in theirs" (p. 265). Homosexuals, according to this theory, seek what they find different and attractive in others, just as do heterosexuals, but what is different and sexually attractive depends on their bio-psycho-social experiences.

Kinsey (1948) had earlier hypothesized a continuum of sexual feeling and attraction, from purely heterosexual to purely homosexual. How a given individual in the middle of the continuum (having both hetero- and homosexual feelings and attractions) expressed his or her sexuality depends on the social context. In a restrictive time, conventional modes of sexuality will likely appear; in times of change, nonconventional modes may appear as well. One instance of changing times occurred in 1973 when the American Psychiatric Association, by majority vote of its membership (58%), decided to remove homosexuality per se from the list of sexual deviations, an act roughly equivalent to the Emancipation Proclamation with regard to slavery, and with as much politics going on during its consideration (see Bayer, 1981).

What lay behind this vote was the fact that homosexuals seemed not to be differentiable from heterosexuals except for their choice of love object (Hooker, 1957; Gonsiorek, 1982). There could be mentally healthy and unhealthy individuals from both groups, and while being gay meant that one had to suffer the stresses and discriminations of the straight society that could lead to problems, this was not a distinctive homosexual characteristic, any more than high blood pressure is a black characteristic even though it is commonly found at high levels among blacks.

In spite of the American Psychiatric Association vote, homosexuality is not out of the woods, let alone the closet. For historic reasons related to religious proscriptions against homosexuality, masturbation, and sex for pleasure rather than for progeny, many people have strong feelings against liberalization in sexual activities and in the discussions about it. A worker must understand the many aspects of the question of human sexuality to be able to deal reasonably and effectively with clients and the public at large on some of the most significant issues of the day that are closely related to those "privy members" and how we use them.

Anthropologists report an almost unbelievable range of ways people express sexual feelings (Ford and Beach, 1951; Gagnon and Henderson, 1975). Almost everything we might consider illegal, immoral, or innovative sexual behavior has been raised to positions of honor in one society or another. Likewise, almost everything we might consider legal, moral, and fun, has been lowered to positions of dishonor in one society or another. Whether societies are sex-permissive or sex-restrictive, an expressive language grows up around bodily and interpersonal functions, frequently demeaning the action or the actors involved. Social workers must be familiar with the meanings of the current crops of "four-letter" words, which may be more familiar to clients than the technical terms for the same functions (see, for example, Gochros and Fischer, 1975).

Now, let us turn to several instances in which this fundamental human experience may become problematic. First, we will consider adolescent sexuality.

UNWANTED ADOLESCENT PREGNANCY: A CONTINUING EPIDEMIC

Adolescence is a fascinating phase of life-span development when biological, psychological, and social growth and development come together in dramatic ways. Not only is the body developing in its reproductive, cardiovascular, and musculoskeletal systems (Slap, 1986), but also there are changes in cognitive (Pestrak and Martin 1985) and affective-moral (Kohlberg, 1983; Gilligan, 1982) areas. The sense of the whole person, moreover, is coming into being (Erikson, 1968; Chilman, 1983). Expectations from society and culture have continuing influence on who and what the adolescent is to become. This is particularly true regarding the ways young people express their sexual feelings.

Sexual activity among teenagers has been steadily increasing with two almost inevitable results. The more visible result is the one million teenage pregnancies annually in the U.S., and the less visible result is the occurrence of sexually transmitted diseases—genital chlamydia, gonorrhea, trichomoniasis in particular, but also herpes and genital warts. Syphilis is less common among teenagers, and, as of the late 1980s, AIDS was rare. Young people mature sexually at earlier ages than did their parents, and the teenagers—of both sexes, white as well as nonwhite adolescents—have begun sexual activities earlier as well (O'Reilly and Aral, 1985; McAnarney and Schreider, 1984; Zelnick and Kantner, 1980).

The fallout of unwanted and unexpected teenage pregnancy is widespread. Roughly speaking, about half of those made pregnant give birth; another third are terminated by abortion, while the rest miscarry (*Teenage Pregnancy: The Problem That Hasn't Gone Away,* 1981). Of those who give birth, the great majority keep their babies (at least in name; many are helped considerably by family and the welfare system). However, having a baby places many limitations on the life development of a young woman who is head of her own household and who may not have been able to complete her high school education (let alone go on for further training). Should she marry the father of her child, chances are not good that the marriage will be long-lasting.

Children who grow up in this limited environment may themselves experience many deprivations, unless the mother is highly adaptive in finding resources to nurture her child. Problems begin immediately after becoming pregnant: health care comes late and irregularly to teenage mothers, and results in medical problems and difficulties in the pregnancy. Young mothers without adequate care during pregnancy are more likely than others to have premature infants, low in birth weight, and sometimes with birth defects. These infants often have to struggle for life. The young mother is often unprepared for the responsibilities of parenthood and does not possess the skills to deal with ordinary stresses of infancy. There is some suggestion in the literature of higher rates of child abuse among this group of unwed mothers, probably reflecting the stresses they face with limited resources and social supports.

About 1,300,000 children live with 1,100,000 teenage mothers (*Teenage Pregnancy,* 1981). Because of their educational and experiential limitations, single parents have difficulties locating good jobs, and they find few child care facilities available to support efforts toward independence (cf. Kahn and Kamerman, 1987). Their children are more likely than their peers to show impaired intellectual functioning, which also has its progressive impact as they grow up and face challenges similar to those their parents faced a generation before. Thus, with some notable exceptions, many single-parent households are locked into a vicious cycle of difficulties.

Adolescent fathers are not as well studied as are mothers, but research from a nationally representative longitudinal study (Marsiglio, 1987) suggests that seven percent of young males 20–27 fathered a child while they were teenagers. Three-quarters of them were not married at the time, but one-half of all these young men lived with their child shortly after the child's birth. Young black men were more likely to have been responsible for a nonmarried first birth, but were least likely to live with their child afterward. Moreover, teenage fathers, regardless of their marital status when their child was conceived, were much more likely to have been high school dropouts than their (nonfathering) peers. More information is needed about teenage fathers as well as the sexually active adolescent male (Robinson, 1988).

Some innovative service programs and natural helping networks have emerged to assist young single parents and those who might be prevented from entering their ranks. First, there are various types of sex education programs, such as the highly successful clinic in the school system at St. Paul, Minnesota, in which a full-spectrum health clinic is established in a school building that deals with everything from giving physicals to discussing contraception. Since students go to the health service for all sorts of reasons, there is no stigma attached. The convenience, confidentiality, and completeness of the services offered have reduced the rates of unwanted teen pregnancy in that area. This model has been widely adopted throughout the country (see Dryfoos, 1988).

Sex education is widely favored; 8 out of 10 Americans support sex education in the schools—including 7 out of 10 who also favor instruction in birth control (*Teenage Pregnancy*, 1981). But only 10 states required or encouraged sex education (as of 1981). Consequently it should come as no surprise that only 4 out of 10 adolescents received any formal sex education. Fewer than 4 out of 10 adolescents knew the time of the month when conception was least likely. Mothers of these school children were no better informed than their daughters when asked the same question (*Teenage Pregnancy*, 1981).

Family planning clinics, however, have been very helpful to many individuals. It is estimated that 689,000 additional births to teenagers would have occurred between 1970 and 1978 (in addition to the 4,800,000 that did occur) if family planning clinics had not been available. While there has been an encouraging rise in the use of such clinics, the need still far exceeds the available resources. Actions by the Reagan administration to curtail the funding of any family planning agency that even talks about abortion options further limited access to that type of service in the 1980s.

There are other innovative programs related to adolescent sexuality. Miller (1982) describes a Teen Advocate Program in which some teenagers are selected and trained to provide informal information to their peers whenever and wherever needed. The 90-hour training program is, of course, helpful to the teen advocates themselves, as well as in their paid efforts to spread accurate information among their peers.

Research by Schinke, Gilchrist, and Small (1979) suggests that information alone is not sufficient to assist teenagers to make effective behavioral choices, particularly in the realm of interpersonal pressures such as those that surround sexual activity. The authors have translated the cognitive-behavioral model to fit the needs of adolescents and thus aid them in preventing unwanted pregnancy. The steps of this model are very useful in a number of interpersonal problems and so are worth noting: (1) Transmit relevant general information on the topic. (This would include basic sex education content, ranging from human anatomy to contraceptive practices to family planning goals. For example, "A condom and foam, appropriately used, is highly effective in preventing conception as well as sexually transmitted diseases.") (2) Test whether this information has been received, stored, and is retrievable as needed. (Testing can be done in any number of ways, including ordinary school testing.) (3) Individualize this general information so that it is comprehended by the client in his or her personal life: "When Jane and I have sex without using a condom, we risk making her pregnant, especially because her periods are irregular." (4) Practice the necessary steps to carry out individualized preventive plans—such as talking with your partner about contraceptives, buying them from the drug store, etc.—all with suitable positive reinforcement for effective actions taken by the teenager.

What factors contribute to unwanted adolescent pregnancy? As you review those selected here, think about how helping professionals might organize a configuration of efforts to counteract them.

1. *Cognitive Factors*
   (a) Lack of knowledge about human anatomy, physiology, and, particularly, about human sexuality as related to conception and contraception. Parents are not much better informed, and peers tend to provide most of the information (misinformation) they obtain.
   (b) Adolescent "myths" about sexuality (e.g., "use it or lose it" or "it can't happen to me" or "it can't happen the first time"). Young people with immature conceptual equipment may not see the broader implications of their actions or understand the full consequences.
   (c) Adolescent difficulties in obtaining effective contraceptive devices because of location, costs, and cultural pressures. They tend not to know about options they have in contraceptives.
   (d) Teenagers may not expect to have sex on a given date, and hence may not be prepared to take preventive actions.

2. *Affective Factors*
   (a) Teenagers may be impulsive in their sexual behaviors, with limited ability to delay gratifications. They may be immature in their self-orientation, although they may develop concern for all parties involved in time. (This is reflected in levels of moral development—see Kohlberg, 1983; Gilligan, 1988). Fantasies about "Prince Charming" and other idealizations may block out reality factors.
   (b) Adolescent anxiety about preparing for sexual behavior in advance. They may not see themselves as sexual beings, or may want to preserve the spontaneity they view as necessary to the act. The defense mechanisms protecting youths against their own impulses may not be well-developed when they are sexually active.
   (c) Masturbation is widely used to relieve sexual tensions, but teenagers may not view it as acceptable because of culturally-generated guilt, or social definitions of appropriate sexual activity.

3. *Behavioral, Interpersonal, and Social Factors*
   (a) Much adolescent sexuality is short-term and episodic and thus hard to plan for in advance. Some teenagers lack interpersonal skills (to say "no" in ways that do not also cut off social contacts). They may lack clear value positions from which to direct their behavior in new contexts.
   (b) Teenagers can exploit one another through unscrupulous actions, particularly when related to the need to be liked by socially power-

ful friends. Teens may not have good role models for appropriate sexual behavior.

(c) Sex may be influenced by the use of illegal substances, and such contexts reduce moral and social controls. Sexuality may be contagious in the sense that it is engaged in for the social status involved more than for the personally satisfying experience as such.

(d) "Unwanted" pregnancy may be positively desired by some adolescents, to gain the social status that comes from being a parent, even though problems abound. Mass media glorifies sexuality without responsibility, and many viewers act out scenes in their own lives.

There are many other possible causes for adolescent pregnancy (see McAnarney and Schreider, 1984). However, it should also be noted that considerably more research needs to be done as the times are rapidly changing. We need to understand in far greater detail how some teens are able to make their way through this period of life without serious problems, even though they experience the same bio-cultural tensions. Recent research suggests that there are personality factors ("hardiness") (Kobasa, Maddi, and Kahn, 1982) and contextual factors (Hull, Van Treuren, and Virnelli, 1987) that interact to enable people to resist succumbing to stress. This configuration of events might become very important in the prevention of a variety of problems, including unwanted teenage pregnancy.

OVERPOPULATION AND THE PROBLEM OF NATURAL THRESHOLDS

It was not until about the year 1850 that the world first experienced the situation where one billion people were alive at the same time. A century later, there were 2.5 billion. And you contributed to the 5 billion mark that was reached 36 years later, in 1986. By the year 2000, there will be over 6 billion inhabitants of this small planet. In raw terms, this means about 225,000 infants come into the world each day; some 83,000,000 people join us each year (Brown, et al., 1987; 1988). The Third World nations (in Asia, Africa, and South America particularly) are increasing populations at alarming rates, doubling in 20 to 35 years, while developed nations (such as the United States) have much slower rates of growth, taking from 50 to 250 years to double their populations.

So this wonderful thing called sexuality has huge implications. How clever of Nature to arrange it that we eagerly want to do what we must do to perpetuate the human species, as Schopenhauer noted. Unfortunately, simply spawning infants does not guarantee the perpetuation of the human race, and indeed, may be strongly counterproductive to that end. The biblical injunction to be fruitful and multiply may not have considered the numerical implications of geometric progressions.

But the good Reverend Thomas Malthus did. In 1798 he wrote one of those provocative and controversial essays whose enduring questions we are still trying to answer appropriately. In his day, families were generally larger than they are today, perhaps having four children. If the first generation has four children and each of these has four children in turn, and in time, all of these also have four children, a total of 84 human beings may be spawned from the two great grandparents. When such geometric expansions are compared to the productivity of the land, for which great efforts were made to have it yield even twice as much as before, we reach Malthus' grim prediction: population will inevitably outrun the means of food production.

Malthus never conceived of innovations such as the green revolution, in which agricultural methods and chemical fertilizers combined to make given lands much more productive; nor did he conceive of the massive use of effective contraceptives that not only set limits on pregnancy, but gave the power of choice to women (and men) as to whether or not to make babies. Yet the issues that Malthus raised still have not been satisfactorily resolved. Our ability to produce enormous amounts of food is not the whole point.

Brown and Postel (1987), in their report on the "state of the world," present some profoundly disturbing information regarding thresholds of change. With three billion young people entering their reproductive period over the next generation, there will be great pressure on population and everything that these numbers affect; for example, Brown and Postel report the crossing of natural thresholds in forests in specific countries—where wood harvesting or damage from burning of fossil fuels exceeds annual forest growth. There has been an expansion of lands devoted to agriculture that has increased the risk of erosion and depletion; more recently, lands have been intensively farmed by means of chemical fertilizers and the use of machinery in food production. "Between 1950 and 1985, the amount of oil used to produce a given unit of grain doubled. By the same date, nearly half of all oil discovered had been consumed." "Current proven U.S. reserves in the United States total 36 billion barrels, enough to supply U.S. needs for less than eight years at current rates of use (Brown and Postel, 1987, pp. 11–12)." With energy consumption rapidly increasing, America becomes dependent on foreign supplies of oil, or development of nuclear power plants, which raises another set of difficult problems.

Other events lead back to Malthus' hypothesis in modern dress. They include the human-caused thinning of the ozone layer that now permits more ultraviolet radiation to reach the earth, retarding crop growth, impairing human immune systems, and causing increased skin cancer and overuse of local water sources, depletion of fishing areas, and other changes in the way foods are prepared and sold. The most disturbing implications of the population explosion involve the exploitation of limited natural resources, the resulting pollution from industry, and the pursuit of short-term political-economic growth at the expense of the environment. As nations try to maintain or improve living standards for their citizens, they are collectively endangering the health of the global ecology. Such are the issues that are ultimately at stake as we snuggle together, enjoying the pleasures of sexual intimacy with our loved one. We five billion.

Estimates of the numbers of people suffering from undernourishment or malnutrition exceed one billion (cf. P. Ehrlich, A. Ehrlich, and J. Holdren, 1973). Those who die from starvation—even in the midst of the green revolution—number somewhere between ten and twenty million a year. A rough estimate suggests that 20 to 40 people are dying of starvation every minute of every day. Beyond the terrible facts of starvation, it is known that malnutrition affects people's ability to learn, to work, and to enjoy life (cf. Birch and Gussow, 1970). The problem of starvation is largely focused in Third World nations, those that are rapidly growing in population, without equally rapid growth in the supporting industries that can supply needed resources. But, as discussed in another chapter, there are pockets of malnutrition and starvation in America as well. The opposite side of the coin is the problem generated by developed nations (especially the United States), which consume a disproportionate amount of the world's resources. Demerath (1976) puts the world population picture into comprehensible terms:

> If the world population were to be compressed into a village of 1,000 with the continents comprising the neighborhoods, there would be roughly: 575 Asians, 200 Europeans, 85 Africans, 85 North Americans (55 U.S. citizens), 55 South Americans—1,000 total. In the village, there would be about 300 whites and 300 professed Christians. Of the total income generated, half would go to the U.S. citizens (pp. 5–6).

AIDS: THE NEW EPIDEMIC

The Actors

Newsweek (August 10, 1987) ran a feature story on AIDS that consisted primarily of the photographs and brief descriptions of 302 men and women and children who had died of AIDS in that past year, a small sampling of the 4,000 who died during the period. These are the actors—more will follow on the drama they were enacting, after we meet a few of them: Philip-Dimitri Galas, age 32, playwright working in San Diego; Michael Distler, age 35, a secretary in New York City; Carmen Joyce, age 25, a dietitian's aide from Atlantic City, New Jersey; Patrick O'Brien, cab driver from Seattle; John Gaffney, aged 13 months, who died in Boston, as did his mother, from a contaminated blood transfusion; Robert Gordy, age 52, an artist from New Orleans; Lance Gregory, 18 years old, a hemophiliac from Miami who was planning to become a doctor; Jerry Smith, age 43, a former pro football star from Maryland; Dominic Vasile, age 53, a street person from Boston who was a Korean War vet, a gifted sax player, and an intravenous drug user; Steven Schlitt, age 35, a cardiologist from Honolulu; David Summers, age 34, a cabaret singer in New York City, and cofounder of the New York City's People with AIDS Coalition; Terry Dolan, age 36, a Washingtonian who founded a conservative political-action group; Eugene Ewins, age 31, a sheet-metal worker in Houston before he committed suicide to escape the pain of AIDS; Richard Bray, age 30, a cowboy from Walnut Creek, California; Calu Lester, age 35, a San Francisco social worker who ran a shelter for the homeless; Donald Howard, age 59, a professor at Stanford who taught Chaucer; Jon Brower, age 31, an artist and ballet composer from Portland, Oregon; Dwight Tipton, age 30, prison inmate in Knoxville; Stewart McKinney, age 56, a liberal Connecticut Republican who had served nine terms in office; Beulah Wright O'Toole, age 87, a retired statistician from Gaitherberg, Maryland, who was infected by a 1984 blood transfusion; Joseph Foulon, age 33, an actor from New York City who devoted the last two years of his life to helping people with AIDS. . . .

Kathleen Weis

Pictured here is a small fragment of the AIDS Quilt, comprised of thousands of 3′ × 6′ panels commemorating those who have died of AIDS. Like the Vietnam War Memorial in Washington, D.C., it brings to life what the mere statistics can never tell. While a growing proportion of AIDS victims come from drug users, the great majority contracted AIDS from unsafe sex practices. This AIDS Quilt is a *memento mori* to us all.

As Peter Goldman (1987) writes of this picture gallery of the dead, "Seeing them gathered here reminds us that they are ours—our kin, our colleagues, our neighbors and friends. . . . We (Americans) are unaccustomed to an epidemic that resists the magic of our medicine, and we have too often held ourselves apart from its sufferers. But our response to AIDS will in important ways define us as a society" (p. 23).

The Stage

These brief biographical sketches present the individual victims, but to understand the scope of the problem we must also see the actors involved from a more general perspective. Epidemiology is the science that studies the distribution of diseases in time and space; it is a powerful tool in understanding what factors are correlated with the disease, which then permits us to take preventive or interventive actions. This is the stage on which the drama of thousands of lives takes place.

As of the latter 1980s, about 1,500,000 Americans had been exposed to the AIDS virus, and more than 34,000 adult and adolescent cases and about 23,000 deaths from AIDS had been reported to the Centers for Disease Control (CDC) in the United States. The number doubles every 12 to 15 months. Of these, 93 percent are men. Kristal reports (1986) that AIDS is the leading cause of death among women ages 25–29 in New York City. In Africa and Haiti, men and women show about the same proportion of reported cases of AIDS. (See Mantell, Schinke, and Akabas, 1988.)

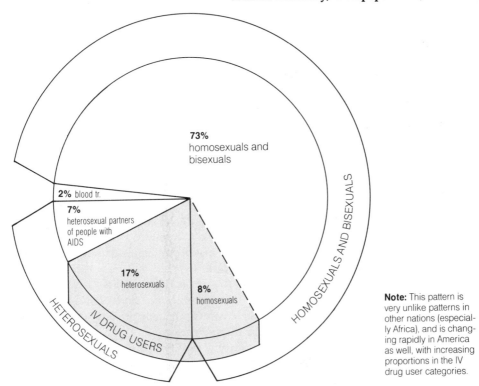

Note: This pattern is very unlike patterns in other nations (especially Africa), and is changing rapidly in America as well, with increasing proportions in the IV drug user categories.

FIGURE 20.1   Distribution of AIDS victims by sexual preference, intravenous drug use, and blood transfusions, United States, 1986

Homosexual and bisexual males compose the largest group of adult AIDS victims (about 73 percent, including 8 percent who are also IV drug users). IV drug users are the second largest group (about 17 percent heterosexual and 8 percent homosexual IV drug users). Hemophiliacs and others receiving blood transfusions represent 2 percent of AIDS victims, while another 7 percent comprise heterosexual partners of people with AIDS (*AIDS—A Public Health Crisis*, 1986). Nearly 500 children under the age of 13 have been afflicted with AIDS (CDC, 1987).

Colburn reports (1987) that AIDS strikes minorities disproportionately. Blacks and Hispanics account for about 39 percent of cases nationally, which is nearly double their proportions in the population. Bakeman, Lumb, Jackson, and Smith (1986) note that among all women with AIDS, blacks account for 51 percent while Hispanics compose another 21.

Worldwide, the estimates of the extent of AIDS are horrendous. It is estimated that about 100,000 persons have AIDS, and there are 300,000 to 500,000 persons with other symptoms of the AIDS virus and between 5 and 10 million persons who are asymptomatic carriers of the disease (*AIDS—A Public Health Crisis*, 1986). The Surgeon General predicted that by the end of 1991, an estimated 270,000 cases of AIDS will have occurred in the United States, with 179,000 deaths during the decade since the disease was first recognized in 1981.

Langone (1985) notes that for men or women in the United States who are straight, who do not take drugs intravenously, and who are not hemophiliacs requiring transfusions, the chances of contracting AIDS is less than one in a million (for comparison, one's chances of dying in a car accident are one in 5,000). However, helping professionals who are on the front lines where AIDS victims are involved (as health care workers in emergency wards of hospitals, or in laboratories assaying blood and other bodily fluids, or police officers on the beat) are at higher risks for contracting AIDS through breakdowns in security procedures, such as a tear in rubber gloves or a puncture wound. Ethical issues are emerging regarding the extent to which one ought to engage in risky helping behaviors.

The Drama

The following information on AIDS is drawn largely from government documents, especially the Surgeon General's dramatic and candid report to the American people on this subject, but also from *Coping with AIDS: Psychological and Social Considerations in Helping People with HTLV-III Infection* (1986). A special section of *Population Reports on AIDS—A Public Health Crisis* (1986) is also very informative. Social workers should understand the nature of this disease and what they can do to contribute to its prevention since there is no cure, nor any hope of one in the near future.

Acquired immune deficiency syndrome (AIDS) is the end-stage of a series of health problems caused by a virus that is passed from one person to another mainly through sexual contact, but also through the sharing of intravenous needles used for "shooting" drugs, and to a much lesser degree, from transfusions with contaminated blood, or when an infected woman transmits the AIDS virus to her fetus or at birth. Scientists have given different names to the AIDS virus (which belongs to a subclass of viruses called retroviruses)—HIV or HTLV-III or LAV—but they all refer to the same submicroscopic agent that attacks white blood cells (T-Lymphocytes or T-helpers or T-4 cells) in human blood.

When an individual's white blood cells are infected with the AIDS virus, the following events occur. First, the AIDS virus antibodies are developed, a fact that permits testing for their presence, which is usually but not totally indicative of having been infected with the virus at one time. One simple and inexpensive test detects antibodies of the AIDS virus (the Enzyme-Linked Immunosorbent Assay or ELISA test), and if it is positive (indicating presence of the antibodies), then a second, more specific test, and much more expensive test (the Western Blot) may be used to make a definitive confirmation. ELISA sometimes gives false positives because of other antibodies that show up on the test, for example, in women who have had several children and who have produced antibodies to these cells during pregnancy.

Second, some people may remain free of symptoms, but are able to infect others. Third, other people may develop a disease that is less serious than AIDS, referred to as AIDS Related Complex (ARC). These persons may continue to suffer from illnesses such as loss of appetite, weight loss, fever, night sweats, skin rashes, diarrhea, tiredness, lack of resistance to infection, or swollen lymph nodes. For reasons not yet understood, other ARC victims appear to recover (although because of the long-term nature of the problem—sometimes the incubation period may be five years or more—it is not certain that recovery is an accurate end-result).

The fourth possibility is that people will get AIDS and other life-threatening conditions that inevitably end in death. There is no known cure for AIDS. Seventy percent of AIDS victims die within two years. The diseases AIDS victims die from emerge because of the opportunity created by the persons' lowered resistance. There appears to be a connection between use of drugs and alcohol—particularly the nitrite inhalants that act in ways to enhance sexual pleasure—which appear to trigger the AIDS virus infecting the immune system (*Acquired Immune Deficiency Syndrome and Chemical Dependency*, 1987). Most commonly occurring diseases are pneumocystis carinni pneumonia and tuberculosis. Others may develop a kind of cancer called Kaposi's sarcoma. In addition, there can be severe neurological disorders such as progressive memory loss, indifference, loss of coordination, partial paralysis, or mental disorder. Other symptoms may include night sweats, fever, fatigue, and two potentially fatal factors—diarrhea and weight loss—all occurring singly or in combinations, intermittently or persistently, with varying degrees of severity (*AIDS—A Public Health Crisis*, 1986).

In addition to these physical symptoms, there are other psychological trauma related to facing death during the prime of life—most AIDS victims are young adults between the ages of 20 and 40. These include ostracism from family and friends, rejection at work or even from helping professionals, reactions to continuing pain, possibly guilt arising from deviant life-style practices, and the anxiety of the unknown (especially by people suffering from ARC diseases, with regard to their getting AIDS). Suicidal ideation is common.

The Script: What Can We Do To Prevent AIDS?

The ways to prevent AIDS are clear. Here is one statement from the Public Health Service:

> Don't have sex with multiple partners or with persons who have had multiple partners (including prostitutes). The more partners you have, the greater your risk of contracting AIDS.
>
> Obviously, avoid sex with persons with AIDS or members of the risk group (homosexual and bisexual men; present or past intravenous drug users; persons with clinical or laboratory evidence of infection—that is, those who test positive on the AIDS virus antibody tests; persons born in countries where heterosexual transmission is thought to play a major role in the spread of the AIDS virus, such as Haiti and Central African countries; male or female prostitutes and their sex partners; persons with hemophilia who have received clotting factor products).
>
> If you do have sex with a person you think may be infected, protect yourself by taking appropriate precautions to prevent contact with the person's body fluids (including blood, semen, urine, feces, saliva, and women's genital secretions). These preventive practices include:
> - use of condoms
> - avoidance of practices that may injure body tissues (such as anal intercourse)
> - avoidance of oral-genital contact
> - avoidance of open-mouthed, intimate kissing
> - Do not use intravenous drugs. However, if you do, don't share needles or syringes.

Even though these precautions are so clear and potentially so effective, there is no guarantee that vulnerable people will heed the advice. With effective communication, however, the effects can be powerful. For example, Abrams (1987) reports that there were 1,500 cases of rectal gonorrhea in San Francisco in the first quarter of 1980, and following an information campaign on its prevention by use of condoms, the incidence fell to 100 cases in the last quarter of 1985. Smith (1987) reports an increase in long-term relationships and healthier life-styles among the nonaddicted gays in San Francisco in the wake of information about AIDS.

Many problems still remain, particularly among intravenous drug users and people living in areas without strong public health campaigns—which is about everywhere except in places with the major concentration of the disease (in New York and California primarily, but also in New Jersey, Florida, and Texas). Young people who are exploring their own sexuality (heterosexual or homosexual) are very vulnerable as well, particularly when these explorations are combined with experimenting with alcohol and drugs. The Surgeon General writes:

> Education about AIDS should start in early elementary school and at home so that children can grow up knowing the behavior to avoid to protect themselves from exposure to the AIDS virus. The threat of AIDS can provide an opportunity for parents to instill in their children their own moral and ethical standards (p. 5). . . . There is no doubt that we need sex education in schools and that it must include information on heterosexual and homosexual relationships. The threat of AIDS should be sufficient to permit a sex education curriculum with a heavy emphasis on prevention of AIDS and other sexually transmitted diseases (p. 31).

In addition to basic education of children, there are many other avenues toward the prevention of AIDS. Mass media is a vital tool, but we must identify the specific audiences that have to be reached in order to develop messages that are appropriate and credible to them. Efforts to date have been minuscule in the United States as compared, for example, to Switzerland, where the government distributed a 10-page pamphlet to all households in the country, and then conducted a random survey to discover that people in 75 percent of the households had read the pamphlets (*AIDS—A Public Health Crisis*, 1986). Opportunities abound to reach audiences such as teenagers through popular radio and television programs, magazines, motion pictures, and even stage productions. (The Johns Hopkins School of Public Health helped to write a pro-family planning song sung by popular Mexican singers, just as a popular American singer was selling her theme song that requested her father not to give her moral sermons about her sexual behavior. Such are the conflicting messages heard by youth.)

Individualized communications and instruction may also be necessary, in health and counseling contexts, but also in nonconventional settings such as the gymnasium, the church, gay bath houses (see Rabin, 1986), singles bars, prisons, military training camps and bases, boarding schools, restaurants, record stores, dance halls, on buses and subways, on billboards, in public toilets, college dorms, well-baby clinics, family planning centers, the workplace, homes for runaway youth, shelters for the homeless, rape crisis centers, community centers, housing projects, places where prostitution takes place, and possibly even the local supermarket, the corner drug store, and pool hall (see Arnold and Cogswell, 1971). In all of these places, people at risk for sexual experimentation must be given clear, accurate, and full information, and be aided to achieve, not "safe sex," because that is impossible, but rather, to achieve "safer sex" (Thompson, 1987). The information must be given in class- and culture-sensitive ways, with due regard to the reading level of the targeted audience.

Influencing changes in basic life-styles is difficult, especially when the person involved has invested so much in breaking out of a conventional mode and is supported by others in the same life-style. However, AIDS is literally wiping out whole neighborhoods of gays and intravenous drug users who had adopted an unprotected, multiple partner approach to sexuality. The cognitive-behavioral methods by Schinke and Gilchrist described earlier may be especially helpful to women in enabling them to negotiate successfully with their partners concerning the use of condoms (cf. Mantell, Schinke, and Akabas, 1988). There are cultural barriers as well, such as the negative labels attached to unmarried Hispanic women who insist that condoms be used, or the opposition by the Catholic Church to condom use even as a preventive barrier for AIDS.

Added to the existing social taboos about discussions of sexual matters is the difficulty even helping professionals may have in presenting low-risk sexual alternatives to persons at high risk of AIDS. [These include direct alternatives such as hugging, petting, mutual masturbation, erotic massage, and the like; nonsexual alternatives for emotional highs might include relaxation exercises, yoga, dance, all sorts of physical recreation, sports, and, indeed, involvement in social causes. See Cohen (1975) on related suggestions.]

Obviously, basic and applied research into the biological nature of AIDS must proceed—and be interpreted to citizens as new information comes along. Screening of blood for transfusions must continue. And standard procedures with regard to helping professionals' contact with bodily fluids of AIDS patients must be carried out. Abrams (1987) reminds us of 14th-century Italian physicians who wore elaborate garments made entirely of leather, from head to foot, with wide-brimmed hats to keep them at a distance from their patients, whom they touched only with a pointer, never by hand. They also had attached to their hoods a long leather beak stuffed with herbs to "purify" the air. The disease they were avoiding then was the bubonic plague. By the way, it worked because the fleas that transmitted the disease couldn't reach them. Today, some health workers, school teachers, police officers, first aiders doing mouth-to-mouth resuscitation, nursery school attendants, ambulance drivers, and others are fearful of AIDS and have refused to help persons known or suspected of the disease. Since there is an element of risk in some of these circumstances, there will need to be retraining of these helpers on managing their work under conditions of the risk of AIDS. The ethics of helping professionals is receiving another major test.

SUMMARY

As the finishing touches were being made on the manuscript for this book, *Ms.* magazine published a special issue on "sex, romance, love and lust in the 90s." The cover showed a couple in what looked to be like a state of ecstacy.

But every Garden of Eden has its snake, and this chapter has reported on some of the problems associated with human sexuality and related matters. Unwanted teenage pregnancy comes from loving too soon and unwisely. Overpopulation comes from loving too often and unwisely. AIDS comes, in part, from loving unsafely—and increasingly, from causes related to use of illegal substances. The very statement of these problems raises value judgments that put any commentator into a moralistic light, whether or not that position is warranted.

The facts of life are brutally clear. Huge numbers of conceptions take place every year, some of which are aborted naturally or artificially. But the great majority are born and of these, many are unloved, unwanted, unprepared for. Their lives are filled with the problems that social workers see under many different labels—delinquency, abuse, whatever.

Because every problem person has to be born, and has to experience deficits in the growing up process that lead to other problems, human sexuality may be the root condition that requires the preventive/promotive attentions of social workers and all citizens. If problems are not prevented, and if well-nourished and much-loved children are not promoted, then we will see no end to social problems.

PART

VIII.

TOOLS OF THE PROFESSION

There are some special tools that every helping professional will need to use often and with considerable skill, so as to take advantage of the vast information system available to him or her, and to evaluate how well that information is serving to resolve the client's problems or fulfill the client's potentials. The first requisite of scientific practice is careful observation, and so Chapter 21 offers some basic principles and a photographic section on which to practice these rules for looking carefully for what is present—and for what is absent.

Chapter 22 introduces social work students to some of the powerful information retrieval tools for finding specific information rapidly and effectively. (I have written about this topic elsewhere, should the student be interested in other aspects of information retrieval. See Bloom, 1975; 1984.)

Evaluation in the technical sense is a specialized business, for which few undergraduate or generic programs offer much exposure. All social workers, however, must have some objective sense about how well their work is going if they are to resolve client problems and fulfill client objectives. So Chapter 23 offers a brief introduction to evaluation of practice. (For further discussions, see Bloom, 1986; Bloom and Fischer, 1982.) This is the age of accountability, at every level of practice.

OUTLINE

Introduction to Systemic Observation
A Photographic Essay

CHAPTER TWENTY-ONE

The Challenge of Observation—
A Photographic Essay

This is the first of three "tool" chapters in which I introduce some important techniques for use in social work thinking and practice. Observation is the basic building block for all practice, but to be able to observe systematically, as a helping professional is called on to do, is something that we must carefully learn and enrich.

INTRODUCTION TO SYSTEMATIC OBSERVATION

Scientific practice begins with careful and thorough observation. From the ancient times when Hippocrates recorded case descriptions of medical illnesses that are still recognizable today, to the meticulous studies of such Nobel prize winners as Madame Curie and Barbara McClintock, observation is of the essence. It has always been so. It will always be so. Exact and exacting observation.

Observation is not the same as seeing. The process of seeing has fascinated philosophers and scientists throughout history. How is it that things in the outer world—ants and elephants, a grain of sand and a mountain range—get transmitted to our eyes all in the right size and in perspective? As wondrous and mystifying as seeing is, so observation—planned and systematic seeing—is more so.

This photo essay presents a series of pictures for you to observe. Except for the first one*, all of the pictures are by the talented photographer-social worker David Antebi, who has sensitively and humanely recorded a small sampling in the flow of human events. Any photograph is perforce an instant in that flow. It is we who impose a history and a future to that picture so as to give it meaning. Giving something a meaning means, in turn, that we know

---

*The first photograph is from the Virginia Shakespeare Festival, the 1984 Production of *Equus*, directed by James J. Christy.

how to behave toward that something, what to feel about it, how to think about it. All of social work action is therefore based on our understanding or giving meaning to what our clients present to us. Thus all of social work begins with observation.

How are we to go beyond seeing, to observing, to giving meaning to events? How can we be sure that the meaning we give to events is accurate, so that we can offer interventions based on accurate information? Professional training is probably the best beginning of learning how to observe carefully and effectively. It will take work on your part and on the part of your instructors. Let's begin with some observation exercises in the following photographs.

Look at the first photograph on page 443. What do you see? Do you trust your eyes? Do you see in the blurred image what appears to be a naked youth falling or leaping onto something? And beyond the blurred images, do you believe what you see—what are these men wearing on their heads? If you look closely, they look like horses' heads. And look at their shoes. What on earth is going on here? What is the meaning of all this?

Let's review what we have just done. We have looked at a photograph of a moment in life, and our eye—that is, our attention—was probably drawn first to the blurred "moving" patch of light that looked familiar if out of place as a naked person. We do not often see nude people except in socially prescribed places—in the gym showers or chiseled in marble in museums—so our attention is drawn to this blurred image, even though the clearer images of men in horse's heads are more unusual, if less erotic.

In general, we tend to see moving figures against still backgrounds. Yet, it is the background context of men in horse's heads that gives meaning to the foreground, the blurred image of the youth. When I tell you that this photograph is a snapshot taken during a theater production of *Equus*, does this "fact" not make all of the pieces fit together in an instant? Having read about the play (in Chapter 1), you now recognize this blurred image to be the climactic point in the drama when the youth leaps upon his beloved gods and blinds them. You know the history (from the painfully slow explorations of the therapist in the play); you know the present moment; and you anticipate the future, one that will free the youth from the psycho-social burdens under which he labors.

In a word, you understand. You have combined a myriad of pieces of observation and conversation (about observations other people have had about the client). The pieces fit together—at least to a degree. You may wonder about some parts of the client's story; you may even doubt other parts. (Everyone retells his or her experiences from a biased perspective!) But this wonderful or awe-ful experience of insight or understanding of how the pieces of a situation fit together meaningfully is the reward of successful observation. Look for it. Demand it of yourself.

Until you get this sense of closure, your observations and data gathering are incomplete. Keep looking. On the other hand, beware of premature closure, of shutting down the observation process too soon, before all of the relevant facts are known. Indeed, observation is an on-going process because new facts, new facets of the client's story may unfold that dramatically change the meaning of the existing story.

What is closure? It probably involves seeing that specific event as an instance of some pattern of events. In other words, it is seeing that the particular is an instance of a general concept. Knowledge itself consists in having conceptual frameworks that describe what we know, that help explain how things work, and that predict what will happen so we can know what to do about it. We add new knowledge to our fund of information by translating specific events into the general concepts of which they are instances.

So, the first rule of observation is to look at a momentary human scene and find a likeness between it and some larger pattern of events of which it is an instance. Locate the concept amid everyday events. (Caution: the same event may be related to more than one concept.)

The second rule of observation is to reduce the number of possible concepts of which that observed event may be an instance. For example, that youth in *Equus* may have been someone who was in fact mentally deranged, or it may have been a fraternity stunt on campus, or a scene from a play. One has to examine the context and history of an event in order to reduce these alternative explanations to the most likely one as the basis for understanding and action. Obviously, we would do different things if that youth were mentally ill or merely play acting on campus or on the stage.

The third rule of observation is to test your interpretation against additional evidence. This could be additional historical evidence, but it is more likely to be concurrent and future evidence. The better the fit to an existing body of evidence, the more comfortable we may be with our interpretation. (Caution: the desire to be comfortable with our values about what ought to be the case may sometimes make us see things that are not there, or not see things that are there.)

Now, turn to the photographs in the rest of this gallery of human events. What do you see? These photographs contain a variety of human beings in various modes of action or inaction, with others or in isolation, and doing things that may be the problem or the solution. You can examine each photograph separately, or in small clusters of "like" persons or events, or altogether as aspects of one humanity. Each of these approaches is the "right" way only because people are themselves unique individuals like others of their kind; they are fundamentally similar as biological species—all at the same time.

As you look at each picture, jot down one impression at a time on a separate line so you can see the progression of your thinking about a given picture. What do you see (and record) first? Is it something about the persons and objects in the picture, or is it something about you, the observer, such as how you feel about these people or in reaction to their circumstances?

As you list your impressions, do you begin to use sociological-anthropological categories, like race, age, gender, socio-economic class—or do you use psychological categories, such as mentally depressed, happy, resigned, assertive? Or do you use qualitative and individualizing impressions such as "this scene disgusts me," "I can't believe people live that way," or "I wish I had the guts to do that." Why do you suppose you respond the way you do, while your neighbor, looking at exactly the same photographs, responds in fundamentally different ways? Is there a "right" way? A way that leads to more "effective and humane helping"? (If there is, please write to me immediately; I would very much like to know what it is.)

Looking at your list of impressions from the first picture after the scene from *Equus*, do you "see" any generalizations or concepts emerging from your impressions? (We do not see or hear concepts as such; they are purely mental constructs that we can use to describe, explain, or predict about real world events.) Are these concepts positive or negative from your point of view, that is, are you aware of how you value these abstractions that you have inferred? The concepts themselves are social categories; do you see any similar valuing in the way society uses these terms? When does a social value become a stereotype or a bias? When does a personal value embody social stereotypes or social biases?

As you look at these pictures, when did you "not know"? That is, when did you admit on your jotted list of observations that you did not know what was going on in the picture? (Some things you cannot know exactly, although you might make some sage guesses. So I assume that there are opportunities for you to "not know," to admit you do not have all of the evidence on which to base an informed judgment. If you didn't have any "not knows" in your list, that's all right; it takes some time and maturity to be wise enough not to know everything. Or rather, to be able to admit it. (Did I catch you on that one? Sorry. I was not playing tricks. "Not knowing" really exists for scientists and others.)

Some problems are portrayed in these pictures, as you probably have discovered. Who is to blame, if anyone or anything? What is to be done? Should we leave these people alone to live their lives freely—as we generally wish others would do to us? Should we invite ourselves into their lives with offers of help, if they would accept it? Or should we force them to be healthy and happy—like us? What are their rights? What are our responsibilities? These are very difficult questions, but, remarkably, they are ones on which many people have strong views. What is the evidence or basis for taking any of these views?

"No man is an island. . . ." Do you see any human groupings? Such groupings are thought to be essential for a satisfying human existence. Who is not present who might be members of these groups? Did you see any social workers (or persons who might be or have been social workers) in these photographs? Did you see any "social problems"—commonalities among the human experiences presented in these photographs? Or any "social victories"? Do you see yourself here?

Scene from the 1984 production of "Equus," directed by James J. Christy, at the College of William and Mary. Photo courtesy of the Virginia Shakespeare Festival.

David Antebi

. . . all of social work begins with observation

observation is not the same as seeing . . .

as wondrous and mystifying as seeing is, so

observation—planned and systematic seeing—is more so

David Antebi

. . . observation is an on-going process . . .

David Anteb

David Antebi

. . . *observation is of the essence*

it has always been so—it will always be so

David Antebi

observation is the basic building block for all practice . . .

to observe systematically

is something that we must carefully learn and enrich

. . . understanding how the pieces of a situation

fit together is the reward of successful observation.

David Antebi

OUTLINE

Introduction to Information Retrieval (IR)
Information Retrieval Strategies for Helping Professionals
A Case Illustration: The Women's Shelter
Translating Scientific Information Back into Practice Hypotheses
One Final Caveat: Let the Reader Beware!

CHAPTER TWENTY-TWO

Information Retrieval
for Helping Professionals

Scientific practice is only as good as the information on which it is based. Therefore social workers and other helping professionals have to consult the scientific and professional literature if they are to discover what others have done successfully (or unsuccessfully) in similar client situations and to be guided to experiment with some practice strategy.

This chapter discusses how workers can retrieve relevant information rapidly and effectively. What it does not say, but what should be obvious, is that this takes practice: The more you use information storage resources like Social Work Research and Abstracts *or* Psychological Abstracts, *the easier it will become to find information that you need.*

INTRODUCTION TO INFORMATION RETRIEVAL (IR)

One of the great moments of American engineering occurred when the two teams of builders of the transcontinental railroad met near Promontory Point, Ogden, Utah, on May 10, 1869. What is fascinating about this feat is that the two teams were working so precisely—over mountains, across rivers, through enormous stretches of prairie, one from the west, the other from the east—that they met exactly at the right place to effect a perfect fit—the single transcontinental railroad.

In a parallel fashion, it is only slightly less miraculous that two teams of workers meet at a common point, coming from vastly different perspectives: Information retrieval combines the needs of the practitioner with the efforts of the scientist. Just as the railway teams used planned procedures to effect that precise meeting, so too do the teams making connections in the realm of scientific information. This chapter explores the strategies for rapid and precise retrieval of the best available information for the helping professional.

To make that precise connection between the messy subjectivities of the client situation with the rigorous but narrow abstractions of the laboratory or field experiment, both teams have to use some common terms and proce-

This girl scout is involved in an experience in perception, taking in information about the world by means of touch, rather than by sight. While this is an interesting experience for this young person, we should recognize that we are roughly in an analogous position in searching for scientific information unless we use effectively all of the modes of information retrieval at our disposal. This chapter discusses some of these methods.

dures. Concepts—generalized and abstracted classes of events—are the common terms. The practitioner has to generalize from his or her single client's situation to the class of events of which these are one instance. Then, taking this generalization and abstraction—that is to say, taking the concept that describes the category of events that is troubling the client—the helping professional scans the information retrieval system to find matching concepts from scientists who have studied (theorized, done research, offered statements of practice wisdom) the same topic. The applied scientist has to relate his or her research variables—which are measurable terms that stand in the place of concepts—to issues of social significance and concern that may be helpful to practitioners. The knowledge that scientists generate must be expressed in a form comprehensible by others, both other scientists who may wish to retest the conclusions and practitioners who may wish to translate the findings into directives guiding their practice with specific clients.

INFORMATION RETRIEVAL STRATEGIES FOR HELPING PROFESSIONALS

Information retrieval involves three parties who come together for a common purpose of sharing information. One party is the scientist who generates the knowledge; another party is the practitioner who seeks specific information; and the third party is the information specialist who arranges for the meeting of the other two. Each speaks his or her own specialized language—research concepts or variables, practice terminology, or the key words for information storage and retrieval. To some extent, each must learn to communicate with the others.

There are some strategies for making the meeting of these parties as easy and rapid as possible, for getting the best available information about particular case situations from the general and abstract scientific information. Table 22.1 presents a brief map for this meeting. It contains (on the left side) the steps a helping professional must take, and (on the right side) the events related to the information that the scientist generates. In the middle column are the information retrieval strategies for making this linkage as easily and painlessly as possible.

A CASE ILLUSTRATION: THE WOMEN'S SHELTER

To illustrate this abstract discussion of information retrieval, the author presents here a case situation (actually two simultaneous situations) of one of his students, suitably disguised to preserve confidentiality. Susan Wellington-Sims (the social work student—abbreviated to SWS) met her client, Miss C, at the downtown women's shelter of a large city. Miss C is a 17-year-old unmarried mother who recently came to the city seeking employment and a new life away from an abusive family and boyfriend. Terry, her 2-year-old, was rather slow and lethargic, and talked only in occasional babbles. Miss C had not finished high school, and although she seemed quite intelligent, she had difficulty locating any job that paid enough for her and her son to live on. Her

TABLE 22.1   Summary of information retrieval strategies for practice

Activities related to the client situation	Information retrieval strategies	Activities related to the information tools
1. What is the problem on which you need information? (Step 1 of the problem-solving process.) Sort out personal factors (strengths and limitations) and contextual factors (stresses and supports from primary and secondary groups, socio-cultural and physical environments).	**1.** FORMULATE A SEARCH SENTENCE: Link the *specific events* from the client situation to their *conceptual categories*. These concepts become the terms in the search sentence.	**1.** The articles listed in the information retrieval tools are "tagged" by key terms taken from their titles or abstracts. These tag words are listed in subject indexes, and directions are given on how to find the whole citation. These tag words are concepts.
2. What are the alternative theoretical conceptualizations on how factors came together to produce the state of affairs the worker sees? These theories may offer suggestions about "centers of gravity" in certain kinds of cases. (Step 2 of the problem-solving process.)	**2.** SELECT MAJOR OPERATIVE TERMS FOR INITIAL RETRIEVAL SEARCH: The "center of gravity" of a client situation indicates the structures or forces determining the problem. Since these are the controlling factors, look for guidance on how others have effectively dealt with them to see if you can use a similar plan of action.	**2.** Study the structures and retrieval procedures of each abstract or bibliography you use. There are several major types plus variations (like the telescoped abstracts in *Psychological Abstracts*; or the paired terms in *Social Work Research and Abstracts* or key word in context as in the *Inventory of Marriage and Family Literature*). (See Bloom, 1984.)
3. Does the consideration of long-term goals or immediate objectives add anything to what information you want to find? (Step 3 of the problem-solving process.)	**3.** ADAPT YOUR PRACTICE-ORIENTED TERMS TO THOSE CONCEPTS USED BY SCIENTISTS: Use a thesaurus (such as the *Thesaurus of Psychological Index Terms—for Psychological Abstracts*) to identify scientific terms corresponding to those you use in describing your clients.	**3.** Use synonyms of your original search terms. Use levels of abstraction approach to increase your usable information: (*a*) Select a more inclusive, higher level abstraction when citations are few; (*b*) Select a more specific, lower level when there are too many to handle.
4. Continue to re-evaluate the information needs of your client as the case develops.	**4.** SELECT ONLY TITLES OF ARTICLES THAT ARE A GOOD FIT TO YOUR SEARCH STATEMENT: Match the major concepts from your search statement to the major concepts in the article title.	**4.** Record clearly the whole citation for future use: author, title, journal, year, volume number, pages. Check to see which journals are available in your library.
5. Implement and simultaneously evaluate the service package. (See generic problem-solving steps in chapter 6.) The worker translates to what degree the information from the literature is applicable and practical in a given client context. If there are sufficient similarities of actors; if similar kinds of service programs can be set up for persons and social groups then the worker might expect some degree of the kind of outcome the research paper reported. One cannot expect precisely the same results because of differences between the client's situation and factors reported in the article. But often such reports provide initial practice suggestions that use available resources.	**5.** FORMULATE A PRACTICE STATEMENT: Link the *concepts and propositions* from the theoretical articles (or the variables and hypotheses from research studies) to the *specific events* in the client situation. In general, such linkages of successful research or theoretical discussions will provide the following information: What actors (client, worker, or others) influence what aspects of the client and what aspects of relevant social environments, by what actions, are intended to have what effects?	**5.** Read original article for a full understanding of the procedures described.

small savings quickly evaporated in the dazzling but expensive city, and so she ended up in the women's shelter—a place that provided room and board for a month, while insisting that residents look for jobs and other living accommodations.

The student's field instructor, Mrs. Felice Inman (FI, for short), pointed out that this type of situation—an unwed and unemployed mother of young children—was unfortunately rather common, and what the SWS did for her client might be used with other clients as well. Here is the critical point: SWS is seeking information on helping her client, while at the same time recognizing that the practice strategies she discovers might be useful for other clients in similar circumstances, either individually or collectively.

Use Table 22.1 as our road map to follow the paths the SWS took to locate information for her client and for the class of clients with similar circumstances. First, as in any problem-solving process, the worker attempted to identify the problem on which she needed information. By following the configural approach, she sorted out the issues according to their personal, primary, and secondary group and socio-cultural and physical environmental contexts—not just because this provides a good overview of relevant topics, but because it presents an approach for information retrieval as well. The basic question in information retrieval is what concept or key word will lead to the best available information in the scientific and professional literature? The emphasis that a practitioner might place on a given case may not be the same as the conceptual perspective of the scientist, or the key terms used by the information specialist. Some topics are of recent origin, and so relatively little research may be in the literature to be retrieved. What information strategies promise is the locating of whatever is available. There is no guarantee of the quality, quantity, or utility of the information retrieved. Let's illustrate the search process with reference to Table 22.2.

Given the analysis of problems and strengths in Table 22.2, step two of the information retrieval strategy asks what factors would the social work student pay attention to? Many workers would focus on the personal factors, possibly combined with the small group (or family) factors—and this may be fine as far as practice is concerned. But in so far as the knowledge-generating scientist and the specialist in information retrieval are concerned, the personal and small group terms may not be the best ones on which to search for information in all cases. We have to get into the mind-set of the scientist and information specialist to see how information might be generated and later stored.

To enter this mind-set, consider once again the idea of a center of gravity in a configuration. What is the "point" among personal, primary, and secondary groups and socio-cultural and physical environments at this time that seems to determine the nature and extent of the client's problem? Another way to phrase this is to ask what is the predominant force in the client's life, the one that combines the pushes and pulls of all the other forces acting on the client?

One such "point" or predominant force in Miss C's life would relate to her socio-economic problem, particularly at an organizational level. It might be argued that if there were well-paying jobs for persons with Miss C's educational and skill levels, and if there were child care facilities available for Terry while she was at work, then some of the other personal problems would disappear—such as "not having enough money." There might be other centers of gravity in Miss C's life that suggest other basic problems, such as Terry's apparent developmental difficulties, Miss C's interpersonal relationships with other adults, and so forth. But let us illustrate the process of information retrieval with this one socio-economic issue.

With a given problem area, we next have to ask at what level or levels of the configuration would information likely be stored? Sometimes a personal level factor might be relevant, such as the problem of the compulsive gambler. But from our analysis of the center of gravity in Miss C's case, it seems likely that organizational and societal factors might be more relevant.

The center of gravity idea also suggests that problems may be embedded within one another. For example, the lack of available jobs and lack of child care facilities in the area are obviously two parts of the same larger problem. Both have to be resolved before changes can be made at the personal level. Stating these problems as centers of gravity also leads the worker to see both the individual and the collective manifestations of the problem. Miss C needs child care support, but so do others in the same situation. Miss C needs a well-paying job, as do others. Miss C needs job training to qualify for a reasonable job; so might others. Indeed, it would be difficult to arrange any of these for one individual alone, and so in effect the worker is guided to look for collective solutions for common problems.

What we have been doing in analyzing this case problem can now be translated into information retrieval terms. We must first formulate a search sentence that describes Miss C's situation, but also is general enough to relate to the common problems that others might be facing as well. Given the discussion of centers of gravity, consider this formulation: *What means of intervention have proven effective in providing employment opportunities for unmarried mothers needing child care?*

Next, we look at the search sentence and select the major operative ideas, those that determine the shape and extent of the client's problem. From the center of gravity discussion, we determined that this major idea would be the socio-economic consideration of employment of women. Obviously, we could qualify the search statement to reflect the particular characteristics of Miss C, such as having a child who may be developmentally delayed. But this would not be helpful at this initial stage of information searching. We should first look for the center of gravity in the situation, the set of forces or structures that strongly determines the scope of the problem; this would be the employment situation. But as we will see, all information is stored in clusters, so the search sentence provides the needed paired ideas, such as employment of mothers. The more detailed we become, the less information we will find that fits precisely, so let's begin with a broad net and see what we catch.

The third step in information retrieval strategies would be to make sure that our language involves practice terms that are compatible with the language of scientists who are generating information on this topic. Fortunately, there are some thesauruses available in psychology and sociology that take the large set of lay language terms and show what smaller set of technical words are used by information specialists to store information generated by scientists. Consider all of the synonyms for employment that we might use, like being out of work, not having a paying job, on the dole, being jobless or

TABLE 22.2   Analysis of a case situation from a configural perspective for information retrieval purposes

WHAT IS THE PROBLEM?

from the personal perspective	from a small group perspective	from an organizational perspective	from the socio-cultural and/or physical environmental perspective
1. Miss C has no money 2. Miss C has no job 3. Miss C does not have a high school diploma 4. Miss C has few marketable skills	1. Miss C receives no support from her family 2. Miss C has few friends in the city, because of her recent move there 3. Terry may be developmentally delayed, with the attendant problems for him and his mother	1. There are no well-paying jobs available for a person with her educational and skill level 2. There are no child care facilities available to Miss C	1. There may be some discriminations against unwed mothers in regard to employment 2. Miss C may be at a considerable distance from job opportunities

WHAT STRENGTHS EXIST IN THIS SITUATION?

from the personal perspective	from a small group perspective	from an organizational perspective	from the socio-cultural and/or physical environmental perspective
1. Miss C seems to be intelligent 2. Miss C is pleasant and makes friends easily	1. Both the mother and son are physically healthy	1. The shelter offers some temporary support and advice on adapting to the new city	1. Some welfare provisions appear to be relevant to Miss C's situation (such as AFDC and food stamps)

unemployed, and so forth. (Some terms are more complicated than "employment," but the same principles apply.)

Now, for the meeting of the two teams at Promontory Point: In searching for information under the key term "employment," the student used *Social Work Research and Abstracts* for 1987, and encountered several citations and their abstracts that might prove useful—all in the matter of a few minutes. Obviously, the student could use other retrieval devices in this and other years, and should do so until some materials are found that fit closely to the ideas in the original search sentence.

Each information retrieval tool has its own organization for locating materials. *Social Work Research and Abstracts* uses the key word and qualifying phrase format: Employment + Some Other Terms or Phrases. For example, one citation linked Employment and Rural Women. (Miss C came from a rural area, and so it seemed to be a good fit.): L. C. Morris wrote a paper abstracted in AFFILIA, *a Journal of Women and Social Work*, 1986, volume 1, number 2, pages 20–29, entitled "The changing and unchanging status of rural women in the work place." (Note the synonym for employment in this title.)

The abstract briefly summarizes the article dealing with the history of rural women entering the work force in 1970–1980. Record numbers became employed, but they entered in low-status and low-paying jobs, especially rural black women. What the student realizes from this article is that what she is seeing in her one client and what the agency is seeing in several of its clients is in fact a general problem in the nation. This brings in other aspects of the social configuration, should the worker wish to do so. There may be other groups studying this problem, developing legislative action at the state or national level—or be interested in doing so. A telephone call to one's congressional representatives might help to locate this information. There is no need to reinvent the wheel; what is important is that the worker make connections with existing organizations seeking to help this kind of client. But how? Where? This article does not say.

The student also looked under the key term "Unemployment" and found different citations. One, for example, reported briefly on the entire issue of the *International Journal of Mental Health* (1984, volume 13, numbers 1 and 2, edited by P. Rayman and R. Liem). Included in the abstract were mentions of several articles on grass roots unemployment networks and a counseling program for dislocated workers—both topics that might be relevant to programs that the Shelter might develop or participate with others in developing. To find out, SWS has to locate the original articles and read carefully for details. But the search for this information has been greatly simplified by locating exactly the papers that seem relevant. By "relevance" I mean a good match in key words between one's search statement and the title of the article. Titles are not always perfect indicators of what is discussed in the paper, but this is the best we have to go on for most research at the current state of technology in information retrieval in the social sciences.

Lest you think that every information search turns up good information, let us finish this case study. SWS also looked for information under the key term, "Child Care." One citation seemed pertinent, a dissertation by I. M. Sevick, entitled "Adequacy in child care: Parenting task performance within an ecological framework" (Toronto, June, 1986). The abstract reports a study in which personal and environmental factors were combined to influence the parenting task (a view compatible with the configural approach of this book). The student thought it might be helpful to be guided in considering the various types of personal and environmental factors involved, as she planned her own interventive strategy. However, dissertations are not easily available, and so accessibility of information has to be considered as one does an information search.

Likewise, another interesting citation in the 1987 *Social Work Research and Abstracts*, "Child care and family benefits: Policies of six industrialized countries" by S. B. Kamerman in the *Monthly Labor Review* for 1980 (vol 103, number 1, pages 23–28) is presented by title only. There is no abstract, and so the title alone must provide the clues to see whether the worker wants to invest the time and energy in reading the original paper. What clues do you see in this citation that would influence your decision?

No information retrieval device is perfect; nor do such devices always present full, clear, and relevant information in accessible journals. This is the best we have at present, and we all have to learn how to make the best of it. For additional suggestions on using information retrieval tools, see Bloom 1984 and 1975.

TRANSLATING SCIENTIFIC INFORMATION BACK INTO PRACTICE HYPOTHESES

The fifth step in the information retrieval strategies is vital and yet it is not often discussed in the professional literature. The issue involves translating scientific information back into a form usable by the helping professional facing a specific client situation. The information in the article is given in scientific language—concepts and empirical statements. These do not refer to any one person, but rather to certain classes of people being studied. The worker has to take this general and abstract information, and translate it back into specific terms for guidance with a specific client.

Let me suggest a brief formula for making this translation: *What actors influencing what aspects of the client and the relevant social environments by what actions are intended to have what effects?* Suppose that we read an abstract that supplied the following information: A not-for-profit organization at a family services center provided a multidisciplinary team approach to resolving the stresses facing parents at risk for child abuse or neglect. The social workers set up support groups among the clients of the agency to talk about and learn how to resolve common stressful situations these parents faced. Other workers set up job-training sessions. Educators arranged for child care services, along with training on parenting skills (presumably to reduce the need for abuse or neglect). The results appear to indicate that this total program has been effective, although expensive, in preventing child abuse and neglect among its participants, as compared with like parties in the same city who were not served by this agency.

Some parts of this report are relevant to Miss C's situation while other parts are probably beyond the means of the Shelter at this time. Let's assume that you have determined that this article is relevant to your client, like Miss C. How should we translate this research study to the specifics that may guide our actions in a case situation? It seems from the paper that the clients studied are similar to Miss C, and so we can assume that what worked or did not work with them stands a reasonable chance of doing the same for our clients, provided we deliver the same services. But at the present, we cannot. In place of the abstract "multidisciplinary group," we have just two professional and some volunteers at the Shelter. The workers know others in the community, however, and perhaps we can translate the situation at the Shelter as similar to a degree to the concept of the multidisciplinary team. We might be able to take pieces of the reported study and get them set up for Miss C and others in her situation, such as organizing a support group at the agency to talk about common problems and effective solutions. Just how the support group was organized and handled in the research report would require further reading and perhaps a telephone call or visit to that agency.

Perhaps the field instructor is aware of other agencies in town that engage in job training, and might be persuaded to cooperate with the shelter on such a project. And, as one benefit from reading in the literature, the student gets the idea of setting up a child care facility at the Shelter in which some mothers would care for the whole group of children (with the help of the staff people on duty), while other mothers would go to look for jobs. The child care mothers would get advice on how to handle the little problems that inevitably arise, and thus would get some parenting instruction as an additional benefit. Possibly, this child care idea might be extended to church groups or settlement houses around the city after the mothers leave this shelter. In general, the student took the statements describing the research project and attempted to see what, if any, fit with what was possible at her agency. Even when some element did not fit, it was possible to imagine some substitute or variation. Will this imaginary program work?

Clearly, the Shelter's plan is a reduced version of the more well-endowed agency described in the article. But since the same aspects of the configuration of problems are being addressed, can we assume as a working hypothesis that the more limited program could attain at least some degree of successful outcome? Such information and imaginings have to be weighed by the staff involved, but at least the information in the literature has stimulated the ideas and offered some guidance on how to set up programs, as well as giving some encouragement that such programs have been effective in a similar circumstance. We must be aware of the limits of transferred information, but such translations from abstractions or other programmatic studies serve as the points of departure for practice hypotheses, and this is a critical function of the applied scientific literature.

ONE FINAL CAVEAT: LET THE READER BEWARE!

Not everything appearing in print, even in professional or scientific journals, is necessarily useful, accurate, clear, and well-written. Most scientific journals are refereed. A would-be author submits a manuscript to an editor of the journal, who then circulates it (without identifying that author) to readers who are specialists in the area discussed in the paper. The readers write a critique of the quality of the research. This "blind" peer review is supposed to eliminate those papers containing poor research or illogical analysis. But this screening method is not foolproof, and some problematic papers do slip through into the journals.

How is the student to know when an article published in a respectable journal by a credentialed author is good or not? This question is difficult, even for experts. In addition to the basic rules of writing—that ideas are presented clearly and supported in an orderly development of an argument or research—I would like to offer a few rules of thumb for your consideration:

1. *Let the reader beware.* Assume every assertion by an author must be tested within your own practice experience, even if it seems overwhelmingly logical and has fancy statistics to back it up.

2. *All research findings are invariably limited.* This rule of thumb means that even strong empirical results may not be applicable to persons in other contexts. Research always deals with a limited portion of the universe, and thus is limited in the types of clients and contexts discussed for that time and place. Every new situation offers additional factors that can influence outcomes.

3. *Don't forget your common sense when considering a theory or the results of research.* Common sense is not always right, but theories have to explain why common sense is not applicable in a given context. In providing useful understanding of a situation, theories have to account for what you see in addition to going beyond what is visible.

4. *Consider what other critics say about a given theory or research finding.* Often issues of a journal will contain critical comments about articles published previously. There are also comparative research studies (when two or more theoretical or practice models are put to the test with similar kinds of clients and workers). Books of reviews of theories and therapies often contain critical discussions that help us to see the strengths and limitations of theories we might use in practice. (See, for example, Corsini and Wedding, 1989; Maddi, 1980)

5. *Knowledge about knowledge is power.* We may expand Bacon's famous dictum, "knowledge is power," by recognizing and mastering the information retrieval tools of our profession as ways of getting to knowledge that may be powerful influences in guiding practice to effective and humane outcomes.

OUTLINE

Introduction to the Logic of Evaluation
   Objective Assessment
   Methods of Comparison
     Major Barbara
     Robert Owen

The Classical Experimental/Control Group

The Single-System Design (And *Major Barbara* Revisited)

Summary

CHAPTER TWENTY-THREE

Evaluation of Practice—
An Introduction

Evaluation is an intrinsic part of human behavior. We continually assess the progress of events in our environment, and we make calculations as to how well we are achieving our desired objectives. But these kinds of evaluations are usually "in our heads," and thus subject to the biases of self-interest—we tend to see what we want to see. The helping professional has to use more objective procedures, to identify and characterize the problems in question and to monitor progress and evaluate outcome—did we achieve the objectives that we set out to achieve? This chapter provides a brief introduction to the logic and methods of conducting such evaluations, both to the classical experimental/control group design and to the recent developments in single-system design.

INTRODUCTION TO THE LOGIC OF EVALUATION

Evaluation involves the comparison of one thing with another. Usually the "one thing" is a current set of experiences: How much time does it take us to swim 50 yards? Or how depressed does the client report feeling during the past week? The "other" is some standard or reference point, such as "best time" we have swum that distance in the past. Or how depressed that client appears as indicated by a score on a depression test, which has been developed by comparing scores of groups of persons who vary on their known status involving depression. Regardless of how many steps there are in developing a standard reference (like psychological tests or socio-economic indicators of large geographic regions), the same basic logic holds: Compare the given event against some standard or reference point.

Obviously, there are two critical parts to evaluation: The objective assessment of the event being studied and the methods of comparison with the standard or reference point. Both are important parts of scientific practice and are necessary for a sensitive and humane understanding of clients' problems.

Objective Assessment

The underlying logic of this part of evaluation involves attaching numbers to things or events being studied. With the swimmer, we simply count the seconds he or she takes to complete a measured length of swimming. With the depressed client, we simply count the responses on the depression questionnaire and apply the rules for interpreting the results. (The art of constructing such tests is another topic entirely and involves considerable skill and knowledge; we will discuss only the use of existing tests and measures.)

The main point of this assessment is that it appears to be very natural to the context. Clients will frequently observe that "this was a very bad week" or "things went pretty well this week"—indicating some sense of evaluation in the process of everyday living. Social workers simply seek to attach some objective number system to these feelings and beliefs. A worker might ask the client, for example, to rate the degree of current feelings of self-esteem, from a 5, which indicates feeling a high sense of self-esteem, to 1, which indicates a low sense. Most clients can cooperate meaningfully in this kind of evaluation process. Moreover, clients are usually willing to repeat these observations (measurements) at each contact with the worker. It may be helpful to explain that such questions are like a "social thermometer" indicating the degree of problems currently facing the client. Such questions can be asked formally (as in paper-and-pencil questionnaires) or informally (the casual but intentional questions the worker asks the client each time the client is seen).

Methods of Comparison

Once some information about the client's state of health or healthy functioning is obtained, it must be compared with some known standard or reference point. Comparing swimming times is easy: simply look at the current time with either that swimmer's own best time, or the best time of his or her competition. This time comparison immediately tells us how well the swimmer is doing: the current time may be less than, equal to, or greater than the best time. Knowing this, the swimmer can be guided to practice harder or be cheered that he or she is making progress. That is important "feedback" for learning how to act in the future.

In the same way, comparing a client's scores on a depression questionnaire or whatever is a way of assessing the client's current status and his or her progress toward some desired objective. By taking repeated measures, we get a kind of moving picture of that client's progress—or lack of it. Depending on these results, the worker is guided to continue the same intervention tactics, to modify them in one fashion or another, or to terminate (if the objective has been stably achieved).

Research may be conducted with one client or large numbers of people. The particular methods will differ, but the same logic—comparing a given set of events against some standard—is the same in both cases. Consider, for example, two approaches to evaluation—the classical approach that uses large groups of subjects, and the more recent single-system design approach in which one person or a small group is followed over the course of their service experience. To get to these two forms of evaluation, while at the same time

Doug Buerlein/Virginia Commonwealth University

How do you know whether or not what you have done in the service of others has actually helped them? Monitoring and evaluating our own practice is a complex challenge. Is it enough to help "the identified client," or must we also be concerned with the effects our services create on all of the other persons involved in this situation? Recently, the Council of Social Work's accreditation standards have mandated that all students at the bachelor's and master's levels should be able to evaluate their own practice. This is not simply an academic skill; it is also a vital aspect in providing accountability for this helping profession.

show the naturalness of making evaluative judgments, we will draw on George Bernard Shaw's lively drama *Major Barbara*. Shaw is an enormously witty and insightful dramatist, and not shy about taking potshots at various professions and social classes, as you will see. Using *Major Barbara* to illustrate evaluation of practice here will probably make Shaw turn over in his grave.

Major Barbara.   The play concerns the Undershaft family, the estranged father who is a munitions factory owner versus all the rest. Undershaft's son and two daughters are facing the delicate stage in life for an upper-class English family circa 1905. For the daughters, this involves marriage and for the son, some occupation, to be determined. Because of the children's talents (or lack of them), the mother wants rich daddy to provide for them in the style to which they have become accustomed, even though they did not know that their life-style was underwritten by the "Prince of Darkness," their father. The younger daughter is engaged to a buffoon, and the older one (Barbara) is engaged to a professor of Greek, and thus is equally suspect.

The mother invites the estranged father to meet his now-grown children and to get him to pay the future bills, but the evening soon turns into a double challenge. Barbara has become Major Barbara of the Salvation Army, fighting in "darkest England" to save souls at a humble shelter in a London slum. She invites her father to see her in action and he agrees, if she and the others will then visit his munitions factory. And why not? The Salvation Army motto,

"Blood and Fire," could as well be the motto of the munitions maker, Mr. Undershaft slyly notes.

The main thesis of the play soon emerges. Who really can save society by ministering to the needs of the populace? The two contrasting paths toward salvation are the individual approach of the Salvation Army (as interpreted with literary license by Shaw) and the collective approach as reflected in the way Shaw's munitions maker operates his factory-village. Indeed, these are like the individual and collective approaches that might be visible in modern social work. So, for the sake of a dramatic example, let's follow the play to see which side wins—or, to cast this into a question closer to an evaluation mode, let's see which approach produces the more desirable outcomes.

We meet an assortment of characters at the Salvation Army shelter. Some are the down-and-out unemployed who are truly pitiable. Some are welfare frauds who have learned their roles well—often from teachers who are the welfare providers! As Shaw has one character say: "Them Salvation Army lasses is dear good girls; but the better you are, the worse they likes to think you were before they rescued you." So that is what the helpers want to hear; let's tell them that.

Barbara is battling for the soul of one aggressive tough guy—this is the "case study" we'll return to shortly, as our example of evaluation of a single case—and appears on the verge of winning, when the leader of the Salvation Army comes to visit and accepts a big donation from Mr. Undershaft, much to his daughter's objections. No tainted money for her, and as the others go off to a religious rally, drums banging, tambourines jingling, and trumpets blaring, Barbara resigns from the service. As de la Rochefoucauld quipped, hypocrisy is the homage that vice pays to virtue. It appears that the munitions makers and their ilk are the ones who underwrite the welfare armies of the land, not out of piety and love but to make life bearable for the masses who work in the factories, and consequently, to make profits for the owners of the factories.

True to their part of the Faustian bargain, the Undershaft entourage decends, as to Hell, to the munitions factory town. And much to their surprise, it looks like a utopian dream come true: all clean and spotless, with libraries and schools, with ballrooms, banquet halls, and nursing homes, with insurance funds, and with pension systems and cooperatives. There is even a William Morris Labor Church. Here is the heart and the future of an industrial society, where workers are content, well-paid, and productive. The "Prince of Darkness" runs a neat ship; the personal motives of profit-making are expressed in a socially humanistic way. Adam Smith could not have said it better. (And Shaw was a Fabian socialist!)

Robert Owen.   If you find it a bit strange that a businessman should appear to be the better doctor to society, then consider the other businessmen of Shaw's day who also were taking a major role in constructing the modern world. The utopian experiments of Robert Owen (1771–1858) were not too far out of the memories of Englishmen.

Owen ran a cotton mill that generated profits while spinning out fibers and cloth. The typical cotton mill of that age had hundreds of young children standing up for more than a dozen hours a day bending over the spinning machines with their tiny spools of cotton thread in 80-degree temperatures (better for the threads) in rooms filled with fiber particles. The picture of these child workers are haunting; most of the children were between six and seven years of age, and were indentured from town workhouses to the factories. They were required to work there for room and board until their maturity (Cole, 1953). What Owen and other reformers began took a hundred years to complete.

But unlike every other mill in the British Isles, Owen's was a model of progressive ideas. He stopped the importing of pauper apprentices from the workhouses and began a series of reform that rocked the business community—while still making a handsome profit! Owen had new and better houses built for the workers in hope of attracting large families to replace the pauper apprentices. He established a central store where workers could buy clothes and good food at low prices. (He also had whiskey sold there, but fined workers who appeared drunk on the streets.) His methods of bulk purchasing later led to food cooperatives.

Owen removed all forms of punishment in his factory as ways to drive people to obey orders. But he did manipulate the environment to his own ends. For example, he wanted village housewives to keep their homes cleaner. So he appointed a committee to inspect homes once a week, without forcing their way in. There was a howl of opposition from housewives. Those homes that passed muster were publicly praised and received small gifts, and soon the holdouts were competing for praise and prizes as well. (This form of paternalism was also typical of Owen, as was the snobbery of presuming to know what was right for others.) He employed a similar system at the factory, an early application of industrial psychology.

In addition, he had schoolrooms built for children and public halls for his workers' adult education. He created what we now would call a nursery school, the first of its kind. Teachers at the nursery school employed kindness as their sole means of discipline—this at a time when whips were common tools of educators. No toys were used; teachers were to stimulate the curiosity of the children with real implements, which required trained teachers—another innovation. His schools included physical exercise and singing in the curriculum, thus anticipating still other 20th-century innovations.

Owen instituted a number of programs at the factory that were also remarkably innovative. He obliged workers to contribute each week to a fund to cover sick pay and retirement benefits. He engaged in what would now be called town planning, with an industrial work area and a Green Belt that separated it from the residential area where workers were to gain a renewal of spirit, not simply a place to eat and sleep. Unfortunately, Owen had some other ideas that were too radical for the times, and even though he was very successful in his New Lanark factory, he never was able to convince the English Parliament to establish his methods throughout England.

Owen also conducted an American utopian experiment at New Harmony, Indiana. It was a spectacular failure—spectacular in stimulating the imaginations of many reformers, but its impracticality and poor management led to economic and social failure nonetheless.

So here we have a powerful story of success (and failure) using social environmental modifications to obtain humanitarian ends, just as Shaw was describing in *Major Barbara*. The "success" was easily measured in pounds and shillings, but what attracted worldwide attention were the social indicators of success: Workers appeared more content, and more productive; they experienced fewer labor disturbances or problems than workers at the other factories of the times. But how can we be sure? How would one go about measuring "worker contentment," "worker productivity," and "labor problems"? How do we know one method of organization was more successful than another?

When we ask these questions—comparing a group of factories experiencing one kind of management against other factories that have a traditional kind of management—we have two broad ways of making the comparison. The first is termed the classical research model; it uses experimental and control groups, that is, those which receive some new experimental intervention program versus those which receive the standard experiences ordinarily in place among such factories or groups. We will review this approach briefly and then consider the second approach, (single-system designs), in which a single system is monitored over time.

THE CLASSICAL EXPERIMENTAL/CONTROL GROUP

Picture yourself talking to Robert Owen (or Mr. Undershaft) about how to test whether a certain approach toward organizing and running a factory group is better than some other approach. The steps you might follow are these: First, look for a population of like groups—such as all of the cotton mills in a given region at a given time. Second, from this group, randomly select some to be experimental (i.e., those which are to receive the new experimental program) and others to be controls (i.e., those which will continue to be run as usual). The random selection will ensure that the results are not systematically biased because of the factories that are put into one or the other category. Certainly, the factories will be different, as all things in the world are different. But if factories are assigned at random to experimental and control groups, then the effects of these individual differences will be randomly divided between the two groups, and we can assume that whatever outcomes occur in the experiment will be caused primarily by the experimental program.

Third, we measure the group of factories in the study before any experimental programs begin. (We can see whether our random assignment has produced any unusual differences—in which case we may have to adjust our study statistically to account for these accidental difference.) The measures we use are important, and will be used again at the end of the study. For example, on "worker contentment," we might ask a random sample of workers about their attitudes toward their work and their life in general. The pattern of answers represents the views of the entire group from which these workers are drawn. It is our best guess how all the other workers would feel, if asked.

After all the selected workers in the selected factories (experimental and control) are surveyed, then the experimental intervention is started. Let's say a Robert Owen-type of manager sets up the kinds of programs described above in the experimental factories, while the managers of the control factories continue to do whatever they have been doing before. Time passes. The researchers keep track of profits and losses, of labor strikes and other difficulties like absenteeism, theft from the factory, and so on. Then, at the end of the study period—probably a long time since it would naturally take some time for the experimental factors to influence the habits of workers—the same workers are once again questioned about their attitudes toward work and family life. The two sets of answers, the before and the after answers, are compared statistically to see whether there are any systematic differences between the experimental group (which received the new management program) and the control group (the business-as-usual group). If whatever differences that emerge favor the experimental group, then, under the logic of this research design, the researcher is entitled to claim that the outcomes were influenced by the experimental program.

If, like that of Owen's New Lanark, a profit was made and the workers and their families were much more content and better off than like workers and families in other mill towns, then the researcher would be able to state in scientific terms that these outcomes occurred. There is a particular way to express these outcomes that is a universal scientific language, which you will see in professional and scientific journals and books. This is the language of probability. Briefly put, probability thinking considers how likely something was to have happened, given its earlier state. For example, how likely is it that workers who had very negative attitudes and behaviors regarding their work situation at the beginning of the study could be showing such positive attitudes now? Not very likely unless something happened to cause that change of heart. When we see such notations as $p < .05$, we are seeing the probability statement that reads "the probability (p) of a given outcome occurring as it did, given its initial state of affairs, could not have happened by chance alone except 5 times in 100." This means that while such results could have happened by chance (namely, about 5 times in 100), this is so unlikely that we can consider alternative explanations for these results. Since we set up a logical design to compare equivalent groups, only one of which received the experimental treatment, we can assume that it was this experience that caused the differences—from a probabilistic point of view.

With the support of the scientific method described above, such statements should have much force in the affairs of people. That is to say, such evidence should be used to influence the policies of both the private and the public sectors in how we ought to arrange the management of cotton mills. Should this type of research be repeated in other settings, then we could begin to generalize the results to a wider range of social organizations. In fact, decision makers (in government and business and elsewhere) use more than scientific facts to make decisions like this. There are values to be considered, resources to be allocated, and other factors.

But the point of this excursion into history and drama is to point out that evaluation is possible even with complex ideas like worker satisfaction and productivity. In your future studies you may go into greater detail on how to apply this basic experimental/control group model to many different topics. In each case, there will be variations on a theme of randomly assigning units (like factories) to experimental and control groups, measuring them initially, then providing the experimental program to the one but not to the other, and ending with repeated measurements to see whether there were any differences between the two groups.

THE SINGLE-SYSTEM DESIGN (AND MAJOR BARBARA REVISITED)

Let's return to Major Barbara (before she had resigned from the Army). In the second Act, we eventually meet a tough guy, Bill Walker, who is looking for his girl, Mog, whom he says was taken from him by the Salvation Army. He orders a young Salvation Army helper, Jenny, to go inside and tell Mog that he wants her outside, or else he will come in and kick her out. To emphasize the point he twists Jenny's arm, and when the old woman who was eating bread and milk provided by the Salvation Army, tries to come to her assistance, he knocks her down. Jenny tries to help her, only to be roughed up and punched by Bill. Jenny goes inside the shelter to call for help, and soon Major Barbara comes outside to meet her adversary.

In a witty exchange, Barbara overwhelms the tough guy with words:

Barbara: Whats your name?
Bill: Whots thet to you? (the play is written in dialect)
Barbara: (calmly making notes) Afraid to give his name. Any trade?
Bill: Oo's afride to give is name? If you want to bring a chawge agen me, bring it. Moy nime's Bill Walker.
Barbara: (as if the name were familiar. . .) Bill Walker? Oh, I know: youre the man that Jenny Hill was praying for inside just now. (She enters his name in her notebook.)
Bill: Oo's Jenny Ill? And wot call as she to pry for me?
Barbara: I dont know. Perhaps it was you that cut her lip. . . .

Barbara later asks Bill what he came to the Salvation Army shelter for (what his objectives were). He tells Barbara that he came to get Mog back and break her jaw. Too bad, says Barbara, but Mog was saved by the Salvation Army and has gone to the army barracks with her new boyfriend, whom she converted. Who is this bloke, asks Bill. It turns out that the new boyfriend is Todger Fairmile, a well-known professional boxer.

Then Barbara has Jenny come out of the shelter, ostensibly to clean up, but really to tell Bill that she bears him no grudge, "bless his heart." Bill is in a daze over whether to risk getting pummeled by the boxer to get back his girl. Just then Barbara's father comes to the shelter, as agreed, and watches her work.

Undershaft: . . . What's the matter with that out-patient over there? (pointing to Bill)
Barbara: Oh, we shall cure him in no time. Just watch. (Turning to Bill, she says:) It would be nice just to stamp on Mog's face, wouldnt it, Bill?
Bill: Oo taold you wot was in moy mawnd (mind)?
Barbara: Only your new friend.

Who is this new friend? Why, the devil, of course. He hangs around people making them miserable, like Bill is, just now. Bill lashes out—leave me alone. But Barbara says it isn't she who is getting at Bill, but someone else who doesn't intend for him to smash women's faces. It is someone who wants to make a man of Bill. He protests that he is a man, but Barbara only says that there is a man somewhere inside him. But why did that man let Bill hit poor Jenny. Bill is tormented; I'm sick of this poor Jenny business; leave me alone.

Barbara, ever on the attack, asks why Bill keeps thinking about it, why he can't let it alone. Is he perhaps getting converted? Not me, says Bill. Barbara retorts: That's right, Bill, don't give up easily. Fight it with all your might, like Todger Fairmile, who fought it with all his heart, before he gave in. But maybe Bill doesn't have a heart. Of course I do, says Bill. Then why did you bash poor Jenny in the face? Bill is in utter torment: Leave me alone, will you? And Barbara delivers the coup de grace:

> Barbara: It's your soul that's hurting you, Bill, and not me. Weve been through it all ourselves. Come with us, Bill. To brave manhood on earth and eternal glory in heaven.

She almost has him, but not quite. Just then her boyfriend comes in and gets introduced to Bill as the man she is going to marry. ("Gawd elp im!" exclaims Bill.) Will Major Barbara win over Bill? Will she convert him? Rather than tell you how this story within the larger play turns out (and thus taking away your pleasure of discovery), let's look again at Bill and Barbara, from the point of view of evaluating Barbara's practice, as if she were a helping professional.

The single-system design is a brief form of evaluation, rather than an extensive form of research (as is the classical experimental/control group design). Essentially, the problems or targets of intervention of one system (a person, a family, whatever) are followed over the time before an intervention and then through the intervention to some point at its conclusion. The evaluation is a comparison of one target in the before picture, with its during or after picture, each measured in exactly the same way.

For example, say Bill has a problem with bashing people. It is problematic because it is illegal and gets him into trouble, as well as being bad for the health of others. We can measure the extent of Bill's hitting behavior as the number of people bashed per day. Then we can observe Bill, or have him report the number of bashing for a period of time before we begin the intervention. (Since we do not want to let the fighting go on, we might use his report of bashing for the past four weeks to represent a baseline or point of reference for the coming weeks.) Then we put Major Barbara to work trying to convert him, and afterward, continue to count in the same way the number of bashings Bill has performed, if any. See these numbers plotted on a graph in Figure 23.1.

We can also graph internal feelings and thoughts—by having the party involved report these inner behaviors, or by using external indicators. If we wanted to measure Bill's level of self-esteem, for example, we could ask him, or we could use some agreed upon measures of self-esteem like Major Barbara's observations that Bill did not seem very happy with himself, that Bill seemed distracted and anxious. These may not be the best scientific measures—see books like Corcoran and Fisher, 1987 for standardized scientific scales and measures for some important psycho-social variables—but this is a literary example, and we are taking some license.

For any such graph, there are various procedures for comparing the before and the after picture. One method of analysis is introduced here; readers may wish to consult other books for further discussion and additional methods (Bloom and Fischer, 1982; Bloom, 1986). Analysis of the data comparing the

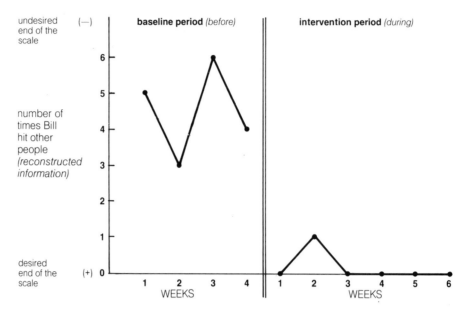

FIGURE 23.1   Imaginary data collected on Bill "before" and "after" his "treatment" by Major Barbara

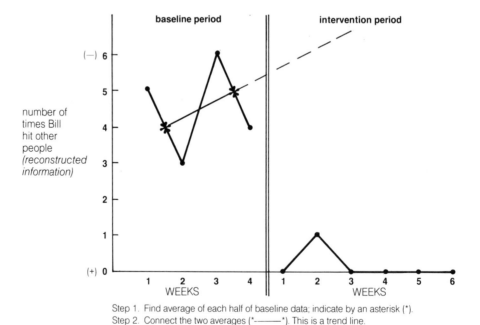

Step 1. Find average of each half of baseline data; indicate by an asterisk (*).
Step 2. Connect the two averages (*———*). This is a trend line.
Step 3. Project trend line into the intervention period (*———*) - - - -.
Step 4. Add data of what really happens during the intervention period.
Step 5. Compare what really happens to what was projected to happen.

FIGURE 23.2   A split-half method of data analysis, comparing the trend line from baseline data projected into the intervention period, with the actual data during the treatment phase

before and after picture is based on the assumption that if there had been no intervention, matters would have continued pretty much as before. This assumption can be put on the graph in the following steps.

First, the before-intervention baseline picture is divided into two parts so that the average of each half can be obtained, as indicated in Figure 23.2. Second, a line connecting the two points is drawn; this represents the typical pattern or trend of problem behavior before the intervention. Third, a dotted line is drawn as an extension of the baseline line to represent the assumption of what would be expected to happen regarding this behavior, had there been no intervention. As you can see, these imaginary data indicate Bill is getting more violent. Fourth, what really happened in the treatment period is also placed on the graph. Fifth, a comparison is made between what might have been expected to occur without the intervention and what did occur. This analysis can be made on the basis of visual inspection, or some simple tables or mathematical procedures. But for this stage of education, I will leave it at the visual analysis level. Let us interpret the imaginary data for Bill Walker and his bashings.

Let's say that by his own statements, he had been quite violent for the past month. This is represented by the numbers of bashings he reported (in Baseline). Then Major Barbara got hold of him, and, let us say, Bill was converted to a gentler way of relating to people. This is indicated in the intervention part of the graph. These graphed behaviors are very different from the projected numbers of bashings that Bill might have been expected to perform, based on his track record of the past month. So, because the differences are so great, we can see that there has been a significant difference. (There are also ways to make mathematical statements to the same effect, which permit use of probability statements—that the observed difference could not have occurred by chance alone except fewer than 5 times in 100. This is the $p < .05$ notation that we met earlier in the experimental/control group design.) This information and the associated probability figure provide some support for thinking that a significant change has occurred. (We cannot assume that Barbara's dialog with Bill was the cause because there are some logical limitations to the measurement design we are using here. Other single-system designs would permit us to test the inference that what the worker did with the client may have been part of the causal picture. Again, this involves some advanced considerations in evaluating practice, covered in other texts.)

There are some obvious similarities and differences between the classical research and the single-system design. Both select portions of the world to observe and influence in order to see whether what happens as a result of the intervention is significantly different from the initial state of affairs. Each uses a control-group idea. For the classical design, however, it is an actual control group, while in the single-system design, the party under study is his/her/their own control group in the sense that the before picture is being compared with the after picture on the same party. These two approaches differ in size— obviously the classical design involves many more parties in the test groups, and may take a longer time to conduct, analyze, and report. The strength of the single-system design is to give rapid and approximate indications of the effectiveness of a given intervention. If the practitioner is on the right track, some encouraging changes should occur as compared with what might have been expected had the intervention not occurred. If the data do not support

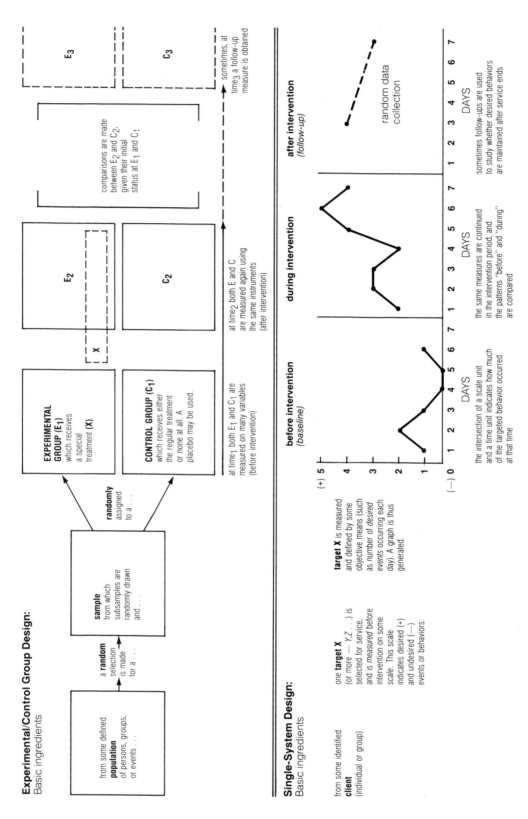

FIGURE 23.3 Schematic diagrams comparing the basic ingredients of Experimental Control Group Designs and Single-System Designs

this hunch, then the worker has information on which to base a change in the intervention.

By beginning to think about practice in the context of evaluation, we can become more objective in determining what our targets of intervention are and whether we have objectively come close to seeing the client attain those objectives. If we do not try some objective evaluation, we are driving in the dark without lights on. It is hazardous to the health of the client, let alone to us and our profession. Evaluation is no longer a choice of the scientific practitioner; it is a necessity, one that we should eagerly endorse for our own as well as our client's benefit. (Figure 23.3 summarizes the basic ingredients of the two general modes of social research.)

SUMMARY

Good evaluation requires good practice, and vice versa. The worker and the client have to work together to identify what problems are facing the client, and what strengths the client has or the environment provides. One way to do this is to indicate the scope or magnitude of the current state of the problem, and then to continue to assess it over time, so as to observe what changes take place during the time of the planned intervention. Ultimately, the basic logic is the comparison of one thing (the current state of the client and environment) compared to another (some ideal or desired state of affairs involving that client and relevant parts of the environment).

We have discussed two major forms of evaluation—first, the classical research approach in which experimental groups are compared with control (or standard treatment) groups in logical combinations so as to assess whether or not the planned interventions had their desired effect on the client. Knowing this is a way of assessing the overall intervention system. Usually, such information involves many people and long periods of time, so that it is not useful in making modifications to individual treatment programs.

The single-system design approach addresses the individual system directly. By observing changes over a period of time, the worker comes to know whether or not his or her intervention program is accomplishing what it was designed to do, and thus, what response to make as a consequence. These responses include continuing the present intervention, modifying it (either more or less or using some different elements), or terminating the service. All of these decisions are based on as objective information as is available. It is a fundamental practice assumption that the better our information, the more likely it is that we can achieve the clients' objectives. This information includes the specific nature and extent of the clients' problems and their changes. Thus evaluation takes its place as a key ingredient in scientific practice.

PART

IX.

SUMMARY

I n the final chapter, we attempt to pull together some of the major themes of the book with regard to the configural approach in social work practice. You will recall that the configuration has served as a checklist of systems that need to be considered in any practice situation—individuals, primary groups, secondary groups, socio-cultural and physical environmental contexts in time. In any given situation, not all of these systems may need to be considered, but the checklist makes us stop and think about possible influences that we need to deal with in practice, and their various valued perspectives.

Another application of the configurations was in thinking about the practice situation as involving a series of centers of gravity. These represent conceptual clusters that may run across the levels of the configuration or which may be focused at one level. These centers of gravity are the focal points of various pushes and pulls on the lives of individuals and groups. The same events may be pushes to one and pulls to another. We come to understand our clients as the sum of the forces pushing them toward some objective or pulling them away from that objective. This understanding is our way of integrating the whole picture of our clients' life situation at this moment. Overlapping memberships may cause some problems unless the parties involved or the helping professionals are able to modify, at one or another level within the configuration, existing centers or construct new ones that lead to a more acceptable balance of events.

A third use of the configural approach involves points of entry to influence desired change. Appropriate but powerful centers of gravity must be found or created to assist clients to help themselves, with the introduction of a minimum of intrusive change. Such intrusions are inherently risky, but when we combine concurrent evaluation with practice, we can monitor change as well as assess the outcomes among all parties in the given configuration.

Thus the configural approach includes a descriptive, explanatory, and predictive (and evaluative) component, the set of which may be useful in social work practice.

OUTLINE

CHAPTER TWENTY-FOUR

The Configural Approach
to Preventive and Interventive Helping

This final chapter attempts to present a summary of the configural perspective in social work. It offers the last chance for me to present another drama in which you might choose to be a vital actor.

ORGANIZING OUR THINKING AND ACTIONS IN THE DRAMA OF SOCIAL WORK: THE CONFIGURAL APPROACH

The professional helper is like a dramatist who creates a configuration of events on the stage of everyday life. The professional helper sets up the props (chairs and tables at the agency) and the overall directions ("Let's talk about the concerns that brought you here today"), and then encourages the actors (clients) to present their feelings, ideas, and actions as fully and truthfully as possible.

As in the theater production, it is the actors or clients who take the center stage. It is their problems and potentials, their lives and actions, their goals and objectives that are the main features of the case. But in addition to those persons who are "on stage" (in the worker's office), there are many others "off stage" who may never been seen directly by the worker. The other players might include the client's co-workers, classmates, relatives and friends, as well as some strangers who may directly affect or be affected by the specific client. All people are functionally interrelated in a society, so that when one person has problems, the ramifications of those problems may affect many others, if only as tax payers, or as persons feeling pity for, or annoyance about, those who are troubled in body, mind, or spirit. Social work services have to take into account the values of these people (the "community at large") as well as the values of clients and the ethics of the profession. So the stage is very crowded with persons directly or indirectly affected by professional helping. How are we to get organized?

Throughout this book, these ideas have been discussed in the light of a conceptual model called the configural approach, intended as a systematic and comprehensive guide to our thinking about social work issues. It is now time to draw these various themes together and to present a summary of the configural perspective in social work.

Description: The Configuration

First, the configuration was used as a checklist describing the basic components of the world in which clients led their lives. People and environments are the principal targets of social work services, and so the basic configuration was described in Figure 1.1 as nested units—the individual, primary groups, secondary groups, culture, society, and physical environmental contexts at given times. (It is to be understood that intraindividual aspects, such as a diseased tissue, a maladaptive habit, or a defective gene are considered in relation to the individual involved as well as to relevant others.) For any social work concern, the configural approach first reminds us of the total array of components that have to be considered for any effective and humane action.

The configuration is entered at any conceptual point—individual, group, organization, environment, whatever—immediately relevant to the question at hand. But as part of the first step of the generic problem-solving process, we must identify the client-system problems and potentials, and thus all parts of the configuration are assessed for their relevance to the given situation.

The helper entered at one point in the client system, but just as that helper begins to relate to the client configuration, so too is the helper just one part in the helping configuration. Other resources are likely to be activated for preventive, treatment, or rehabilitative purposes. A configural analysis calls to the worker's attention what other systems may need to be activated in the effort of collaborative problem solving. No helping professional is ever alone in the complex business of assisting people in need.

The checklist function of the configuration makes several contributions to helping. First, there is less likelihood that some significant actor in the situation will be overlooked. Second, the points of view—and hence the values—of the relevant parties are brought into the picture as entities about which the final plans must take into consideration. Third, because of this multiple perspective, we have to explore how each party relates to every other party, so that each of these systems is viewed more nearly completely. This is a critical point as we come to recognize each person's strengths and limitations as part of the total configuration. Professional practice that is effective and humane must emerge from considerations of the strengths and limitations of involved persons and groups, as well as from the resources and limitations of cultural and physical environments. We can summarize this section by revising Lewin's important equation (behavior is a function of the person and the psychological environment) by specifying the several real and perceived environments involved:

Behavior   = (f)
(thoughts, feelings, actions   Person(s) $\times$ Primary Groups
of individuals or groups $\times$ Secondary Groups $\times$ Culture
conceived as the actor $\times$ Society $\times$ Physical Environment
involved)   (at a given historical time)

Carolyn Baker/Virginia Commonwealth University

Infants, adults; individuals, groups, institutions; helpers, persons in need of help; now and the future—all these are parts of the human configuration. As professional helpers, we seek to find the center of gravity of the events making up a client's life, pushing and pulling the client away from desired goals. When we find this center of gravity, we introduce changes to neutralize the opposing forces and to mobilize the constructive forces that will enable the client to achieve his or her goals within the ecological context.

Both the strengths and the limitations of each element in the equation are considered as aspects of a force field pushing and pulling in different directions with respect to the actor in question. The actor's behavior is the product of the resultant force, that is, the ultimate resolution of various pushes and pulls by involved parties regarding a particular target.

Explanation: Centers of Gravity

A second major feature of the configural approach concerns the concept of "centers of gravity," which serves as an explanatory tool. Obviously, each component of the configuration (persons, groups, organizations) is an active agent. The conventional social sciences study each level separately. Psychology studies the individual and interpersonal levels; sociology and anthropology study the organizational and the socio-cultural levels; culturology (White, 1949) studies the culture and technology viewed as dominant causal agents in the affairs of people. And so on. Social work as an applied social science inevitably has to work at all levels simultaneously, however, and is left to fill in the gaps between levels when theoretical tools are not available.

The purpose of the centers of gravity concept is to provide professional helpers with a way of conceptually combining different aspects of the many biopsychosocial systems that influence client behavior. It is a way of putting a marker around all of the interacting factors that appear to be influencing a client's problems or potentials so that the worker can act to reduce the negative or harmful forces while encouraging the constructive forces that will enable the client to attain desired objectives. But since the parties influencing the client are at different conceptual levels, it is difficult to form one large concept of them all. Instead, this author has chosen to view these various systems from the center, so to speak, from the perspective of a given actor, the client. A center of gravity is the conceptual point where forces emanating from different configural components are concentrated in one situation from the perspective of a given actor. Viewed over time, these forces indicate the movement of the client in a given direction. To change that line of movement, the worker must influence the center of gravity, that is, the worker must, in accord with a plan, influence all of the salient factors in the client's configuration. (Only some aspects of the total configuration are relevant for a given person in a given situation.) Some of these factors must be encouraged to continue their positive contributions to the client; others must be discouraged or changed from exerting a negative influence on the client's actions. And the actors (or clients) must be aided to perceive these constructive changes because their perception is a key motivation for continuing and sustaining change.

You will recall in Chapter 3 how the social worker became aware of the relevant clusters of social events that were active in the case of the rebellious teenager. There was the Landsma family itself (father, mother, and son, Richard) and there was the peer group composed of Richard and a small number of his friends. There were also the families of other teenagers, business realms in which they worked, the settings where they socialized, and the cultural conditions underlying all the others. Social-class-related factors were brought into the picture when the youths would use invidious comparisons between themselves and more wealthy peers as a way of extracting money from their parents. After trying some conventional approaches to resolve the Landsma problem, which were not successful, the creative social worker set up a social entity that exerted a new constructive force by combining components of relatively weak units—the several families that were unable to control their teenage sons—into a fathers' support group. That support group provided the forum to share information and sustain the individual member's willpower to exert sensitive control over their sons. This control attempted to encourage constructive maturation rather than let the destructive movements toward independence cause more problems than they solved.

How are we to recognize a center of gravity and how do we create new constructive components to counterbalance destructive ones? One approach is to go back to the configural checklist to see what components are perceived by the actors involved that might be combined. Also, what factors are conceivable that are not present, but might be brought into being, to support existing people or groups. Then, by comparing the existing configuration with projected ideal ones that would have the components needed to resolve the client's problems and enhance the client's objectives, we have some clearer sense of the actor's problems and goals and what we might do about them. This would include promoting some factors, preventing others from coming into being, and neutralizing still others.

Another approach might be called "reverse problem solving," which involves imagining that the objective has been reached, and then conceptualizing what set of intermediary events or forces would have had to be present to achieve that end point. Then, we have to conceptualize what components were needed to achieve that intermediary event or force, and so on. The practitioner works backward from each of these intermediate objectives until he or she discovers some planned action that gets the ball rolling. Thus the worker acts to bring about the immediate objective in a planned scenario. If this first action in fact succeeds in attaining the desired initial objective, then further actions are attempted to see whether they attain their sequential objectives. Obviously, many actions can lead to a given outcome, so the process has to be continually monitored. If one planned action does not achieve its desired intermediary objective, then another intervention (the next most probable) might be tried to do so. Many theories are available as road maps for constructing such sequences of events. When theories are not available, however, we have to map our own way.

Prediction: Measuring Changes in Resultant Forces

A third major function of the configural perspective in social work is the possibility of using the checklist and the centers of gravity concept as predictors of relevant force fields for planned interventions. In the case of the rebellious teenager, the worker moved from his tentative understanding of the existing centers of gravity to his risky guess as to what new social components might exert a preponderant force in desired directions, thus changing the center of gravity acting on the client. This is a prediction based on the general principle that resultant forces act to move a system in a given direction (Lewin, 1951). The notion of resultant forces involves a combining of pushes and pulls from various directions into one overall movement. Such a concept theoretically permits quantification of the component forces as a predictor of the strength and direction of the resultant force.

Interventions, by their very nature, are predictions of future events given changes in existing events, some of which are caused by the worker. Workers always assess how well matters in the case are proceeding, although frequently in subjective and casual ways. I would add that all workers can become more objective and systematic in these assessments by employing some of the new technologies for evaluating cases in field situations and using on-the-spot feedback to make appropriate corrections. In particular, the methodology of single-system design offers the intrinsic possibility of simultaneous evaluation of multiple targets in multiple systems so as to monitor on a continuing basis how useful a worker's intervention is in relation to the prediction that is derived from the practice theory.

Any theory will lead the worker to influence some portions of the client's centers of gravity. For example, a learning theory that generates an assertiveness training program will likely lead to changes in the student's thoughts, feelings, and behaviors. However, these changes will probably affect that person's relationship to family, friends, co-workers and others. Some effects will be desirable (from the client's point of view) while others may be undesirable (including the same action as interpreted by another party). The professional helper may have to fine-tune this skill training by helping the client moderate his or her behaviors in certain contexts so that, overall, the learning will have a maximum of desired outcomes and a minimum of undesired ones for all parties involved. This leads to some sharp ethical issues. Who is asked to accommodate to whom and to what degree? What do those who are presently in an advantageous situation stand to gain if they give up some prerogative or good in the course of this social transaction? The configural checklist indicates what parties are affected by a given situation.

The centers of gravity concept indicates the values or choices of these several parties by identifying the persisting patterns of their actions. The predictive aspect of the configural force fields asks what combination of changes will produce the optimal desired effects (especially for the targeted client) while leading to the fewest undesirable effects that would be acceptable to the other parties involved. This is not a situation where what one actor gains, another actor loses. In the Landsma case, for example, both families and peer group gained because of the worker's efforts, although it was a value decision regarding who was to gain what.

A theory leads the worker to conceptualize and to generate a new center of gravity within relevant force fields that opposes the harmful aspects and supports the constructive aspects of the clie0t's existing state. However, most theories are focused on one conceptual level, while the concept of centers of gravity urges workers to combine multiple levels for the sake of harnessing the appropriate and sufficient force to help the clients attain their goals. The centers of gravity concept also recognizes that other systems have to receive different incentives or reinforcements if they give up prerogatives or goods. Thus the configural approach is a theory-coupler, a combiner of hypothesized forces at different levels into one unified force field. The configural approach tries to link theories from different levels of abstraction. It does so, first, conceptually, by indicating what factors are presumed to be affecting other systems. Second, the configural approach can link different conceptual levels by means of the methodology of the single-system design that shows the resultant actions of the various involved parties based on the configural predictions.

Social work is the profession par excellence that combines force fields toward one united objective. This action helps clients resolve complex problems using the many strengths and resources of the persons and environments involved, while neutralizing opposing forces (limitations of persons, stresses from environments).

A CASE SITUATION: A VIETNAMESE REFUGEE FAMILY

We consider here one final case to which we may apply the configural approach. The Nguyen family fled Vietnam near the end of the war, and made their way to a refugee camp in Thailand. They lived there until a church group sponsored their immigration to the United States. It was a "trail of tears," leaving their beloved homeland in flames, their careers in ruin, and the fate of several family members and friends unknown. (Some may have been lost at sea when they tried to reach Thailand in flimsy boats.)

Mr. and Mrs. Nguyen (ages 38 and 35) and their children (daughters aged 14 and 10) went to an East coast town where their sponsoring church was located. They were met at the plane by a social worker, escorted to temporary housing (a small apartment), given food, appropriate winter clothing, and also some toys for the children. It was a warm welcome, much appreciated by the tired travelers.

Mr. Nguyen spoke English, so no interpreter was needed. He had held a responsible position in Saigon that involved business transactions with the U.S. military. The Nguyens had lived prosperously in a suburb of Saigon. By mutual agreement, Mrs. Nguyen stayed home to raise the children, even though other Vietnamese women of her class worked.

The first few weeks of their life in the United States were intense. There were public health screenings (for possible contagious diseases). There were introductions to public welfare and arrangements for food stamps and other aids were set up to augment what the church group could supply. The social worker invited the Nguyens to an orienting group that met in a high school classroom at night to discuss common concerns in their new country—clothing and the weather, health and the health-care system, nutrition and the use of new and strange foods, and the like. Several new Vietnamese families were invited to these friendly gatherings, but they lived at some distance from one another and so it was difficult to maintain continuing contacts.

After the orienting sessions and the flurry of welcomes, people returned to their ordinary affairs. The Nguyens were left on their own. Mr. Nguyen had difficulty finding work, as the economic situation in that state had taken a downward turn. He took several jobs, one as night watchman at a local factory, another as part-time janitor in another business. Neither paid well, and he felt humiliated to have to do that sort of work. Also, he began to feel anxious and depressed about the future. He began to experience some physical pains, but he told no one since he did not want to worry anybody. Mrs. Nguyen did some housekeeping for neighbors in the daytime, which only added to Mr. Nguyen's discomfort, since he had assumed that they would maintain their prior agreement that she was to stay home to tend the family. Objectively, they needed the money, and so she continued working part-time. Their temporary apartment became their full-time residence.

Some more difficult problems awaited the Nguyens as their daughters became acculturated to the new community. They picked up English rapidly in language classes and at school—Mrs. Nguyen was having a more difficult time. They also picked up some cultural traits that were contrary to traditional Vietnamese behavior. The older daughter, who was very attractive, appeared to have acquired an admirer at school, an American boy. She began to disobey orders (such as returning home immediately from school), and what was most distressing to her parents, she began to talk back to them. (She called this "discussing options," but her parents saw it as disrespectful behavior.) The younger daughter became increasingly fearful of many aspects of the new culture. She was a very shy person, and did not make friends easily. Her mother walked her to school, and made excuses when she claimed to have a stomachache and did not want to go to school. The school truant officer visited the Nguyens about the younger daughter's school-phobic problems, which frightened them thoroughly. They felt that the whole family had been disgraced because the truant officer visited them (Land and Nishimoto, 1988). They tried to maintain "face" before threatening social forces.

The truant officer noticed some parallels among other refugee children in the school system, and called the social worker at the church agency that had sponsored the Nguyens to ask him to look into the situation. The social worker had been seeing the Nguyens as well as the other Vietnamese refugee families about once a month following the initial orienting period. None of the families had revealed any significant problems during several prior visits, but the worker was picking up clues from various sources (including the school) that not all was going well for these families. He visited the Nguyens and told them that he knew about the school problem, and wanted to be of assistance in dealing with the American culture. He said that he recognized and appreciated the Vietnamese way of trying to solve one's own problems on one's own, but this situation involved some social and cultural problems that were getting out of hand. Hesitantly, the Nguyens told him their story. He tried to respond sensitively from what he understood of their culture, but also effectively, in terms of what he thought would be most helpful to them. Let's follow his efforts as a way of reviewing the configural approach.

The social worker was using a reverse problem-solving approach in which he imagined an ideal situation for the Nguyens. This might be something that approximated being back in Saigon among family and friends, holding a prestigious and well-paying job, and following the traditional ways of family relationships and courtship that were strongly supported by the entire community. Under these conditions, the worker imagined that the Nguyens' current problems would probably disappear. Obviously, no one can turn back history, but this image described an ideal situation. Is there any way to approximate it for the Nguyens in America? What the worker was looking for was a combination of social, cultural, and personal factors that could approximate the ideal—this involved a search for a new center of gravity in their lives to pull them, as it were, closer to their valued objective.

The social worker began to speculate about what entity might serve to influence this new center of gravity. He wondered about involving all of the other Vietnamese families in the community to recreate a Vietnamese subculture within the dominant American culture for the purpose of gaining personal and social renewal, although he recognized the logistic difficulties. Each family had its own types of strengths and limitations, and together they could probably offer each other some mutual aid.

Nothing exactly like it existed in the community. But he knew about a Vietnamese mutual assistance association in a large city in the state, which provided recreational and social services. They celebrated Vietnamese holidays, prepared regional foods, and in general, provided a strong cultural experience for Vietnamese away from home. They also had workshops on various topics, from finding jobs to dealing with American schools. He called that organization, which was being run by paraprofessionals, including many Vietnamese, and they expressed interest in having the Nguyens and others join their program as often as possible.

The next step in the worker's thinking was to imagine what entity might bring the handful of Vietnamese families in this community together so that they could participate in the mutual assistance association activities. The worker was in effect looking for a social component that would influence individual participants in such ways that the whole group would benefit. The worker also realized that any social component he proposed would have to constitute the least intrusive change possible and still be capable of producing the changes desired. He did not want to create any new stresses for the families, even as part of initiating solutions to common problems.

It slowly dawned on him that the church-related agency had once served as a strong component in a constructive center of gravity, having had a history of sponsoring people to the new country, and having socialized them in the first few weeks of orientation. However, he recognized that the agency needed to assume a long-term responsibility in acculturating the refugees, even though the agency had only initially recognized a short-term role. So he explored this issue with his supervisor, who agreed with his assessment and offered to continue the agency support toward helping the families get together locally at least.

The social worker thought he was at a point at which he should involve the Vietnamese families in thinking about common problems and possible solutions (such as transportation to the city for special Vietnamese occasions). This intentionally did not address individual or family problems (like school phobia, marital disputes, or depression); rather, the configural intervention was framed as a cultural and educational experience that would motivate the families to participate in efforts to solve their own problems.

Once cultural pride and support could be revitalized, the worker speculated, some of the other problems would disappear, such as the older Nguyen daughter's too rapid Americanization, or the younger daughter's excessive fears. He would have to monitor this prediction carefully by observing what additional changes occurred in the lives of these people. The worker also recognized that more extensive effort would have to be expended regarding employment, particularly because of the level of the general economy in that state. That required another round of analysis that he would plan as soon as the first round went into effect.

•   •   •

We conclude this book with a small drama that is still to be enacted. We have drawn on the insights of the dramatist to aid us in our study of some old and some new tools of the scientific practitioner. May they enhance your understanding of life's drama and help you to influence its course of events. I wish you well in this great endeavor.

Glossary

Accurate empathy.   A term originated by Carl Rogers and colleagues that refers to a skill of an interviewer who is accurately aware of the client's feelings and thoughts with regard to a given situation and is able to convey those understandings to the client during the course of the interview. Clients who believe that interviewers accurately understand how they are feeling and what they are thinking are presumed to be able to move ahead more effectively in resolving their problems through discussions. (See Chapter 2.)

Administration.   One form of social work practice in which services are organized within a bureaucratic structure and delivered to a client population. The services include personnel and resources coordinated in the effective and humane solution of social and personal problems. (See Chapter 8.)

AIDS.   Acronym of the acquired immune deficiency syndrome, an end-stage of a series of health problems caused by a virus. The virus is passed from one person to another mainly through sexual contact, but also through sharing intravenous needles used for "shooting" drugs and, to a much lesser degree, from transfusions with contaminated blood, or when an infected woman transmits the AIDS virus to her fetus at birth. The AIDS virus belongs to a subclass of viruses called retroviruses, and have been labeled HIV or HTLV-III or LAV by different investigators; all refer to the same submicroscopic agent that attacks white blood cells in the human blood. The white blood cells are then not able to protect that person from diseases that take the opportunity to attack and ultimately kill the person. There is no known cure, although some medication slows down the deadly process. Prevention is the only feasible response to this disease. (See Chapter 20.)

Alienation.   A condition in which a person or a whole group (such as a social class) is separated or isolated from meaningful and effective association with others in the society or culture. There are two major aspects to alienation. One involves isolation from the values and norms of the majority, resulting in a feeling of meaninglessness; the alienated individual feels no involvement or connection with the common values of society. The second involves isolation from the roles and structures of the society, resulting in a feeling of powerlessness; the alienated individual feels unable to control his or her own destiny.

Behavior. Comprises thoughts, feelings, and actions that one party communicates internally and/or externally. Social behavior involves reciprocated communications in which the behavior of one party influences the behavior of another. The term party refers to individuals acting for themselves or in their capacity as a member of some group.

Behavioral theory. One approach to understanding human behavior. The basic ingredients include the belief that all significant social behaviors are learned through stimuli conditioning the person (a Pavlovian approach), or as a result of the consequences of a behavior encouraging or discouraging the person to repeat a given action (a Skinnerian approach), or through one person modeling the behaviors of another (a Bandurian approach). (See Chapter 9.)

Bureaucratic model. A theory of social organizations originally stated by Max Weber, who conceived of a ideal type of social problem-solving machine whose parts (positions in the organization) are arranged so as to achieve some goal in the most orderly and efficient manner possible. Qualified people are recruited on the basis of merit; like positions are rewarded equally. The organization chart represents the channels of communication among these role holders who follow formal rules to achieve goals. All real organizations differ by degrees from this ideal picture. (See Chapter 8.)

Center of gravity. See Configuration

Civil rights/civil liberties. The rights that belong to people under the laws of the land as basic to the nature of being a human being, and thus are not to be taken away arbitrarily. The United States Constitution, for example, guarantees such fundamental rights as life, liberty, and the pursuit of happiness. The interpretation of the meaning of these rights is an on-going judicial task, and requires "eternal vigilance" on the part of citizens to protect the spirit as well as the letter of the law.

Cognitive-behavior theory. A theory of human behavior associated with the work of Donald Meichenbaum, Albert Ellis, Albert Bandura, and many others that combines both the behavioral theory and the cognitive theory in order to account more effectively for a broad range of human behaviors. Not only are stimuli and consequences presumed to affect behavior, but so also are the thoughts, memories, values, and expectancies in the person's mind.

Communication. The transmission of information from one party to another through shared symbols (e.g., words, signs, gestures) or physical forms (e.g., the genetic code passed in seminal materials). Communication is effective to the degree that the intention of one party is understood by the other. This mutuality in information exchange involves a cycle of communications. Cycles of shared meanings cumulate to become the shared experiences of individuals and the culture of the group of related persons.

Community development. See Community organization

Community organization. One form of social work practice that deals with persons and groups at the community level. Jack Rothman distinguishes three major approaches within this mode of practice: (1) Community Development, which involves a practitioner facilitating local citizen involvement in determining the problems and forming solutions in their own way; (2) Social Planning, which involves an expert assembling information about a problem and then constructing a plan of action to resolve it; (3) Social Action or Reform, which involves a practitioner helping some victimized group mobilize strong collective action against entrenched power interests. Most community organizations combine elements of these three approaches, as situations and circumstances dictate. (See Chapter 8.)

Concepts; constructs.   Concepts are arbitrary symbols (that is, made by people) referring to some class of events. Concepts abstract general features which are common to all members of that class but different from any specific member. Concepts are the building blocks of larger conceptual terms (propositions, theories). They are neither true or false, merely better or worse guides to reality. Constructs are abstractions of concepts, and tend to be more general symbols than concepts.

Configuration or configural perspective.   The perspective offered in this text regarding how individuals, groups, cultures, societies, and environments may be viewed as one interactive system. The configuration is the largest field of structures and forces acting on one another to produce the behaviors we see. As such, it becomes our unit of study for understanding human behavior; we mentally check each component of the configuration for how it affects the client, and how it is affected by the client. The configuration can also be used as a guide for changing behaviors to attain valued objectives. The term Center of Gravity has been offered to represent the resultant of forces pushing and pulling an actor toward/away from some objective. Practitioners have to recognize this center of gravity in any given case situation so as to encourage constructive forces while neutralizing destructive ones. Careful empirical monitoring of changes in the configuration help the practitioner to keep moving toward goal attainment. (See Chapters 1 and 24.)

Contract.   In social work contexts, formal or informal arrangements made between a practitioner and a client (plus significant others) in which the verbal understanding between (among) them is stated explicitly as to who is to do what with whom under what conditions and to what end. (See Chapter 6.)

Core professional conditions.   As identified by Carl Rogers, Allen Ivey, Joel Fischer and others, Accurate Empathy, Warmth/Respect, and Facilitative Genuinessness form the basic core of ingredients necessary to effective interviewing in the helping context. (See Chapter 2.)

Culturally-sensitive social work.   A goal to be approximated, in which a social work practitioner who embodies his or her own cultural experiences seeks to serve a client who will differ culturally to a greater or lesser extent. Cultural differences may interfere with effective and humane services, and so to the extent that a practitioner is aware of his or her own cultural beliefs and expectations, especially with regard to the culture of the client, to that degree there is hope for practice that will use the strengths of the person and culture without harming or offending the client. (See Chapters 17 and 18.)

Culture; subculture.   Culture is the total way of life of a people and all the material and nonmaterial products that are transmitted from one generation to the next. Culture includes the set of thoughts, feelings, and actions of all of the people acquired as members of a society that are communicated through symbols, artifacts, or social arrangements in the present and succeeding generations. Subculture, a more limited term, refers to a relatively distinctive way of life of people who share some common characteristics, history, geography, and/or language. Members of such a subculture often influence one another to exhibit these common characteristics, such as dress codes or language.

Direct practice.   Services provided by a social worker to individuals, families, and small groups who are the clients, generally on a face-to-face basis. Contrasted with *indirect practice*, which involves services provided by social workers to populations at risk through intermediaries. For example, in community organization, social workers will seek to aid and inform natural leaders in a neighborhood to attain some objective, but the practitioners may not themselves become directly a part of these actions. In primary prevention, social workers may institute practices or generate resources by which citizens may avail themselves to prevent problems or to promote desired objectives.

Empathy.   See Accurate empathy

Epidemiology.   The study of the distribution in time and space of factors describing illness or health. This can be simply a description of such factors, or the information can be used in understanding possible causal patterns as the basis of preventive or interventive actions.

Epistemology.   The study of knowledge itself, its origin, nature, limits, and the language by which knowledge is expressed.

Ethics and values.   Values are the relatively persistent preferences people form that guide the means and ends of action. For example, people may seek as an end or goal the value of material success; they may use the value of honesty as means to attain that end. Ethics are the rules by which people prioritize how to attain certain ends by using certain means. Professional codes of ethics, in particular, attempt to state the guiding principles through which practitioners will act so as to help clients attain their goals. Such codes of ethics may suggest ways to resolve conflicts between valued objectives. (See Chapter 10.)

Evaluation.   See Research

Facilitative genuineness.   A term originated by Carl Rogers and his colleagues referring to an attribute of the interviewer to present him or herself as a person fully open and interested in the client, such that this method of openness and honesty facilitates the client's presenting the problems in a full and comprehensible manner. (See Chapter 2.)

Fields of practice.   The general territory in which social workers practice is traditionally divided into domains that have common elements, such as specific setting (medical social work) or common methods (mental health practices). Three illustrative fields of practice are covered in this book in detail; many others are mentioned in other chapters. (See Part VI and Chapters 14, 15, and 16.)

Generic problem-solving approach.   Common to social work practice at the individual, group, and organizational or community levels is a sequence of logical steps for understanding the presenting problems and working toward solutions. These commonalities are termed the generic problem-solving approach in recognition of their broad applicability. Beginning social workers and advanced practitioners alike use these basic ideas, albeit with more or less depth and scope. (See Chapter 6 for specific steps.)

Genuinessness.   See Facilitative genuineness

Goals and objectives.   Goals are the long-term ends clients seek; objectives are what clients seek as intermediatary to goals. It is possible to map out both the short-term and the long-range states of affairs clients desire as part of the overall planning for the case. Evaluation involves comparing each successive state of affairs during intervention with clients' stated objectives and goals in order to understand how the intervention is working and to know when to terminate practice.

Group work and work with people in groups.   Social workers frequently work with clients and others in group situations, that is, when the client and others are present together in seeking solutions to problems. But group work is more than just that; group work involves the planned use of the group structure and dynamics to influence individual and collective goal attainment. (See Chapter 8.)

Human relations.   A theory of social organization that emphasizes the personal or informal aspect of every formal bureaucracy. Such informal groups influence the productivity of the formal organization, and affect the level of satisfaction of its members. (See Chapter 8.)

Human services.   A relatively new term that is intended to convey the general category of services social workers and other helping professionals provide that are related to personal and interpersonal problems (as contrasted with financial or medical problems, for example). Some authors use the phrase personal services to refer to this same domain, while the older term, general welfare, covered much the same territory.

Humanist theory.   A theory of human behavior that emphasizes the values of the individual to determine his or her own goals and actions, and the active part the individual plays in every aspect of behavior. This theory is often contrasted with the radical behavioral approach in which the individual is fully determined by environmental events and consequences. (See Chapter 9.)

Information retrieval.   Procedures for locating scientific information needed by helping professionals as the basis of informed action. These procedures are derived from information science, which seeks to understand the nature of information and communication so as to make optimal use of cumulative knowledge in advancing science and practice.

Intervention.   See Primary prevention, Treatment, and Rehabilitation.

Learning theory.   See Behavioral theory

Mental health and mental illness.   These broad labels refer to the nature of people's adapting to their ordinary environments in socially acceptable ways. Mental disorders or mental illnesses are to be distinguished from mental retardation in that the former are primarily emotional disturbances (usually related to untoward life experiences or possibly genetic inheritance), while the latter is related to cognitive functioning that is persistently below the level of performance of persons of the same age (often due to biological or genetic problems). (See Chapter 12.)

Model.   See Theory

Person-centered therapy or client-centered therapy.   See Humanist theory

Philosophy of science and philosophy of scientific practice.   A philosophy of science is an analytic activity concerning the nature of scientific activity and how scientists practice that activity. It examines how we know and what tools we use by which to know. It considers the language by which we express scientific problems and solutions, as well as the values involved in these activities. All of these considerations are treated at abstract levels. In contrast, a philosophy of scientific practice considers related issues all from the perspective on how this information may be used in practice contexts. For example, theories are reconsidered with regard to how their concepts and propositions may be translated into strategies for action. (See Chapter 3.)

Policy.   See Social policy

Post-traumatic stress disorder.   A new label for an old condition, the delayed reaction to traumatic stress (such as military combat or a bad accident) that is exhibited in many forms of problematic behaviors such as tensions, restlessness, psychosomatic symptoms, and impulsive behaviors. New methods of treatment are being developed that have proven to be effective. (See Chapter 19.)

Poverty line.   An arbitrary determination of an economic level below which people are considered poor, which in turn means that their economic condition cannot support a level or quality of life deemed necessary in a given society. Depending on who defines what level of income or wealth constitutes the poverty line, millions of people are defined as poor or nonpoor. The poor may be eligible for certain welfare benefits, and so this designation takes on immense political and economic importance.

Primary prevention. This helping modality seeks to prevent predictable problems, to protect existing states of health and healthy functioning, and to promote desired goals and objectives. Primary prevention is practiced before specific problems occur, in order to prevent the suffering that knowingly occurs with problems. Primary prevention works with the strengths of clients and environments, rather than focusing mainly on weaknesses and problems of each.

Problem-solving process. See Generic problem-solving process

Profession. A high-status occupation whose members undergo extensive training to learn the knowledge, skills, and values of this group at some requisite level. Professionals are entrusted by society to deal with individuals' personal problems as well as the collective problems of groups, and thus require a code of ethics to guide and monitor their largely autonomous behavior.

Psychodynamic theory. A theory of human behavior initially formulated by Sigmund Freud and developed by many of his colleagues and opponents. It emphasizes the place of unconscious conflicts stemming from experiences largely within the first five years of life that play out their warping effects at later stages.

Reform. See Community organization

Rehabilitation. A helping modality that begins after the major effects of a problem or illness have run their course. The goals of rehabilitation are to return the client to the highest levels of functioning possible. Sometimes this involves prostheses, temporary or permanent aids that help clients adapt to the environment.

Relationship or rapport. One of two major activities of any helping effort (the other being dealing with the task); relationship involves the psycho-social connections made between client and practitioner on a human level (as contrasted with a technological or expertise level for task functions). These psycho-social connections involve trust (due to the personal and confidential nature of the discussions); honesty (because of the need to have truthful communications for effective problem resolution); and some minimal degree of liking to maintain the relationship over a time-limited period sufficient to achieve client objectives. Different theories of behavior change put more (the psychodynamic approach) or less (the behavioral approach) emphasis on relationship as central to the behavior change process. (See Chapter 7.)

Research. In the form of surveys or experimental/control group designs that are often used to describe situations or to add to basic knowledge, research should be distinguished from evaluation, in which rapid and approximate feedback is obtained for the purpose of correcting on-going practice. (See Chapter 23.)

Resistance. As used in psychotherapy, the forces within the client, knowingly or not, that oppose the therapeutic activities of the practitioner. Critics of therapy point out that resistance is often used as a label for any client activity that does not fit with the practitioner's desires. This may be a "blame-the-victim" stance when the practitioner is unable to influence the situation appropriately, and merely blames the client for the failure. (See Chapter 7.)

Single-system designs. Evaluation methods by which practitioners can monitor the process of their practice and evaluate the outcomes against client goals (also single-case designs, N=1 designs, etc.). (See Chapter 23.)

Social action or reform.   See Community organization

Social change.   Significant modifications in the social structure, and hence, in the roles or in the norms of which that structure is composed. The tendency to social change runs counter to the tendency toward social stability, resulting in a dynamic or dialectic (interactive and spiraling) relationship between these processes.

Social class.   A large group of persons all of whom have a similar socioeconomic status in a society and related similarities in life-style and life chances.

Social functioning.   Comprises the processes by which social roles and norms are made manifest by the behavior of the people involved in social structures.

Social institutions.   Clusters of social structures that are actively involved in meeting persisting social needs. The typical institutions are the family, the economic system, the political system, the military system, and the religious system. Some authors extend this list to include health, education, art, among others.

Social norms.   Affective expectations that develop around roles in given social contexts. In effect, these norms involve a given group's awareness of the positive and negative sanctions related to acceptable or nonacceptable ranges of behaviors. Norms are independent of the individual who is aware of their sanctions.

Social planning.   See Community organization

Social policy.   Plans for the attainment of social goals and objectives through the organized expenditure of resources by identified personnel for populations at risk.

Social problems.   At the level of a major social concern, those problems that affect a relatively large number of persons in ways that have relatively serious social consequences, and are perceived by persons able and willing to seek collective changes to correct the difficulties.

Social roles.   Involving a set of behaviors that are expected of a person in a given social position, social roles are independent of the individual who is performing these behaviors at a particular time.

Social stratification.   Involving the relatively stable ranking of roles in a given society according to differential power, prestige, or privilege, this ranking expresses inequality and differences in life-style and in life chances.

Social structure.   The relatively stable systems of relationships between roles and norms at a given time and within a given culture. Social structures are independent of the people who originated them or who currently are involved in them. These social structures are sometimes called social organizations or social groups.

Social system.   A broad social structural term used particularly in the comparative sense when referring to supersystems and subsystems, that is, the ecological context in which social life occurs. Systems contain interdependent parts viewed as a single entity such that changes in one produce changes in the others.

Social welfare.   Society's organized ways to provide for the persistent needs of all people—for health, education, socio-economic support, personal rights, and political freedom. Social welfare is manifested through many programs and services from public (governmental) and private sources.

Social work.   Consists of the activities of persons trained to help individuals, groups, families, or communities to enhance or to restore their capacity for effective social functioning, and to create the societal conditions that are favorable to this goal.

Task functions.   One of two major activities of any helping effort (the other being the relationship function). Task functions involve the specific efforts clients and practitioners have to perform in order to attain identified objectives. The generic problem-solving process is an operational statement of how tasks may be effectively and humanely attained. (See Chapter 6.)

Theory.   A logical system of interrelated concepts and propositions that describe, explain, and predict some things about some portion of the universe in a parsimonious way. Theories embody assumptions about how the world operates, so as to propose certain logical relationships about a portion of that world. Propositions (hypotheses) are derived from the theory and are tested in the real world. Tested results and new ideas may be abstracted (that is, new concepts may be formed) and become part of the changing theory. (See Chapter 3.)

Theory of behavior and theory of behavior change.   A theory of behavior, which describes how some person or group behaves, should be distinguished from a theory of behavior *change*, which describes the action steps needed to produce a change in a given behavior. Practitioners often hold one theory of behavior and another theory of behavior change, which may lead to conceptual ambiguity.

Treatment.   Helping modality of work with clients who have identified problems or limitations that seeks to help them help themselves. Treatment may supply missing resources or reorganize available resources; it may also involve changes in the environment.

Values.   See Ethics and values

Warmth/respect.   Originated by Carl Rogers and his colleagues, term referring to an aspect of the interviewer in relationship to the client. The interviewer conveys in words and gestures his or her interest in and respect for the client. It should be noted that maintaining a friendly concern *for* the client is not the same as being a friend *to* the client; the practitioner maintains a professional relationship (for perspective on solving problems) while being a warm human being (to maintain a working relationship). (See Chapter 2.)

Welfare.   See Social welfare

Whistle blower.   A person who notifies outside authorities that there is some problem in his or her own agency with the goal of gaining the necessary leverage to be able to correct the situation, or have that situation corrected by others.

Bibliography

Abrams, D. I. "The nature of AIDS." In *Acquired Immune Deficiency Syndrome and Chemical Dependency*. DHHS Publication No. (ADM) 87–1513, 1987.

Acquired Immune Deficiency Syndrome and Chemical Dependency. Department of Health and Human Services. Publication No. (ADM) 87–1513, 1987.

AIDS—A Public Health Crisis. Population Reports. 1986, Series L, No. 6, pp. L. 194–L. 228.

"AIDS in the United States." Health Section. *Washington Post*, June 2, 1987, 5.

Akabas, S. H. "Women, work and mental health: Room for improvement." *Journal of Primary Prevention*, 1988, 9:1 & 2, 130–140.

Akabas, S. H., and Kurzman, P. A. (Eds.). *Work, Workers, and Work Organizations: A View of Social Work*. Englewood Cliffs, N.J.: Prentice-Hall, 1982.

Albee, G. W. "Psychopathology, prevention, and the just society." *Journal of Primary Prevention*, 1983, 4:1, 5–40.

Allman, L. R. "The aesthetic preference: Overcoming the pragmatic error." *Family Process*. 1982, 21:1, 43–56.

Alpert, G. P. *The American System of Criminal Justice*. Vol. 1. Law and Criminal Justice Service. Beverly Hills, Calif.: Sage, 1985.

American Humane Society. *National Analysis of Official Child Neglect and Abuse Reporting*. Denver: The Society, 1983.

Aptheker, H. (Ed.). *A Documentary History of the Negro People in the United States*. New York and Secaucus, N.J.: Citadel Press, 1951–1974.

Argandona, M., and Kiev, A. *Mental Health in the Developing World: A Case Study in Latin America*. New York: Free Press, 1972.

Armour, P. K. *The Cycles of Social Reform: Mental Health Policy Making in the United States, England, and Sweden*. Washington, D.C.: University Press of America, 1986.

Arnold, C. B., and Cogswell, B. E. "A condom distribution program for adolescents: The findings of a feasibility study." *American Journal of Public Health*. 1971, 61:4, 739–750.

Aronson, E. *The Social Animal*. 4th Ed. New York: Freeman, 1984.

Ashton, D. N. *Unemployment Under Capitalism: The Sociology of British and American Labour Markets*. Westport, Conn.: Greenwood Press, 1986.

Auletta, K. *The Underclass*. New York: Random House, 1982.

Ayllon, T., and Azrin, N. H. *The Token Economy: A Motivational System for Therapy and Rehabilitation.* New York: Appleton-Century-Crofts, 1968.

Bachrach, L. L. "Psychiatric services in rural areas: A sociological overview." *Hospital and Community Psychiatry,* 1983, 34, 215–226.

Bagarozzi, J. I., and Bagarozzi, D. A. "Family financial counseling." In D. Myers (Ed.). *Employee Problem Prevention and Counseling.* Westport, Conn.: Quorum Books, 1985.

Baily, T. F., and Baily, W. H. *Child Welfare Practice: A Guide to Providing Effective Services for Children and Families.* San Francisco: Jossey-Bass, 1983.

Bakeman, R., Lumb, J. R., Jackson, R. E., and Smith, D. W. "AIDS risk-reduction group profiles in whites and members of minority groups." *The New England Journal of Medicine,* 1986, 315:3, 191–2.

Bandura, A. *Social-Learning Theory.* Englewood Cliffs, N.J.: Prentice-Hall, 1977.

Bane, M. J. "Household composition and poverty." In S. Danziger and D. Weinberg (Eds.). *Fighting Poverty.* Cambridge, Mass.: Harvard University Press, 1986.

Bard, M. *Training Police as Specialists in Family Crisis Intervention.* Washington, D.C.: U.S. Government Printing Office, 1970.

Barker, J. G. "Are microskills worth teaching?" *Journal of Social Work Education,* 1988, 24:1, 3–12.

Barker, R. L. *The Social Work Dictionary.* Silver Spring, Md.: NASW, 1987.

Barth, R. P. *Social and Cognitive Treatment of Children and Adolescents.* San Francisco: Jossey-Bass, 1986.

Bassi, J. J., and Ashenfelter, O. "The effect of direct job creation and training programs on low-skilled workers." In S. Danziger and D. Weinberg (Eds.). *Fighting Poverty.* Cambridge, Mass.: Harvard University Press, 1986.

Bassuk, E. "Is homelessness a mental-health problem?" *American Journal of Psychiatry,* 1984, 141:12, 1546–1550.

Bateson, G. *Steps to an Ecology of Mind.* New York: Ballantine, 1975.

Baumer, D. C., and Van Horn, C. E. *The Politics of Unemployment.* Washington, D.C.: Congressional Quarterly Press, 1985.

Baxandall, R., Gordon, L., and Reverby, S. (Eds.). *America's Working Women: A Documentary History—1600 to the Present.* New York: Random House, 1976.

Bayer, R. *Homosexuality and American Psychiatry: The Politics of Diagnosis.* New York: Basic Books, 1981.

Beccaria (Cesare). *On Crimes and Punishments.* (Translated by Henry Paolucci.) Indianapolis, Indiana: Bobbs-Merrill, 1963.

Beck, A. T., Resnik, H. L. P., and Lettieri, D. J. *The Prediction of Suicide.* Bowie, Md.: Charles Press, 1974.

Beeghley, L. *Social Stratification in America: A Critical Analysis of Theory and Research.* New York: Random House, 1978.

Beeghley, L. *Living Poorly in America.* New York: Praeger Publishers, 1983.

Beers, C. W. *A Mind That Found Itself.* Pittsburgh: University of Pittsburgh Press, 1981 (reprint of 1907 book).

Bell, A. P. "Sexual preference: A postscript." *SIECUS Reports,* 1982, XI:2, 1–3.

Bell, A. P., Weinberg, M. S., and Hammersmith, S. K. *Sexual Preference: Its Development in Men and Women.* Bloomington, Ind.: Indiana University Press, 1981.

Bell, A. P., Weinberg, M. S., and Hammersmith, S. K. *Homosexualities: A Study of Diversity Among Men and Women.* New York: Simon and Schuster, 1978.

Belloc, N., and Breslow, L. "A study of longevity and health factors," mentioned in A. F. Ehrbar. "A radical prescription for medical care." *Fortune,* 1977 (February), p. 169.

Belsky, J., and Benn, J. "Beyond bonding: A family-centered approach to enhancing early parent-infant relations." In L. A. Bond and J. M. Joffe (Eds.). *Facilitating In-*

fant and Early Childhood Development. Hanover, N.H.: University Press of New England, 1982.

Bem, S. L. "Masculinity and femininity exist only in the mind of the perceiver." In J. M. Reinisch, L. A. Rosenblum, and S. A. Sanders (Eds.). *Masculinity/Femininity: Basic Perspectives.* New York: Oxford University Press, 1987.

Berger, R. M. "Homosexuality: Gay Men." In A. Minahan et al. (Eds.). *Encyclopedia of Social Work.* 18th Ed. Silver Spring, Md.: NASW, 1987.

Bergmann, B. R. *The Economic Emergence of Women.* New York: Basic Books. 1986.

Bernard, J. *The Future of Marriage.* New York: Bantam, 1972.

Bernstein, B. J. "The dropping of the A-bomb: How decisions are made when a nation is at war." *The Center Magazine,* 1983 (March/April), 7–15. (Center for the Study of Democratic Institutions, Santa Barbara, Calif.)

Beverly, D. P., and McSweeney, E. A. *Social Welfare and Social Justice.* Englewood Cliffs, N.J.: Prentice-Hall, 1987.

Biller, H. B., and Solomon, R. S. *Child Maltreatment and Paternal Deprivation: A Manifesto for Research, Prevention, and Treatment.* Lexington, Mass.: Lexington Books, 1986.

Birch, H., and Gussow, J. D. *Disadvantaged Children: Health, Nutrition, and School Failure.* New York: Harcourt, Brace, and World, 1970.

Black, B. "Milieu Therapy." In John B. Turner et al. (Eds.). *Encyclopedia of Social Work,* 17th Ed. New York: NASW, 1977.

Blau, P. S. *Old Age in a Changing Society.* New York: New Viewpoints, 1973.

Bloom, A. *The Closing of the American Mind.* New York: Touchstone Books, 1988.

Bloom, B. L. *Community Mental Health: A General Introduction.* 2nd edition. Monterey, Calif.: Brooks/Cole, 1984.

Bloom, L. Z., Coburn, K., and Pearlman, J. *The New Assertive Woman.* Delacorte Press, 1975.

Bloom, M. *Paradox of Helping: Introduction to the Philosophy of Scientific Practice.* New York: Wiley, 1975.

Bloom, M. *Primary Prevention: The Possible Science.* Englewood Cliffs, N.J.: Prentice-Hall, 1981.

Bloom, M. *The Experience of Research.* New York: Macmillan, 1986.

Bloom, M. "Prevention." In A. Minahan et al. (Eds.). *Encyclopedia of Social Work.* 18th Ed. Silver Spring, Md.: NASW, 1987.

Bloom, M., and Fischer, J. *Evaluating Practice: Guidelines for the Helping Professional.* Englewood Cliffs, N.J.: Prentice-Hall, 1982.

Bloom, M., Siefert, K., and Akabas, S. H. (Eds.). "Prevention and women's concerns." *Journal of Primary Prevention,* 1988, 9:1 & 2, whole issue.

Blue Cross and Blue Shield Guide to Staying Well. Chicago: Contemporary Books, 1982.

Bockoven, J. S. *Moral Treatment in American Psychiatry.* New York: Springer, 1963.

Bohr, N. "Memorandum to President Roosevelt, July, 1944." Reprinted in Gregory, 1986.

Boles, S. M., Bellamy, G. T., Horner, R. H., and Mank, D. M. "Specialized training programs: The structured employment model. In S. C. Paine, et al. (Eds.). *Human Services that Work: From Innovation to Standard Practice.* Baltimore: Paul H. Brookes Publishing Co., 1984.

Bond, L., and Joffe, J. M. (Eds.). *Facilitating Infant and Early Childhood Development.* Hanover, N.H.: University Press of New England, 1982.

Bond, L., and Wagner, B. (Eds.). *Families in Transition: Primary Prevention Programs that Work.* Vol. 11. Beverly Hills, Calif.: Sage, 1988.

Bowers, J. Z., and Purcell, E. F. (Eds.). *Medicine and Society in China.* New York: Josiah Macy, Jr. Foundation, 1974.

Brace, C. L. *The Dangerous Classes of New York and Twenty Years Work Among Them.* New York: Wynkoop and Hallenbeck, 1872.

Brecht, B. "Galileo." In J. Gassner (Ed.). *Best Plays of the Modern American Theater.* New York: Crown Publisher, 1947.

Bremner, R. H. *From the Depths: The Discovery of Poverty in the United States.* New York: New York University Press, 1956.

Bremner, R. H. *American Philanthropy.* Chicago: University of Chicago Press, 1960.

Bremner, R. H. (Ed.). *Children and Youth in America: A Documentary History.* Cambridge, Mass.: Harvard University Press. Volume 1, 1970; Volume II, Parts I and II, 1971; Volume III, Parts I and II, 1974.

Bremner, R. H., and Reichard, G. W. (Eds.). *Reshaping America: Society and Institutions 1945–1960.* Columbus, Ohio: Ohio State University Press, 1982.

Bremner, R. H., Reichard, G. W., and Hopkins, R. J. (Eds.). *American Choices: Social Dilemmas and Public Policy since 1960.* Columbus, Ohio: Ohio State University Press, 1986.

Brenner, M. H. "Estimating the Costs of National Economic Policy: Implications for Mental and Physical Health and Aggression." Study prepared for the Joint Economic Committee, U.S. Congress, 94th Congress, 2nd Session, 1976. (Cited in Ginsburg, 1983.)

Briar, K. H. *The Effect of Long-Term Unemployment on Workers and Their Families.* San Francisco: R and E Research Associates, 1978.

Briar, K. H. "Unemployment and Underemployment." In A. Minahan et al. (Eds.). *Encyclopedia of Social Work.* 18th Ed. Silver Spring, Md.: NASW, 1987.

Brieland, D., Costin, L. B., and Atherton, C. R. *Contemporary Social Work.* New York: McGraw-Hill, 1985.

Brieland, D., and Goldfarb, S. Z. "Legal issues and legal services." In A. Minahan et al. (Eds.). *Encyclopedia of Social Work.* 18th ed. Silver Spring, Md.: NASW, 1987.

Brockway, B., Werking, J., Fitzgibbons, K., and Butterfield, W. "Social work at the grass roots: Practicing in the doctor's office" (unpublished manuscript, no date).

Brody, E. M. and Brody, S. J. "Aged: Services." In A. Minahan et al. (Eds.). *Encyclopedia of Social Work,* 18th Ed. Silver Spring, Md.: NASW, 1987.

Brody, J. *Jane Brody's Good Food Book.* New York: Norton, 1985.

Brokowski, A., Marks, E., and Budman, S. H. (Eds.). *Linking Health and Mental Health.* Beverly Hills, Calif.: Sage, 1981.

Bromley, D. B. *The Psychology of Human Aging.* Penguin Books, 1966.

Bronfenbrenner, U. "Is early intervention effective? Facts and principles of early intervention: A summary." *A Report on Longitudinal Evaluation of Preschool Programs. Vol 2. Is Early Intervention Effective?* Washington, D.C.: HEW Publication No. (OHD) 74–25, 1974.

Bronowski, J. *The Origins of Knowledge and Imagination.* New Haven: Yale University Press, 1978.

Brookman, R. R. "Adolescent sexuality and related health problems." In A. Hofman (Ed.). *Adolescent Medicine.* Menlo Park, Calif.: Addison-Wesley, 1983.

Brown, L. R., and others (Eds.). *State of the World,* 1988. New York: Norton, 1988.

Brown, L. R., and Postel, S. "Thresholds of change." In L. R. Brown and others (Eds.). *State of the World,* 1987. New York: Norton, 1987.

Brown, P. "Women and competence." In A. N. Maluccio (Ed.). *Promoting Competence in Clients: A New/Old Approach to Social Work Practice.* New York: Free Press, 1981.

Brown, R. C. "Family and marriage counseling in industry." In D. Myers (Ed.). *Employee Problem Prevention and Counseling.* Westport, Conn.: Quorum Books, 1985.

Brown, K. S., and Ziefert, M. "Crisis resolution, competence, and empowerment: A service model for women." *Journal of Primary Prevention,* 1988, 9:1 & 2, 92–103.

Browning, E. K. *Redistribution and the Welfare System*. Washington, D.C.: American Enterprise Institute, 1975.

Brownmiller, S. *Against our Will: Men, Women, and Rape*. New York: Bantam Books, 1975.

Buckner, J., Trickett, E. J., and Corse, S. J. *Primary Prevention in Mental Health: An Annotated Bibliography*. Washington, D.C.: GPO, 1985.

Bundy, M., Kennan, G. F., McNamara, R. S., and Smith, G. "The President's choice: Star wars or arms control." *Foreign Affairs*, 1984/85 (Winter), 277–292.

Burtless, G. "Public spending for the poor: Trends, prospects, and economic limits. In S. Danziger and E. Weinberg (Eds.). *Fighting Poverty*. Cambridge, Mass.: Harvard University Press, 1986.

Burtt, E. A. *Metaphysical Foundations of Modern Physical Science*. 2nd Ed. Atlantic Highlands, N.J.: Humanities, 1967 reprint.

Butler, R. N. *Why Survive? Being Old in America*. New York: Harper and Row, 1975.

Carkoff, R. *Helping and Human Relations* (Vols. I and II). New York: Holt, Rinehart and Winston, 1969.

Carter, L. F. "The sustaining effects study of compensatory and elementary education." *Educational Researcher*, 1984, 13L7, 4–13.

Cartwright, F. F. *A Social History of Medicine*. London: Longman, 1977.

Case, J., and Taylor, R. C. R. *Co-ops, Communes, and Collectives: Experiments in Social Change in the 1960s and 1970s*. New York: Pantheon Books, 1979.

Castelle, G. "Juvenile offender institutions." In A. Minahan et al. (Eds.). *Encyclopedia of Social Work*. 18th Ed. Silver Spring, Md.: NASW, 1987.

Centers for Disease Control. "Acquired immunodeficiency syndrome (AIDS) among blacks and Hispanics—United States." *Morbidity and Mortality Weekly Report*, 1986, 35, 655–658, 633–666.

Centers for Disease Control. "AIDS Program, Center for Infectious Diseases." *AIDS Weekly Surveillance Report—United States*. 1987.

Chafetz, J. S. *Feminist Sociology: An Overview of Contemporary Theories*. Itasca, Ill.: Peacock, 1988.

Chambers, C. *Seedtime of Reform: American Social Service and Social Action, 1918–1933*. Minneapolis: University of Minnesota Press, 1963.

Chilman, C. S. *Adolescent Sexuality in a Changing American Society*. New York: Wiley, 1983.

Clark, M. *Health in the Mexican-American Culture: A Community Study*. Berkeley: University of California Press, 1970.

Cohen, A. Y. *Alternatives to Drug Abuse: Steps Toward Prevention*. Washington, D.C.: DHEW Publication No. (ADM) 75–79, 1975.

Colburn, D. "AIDS—The growing impact." "Health": *Washington Post*, June 2, 1987, p. 12.

Colburn, D. "The black-white health gap: Why medical progress leaves some behind." "Health": *Washington Post*, April 4, 1988, 11–15.

Cole, E. S. "Adoption." In A. Minahan et al. (Eds.). *Encyclopedia of Social Work*. 18th Ed. Silver Spring, Md.: NASW, 1987.

Coles, R. *Children of Crisis*. Vol. 1. Boston: Little, Brown, 1964.

Coles, R. *The Privileged Ones*. Boston: Little, Brown, 1977.

Collins, A. H. and Pancoast, D. *Natural Helping Networks: A Strategy for Prevention*. Washington, D.C.: NASW, 1976.

Compton, B. R. *Introduction to Social Welfare and Social Work: Structure, Function, and Process*. Homewood, Ill.: Dorsey Press, 1980.

Conklin, J. J. "Homelessness and de-institutionalization." *Journal of Sociology and Social Welfare*, 1985, 12:1, 41–61.

Connell, S. "Homelessness." In A. Minahan et al. (Eds.). *Encyclopedia of Social Work.* 18th Ed. Silver Spring, Md.: NASW, 1987.

Coping with AIDS: Psychological and Social Considerations in Helping People with HTLV-III Infection. U.S. Department of Health and Human Services. DHSS Publication No. (ADM) 85–1432, 1986.

Corcoran, K., and Fischer, J. *Measures for Clinical Practice: A Sourcebook.* New York: Free Press, 1987.

Corsini, R. J., and Wedding, D. *Current Psychotherapies.* 4th Ed. Itasca, Ill.: Peacock Publications, 1989.

Cox, T. *Stress.* Baltimore: University Park Press, 1978.

Coyne, J. C., Denner, B., and Ransom, D. C. "Undressing the fashionable mind." *Family Process,* 1982, 21, 391–396.

Cronk, S. D., Jankovic, J., and Green, R. K. (Eds.). *Criminal Justice in Rural America.* Washington, D.C.: U.S. Department of Justice, 1982.

Csikszentmihalyi, M. *Beyond Boredom and Anxiety.* San Francisco: Jossey-Bass, 1975.

Cuomo, M. *1933/1983—Never Again. Report to the National Governers' Conference Task Force on the Homeless,* Portland, Maine, 1983. (Reported in Connell, 1987.)

D'Angelo, R. "Runaways." In A. Minahan et al. (Eds.). *Encyclopedia of Social Work.* 18th Ed. Silver Spring, Md.: NASW, 1987.

Danziger, S. H., Haveman, R. H., and Plotnick, R. D. "Antipoverty policy: Effects on the poor and the nonpoor." In S. Danziger and D. Weinberg (Eds.). *Fighting Poverty.* Cambridge, Mass.: Harvard University Press, 1986.

Danziger, S. H., and Weinberg, D. H. (Eds.). *Fighting Poverty: What Works and What Doesn't.* Cambridge, Mass.: Harvard University Press, 1986.

Darlington, R. B., et al. "Preschool programs and later school competence of children of low income families." *Science,* 1980, 208, 202–204.

David, H. P. (Ed.). *International Trends in Mental Health.* New York: McGraw-Hill, 1966.

Davidson, M. J., and Cooper, C. L. (Eds.). *Working Women: An International Survey.* New York: Wiley, 1984.

Davis, N. J. "Prostitution." In A. Minahan et al. (Eds.). *Encyclopedia of Social Work.* 18th Ed. Silver Spring, Md.: NASW, 1987.

de Jesus, C. M. *Child of the Dark: Diary of Carolina Maria DeJesus.* New York: Mentor Books, 1962.

Dell, P. F. "Beyond homeostasis: Toward a concept of coherence." *Family Process,* 1982, 21, 21–41.

Demerath, N. *Birth Control and Foreign Policy: The Alternatives to Family Planning.* New York: Harper and Row, 1976.

de Valdez, T. A., and Gallegos, J. "The Chincano familia in social work." In J. W. Green (Ed.). *Cultural Awareness in Human Services.* Englewood Cliffs, N.J.: Prentice-Hall, 1982.

Devore, W., and Schlesinger, E. G. *Ethnic-Sensitive Social Work Practice.* 2nd Ed. Columbus, Ohio: Merrill Publishing Company, 1987.

DeWeaver, K. L., and Johnson, P. J. "Case management in rural areas for the developmentally disabled." *Human Services in the Rural Environment,* 1983, 8:4, 23–31.

Dewey, J. *The School and Society.* Rev. Ed. Chicago: University of Chicago Press (1899) 1915.

Diagnostic and Statistical Manual of Mental Disorders—3rd Edition, Revised. Washington D.C.: American Psychiatric Association, 1987.

DiNitto, D., and Dye, T. *Social Welfare, Politics and Public Policy.* 3rd Ed. Englewood Cliffs, N.J.: Prentice-Hall, 1989.

Draper, E., and Margolis, P. "A psychodynamic approach to suicide prevention." *Community Mental Health Journal,* 1976, 12:4, 376–382.

Dryfoos, J. G. "School-based health clinics: Three years' experience." *Family Planning Perspectives*, 1988, 20:4, 193–200.

Duffy, J. *A History of Public Health in New York City, 1625–1866*. New York: Russell Sage Foundation, 1968.

Durkheim, E. *Suicide*. New York: Free Press, 1952.

Edmondson, J. E., Holman, T. B., and Morrell, W. R. "The need for and effectiveness of surrogate role models among single-parent children." *Journal of Primary Prevention*, 1984, 5:2, 111–123.

Ehrbar, A. F. "A radical prescription for medical care." *Fortune*, February, 1977, p. 169. (Quoted in Zastrow, 1986.)

Ehrlich, P. R., Ehrlich, A. H., and Holdren, J. P. *Human Ecology: Problems and Solutions*. San Francisco: W. H. Freeman, 1973.

Einstein, A. "Letter to President Roosevelt, August 2, 1939." Reprinted in Gregory, 1986.

Elliot, D. S., and Voss, H. *Delinquency and Dropout*. Lexington, Mass.: Lexington Books, 1974.

Ellis, A. *Reason and Emotion in Psychotherapy*. New York: Lyle Stuart, 1962.

Ellis, A. *Growth Through Reason: Verbatim Cases in Rational-Emotive Therapy*. Palo Alto, Calif.: Science and Behavior Books, 1971.

Ellis, A. "Rational-emotive therapy." In R. J. Corsini (Ed.). *Current Psychotherapies*. 3rd Ed. Itasca, Ill.: Peacock, 1984.

Ellwood, D. T., and Summers, L. H. "Poverty in America: Is welfare the answer or the problem?" In S. Danziger and D. Weinberg (Eds.). *Fighting Poverty*. Cambridge, Mass.: Harvard University Press, 1986.

Engel, K. C., and Gabel, K. "Female offenders." In A. Minahan et al. (Eds.). *Encyclopedia of Social Work*. 18th Ed. Silver Spring, Md.: NASW, 1987.

Epp, J. *Achieving Health for All*. Canadian Government Printing Office. 1986.

Epstein, L. *Helping People: The Task-Centered Approach*. 2nd ed. Columbus, Ohio: Merrill Publishing Co, 1988.

Erikson, E. H. *Childhood and Society*. New York: Norton, 1950.

Erikson, E. H. "Life cycle." In *The International Encyclopedia of the Social Sciences*. New York: Crowell, Collier, and Macmillan, 1968.

Eron, L. D. "Parent-child interaction, television violence, and aggression of children." *American Psychologist*, 1982, 37:2, 197–211.

Estrich, S. *Real Rape*. Cambridge, Mass.: Harvard University Press, 1987.

Faberow, N. L. *The Many Faces of Suicide: Indirect Self-Destructive Behavior*. New York: McGraw-Hill, 1979.

Faberow, N. L. and Shneidman, E. S. (Eds.). *The Cry for Help*. New York: McGraw-Hill, 1961.

Fairweather, G. W. *The Fairweather Lodge: A Twenty-five Year Retrospective*. San Francisco: Jossey-Bass, 1980.

Farmer, R., and Hirsch, S. (Eds.). *The Suicide Syndrome*. London: Croom Helm, 1980.

"Federal Emergency Management Agency. Shelter Management Handbook. 1984." Excerpt reprinted in Gregory, 1986.

Feinman, C. *Women in the Criminal Justice System*. New York: Praeger, 1980.

Feldman, R. A., Capinger, T. E., and Wodarski, J. S. *The St. Louis Conundrum: The Effective Treatment of Antisocial Youths*. Englewood Cliffs, N.J.: Prentice-Hall, 1983.

Fiedler, F. E. "A contingency model of leadership effectiveness." In L. Berkowitz (Ed.). *Advances in Experimental Social Psychology*. New York: Academic Press, 1964, 1.

Figley, C. R. (Ed.). *Stress Disorders among Vietnam Veterans: Theory, Research and Treatment*. New York: Brunner/Mazel, 1978.

Figley, C. R. (Ed.). *Trauma and its Wake: The Study and Treatment of Post-Traumatic Stress Disorder*. New York: Brunner/Mazel, 1985.

Finckenauer, J. O. *Scared Straight! and the Panacea Phenomenon.* Englewood Cliffs, N.J.: Prentice-Hall, 1982.

Fineman, S. *White Collar Unemployment: Impact and Stress.* New York: Wiley, 1983.

Fischer, J. *Effective Social Work Practice: An Eclectic Approach.* New York: McGraw-Hill, 1978.

Ford, C. S., and Beach, F. A. *Patterns of Sexual Behavior.* New York: Harper and Row, 1951.

Forsberg, R. *Nuclear Arms: A Brief History.* Brookline, Mass.: Institute for Defense and Disarmament Studies, 1982. (Original title: "A nuclear freeze and non-interventionary conventional policy.")

Fortune, A. *Task-Centered Practice with Families and Groups.* New York: Springer, 1985.

Fradd, S. "Bilingualism, cognitive growth, and divergent thinking skills." *Educational Forum,* 1982, 46:4, 469–474.

Frankl, V. *Man's Search for Meaning: An Introduction to Logotherapy.* New York: Washington Square Press, 1963.

Freeman, R. B., and Holzer, H. J. (Eds.). *The Black Youth Employment Crisis.* Chicago: University of Chicago Press, 1986.

French, J. R. P., and Raven, B. "The bases of social power." In D. Cartwright (Ed.). *Studies in Social Power.* Ann Arbor: University of Michigan Press, 1959.

Freud, A. *The Ego and Mechanisms of Defense.* New York: International Universities Press, 1936.

Friedan, B. *Feminine Mystique.* New York: Dell, 1963.

Fries, M., and Siverman, M. "Issues of prediction and prevention in a longitudinal study: Birth to forty-five years." *Journal of Preventive Psychiatry,* 1981, 1:2, 207–217.

Gagon, J., and Henderson, B. *Human Sexuality: The Age of Ambiguity.* Boston: Little, Brown, 1975.

Galper, J. *The Politics of Social Services.* Englewood Cliffs, N.J.: Prentice-Hall, 1974.

Gambrill, E. *Casework: A Competency-based Approach.* Englewood Cliffs, N.J.: Prentice-Hall, 1983.

Gans, H. "The positive functions of poverty." *American Journal of Sociology,* 1972, 78, 275–289.

Garvin, C. D. *Contemporary Group Work.* Englewood Cliffs, N.J.: Prentice-Hall, 1987.

Gavin, C., Smith, A., and Reid, W. (Eds.). *The Work Incentive Experience.* Montclair, N.J.: Allenheld, Osmun, and Company, 1978.

Gelfand, M. I. "Elevating or ignoring the underclass." In R. Bremner et al. (Eds.). *American Choices.* Columbus, Ohio: Ohio State University Press, 1986.

Gelles, R. J. "Violence in the family: A review of research in the seventies." *Journal of Marriage and the Family,* 1980, 42:4, 873–885.

Gentry, W. D. (Ed.). *Handbook of Behavioral Medicine.* New York: Guilford Press, 1984.

Germain, C. B. (Ed.). *Social Work Practice: People and Environments.* New York: Columbia University Press, 1979.

Germain, C. B. *Social Work Practice in Health Care: An Ecological Perspective.* New York: Free Press, 1984.

Germain, C. B., and Gitterman, A. *The Life Model of Social Work Practice.* New York: Columbia University Press, 1980.

Germain, C. B., and Gitterman, A. "Ecological perspective." In A. Minahan et al. (Eds.). *Encyclopedia of Social Work.* 18th Ed. Silver Spring, Md.: NASW, 1987.

Gewirth, A. *Reason and Morality.* Chicago: University of Chicago Press, 1978.

Gibson, G. "Chicanos and their support systems in interaction with social institutions." In M. Bloom (Ed.). *Life Span Development.* 2nd Ed. New York: Macmillan, 1985.

Gill, D. *Violence Against Children: Physical Abuse in the United States.* Cambridge, Mass.: Harvard University Press, 1973.

Gillespie, D. F. (Ed.). "Burnout among social workers." *Journal of Social Service Research,* 1986, 10:1, entire issue 1–105.

Gilligan, C. *In a Different Voice: Psychological Theory and Women's Development.* Cambridge, Mass.: Harvard University Press, 1982.

Gilligan, C., and Attanucci, J. "Two moral orientations: Gender differences and similarities." *Merrill-Palmer Quarterly,* 1988, 34:3, 223–237.

Ginsberg, H. *Full Employment and Public Policy: The United States and Sweden.* Lexington, Mass.: Lexington Books, 1983.

Ginzberg, E. (Ed.). *Employing the Unemployed.* New York: Basic Books, 1980.

Glasser, D. *Strategic Criminal Justice Planning.* Rockville, Md.: NIMH Center for Studies in Crime and Delinquency, 1975.

Glazer, N. "Education and training programs and poverty." In S. Danziger and D. Weinberg (Eds.). *Fighting Poverty.* Cambridge, Mass.: Harvard University Press, 1986.

Gochros, H. "Sexuality." In A. Minahan et al. (Eds.). *Encyclopedia of Social Work.* 18th Ed. Silver Spring, Md.: NASW, 1987.

Gochros, H., and Fischer, J. *Planned Behavior Change: Behavior Modification in Social Work.* New York: Free Press, 1975.

Goffman, E. *Asylums: Essays on the Social Situation of Mental Patients and Other Inmates.* Garden City, N.Y.: Doubleday, 1961.

Gold, M. "Undetected delinquent behavior." *The Journal of Research in Crime and Delinquency,* 1966, January, 27–46.

Goldman, P. (with bureau reports). "The face of AIDS: One year in the epidemic." *Newsweek,* August 10, 1987, p. 22–37.

Goldstein, J., Freud, A., and Solnit, A. J. *Beyond the Best Interests of the Child.* New York: Free Press, 1973.

Goldstein, J., Freud, A., and Solnit, A. J. *Before the Best Interests of the Child.* New York: Free Press, 1979.

Gondolf, E. W. "Changing men who batter: A developmental model of integrated intervention." *Journal of Family Violence,* 1987, 2:4, 345–359.

Gonsiorek, J. C. "Results of psychological testing on homosexual populations." In W. Paul et al. (Eds.). *Homosexuality: Social, Psychological, and Biological Issues.* Beverly Hills, Calif.: Sage Publications, 1982.

Googins, B., and Godfrey, J. *Occupational Social Work.* Englewood Cliffs, N.J.: Prentice-Hall, 1987.

Gothard, S. "Juvenile justice system." In A. Minahan et al. (Eds.). *Encyclopedia of Social Work.* 18th Ed. Silver Spring, Md.: NASW, 1987.

Gottlieb, B. H. (Special Issue Editor on Social Support and Risk Reduction). *Journal of Primary Prevention,* 1982, 3:2, whole issue.

Gottman, J. M., and Leiblum, S. R. *How to Do Psychotherapy and How to Evaluate It.* New York: Holt, Rinehart and Winston, 1974.

Gould, S. J. *Mismeasure of Man.* New York: Norton, 1981.

Grannis, G. F. "Demographic perturbations secondary to cigarette smoking." *Journal of Gerontology,* 1970, 25:1, 55–63.

Gray, E. B. "Perinatal support programs: A strategy for the primary prevention of child abuse." *Journal of Primary Prevention,* 1982, 2:3, 138–152.

Green, B., Parham, I. A., Kleff, R., and Pilisuk, M. (Issue Editors). "Old age: Environmental complexity and policy intervention." *Journal of Social Issues,* 1980, 36:2, whole issue.

Green, B. L., Wilson, J. P., and Lindy, J. D. "Conceptualizing post-traumatic stress disorder: A psychosocial framework." In C. R. Figley (Ed.). *Trauma and its Wake*. New York: Brunner/Mazel, 1985.

Green, J. W. *Cultural Awareness in the Human Services*. Englewood Cliffs, N.J.: Prentice-Hall, 1982.

Green, S. *The Curious History of Contraception*. New York: St. Martin's Press, 1971.

Greene, R. R. *Social Work with the Aged and Their Families*. New York: Aldine de Gruyter, 1986.

Gregory, D. U. (Ed.). *The Nuclear Predicament: A Source Book*. New York: St. Martin's Press, 1986.

Gross, B. *Friendly Fascism*. New York: Evans, 1980. From Ginsberg, 1983.

Gross, J. "What medical care the poor can have: Lists are drawn up." *New York Times*, March 27, 1989, P.B.1, 14.

Gurman, A. S., Kniskern, D. P., and Pinsof, W. M. "Research on the process and outcome of marital and family therapy." In S. Garfield and A. Bergin (Eds.). *Handbook of Psychotherapy and Behavior Change*. 3rd Ed. New York: Wiley, 1986.

The Alan Guttmacher Institute. *Teenage Pregnancy: The Problem That Hasn't Gone Away*. New York: Guttmacher Institute, 1980.

Hackler, J. C., and Hagen, J. L. "Work and teaching machines as delinquency prevention tools: A four-year follow-up." *Social Service Review*, 1975, 49:1, 92–106.

Haley, J. *Strategies of Psychotherapy*. New York: Grune-Stratton, 1963.

Haley, S. A. "Treatment implications of post-combat stress response syndromes for mental health professionals." In C. R. Figley (Ed.). *Stress Disorders among Vietnam Veterans*. New York: Brunner/Mazel, 1978.

Handal, P. J., and Moore, C. "The influence of physical, psychosocial, and sociocultural supplies on mental health and life satisfaction: A test of Caplan's supply model." *Journal of Primary Prevention*, 1987, 7:3, 132–142.

Hanley, C., Banks, C., and Zimbardo, P. "Interpersonal dynamics in a simulated prison." *International Journal of Criminology and Penology*, 1973, 1, 69–97.

Hanlon, M. D. "Primary group assistance during unemployment." *Human Organization*, 1982, 41:2, 156–161.

Harrington, M. *The Other America: Poverty in the United States*. New York: Penguin, 1962.

Harrington, M. *The New American Poverty*. New York: Holt, Rinehart and Winston, 1984.

Harrington, M. *The Long-Distance Runner: An Autobiography*. New York: Holt, Rinehart and Winston, 1988.

Hasenfeld, Y. *Human Service Organizations*. Englewood Cliffs, N.J.: Prentice-Hall, 1983.

Hawking, S. W. *A Brief History of Time: From the Big Bang to Black Holes*. New York: Bantam, 1988.

Hawkins, G., and Zimring, F. E. (Eds.). *The Pursuit of Criminal Justice: Essays from the Chicago Center*. Chicago: University of Chicago Press, 1984.

Hawkins, J. D., and Doueck, H. J. "Juvenile offender diversion and community-based services." In A. Minahan et al. (Eds.). *Encyclopedia of Social Work*. 18th Ed. Silver Spring, Md.: NASW, 1987.

Hawkins, J. D., and Weis, J. G. "The social development model: An integrated approach to delinquency prevention." *Journal of Primary Prevention*, 1985, 6:2, 73–79.

Heber, F. R. "Sociocultural mental retardation: A longitudinal study." In D. Forgays (Ed.). *Primary Prevention of Psychopathology*. Vol II. *Environmental Influences*. Hanover, N.H.: University Press of New England, 1978.

Heclo, H. "The political foundations of antipoverty policy." In S. Danziger and D. Weinberg (Eds.). *Fighting Poverty.* Harvard, 1986.

Heffernan, J., Shuttlesworth, G., and Ambrosino, R. *Social Work and Social Welfare: An Introduction.* St. Paul, Minnesota: West Publishing Co., 1988.

Heitler, J. B. "Preparatory techniques in initiating expressive psychotherapy with lower-class, unsophisticated patients." *Psychological Bulletin,* 1976, 83:2, 339–352.

Hellenbrand, S. "Termination of direct practice." In A. Minahan et al. (Eds.). *Encyclopedia of Social Work.* 18th Ed. Silver Spring, Md.: NASW, 1987.

Heller, K., and Swindle, R. W. "Social networks, perceived social support, and coping with stress." In R. D. Felner et al. (Eds.). *Preventive Psychology: Theory, Research and Practice.* New York: Pergamon Press, 1983.

Hendrickson, P. "Mississippi's longest summer: 20 years after the civil rights murders, a town guards its memories." *Washington Post,* July 10, 1984, p. C1, C2, C3.

Hendricks, J., and Hendricks, C. D. *Aging in Mass Society: Myths and Realities.* Cambridge, Mass.: Winthrop Publishers, 1977.

Henig, R. M. "When sadness doesn't go away: New tools to fight depression in children." "Health": *Washington Post,* March 3, 1987, 12–17.

Henry, A. F., and Short, J. F. *Suicide and Homicide.* Glencoe, Ill.: Free Press, 1954.

Herzberg, F. *The Managerial Choice: To Be Efficient and To Be Humane.* 2nd ed. Salt Lake City: Olympus, 1982.

Hilbert, M. S. "Prevention." *American Journal of Public Health,* 1977, 67:4, 353–356.

Hill, C. *Subsistence U.S.A.* New York: Holt, Rinehart and Winston, 1973.

Hill, R. "Social stresses in the family." In M. Sussman (Ed.). *Sourcebook in Marriage and the Family.* Boston: Houghton-Mifflin, 1968.

Hill, R. *The Strengths of Black Families.* New York: National Urban League, 1971.

Hirsch, E. D., Jr. *Cultural Literacy: What Every American Needs to Know.* New York: Houghton-Mifflin, 1987.

Hirsch, K. "Who will save the homeless?" *The Washington Post Magazine,* Nov. 2, 1986, 18–25, 48–51.

Hofferth, S. L., and Phillips, D. A. "Child care in the United States 1970–1995." *Journal of Marriage and the Family,* 1987, 49:3, 559–571.

Hollingshead, A. B., and Redlich, F. C. *Social Class and Mental Illness.* New York: Wiley, 1958.

Holmes, T. H., and Rahe, R. H. "The social readjustment rating scale." *Journal of Psychosomatic Research,* 1967, 11, 213–218.

Hooker, E. "The adjustment of the male overt homosexual." *Journal of Projective Techniques,* 1957, 21, 18–31.

Horowitz, M. J. *Stress Response Syndromes.* New York: Jason Aronson, 1976.

Horowitz, M. J. "Psychological response to serious life events." In V. Hamilton and Warburton, D. M. (Eds.). *Human Stress and Cognition.* New York: Wiley, 1979.

Hotelling, K., and Forrest, L. "Gilligan's theory of sex-role development: A perspective for counseling." *Journal of Counseling and Development,* 1985, 64:3, 183–186.

Howard, E. R. *School Discipline Desk Book.* West Nyack, New York: Parker Publishing Company, 1978.

Howard, M. "Postponing sexual involvement among adolescents: An alternative approach to prevention of sexually transmitted diseases." *Journal of Adolescent Health Care,* 1985, 6, 271–277.

Hraba, J. *American Ethnicity.* Itasca, Ill.: Peacock, 1979.

Hull, J. G., Van Treuren, R. R., and Virnelli, S. "Hardiness and health: A critique and alternative approach." *Journal of Personality and Social Psychology,* 1987, 53:3, 518–530.

Hunt, M. *The Mugging.* New York: Atheneum, 1972.

Hunt, McV. J. "Plasticity in the rates of achieving cognitive and motivational landmarks." In D. Forgays (Ed.). *Primary Prevention of Psychopathology.* Vol II. Environmental Influences. Hanover, N.H.: University Press of New England, 1978.

Hurley, R. *Poverty and Mental Retardation: A Causal Relationship.* New York: Vintage Books, 1969.

Hutchinson, W., Searight, P., and Stretch, J. J. "Multidimensional networking: A response to the needs of homeless families." *Social Work,* 1986, 31:6, 427–431.

Ibsen, H. *Enemy of the People.* In B. Cerf and D. Klopfer (Eds.). *Eleven Plays of Ibsen.* New York: Modern Library, 1935.

Irons, P. *Justice at War: The Story of the Japanese American Internment Cases.* New York: Oxford University Press, 1983.

Ishisaka, H., et al. "Family structure and marital treatment." Discussed in J. W. Green (Ed.). *Cultural Awareness in Human Services.* Englewood Cliffs, N.J.: Prentice-Hall, 1982.

Ivanoff, A. M. "Suicide." In A. Minahan et al. (Eds.). *Encyclopedia of Social Work.* 18th Ed. Silver Spring, Md.: NASW, 1987.

Ivey, A. E., and Authier, J. *Microcounseling: Innovations in Interviewing, Counseling, Psychotherapy, and Psychoeducation.* 2nd Ed. Springfield, Ill.: Charles C. Thomas, 1978.

Jackson, J. S., Tucker, M. B., and Bowman, P. J. "Conceptual and methodological problems in survey research on black Americans." In W. T. Lie (Ed.). *Methodological Problems in Minority Research.* Occasional Paper No. 7. The Pacific/Asian American Mental Health Research Center, 1982.

Jansen, G. *The Doctor-Patient Relationship in an African Tribal Society.* Assen, the Netherlands: Van Gorcum & Company, B. V., 1973.

Janson, L. A., Hess, R. E., Felner, R. D., and Moritsugu, J. N. (Eds.). "Prevention: Toward a multidisciplinary approach." *Prevention in Human Services,* 1987, 5:2, whole issue.

Jason, L. A., La Pointe, A., and Billingham, S. "The media and self-help: A preventive community intervention." *Journal of Primary Prevention,* 1986, 6:3, 156–167.

Jayaratne, S. "Child abusers as parents and children: A review." *Social Work,* 1977, 22:1, 5–9.

Johnson, G., Bird, T., and Little, J. W. *Delinquency Prevention: Theories and Strategies.* Washington, D.C.: U.S. Department of Justice, 1979.

Johnson, L. B. *Public Papers of the President, 1963–1964.* Vol. 2. Washington, D.C.: U.S. Government Printing Office, 1972.

Johnson, L. C., and Schwartz, C. L. *Social Welfare: A Response to Human Need.* Boston: Allyn and Bacon, Inc., 1988.

Jones, E., and Prescott, E. "Day care: Short- or long-term solution?" *The Annals of the American Academy of Political and Social Science,* AAPSS, 1982 (May), 461, 91–101.

Jones, L. R. W. "Unemployment compensation and workers' compensation programs." In A. Minahan et al. (Eds.). *Encyclopedia of Social Work.* 18th Ed. Silver Spring, Md.: NASW, 1987.

Jordon, M. "Help from closer to home: Local nonprofit groups expand role." *Washington Post,* 1987, March 30, pp. A1, A6, A7.

Kadushin, A. "Child welfare strategy in the coming years: An overview." *Child Welfare Strategy in the Coming Years.* Washington, D.C.: DHEW, 1978.

Kadushin, A. *Child Welfare Services.* 3rd Ed. New York: Macmillan, 1980.

Kadushin, A. "Child welfare services." In A. Minahan et al. (Eds.). *Encyclopedia of Social Work.* 18th Ed. Silver Spring, Md.: NASW, 1987.

Kahn, A. J. "New policies and service models: The next phase." *American Journal of Orthopsychiatry,* 1965, 35:4, 652–662.

Kahn, A. J., and Kamerman, S. B. *Child-Care in Nine Countries: A Report Prepared for the OECD Working Party on the Role of Women in the Economy.* Washington, D.C.: DHEW Publication No. (OHD) 76–30080, 1976.

Kahn, A. J., and Kamerman, S. B. *Not for the Poor Alone: European Social Services.* New York: Harper Colophon Books, 1977.

Kahn, A. J., and Kamerman, S. B. *Helping America's Families.* New York: Temple University Press, 1982.

Kahn, A. J., and Kamerman, S. B. *Child Care: Facing the Hard Choices.* Dover, Mass.: Auburn House Publishing Company, 1987.

Kalven, H., and Zeisel, H. *The American Jury.* Boston: Little, Brown, 1966.

Kamerman, S. B., and Kahn, A. J. (Eds.). *Family Policy: Government and Family in Fourteen Countries.* New York: Columbia University Press, 1978.

Kanfer, F. H., and Phillips, S. *Learning Foundations of Behavior Therapy.* New York: Wiley, 1970.

Karlen, N., Agrest, S., Robins, K., and Greenberg, K. F. "Homeless kids: 'Forgotten faces'." *Newsweek,* January 6, 1986, 20.

Karoly, P. (Ed.). *Measurement Strategies in Health Psychology.* New York: Wiley, 1985.

Kasl, S. V., Gore, S., and Cobb, S. "The experience of losing a job: Reported changes in health, symptoms, and illness behavior." *Psychosomatic Medicine,* 1975, 37, 106–122.

Kastenbaum, R. J. *Death, Society, and Human Experience.* 3rd Ed. Columbus, Ohio: Charles E. Merrill Publishing Co., 1986.

Katz, J. (Ed.). *Gay American History: Lesbians and Gays in the U.S.A.* New York: Thomas Y. Crowell, 1976.

Keane, T. M., Fairbank, J. A., Caddell, J. M., Zimering, R. T., and Bender, M. E. "A behavioral approach to assessing and treating post-traumatic stress disorder in Vietnam veterans." In C. R. Figley (Ed.). *Trauma and its Wake.* New York: Brunner/Mazel, 1985.

Keeney, B. P. and Sprenkle, D. H. "Ecosystemic epistemology: Critical implications for the aesthetics and pragmatics of family therapy." *Family Process,* 1982, 211:1, 1–19.

Keller, E. F. *A Feeling for the Organism: The Life and Work of Barbara McClintuck.* New York: Freeman, 1983.

Kessler, R. C., and Cleary, P. D. "Social class and psychological distress." *American Sociological Review,* 1980, 45, 465–478.

Kinard, E. M. "Child abuse and neglect." In A. Minahan et al. (Eds.). *Encyclopedia of Social Work.* 18th Ed. Silver Spring, Md.: NASW, 1987.

Kinsey, A. C. and others. *Sexual Behavior in the Human Male.* Philadelphia: W. B. Saunders, 1948.

Kinsey, A. C., and others. *Sexual Behavior in the Human Female.* Philadelphia: W. B. Saunders, 1953.

Klein, N. C., Alexander, J. F., and Parsons, B. V. "Impact of family systems intervention on recidivism and sibling delinquency: A model of primary prevention and program evaluation." *Journal of Consulting and Clinical Psychology,* 1977, 45:3, 469–474.

Kleinman, A. "Clinical relevance of anthropological and cross-cultural research: Concepts and strategies." *American Journal of Psychiatry,* 1978, 135:4, 427–431.

Klerman, G. L. (Ed.). *Suicide and Depression among Adolescents and Young Adults.* Washington, D.C.: American Psychiatric Press, 1986.

Kluckhohn, C., and Murray, H. A. *Personality in Nature, Society, and Culture.* New York: Knopf, 1953.

Kobasa, S. C., Maddi, S. R., and Kahn, S. "Hardiness and health: A prospective study." *Journal of Personality and Social Psychology,* 1982, 42, 168–177.

Kohlberg, L. *The Psychology of Moral Development.* New York: Harper and Row, 1983.

Konle, C. *Social Work Day-to-Day, The Experience of Generalist Social Work Practice.* New York: Longman, 1982.

Kosterlitz, J. "Educating about AIDS." *National Journal,* 118/30, 1986, 2044–2049.

Kreipe, R. E., and McAnarney, E. R. "Psychosocial aspects of adolescent medicine." *Seminars in Adolescent Medicine,* 1985, 1:1, 33–45.

Kristal, A. "The impact of the acquired immunodeficiency syndrome on patterns of premature death in New York City." *Journal of the American Medical Association,* 1986 (May 2), 255, 2306–2310.

Kroeber, A. L., and Kluckhohn, C. *Culture: A Critical Review of Concepts and Definitions.* Anthropological Papers, Peabody Museum, 1952, 47.

Kuhn, T. S. *The Structure of Scientific Revolutions.* 2nd Ed. Chicago: University of Chicago Press, 1970.

Kurtz, H. "New York child died because system failed." *Washington Post,* Nov. 7, 1987, pp. A1, A7.

Lamberts, M. B., Cudaback, D. J., and Claesgens, M. A. "Helping teenage parents: Use of age-paced parent education newsletter." *Journal of Primary Prevention,* 1985, 5:3, 188–199.

Land, H., Nishimoto, R., and Chau, K. "Interventive and preventive services for Vietnamese Chinese refugees." *Social Service Review,* 1988, 62:3, 468–484.

Lane, T. W., Lane, M. Z., Friedman, B. S., Goetz, E. M., and Pinkston, E. M. "A creativity enhancement program for preschool children in an inner city child-parent center." In E. M. Pinkston et al. (Eds.). *Effective Social Work Practices: Advanced Techniques for Behavioral Intervention with Individuals, Families, and Institutional Staff.* San Francisco: Jossey-Bass, 1982.

Langone, J. "Discover AIDS." *Discover,* 1985 (December).

Larwood, L., and Gutek, B. A. "Women at work in the USA." In M. Davidson and C. Cooper (Eds.). *Working Women: An International Survey.* New York: Wiley, 1984.

Lawton, M. J. "Chemical dependency counseling." In D. Myers (Ed.). *Employee Problem Prevention and Counseling.* Westport, Conn.: Quorum Books, 1985.

Lazar, I. "Early intervention is effective." *Educational Leadership,* 1981, 38, 303–305.

Leacock, E. B. *The Culture of Poverty: A Critique.* New York: Simon and Schuster, 1971.

Lebacqz, K. *Six Theories of Justice: Perspectives from Philosophical and Theological Ethics.* Minneapolis: Augsburg Publishing House, 1986.

Leigh, J. W., and Green, J. W. "The structure of the black community: The knowledge base for social services." In J. W. Green (Ed.). *Cultural Awareness in the Human Services.* Englewood Cliffs, N.J.: Prentice-Hall, 1982.

Leinen, S. *Black Police, White Society.* New York: New York University Press, 1984.

Lens, S. *Poverty: America's Enduring Paradox: A History of the Richest Nation's Unwon War.* New York: Crowell, 1971.

Lerman, P. *Deinstitutionalization and the Welfare State.* New Brunswick, N.J.: Rutgers University Press, 1982.

Lerner, G. *Black Woman in White America.* New York: Vintage, 1972.

Levenstein, P. "Cognitive growth in preschoolers through verbal interaction with mothers." *American Journal of Orthopsychiatry,* 1970, 40, 426–432.

Lewin, K. *Field Theory in Social Science: Selected Theoretical Papers.* Edited by D. Cartwright. New York: Harper and Row, 1951.

Lewis, O. "The culture of poverty." In D. Moynihan (Ed.). *On Understanding Poverty.* New York: Basic Books, 1969.

Libassi, M. F., and Maluccio, A. N. "Competence-centered social work: Prevention in action." *Journal of Primary Prevention*, 1986, 6:3, 168–180.

Liebert, R. M., and Schwartzberg, N. S. "Effects of mass media." In M. R. Rosenzweig and L. W. Porter (Eds.). *Annual Review of Psychology.* Vol 28. Palo Alto, Calif.: Annual Reviews, 1977.

Lifton, R. J. "Advocacy and corruption in the healing process." In C. R. Figley (Ed.). *Stress Disorders among Vietnam Veterans.* New York: Brunner/Mazel, 1978.

Light, R. J. "Abused and neglected children in America: A study of alternative policies." *Harvard Educational Review*, 1973, 43:4, 556–598.

Likert, R. *New Patterns of Management.* New York: McGraw-Hill, 1961.

Lin-Fu, J. S. "Lead poisoning in children: An eradicable disease." *Children*, 1970, 17:1, 2–9.

Longres, J. F. "Juvenile offenders and delinquency." In A. Minahan et al. (Eds.). *Encyclopedia of Social Work.* 18th Ed. Silver Spring, Md.: NASW, 1987.

Lugo, J. O., and Hersey, G. L. *Human Development: A Psychological, Biological, and Sociological Approach to the Life Span.* 2nd Ed. New York: Macmillan, 1979.

Lum, D. *Social Work Practice and People of Color: A Process-Stage Approach.* Monterey, Calif.: Brooks/Cole, 1986.

Lum, D. "Health Service System." In A. Minahan et al. (Eds.). *Encyclopedia of Social Work.* 18th Ed. Silver Spring, Md.: NASW, 1987.

Maddi, S. R. *Personality Theories: A Comparative Analysis.* 4th Ed. Homewood, Ill.: Dorsey Press, 1980.

Maidman, F. (Ed.). *Child Welfare: A Source Book of Knowledge and Practice.* New York: Child Welfare League of America, 1984.

Maldonado, D., Jr. "Aged." In A. Minahan et al. (Eds.). *Encyclopedia of Social Work.* 18th Ed. Silver Spring, Md.: NASW, 1987.

Maluccio, A. N. *Promoting Competence in Clients: A New/Old Approach to Social Work Practice.* New York: Macmillan, 1981.

Mantell, J. E., Schinke, S. P., and Akabas, S. H. "Women and AIDS prevention." *Journal of Primary Prevention*, 1988, 9:1 & 2, 18–40.

Marcus, L. J. "Health Care Financing." In A. Minahan et al. (Eds.). *Encyclopedia of Social Work.* 18th Ed. Silver Spring, Md.: NASW, 1987.

Markides, K. S., and McFarland, C. "A note on recent trends in the infant mortality–socioeconomic status relationship." *Social Forces*, 1982, 61, 286–96.

Marsiglio, W. "Adolescent fathers in the United States: Their initial living 0arrangements, marital experiences and educational outcomes." *Family Planning Perspectives*, 1987, 19:6, 240–251.

Martin, E. P., and Martin, J. M. *The Black Extended Family.* Chicago: University of Chicago Press, 1978.

Masi, D. A. *Human Services in Industry.* Lexington, Mass.: Lexington Books, 1982.

Masi, D. A. *Designing Employee Assistance Programs.* New York: American Management Associations, 1984.

Masters, W. H., and Johnson, V. E. *Human Sexual Response.* Boston: Little, Brown, 1966.

Masters, W. H., and Johnson, V. E. *Human Sexual Inadequacy.* Boston: Little, Brown, 1970.

Mathews, M. A. *The Social Work Mystique: Toward a Sociology of Social Work.* Washington, D.C.: University Press of America, 1981.

Mayer, J. E., and Timms, N. *The Client Speaks.* London: Routledge, 1970.

McAnarney, E. R., and Schreider, C. *Identifying Social and Psychological Antecedents of Adolescent Pregnancy: The Contribution of Research to Concepts of Prevention.* New York: William T. Grant Foundation, 1984.

McCartney, K., Scarr, S., Phillips, D., Grajek, S., and Schwarz, J. C. "Environmental differences among day care centers and their effects on children's development." In E. Zigler and E. Gordon (Eds.). *Day Care: Scientific and Social Policy Issues*. Boston: Auburn House Publishing Co, 1982.

McGovern, C. *Masters of Madness: Social Origins of the American Psychiatric Profession*. Hanover, N.H.: University Press of New England, 1985.

McGowan, B. G., and Meezan, W. *Child Welfare: Current Dilemmas. Future Directions*. Itasca, Ill.: Peacock, 1983.

Meador, B. D., and Rogers, C. R. "Person-centered therapy." In R. J. Corsini (Ed.). *Current Psychotherapies*. 3rd Ed. Itasca, Ill.: Peacock, 1984.

Mechanic, D. *Mental Health and Social Policy*. 3rd Ed. Englewood Cliffs, N.J.: Prentice-Hall, 1986.

Mechanic, D. *From Advocacy to Allocation: The Evolving American Health Care System*. New York: Free Press, 1988.

Meichenbaum, D. *Cognitive-Behavioral Modification: An Integrative Approach*. New York: Plenum, 1977.

Menninger, K. *Man Against Himself*. New York: Harcourt, Brace, 1938.

Mercer, J. R. *Labeling the Mentally Retarded: Clinical and Social System Perspectives on Mental Retardation*. Berkeley, Ca.: University of California Press, 1973.

Middleman, R. R., and Goldberg, G. *Social Service Delivery: A Structural Approach to Social Work Practice*. New York: Columbia University Press, 1974.

Miller, A. *The Crucible*. New York: Viking, 1953.

Miller, A. *Death of a Salesman*. Text and Criticism, edited by G. Weales. New York: Viking Press, 1949/1967.

Miller, L. M. "Teen advocate program." *The Journal of School Health*, 1982 (December), 605–607.

Miller, N. B. "Social work services to urban Indians." In J. W. Green (Ed.). *Cultural Awareness in Human Services*. Englewood Cliffs, N.J.: Prentice-Hall, 1982.

Miller, S. O., O'Neal, G. S., and Scott, C. A. *Primary Prevention Approaches to the Development of Mental Health Services for Ethnic Minorities: A Challenge to Social Work Education and Practice*. New York: CSWE, 1982.

Millett, K. *Sexual Politics*. New York: Doubleday, 1970.

Minuchin, S. *Family Kaleidoscope*. Cambridge, Mass.: Harvard University Press, 1974.

Montague, A. *The Nature of Human Aggression*. New York: Oxford University Press, 1976.

Moore, E. "Day care: A black perspective." In E. Zigler and E. Gordon (Eds.). *Day Care: Scientific and Social Policy Issues*. Boston: Auburn House Publishing Co, 1982.

Moore, P. S. *Useful Information on Suicide*. U.S. Department of Health and Human Services. Publication No. (ADM) 86–1489, 1986.

Moore, T. W. "Prophylaxis as facilitation: Some implications of a longitudinal psychodevelopmental research." *Journal of Preventive Psychiatry*, 1981, 1:2, 189–205.

Moos, R. H., and Fuhr, R. "The clinical use of social-ecological concepts: The case of an adolescent girl." *American Journal of Orthopsychiatry*, 1982, 52:1, 111–122.

Moos, R. H., and Insel, P. M. (Eds.). *Issues in Social Ecology: Human Milieus*. Palo Alto, Calif.: National Press Books, 1974.

Mora G. "On the 400th anniversary of Johann Weyer's 'De Praestigiis Daemonum'— Its significance for today's psychiatry." *American Journal of Psychiatry*, 1963, 120:5, 417–428.

Morganthau, T., Agrest, S., Greenberg, N. F., Doherty, S., and Raine, G. "Abandoned." *Newsweek*, January 6, 1986, 14–19.

Moynihan, D. P. *The Negro Family: A Case for National Action*. Washington, D.C.: U.S. Department of Labor, Office of Policy, Planning and Research, 1965.

Moynihan, D. P. (Ed.). *On Understanding Poverty: Perspective from the Social Sciences.* New York: Basic Books, 1968.

Moynihan, D. P. *Family and Nation.* San Diego: Harcourt Brace Jovanovich Publishers, 1986.

Muller, H. J. *The Uses of the Past: Profiles of Former Societies.* New York: Mentor Books, 1952.

Mullin, S. P., and Summers, A. A. "Is more better? The effectiveness of spending on compensatory education." *Phi Delta Kappan,* 1983, 64, 339–347.

Murray, C. *Losing Ground: American Social Policy, 1959–1980.* New York: Basic Books, 1984.

Mussen, P., and Eisenberg-Berg, N. *Roots of Caring, Sharing, and Helping: The Development of Prosocial Behavior in Children.* San Francisco: Freeman, 1977.

Myers, D. W. (Ed.). *Employee Problem Prevention and Counseling: A Guide for Professionals.* Westport, Conn.: Quorum Books, 1985.

Myers, D. W., and Reynolds, R. P. "Leisure lifestyle development." In D. Myers (Ed.). *Employee Problem Prevention and Counseling.* Westport, Conn.: Quorum Books, 1985.

Naditch, M. P. "Industry-based wellness programs." In D. Myers (Ed.). *Employee Problem Prevention and Counseling.* Westport, Conn.: Quorum Books, 1985.

Nadler, S. *Good Girls Gone Bad: American Women in Crime.* New York: Freundlich Books, 1987.

National Center on Child Abuse and Neglect. *Study Findings: National Study of the Incidence and Severity of Child Abuse and Neglect.* Department of Health and Human Services. No. 81–30325. Washington, D.C.: DHHS, 1981.

Nelson, J. R., Jr. "The politics of federal day care regulations." In E. Zigler and E. Gordon (Eds.). *Day Care: Scientific and Policy Issues.* Boston: Auburn House Publishing Co., 1982.

Netherland, W. "Corrections system: Adult." In A. Minahan et al. (Eds.). *Encyclopedia of Social Work.* 18th Ed. Silver Spring, Md.: NASW, 1987.

Newsweek, August 10, 1987 (on AIDS).

Nielsen, M., Blenkner, M., Bloom, M., Downs, T., and Beggs, H. "Older persons after hospitalization: A controlled study of home aide services." *American Journal of Public Health,* 1972, 62:8, 1094–1101.

Nikelly, A. G. "Prevention in Sweden and Cuba: Implications for policy research." *Journal of Primary Prevention,* 1987, 7:3, 117–131.

Northern, H. *Social Work with Groups.* New York: Columbia University Press, 1969.

Nozick, R. *Anarchy, State, and Utopia.* New York: Basic Books, 1974.

O'Donnell, M. P., and Ainsworth, T. H. (Eds.). *Health Promotion in the Workplace.* New York: Wiley, 1984.

Okie, S. "Smoking's contribution of U.S. deaths." *Washington Post,* 1987, Oct. 30, p. A23.

Oldenburg, D. "Born to run." *Washington Post Magazine.* May 15, 1988, 20–28.

O'Neill, C. "No tomorrow: Teen suicide in America." "Health": *Washington Post,* April 23, 1986, 12–15.

O'Reilly, K. R., and Aral, S. O. "Adolescence and sexual behavior. Trends and implications for STD." *Journal of Adolescent Health Care,* 1985, 6: 262–270.

Orme, J. G., and Stuart, P. "The habit clinics: Behavioral social work and prevention in the 1920s." *Social Service Review,* 1981, 55:242–255.

Osborn, A. F. *Applied Imagination.* New York: Scribner, 1957.

Ostrow, D. G. "Barriers to the recognition of links between drugs and alcohol abuse and AIDS." In *Acquired Immune Deficiency Syndrome and Chemical Dependency.* DHHS Publication No. (ADM) 87–1513. 1987.

Our Bodies, Ourselves. The Boston Women's Health Book Collective, 1979.

Oxley, G. B. "Promoting competence in involuntary clients." In Anthony N. Maluccio (Ed.). *Promoting Competence in Clients: A New/Old Approach to Social Work Practice.* New York: Free Press, 1981.

Ozawa, M. "Development of social services in industry: Why and how?" *Social Work,* 1980, 25:6, 464–470.

Ozawa, M. "The nation's children: Key to a secure retirement." *New England Journal of Human Services,* 1986, 6:3, 12–19.

Paglin, M. *Poverty and Transfer In-Kind.* Stanford, Calif.: Hoover Institution Press, 1980.

Palmore, E. B., and Manton, K. "Ageism compared to racism and sexism." *Journal of Gerontology,* 1973, 28:3, 363–369.

Papachristou, J. *Women Together: A History in Documents of the Women's Movement in the United States.* New York: Knopf, 1976.

Pappenfort, D. M., and Young, T. M. "Uses of Secure Detention for Juveniles, and Alternatives to Its Use." *National Study of Juvenile Detention.* Washington, D.C.: U.S. Department of Justice, 1980.

Parson, E. R. "Ethnicity and traumatic stress: The intersecting point in psychotherapy." In C. R. Figley (Ed.). *Trauma and Its Wake.* New York: Brunner/Mazel, 1985.

Patrick, L. F., and Minish, P. A. "Child-rearing strategies for the development of altruistic behavior in young children." *Journal of Primary Prevention,* 1985, 5:3, 154–168.

Perez, V., Gesten, E. L., Cowen, E. L., Weissberg, R. P., Rapkin, B., and Boike, M. "Relationship between family background problems and social problem solving skills of young normal children." *Journal of Primary Prevention,* 1981, 2:2, 80–90.

Perry, S. W., and Markowitz, J. "Psychiatric interventions for AIDS-spectrum disorders." *Hospital and Community Psychiatry,* 1986, 37:10, 1001–1006.

Pestrak, V. A., and Martin, D. "Cognitive development and aspects of adolescent sexuality." *Adolescence,* 1985, XX:80, 981–987.

Philip, C. O. (Ed.). *Imprisoned in America: Prison Communications: 1776 to Attica.* New York: Harper and Row, 1973.

Physician Task Force on Hunger in America. *Hunger in America: The Growing Epidemic.* Middletown, Conn.: Wesleyan University Press, 1985.

Pilalis, J., and Anderson, J. "Feminist theory and family therapy: A possible meeting point." *Journal of Family Therapy,* 1986, 8:2, 99–114.

Pilisuk, M., and Parks, S. H. *The Healing Web: Social Networks and Human Survival.* Hanover, N.H.: University Press of New England, 1986.

Pilisuk, M., Parks, S. H., Kelly, J., and Turner, E. "The helping network approach: Community promotion of mental health." *Journal of Primary Prevention,* 1982, 3:2, 116–132.

Piven, F. F., and Cloward, R. *Regulating the Poor: The Functions of Public Welfare.* New York: Vintage Books, 1971.

Plato. *Complete Works of Plato* (Jowett translation). New York: Tudor Publishing, 1965.

Population in the United States, 1987. U.S. Department of Commerce, Current Population Report, Consumer Income, Series P-60, #163, 1989.

Porter, R. "Ecological strategies of prevention in rural community development." *Journal of Primary Prevention,* 1983, 3:4, 235–243.

The President's Commission on Mental Health. *Report to the President from the President's Commission on Mental Health.* Washington, D.C.: Government Printing Office, 1978.

"A Profile of Older Americans, 1987." Brochure developed by the American Association of Retired Persons.

Pumphrey, R., and Pumphrey, M. (Eds.). *The Heritage of American Social Work.* New York: Columbia University Press, 1961.

Quick, J. D., Kertesz, J. W., Nelson, D. L., and Quick, J. C. "Preventive management of stress." In D. Myers (Ed.). *Employee Problem Prevention and Counseling.* Westport, Conn.: Quorum Books, 1985.

Rabin, J. A. "The AIDS epidemic and gay bathhouses: A constitutional analysis." *Journal of Health Politics, Policy and Law,* 1986, Winter, 10:4m, 729–748.

Ramey, C. T., MacPhee, D., and Yeates, K. O. "Preventing developmental retardation: A general systems approach." In L. Bond and J. Joffe (Eds.). *Facilitating Infant and Early Childhood Development.* Hanover, N.H.: University Press of New England, 1982.

Rampersad, A. *The Life of Langston Hughes.* Vol. I. 1902–1941. I, Too, Sing America. New York: Oxford, 1986.

Rampersad, A. *The Life of Langston Hughes.* Vol. II. 1941–1967. I Dream a World. New York: Oxford, 1988.

Rasnic, C. D. "Counseling employees with legal problems." In D. Myers (Ed.). *Employee Problem Prevention and Counseling.* Westport, Conn.: Quorum Books, 1985.

Rawls, J. *A Theory of Justice.* Cambridge, Mass.: Belknap Press of Harvard University Press, 1971.

Reamer, F. G. *Ethical Dilemmas in Social Services.* New York: Columbia University Press, 1982.

Reid, W. J. *Family Problem Solving.* New York: Columbia University Press, 1985.

Reid, W. J., and Epstein, L. *Task-Centered Casework.* New York: Columbia University Press, 1972.

Rensberger, B. "All family trees lead to 'Eve,' an African, scientists conclude." *Washington Post,* January 13, 1987, p. A3.

Rescorla, L. A., Provence, S., and Naylor, A. "The Yale Child Welfare Program: Description and results." In E. Zigler and E. Gordon (Eds.). *Day Care: Scientific and Social Policy Issues.* Boston: Auburn House Publishing Co., 1982.

Richardson, B. L., and Kaufman, D. R. "Social science inquiries into female achievement: Recurrent methodological problems." In B. Richardson and J. Wirtenberg (Eds.). *Sex Role Research: Measuring Social Change.* New York: Praeger Publishers, 1983.

Richmond, J. B., and Janis, J. M. "Health care services for children in day care programs." In E. Zigler and E. Gordon (Eds.). *Day Care: Scientific and Social Policy Issues.* Boston: Auburn House Publishing Co., 1982.

Richmond, J., Zigler, E., and Stipek, D. "Head Start: The first decade." In M. Bloom (Ed.). *Life Span Development: Bases of Preventive and Interventive Helping.* New York: Macmillan, 1980.

Riessman, F. "The "helper" therapy principle." *Social Work,* 1965, 10:2, 27–32.

Ringenback, P. T. *Tramps and Reformers 1873–1916: The Discovery of Unemployment in New York.* Westport, Conn.: Greenwood Press, 1973.

Robinson, B. *Teenage Fathers.* Lexington, Mass.: Lexington Books, 1988.

Roethlisberger, F. J., and Dickson, W. J. *Management and the Worker.* Cambridge: Harvard University Press, 1939.

Rogers, C. R. "A theory of therapy, personality, and interpersonal relationships as developed in the client-centered framework." In S. Koch (Ed.). *Psychology: A Study of Science.* New York: McGraw Hill, 1959, 184–256.

Roman, P. M., and Trice, H. "Alcohol abuse and work organization." In B. Kissin and H. Begleiter (Eds.). *The Biology of Alcoholism.* New York: Plenum, 1976.

Romig, D. A. *Justice for Our Children.* Lexington, Mass.: Lexington Books, 1978.

Roosens, E. *Mental Patients in Town Life: Geel, Europe's First Therapeutic Community.* Beverly Hills, Calif.: Sage, 1979.

Rose, S. D. *Treating Children in Groups: A Behavioral Approach.* San Francisco: Jossey-Bass, 1972.

Rosen, G. *Preventive Medicine in the United States 1900–1975: Trends and Interpretations.* New York: Science History Publications, 1975.

Rosen, S. M., Fanshel, D., and Lutz, M. *Face of the Nation.* Vol. III of the *Encyclopedia of Social Work,* 18th Ed. Silver Spring, Md.: NASW, 1987.

Rosenberg, R. *Beyond Separate Spheres: Intellectual Roots of Modern Feminism.* New Haven: Yale, 1982.

Rosenfeld, A., Caplan, G., Yaroslavsky, A., Jacobowitz, J., Yuval, Y., and LeBow, H. "Adaptation of children of parents suffering from cancer: A preliminary study of a new field for primary prevention research." *Journal of Primary Prevention,* 1983, 3:4, 244–250.

Rothman, J. "Three models of community organization practice." In F. M. Cox et al. (Eds.). *Strategies of Community Organization.* 3rd Ed. Itasca, Ill.: Peacock, 1979.

Rowland, J. *The Ultimate Violation.* Garden City, New York: Doubleday, 1985.

Ruopp, R. R., and Travers, J. "Janus faces day care: Perspectives on quality and cost." In E. Zigler and E. Gordon (Eds.). *Day Care: Scientific and Social Policy Issues.* Boston: Auburn House Publishing Co., 1982.

Russell, A. B., and Trainor, C. M. *Trends in Child Abuse and Neglect: A National Perspective.* Denver: American Humane Association, 1984.

Russell, G. "Spectator moods at an aggressive sports event." *Journal of Social Psychology,* 1981, 3, 217–227.

Russell, L. B. *Is Prevention Better than Cure?* Washington, D.C.: The Brookings Institution, 1986.

Rutter, M. "Socio-emotional consequences of day care for preschool children." In E. Zigler and E. Gordon (Eds.). *Day Care: Scientific and Social Policy Issues.* Boston: Auburn House Publishing Co., 1982.

Ryan, W. *Blaming the Victim.* Rev. Ed. New York: Vintage, 1976.

Ryan, W. *Equality.* New York: Pantheon, 1981.

Sagan, C. "Nuclear winter." *Parade Magazine,* October 30, 1983, 4–7.

Sanger, M. *An Autobiography.* New York: Dover Publishers, 1971.

Satir, V. *Conjoint Family Therapy: A Guide to Therapy and Technique.* Palo Alto, Calif.: Science and Behavior Books, 1964.

Scales, P., and Kirby, D. "A review of exemplary sex education programs for teenagers offered by nonschool organizations." *Family Relations,* 1981, 30, 238–245.

Scanlon, W. E. *Alcoholism and Drug Abuse in the Workplace: Employee Assistance Programs.* New York: Praeger, 1986.

Scheingold, S. A. *The Politics of Law and Order: Street Crime and Public Policy.* New York: Longman, 1984.

Schell, J. *The Fate of the Earth.* New York: Knopf, 1982.

Schinke, S. P., and Gilchrist, L. *Life Skills Counseling with Adolescents.* Baltimore: University Park Press, 1984.

Schinke, S. P., Gilchrist, L. D., and Small, R. W. "Preventing unwanted adolescent pregnancy: A cognitive-behavioral approach." *American Journal of Orthopsychiatry,* 1979, 49:1, 81–88.

Schlesinger, A. M., Jr. (Ed.). *The Almanac of American History.* New York: Bramhall House, 1983.

Schultz, J. L. *White Medicine, Indian Lives . . . As Long As the Grass Shall Grow . . .* Department of Anthropology, Colorado State University, n.d.

Schultz, L. G. "Victimization programs and victims of crime." In A. Minahan et al. (Eds.). *Encyclopedia of Social Work.* 18th Ed. Silver Spring, Md.: NASW, 1987.

Scurfield, R. M. "Post-trauma stress assessment and treatment: Overview and formulations." In C. R. Figley (Ed.). *Trauma and Its Wake.* New York: Brunner/Mazel, 1985.

Searight, H. R., and Handal, P. J. "Premature birth and its later effects: Towards preventive intervention." *Journal of Primary Prevention*, 1986, 7:1, 3–16.

Seligman, M. E. P. *Helplessness: On Depression, Development, and Death*. San Francisco: Freeman, 1975.

Seyle, H. *The Stress of Life*. New York: McGraw-Hill, 1956.

Shaffer, P. *Equus, a Play*. London: Deutsch, 1973.

Shain, M., and Groeneveld, J. *Employee-Assistance Programs: Philosophy, Theory, and Practice*. Lexington, Mass.: Lexington Books, 1980.

Shain, M., Suurvali, H., and Boutilier, M. *Healthier Workers: Health Promotion and Employee Assistance Programs*. Lexington, Mass.: Lexington Books, 1986.

Shakespeare, W. *Hamlet, Prince of Denmark* (Edited by P. Edwards). Cambridge: Cambridge University Press, 1985.

Shatan, C. F. "Stress disorders among Vietnam veterans: The emotional content of combat continues." In C. R. Figley (Ed.). *Stress Disorders among Vietnam Veterans*. New York: Brunner/Mazel, 1978.

Shaw, M. E. *Group Dynamics: The Psychology of Small Group Behavior*. New York: McGraw Hill, 1981.

Shelter Management Handbook, 1984. Quoted in D.U. Gregory (Ed.). *The Nuclear Predicament: A Source Book*. New York: St. Martin's Press, 1986.

Sherman, M., and Hawkins, G. *Imprisonment in America: Choosing the Future*. Chicago: University of Chicago Press, 1981.

Shibano, M., Cox, W. H., Rzepnicki, T. L., and Pinkston, E. M. "A single-parent intervention to increase parenting skills over time." In E. M. Pinkston et al. (Eds.). *Effective Social Work Practice*. San Francisco: Jossey-Bass, 1982.

Showalter, E. *The Female Malady: Women, Madness, and English Culture, 1830–1980*. New York: Pantheon Books, 1985.

Shneidman, E., Faberow, N., and Litman, R. *The Psychology of Suicide*. New York: Aronson, 1983.

Siefert, K. "Nuclear war and disarmament." In A. Minahan et al. (Eds.). *Encyclopedia of Social Work*. 18th Ed. Silver Spring, Md.: NASW, 1987.

Siegel, J. M. "A brief review of the effects of race in clinical service intervention." *American Journal of Orthopsychiatry*, 1974, 44:4, 555–562.

Sigerist, H. E. *Landmarks in the History of Hygiene*. London: Oxford, 1956.

Silberman, C. E. *Criminal Violence, Criminal Justice*. New York: Random House, 1978.

Simmel, G. *The Sociology of Georg Simmel*. Translated and edited by K. H. Wolff. New York: Free Press, 1950.

Simon, B. L. "The feminization of poverty: A call for primary prevention." *Journal of Primary Prevention*, 1988, 9:1 and 2, 6–17.

Simonsen, C. E., and Gordon, M. S. *Juvenile Justice in America*. 2nd ed. New York: Macmillan, 1982.

Sinzinger, K. "Giving whistle-blowers a champion." *Washington Post*, September 18, 1986, p. A 23.

Sivard, R. L. *World Military and Social Expenditures 1983*. World Priorities, Box 25140, Washington, D.C. 1983.

Skidmore, R. A., Balsam, D., and Jones, O. F. "Social work practice in industry." *Social Work*, 1974 (May), 280–286.

Skolnick, J. H., Forst, M. L., and Scheiber, J. L. (Eds.). *Crime and Justice in America*. Del Mar, Calif.: Publisher's Inc., 1977.

Slap, G. B. "Normal physiological and psychosocial growth in the adolescent." *Journal of Adolescent Health Care*. 1986.

Slater, P. E. "Contrasting correlates of group size." *Sociometry*, 1958, 25, 129–139.

Smeeding, T. *Alternative Methods for Valuing Selected In-Kind Transfer Benefits and Measuring Their Effect on Poverty*. Washington, D.C.: U.S. Bureau of the Census, 1982.

Smith, D. E. "Chemical dependency and AIDS." In *Acquired Immune Deficiency Syndrome and Chemical Dependency.* DHHS Publication No. (ADM) 87–1513. 1987.

Smith, D. *Dennis Smith's History of Firefighting in America: 300 Years of Courage.* New York: Dial Press, 1978.

Solomon, B. *Black Empowerment.* New York: Columbia, 1976.

Solzhenitsyn, A. I. *Cancer Ward.* New York: Farrar, Straus and Girboux, 1969.

Sowell, T. *Ethnic America: A History.* New York: Basic Books, 1981.

Specter, M. "Rising costs of treatment force Oregon to 'play god'." *Washington Post,* February 5, 1988, p. A1, 6, 7.

Stage, S. *Female Complaints: Lydia Pinkham and the Business of Women's Medicine.* New York: W. W. Norton, 1979.

Star, B. "Domestic violence." In A. Minahan et al. (Eds.). *Encyclopedia of Social Work.* 18th Ed. Silver Spring, Md.: NASW, 1987.

Starr, P. "Health care for the poor: The past twenty years." In S. Danziger and D. Weinberg. *Fighting Poverty.* Cambridge, Mass.: Harvard University Press, 1986.

Statistical Abstracts of the United States (various years). U.S. Department of Commerce, Bureau of the Census. Washington, D.C.: GPO.

Steffens, L. *The Shame of the Cities.* New York: Hill and Wang, 1957.

Stehno, S. M. "Juvenile courts, probation, and parole." In A. Minahan et al. (Eds.). *Encyclopedia of Social Work.* 18th Ed. Silver Spring, Md.: NASW, 1987.

Stein, T. "Foster care for children." In A. Minahan et al (Eds.). *Encyclopedia of Social Work.* 18th ed. Silver Spring, Md.: NASW, 1987.

Stellman, J. M., and Daum, S. M. *Work is Dangerous to Your Health: A Handbook of Health Hazards in the Workplace and What You Can Do About Them.* New York: Vintage Books, 1973.

Stockholm International Peace Research Institute. *World Armaments and Disarmament.* London: Taylor and Francis, 1982.

Stolberg, A. L. "Prevention programs for divorcing families." In L. A. Bond (Ed.). *Families in Transition: Primary Prevention Programs that Work.* Hanover, N.H.: University Press of New England, 1987.

Stolberg, A. L., and Garrison, K. M. "Evaluating a primary prevention program for children of divorce." *American Journal of Community Psychology,* 1985, 13:2, 111–124.

Strodtbeck, F. L. "Husband-wife interactions over revealed differences." *American Sociological Review,* 1951, 16, 468–473.

Surgeon General's Report on Acquired Immune Deficiency Syndrome. U.S. Department of Health and Human Services, n.d.

Sutherland, E. H., and Cressey, D. R. *Principles of Criminology.* 8th ed. Philadelphia: Lippincott, 1970.

Swardson, A. "Jobless rate drops to 6% in July." *Washington Post,* August 8, 1987. pp. A1, A11.

Szasz, T. *The Myth of Mental Illness.* American Psychologist, 1960, 15, 113–118.

Szasz, T. *The Myth of Mental Illness.* New York: Hoeber-Harper, 1961.

Taggart, R. *A Fisherman's Guide: An Assessment of Training and Remediation Strategies.* Kalamazoo, Mich.: Upjohn Institute for Employment Research, 1981.

Talbott, J. A. "Toward a public policy on the chronically mentally ill patient." *American Journal of Orthopsychiatry,* 1980, 50:1.

Teenage Pregnancy: The Problem that Hasn't Gone Away. New York: Alan Guttmacher Institute, 1981.

Thompson, L. "Safe sex in the era of AIDS." "Health": *Washington Post,* March 31, 1987, 10–14.

Thurow, L. C. "A surge of inequality." *Scientific American,* 1987, May, 30–37.

Timms, N. *Social Work Values: An Enquiry.* London: Routledge and Kegan Paul, 1983.

Titchener, J. L., and Kapp, F. "Post-traumatic decline." Paper presented at the American Psychoanalytic Association Meeting, New York, 1978. Reported in Green et al., 1985.

Tobias, S. *Overcoming Math Anxiety.* New York: Norton, 1978.

Toch, H. *Living in Prison: The Ecology of Survival.* New York: Free Press, 1977.

Toffler, A. *The Third Wave.* New York: Bantam, 1980.

Toomey, B. G. "Sexual assault services." In A. Minahan et al. (Eds.). *Encyclopedia of Social Work,* 18th Ed. Silver Spring, Md.: NASW, 1987.

Trattner, W. I. *From Poor Law to Welfare State: A History of Social Welfare in America.* 3rd ed. New York: Free Press, 1984.

Treger, H. "Police social work." In A. Minahan et al. (Eds.). *Encyclopedia of Social Work.* 18th Ed. Silver Spring, Md.: NASW, 1987.

Trickett, P. K., Apfel, N. H., Rosenbaum, L. K., and Zigler, E. "A five-year follow-up of participants in the Yale Child Welfare Research Program." In E. Zigler and E. Gordon (Eds.). *Day Care: Scientific and Social Policy Issues.* Boston: Auburn House Publishing Co., 1982.

Tropman, J. E. "Value conflicts and decision making: Analysis and resolution." *Community Development Journal,* 1981, 16:3. Republished in F. M. Cox et al. (Eds.). *Tactics & Techniques of Community Practice,* Itasca, Ill.: F. E. Peacock Publishers, 1984, pp. 89–98.

Tuchman, B. *The March of Folly: From Troy to Vietnam.* New York: Ballantine, 1985.

Tymchuk, A. J. "Ethical Decision Making and Psychological Treatment." *Journal of Psychiatric Treatment and Evaluation,* 1981, 3, 507–513.

United Nations Secretary-General. *General and Complete Disarmament: Comprehensive Study on Nuclear Weapons: Report of the Secretary-General,* Fall, 1980.

U.S. Bureau of the Census. *Statistical Abstracts of the United States.* Washington, D.C.: U.S. Department of Commerce, various editions.

U.S. Council of Economic Advisers. *1964 Economic Report of the President.* Washington, D.C.: U.S. Government Printing Office, 1964.

U.S. Department of Justice. *Crime in the United States.* Washington, D.C.: GPO, 1981.

U.S. Office of Management and the Budget, 1984. *Major Themes and Additional Budget Details, FY 1985.* Washington, D.C.: Government Printing Office, 1984.

Ursano, R., Boydstun, J., and Weatley, R. "Psychiatric illness in U.S. air force Vietnam prisoners of war: A five-year follow-up." *American Journal of Psychiatry,* 1981, 138, 310–314.

Valentine, C. *Culture and Poverty.* Chicago: University of Chicago Press, 1978.

Valentine, D. P., and Andreas, T. "An expanding view of respite care: Supporting families." *Journal of Primary Prevention,* 1984, 5:1, 27–35.

Van Den Bergh, N., and Cooper, L. B. "Feminist social work." In A. Minahan et al. (Eds.). *Encyclopedia of Social Work.* 18th Ed. Silver Spring, Md.: NASW, 1987.

Vaught, B. C., Hoy, F., and Buchanan, W. W. *Employee Development Programs: An Organizational Approach.* Westport, Conn.: Quorum Books, 1985.

Vaz Pato, M., and Williamson, J. "Socioeconomic achievement: The case of the working poor." *Journal of Sociology and Social Welfare,* 1979, 6, 245–264.

Veatch, R. *A Theory of Medical Ethics.* New York: Basic Books, 1981.

Wagenfeld, M. O., Lemkau, P. V., and Justice, B. (Eds.). *Public Mental Health: Perspectives and Prospects.* Beverly Hills: Sage, 1982.

Waldon, I., and Johnston, S. "Why do women live longer than men?" *Journal of Human Stress,* 1976, 2 (pt 1) 2–13; 1976, 2 (pt 2) 19–30.

Walker, S. *Popular Justice: A History of American Criminal Justice.* New York: Oxford University Press, 1980.

Waxman, C. I. *The Stigma of Poverty: A Critique of Poverty Theories and Policies.* New York: Pergamon Press, 1983.

Weiner, H., Akabas, S., and Sommer, J. J. *Mental Health Care in the World of Work.* New York: Association Press, 1973.

Weitzman, L. J. *The Divorce Revolution: The Unexpected Social and Economic Consequences for Women and Children in America.* New York: Free Press, 1985.

Welfare Programs for Families with Children. Staff of the Committee on Finance, U.S. Senate, Lloyd Bentsen, Chair. 100th Congress, 1st Session. Committee Print. S Prt. 100-20, March 1987.

Welu, T. C. "Broadening the focus of suicide prevention activities utilizing the public health model." *American Journal of Public Health,* 1972, 62:12, 1625–1628.

Wertz, R. W., and Wertz, D. C. *Lying-in: A History of Childbirth in America.* New York: Free Press, 1977.

White House Paper. *The President's Strategic Defense Initiative.* Washington, D.C.: U.S. President, 1985, 10 pp.

Wilensky, H. L., and Lebeaux, C. N. *Industrial Society and Social Welfare.* New York: Free Press, 1965.

Williams, J. "Nation's poverty increasingly wears a child's face." *Washington Post,* June 9, 1985, p. A1, 14.

Wilson, J. Q. *Thinking about Crime.* New York: Basic Books, 1975.

Wilson, J. Q. *Crime and Human Nature.* New York: Simon and Schuster, 1985.

Wilson, J. P., Smith, W. K., and Johnson, S. K. "A comparative analysis of PTSD among various survivor groups." In C. R. Figley (Ed.). *Trauma and Its Wake.* New York: Brunner/Mazel, 1985.

Wilson, S. *Confidentiality in Social Work.* New York: Free Press, 1978.

Wilson, W. J., and Neckerman, K. M. "Poverty and family structure: The widening gap between evidence and public policy issues." In S. Danziger and D. Weinberg (Eds.). *Fighting Poverty.* Cambridge, Mass.: Harvard University Press, 1986.

Winkler, A. M. "The nuclear question." In R. Bremner et al. (Eds.). *American Choices.* Columbus, Ohio: Ohio State University Press, 1986.

Winslow, G. R. *Triage and Justice.* Berkeley, Calif.: University of California Press, 1982.

Wodarski, J. S. *Rural Community Mental Health Practice.* Baltimore: University Park Press, 1983.

Woodman, N. J. "Homosexuality: Lesbian women." In A. Minahan et al. (Eds.). *Encyclopedia of Social Work.* 18th Ed. Silver Spring, Md.: NASW, 1987.

Woodson, R. L. (Ed.). *Black Perspectives on Crime and the Criminal Justice System.* Boston: G. K. Hall, 1977.

World Health Organization. "The economics of health and disease." *WHO Chronicle,* 1971, 25, 20–24.

Worthington, R. "Demographic and pre-service variables as predictors of post-military service adjustment." In C. R. Figley (Ed.). *Stress Disorders among Vietnam Veterans.* New York: Brunner/Mazel, 1978.

Wrightsman, L. S., and Deaux, K. *Social Psychology in the 80's.* 3rd Ed. Monterey, Calif.: Brooks/Cole, 1981.

Young, R. L., and Adams, G. R. "The 4-H youth organization: Primary prevention though competency promotion." *Journal of Primary Prevention,* 1984, 4:4, 225–239.

Zastrow, C. *Introduction to Social Welfare Institutions: Social Problems, Services, and Current Issues.* 4th Ed. Belmont, CA: Wadsworth, 1990.

Zeisel, H. *The Limits of Law Enforcement.* Chicago: University of Chicago Press, 1982.

Zelnick, M., and Kantner, J. "Sexual activity, contraceptive use and pregnancy among metropolitan-area teenagers: 1971–1979." *Family Planning Perspectives,* 1980, 12: 230–237.

Zigler, E. F., and Gordon, E. W. (Eds.). *Day Care: Scientific and Social Policy Issues.* Boston: Auburn House Publishing Company, 1982.

Zimbardo, P. G. "A Pirandellian prison." *New York Times Sunday Magazine,* April 8, 1973, 38–60.

Zuckerman, E. *The Day After World War III.* New York: Penguin (Viking) 1984.

Zwelling, S. S. *Quest for a Cure: The Public Hospital in Williamsburg, 1773–1885.* Williamsburg, Va.: The Colonial Williamsburg Foundation, 1985.

Author Index

Subject Index

About the Author

Martin Bloom, Professor of Social Work at Rutgers University, earned a Ph.D. in Social Psychology at the University of Michigan, and a Certificate in Social Study (Social Work) at the University of Edinburgh. His career began as a Research Associate in Gerontological Research at the Benjamin Rose Institute (Cleveland), followed by faculty appointments in schools of social work at Indiana University (Indianapolis), Washington University (St. Louis), and Virginia Commonwealth University (Richmond). Dr. Bloom has taught in bachelors, masters, and doctoral programs.

Dr. Bloom's numerous publications include *Configurations of Human Behavior* (1984); *Life Span Development* (1985); *Evaluating Practice,* with Joel Fischer (1982); *The Experience of Research* (1986); *Primary Prevention* (1981); and *The Paradox of Helping* (1975). He has also contributed papers and chapters to many books and journals, including *Social Service Review, Social Work,* and *Journal of Primary Prevention.*

INTRODUCTION TO THE DRAMA OF SOCIAL WORK

Composition by Compositors Corporation, Cedar Rapids, Iowa
Printed and bound by Arcata Graphics, Kingsport, Tennessee
Designed by Willis Proudfoot, Mt. Prospect, Illinois
Production supervision by Robert H. Grigg, Chicago, Illinois
The text is set in Palatino